official guides to **quality**

Britain's

camping + caravan parks

2005

GW00506054

visit **Britain**
publishing

Contents

Key to symbols

Accommodation symbols
A key to symbols can be found on the inside back cover. Keep it open for easy reference.

Above Ogmore Castle, Bridgend **Right** Whitecliff Bay Holiday Park, Bembridge

The guide is divided into 12 sections

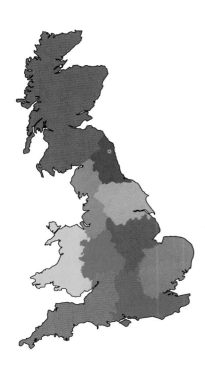

VisitBritain

VisitBritain is the organisation created to market Britain to the rest of the world, and England to the British. Formed by the merger of the British Tourist Authority and the English Tourism Council, its mission is to build the value of tourism by creating world-class destination brands and marketing campaigns.

It will also build partnerships with – and provide insights to – other organisations which have a stake in British and English tourism.

welcome

to the new and fully updated
edition of Camping and
Caravan Parks in Britain

The guide that gives you more

This guide is packed with information from where to stay, to how to get there and what to do. In fact, everything you need to know to enjoy Britain.

Quality accommodation

Choose from a wide choice of quality-assured accommodation to suit all budgets and tastes. This guide contains an exclusive listing of all camping, caravan parks and holiday villages participating in The British Graded Holiday Parks Scheme.

Visitor attractions

Ideas for places to visit, highlighting those receiving our quality assurance marque, are detailed in each regional section.

Tourist Information Centres

For local information call a Tourist Information Centre. Telephone numbers are shown in the blue bands next to the place names in accommodation entries.

Guides and maps

We list free and saleable tourism publications available from regional tourism organisations.

Town descriptions

At the end of each section is a brief description of the main places where accommodation is listed.

Finding accommodation is easy

Regional listings

The guide is divided into 12 areas, and accommodation is listed alphabetically by place name within each section. Additionally ALL VisitBritain assessed camping, caravan parks and holiday villages are listed in the back of the guide.

Colour maps

Use the colour maps, starting on page 19, to find the location of all accommodation featured in the regional sections. Then refer to the town index at the back of the guide to find the page number. The index also includes tourism areas such as the New Forest or the Cotswolds.

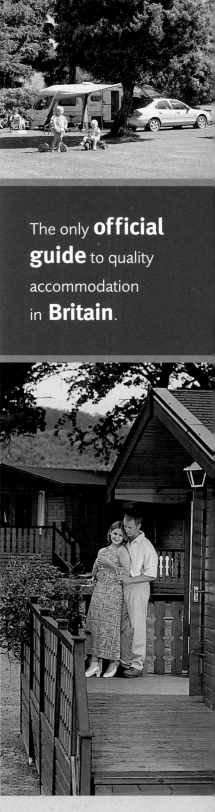

The only **official guide** to quality accommodation in **Britain**.

Left River Isis, Oxford **Right, from top** Langstone Manor Camping and Caravan Park, Tavistock; Crowhurst Park, Battle

Touring Britain

Britain is a country of beautiful landscapes and historic interest where the traveller can enjoy a great variety of scenery within short distances.

Camping or caravanning is a good way to see Britain. You can go as you please without sticking to a set programme, enjoy the country air and have a lot of fun. Wherever you stay, you can use your park as a base for sightseeing and touring the surrounding area.

As the birthplace of camping, Britain has a large number of places to stay of every kind – from small, quiet spots to big, lively parks offering a wide range of facilities and entertainment. Many have a restaurant, bar, nightclub, regular barbecues and evening entertainment (eg dinner dance, cabaret).

An increasing number of parks now make ideal centres for an activity holiday. Fishing, sailing and golfing are just three of the more popular activities on offer. Many parks also have indoor swimming pools, tennis courts and games room, and provide a wide range of facilities and activities to keep the children amused.

Most parks admit tents, touring and motor caravans and provide a wide range of central facilities for the tourer. Many have caravan holiday homes for hire. These are often very spacious, luxurious and well equipped with two to three good-sized bedrooms, a lounge with comfortable furnishings and a separate dining area.

Left Whitecliff Bay Holiday Park, Bembridge
Right, from top enjoy a country walk in Powys; Brixham Holiday Park, Brixham

Many have modern conveniences such as colour televisions, fridges, hot showers, en suite bathrooms and microwaves. In addition to caravan holiday homes, many parks also have chalets and lodges for hire, designed and equipped to the same standard as the caravans. All are truly a home from home, giving you the facilities and freedom you need to enjoy your holiday.

To help you select the type of park to suit you, with the facilities and standards you require, the British Graded Holiday Parks Rating Scheme will be of great assistance. Each park involved in this scheme has been visited by an independent assessor and given a rating based on cleanliness, environment and the quality of facilities and services provided.

Many parks are open all year and can be an excellent way to enjoy a short break in the spring, autumn and even in the winter months. Prices will be cheaper than during the main season and many facilities will still be available (although it might be wise to check).

If you intend to stay in a popular holiday area during the main season (June to September), you are advised to book in advance. It is essential either to send written confirmation of any reservations made or to arrive very early at your chosen park.

Le tourisme en Grande-Bretagne
(Voir page 8)

Unterwegs in Großbritannien
(Lesen Sie Seite 10)

Rondtrekken in Groot-Brittannië
(Zie pag 12)

Alla scoperta della Gran Bretagna
(Vedi 14)

Le tourisme en Grande-Bretagne

La Grande-Bretagne est un pays qui abonde en panoramas superbes et en sites d'intérêt historique, où les touristes n'ont pas besoin de parcourir des kilomètres pour pouvoir admirer des paysages très variés.

Le camping et le caravaning sont d'excellents moyens d'explorer la Grande-Bretagne. On peut aller où on le désire sans adhérer à un plan fixe, profiter du bon air de la campagne et se divertir. Quelle que soit la région où se trouve le terrain dans lequel on séjourne, on peut s'en servir comme point de chute pour faire du tourisme et rayonner dans la région.

C'est en Grande-Bretagne qu'est né le camping, on y trouve donc un grand nombre de terrains de toutes sortes, allant de petits terrains tranquilles à de grands parcs pleins d'animation proposant une vaste gamme d'équipements et de distractions. Un grand nombre de terrains possèdent des restaurants, bars, night-clubs, et organisent régulièrement des barbecues et des distractions nocturnes (par ex. dîners dansants, spectacles de cabaret). Les terrains de camping sont des endroits merveilleux pour passer des vacances à thème, et un nombre de plus en plus important de terrains proposent cette formule. La pêche, la navigation de plaisance et le golf, entre autres, font partie des activités les plus populaires qu'on peut pratiquer dans des terrains de plus en plus nombreux. Un grand nombre de terrains mettent également à la disposition des vacanciers des piscines couvertes chauffées, des courts de tennis, des salles de jeux, et proposent une large gamme d'installations et d'activités destinées aux enfants.

La plupart de terrains acceptent les tentes, les caravanes de tourisme et les camping-cars, et mettent un vaste éventail d'équipements à la disposition des vacanciers. Un grand nombre de terrains louent des caravanes fixes, qui sont souvent très spacieuses, luxueuses et bien aménagées, comportant deux ou trois belles chambres à coucher, un salon confortable et un coin salle à manger séparé. Un grand nombre de ces logements de vacances ont tout le confort moderne: télévision couleur, réfrigérateur, douche avec eau chaude, salle de bains et four à micro-ondes. En plus des caravanes de vacances, de nombreux terrains louent également des chalets et des pavillons, conçus et équipés avec le même soin et dotés du même confort. Vous vous sentirez comme chez vous dans tous ces terrains et vous y trouverez les aménagements et la liberté dont vous avez besoin pour profiter au mieux de vos vacances.

Pour sélectionner le meilleur terrain/centre offrant les services et normes dont vous avez besoin, le British Graded Holiday Parks Rating Scheme (système d'évaluation des centres de vacances/terrains de camping britanniques) vous sera très utile. Des inspecteurs indépendants ont visité chaque terrain participant à ce projet et les ont classés selon la propreté, l'environnement et la qualité de leurs services.

De nombreux terrains sont ouverts toute l'année, et permettent ainsi de prendre quelques jours de vacances agréables au printemps, en automne et même en hiver. Les tarifs sont moins élevés que pendant la haute saison, et de nombreux équipements sont encore à la disposition des vacanciers (il est toutefois prudent de vérifier).

Si vous avez l'intention de séjourner, en haute saison (de juin à septembre), dans une région de villégiature très fréquentée, nous vous conseillons de réserver à l'avance. Il est indispensable soit de confirmer toute réservation par écrit, soit d'arriver très tôt au terrain de votre choix.

Left historical day out in Windsor **Right, from top** picturesque Winsford, Somerset; enjoy a day by the sea – any time of the year

Unterwegs in Großbritannien

Großbritannien ist reich an schönen Landschaften und historischen Stätten und die Natur zeigt sich dem Besucher innerhalb weniger Kilometer von ihrer abwechslungsreichsten Seite.

Die Übernachtung auf dem Campingplatz oder im Wohnwagen eignet sich gut, um Großbritannien kennen zu lernen. Sie können nach Lust und Laune ins Blaue fahren, die würzige Landluft genießen und viel Interessantes erleben.Wo Sie sich auch aufhalten mögen, Ihr Platz ist stets ein idealer Ausgangsort für Besichtigungstouren und Ausflüge in die Umgebung.

Großbritannien ist der Geburtsort des Zeltens und bietet eine große Anzahl an Plätzen jeder Art – von kleinen, ruhigen bis zu großen, lebhaften Plätzen mit einer großen Auswahl an Einrichtungen und einem reichen Unterhaltungsprogramm. Zahlreiche Plätze verfügen über ein Restaurant, eine Bar, einen Nachtklub und veranstalten regelmäßige Grillpartys und Abendunterhaltung (z.B. Abendessen mit Tanz, Kabarett).

Immer mehr Plätze sind ideale Ferienorte für Aktivferien. Angeln, Segeln und Golf, nur drei der beliebtesten Aktivitäten, werden von einer wachsenden Zahl von Plätzen angeboten. Viele verfügen auch über ein Hallenbad, Tennisplätze, Spielzimmer und bieten eine große Auswahl an Einrichtungen und Aktivitäten für Kinder.

Die meisten Plätze sind für Zelte, Wohnwagen und Wohnmobile eingerichtet und bieten dem Besucher eine Reihe von Einrichtungen. Zahlreiche Plätze vermieten Wohnwagen. Diese sind oft äußerst geräumig, luxuriös und gut ausgestattet und verfügen über zwei oder drei Schlafzimmer, ein Wohnzimmer mit komfortablen Möbeln und einen getrennten Essbereich. Viele bieten auch Farbfernseher, Kühlschrank, Dusche mit warmem Wasser, Bad und Mikrowellenherd. Zusätzlich zu den Wohnwagen gibt es auf zahlreichen Plätzen auch Chalets und Hütten mit demselben Komfort. Alle sind in der Tat ein zweites Zuhause und bieten die Einrichtungen und die Unabhängigkeit, die für erfolgreiche Ferien unerlässlich sind.

Um Ihnen bei der Auswahl des Parktyps zu helfen, dessen Standards und Leistungsumfang Ihren Anforderungen und Wünschen am besten entspricht, wird Ihnen das British Graded Holiday Parks Rating Scheme (Beurteilungssystem für britische Ferienparks) von großem Nutzen sein. Alle an diesem System beteiligten Parks sind von unabhängigen Gutachtern besucht und im Hinblick auf Sauberkeit, Umwelt und Qualität von Angebot und Service beurteilt worden.

Zahlreiche Plätze sind ganzjährig geöffnet und ideal für Kurzurlaube im Frühling, Herbst oder auch Winter. Die Preise sind während der Nebensaison billiger als während der Hochsaison und zahlreiche Einrichtungen sind immer in Betrieb (es ist jedoch ratsam, sich zuerst zu erkundigen).

Falls Sie während der Hochsaison (Juni bis September) eine beliebte Feriendestination wählen, ist es ratsam, im Voraus zu buchen. Sie müssen die Buchung entweder schriftlich bestätigen oder sehr früh auf dem Platz Ihrer Wahl eintreffen.

Left imposing Alnwick Castle, Northumberland
Right, from top explore the seaside, Woolacombe; a romantic stroll in peaceful countryside

Rondtrekken in Groot-Brittannië

In Groot-Brittannië vindt u prachtige landschappen en een interessante geschiedenis. De reiziger treft op korte afstand van elkaar allerlei verschillende gebieden aan, en kamperen met de tent of de caravan is de ideale manier om echt van Groot-Brittannië te genieten.

Ga en sta waar u wilt, zonder aan een programma vast te zitten, geniet van de frisse lucht en maak plezier! Waar u ook bent, u kunt uw kampeerplaats uw basis maken en in het omliggende gebied rondtrekken.

Groot-Brittannië is het geboorteland van het kamperen, en wij hebben dan ook een groot aantal terreinen in allerlei soorten en maten: vanaf kleine rustige terreintjes tot en met grote gezellige parken met allerlei faciliteiten en amusement. Vele hebben een restaurant, bar, nachtclub, en organiseren regelmatig barbecues en amusement 's avonds (zoals diner dansant, cabaret).

Steeds meer parken vormen tegenwoordig een ideaal centrum voor een actieve vakantie. Vissen, zeilen en golfen zijn slechts drie mogelijkheden die steeds meer terreinen organiseren. Vaak vindt u ook overdekte zwembaden, tennisbanen, spellenkamers en allerlei faciliteiten en activiteiten om de kinderen bezig te houden.

Op de meeste terreinen worden tenten, trekcaravans en kampeerauto's toegelaten en vindt u een groot aantal centrale faciliteiten voor de trekker. Ook zijn er vaak stacaravans te huur: deze zijn vaak zeer ruim, luxueus en goed uitgerust, met twee of drie ruime slaapkamers, een zitkamer met gerieflijk meubilair en een aparte eetkamer. Vaak vindt u er ook moderne gemakken zoals kleuren t.v., ijskast, warme douches, en-suite badkamers en magnetronovens.

Vele parken bieden niet alleen stacaravans maar ook huisjes te huur, die al net zo goed zijn ingericht en uitgerust. Geniet van de faciliteiten en de vrijheid om echt vakantie te vieren.

Om u te helpen met het selecteren van een bepaald type park metvoorzieningen en op het niveau dat u zoekt, zal het British Graded Holiday Parks Rating Scheme u zeker van pas komen. Elk park dat aan dit systeem meedoet is bezocht door een onafhankelijke controleur en heeft een classificatie gekregen op basis van hygiëne, omgeving en de kwaliteit van de voorzieningen en diensten die er aanwezig zijn.

Vele parken zijn het hele jaar open en bieden de ideale manier om er even tussenuit te gaan in de lente, herfst of zelfs in de winter. De prijzen zijn dan lager dan in het hoogseizoen, terwijl toch vele faciliteiten beschikbaar zijn (het is wel raadzaam dit van te voren na te gaan).

Als u in een populair vakantiegebied denkt te verblijven in het hoogseizoen (juni tot september), raden wij u aan van te voren te reserveren. Bevestig de reservering schriftelijk of kom zeer vroeg aan op het terrein.

Left an energetic cycle around Kielder Water
Right, from top be inspired at the Tate St Ives; seaside stroll, Southwold

Alla scoperta della Gran Bretagna

La Gran Bretagna è uno stupendo paese di grande interesse storico che offre un'ampia varietà di paesaggi.

Il campeggio in tenda o roulotte è uno dei modi più efficaci di visitare la Gran Bretagna, dato che consente di viaggiare quando e dove si vuole, senza dover rispettare un itinerario prestabilito, divertendosi e respirando l'aria fresca della campagna. Ovunque si decida di andare, il campeggio può servire da base dalla quale il turista può visitare la zona circostante.

Il campeggio è un'invenzione britannica, ne consegue che in Gran Bretagna vi sono numerosissimi campeggi di tutti i tipi: da quelli piccoli e tranquilli a quelli grandi e animatissimi che offrono un'ampia gamma di strutture e intrattenimenti. Molti campeggi offrono anche ristoranti, bar, locali notturni, banchetti all'aperto con barbecue e spettacoli serali (p.es. serate di ballo, cabaret).

Molti campeggi sono ideali per trascorrere periodi di vacanza di tipo più dinamico, dato che un numero sempre maggiore di essi offre la possibilità, ad esempio, di pescare, praticare la vela o giocare al golf. Molti dispongono di piscine, campi da tennis e palestre al coperto e di numerose strutture e attività per il divertimento dei bambini.

La maggior parte dei campeggi accetta tende, campers e roulottes e offre un'ampia gamma di strutture centralizzate per il campeggiatore. Molti offrono anche roulottes a noleggio Queste roulottes sono spesso spaziosissime, lussuose e ben attrezzate con due o tre camere doppie, un salotto comodamente ammobiliato e una sala da pranzo separata. Molte offrono anche altre moderne comodità come televisioni a colori, frigoriferi, docce calde, camere con bagno e forni a microonde. Oltre alle roulottes a noleggio, molti campeggi offrono anche chalet e casette a noleggio progettate e attrezzate con gli stessi criteri. Sono tutte abitazioni dove ci si sente come a casa propria, e che offrono libertà e tutte le attrezzature necessarie a godersi la propria vacanza.

Per aiutare a scegliere il tipo di parco più adatto, che offra i requisiti e gli standard richiesti, sarà molto utile il British Graded Holiday Parks Rating Scheme (progetto di assegnazione di punteggio ai parchi vacanze del Regno Unito). Ogni parco iscritto viene ispezionato da ispettori indipendenti, con assegnazione di punteggio sulla base dei criteri di pulizia, qualità dell'ambiente e delle risorse e dei servizi offerti.

Molti dei campeggi sono aperti tutto l'anno e sono dunque ideali per trascorrere una breve vacanza anche in primavera, in autunno o in inverno, stagioni in cui i prezzi sono più bassi che durante i mesi di alta stagione, anche se restano disponibili molte delle strutture (consigliamo comunque di controllare prima dell'arrivo).

Si consiglia a chi intenda trascorrere una vacanza in una delle località turistiche più frequentate durante i mesi di alta stagione (da giugno a settembre) di prenotare in anticipo. È essenziale confermare la prenotazione per iscritto o arrivare molto presto al campeggio prescelto.

Left take a stroll by the river in Ross-on-Wye
Right, from top family fun, St Ives; flying high on Holy Island

COMPETITION

WIN A WEEK'S STAY
in London
with
The Caravan Club

The Club's Crystal Palace site

The Caravan Club is delighted to offer you the opportunity to win a pitch for a 7-night family holiday for up to 2 adults and 2 children at one of its two key London sites - Abbey Wood or Crystal Palace. There will be 2 runners up prizes of 2-night stays at either site.

Abbey Wood and Crystal Palace are ideally situated for visiting the London sights and shows, with Abbey Wood only a stone's throw away from Greenwich which is home to many of the SeaBritain events during 2005.

The winner and runners up will be selected at random from correct entries received by the closing date. Please send your answers on a postcard, including your full name and address to:

Sites Marketing,
The Caravan Club
East Grinstead House,
East Grinstead
West Sussex RH19 1UA

Closing date: 31st August 2005.

For your chance to win, just answer the following question:
How many sites does The Caravan Club have in London?

THE CARAVAN CLUB

For sites information visit www.caravanclub.co.uk
or telephone today on 0800 521 161 quoting WTS05

enjoyEngland™
Excellence Awards

Enjoy England Excellence Awards are all about blowing English tourism's trumpet and telling the world what a fantastic place England is to visit, whether it's for a day trip, a weekend break or a fortnight's holiday.

The Awards, now in their 6th year, are run by Enjoy England in association with England's regional tourism organisations. This year there are 10 categories including Caravan Holiday Park of the Year, Visitor Attraction of the Year, and an award for the best tourism website.

Winners of the 2005 awards will receive their trophies at a ceremony on 19 April 2005. The day will celebrate excellence in tourism in England.

For more information about the Enjoy England Excellence Awards visit www.visitengland.com

enjoyEngland™
Excellence
Awards 2005

The winners of the 2004 Caravan Holiday Park of the Year are:

- **Gold winner:**
  Far Grange Caravan Park, Skipsea, North Yorkshire
- **Silver winner:**
  Blackmore Camping and Caravanning Club Site, Hanley Swan, Worcestershire

  Searles Leisure Resort, Hunstanton, Norfolk

Left Far Grange Caravan Park receiving their award from Sue Lawley and HRH The Duke of Kent

MAP 1

Location
Maps

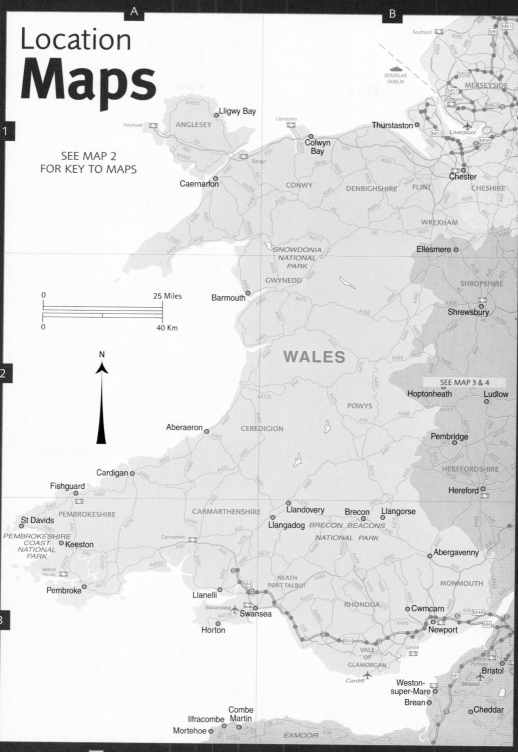

A

B

SEE MAP 2
FOR KEY TO MAPS

Holyhead

ANGLESEY

Lligwy Bay

Llandudno

Colwyn
Bay

Southport

DOUGLAS
DUBLIN

MERSEYSIDE

Liverpool

Thurstaston

Liverpool

1

Caernarfon

Bangor

CONWY

DENBIGHSHIRE

FLINT

Chester

CHESHIRE

WREXHAM

Ellesmere

SHROPSHIRE

SNOWDONIA
NATIONAL
PARK

GWYNEDD

0   25 Miles

0   40 Km

Barmouth

Shrewsbury

WALES

N

2

SEE MAP 3 & 4

Hoptonheath

Ludlow

POWYS

Aberaeron

CEREDIGION

Pembridge

HEREFORDSHIRE

Cardigan

Hereford

Fishguard

PEMBROKESHIRE

CARMARTHENSHIRE

Llandovery

Brecon

Llangorse

St Davids

Llangadog

BRECON BEACONS

PEMBROKESHIRE
COAST
NATIONAL
PARK

Keeston

Carmarthen

NATIONAL PARK

Abergavenny

Milford
Haven

MONMOUTH

Pembroke

Llanelli

NEATH
PORT TALBOT

Swansea

M4

RHONDDA

Cwmcarn

M48

M4

3

Horton

Swansea

Cardiff

Newport

VALE
OF
GLAMORGAN

Cardiff

Bristol

Bristol

Weston-
super-Mare

M5

Combe
Martin

Brean

Cheddar

Ilfracombe

Mortehoe

EXMOOR

Key to regions: Wales

All place names in black offer parks in this guide.

MAP 2

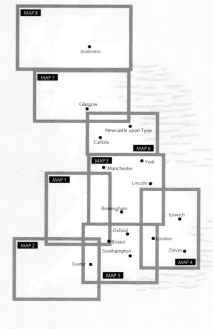

A   B

1

MAP 8

Inverness

MAP 7

Glasgow

Newcastle upon Tyne

Carlisle

MAP 6

MAP 5

Manchester   York

MAP 1

Lincoln

2

Birmingham

Ipswich

Oxford

MAP 2

Bristol   London

Southampton

Dover

MAP 4

Exeter

MAP 3

Every place name featured in the regional accommodation sections of this Enjoy England guide has a map reference to help you locate it on the maps which follow. For example, to find Colchester, Essex, which has 'Map ref 3B2', turn to Map 3 and refer to grid square B2.

All place names appearing in the regional sections are shown in black type on the maps. This enables you to find other places in your chosen area which may have suitable accommodation – the town index (at the back of this guide) gives page numbers.

Tintagel

Camelford

Polzeath

Padstow

Newquay

CORNWALL

Newquay   White Cross

Luxulyan

Fowey

St Agnes   St Austell

Polruan-by-Fowey

Blackwater

Portreath

Redruth

St Ives

St Just in Roseland

Penzance

Hayle

Relubbus

Land's End (St Just)

Penzance

Rosudgeon

Lands End

3

Tresco

Isles of Scilly

Ruan Minor

Key to regions: South West England

MAP 2

C   D

VALE
OF
GLAMORGAN

Cardiff

Cardiff

Weston-
super-Mare

Brean

Cheddar

Combe
Martin
Ilfracombe
Mortehoe

EXMOOR
NATIONAL

Croyde Bay
Braunton

PARK

Winsford

Westward Ho!

South
Molton

Dulverton

Taunton

Langport

Muchelney

SOMERSET

Bude

DEVON

Kentisbeare

Beetham

Axminster

Charmouth

Exeter

Sidbury

Exeter

Sidmouth

Tavistock

DARTMOOR
NATIONAL
PARK

Teigngrace
Bickington

Exmouth
Dawlish

Torquay

Landrake

Plymouth

Plymouth

Paignton

Brixham

ROSCOFF
SANTANDER

Salcombe

| 0 | | 25 Miles |
| 0 | | 40 Km |

N

All place names in black offer parks in this guide.

MAP 3

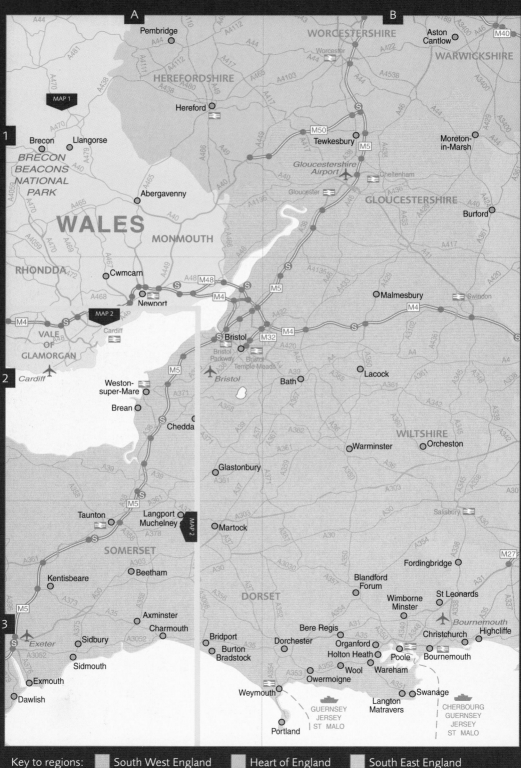

Key to regions:　South West England　Heart of England　South East England

MAP 3

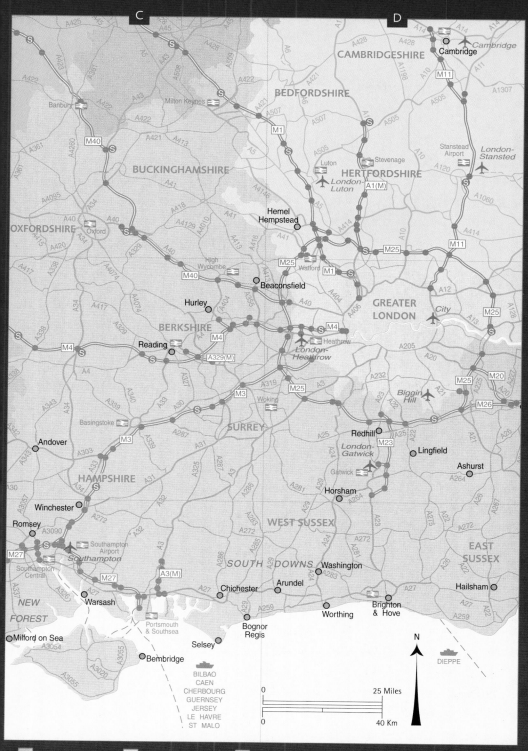

East Midlands   East of England   London

All place names in black offer parks in this guide.

MAP 4

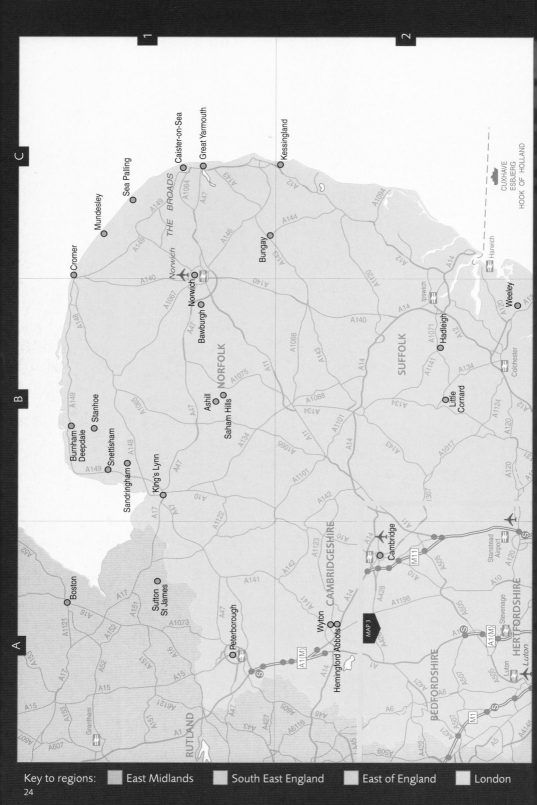

Key to regions: ⬛ East Midlands ⬛ South East England ⬛ East of England ⬛ London

MAP 4

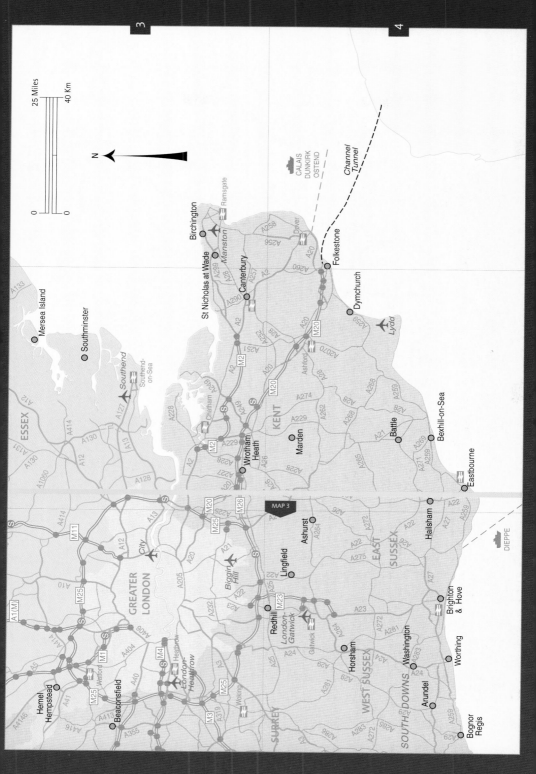

All place names in black offer parks in this guide.

MAP 5

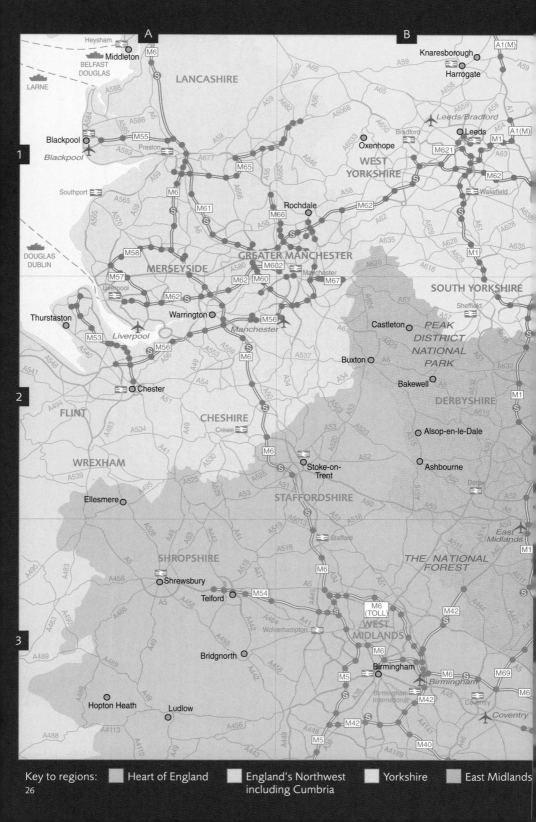

Key to regions:　　Heart of England　　　England's Northwest　　　Yorkshire　　　East Midlands
including Cumbria

MAP 5

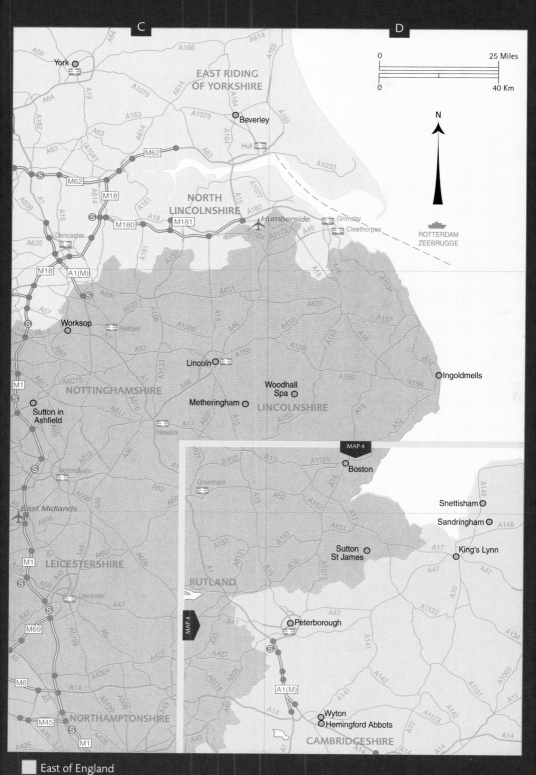

East of England

All place names in black offer parks in this guide.

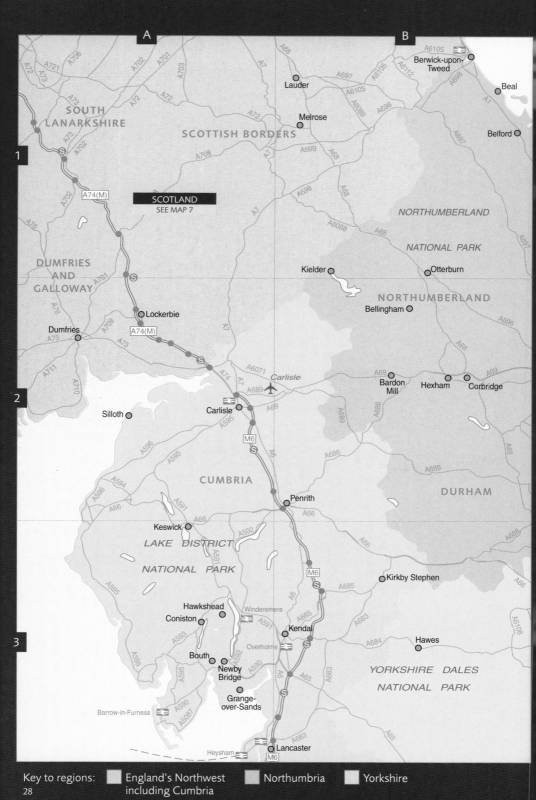

MAP 6

A   B

A706   A721   A72   A702   A701   A702   A703

A6105   Berwick-upon-Tweed

Beal

A72   A73

SOUTH LANARKSHIRE

A73   A702

Lauder

A697   A6105   A6112

1

A74(M)

SCOTTISH BORDERS

Melrose

A6089   A698

A1

Belford

A697

A72   A7

A699   A68

SCOTLAND
SEE MAP 7

A708

A698   A68

NORTHUMBERLAND

A76

A701

DUMFRIES AND GALLOWAY

A6088   A68

NATIONAL PARK

A497

Kielder

Otterburn

NORTHUMBERLAND

Lockerbie

A709   A74(M)

Bellingham

A696

Dumfries

A75   A709   A75

A7

A711

A710

A74

A6071   *Carlisle*

A689

A69

Bardon Mill

Hexham

Corbridge

A69

2

Silloth

Carlisle

A595

A69

A686

A689

A689

A596

M6

A6

A686

DURHAM

A596   A594

CUMBRIA

A66

A591

Penrith

A66

A689

A688

Keswick

A592

A66

LAKE DISTRICT

A591

Kirkby Stephen

A66

A66

NATIONAL PARK

M6

A685

Hawkshead

Windermere

A591

Coniston

A593

A685   A683

Hawes

3

Bouth

Kendal

A684

Overholme

YORKSHIRE DALES

Newby Bridge

A590

A65

A683

NATIONAL PARK

A595

Grange-over-Sands

A6

Barrow-in-Furness

A5087

A590

Heysham   Lancaster

A683

A65

M6

England's Northwest including Cumbria   Northumbria   Yorkshire

MAP 6

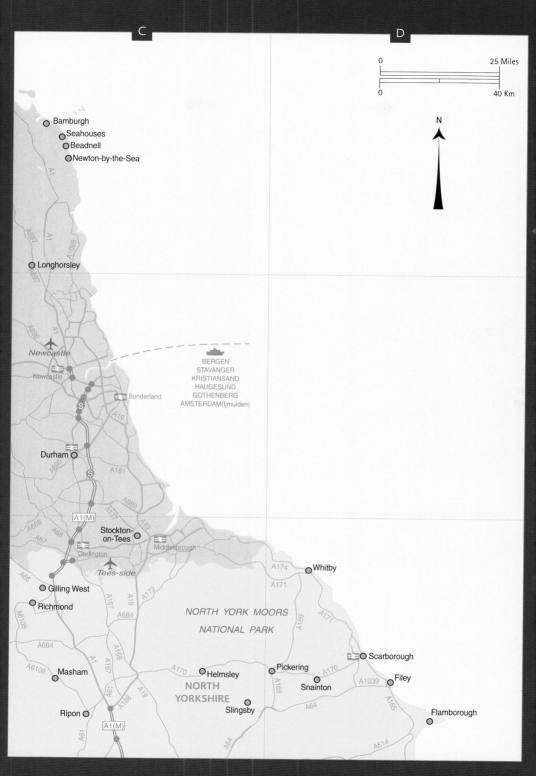

All place names in black offer parks in this guide.

MAP 7

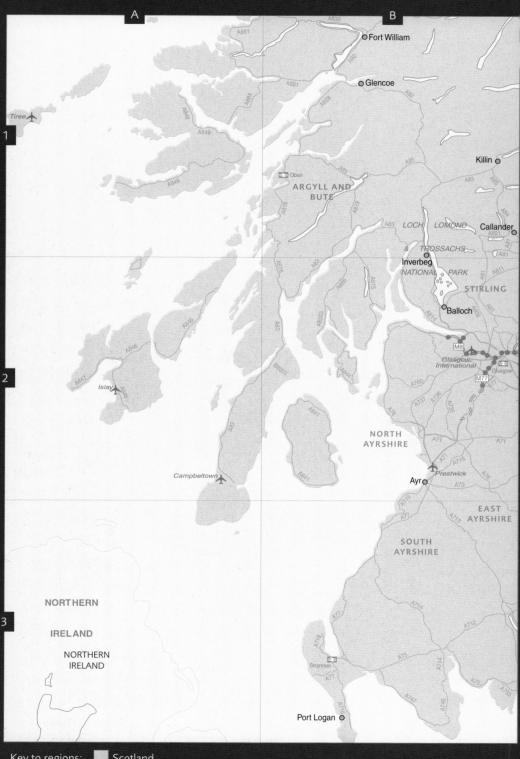

Key to regions: ▢ Scotland

MAP 7

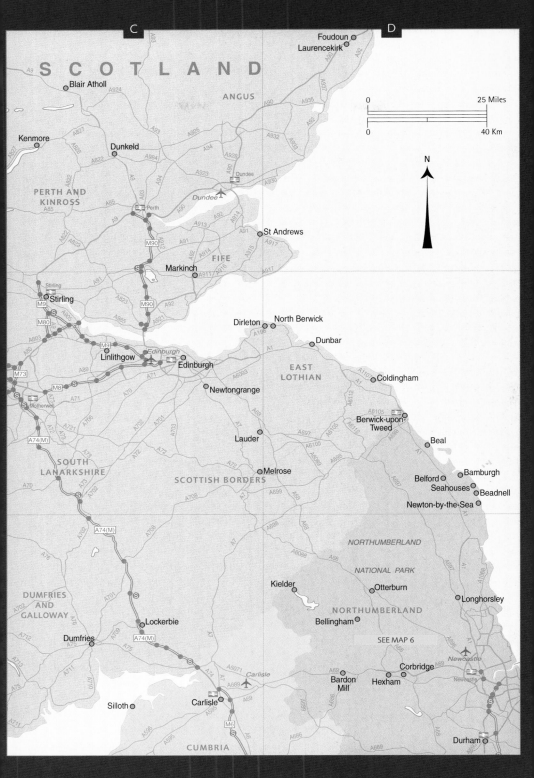

C   D

S C O T L A N D

Foudoun
Laurencekirk

Blair Atholl

ANGUS

0   25 Miles

0   40 Km

Kenmore

Dunkeld

N

Dundee

PERTH AND
KINROSS

Perth

St Andrews

FIFE

Markinch

Dirleton   North Berwick

Stirling

Dunbar

EAST
LOTHIAN

Coldingham

Linlithgow

Edinburgh

Newtongrange

Berwick-upon-Tweed

Motherwell

Lauder

Beal

SOUTH
LANARKSHIRE

Melrose

Belford   Bamburgh
Seahouses
Beadnell

SCOTTISH BORDERS

Newton-by-the-Sea

NORTHUMBERLAND

NATIONAL PARK

DUMFRIES
AND
GALLOWAY

Kielder

Otterburn

Longhorsley

NORTHUMBERLAND

Lockerbie

Bellingham

SEE MAP 6

Dumfries

Newcastle

Corbridge

Carlisle

Bardon
Mill

Hexham

Silloth

Carlisle

Durham

M6

CUMBRIA

MAP 8

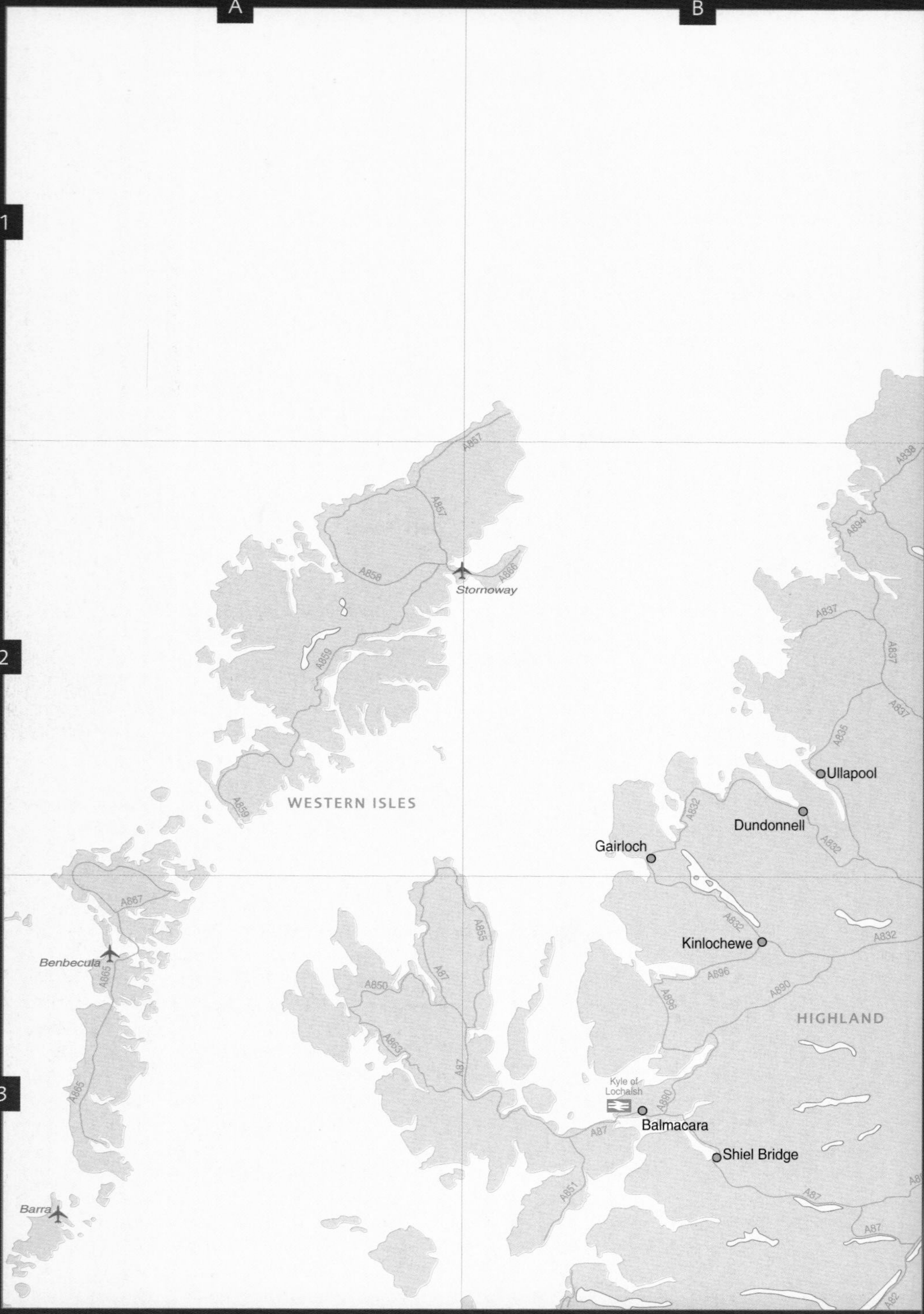
A
B
1
2
3
Stornoway
A857
A858
A859
A866
WESTERN ISLES
A867
Benbecula
A865
Barra
A838
A894
A837
A835
Ullapool
Dundonnell
A832
Gairloch
Kinlochewe
A896
A890
HIGHLAND
A855
A850
A863
A87
Kyle of Lochalsh
Balmacara
Shiel Bridge
A851
A82

Key to regions: Scotland

MAP 8

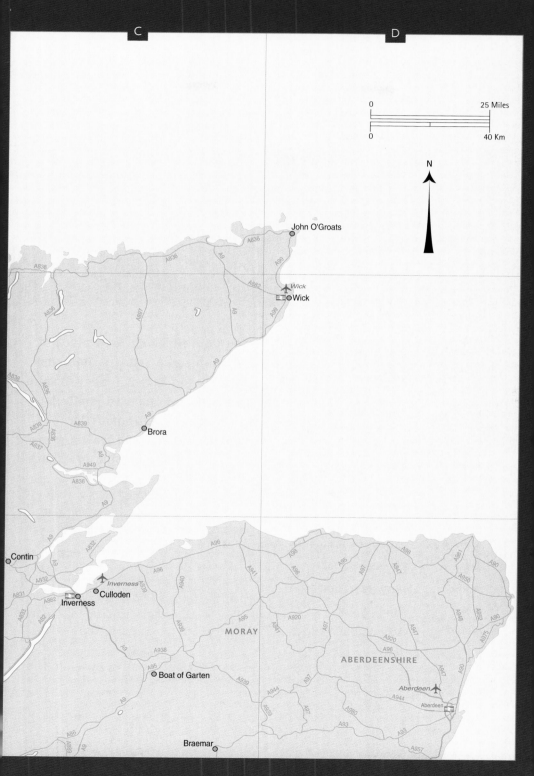

All place names in black offer parks in this guide.

Ratings **you** can trust

When you're looking for a place to stay, you need a rating system you can trust. The British Graded Holiday Parks Scheme, operated jointly by the national tourist boards for England, Scotland and Wales, gives you a clear guide of what to expect.

Based on the internationally recognised rating of one to five stars, the system puts great emphasis on quality and reflects customer expectations.

Parks are visited annually by trained, impartial assessors who award a rating based on cleanliness, environment and the quality of services and facilities provided.

STAR QUALITY

★★★★★ Exceptional quality

★★★★ Excellent quality

★★★ Very good quality

★★ Good quality

★ Acceptable quality

How to use this guide

Camping and caravan parks listed in this guide have accommodation for touring caravans or tents, or both, and most welcome motor caravans. Many parks also have caravan holiday homes to let.

The Quality Assurance Standard

When you're looking for a place to stay, you need a rating system you can trust. The British Graded Holiday Parks Scheme gives you a clear guide of what you can expect, in an easy-to-understand form. The scheme has quality at its heart and reflects consumer expectations.

VisitBritain uses stars to show the quality rating of parks participating in the scheme. Parks are visited annually by trained, impartial assessors who award a rating from one to five stars. These are based on cleanliness, environment and the quality of facilities and services provided.

Parks are also given a designator so you can identify the type of site at a glance – a Holiday Park, a Touring Park or a Camping Park, for example. (If no rating or designator is shown, the park was awaiting assessment at the time of going to press.)

The British Graded Holiday Parks Scheme was devised jointly by the national tourist boards for England, Northern Ireland, Scotland and Wales in association with the British Holiday and Home Parks Association (see page 56) and the National Caravan Council (see page 62).

Facilities

Facilities are indicated by means of the at-a-glance symbols explained on the fold-out back cover flap.

Prices

Prices given for touring pitches are based on the minimum and maximum charges for one night for two persons, car and either caravan or tent. It is more usual in Britain to charge simply for the use of the pitch, but a number of parks charge separately for car, caravan or tent, and for each person. Some parks may charge extra for caravan awnings. Minimum and maximum prices for caravan holiday homes are given per week. Prices quoted are those supplied to us by the park operators concerned, and are intended to give an indication of the prices which will be charged during the currency of this publication. Prices are shown in pounds (£) and pence (p). VAT (Value Added Tax) at 17.50% is included in the prices shown. In order to avoid misunderstandings, it is particularly advisable to check prices with the park concerned when making reservations.

Making a booking

When enquiring about accommodation, as well as checking prices and other details, you will need to state your requirements clearly and precisely, for example:

- arrival and departure dates with acceptable alternatives if appropriate.
- the accommodation you need.
- tell the management about any particular requirements.

Above Crowhurst Park, Battle

Misunderstandings can occur very easily over the telephone so we recommend that all bookings be confirmed in writing if time permits. Remember to include your name and address and please enclose a stamped addressed envelope or an international reply coupon (if writing from outside Britain) for each reply.

Deposits and advance payments
In the case of caravan, camping and chalet parks and holiday centres the full charge often has to be paid in advance. This may be in two instalments – a deposit at the time of booking and the balance by, say, two weeks before the start of the booked period.

Cancellations
When you accept offered accommodation, in writing or on the telephone, you are entering into a legally binding contract with the proprietor of the establishment. This means that if you cancel a reservation, fail to take up the accommodation or leave prematurely (regardless of the reasons) the proprietor may be entitled to compensation if it cannot be re-let for all or a good part of the booked period. If a deposit has been paid it is likely to be forfeited and an additional payment may be demanded.

It is therefore in your interest to advise the management immediately if you have to change your travel plans, cancel a booking or leave prematurely.

Electric hook-up points
Most parks now have electric hook-up points for caravans and tents. Voltage is generally 240v AC, 50 cycles, although variations between 200v and 250v may still be found. An adaptor for use with hook-ups may be necessary. Parks will usually charge extra for this facility, and it is advisable to check rates when making a booking.

Finding your park
Parks in this guide are listed in England by region followed by Scotland and Wales. They are listed alphabetically under the name of the town in or near which they are situated.

The town index on page 298 and colour location maps at the front of the guide show all cities, towns and villages with detailed entries. Use these as a quick and easy way to find suitable accommodation. If you know which park you wish to stay at, check under the Index to Parks on page 294.

If the place you wish to stay is included in the town index, turn to the page number given to find the parks available there. The town names appear in black on the maps at the front of the guide as indicated by the map reference in the entry. Also check on the colour maps to find other places nearby which also have parks listed in this guide. If the place you want is not in the town index – or you only have a general idea of the area in which you wish to stay – use the colour location maps.

The maps show all place names under which a park is listed in this guide. For a precise location read the directions in each entry. If you have any difficulties finding a particular park, we suggest that you ask for final directions within the neighbourhood.

 The International Direction Signs shown here are in use in Britain and are designed to help visitors find their park. They have not yet been erected for all parks and do not display the name of any particular one. They do show, however, whether the park is for tents or caravans or both. The International Camping Carnet is rarely recognised in Britain except at parks organised by the major clubs.

London sites
London is a great attraction to many visitors, so the camping and caravan parks in the Greater London area tend to become full very quickly, and early booking is required. Parks are also available at most ports of entry to the country and many of these are listed in this guide and marked on the maps at the front.

Park-finding services

Tourist Information Centres throughout Britain (see end pages) are able to give campers and caravanners information about parks in their areas. Some Tourist Information Centres have camping and caravanning advisory services which provide details of park availability and often assist with park booking.

Avoiding peak season

In the summer months of June to September, parks in popular areas such as North Wales, Cumbria, the West Country or the New Forest in Hampshire may become full. Campers should aim to arrive at parks early in the day or, where possible, should book in advance. Some parks have overnight holding areas for visitors who arrive late. This helps to prevent disturbing other campers and caravanners late at night and means that fewer visitors are turned away. Caravans or tents are directed to a pitch the following morning.

Other caravan and camping places

If you enjoy making your own route through Britain's countryside, it may interest you to know that the Forestry Commission operates forest camp parks in Britain's Forest Parks as well as in the New Forest. Some offer reduced charges for youth organisations on organised camping trips, and all enquiries about them should be made, well in advance of your intended stay, to the Forestry Commission.

Pets

Many places accept guests with dogs, but we do advise that you check this when you book, and ask if there are any extra charges or rules about exactly where your pet is allowed. The acceptance of dogs is not always extended to cats and it is strongly advised that cat owners contact the establishment well in advance. Some establishments do not accept pets at all. Pets are welcome where you see this symbol ✟.

Bringing pets to Britain

The quarantine laws have changed in England, and a Pet Travel Scheme (PETS) is currently in operation. Under this scheme pet dogs, cats and ferrets are able to come into Britain from over 50 countries via certain sea, air and rail routes into England as long as they meet the rules.

Dogs, cats and ferrets that have been resident in these countries for more than six months may enter the UK under the scheme, providing they are accompanied by the appropriate documentation. Pets from other countries will still have to undergo six months' quarantine. For dogs, cats and ferrets to be able to enter the UK without quarantine under PETS they will have to meet certain conditions and travel with official documentation.

On 3 July 2004 a new European Regulation on moving pets between European Union (EU) countries and into the EU took effect. The UK will continue to operate the Pet Travel Scheme, but there will be some changes to the scheme in terms of documentation, countries involved and types of animals covered.

For details of the rules, participating countries, routes, operators and further information about the scheme and the new EU Regulation, please contact the PETS Helpline or write to DEFRA (Department for Environment, Food and Rural Affairs), 1a Page Street, London SW1P 4PQ
Tel: + 44 (0) 870 241 1710
Fax: +44 (0) 20 7904 6206
Email: pets.helpline@defra.gsi.gov.uk,
or visit their website at
www.defra.gov.uk/animalh/quarantine/index.htm

Drugs warnings for incoming tourists

The United Kingdom has severe penalties against drug smuggling. Drug traffickers may try to trick travellers. If you are travelling to the United Kingdom avoid any involvement with drugs. Never carry luggage or parcels through customs for someone else.

Legal points

The best source of legal advice for motorists in Britain will be your motoring organisation. What the caravanner or camper needs to know in addition is relatively simple. If you are towing a caravan or camping trailer you must not exceed 96 kph (60 mph) on dual carriageways and motorways, 80 kph (50 mph) on single carriageways, and on a motorway with three lanes each side you must not enter the third (fastest) lane. Do not light cooking stoves in motorway service areas.

In most towns parking is restricted both by regulations and practical difficulties. Cars with trailers may not use meter-controlled parking spaces, and many town car parks are designed with spaces for single vehicles only. However, a number can accommodate long vehicles as well as cars. At night a trailer or a car attached to a trailer, if parked on the roadway, must show two front and two rear lights even where a car by itself would be exempt.

The brakes, lights, weight etc of foreign vehicles do not have to comply with British technical requirements. However, a trailer must not exceed the British size limits – 7 metres (23 feet) long and 2.3 metres (7 feet 6 inches) wide. They must carry your national identification plates. Do not stop overnight on roadside grass verges or lay-bys, because these are considered by law to be part of the road.

Finally, it is important to find out the time you are expected to vacate your pitch on your departure day. You should then leave in good time in the morning, or you may be asked to pay an extra day's charge.

Advice for visitors

VisitBritain welcomes your comments on any aspects of your stay in Britain, whether favourable or otherwise. We hope that you will have no cause to complain, but if you do, the best advice is to take up the complaint immediately with the management of the enterprise concerned: for example the park, shop or transport company. If you cannot obtain satisfaction in this way, please let us know and we ourselves may investigate the matter or suggest what action you might take.

You may bring currency in any denomination and up to any amount into Britain and there is no restriction on the number of travellers' cheques you can change. If you need to change money when the banks are closed you can do so at some large hotels, travel agents and stores or at independent bureaux de change. Be sure to check in advance the rate of exchange and the commission charges. All large shops, department stores and most hotels and restaurants will accept the usual internationally recognised credit cards. If you go shopping in local street markets, patronise only the large, recognised ones, and examine goods carefully.

Always ask the price of goods and services before committing yourself. Beware of pick-pockets in crowded places. If your possessions are stolen or if you are involved in an accident or fire, telephone 999 (no charge will be made) and ask for the police, the ambulance service or the fire brigade.

Every effort has been made by VisitBritain to ensure accuracy in this publication at the time of going to press. The information is given in good faith on the basis of information submitted to VisitBritain by the promoters of the caravan parks listed. However, VisitBritain cannot guarantee the accuracy of this information and accepts no responsibility for any error or misrepresentation. All liability for loss, disappointment, negligence or other damage caused by reliance on the information contained in this guide or in the event of the bankruptcy or liquidation of any company, individual or firm mentioned, or in the event of any company, individual or firm ceasing to trade, is hereby excluded. It is advisable to confirm the information given with the establishments concerned at the time of booking.

All parks in this guide conform to VisitBritain standards. A list of these standards for camping and caravan parks can be found on page 266. All the establishments included in the full colour section of this guide have paid for inclusion.

Mode d'emploi du guide

La plupart des terrains répertoirés ici possèdent des emplacements pour les caravanes de tourisme ou les tentes, ou les deux, et la plupart accueillent volontiers les camping-cars. De nombreux terrains ont aussi des caravanes fixes à louer.

La Norme d'Assurance-Qualité

Lorsque vous cherchez un endroit où faire étape, vous voulez un système d'évaluation de confiance. Le British Holiday Parks Scheme vous indique clairement et en toute simplicité à quoi vous attendre. La qualité reste la préoccupation principale de ce système, en réponse aux exigences des consommateurs.

VisitBritain utilise des etoiles pour indiquer la qualité des terrains et centres de vacances participant à ce système. Des inspecteurs agréés et impartiaux visitent ces terrains chaque année et les récompensent de une à cinq etoiles. Celles-ci indiquent la propreté, l'environnement et la qualité des services fournis.

Les terrains reçoivent également un symbole pour vous permettre d'identifier le type de terrain en un clin d'œil – centre de vacances familial, terrain de camping ou de caravanes, par exemple (si aucun symbole/aucune étoile n'est indiqué pour un terrain/centre particulier, celui-ci n'a pas encore reçu son évaluation à l'heure de mise sous presse).

Le British Graded Holiday Parks Scheme (système d'évaluation des centres de vacances/terrains de camping britanniques) a été conçu par les agences de tourisme d'Angleterre, d'Irlande du Nord,

Signes conventionnels

BH&HPA	British Holiday & Home Parks Association (voir page 56)
NCC	National Caravan Council (voir page 62)
🚐	Caravanes admises (suivi du nombre d'emplacements et des tarifs)
🚍	Camping-cars admis (suivi du nombre d'emplacements et des tarifs). Dans certains cas, les emplacements pour camping-cars sont compris dans le total des emplacements pour caravanes
▲	Tentes admises (suivi du nombre d'emplacements et des tarifs)
🏕	Nombre de caravanes disponibles pour la location (voir la rubrique 'emplacements' ci-dessous)
🛏	Location de bungalows et logements similaires
🅰	Aire de séjour d'une nuit
🔌	Branchements électriques
🚗	Stationnement à côté de l'emplacement
🚿	Douches
🚽	Décharge pour WC chimiques
🚐	Décharge pour véhicules automobiles
⛽	Service de remplacement des bouteilles de gaz butane ou propane
🛒	Magasin d'alimentation fixe/itinérant
✕	Café/restaurant
🍷	Club avec bar
📺	Salle de télévision couleur
☎	Cabine(s) teléphonique(s)
🧺	Laverie
⊙	Prises pour rasoirs électriques
🎱	Salle de jeux
🛝	Aire de jeux pour enfants
🚲	Location de vélos
🏊	Piscine couverte chauffée sur le terrain
🏊	Piscine de plein air sur le terrain
∪	Equitation/randonnée à dos de poney depuis le terrain
🎾	Tennis sur le terrain
🎣	Pêche sur le terrain
⛳	Golf sur le terrain ou à proximité
🐕	Les chiens sont acceptés
🎵	Distractions nocturnes
☀	Il est recommandé de réserver en été

d'Ecosse et du Pays de Galles en collaboration avec The British Holiday & Home Parks Association (l'Association britannique des centres familiaux de vacances et de terrains de camping) (voir page 56) et le National Caravan Council (le bureau national des caravaniers) (voir page 62).

Equipements

Les installations sont indiquées au moyen de symboles illustratifs, dont la légende est donnée ici.

Tarifs

Les tarifs indiqués pour les emplacements sont établis sur la base du tarif minimum et du tarif maximum pour une nuitée et pour 2 personnes accompagnées d'une voiture et d'une tente ou d'une caravane La pratique générale veut qu'en Grande-Bretagne on ne fasse payer que l'emplacement, mais certains terrains de camping pratiquent des tarifs séparés pour la voiture, la tente ou la caravane ainsi que pour chaque personne. Certains terrains appliquent parfois des suppléments pour les auvents des caravanes.

Les tarifs minimum et maximum de location des caravanes sont donnés par semaine. Les prix indiqués nous ont été fournis par les responsables des terrains concernés, et ont pour but de donner une idée des prix en vigueur au moment de la publication de ce guide. Les prix sont libellés en livres (£) et pence (p). La T.V.A. (Taxe à la Valeur Ajoutée) de 17,5% est comprise dans les tarifs indiqués Afin d'éviter tout malentendu, il est fortement conseillé de vérifier les prix auprès du terrain de camping concerné au moment d'effectuer les réservations.

Modalités de réservation

Lorsque vous vous renseignerez sur l'hebergement offert ainsi que sur les tarifs et autres détails, vous devrez énoncer avec clarté et précision quels sont vos besoins, notamment;

- dates d'arrivée et de départ, avec dates de remplacement acceptables le cas échéant.
- type d'hebergement requis.
- autres besoins particuliers à signaler à la direction.

Les malentendus sont très courants par téléphone, aussi vous est-il recommandé de confirmer par écrit toutes vos réservations si les délais vous le permettent. N'oubliez pas de mentionner votre nom et votre adresse et prenez soin de joindre une enveloppe timbrée à votre adresse ou un coupon-réponse international (si vous écrivez depuis l'étranger) pour la réponse.

Arrhes et paiements anticipés

Les terrains de camping, de caravaning, ou avec bungalows, ainsi que les centres de vacances exigent souvent le versement intégral du paiement à l'avance. Celui-ci peut s'effectuer en deux fois: vous devez payer des arrhes lors de la réservation et vous acquitter du solde deux semaines avant le début de la période de location, par exemple.

Annulations

Lorsque vous acceptez l'hébergement qui vous est offert par écrit ou par téléphone, bous êtes lié par contrat avec le propriétaire de l'établissement. Cela signifie que si vous annulez une réservation, si vous ne venez pas prendre possession du logement ou si vous partez plus tôt que prévu (quelle qu'en soit la raison), le propriétaire est en droit d'exiger un dédommagement s'il ne peut pas relouer pour la durée totale ou une grande partie de la location. Si vous avez versé des arrhes, vous ne serez probablement pas remboursé, et l'on peut vous demander de payer une somme supplémentaire.

Vous avez donc intérêt à aviser immédiatement la direction si vous devez changer vos projets de voyage, annuler une réservation ou partir plus tôt que prévu.

Point de branchement électrique

La plupart des terrains ont à présent des points de branchement électrique pour les caravanes et les tentes. Le voltage est en général de 240v 50Hz en courant alternatif, bien qu'on puisse encore trouver des courants variant entre 200v et 250v. Il se peut qu'un adaptateur soit nécessaire pour le branchement. En général, les terrains font payer un supplément pour ce service, et il est conseillé de se renseigner sur les tarifs en vigueur au moment de la réservation.

Comment choisir un terrain

Les terrains sont répertoriés dans ce guide en plusieurs sections : Angleterre (par région), Écosse et Pays de Galles. Dans chaque section, ils sont répertoriés par ordre alphabétique selon le nom de la ville la plus proche. L'Index des Villes en page 298 ainsi que les cartes en couleur au début du guide vous indiquent toues les villes et villages pour lesquels un terrain apparaît dans ce guide. Utilisez-les pour trouver un terrain rapidement et très facilement. Si vous savez quel est le terrain où vous voulez séjourner, vous le trouverez immédiatement en consultant l'index des terrains en page 294.

Si le lieu où vous désirez séjourner figure dans l'index des villes, reportez-vous au numéro de page indiqué pour voir quels terrains y sont disponibles. Le nom de la ville est indiqué en noir sur les cartes au début du guide à l'endroit indiqué par la référence carte donnée dans chaque entrée. Consultez également les cartes en couleur pour trouver des lieux proches pour lesquels des terrains sont également répertoriés dans ce guide.

Si le lieu où vous désirez séjourner ne figure pas dans l'index des villes (ou bien si vous avez seulement une idée générale du lieu dans lequel vous désirez séjourner), utilisez les cartes en couleur. Certaines régions apparaissent sur plus d'une carte mais les noms de villes (imprimés en noir sur les cartes) sont indiqués une fois seulement.

Toutes les localités dans lesquelles un terrain est répertorié dans le guide figurent sur la carte. Pour avoir la position précise du terrain, veuillez consultez la rubrique qui lui est consacrée. Si vous avez des difficultés pour trouver un terrain donné, nous vous suggérons de demander votre chemin dans le voisinage.

 Pour aider les visiteurs à trouver leur terrain de camping, la Grande-Bretagne emploie les panneaux de signalisation internationaux ci-contre. Tous les terrains ne sont pas encore signalés de cette manière et les panneaux n'affichent pas le nom de terrains particuliers. Ces panneaux indiquent en revanche si le terrain peut accueillir des tentes, des caravanes ou les deux. L'International Camping Carnet est rarement reconnu en Grande-Bretagne sauf dans les terrains gérés par les grands clubs.

Sites à Londres

Londres attire de nombreux visiteurs, aussi les terrains de Camping-caravaning du Grand Londres ont-ils tendance à se remplir tres rapidement. Des terrains sont également disponibles dans la plupart des ports d'entrée du pays: bon nombre d'entre eux sont répertoriés dans ce guide et indiqués sur les cartes au début du guide.

Services-conseils disponibles

Les Centres d'Information Touristique de toute la Grande-Bretagne (voir dernières pages) sont en mesure de donner aux campeurs et au caravaniers des renseignements sur les terrains de leur région.

Certains Centres d'Information Touristique possèdent des services-conseils pour le camping-caravaning qui vous donneront des détails sur les terrains disponibles et pourront souvent vous aider à effectuer votre réservation.

Précautions à prendre en haute saison

Lors des mois d'été, de juin à septembre, les terrains situés dans des régions très fréquentées comme le Nord Gallois, le Cumbria, le Sud-Ouest de l'Angleterre ou la New Forest, dans le Hampshire, risquent d'être complets. Les campeurs doivent s'efforcer d'arriver sur les terrains de bonne heure dans la journée ou, si c'est possible, de réserver à l'avance. Certains terrains ont des aires de séjour temporaire ou les visiteurs arrivant tard le soir peuvent passer la nuit. Cela permet de ne pas déranger les autres campeurs et caravaniers pendant la nuit et d'accepter un plus grand nombre de vacanciers.

Les caravanes et les tentes se voient attribuer un emplacement le lendemain matin.

Autres terrains de camping-caravaning

Si vous souhaitez suivre votre propre itinéraire dans la campagne britannique, il peut vous être utile de savoir que la Forestry Commission gère des terrains de camping en forêt dans les sept Parcs forestiers de Grande-Bretagne ainsi que dans la New Forest. Certains terrains offrent des tarifs réduits pour les organisations de jeunesse effectuant des séjours de groupes: il vous est conseillé de vous renseigner à ce sujet auprès de la Forestry Commission très à l'avance.

Les animaux

De nombreux terrains acceptent les chiens, mais nous vous conseillons de vérifier si c'est bien le cas lorsque vous réservez. Demandez également s'il y a des frais supplémentaires et si votre chien sera exclu de certaines zones. Lorsque les chiens sont acceptés, les chats ne le sont pas automatiquement et nous conseillons vivement aux propriétaires de chats de contacter l'établissement longtemps à l'avance. Certains terrains n'acceptent aucun animal familier. Les chiens sont acceptés lorsque vous voyez ce symbole 🐾.

Amener vos animaux familiers en Grande-Bretagne

Les lois sur la quarantaine ont changé en Angleterre. Un système appelé Pet Travel Scheme (PETS) est actuellement utilisé. Ce système autorise les chiens, les chats et les furets domestiques de plus de 50 pays d'entrer en Angleterre par certaines voies maritimes, aériennes et ferroviaires, du moment qu'ils respectent certaines règles.

Les chiens, les chats et les furets ayant résidé dans ces pays pendant plus de six mois peuvent entrer au Royaume-Uni du moment qu'ils ont certains documents. Les animaux d'autres pays doivent passer six mois en quarantaine.

Pour que les chiens, les chats et les furets puissent entrer au Royaume-Uni sans quarantaine, le système PETS exige qu'ils respectent certaines conditions et qu'ils voyagent avec des documents officiels.

Le 3 juillet 2004, une nouvelle réglementation européenne sur le mouvement des animaux domestiques entre les différents pays de l'Union Européenne et depuis les autres pays est entrée en vigueur. Le Royaume-Uni continuera à utiliser le Pet Travel Scheme, mais le système sera modifié au niveau de la documentation demandé, des pays participants et des animaux concernés.

Pour avoir la liste des pays participant à ce programme, ainsi que la liste des points d'entrée et des opérateurs, ou pour tout complément d'information sur le projet pilote PETS et la nouvelle réglementation européenne veuillez contacter le téléphone rouge PETS, DEFRA (Department for Environment, Food and Rural Affairs), 1a Page Street, London SW1P 4PQ
Tel: +44 (0) 870 241 1710
Fax: +44 (0) 20 7904 6206
Email: pets.helpline@defra.gsi.gov.uk,
ou consultez le site web
www.defra.gov.uk/animalh/quarantine/index/htm

Réglementation contre la drogue

Le Royaume-Uni applique des sanctions sévères contre la contrebande de la drogue. Les trafiquants de drogue peuvent essayer de duper les voyageurs. Si vous voyagez à destination du Royaume-Uni, ne soyez pas mêlé au trafic de drogue. Ne passez jamais de bagages ou de colis pour autrui par les douanes.

Right Shaftesbury, Dorset; try a new or favourite pastime

Aspects juridiques

La meilleure source de renseignements juridiques pour les automobilistes voyageant en Grande-Bretagne reste l'association des automobilistes de leur pays d'origine. Les détails supplémentaires que doivent connaître le campeur ou le caravanier sont relativement simples.

Si vous tractez une caravane ou une remorque de camping, vous ne devez pas dépasser 96 km/h sur les voies express ou sur les autoroutes, 80 km/h sur les routes à deux voies; en outre, sur les autoroutes ayant trois voies dans chaque direction, vous ne devez pas rouler sur la troisième voie (la plus rapide). N'allumez pas de réchauds à gaz sur les aires de service des autoroutes.

Dans la plupart des villes, le stationnement est limité à la fois par la réglementation et par le manque de place. Les voitures dotées de remorques ne peuvent pas occuper les espaces de stationnement limité à parcmètres et de nombreux parcs de stationnement de ville ne sont conçus que pour accueillir des véhicules indépendants. Toutefois, certains parcs peuvent accueillir des véhicules plus longs en plus des voitures.

La nuit, les remorques ou les voitures dotées de remorques, lorsqu'elles sont en stationnement au bord de la route, doivent avoir les deux feux avant et les deux feux arrière allumés même dans le cas où cela n'est pas jugé nécessaire pour une voiture seule.

Les freins, l'éclairage, le poids, etc. des véhicules étrangers n'ont pas à respecter les prescriptions techniques britanniques. Toutefois, une remorque ne doit pas dépasser les limites dimensionnelles britanniques: 7m de long et 2,3m de large. Elle doit être munie de votre plaque d'immatriculation nationale. Vous ne devez pas vous arrêter pour la nuit sur les accotements ou sur les petites aires de stationnement des bas-côtés car la loi stipule que ces emplacements font partie de la route.

Enfin, il est important de vous renseigner sur l'heure à laquelle il vous est demandé de libérer votre emplacement le jour du départ. Vous devrez prévoir de partir assez tôt, sans quoi vous risquez d'avoir à payer une journée de location supplémentaire.

Conseils aux visiteurs

VisitBritain vous invite à formuler vos observations sur tout aspect de votre séjour en Grande-Bretagne, qu'elles soient favorables ou non. Nous espérons que vous n'aurez pas lieu de vous plaindre, mais dans l'affirmative, il vous est conseillé de faire part de votre mécontentement immédiatement auprès de la direction de l'établissement concerné comme par exemple: camping, magasin ou société de transport. Si vous ne pouvez pas obtenir satisfaction de cette manière, veuillez nous le faire savoir et nous examinerons la question nous-mêmes ou nous vous suggèrerons une procédure éventuelle à suivre.

Vous pouvez emporter en Grande-Bretagne les devises de votre choix en quantité illimitée et aucune restriction ne s'applique a la quantité de chèques de voyage changés. Si vous avez besoin de devises britanniques pendant les heures de fermeture des banques, vous pouvez vous les procurer dans certains grands hôtels, agences de voyages, grands magasins ou dans les bureaux de change indépendants. Ne manquez pas de vérifier à l'avance le taux de change et la commission appliqués.

Tous les grands magasins et boutiques et la plupart des hôtels et restaurants accepteront les cartes de crédit usuelles reconnues dans le monde entier. Si vous aimez faire vos achats au marché, limitez-vous aux grands marchés de rue officiels et examinez toujours les articles soigneusement.Demandez toujours le prix des marchandises avant de vous engager. Prenez garde aux pickpockets en cas d'affluence. Si l'on vous vole des objets personnels ou si vous vous trouvez sur le lieu d'un incendie ou d'un accident, composez le 999 (numéro gratuit) et demandez la police, les services d'ambulance ou les pompiers.

VisitBritain a pris toutes les dispositions nécessaires pour assurer l'exactitude des Informations contenues dans la présente publication au moment de mettre sous presse.

Ces Informations sont fournies en toute bonne foi sur la base des renseignements donnés à VisitBritain par les exploitants des terrains de camping répertoriés. Toutefois, VisitBritain ne peut garantir l'exactitude de ces renseignements et décline toute responsabllité en cas d'erreur ou de déformation des faits. Toute responsabilité est également déclinée pour toutes pertes, déceptions, négligences ou autres dommages que pourrait subir quiconque se fie aux renseignements contenus dans le présent guide, pour les cas de faillite ou de liquidation de toute personne morale ou physique mentionnée, et pour les cas de cessation d'activités de toute personne morale ou physique. Il est conseillé de se faire confirmer les renseignements fournis par les établissements concernés lors de la réservation.

Tous les terrains inclus dans ce guide respectent les normes VisitBritain. On trouvera à la page 266 une liste de ces normes relatives aux terrains de camping-caravaning.

Tous les établissements répertoriés dans la section eu couleurs figurent dans le présent guide à titre payant.

Above savouring the views across the Malvern Hills

Benutzung dieses Reiseführers

Die meisten der hier aufgeführten Parks verfügen über Stellplätze für Wohnwagen bzw. Zelte oder beides und die meisten nehmen auch Wohnmobile auf. Des Weiteren vermieten viele Parks auch Ferienwohnwagen.

Das Qualitätssicherungssystem

Bei der Suche nach einer geeigneten Unterkunft braucht man ein verlässliches Einstufungssystem. Das 'British Graded Holiday Parks Scheme' (britisches Beurteilungssystem für Ferienparks) vermittelt Ihnen in leicht verständlicher Form einen klaren Eindruck von dem, was Sie erwarten können. Das System spiegelt die Kundenerwartungen und beurteilt in erster Linie die Qualität.

VisitBritain kennzeichnet die Qualitätsstufe der an diesem Programm teilnehmenden Parks durch die Vergabe von Sternen. Die betreffenden Parks werden jährlich von sachlich geschulten, unparteiischen Prüfern inspiziert und dann mittels einer Skala von einem bis fünf Sterne eingestuft. Die Anzahl der vergebenen Sterne hängt von der Sauberkeit, dem Ambiente sowie der Qualität der vorhandenen Einrichtungen und gebotenen Dienstleistungen ab.

Außerdem werden die einzelnen Parks nach Typ gekennzeichnet, so dass man auf einen Blick erkennt, um was für eine Art von Gelände es sich handelt - z.B. Ferienpark, Touringpark oder Campingpark. (Weist der Park keine Einstufung oder Kennzeichnung auf, so bedeutet das, dass die Beurteilung zum Zeitpunkt der Drucklegung noch nicht stattgefunden hat.)

Zeichenerklärung

BH&HPA	British Holiday & Home Parks Association (siehe Seite 56)
NCC	National Caravan Council (siehe Seite 62)
	Wohnwagen zugelassen (mit Anzahl der Stellplätze und Preisen)
	Wohnmobile zugelassen (mit Anzahl der Stellplätze und Preisen)
	Zelte zugelassen (mit Anzahl der Stellplätze und Preisen)
	Anzahl der vermietbaren Ferienwohnwagen (mit Anzahl und Preisen)
	Bungalows, Chalets, Wohnkabinen zum Vermieten
	Auffangstelle für spät im Park eintreffende Gäste
	Stromanschluß
	Parkmöglichkeit neben dem Stellplatz
	Duschen
	Chemische Toiletten
	Sanitäre Entsorgungsstelle
	Umtauschstelle für Butan- /oder Propangaszylinder
	Lebensmittelgeschäft/Wagen für
	Lebensmittelverkauf
	Restaurant
	Clubhaus mit Bar
	Aufenthaltsraum mit Farbfernseher
	Öffentliche Fernsprecher
	Wäscherei
	Anschlüsse für Elektrorasierer
	Hallenspiele
	Kinderspielplatz
	Fahrradverleih
	Hallenbad
	Freibad
	Reiten/Ponyreiten in der Nähe
	Tennis
	Angeln
	Golf im Park oder in der Nähe
	Haustiere willkommen
	Abendunterhaltung
	Reservierung im Voraus im Sommer ratsam

Das 'British Graded Holiday Parks Scheme' entstand in partnerschaftlicher Zusammenarbeit der nationalen Fremdenverkehrsstellen für England, Nordirland, Schottland und Wales, in Verbindung mit der British Holiday & Home Parks Association (siehe Seite 56) und dem National Caravan Council (siehe Seite 62).

Einrichtungen

Die jeweiligen Einrichtungen sind durch Symbole bezeichnet, deren Bedeutung Sie der Zeichenerklärung auf einen Blick entnehmen können.

Preise

Die angegebenen Preise für Stellplätze beruhen auf den Mindest- bzw. Höchstgebühren pro Nacht für zwei Personen, ein Auto und einen Wohnwagen bzw. ein Zelt. In Großbritannien ist es im Allgemeinen üblich, einfach eine Gebühr für die Nutzung des Stellplatzes zu berechnen, allerdings erheben einige Parks separate Gebühren für das Auto, den Wohnwagen bzw. das Zelt und pro Person. Manche Parks verlangen unter Umständen eine Zusatzgebühr für am Wohnwagen angebrachte Sonnenzelte. Die Mindest- und Höchstpreise für Ferienwohnwagen sind pro Woche angegeben. Die Preise wurden jeweils von der betreffenden Parkleitung zur Verfügung gestellt und bilden lediglich eine Richtschnur für die tatsächlich berechneten Preise während der Gültigkeit der vorliegenden Veröffentlichung. Die Preise sind in Pfund Sterling (£) und Pence (p) angegeben. Die Mehrwertsteuer (VAT) zum Satz von 17,5% ist im Preis enthalten. Um etwaigen Missverständnissen vorzubeugen, ist es ratsam, sich bei der Reservierung nach den genauen Preisen zu erkundigen.

Reservierungen

Bei Anfragen über mögliche Unterkünfte, Preise und weitere Angaben sollten Sie Ihre Wünsche klar und genau angeben – zum Beispiel:

- Ankunfts- und Abreisetermin, falls möglich mit akzeptablen Ausweichterminen
- gewünschte Unterkunft
- Teilen Sie der Parkleitung mit, falls Sie besondere Anforderungen haben.

Bei Telefongesprächen kommt es leicht zu Missverständnissen. Deshalb empfehlen wir Ihnen, Ihre Reservierung schriftlich zu bestätigen, falls dies zeitlich möglich ist. Denken Sie bitte daran, Ihren Namen und Ihre Anschrift anzugeben und einen adressierten Freiumschlag, bei Anfragen aus dem Ausland einen internationalen Antwortschein, beizulegen

Anzahlungen und Vorauszahlungen

Bei Wohnwagen-, Camping-, Chaletparks und Ferienzentren ist der gesamte Betrag häufig im Voraus zu entrichten. Die Zahlung kann in zwei Raten erfolgen: bei der Reservierung wird eine Anzahlung fällig und der Restbetrag ist zwei Wochen vor Beginn des Aufenthalts zu leisten.

Stornierungen

Wenn Sie ein Unterkunftsangebot schriftlich oder telefonisch akzeptieren, gehen Sie mit dem Besitzer der betreffenden Unterkunft einen rechtlich bindenden Vertrag ein. Das hat zur Folge, dass der Besitzer, wenn Sie eine Reservierung stornieren, nicht wahrnehmen oder

Left hire a rowing boat on the river Isis, Oxfordshire **Right** Leeds Castle, Maidstone

die Unterkunft (gleichgültig aus welchen Gründen) vorzeitig räumen, unter Umständen berechtigt ist, Schadensersatz zu verlangen, sofern er nicht in der Lage ist, die Unterkunft für den ganzen bzw. einen Teil des gebuchten Zeitraums weiterzuvermieten. Falls eine Anzahlung geleistet wurde, wird sie wahrscheinlich hierfür angerechnet und unter Umständen erfolgt eine weitere Zahlungsforderung.

Es ist daher in Ihrem Interesse, die Geschäftsleitung umgehend zu benachrichtigen, wenn Sie Ihre Reisepläne ändern, eine Reservierung stornieren oder die Unterkunft vorzeitig verlassen möchten.

Anschluss ans Stromnetz
Die meisten Parks verfügen inzwischen über Stromanschlussstellen für Wohnwagen und Zelte. Es handelt sich dabei im Allgemeinen um Wechselstrom mit einer Spannung von 240 Volt, 50 Schwingungen, allerdings können Spannungsschwankungen zwischen 200 V und 250 V auftreten. Unter Umständen benötigen Sie einen Adapter. Die Parks erheben normalerweise eine Zusatzgebühr für diesen

Service und es ist ratsam, sich bei der Reservierung nach deren Höhe zu erkundigen.

So finden Sie Ihren Park

In der vorliegenden Broschüre sind die Parks in England nach Region, danach die Parks in Schottland und Wales aufgeführt. Sie sind in alphabetischer Reihenfolge unter dem Namen der Ortschaft, in der oder in deren Nähe sie liegen, verzeichnet. Im Ortsverzeichnis auf Seite 298 und auf den farbigen Lagekarten am Anfang dieser Veröffentlichung sind alle Städte, Ortschaften und Dörfer aufgeführt, die in dieser Broschüre mit einem Park vertreten sind. Anhand des Verzeichnisses und der Karten finden Sie schnell und mühelos eine geeignete Unterkunft. Wenn Sie bereits wissen, in welchem Park Sie übernachten möchten, schlagen Sie im Verzeichnis der Parks auf Seite 294 nach.

Wenn die Ortschaft, in der Sie übernachten möchten, im Ortsverzeichnis aufgeführt ist, schlagen Sie auf der angegebenen Seite nach, wo die dort vorhandenen Parks verzeichnet sind. Die Namen der Ortschaften sind gemäß des beim betreffenden Eintrag genannten Planquadrats auf den Karten am Anfang dieses Reiseführers schwarz gedruckt. Sehen Sie auch auf den farbigen Karten nach, um Ortschaften in der Nähe zu finden, wo sich ebenfalls Parks befinden, die in dieser Veröffentlichung aufgeführt sind.

Falls die Ortschaft, in der Sie übernachten möchten, nicht im Ortsverzeichnis aufgeführt ist oder Sie nur eine ungefähre Vorstellung von der Gegend haben, in der Sie übernachten möchten, so benutzen Sie die farbigen Lagekarten.

Auf den Karten sind alle Orte verzeichnet, die in der vorliegenden Veröffentlichung mit einem Park vertreten sind. Die genaue Lage ist jeweils in den betreffenden Einträgen beschrieben. Sollten Sie Schwierigkeiten haben, einen bestimmten Park zu finden, so schlagen wir vor, dass Sie sich vor Ort eine genaue Wegbeschreibung geben lassen.

 Die hier abgebildeten internationalen Hinweisschilder, die in Großbritannien vielfach zu finden sind, erleichtern Ihnen das Auffinden eines Parks. Allerdings sind sie noch nicht für alle Camping-, Wohnwagen- bzw. Ferienparks vorhanden und geben nicht den Namen des Parks an, doch zeigen sie, ob es sich um einen Park für Wohnwagen, Zelte oder beides handelt. Der internationale Campingausweis ist in Großbritannien nur in Parks gültig, die von größeren Klubs verwaltet werden.

Plätze in London
Da London ein großer Anziehungspunkt für Besucher ist, sind die Camping- und Wohnwagenparks im Umkreis der britischen Hauptstadt schnell ausgebucht, daher ist eine frühzeitige Reservierung ratsam. Auch in den meisten Einreisehäfen gibt es entsprechende

Parks, von denen viele in dieser Veröffentlichung aufgeführt und auf den Karten am Anfang verzeichnet sind.

Informationsdienste

Die Touristeninformationszentren in allen Teilen Großbritanniens (auf den letzten Seiten aufgeführt) geben Ihnen gerne Auskunft über die Camping- und Wohnwagenparks in ihrem Gebiet.

Einige Touristeninformationszentren haben einen Wohnwagen- und Camping-Beratungsdienst, der über freie Plätze Auskunft geben und häufig auch Reservierungen vornehmen kann.

Vermeiden von Problemen in der Hochsaison

In den Sommermonaten Juni bis September sind die Camping- und Wohnwagenparks in den beliebten Urlaubsgebieten wie etwa Nordwales, Cumbria, im West Country oder im New Forest in Hampshire schnell ausgebucht. Treffen Sie daher frühzeitig am Tag am Park ein oder buchen Sie nach Möglichkeit im Voraus. Manche Parks verfügen über Auffangstellen für spät eintreffende Gäste. Auf diese Weise werden die anderen Gäste zu fortgeschrittener Stunde nicht gestört und es werden weniger Besucher abgewiesen. Es wird dann am nächsten Morgen ein Stellplatz zugewiesen.

Sonstige Wohnwagen- und Campingplätze

Wenn Sie Ihre Reiseroute durch die britische Landschaft lieber auf eigene Faust planen, dürften Sie an den Campingplätzen in Waldgebieten interessiert sein, die von der Forestry Commission verwaltet werden. Hierzu gehören sieben Forest Parks und der New Forest. In einigen erhalten Jugendorganisationen beim Campingurlaub Preisermäßigungen. Alle diesbezüglichen Anfragen sind frühzeitig im Voraus an die Forest Commission zu richten.

Haustiere

In vielen Unterkünften werden Gäste mit Hunden aufgenommen, allerdings raten wir Ihnen, sich bei der Reservierung danach zu erkundigen. Außerdem sollten Sie fragen, ob für den Hund eine zusätzliche Gebühr berechnet wird, und ob es Regeln gibt, wo genau Ihr Haustier sich aufhalten darf. Der Umstand, dass Hunde aufgenommen werden, bedeutet nicht unbedingt, dass das Gleiche auch für Katzen gilt und wir raten Katzenbesitzern dringend, sich diesbezüglich frühzeitig mit der betreffenden Unterkunft zu verständigen. Manche Unterkünfte lassen überhaupt keine Haustiere zu. Wo Sie das Zeichen 🐕 sehen, sind Haustiere willkommen.

Das Mitbringen von Haustieren nach Großbritannien

Die Quarantänevorschriften in England wurden geändert und momentan ist das so genannte Pet Travel Scheme (PETS) in Kraft. Im Rahmen dieser Aktion können Hunde, Katzen und Frettchen, die als Haustiere gehalten werden, aus mehr als 50 Ländern auf dem See-, Luft- und Schienenweg nach Großbritannien mitgebracht werden, vorausgesetzt, dass sie den geltenden Bestimmungen gerecht werden.

Hunde, Katzen und Frettchen, die in diesen Ländern seit über sechs Monaten gehalten werden, können im Rahmen dieser Aktion nach Großbritannien mitgebracht werden, wenn bei der Einreise die entsprechenden Unterlagen vorhanden sind. Haustiere aus anderen Ländern müssen nach wie vor sechs Monate in Quarantäne gegeben werden.

Hunde, Katzen und Frettchen müssen bestimmte Bedingungen erfüllen und bei der Einreise müssen die amtlich erforderlichen Unterlagen vorliegen, damit sie im Rahmen der Aktion PETS ohne Quarantäneauflagen nach Großbritannien mitgebracht werden dürfen.

Right Crowhurst Park, Battle; Whitecliff Bay Holiday Park, Bembridge

Am 3. Juli 2004 trat eine neue Europäische Bestimmung bezüglich des Transports von Haustieren zwischen Ländern der Europäischen Union (EU) und der Einführung von Haustieren in die EU in Kraft. In Großbritannien läuft das Pet Travel Scheme weiter, allerdings sind in Bezug auf die erforderlichen Unterlagen, die betroffenen Länder und die zulässigen Tiere einige Änderungen zu erwarten.

Für weitere Auskünfte über die an dieser Aktion teilnehmenden Länder, die Strecken, Reiseunternehmer sowie ausführlichere Informationen über die Aktion PETS und die neuen EU-Bestimmungen wenden Sie sich bitte an die PETS Helpline, DEFRA (Department for Environment, Food and Rural Affairs), 1a Page Street, London SW1P 4PQ
Tel: +44 (0) 870 241 1710
Fax: +44 (0) 20 7904 6206
E-Mail: pets.helpline@defra.gsi.gov.uk oder schauen Sie auf der Website vorbei:
www.defra.gov.uk/animalh/quarantine/index/htm

Drogenwarnung für einreisende Touristen

Großbritannien geht gegen Rauschgiftschmuggel sehr scharf vor. Drogenhändler versuchen häufig, unschuldige Reisende in ihre Geschäfte zu verwickeln. Seien Sie daher bei der Reise nach Großbritannien sehr auf der Hut und tragen Sie niemals Gepäckstücke für andere Personen durch die Zollkontrolle.

Rechtliches

Wenden Sie sich vor dem Antritt Ihrer Reise am besten an Ihren Automobilverband, der Ihnen gerne Auskunft über alle rechtlichen Fragen in Bezug auf Reisen in Großbritannien gibt. Wenn Sie mit dem Wohnwagen oder Zelt unterwegs sind, sollten Sie zusätzlich ein paar einfache Regeln beachten.

Wenn Sie mit einem Wohnwagen oder einem Camping-Anhänger unterwegs sind, dürfen Sie auf vierspurigen Fernstraßen und Autobahnen höchstens 96 km/h fahren. Auf zweispurigen Fernstraßen gilt das Tempolimit 80 km/h. Auf sechsspurigen Autobahnen dürfen Sie niemals – auch nicht zum Überholen – in der dritten (schnellsten) Spur fahren. Auf den Raststätten an der Autobahn dürfen keine Kochöfen angezün det werden.

In den meisten Städten ist das Parken durch gesetzliche Bestimmungen oder praktische Probleme stark eingeschränkt. Autos mit Anhängern dürfen nicht an Parkuhren parken. Ferner nehmen die meisten Parkplätze nur Wagen ohne Anhänger auf. Allerdings sind einige Parkplätze vorhanden, die überlange Fahrzeuge und Fahrzeuge mit Anhängern zulassen.

Nachts müssen auf der Straße geparkte Anhänger bzw. Autos mit Anhänger vorn und hinten jeweils zwei Lampen aufweisen. Dies gilt auch an Stellen, wo ein Auto ohne Anhänger davon ausgenommen wäre.

Die britischen Vorschriften über Bremsen, Beleuchtung, zulässiges Gewicht und sonstige technische Punkte gelten nicht für ausländische Fahrzeuge. Ein Anhänger muss jedoch die britischen Vorschriften erfüllen und darf nicht länger als 7 m und nicht breiter als 2,30 m sein. Anhänger müssen mit den amtlichen Zulassungsschildern Ihres Heimatlandes versehen sein. Übernachten Sie nicht auf dem Grasrand einer Straße oder in einer Ausweichbucht, weil diese Stellen als zur Straße gehörig angesehen werden.

Abschließend sei betont, wie wichtig es ist, dass Sie sich erkundigen, wann Sie den Stellplatz in einem Camping- oder Wohnwagenpark am Abreisetag räumen müssen. Reisen Sie morgens rechtzeitig ab, sonst müssen Sie vielleicht die Gebühr für einen weiteren Tag bezahlen.

Ratschläge für Besucher

VisitBritain würde sich über Ihren Kommentar hinsichtlich aller Gesichtspunkte Ihres Aufenthalts in Großbritannien freuen, ganz gleich, ob er positiv oder negativ ausfällt. Wir hoffen, dass Sie keinen Grund zur Beanstandung haben, falls Sie aber doch Anlass zu Beschwerden haben sollten, ist es am besten, sich sofort an die Leitung des entsprechenden Unternehmens zu wenden, z. B. des Parks, des Geschäfts oder der Verkehrsgesellschaft. Wenn Sie mit der Behandlung, die Sie dort erfahren, nicht zufrieden sind, so geben Sie uns bitte Bescheid. Wir werden dann der Angelegenheit entweder selbst nachgehen oder Sie darüber beraten, welche Maßnahmen Sie ergreifen können.

Sie können Währungen jeder Art in beliebiger Höhe nach Großbritannien mitbringen. Reiseschecks werden in beliebiger Anzahl eingelöst. Wenn Ihnen das Bargeld ausgeht, wenn die Banken geschlossen sind, so können Sie Geld in einigen großen Hotels, Reisebüros, Kaufhäusern und in unabhängigen Wechselstuben umtauschen. Prüfen Sie vor dem Geldumtausch, welcher Wechselkurs Anwendung findet und wie hoch die Bearbeitungsgebühr ist. Alle größeren Geschäfte, Kaufhäuser und die meisten Hotels

und Restaurants akzeptieren international gängige Kreditkarten als Zahlungsmittel. Wenn Sie auf örtlichen Straßenmärkten einkaufen, so halten Sie sich an die großen, bekannten Märkte und prüfen Sie die Waren sorgfältig.

Erkundigen Sie sich vor dem Kauf stets nach dem Preis der Waren oder Dienstleistungen. Nehmen Sie sich in Menschenmengen vor Taschendieben in Acht Wenn Sie Opfer eines Diebstahls oder Zeuge eines Unfalls oder Brands werden, wählen Sie den Notruf unter der Nummer 999 (der Anruf ist kostenlos) und verlangen Sie die Polizei (police), einen Krankenwagen (ambulance) oder die Feuerwehr (fire brigade).

VisitBritain hat sich alle erdenkliche Mühe gegeben, die Richtigkeit der in der vorliegenden Veröffentlichung gemachten Angaben zum Zeitpunkt der Drucklegung zu gewährleisten. Die Informationen werden in gutem Glauben erteilt und beruhen auf den Angaben, die VisitBritain von den aufgeführten Wohnwagenparks erteilt wurden. VisitBritain gibt jedoch keine Garantie für die Genauigkeit der Angaben und übernehmen keinerlei Verantwortung für Fehler oder fälschliche Darstellungen. Hiermit ausgeschlossen wird die Haftung für Verluste, nicht erfüllte Erwartungen, Fahrlässigkeit oder andere Schäden, die sich daraus ergeben, dass sich Leser auf die Informationen in der vorliegenden Veröffentlichung verlassen, oder die sich daraus ergeben, dass in der Veröffentlichung genannte Unternehmen, Firmen oder Einzelpersonen Konkurs anmelden, in Liquidation gehen oder ihre Geschäftätigkeit einstellen. Es wird empfohlen, sich die in der vorliegenden Veröffentlichung gemachten Angaben bei der Reservierung von den betreffenden Stellen bestätigen zu lassen. Alle in diesem Reiseführer genannten Parks entsprechen den Standards von VisitBritain. Eine Liste der Standardbedingungen für Camping- und Wohnwagenparks befindet sich auf Seite 266.

Sämtliche im farbigen Teil dieser Veröffentlichung genannten Stellen haben für die Aufnahme eine Gebühr entrichtet.

Hoe u deze gids moet gebruiken

Op de meeste vermelde terreinen zijn trekcaravans, tenten of kampeerauto's of alledrie welkom. Bij de meeste zijn vakantiecaravans te huur.

Programma van kwaliteitsgarantie

Als u een verblijfsplaats zoekt, dan heeft u een classificatiesysteem nodig dat u kunt vertrouwen. De British Graded Holiday Parks Scheme geeft u een duidelijk overzicht van wat u kunt verwachten in een gemakkelijk te begrijpen vorm. Het systeem houdt kwaliteit hoog in het vaandel en weerspiegelt de verwachtingen van de consument.

VisitBritain gebruikt sterren om de kwaliteitsclassificatie van de deelnemende parken weer te geven. De parken worden jaarlijks door getrainde, onafhankelijke controleurs bezocht, die 1 tot 5 sterren toekennen. Deze zijn gebaseerd op hygiëne, omgeving en kwaliteit van de voorzieningen en diensten, die er aanwezig zijn.

De parken hebben ook een 'aanwijzer' zodat u het type standplaats in één oogopslag kunt herkennen b.v. een vakantie park, een tourcaravan park en een camping. (Als er geen gradatie of aanwijzer is gegeven dan is men in afwachting van een classifcatie ten tijde van het drukken van deze brochure.)

Verklaring van de tekens

BH&HPA	British Holiday & Home Parks Association (zie blz 56)
NCC	National Caravan Council (zie blz 62)
	caravans toegestaan (met aantal staanplaatsen en tarieven)
	kampeerauto's toegestaan (met aantal staanplaatsen en tarieven) In sommige gevallen is het aantal plekjes voor kampeerauto's opgenomen in het totaal voor toercaravans
	tenten toegestaan (met aantal plekjes en tarieven)
	aantal vakantiecaravans te huur (Zie 'Vakantiecaravans')
	bungalows/chalets/huisjes te huur
	terrein voor late aankomers op het park
	elektrische aansluiting
	parkeerruimte naast plaats
	douches
	lozing van chemische toiletten mogelijk
	lozing chemische toiletten van motorvoertuigen
	omwisseling van butaan- en propaangasflessen
	levensmiddelenwinkel/rijdende winkel
	café/restaurant
	clubhuis met bar
	zitkamer met kleurentelevisie
	openbare telefoons
	wasserette of terrein aanwezig
	stopcontacten voor scheerapparaten
	recreatiekamer
	kinderspeeltuin
	fietsenverhuur
	verwarmd binnenbad op park
	openluchtbad op park
	manège (paard/pony) op terrein
	tennis op terrein
	vissen op terrein
	golf op of bij park
	huisdieren welkom
	amusement 's avonds
	in de zomer is reserveren aanbevolen

The British Graded Holiday Parks Scheme is gezamenlijk ontworpen door de nationale toeristencentra van Engeland, Noord-Ierland, Schotland en Wales en de British Holiday & Home Parks Association (zie pagina 56) en de National Caravan Council (zie pagina 62).

Faciliteiten

De faciliteiten worden aangeduid d.m.v. de hieronder in het kort verklaarde tekens.

Prijzen

De vermelde tarieven zijn de minimale en maximale prijzen voor een overnachting voor 2 personen, auto plus caravan of tent. Over het algemeen berekent men in Groot-Brittannië voor de staanplaats, maar een aantal terreinen belast u apart voor de auto, caravan of tent, en elke persoon. Bij sommige parken moet u eventueel extra betalen voor een tent of voortent die aan een caravan vastgebouwd is. Minimale en maximale tarieven voor vakantiecaravans zijn per week. Vermelde prijzen werden verstrekt door de terreinbeheerders en dienen als richtlijn voor de prijzen die tijdens de geldendheid van dit boekje gerekend zullen worden. Vermelde prijzen zijn in ponden (£) en pence (p). VAT (BTW) à 17,5% is bij de prijzen inbegrepen. Om misverstanden te vermijden, raden wij u dringend aan de prijzen te controleren als u een reservering maakt.

Reserveren

Bij het maken van een reservering, of het inwinnen van inlichtingen, moet u vooral duidelijk en precies aangeven wat u wilt – bij voorbeeld:

- aankomst- en vertrekdata met mogelijke alternatieven.
- gewenste accommodatie.
- vertel de beheerder vooral wat voor speciale wensen of eisen u heeft.

Misverstanden kunnen heel gemakkelijk voorkomen over de telefoon en wij raden u daarom aan alle reserveringen, als de tijd dat toelaat, schriftelijk te bevestigen. Vergeet vooral niet uw naam en adres te vermelden en een aan

uzelf geadresseerde envelop met postzegel of internationale antwoordcoupon (als u uit het buitenland schrijft) in te sluiten voor elk antwoord.

Aan- en vooruitbetalingen

Campings, caravanterreinen, bungalow- en vakantieparken moeten meestal van tevoren geheel betaald worden. Dit kan gedaan worden in tweeën – een aanbetaling bij de reservering en betaling van het saldo bijvoorbeeld twee weken voor de aanvang van de geboekte periode.

Annuleren

De aanvaarding van geboden accommodatie, hetzij schriftelijk of telefonisch, wordt over het algemeen beschouwd als een wettelijk bindend contract. Dit betekent dat als u annuleert, niet verschijnt op het park, of vroegtijdig het park verlaat (het geeft niet om welke reden), de eigenaar compensatie van u kan verlangen als de staanplaats voor het overgrote deel van de geboekte periode niet opnieuw verhuurd kan worden. Als u een aanbetaling gedaan heeft, kan deze vervallen worden verklaard en een aanvullend bedrag van u verlangd worden.

Het is daarom in uw eigen belang de bedrijfsleiding onmiddelijk in kennis te stellen, als u uw reisplannen moet wijzigen, een boeking moet annuleren, of voortijdig moet vertrekken.

Elektrische aansluiting

De meeste parken hebben elektrische aansluitpunten voor caravans en tenten. De voltage is meestal 240v AC, 50Hz, hoewel nog steeds voltages tussen 200v en 250v kunnen worden aangetroffen. Het kan zijn dat u een adaptor nodig heeft voor de aansluiting. Meestal moet u extra betalen voor deze faciliteit. Het is raadzaam de tarieven na te vragen voor u reserveert.

Het vinden van een park of terrein

De parken in dit gidsje zijn ingedeeld in Engeland per regio, gevolgd door Schotland en Wales. Zij staan in alfabetische volgorde onder de naam van

de meest nabijgelegen plaats. De index van plaatsen op blz 298 en de gekleurde lokatiekaarten voorin de gids vertonen alle steden, plaatsen en dorpen met parken die in deze gids voorkomen. Zo kunt u snel en gemakkelijk ergens een park vinden. Als u al weet op welk park u wilt staan, kunt u de index van parken raadplegen op blz 294.

Als uw bestemming in de index van plaatsen voorkomt, raadpleeg dan de gegeven bladzij, waar de aldaar gevestigde parken worden vermeld. De plaatsnamen staan in zwart op de kaarten voorin het gidsje, aangeduid met coördinaten bij de vermelding. Ook kunt u de kleurenkaarten raadplegen om nabijgelegen plaatsen te vinden die ook in de gids voorkomende parken hebben.

Als uw bestemming niet in de index van plaatsen voorkomt, of als u alleen een vaag idee heeft van het gebied dat u wilt bezoeken, kunt u eveneens de kleurenkaarten raadplegen. De kaarten bevatten alle plaatsnamen waaronder een park in het gidsje wordt vermeld. Voor de precieze locatie dient u de routebeschrijvingen bij iedere vermelding te raadplegen. Heeft u moeite met het vinden van een bepaald park, dan raden wij u aan in de buurt om verdere aanwijzingen te vragen.

 De hiernaast vertoonde internationale verkeersborden worden in Groot-Brittannië gebruikt en zijn speciaal ontworpen voor het gebruik van de

parkbezoekers en kampeerders. Ze zijn nog niet bij alle parken opgesteld en vermelden niet de naam van een park of camping. Ze duiden echter wel aan of het park geschikt is voor caravans, tenten of beide.

Het Internationale Kampeerkarnet wordt maar weinig in Groot-Brittannië erkend, behalve op terreinen die beheerd worden door de grote clubs.

Campings bij Londen

Londen is een grote trekpleister voor toeristen en daarom raken de campings en caravanterreinen in de streek van Greater London erg snel vol en boeking ver van tevoren is daarom noodzakelijk. Bij de meeste aankomsthavens zijn ook campings te vinden en de meeste worden vermeld in deze gids en aangeduid op de kaarten voorin.

Hulp bij het vinden van een park

De Toeristische Informatiecentra over heel Groot-Brittannië (zie aan het einde van deze gids) kunnen kampeerders en caravaneigenaars informatie verschaffen over lokale parken en terreinen. Een aantal Toeristische Informatiecentra biedt ook een adviesdienst, die inlichtingen kan geven over mogelijke plaats op campings en vaak kan helpen met het maken van een reservering.

Left an exhilarating day out at a water park **Right** take a trip on a steamboat in the Lake District

Vermijding van problemen in het hoogseizoen

In de zomermaanden juni t/m september kunnen parken in populaire gebieden, zoals Noord-Wales, Cumbria, de West Country en het New Forest in Hampshire bijzonder vol raken. Bezoekers moeten proberen zo vroeg mogelijk op de dag bij het park aan te komen, of nog beter, van tevoren boeken. Een aantal parken heeft een speciaal terrein voor bezoekers die laat in de avond arriveren. Dit is om te voorkomen dat andere bezoekers in hun slaap gestoord worden en minder kampeerders weggestuurd worden. De volgende morgen worden de caravans en tenten dan een juiste plek gegeven.

Andere mogelijkheden voor caravans en tenten

Als u ervan houdt om door landelijke streken in Groot-Brittanië te trekken, vindt u het misschien interessant te weten, dat de Forestry Commission (staatsbosbeheer) bos-kampeerterreinen in zeven van Groot-Brittanië's Forest Parks en het New Forest beheert. Sommige bieden gereduceerde tarieven voor jeugdorganisaties op georganiseerde kampeertochten, en alle inlichtingen hierover moeten ver van tevoren ingewonnen worden bij de Forestry Commission.

Huisdieren

Op veel parken zijn honden toegestaan, maar we raden u aan voor het reserveren na te vragen of dit het geval is, of er een extra tarief wordt geheven, en waar uw hond precies is toegestaan. Als er honden worden toegelaten, wil dit niet altijd zeggen dat ook katten toegestaan zijn, en we raden u ten sterkste aan van te voren contact op te nemen met het etablissement als u uw kat mee wilt nemen. Op sommige parken zijn huisdieren in het geheel niet toegestaan. Honden zijn toegestaan als u dit symbool ziet 🐾.

Huisdieren mee op vakantie in Groot-Brittannië

De Engelse quarantainewet is veranderd. Er is tegenwoordig een zogenaamd Pet Travel Scheme (PETS-regeling) van kracht. Onder deze regeling mogen honden, katten en fretten uit 50 landen via bepaalde zee-, lucht- en treinroutes Groot-Brittannië binnen wanneer zij aan bepaalde voorwaarden voldoen.

Honden, katten en fretten die langer dan zes maanden in een van deze 50 landen zijn geweest kunnen Groot-Brittannië in met de juiste documenten. Huisdieren uit andere landen moeten zes maanden in quarantaine.

Honden, katten en fretten die u zonder quarantaine wilt meenemen naar Groot-Brittannië onder de PETS-regeling moeten aan bepaalde voorwaarden voldoen en de juiste papieren hebben.

Op 3 juli 2004 is er een nieuw Europees Voorschrift van kracht geworden wat betreft het verplaatsen van huisdieren naar en binnen landen in de Europese Unie. Groot-Brittannië blijft het Pet Travel Scheme hanteren, maar er zullen enkele wijzigingen optreden wat betreft documentatie, betrokken landen en de dieren die er onder vallen.

Neem voor meer informatie over deelnemende landen, toegestane routes, reisoperators andere details van het PETS-systeem en de nieuwe EU-voorschriften contact op met de PETS-lijn, DEFRA (Department for Environment, Food and Rural Affairs),1a Page Street, Londen, SW1P 4PQ, Engeland.
Tel: +44 (0) 870 241 1710
Fax: +44 (0) 20 7904 6206
E-mail: pets.helpline@defra.gsi.gov.uk, of bezoek hun website op
www.defra.gov.uk/animalh/quarantine/index.htm

Drugswaarschuwing voor inkomende toeristen

In het Vereningd Koninkrijk staan er zware straffen op het illegaal invoeren van drugs. Drugshandelaars proberen onschuldige reizigers te misleiden en wij raden u daarom aan alle betrokkenheid met drugs te vermijden. Draag nooit pakjes of bagage door de douane die niet van uzelf zijn.

Wettelijke bepalingen

De allerbeste bron van wettelijk advies voor automobilisten is een Club voor Automobilisten (b.v. ANWB). Wat de kampeerder of caravaneigenaar nog meer moet weten is betrekkelijk eenvoudig. Als u een caravan of kampeerwagentje achter de auto heeft, mag u niet meer dan 96 km (60 mijl) per uur rijden op tweebaanswegen of snelwegen, 80 km (50 mijl) per uur op eenbaanswegen, en op snelwegen met drie banen aan elke kant mag u niet in de derde (snelste) baan. Kooktoestellen mogen niet bij een wegrestaurant met benzinestation aangestoken worden.

In de meeste steden is parkeren beperkt, zowel door wettelijke bepalingen als uit praktische overwegingen. Auto's met aanhangende caravans mogen niet parkeren bij een parkeermeter en vele stadsparkeerterreinen zijn alleen geschikt voor auto's zonder aanhangende caravans of kampeerwagentjes.

's Nachts moet een kampeerwagen, of een auto verbonden met een aanhangwagen, die aan de weg geparkeerd staat, zowel z'n twee voorlichten als z'n achterlichten aanhebben, terwijl een auto alleen dit niet hoeft.

De remmen, lampen, het gewicht, etc. van buitenlandse voertuigen hoeven niet te voldoen aan de Britse technische voorschriten. Hoe dan ook, een aanhangwagen mag de Britse wettelijke afmetingsbepalingen – 7m lang en 2,3m breed – niet overschrijden. Ze moeten het internationale kenteken (NL of B) voeren en niet overnachten in de berm of op de parkeerhavens, daar deze wettelijk onderdeel uitmaken van de weg.

Tenslotte is het ook heel belangrijk van tevoren uit te vinden hoe laat u op de dag van vertrek moet opbreken. U moet zich daar aan houden, anders kan men u een extra dag in rekening brengen.

Advies aan bezoekers

VisitBritain stelt er prijs op uw op- of aanmerkingen op uw verblijf in Groot-Brittannië te vernemen. wij hopen dat u geen reden tot klagen heeft, maar mocht dit toch het geval zijn, raden wij u dringend aan om uw klacht onmiddellijk kenbaar te maken aan de leiding van het desbetreffende park, de winkel of vervoersmaatschappij. Indien u hieruit geen genoegdoening verkrijgt, laat u ons dit dan weten, zodat wij zelf een onderzoek kunnen instellen, of u kunnen adviseren over eventuele verder te nemen stappen.

U mag het geeft niet hoeveel geld, en in welke munteenheid dan ook, meenemen en er bestaan geen beperkingen op het aantal inwisselbare reischeques. Als u geld wilt wisselen als de banken gesloten zijn, kunt u dit doen bij de grotere hotels, reisbureaus en warenhuizen of bij onafhankelijke wisselkantoren. Controleer vooral van tevoren de berekende wisselkoers en commissietarieven.

Alle grote winkels, warenhuizen, en de meeste hotels en restaurants accepteren de gebruikelijke, internationaal erkende credit cards. Als u ook graag op markten winkelt, koop dan alleen op grote, erkende markten, en bekijk de artikelen eerst zorgvuldig.

Vraag altijd wat de prijs is voor u tot de aankoop overgaat. Pas op voor zakkenrollers in drukke menigten.

Indien u bestolen bent, of betrokken bent bij een ongeval of brand, bel dan 999 (waarvoor geen geld nodig is) en vraag om de 'police' (politie), 'ambulance service' (ambulance) of de 'fire brigade' (brandweer).

VisitBritain heeft alle pogingen in het werk gesteld om deze publicatie bij het ter perse gaan van nauwkeurigheid te verzekeren. De informatie werd in goed vertrouwen verstrekt, gebaseerd op inlichtingen gegeven aan VisitBritain door de organisatoren van de vermelde caravanparken en campings. VisitBritain kan echter niet garanderen dat deze informatie correct is en kan geen verantwoording aanvaarden voor foute of onjuiste voorstellingen. VisitBritain kan beslist niet verantwoordelijk worden gesteld voor verlies, teleurstelling, nalatigheid of enige andere schade die voortvloeit uit het vertrouwen in de informatie in deze gids, of problemen voortkomend uit het faillisement of liquidatie van enige vermelde maatschappij, individu of bedrijf, of indien een maatschappij, individu of bedrijf ophoudt handel te drijven. Het is daarom raadzaam de gegeven informatie bij het maken van een reservering goed te controleren.

Alle parken in deze gids houden zich aan de richtlijnen van VisitBritain. Een lijst van de aan de campings en caravanparken gestelde eisen kunt u vinden op pagina 266.

All genoemde instellingen in het gedeelte in kleur hebben betaald voor hun vermelding in deze gids.

British Holiday and Home Parks Association

The Association represents commercial operators of all kinds throughout Britain. Its aim is to ensure a high standard of excellence in members' parks for the satisfaction of the visitor.

Parks listed in this guide all conform to the standards set by VisitBritain but BH&HPA Members' Parks, which are identified in the Guide by (BH&HPA), must also abide by the BH&HPA Code of Conduct. This gives the visitor an assurance of a high standard of facilities and reliability.

The BH&HPA works with VisitBritain and the national and regional tourism organisations to safeguard tourist interests. It also works with Government and local government authorities to ensure that all aspects of legislation and control are applied and that proper safety measures are carried out for the comfort and protection of the visitor.

The BH&HPA will investigate problems encountered by visitors and can provide details of self-catering holidays and residential parks.

British Holiday and Home Parks Association Ltd,
Chichester House, 6 Pullman Court, Great Western Road,
Gloucester GL1 3ND
Tel: (01452) 526911 Fax: (01452) 508508

Above Park Coppice Caravan Club Site, Coniston

Come usare questa Guida

I campeggi elencati in questa guida sono per la maggior parte aperti sia alle roulottes che alle tende e molti di essi accolgono anche i camper e le motorhome. Molti campeggi dispongono anche di roulottes a noleggio.

Il progetto di assicurazione di qualità

Per chi va in cerca di un posto dove soggiornare, è necessario un sistema di classificazione affidabile. Il programma britannico di classificazione dei parchi vacanze (British Graded Holiday Parks Scheme) del 2000 offre una guida chiara e comprensibile su ciò che ci si può aspettare. Il programma è sempre imperniato sulla qualità e rispecchia le aspettative del cliente.

VisitBritain utilizza ora delle stelle per illustrare le categorie dei parchi partecipanti al programma. I parchi vengono ispezionati annualmente da funzionari competenti e imparziali, che assegnano una classificazione da una a cinque stelle, basandosi sulla pulizia, sull'ambiente e sulla qualità delle strutture e dei servizi offerti.

Inoltre, i parchi vengono ora contrassegnati da un simbolo, in modo che se ne possa identificare immediatamente il tipo – ad esempio Parco Vacanze, Parco Turistico o Campeggio. (L'assenza di classifica o contrassegno significa che il parco in oggetto non è stato ancora valutato al momento di andare in stampa).

Spiegazione dei Simboli

BH&HPA	British Holiday & Home Parks Association (v. pagina 56)
NCC	National Caravan Council (v. pagina 62)
	Roulottes ammesse (con numero di posteggi e prezzi)
	Camper/motorhome ammessi (con numero di posteggi e prezzi) In alcuni casi il numero di posteggi per camper/motorhome è compreso nel numero di posteggi per roulottes
	Tende ammesse
	Numero di roulottes a noleggio (v. posteggi per roulottes a noleggio a seguito)
	Bungalow/chalet/casette a noleggio
	Zona di pernottamento temporaneo
	Allacciamento elettrico
	Parcheggio accanto all'unità
	Docce
	WC a trattamento chimico
	Allacciamento alla fognatura per camper/motorhome
	Cambio di bombole di gas butano o propano
	Negozio/negozio ambulante di alimentari
	Bar/ristorante
	Club con bar
	Salone con televisione a colori
	Telefono pubblico
	Lavanderia sul posto
	Prese per rasoio elettrico
	Sala giochi
	Zona giochi per bambini
	Locazione biciclette
	Piscina riscaldata al coperto sul posto
	Piscina all'aperto sul posto
	Equitazione/escursioni a dorso di pony partendo dal campeggio
	Tennis sul posto
	Pesca sul posto o nelle vicinanze
	Golf sul posto o nelle vicinanze
	Si accettano animali domestici
	Spettacoli/intrattenimenti serali
	Consigliata la prenotazione in estate

Il programma di classificazione è stato ideato congiuntamente dagli enti nazionali per il turismo dell'Inghilterra, dell'Irlanda del Nord, della Scozia e del Galles in collaborazione con l'associazione britannica dei parchi per roulotte e vacanze (British Holiday & Home Parks Association) (vedere a pagina 56) e con l'organo nazionale per le roulotte (National Caravan Council) (vedere a pagina 62).

Strutture

Le strutture vengono indicate per mezzo di simboli, comprensibili a prima vista, spiegati qui di seguito.

Prezzi

I prezzi indicati per i posteggi sono il prezzo minimo e il prezzo massimo di un pernottamento per 2 persone, un'automobile e una tenda o una roulotte. I campeggi britannici preferiscono in genere includere tutto in un solo prezzo, benché in alcuni vi siano prezzi separati per automobili, roulottes o tende e per ogni persona. In alcuni campeggi possono essere richiesti supplementi per i tendoni delle roulottes. I prezzi minimi e massimi delle roulottes a noleggio sono i prezzi per settimana. I prezzi indicati sono quelli forniti dagli esercenti dei campeggi in questione e sono un'indicazione dei prezzi che verranno praticati per il periodo di validità di questa pubblicazione. I prezzi indicati sono in sterline (£) e pence (p). L'IVA (Imposta sul Valore Aggiunto) al 17,5% è compresa nei prezzi indicati. Per evitare qualsiasi equivoco, si consiglia vivamente di controllare i prezzi al momento di effettuare la prenotazione.

Prenotazione

Nel richiedere informazioni sulle possibilità di sistemazione, è necessario, oltre a controllare il prezzo, illustrare chiaramente le proprie esigenze, per esempio:

- date di arrivo e partenza, e se possibile date alternative;
- tipo di sistemazione richiesto;
- qualsiasi particolare esigenza.

Quando si prenota per telefono c'è sempre il rischio di errori. Tempo permettendo, si consiglia dunque di confermare sempre le prenotazioni per iscritto. Ricordarsi di indicare il proprio nome e indirizzo e di accludere, per ogni risposta, una busta preindirizzata e preaffrancata o un buono internazionale per riposta pagata.

Anticipi

Per la prenotazione di posti nei campeggi per tende, roulottes e chalets, il prezzo intero va normalmente versato in anticipo. Il versamento può normalmente essere effettuato in due rate: un anticipo al momento della prenotazione e il saldo circa due settimane prima dell'inizio del periodo prenotato.

Annullamenti

Nel Regno Unito, l'accettazione di un alloggio offerto, sia per iscritto che per telefono, equivale per legge alla firma di un contratto vincolante tra l'inquilino e il proprietario dell'alloggio. Ciò significa che se l'inquilino annulla la propria prenotazione, non prende domicilio o parte prima del previsto (per qualsiasi ragione), il proprietario potrebbe avere diritto a un risarcimento qualora non riuscisse a riaffittare l'alloggio per tutto o parte del periodo prenotato. Se è stato versato un anticipo, è probabile che venga ritenuto dal proprietario, il quale potrebbe anche esigere un ulteriore addebito.

È consigliabile dunque avvisare immediatamente il proprietario sia di qualsiasi cambiamento di itinerario, sia dell'intenzione di annullare una prenotazione o di partire prima del previsto.

Prese di allacciamento elettrico

I campeggi dispongono per la maggior parte di prese di allacciamento alla rete di distribuzione dell'energia elettrica adoperabili sia per la roulottes che per le tende. La tensione è di 240V circa e 50Hz, benché in alcuni casi possa ancora variare tra 200V e 250V. In alcuni campeggi potrebbe essere necessario un adattatore per l'allacciamento. La fornitura di energia elettrica è normalmente soggetta ad un addebito supplementare e si consiglia di controllare le tariffe al momento della prenotazione.

Come trovare il campeggio prescelto

I campeggi in questa guida sono raggruppati per regione in Inghilterra, seguiti dalle liste relative a Scozia e Galles, e sono stati elencati in ordine alfabetico sotto il nome della città in cui si trovano, o vicino a cui si trovano. L'Indice delle Città a pagina 298 e le Mappe a colori all'inizio della guida riportano tutte le città, i centri e i villaggi che hanno un campeggio elencato in questa guida. Usate questi riferimenti per trovare in un modo facile e veloce un alloggio adatto. Se sapete in quale campeggio volete stare, controllate l'Indice dei Campeggi a pagina 294.

Se il luogo dove volete stare è compreso nell'indice delle città, andate alla pagina indicata per trovarvi i campeggi disponibili. I nomi delle città appaiono in nero sulla mappa all'inizio della guida nel modo in cui sono stati indicati dal riferimento alla mappa nella voce relativa. Controllate anche le mappe a colori per trovarvi altri luoghi vicini che hanno anche dei campeggi elencati in questa guida.

Se il luogo dove volete stare non si trova nell'indice delle città – o avete solo un'idea generale della zona in cui volete stare – usate le cartine a colori.

Le cartine illustrano tutti i nomi delle località in cui viene elencato un campeggio nella guida. Per trovare la località precisa leggete le indicazioni di ogni voce. In caso di difficoltà è consigliabile chiedere indicazioni a qualcuno nelle vicinanze del campeggio.

   I segnali internazionali indicati qui vengono usati in Gran Bretagna per aiutare i visitatori a trovare i campeggi. Non sono ancora stati installati per tutti i campeggi e non indicano il nome di nessun campeggio. Indicano però se il campeggio è per tende, roulottes o ambedue. Il carnet internazionale del campeggiatore è raramente riconosciuto in Gran Bretagna, salvo nei campeggi organizzati dai principali club.

Campeggi di Londra

Londra rappresenta una grande attrazione per molti visitatori, per cui i campeggi per tende e roulotte nell'area della Greater London tendono a riempirsi molto rapidamente, e bisogna prenotare molto in anticipo.

Sono anche disponibili campeggi presso la maggior parte dei porti d'entrata nel paese, e molti di questi sono elencati in questa guida e indicati sulla mappa all'inizio.

Servizi di ricerca campeggi

I Tourist Information Centre di tutta la Gran Bretagna (v. pagine finali) possono fornire ai campeggiatori informazioni sui campeggi nelle loro zone di responsabilità. Alcuni Tourist Information Centre offrono servizi di ricerca campeggi che forniscono informazioni sulla disponibilità di posteggi e spesso aiutano a effettuare le prenotazioni.

Left cruise along the Rochdale Canal **Right** steeped in history at Ightham Mote, Sevenoaks

Come evitare i problemi dell'alta stagione

Nei mesi estivi, da giugno a settembre, i campeggi nelle zone più frequentate del paese: Galles settentrionale, Cumbria, Inghilterra sud-occidentale e la New Forest nel Hampshire, registrano molto presto il tutto esaurito.

Si consiglia ai campeggiatori di arrivare presto o, se possibile, di prenotare in anticipo. Alcuni campeggi dispongono di zone di pernottamento temporaneo per i campeggiatori che arrivano tardi. Queste zone di pernottamento consentono di non disturbare gli altri campeggiatori durante la notte e di accogliere un maggior numero di nuovi arrivati, i quali vengono condotti a uno dei posti liberi la mattina seguente.

Altri luoghi di campeggio

A chi preferisce seguire il proprio itinerario attraverso la campagna britannica potrebbe interessare sapere che la Forestry Commission gestisce dei campeggi forestali nei sette parchi forestali del paese e nella New Forest. Alcuni offrono tariffe ridotte a gruppi organizzati di giovani in campeggio. Tutte le richieste d'informazioni vanno indirizzate direttamente alla Forestry Commission con qualche mese di anticipo sulla data di arrivo.

Animali domestici

Molti campeggi accettano ospiti con cani, ma si consiglia di controllare al momento della prenotazione e di chiedere se è necessario versare un supplemento o se esistono delle regole particolari per l'ammissione degli animali domestici. Spesso anche se sono ammessi i cani, non è consentito portare gatti; è consigliabile per i proprietari di gatti contattare l'esercizio in anticipo. Gli esercizi che accettano animali domestici sono contrassegnati dal simbolo 🐾.

Animali domestici in Gran Bretagna

La normativa sulla quarantena degli animali è cambiata in Inghilterra e attualmente è in vigore il PETS (Pet Travel Scheme). Nell'ambito di questo progetto è consentito l'ingresso in Inghilterra di cani, gatti e furetti provenienti da 50 Paesi diversi attraverso determinati itinerari per mare, aria e ferrovia a condizione che venga rispettata la normativa.

Ai sensi del progetto è consentito l'ingresso nel Regno Unito di cani, gatti e furetti residenti da più di sei mesi in questi paesi, a condizione che siano accompagnati dalla documentazione appropriata. Gli animali domestici di altri Paesi continueranno a essere sottoposti a sei mesi di quarantena.

Per l'ingresso di cani, gatti e furetti nel Regno Unito senza quarantena ai sensi del progetto PETS è necessario che siano soddisfatti determinati requisiti e che gli animali viaggino con la documentazione ufficiale.

Il 3 luglio 2004 è entrata in vigore una nuova normativa europea sul trasferimento degli animali domestici tra i paesi dell'Unione Europea (UE) all'interno della UE. Nel Regno Unito rimane in vigore il Pet Travel Scheme, che subirà alcune modifiche per quanto riguarda documentazione, paesi interessati e tipi di animali coperti.

Per particolari sui paesi partecipanti, gli itinerari, gli operatori e altre informazioni sul programma PETS e sulle nuove norme comunitarie, rivolgersi a: PETS Helpline, DEFRA (Department for Environment, Food and Rural Affaris), 1a Page Street, London SW1P 4PQ
Tel: +44 (0) 870 241 1710
Fax: +44 (0) 20 7904 6206
Email: pets.helpline@defra.gsi.gov.uk
www.defra.gov.uk./animalh/quarantine/index.htm

Avvertimento sugli stupefacenti per i turisti in arrivo

Le leggi britanniche sul contrabbando di stupefacenti prevedono delle sanzioni estremamente severe per i trasgressori. I trafficanti di droga tentano a volte di ingannare i viaggiatori. Si consiglia a chiunque abbia deciso di visitare il Regno Unito di evitare qualsiasi coinvolgimento con lo spaccio di stupefacenti e di non attraversare mai la dogana portando le valige o i pacchi di altri viaggiatori.

Aspetti giuridici

La migliore fonte d'informazioni per gli automobilisti che intendono visitare la Gran Bretagna è l'organizzazione automobilistica del paese di origine. Le regole che deve conoscere l'automobilista campeggiatore sono relativamente semplici.

Le automobili con roulotte o rimorchi al traino non devono superare i 96 chilometri orari (60 miglia all'ora) sulle strade a doppia carreggiata e sulle autostrade, e gli 80 chilometri orari (50 miglia all'ora) sulle strade normali. Sulle autostrade a tre carreggiate in ogni direzione, le roulotte ed i rimorchi non sono ammessi nella terza carreggiata (la più veloce). È vietato accendere fornelli nelle aree di servizio autostradali.

Nella maggior parte delle città, parcheggiare è reso difficile sia dai regolamenti che da difficoltà pratiche. Alle automobili con rimorchio è vietato l'uso di spazi con parchimetri e i posteggi di molti parcheggi cittadini sono intesi per automobili senza rimorchio, sebbene in alcuni di essi vi siano spazi anche per veicoli più lunghi.

Se parcheggiati sulla strada di notte, i rimorchi, o le automobili attaccate ai rimorchi, devono avere due luci anteriori e due luci posteriori accese, anche dove l'automobile senza il rimorchio sarebbe esonerata da quest'obbligo.

I freni, le luci, il peso ecc. dei veicoli provenienti dall'estero non devono soddisfare i criteri tecnici delle norme britanniche. I rimorchi tuttavia non devono superare i limiti britannici, che sono: 7 metri di lunghezza e 2,3 metri di larghezza. I rimorchi devono recare il numero di targa del paese di provenienza. È vietato sostare di notte sui lati erbosi o nelle piazzole di sosta delle strade, dato che queste zone sono per legge considerate parti della strada.

Per concludere, è importante sapere l'ora entro la quale si è obbligati a liberare il posteggio nel giorno previsto per la partenza. Si consiglia di partire presto la mattina per evitare di dover pagare il prezzo di una giornata in più.

Consigli per i visitatori

VisitBritain è sempre lieta di ricevere i commenti e le osservazioni dei turisti su qualsiasi aspetto del loro soggiorno in Gran Bretagna, che siano o meno favorevoli. Ci auguriamo che chiunque visiti il nostro paese non abbia mai occasione di lamentarsi. Se vi fosse ragione di lamentarsi, il consiglio è di rivolgersi in primo luogo alla gestione del campeggio, negozio o società di trasporti. Qualora la risposta non sia soddisfacente, consigliamo ai turisti di rivolgersi a VisitBritain che prenderà in esame la questione o suggerirà le misure da prendere.

Si possono portare in Gran Bretagna valute di qualsiasi denominazione senza limiti di quantità. Si può cambiare anche qualsiasi numero di traveller's cheque. Per cambiare le valute straniere durante le ore di chiusura delle banche ci si può rivolgere alle ricezioni di alcuni grandi alberghi, alle agenzie di viaggio, alle agenzie di cambiavalute indipendenti. Raccomandiamo di

Left Crowhurst Park, Battle **Right** picturesque East Wales

controllare il tasso e la commissione di cambio prima di cambiare i soldi.

Tutti i grandi negozi, i grandi magazzini la maggior parte degli alberghi e dei ristoranti accettano le carte di credito normalmente riconosciute nel mondo. A chi decida di fare spese nei mercati consigliamo di comprare solo in quelli grandi e riconosciuti e di esaminare accuratamente gli articoli prima di acquistarli. Consigliamo di chiedere sempre il prezzo dei beni e dei servizi prima di impegnarsi all'acquisto e di fare attenzione ai borsaioli nei luoghi affollati.

Chiunque sia vittima di un furto, o coinvolto in un incidente o un incendio può telefonare al 999 (chiamata gratuita) e chiedere la polizia, il servizio ambulanze o i vigili del fuoco.

VisitBritain ha fatto del tutto per garantire l'esattezza delle informazioni contenute in questa pubblicazione al momento di andare in stampa. Le informazioni vengono date in buona fede in base ai dati forniti a VisitBritain dai promotori del campeggi elencati. VisitBritain tuttavia non può né garantire l'esattezza delle informazioni né assumersi la responsabilltà di qualsiasi errore o falsità. È esclusa tutta la responsabilità di perdite, delusioni, negligenza o di altri danni che risultino dall'aver fatto affidamento sulle informazioni contenute in questa guida o dal fallimento o dalla liquidazione di qualsiasi società, individuo o ditta, o dalla cessazione delle attività di qualsiasi società, individuo o ditta. Si consiglia di verificare l'esattezza delle informazioni al momento di effettuare la prenotazione.

Tutti i parchi elencati in questa guida sono conformi agli Standard di VisitBritain. A pagina xxx riportiamo un elenco di queste norme applicabili ai campeggi per tende e roulottes. Tutti i campeggi elencati nella seqione a colori hanno pagato per la loro inserzione nella guida.

The National Caravan Council

The National Caravan Council is the trade body for the British caravan industry – touring caravans, motorhomes and caravan holiday-homes.

The Council operates an approval system for caravans, certifying that they are manufactured in accordance with the relevant European Standard. All dealer and park operator members, which are identified in the guide by (NCC), agree to comply with Conditions of Membership which require them to provide their customers with a high standard of service.

The Council works closely with the VisitBritain, national and regional tourism organisations to promote tourism and particularly to promote the important role which all kinds of caravans play in providing tourists with modern facilities to enjoy the outdoors.

Full information on its members and its activities together with assistance on any difficulties encountered can be obtained from:

The National Caravan Council, Catherine House, Victoria Road, Aldershot, Hampshire GU11 1SS.
Telephone: (01252) 318251 Fax: (01252) 322596
E-mail: info@nationalcaravan.co.uk www.thecaravan.net

Right Whitecliff Bay Holiday Park, Bembridge

Caravan Holiday Home Award Scheme

Rose Award
VisitBritain,
Thames Tower, Blacks Road,
Hammersmith,
London W6 9EL

Thistle Award
VisitScotland,
Thistle House, Beechwood Park North,
Inverness IV2 3ED

Dragon Award
Wales Tourist Board,
Brunel House, 2 Fitzalan Road,
Cardiff CF24 0UY

VisitBritain and the national tourist boards for Scotland and Wales run similar award schemes for holiday caravan homes on highly graded caravan parks. They recognise high standards of caravan accommodation and enable you to step into a comfortable, fully furnished holiday home set amongst landscaped surroundings with all the amenities you could wish for.

All the caravan parks included in the award scheme have been inspected and meet the criteria demanded by the scheme. In addition to complying with joint tourist board standards for Holiday Caravan Parks and Caravan Holiday Homes all award caravans must have a shower or bath, toilet, mains electricity and water heating (at no extra charge) and a refrigerator (many also have a colour television).

A complete list of the parks in each country, plus further information about them, can be obtained free from the national tourist boards (see page 284). Look out for these plaques displayed by all award-winning parks, and by each caravan which meets the required standards. Many parks listed in this guide are participating in these schemes and are indicated accordingly.

London

Looking for some inspiration? Here are a few ideas to get you started in London. **experience** Dragon Boat racing – 20 people, a 40-foot-long boat and a drummer. **discover** your artistic side in five new suites at the Victoria & Albert Museum. **explore** the Thames by bike, on foot or on a barge. **relax** on a 40-minute trip around Kew Gardens on the Kew Explorer.

THE REGION
Greater London, comprising the 32 London Boroughs

CONTACT
▸ VISIT LONDON
6th Floor, 2 More London Riverside, London SE1 2RR
T: (020) 7234 5800
F: (020) 7378 6525
www.visitlondon.com

One of the most dynamic and cosmopolitan cities in the world, London is a unique mix of the historical and the contemporary. Enjoy the peace of the many parks, or soak up the buzz and bustle of the busy West End. There's always something new and exciting to experience.

Park life

London's parks and gardens are an oasis of pleasure. Delight in regal Regent's Park and watch a play in the open-air theatre; go swimming on tranquil Hampstead Heath; or play a round of golf in rolling Richmond Park.

For more outdoor entertainment get tickets for Shakespeare's Globe near Southwark Bridge. Audiences at this theatre sit in a gallery or stand in the yard, just as they did 400 years ago. Royal connections are everywhere and Clarence House – the London residence of the Prince of Wales – recently opened to the public for the first time.

Culture capital

Get a flavour of London's opulence in the private rooms of Burlington House. Restored to their original 18th-century glory, they house some of the Royal Academy's finest works. More paintings and art can be viewed at the Hayward Gallery and Barbican, and at the Saatchi Gallery on the South Bank. The Thames is inextricably linked with London's fortunes and you can discover its dramatic 2000-year history at the newly opened Museum in Docklands. Also new is the UK's first Fashion and Textile Museum, dedicated to contemporary works.

Follow the thread, and take in the Vivienne Westwood exhibition at the V&A. If you enjoy classical music, the Handel House Museum celebrates Handel's life and works in his finely restored house at 25 Brook Street.

Lucky dip

For two weeks every summer tennis fever takes hold as Wimbledon hosts the world's most famous tournament. When the covers go back on, you can still enjoy a taste of the action at the Wimbledon Lawn Tennis Museum. Turn your attention to shopping, and you'll find London hits the mark – from Harrods, with its famous food hall, to major new developments at Kingly Court and Duke of York Square. And if you enjoy fine dining with plenty of variety, there really is no better place. Every taste is catered for: from Japanese to Russian, and from restaurants run for the stars – like the fashionable Ivy – to those run by the stars, like Jamie Oliver's Fifteen.

Getting around

Travel in London is easy as the city has a massive transport network: Underground trains, buses, taxis, riverboats and trams, as well as connections to national rail services. Whether touring the sights in the centre of town or exploring areas at the edge of the city, you'll find yourself within easy distance of transport links.

Left, from top set your watch by Big Ben; journey towards Buckingham Palace; share in the excitement of the capital at Trafalgar Square **Right** Yeoman Warder stands guard

Places to visit

 Awarded VisitBritain's Quality Assured Visitor Attraction marque.

Bank of England Museum
Threadneedle Street, EC2R 8AH
Tel: (020) 7601 5491
www.bankofengland.co.uk/museum
Marvel at ancient gold bars, historic bank notes and documents belonging to famous, past customers like Horatio Nelson and George Washington – just a few of the exhibits in the nation's central bank.

BBC Television Centre Tours
BBC Television Centre, Wood Lane, W12 7RJ
Tel: 0870 603 0304
www.bbc.co.uk/tours
Go behind the scenes at the BBC. Your tour will be planned around what is happening on the day, and may include the News Centre, dressing rooms and studios.

British Airways London Eye
Jubilee Gardens, South Bank, SE1 7PB
Tel: 0870 500 0600
www.ba-londoneye.com
From your glass pod on the world's largest observation wheel you'll enjoy the most spectacular views of London – see over 55 famous landmarks in just 30 minutes.

British Library
Euston Road, NW1 2OB
Tel: (020) 7412 7332
www.bl.uk
Visit the UK's national library and browse galleries displaying famous written and printed works, including the Magna Carta, Shakespeare's first folio and a da Vinci notebook.

The British Museum
Great Russell Street, WC1B 3DG
Tel: (020) 7323 8299
www.thebritishmuseum.ac.uk
One of the great museums of the world, showing the works of man from prehistoric to modern times with collections drawn from all over the globe.

Cabinet War Rooms
Clive Steps, King Charles Street, SW1A 2AQ
Tel: (020) 7930 6961
www.iwm.org.uk
Experience the atmosphere in the underground headquarters used by Winston Churchill and the British Government during World War II. Includes Cabinet Room, Transatlantic Telephone Room and Map Room.

Hampton Court Palace
Hampton Court, East Molesey
Tel: 0870 752 7777
www.hrp.org.uk
Step back into history at the oldest Tudor palace in England. The many attractions include the State Apartments and King's Apartments, Tudor kitchens, tennis courts and maze.

Handel House Museum
Brook Street, W1K 4HB
Tel: (020) 7495 1685
www.handelhouse.org
Home to composer George Frideric Handel from 1723 until his death in 1759, the Museum celebrates his life with live music and special exhibitions in an evocative 18th century setting.

Imperial War Museum
Lambeth Road, SE1 6HZ
Tel: (020) 7416 5000
www.iwm.org.uk
This national museum is dedicated to the history of 20thC warfare, with exhibits ranging from tanks and aircraft to personal letters, plus films and sound recordings.

Kensington Palace State Apartments
Kensington Gardens, W8 4PX
Tel: 0870 751 5170
www.hrp.org.uk
Tread where royalty have passed and view the King's Apartment, magnificent Old Master paintings and the Royal Ceremonial Dress Collection, with dresses worn by the Queen and Princess Diana.

Kew Gardens (Royal Botanic Gardens)

Kew, Richmond
Tel: (020) 8332 5655
www.kew.org
121-ha (300-acre) garden in a beautiful setting by the River Thames with stunning vistas, six magnificent glasshouses and over 30,000 plants from all over the world.

The London Dungeon

Tooley Street, SE1 2SZ
Tel: (020) 7403 7221
www.thedungeons.com
This historic horror experience is dead good fun! Descend into the dark Dungeon, relive the Great Fire of London, unmask Jack the Ripper and take the Boat ride to Hell.

London Wetland Centre

Queen Elizabeth's Walk, Barnes, SW13 9WT
Tel: (020) 8409 4400
www.wwt.org.uk
Spot hundreds of birds and other wildlife in this newly created nature reserve of over 40 ha (105 acres) of wetland habitats, developed on the site of disused Victorian reservoirs.

London Zoo

Regent's Park, NW1 4RY
Tel: (020) 7722 3333
www.londonzoo.co.uk
For an action-packed day out, why not escape the stress of city life and visit the amazing animals at the world-famous London Zoo.

London's Transport Museum

Covent Garden Piazza, WC2E 7BB
Tel: (020) 7379 6344
www.ltmuseum.co.uk
The history of transport for everyone, from spectacular vehicles, special exhibitions, actors and guided tours to film shows, gallery talks and children's craft workshops.

Madame Tussauds and the London Planetarium

Marylebone Road, NW1 5LR
Tel: 0870 400 3000
www.madame-tussauds.com
Come face-to-face with your heros in this world-famous collection of wax figures. Themed settings include The Garden Party, Superstars, The Grand Hall, The Chamber of Horrors and The Spirit of London.

Museum of London

London Wall, EC2Y 5HN
Tel: 0870 444 3851
www.museumoflondon.org.uk
Over 2000 years of London's history come alive here, with highlights including the Roman Gallery, Victorian shops, the Great Fire Experience and Elizabethan jewellery.

National Army Museum

Royal Hospital Road, Chelsea, SW3 4HT
Tel: (020) 7730 0717
www.national-army-museum.ac.uk
Learn the story of the British soldier in peace and war, through five centuries. Exhibits range from paintings to uniforms and from the English Civil War to Kosovo.

National Gallery

Trafalgar Square, WC2N 5DN
Tel: (020) 7747 2885
www.nationalgallery.org.uk
Observe stunning works by Botticelli, Leonardo da Vinci, Rembrandt, Gainsborough, Turner, Renoir, Cezanne and Van Gogh in this absorbing gallery, displaying Western European painting from about 1250 to 1900.

National Maritime Museum

Greenwich, SE10 9NF
Tel: (020) 8312 6565
www.nmm.ac.uk
Understand an island's seafaring heritage – Britain's world-wide influence explained through its explorers, traders, migrants and naval power. Features on ship models, costume, and ecology of the sea.

Natural History Museum

Cromwell Road, SW7 5BD
Tel: (020) 7942 5000
www.nhm.ac.uk
Discover the wonders of the natural world from 'Creepy-Crawlies' to dinosaurs, earthquakes to ecology, through hundreds of interactive exhibits.

Royal Air Force Museum Hendon

Grahame Park Way, Hendon, NW9 5LL
Tel: (020) 8205 2266
www.rafmuseum.org
Fly with the best on the Simulator ride! While waiting to take off, take in an amazing display; aircraft, film shows, interactives and more.

Royal Observatory Greenwich

Greenwich, SE10 9NF
Tel: (020) 8858 4422
www.nmm.ac.uk
Museum of time and space and site of the Greenwich Meridian. Working telescopes and planetarium, timeball, Wren's Octagon Room and intricate clocks and computer simulations.

The Saatchi Gallery

County Hall, South Bank, SE1 2SZ
Tel: (020) 7823 2363
www.saatchi-gallery.co.uk
Contemplate contemporary art from the famous Saatchi collection, with shows by the Chapman brothers, Tracey Emin, Damien Hirst and Sarah Lucas.

Left take a flight on the London Eye; face-to-face with The Beatles at Madame Tussauds

Places to visit

Awarded VisitBritain's Quality Assured Visitor Attraction marque.

St Paul's Cathedral
St Paul's Churchyard, EC4M 8AD
Tel: (020) 7246 8348
www.stpauls.co.uk
Experience the splendour of Wren's famous cathedral church of the diocese of London, incorporating the Crypt, Ambulatory and Whispering Gallery.

Science Museum
Exhibition Road, SW7 2DD
Tel: 0870 870 4868
www.sciencemuseum.org.uk
See, touch and experience the major scientific advances of the last 300 years at the largest museum of its kind in the world.

Shakespeare's Globe Exhibition and Tour
New Globe Walk, Bankside, SE1 9DT
Tel: (020) 7902 1500
www.shakespeares-globe.org
A fascinating introduction to the world-famous Globe Theatre and daily existence in Shakespeare's London, brought vividly to life by a story-teller guide.

Somerset House
Strand, WC2R 1LA
Tel: (020) 7845 4600
www.somerset-house.org.uk
Home to the Courtauld Institute's collection of world-famous paintings, the Gilbert Collection of decorative art and the Hermitage Rooms, containing treasures from Russia's Hermitage Museum.

Tate Britain
Millbank, SW1P 4RG
Tel: (020) 7887 8008
www.tate.org.uk
The national gallery of British art from the Tudors to the Turner Prize, including works by Constable, Gainsborough and Turner, through to Hodgkin, Moore and Hockney.

Tate Modern
Bankside, SE1 9TG
Tel: (020) 7887 8008
www.tate.org.uk
For aspiring connoisseurs of modern art, Britain's national museum houses major works by Matisse, Picasso and Rothko as well as contemporary works by Richard Deacon, Mariko Mori and Gerhard Richter.

Theatre Museum
Russell Street, WC2E 7PA
Tel: (020) 7943 4700
www.theatremuseum.org
The museum's galleries explore British theatre and performers from Shakespeare's time, brought to life with imaginative exhibitions and events.

Tower of London
Tower Hill, EC3N 4AB
Tel: 0870 756 6060
www.hrp.org.uk
Chat with a Beefeater and see the legendary ravens. The Tower of London spans 900 years of British history and displays the nation's Crown Jewels, regalia and armoury robes.

Victoria and Albert Museum
Cromwell Road, SW7 2RL
Tel: (020) 7942 2000
www.vam.ac.uk
The V&A holds one of the world's largest and most diverse collections of the decorative arts, dating from 3000BC to the present day.

Vinopolis – London's Wine Tasting Visitor Attraction
Bank End, SE1 9BU
Tel: 0870 241 4040
www.vinopolis.co.uk
One of the few attractions where guests grow merrier as they walk through! Discover wine cultures from around the world and the origins of the art of winemaking.

Above hi-tech discovery at the Science Museum; take time out at the Tate Modern

This is just a selection of attractions available. Contact any Tourist Information Centre in London for more ideas.

Visit London

6th Floor, 2 More London Riverside,
London SE1 2RR
T: (020) 7234 5800 F: (020) 7378 6525
www.visitlondon.com

Need more information?

Call '0870 1 LONDON' **for the following:**

A London tourist information pack

Tourist information on London – speak to an expert for information and advice on museums, galleries, attractions, riverboat trips, sightseeing tours, theatre, shopping, eating out and much more!

Accommodation reservations

Or visit one of London's Tourist Information Centres listed overleaf.

Which part of London?

The majority of tourist accommodation is situated in the central parts of London and is therefore very convenient for most of the city's attractions and nightlife.

However, there are many establishments in outer London which provide other advantages, such as easier parking. In the accommodation pages which follow, you will find establishments listed under INNER LONDON (covering the E1 to W14 London Postal Area) and OUTER LONDON (covering the remainder of Greater London). Colour maps 6 and 7 at the front of the guide show place names and London Postal Area codes and will help you to locate accommodation in your chosen area of London.

Travel information

By road:
Major trunk roads into London include: A1, M1, A5, A10, A11, M11, A13, A2, M2, A23, A3, M3, A4, M4, A40, M40, A41, M25 (London orbital). London Transport is responsible for running London's bus services and the underground rail network. (020) 7222 1234 (24-hour telephone service; calls answered in rotation).

By rail:
Main rail termini: Victoria/Waterloo/Charing Cross – serving the South/South East; King's Cross – serving the North East; Euston – serving the North West/Midlands; Liverpool Street – serving the East; Paddington – serving the Thames Valley/West.

Tourist Information Centres

Inner London

Britain and London Visitor Centre
1 Regent Street, Piccadilly Circus, SW1Y 4XT
Open: Mon 0930-1830,Tue-Fri 0900-1830, Sat & Sun
1000-1600; Jun-Oct, Sat 0900-1700.

Greenwich TIC
Pepys House, 2 Cutty Sark Gardens,
Greenwich, SE10 9LW
Tel: 0870 608 2000 Fax: (020) 8853 4607
Open: Daily 1000-1700.

Lewisham TIC
Lewisham Library,199-201 Lewisham High Street, SE13 6LG
Tel: (020) 8297 8317 Fax: (020) 8297 9241
Open: Mon 1000-1700, Tue-Fri 0900-1700,
Sat 1000-1600.

London Visitors Centre
Arrivals Hall, Waterloo International Terminal, SE1 7LT
Open: Daily 0830-2230.

Southwark TIC
Vinoplois, 1 Bank End, SE1 9BU
Tel: (020) 7357 9168
Open: Tues-Sun 1000-1800.

Outer London

Bexley Hall Place TIC
Bourne Road, Bexley, Kent, DA5 1PQ
Tel: (01322) 558676 Fax (01322) 522921
Open: Mon-Sat 1000-1630, Sun 1400-1730.

Croydon TIC
Katharine Street, Croydon, CR9 1ET
Tel: (020) 8253 1009 Fax: (020) 8253 1008
Open: Mon-Wed & Fri 0900-1800, Thu 0930-1800,
Sat 0900-1700, Sun 1400-1700.

Harrow TIC
Civic Centre, Station Road,
Harrow, HA1 2XF
Tel: (020) 8424 1103 Fax: (020) 8424 1134
Open: Mon-Fri 0900-1700.

Hillingdon TIC
Central Library, 14-15 High Street, Uxbridge, UB8 1HD
Tel: (01895) 250706 Fax: (01895) 239794
Open: Mon, Tue & Thu 0930-2000, Wed 0930-1730,
Fri 1000-1730, Sat 0930-1600.

Hounslow TIC
The Treaty Centre, High Street, Hounslow, TW3 1ES
Tel: 0845 456 2929 Fax: 0845 456 2904
Open: Mon, Tues & Thurs 0930-2000,
Wed, Fri & Sat 0930-1730, Sun 1130-1600.

Kingston TIC
Market House, Market Place,
Kingston upon Thames, KT1 1JS
Tel: (020) 8547 5592 Fax: (020) 8547 5594
Open: Mon-Sat 1000-1700.

Richmond TIC
Old Town Hall, Whittaker Avenue,
Richmond, TW9 1TP
Tel: (020) 8940 6899 Fax: (020) 8940 6899
Open: Mon-Sat 1000-1700;
May-Sep, Sun 1030-1330.

Swanley TIC
London Road, Swanley, BR8 7AE
Tel: (01322) 614660 Fax: (01322) 666154
Open: Mon-Thu 0930-1730, Fri 0930-1800,
Sat 0900-1600.

Twickenham TIC
The Atrium, Civic Centre, York Street, Twickenham,
Middlesex, TW1 3BZ
Tel: (020) 8891 7272; Fax: (020) 8891 7738
Open: Mon-Thu 0900-1715, Fri 0900-1700.

Above experience the splendour of St Paul's Cathedral; explore the underwater world at the London Aquarium

Where to stay in
London

Entries in this region are listed under Inner London (postcode areas E1 to W14).

Please refer to the colour location maps 6 and 7 at the front of this guide.

Accommodation symbols

Symbols give useful information about services and facilities. Inside the back cover flap you can find a key to these symbols. Keep it open for easy reference.

INNER LONDON
LONDON N9

★★★★

TOURING &
CAMPING PARK

LEE VALLEY CAMPING AND CARAVAN PARK
Picketts Lock Lane, London N9 0AS
T: (020) 8803 6900
F: (020) 8884 4975
E: leisurecentre@leevalleypark.org.uk
I: www.leevalleypark.org.uk

OPEN All Year except
Christmas and New Year
Payment accepted: Delta,
Mastercard, Switch, Visa

100	🚐	£12.00–£18.00
100	🚃	£12.00–£18.00
60	⛺	£12.00–£18.00
160 touring pitches		

Turn from the A406 onto Montagu Road, which leads into Meridian Way. From the M25 take the A10 towards London and then turn left onto the A1055. The site is about 5 miles along the A1055.

LONDON SE2

★★★★★

TOURING &
CAMPING PARK

BH&HPA

See Ad on inside back cover

ABBEY WOOD CARAVAN CLUB SITE

Federation Road, Abbey Wood, London SE2 0LS
T: (020) 8311 7708
F: (020) 8311 1465
I: www.caravanclub.co.uk

Recently redeveloped to the highest standards, this site is the ideal base for exploring the capital. A green, gently sloping site with mature trees screening its spacious grounds. Special member rates mean you can save your membership subscription in less than a week. Visit www.caravanclub.co.uk to find out more.

OPEN All Year
Payment accepted: Delta, Mastercard, Switch, Visa

On M2 turn off at A221. Then turn right into McLeod Road, right into Knee Hill and the site is the 2nd turning on the right.

220	🚐	£18.00–£23.00
220	🚃	£18.00–£23.00
	⛺	On application
220 touring pitches		

Credit card bookings

If you book by telephone and are asked for your credit card number it is advisable to check the proprietor's policy should you cancel your reservation.

★★★★★
TOURING &
CAMPING PARK

BH&HPA

See Ad on inside back cover

CRYSTAL PALACE CARAVAN CLUB SITE

Crystal Palace Parade, London SE19 1UF
T: (020) 8778 7155
F: (020) 8676 0980
I: www.caravanclub.co.uk

Popular with European families in the summer, a friendly site on the edge of a pleasant park, in close proximity to all of London's attractions. Special member rates mean you can save your membership subscription in less than a week. Visit www.caravanclub.co.uk to find out more.

84	🚐	£17.00–£22.00
84	🚐	£17.00–£22.00
66	⚊	On application
150 touring pitches		

OPEN All Year
Payment accepted: Delta, Mastercard, Switch, Visa

Turn off the A205, South Circular Road at West Dulwich into Croxted Road. The site is adjacent to the BBC television mast.

Use your *i*s

There are more than 750 Tourist Information Centres throughout England, Scotland and Wales, offering friendly help with accommodation and holiday ideas as well as suggestions of places to visit and things to do. You'll find addresses in the local phone book.

enjoyEngland™
official guides to **quality**

Hotels, Townhouses, Travel Accommodation and Restaurants with Rooms in England 2005
£10.99

Bed & Breakfasts, Guesthouses, Small Hotels, Farmhouses, Inns, Campus Accommodation and Hostels in England 2005
£11.99

Self-Catering Holiday Homes and Boat Accommodation in England 2005
£11.99

Touring Parks, Camping, Holiday Parks and Villages in Britain 2005
£8.99

Somewhere Special in England 2005
£8.99

Families and Pets Welcome in England 2005
£11.99

Explore **fashionable** Manchester, **nautical** Liverpool and **bustling** Blackpool.

England's Northwest

Looking for some inspiration? Here are a few ideas to get you started in England's Northwest. **experience** the atmosphere of anticipation at the Grand National. **discover** the most exciting modern art gallery outside London at Tate Liverpool. **explore** the varied coastline with its unspoilt estuaries and seaside entertainment. **relax** and watch the world go by on a canal-boat holiday through the beautiful Cheshire countryside.

THE REGION
Cheshire, Greater Manchester, Lancashire, Merseyside and Cumbria – The Lake District (see page 84)

CONTACT
▸ **ENGLAND'S NORTHWEST**
   www.visitenglandsnorthwest.com
   Cheshire and Warrington Tourism Board
   T: (01244) 346543 www.visit-cheshire.com
   The Lancashire & Blackpool Tourist Board
   T: (01257) 226600 www.lancashiretourism.com
   or www.visitblackpool.com
   Marketing Manchester – The Tourist Board for Greater Manchester
   T: (0161) 237 1010
   www.destinationmanchester.com
   The Mersey Partnership – The Tourist Board for Merseyside
   T: (0151) 227 2727 www.visitliverpool.com

Explore Cumbria's soaring peaks, with their mirror-perfect reflections in the waters of the lakes (see page 84), or discover the rounded hills and plains of Cheshire. Relax on inland waterways or on Lancashire's sandy beaches. Experience the buzz and excitement of Manchester and Liverpool or the thrill of a rollercoaster ride in Blackpool – it's all possible in England's Northwest.

A black-and-white picture

Tour through the Cheshire countryside and you'll come across pretty black-and-white timbered buildings like 15th-century Little Moreton Hall. At Lyme Park you might get a sense of déjà vu – it was the setting for BBC's Pride and Prejudice. Relax on Cheshire's waterways and experience the thrill as you rise up on the giant Anderton Boat Lift or let a Roman centurion guide you around the walled city of Chester, with its two-tier shops known as The Rows, and the Dewa Roman Experience.

A city reborn

Take in Manchester's amazing vistas from the top of the all-glass Urbis before visiting the museum below. This is just one of 50 fascinating free museums and stunning art galleries in the Greater Manchester area. Head for the Quays and the paintings of LS Lowry or the stunning Imperial War Museum North. Indulge yourself in the city's many restaurants, cafés and bars, in particular the Curry Mile. Or there's music and theatre, festivals and carnivals, superb shopping and, of course, football!

Capital of Culture

More choices to make when you visit Liverpool, named European Capital of Culture 2008. And you can see why. You've hit the jackpot with the largest collection of national museums and galleries outside London. Dine and dance, listen to music, shop 'til you drop, enjoy the theatre and, of course, search out the Beatles' haunts. For a sporting experience, walk through the tunnel to the sound of the crowd at Anfield or test your riding skills on the Grand National simulator at Aintree.

Fairways and candy floss

Like to be active? England's Golf Coast stretches for miles from the Wirral to Cumbria and boasts over 40 links courses to test all handicaps, but for non-golfers there's wonderful walks along stunning beaches or inland on the footpaths of the Forest of Bowland. You'll enjoy historic Lancaster and Preston's National Football Museum, but if it's thrills you want, Blackpool's the place. Take in the spectacular views from the Tower, scream with excitement on the white-knuckle rides of the Pleasure Beach, build sandcastles on the beach or ride a tram along the seafront.

Left, from top feel the thunder of hooves at the Grand National, Aintree; reflections of Liverpool; wander around the gardens at Arley Hall, Northwich **Right** watch the sun go down over Morecambe Bay

Places to visit

Albert Dock
Liverpool, Merseyside
Tel: (0151) 708 7334
www.albertdock.com
Something for everyone at Britain's largest Grade I Listed historic building. Restored four-sided dock including shops, bars, restaurants, entertainment, Maritime Museum, Tate Gallery and marina.

Arley Hall and Gardens
Northwich, Cheshire
Tel: (01565) 777353
www.arleyhallandgardens.com
Early Victorian country house set in 5ha (12 acres) of magnificent gardens, with a 15thC Grade I tithe barn. Plant nursery, gift shop and restaurant. A plantsman's paradise!

The Beatles Story Ltd
Albert Dock, Liverpool, Merseyside
Tel: (0151) 709 1963
www.beatlesstory.com
Award-winning visitor attraction revealing the many chapters of The Beatles story. Relive the group's early days in Hamburg, and the heady days of the Cavern Club.

Beeston Castle (English Heritage)
Chapel Lane, Beeston, Cheshire
Tel: (01829) 260464
www.english-heritage.org.uk
Soak up the history at this ruined 13thC castle set on top of the Peckforton Hills, with dramatic views of the surrounding countryside. Exhibitions are also held telling of the castle's past.

Blackpool Pleasure Beach
Ocean Boulevard, Blackpool, Lancashire
Tel: 0870 444 5566
www.blackpoolpleasurebeach.com
Endless fun for all! Blackpool Pleasure Beach offers over 145 rides and attractions, plus spectacular shows.

Blackpool Tower and Circus
The Promenade, Blackpool, Lancashire
Tel: (01253) 622242
www.blackpooltower.co.uk
A world of entertainment – inside Blackpool Tower you'll find the UK's best circus, the famous Tower Ballroom, Jungle Jim's Playground, Tower Top Ride and Undersea World.

Boat Museum
South Pier Road, Ellesmere Port, Cheshire
Tel: (0151) 355 5017
www.boatmuseum.org.uk
Brush up on the history of the canals at this historic dock complex on the Shropshire Union Canal. Home to the UK's largest collection of inland waterway craft, Power Hall, Pump House and seven exhibitions of industrial heritage.

Botany Bay Villages and Puddletown Pirates
Canal Mill, Chorley, Lancashire
Tel: (01257) 261220
www.botanybay.co.uk
A shopping, leisure and heritage experience including Puddletown Pirates, the largest indoor adventure play centre in the Northwest.

Bridgemere Garden World
Bridgemere, Cheshire
Tel: (01270) 521100
www.bridgemere.co.uk
Inspiration for greenfingers – 10 fascinating hectares (25 acres) of plants, gardens, greenhouses and a shop. Over 20 different display gardens, incorporating many Chelsea Flower Show Gold Medal winners.

Camelot Theme Park
Park Hall Road, Charnock Richard, Lancashire
Tel: (01257) 453044
www.camelotthemepark.co.uk
The Magical Kingdom of Camelot, voted Lancashire's Family Attraction of the Year 2002, is a world of thrilling rides, fantastic entertainment and family fun.

This is just a selection of attractions available. Contact any Tourist Information Centre in the region for more ideas.

Chester Zoo

Chester, Cheshire
Tel: (01244) 380280
www.chesterzoo.org.uk
Observe over 7000 animals in spacious and natural
enclosures at one of Europe's leading conservation zoos.
Now featuring the 'Tsavo' African Black Rhino Experience.

Croxteth Hall and Country Park

Croxteth Hall Lane, Liverpool, Merseyside
Tel: (0151) 228 5311
www.croxteth.co.uk
An Edwardian stately home set in 200ha (500 acres) of
countryside, featuring a Victorian walled garden and large
collection of rare, farm animal breeds.

Dunham Massey Hall Park and Garden (National Trust)

Altrincham, Cheshire
Tel: (0161) 941 1025
www.nationaltrust.org.uk
Spend the day at this 18thC mansion, with furniture,
paintings and silver, set in a wooded deer park with a 10-ha
(25-acre) informal garden.

East Lancashire Railway

Bolton Street Station, Bury, Lancashire
Tel: (0161) 764 7790
www.east-lancs-rly.co.uk
Journey back in time on this steam-hauled railway running
along the Irwell Valley, north from Bury to Ramsbottom and
Rawtenstall. Spectacular views of the West Pennine Moor.

Gawsworth Hall

Gawsworth, Cheshire
Tel: (01260) 223456
www.gawsworthhall.com
Beautiful, Tudor, half-timbered manor house with tilting
ground. Inside are pictures, sculpture and furniture. Book
your seat at one of the summer plays performed in the
open-air theatre.

Gulliver's World Family Theme Park

Off Shackleton Close, Warrington, Cheshire
Tel: (01925) 444888
www.gulliversfun.co.uk
A theme park for the whole family, offering over 50 rides
and attractions from log flumes to roller-coasters and
dinosaurs. Suitable for children aged two and over.

Jodrell Bank Visitor Centre

Lower Withington, Macclesfield, Cheshire
Tel: (01477) 571339
www.jb.man.ac.uk/scicen
Home of the Lovell radio telescope, plus 3D theatre, small
exhibition, observational pathway and 14-ha (35-acre)
arboretum. Shop and space café.

Knowsley Safari Park

Prescot, Merseyside
Tel: (0151) 430 9009
www.knowsley.com
Enjoy, if you dare, a five-mile safari through 200ha (500
acres) of rolling countryside and see the world's wildest
animals roaming free.

Lady Lever Art Gallery

Port Sunlight Village, Higher Bebington, Cheshire
Tel: (0151) 478 4136
www.ladyleverartgallery.org.uk
A chance to admire the 1st Lord Leverhulme's magnificent
collection of British paintings dating from 1750-1900, British
furniture, Wedgwood pottery and oriental porcelain.

Lyme Park (National Trust)

Disley, Stockport
Tel: (01663) 762023
www.nationaltrust.org.uk
Set in a country estate of over 550ha (1377 acres) of
moorland, woodland and park, this magnificent house will
appeal to those who appreciate Elizabethan, Georgian and
Regency architecture.

Macclesfield Silk Museum

The Heritage Centre, Macclesfield, Cheshire
Tel: (01625) 613210
www.silk-macclesfield.org
Set in the former Sunday School built for child workers
in the silk industry, the museum tells the story of silk in
Macclesfield through an award-winning audio-visual
programme.

Merseyside Maritime Museum

Albert Dock, Liverpool, Merseyside
Tel: (0151) 478 4499
www.merseysidemaritimemuseum.org.uk
The museum tells the story of one of the world's greatest
ports and the people who used it, reflecting the international
importance of Liverpool as a gateway to the world.

The Museum of Science & Industry in Manchester

Liverpool Road, Manchester
Tel: (0161) 832 2244
www.msim.org.uk
Get interactive in the brand new Xperiment gallery, see the
wheels of industry turning in the Power Hall and marvel at
the planes that made history in the Air and Space Hall.

The National Football Museum

Deepdale Stadium, Preston, Lancashire
Tel: (01772) 908442
www.nationalfootballmuseum.com
The history of football at your fingertips with hands-on
exhibits and the magnificent FIFA collection, the finest
collection of historic football memorabilia in the world.

Left take a ride to the top of Blackpool Tower; admire the collection at Lady Lever Art Gallery, Port Sunlight

Places to visit

Awarded VisitBritain's Quality Assured Visitor Attraction marque.

Norton Priory Museum and Gardens
Tudor Road, Runcorn, Cheshire
Tel: (01928) 569895
www.nortonpriory.org
Medieval priory remains with a purpose-built museum, St Christopher's statue, sculpture trail and award-winning walled garden, all set in 15ha (38 acres) of beautiful gardens.

Pleasureland Theme Park
Marine Drive, Southport, Merseyside
Tel: 0870 220 0204
www.pleasureland.uk.com
Over 100 rides and attractions, including the classic Cyclone coaster, TRAUMAtizer and the Lucozade Space Shot. Not for the fainthearted!

Quarry Bank Mill (National Trust)
Styal, Cheshire
Tel: (01625) 527468
www.quarrybankmill.org.uk
A Georgian water-powered cotton spinning mill with five floors of award-winning displays and demonstrations and 120ha (300 acres) of parkland surroundings.

Sandcastle Tropical Waterworld
South Promenade, Blackpool, Lancashire
Tel: (01253) 343602
www.sandcastle-waterworld.co.uk
Prepare to get wet ... complete with wave pool, fun pools, giant water flumes, sauna, white-knuckle water slides, children's safe harbour, play area, catering, bar shops and amusements.

Sea Life Blackpool
The Promenade, Blackpool, Lancashire
Tel: (01253) 621258
www.sealifeeurope.com
Experience the enchanting world of the Amazon, one of the world's greatest rainforests, featuring electric eels and piranhas, and discover the lost city of Atlantis.

Smithills Hall
Smithills Dean Road, Bolton, Lancashire
Tel: (01204) 332377
www.smithills.org
Budding historians will appreciate one of the oldest manor houses in Lancashire. Smithills Hall has a great hall dating back to the 14thC, plus 16thC and Victorian additions.

Tate Liverpool
Albert Dock, Liverpool, Merseyside
Tel: (0151) 702 7400
www.tate.org.uk/liverpool/
Exhibiting the National Collection of Modern Art, Tate Liverpool is well worth a visit.

Tatton Park (National Trust)
Knutsford, Cheshire
Tel: (01625) 534400
www.tattonpark.org.uk
Fine Georgian mansion full of art treasures and furniture with a garden, traditional working farm and Tudor manor house, all set in a 400-ha (1000-acre) deer park.

Wigan Pier
Trencherfield Mill, Wigan
Tel: (01942) 323666
www.wiganmbc.gov.uk
With old favourites 'The Way We Were' and 'Victorian Schoolroom', plus the new attraction 'The Museum of Memories', our social history is explored in Wigan Pier's unique style.

Wildfowl and Wetland Trust Martin Mere
Burscough, Lancashire
Tel: (01704) 895181
www.wwt.org.uk
Twenty-hectare (50-acre) landscaped Waterfowl Gardens, home to over 1600 ducks, geese and swans, including some of the world's rarest and most endangered species.

Above the inspired Trois Danseusses by Pablo Picasso, Tate Liverpool; enjoy the high life on Blackpool's Central Pier
Right marvel at The Lowry arts centre, The Quays, Salford

This is just a selection of attractions available. Contact any Tourist Information Centre in the region for more ideas.

England's Northwest
www.visitenglandsnorthwest.com

There are various publications and guides about England's Northwest available from the following Tourist Boards:

Cheshire and Warrington Tourism Board
Grosvenor Park Lodge, Grosvenor Park Road
Chester CH1 1QQ
T: (01244) 346543
E: info@cwtb.co.uk
www.visit-cheshire.com

The Lancashire & Blackpool Tourist Board
St Georges House, St Georges Street
Chorley PR7 2AA
T: (01257) 226600
Brochure request: (01772) 533369
E: info@lancashiretourism.com
www.lancashiretourism.com or www.visitblackpool.com

Marketing Manchester – The Tourist Board for Greater Manchester
Churchgate House, 56 Oxford Street
Manchester M1 6EU
T: (0161) 237 1010
Brochure request: 0870 609 3013
F: (0161) 228 2960
E: Manchester_visitor_centre@notes.manchester.gov.uk
www.destinationmanchester.com

The Mersey Partnership – The Tourist Board for Merseyside
12 Princes Parade, Liverpool L3 1BG
T: (0151) 227 2727
F: (0151) 227 2325
Overseas: 00 44 151 709 8111
Tourist Information Centre: (0151) 709 3285
Accommodation booking service: 0845 601 1125
E: info@visitliverpool.com
www.visitliverpool.com

Travel information

By road:
Motorways intersect within the region which has the best road network in the country. Travelling north or south use the M6, and east or west the M62.

By rail:
Most Northwest coastal resorts are connected to InterCity routes with trains from many parts of the country, and there are through trains to major cities and towns.

Where to stay in
England's Northwest

All place names in the blue bands, under which accommodation is listed, are shown on the maps at the front of this guide.

A complete listing of all VisitBritain assessed accommodation covered by this guide appears at the back.

Accommodation symbols

Symbols give useful information about services and facilities. Inside the back cover flap you can find a key to these symbols. Keep it open for easy reference.

BLACKPOOL, Blackpool Map ref 5A1 *Tourist Information Centre Tel: (01253) 478 222*

★★★
TOURING PARK

RICHMOND HILL CARAVAN PARK
352 St Annes Road, South Shore, Blackpool
FY4 2QN
T: (01253) 344266
E: bookings@richmond-hill.freeserve.co.uk
I: www.richmond-hill.freeserve.co.uk

20		£12.00–£17.50
20		£12.00–£17.50
20 touring pitches		

Follow signs for Squires Gate and airport. At traffic lights at the Halfway House pub turn right onto St Annes Road. Richmond Hill is 200yds on right, between Faringdon and Ivy Avenue. Entrance on Ivy Avenue.

CHESTER, Cheshire Map ref 5A2 *Tourist Information Centre Tel: (01244) 402111*

★★★★★
**TOURING &
CAMPING PARK**

BH&HPA

See Ad on inside back cover

CHESTER FAIROAKS
CARAVAN CLUB SITE

Rake Lane, Chester CH2 4HS
T: (0151) 355 1600
I: www.caravanclub.co.uk

A tranquil site only six miles from the walled city of Chester with its famous zoo, historic sites, top-class entertainment and excellent shopping. Special member rates mean you can save your membership subscription in less than a week. Visit www.caravanclub.co.uk to find out more.

OPEN All Year
Payment accepted: Delta, Mastercard, Switch, Visa

99		£17.00–£22.00
99		£17.00–£22.00
	▲	On application
99 touring pitches		

From the M53 take jct 10 and join the A5117. Travel towards Queensferry, follow the brown signs. Turn left in Little Stanney at signpost Chorlton. Site 0.25 miles on left.

THE CARAVAN CLUB

LANCASTER, Lancashire Map ref 6A3 *Tourist Information Centre Tel: (01524) 32878*

★★★
**TOURING &
CAMPING PARK**

BH&HPA

NEW PARKSIDE FARM CARAVAN PARK
Denny Beck, Caton Road, Lancaster
LA2 9HH
T: (01524) 770723
I: www.ukparks.co.uk/newparkside

30		£9.50–£11.50
5		£9.50–£11.50
5	▲	£6.00–£8.00
40 touring pitches		

Leave the M6 at jct 34 and go onto the A683 towards Caton and Kirkby Lonsdale, 1 mile from jct.

LANCASTER continued

★★★
TOURING &
CAMPING PARK

WYRESIDE LAKES FISHERY
Sunnyside Farmhouse, Gleaves Hill Road,
Lancaster LA2 9DQ
T: (01524) 792093
F: (01524) 792093
E: wyreside2003@yahoo.co.uk
I: www.wyresidelakes.co.uk

OPEN All Year except
Christmas
Payment accepted: Amex,
Delta, Mastercard, Switch,
Visa

26 🚐	£9.00–£11.00
26 🚙	£9.00
50 ▲	£9.00
52 touring pitches	

Jct 33 on M6, turn left at roundabout then take an immediate left down Hampson Lane. Turn right at T-junction and over 2 crossroads. Turn right at next crossroads. Fishery on the left.

MIDDLETON, Lancashire Map ref 5A1

★★★
HOLIDAY, TOURING
& CAMPING PARK

BH&HPA

MELBREAK CARAVAN PARK
Carr Lane, Middleton, Morecambe LA3 3LH
T: (01524) 852430

6 🚐	£10.50–£10.50
6 🚙	£10.50–£10.50
10 ▲	£8.20–£8.20
16 touring pitches	

Leave the M6 at jct 34 and take the A683 for 7 miles to Middleton. Turn right towards the beach. The site is 0.5 miles on the left.

ROCHDALE, Greater Manchester Map ref 5B1 *Tourist Information Centre Tel: (01706) 864928*

★★★
TOURING &
CAMPING PARK

BH&HPA

HOLLINGWORTH LAKE CARAVAN PARK
Roundhouse Farm, Hollingworth Lake,
Littleborough OL15 0AT
T: (01706) 378661

OPEN All Year

30 🚐	£10.00–£14.00
10 🚙	£8.00–£14.00
10 ▲	£5.00–£14.00
50 touring pitches	

From M62 jct 21 follow Hollingworth Lake Country Park signs to the Fishermans Inn. Take Rakewood Road. Then second on right.

THURSTASTON, Wirral Map ref 5A2

★★★★
TOURING &
CAMPING PARK

BH&HPA

See Ad on inside back cover

WIRRAL COUNTRY PARK CARAVAN CLUB SITE
Station Road, Thurstaston, Wirral CH61 0HN
T: (0151) 648 5228
I: www.caravanclub.co.uk

The site is set in 2,000 acres of unspoilt landscape in a country park from where you can explore the beautiful Wirral peninsula. Open 2 April to 1 November. Special member rates mean you can save your membership subscription in less than a week. Visit www.caravanclub.co.uk to find out more.

Payment accepted: Delta, Mastercard, Switch, Visa

On the A540 in the village of Thurstaston, heading north from Heswall, turn left into Station Road at the sign stating Wirral Country Park Centre.

92 🚐	£14.60–£20.60
92 🚙	£14.60–£20.60
92 touring pitches	

★ Ratings All accommodation in this guide has been rated, or is awaiting a rating, by a trained VisitBritain assessor.

WARRINGTON, Warrington Map ref 5A2 *Tourist Information Centre Tel: (01925) 632571*

★★★★	**HOLLY BANK CARAVAN PARK**		62		£15.00–£17.00
TOURING PARK	Warburton Bridge Road, Rixton,	OPEN All Year	3		£15.00–£17.00
	Warrington WA3 6HU		10		£13.00–£15.00
BH&HPA	T: (0161) 775 2842		75 touring pitches		

*Two miles east of jct 21 off the M6 onto the A57 Irlam. Turn right at the lights onto Warburton Bridge Road.
Entry to the site is on the left.*

Use your *i*s

There are more than 750
Tourist Information Centres
throughout England, Scotland
and Wales, offering friendly
help with accommodation and
holiday ideas as well as
suggestions of places to visit
and things to do. You'll find
addresses in the local
phone book.

A brief guide to the main towns and villages offering accommodation in **England's Northwest**

BLACKPOOL, Blackpool
Britain's largest fun resort, with Blackpool Pleasure Beach, three piers and the famous Tower. Host to the spectacular autumn illuminations.

CHESTER, Cheshire
Roman and medieval walled city rich in treasures. Black and white buildings are a hallmark, including The Rows – two-tier shopping galleries. The famous Chester Zoo and 900-year-old cathedral.

ROCHDALE, Greater Manchester
An ancient crossroads for trade, today Rochdale's town centre is dominated by the spectacular Victorian Gothic Town Hall, fronted by the broad Esplanade, thought to be the widest road bridge in Europe. The medieval St Chad's Parish Church and Broadfield Park provide a stunning backdrop. The historic conservation area of Toad Lane, site of the first Co-op Shop, is nearby.

LANCASTER, Lancashire
Interesting old county town on the river Lune with history dating back to Roman times. Norman castle, St Mary's Church, Customs House, City and Maritime Museums, Ashton Memorial and Butterfly House are among places of note. Good centre for touring the Lake District.

WARRINGTON, Warrington
Has prehistoric and Roman origins. Once the beer capital of Britain because so much beer was brewed here. Developed in the 18th and 19thC as a commercial and industrial town. The cast-iron gates in front of the town hall were originally destined for Sandringham.

Above dramatic Healey Dell, Rochdale

Tourist Information Centres

When it comes to your next English break, the first stage of your journey could be closer than you think. You've probably got a tourist information centre nearby which is there to serve the local community – as well as visitors. Knowledgeable staff will be happy to help you, wherever you're heading.

Many tourist information centres can provide you with maps and guides, and often it's possible to book accommodation and travel tickets too.

Across the country there are more than 550 TICs. You'll find the address of your nearest centre in your local phone book.

Awesome views and calm lakes; the **great outdoors** doesn't get much **grander** than in Cumbria.

Cumbria –
The Lake District

Looking for some inspiration? Here are a few ideas to get you started in Cumbria – The Lake District. **experience** Roman history along Hadrian's Wall. **discover** the narrow gauge steam railway running through the Eskdale Valley. **explore** England's highest mountain and deepest lake – Scafell Pike and Wastwater. **relax** on a romantic break in a lakeside hotel.

CONTACT

▸ **CUMBRIA TOURIST BOARD**
Ashleigh, Holly Road,
Windermere, Cumbria LA23 2AQ
T: (015394) 44444
F: (015394) 44041
E: info@golakes.co.uk
www.golakes.co.uk
www.lakedistrictoutdoors.co.uk

Rewarding walks, energetic climbs, awesome views and calm lakes: Cumbria offers a spectacular variety of pursuits and a refreshing quality of life. Roman remains, outdoor adventure, colourful gardens and good food and drink will ensure you're fully satisfied with your stay.

Floral inspiration

Visit in springtime to see the hosts of golden daffodils that inspired Wordsworth to write his famous poem 200 years ago. In Cockermouth you can visit his birthplace and see the garden he loved so much. A new centre near Grasmere houses Wordsworth's books, manuscripts, paintings and drawings, and includes a space for poetry reading. Explore the magnificent grounds surrounding 800-year-old Muncaster Castle, wander through the national award-winning gardens at Holker Hall or let the children run free in the lakeside parkland of Fell Foot Country Park.

High excitement

The great outdoors doesn't get much grander than the Lake District where you can experience some of the best walking and outdoor activities in England. Go Ape! on a forest adventure course, go sailing, rock climbing or paragliding. Walk alongside Hadrian's Wall – you'll find spectacular views and a visitor centre explaining its 1800 year history at Birdoswald Roman Fort, set high on a spur overlooking the river Irthing.

Then discover the diverse wildlife, scenic qualities and world-class geological heritage which has earned the North Pennines its status as the first European Geopark in Britain. For something more leisurely take a cruise across one of the many lakes. Lake Windermere is the most popular, with a 10-mile boat trip in wonderful scenery.

Festivals and food

Cumbria is awash with festivals and events, including the Barrow Festival of the Sea, the Whitehaven Maritime Festival, Words by the Water, the Lake District Summer Music Festival and a variety of country shows. If you're a connoisseur of local produce, don't miss The Cumbria and Lake District Food and Drink Festival including a series of events at award-winning Rheged – The Village in the Hill – where you can sample the excellent and diverse range of food from across the county.

Left, from top top take a scenic drive along a Cumbrian country lane, Haweswater Beck; deserted coastline, St Bees; discover the world of Wordsworth at Dove Cottage, Grasmere **Right** a gentle stroll, Ashness Bridge

Places to visit

 Awarded VisitBritain's
Quality Assured Visitor
Attraction marque.

Aquarium of the Lakes
Lakeside, Newby Bridge, Cumbria
Tel: (01539) 530153
www.aquariumofthelakes.co.uk
Set on the southern shores of Lake Windermere, this
fascinating aquarium is the UK's largest collection
of freshwater fish, with over 30 naturally themed displays.

The Beacon
West Strand, Whitehaven, Cumbria
Tel: (01946) 592302
www.thebeacon-whitehaven.co.uk
Award-winning attraction and museum telling the story
of historic Whitehaven, superbly situated overlooking
the Georgian harbour.

Birdoswald Roman Fort
Gilsland, Cumbria
Tel: (01697) 747602
www.birdoswaldromanfort.org
Remains of a Roman fort on one of the best parts of
Hadrian's Wall with excellent views of the Irthing Gorge.
Exhibition, shop, tearoom and excavations.

Brantwood, Home of John Ruskin
Coniston, Cumbria
Tel: (015394) 41396
www.brantwood.org.uk
Discover a wealth of things to do at Brantwood, the most
beautifully situated house in the Lake District, and home
of John Ruskin from 1872 until 1900.

Cars of the Stars Motor Museum
Standish Street, Keswick, Cumbria
Tel: (017687) 73757
www.carsofthestars.com
See many famous TV and film vehicles including the
Batmobile, Chitty Chitty Bang Bang, the James Bond
Aston Martin, Herbie and Thunderbird's FAB 1.

The Dock Museum
North Road, Barrow-in-Furness, Cumbria
Tel: (01229) 894444
www.dockmuseum.org.uk
A spectacular modern museum built over an original
Victorian dry dock. Galleries include multi-media
interactive exhibits and impressive ship models.

Dove Cottage and Wordsworth Museum
Town End, Grasmere, Cumbria
Tel: (015394) 35544
www.wordsworth.org.uk
Wordsworth's home during his most creative period.
Cottage guided tours, original manuscripts in the museum
and contemporary art in the 3°W art gallery.

Eden Ostrich World
Langwathby, Cumbria
Tel: (01768) 881771
www.ostrich-world.com
Meet ostriches and many other animals. Also enjoy the
tearoom, hayloft galleries, play areas, including soft
play mania, riverside walk, Zebroid foal and a sheep
milking parlour.

Gleaston Water Mill
Gleaston, Ulverston, Cumbria
Tel: (01229) 869244
www.watermill.co.uk
A truly rural experience – a water cornmill, artefacts,
traditions, folklore, great home-cooked food, and of
course, the acclaimed Pig's Whisper country store.

Heron Glass
Ulverston, Cumbria
Tel: (01229) 581121
www.herongiftware.com
Displays of making hand-blown glass giftware and lead
crystal, plus the Gateway to Furness Exhibition, which
provides a fascinating snapshot of the history of the
Furness Peninsula. Lighthouse café and restaurant.

Hill Top (National Trust)
Near Sawrey, Ambleside, Cumbria
Tel: (015394) 36269
www.nationaltrust.org.uk
Beatrix Potter wrote many of her popular Peter Rabbit stories and other books in this charming little house which still contains her own china and furniture.

Holker Hall and Gardens
Cark in Cartmel, Cumbria
Tel: (015395) 58328
www.holker-hall.co.uk
An impressive historic house with new Victorian wing, award-winning formal and woodland gardens, deer park, motor museum, adventure playground, café and gift shop.

Jennings Brothers plc
The Castle Brewery, Cockermouth, Cumbria
Tel: 0845 129 7185
www.jenningsbrewery.co.uk
Take a guided tour of this traditional brewery and sample the ales in the Old Cooperage Bar.

The Lake District Coast Aquarium Maryport
South Quay, Maryport, Cumbria
Tel: (01900) 817760
www.lakedistrict-coastaquarium.co.uk
Independent aquarium with over 35 displays, including walk-over ray pool and hands-in rock pool. Largest collection of native marine species in Cumbria.

The Lake District Visitor Centre
Brockhole, Windermere, Cumbria
Tel: (015394) 46601
www.lake-district.gov.uk
An Edwardian house on the shores of Windermere with extensive landscaped gardens and stunning views. Lake cruises, adventure playground, walks, events and activities.

Lakeland Motor Museum
Holker Hall and Gardens, Cark in Cartmel, Cumbria
Tel: (015395) 58509
www.lakelandmotormuseum.co.uk
Over 25,000 exhibits including rare motoring automobilia, a 1930s garage re-creation and the Campbell Legend Bluebird Exhibition.

Lakeland Sheep and Wool Centre
Egremont Road, Cockermouth, Cumbria
Tel: (01900) 822673
www.sheep-woolcentre.co.uk
Live farm show including cows, sheep, dogs and geese, all displaying their working qualities. Large gift shop and licensed café/restaurant. All weather attraction.

Lakeland Wildlife Oasis
Hale, Cumbria
Tel: (015395) 63027
www.wildlifeoasis.co.uk
A wildlife exhibition where both living animals and hands-on displays are used to illustrate evolution in the animal kingdom. Includes gift shop and café.

Lakeside and Haverthwaite Railway
Haverthwaite Station, Ulverston, Cumbria
Tel: (015395) 31594
Standard-gauge steam railway operating a daily seasonal service through the beautiful Leven Valley. Steam and diesel locomotives on display.

Levens Hall
Levens, Cumbria
Tel: (015395) 60321
www.levenshall.co.uk
Elizabethan home of the Bagot family with 13thC pele tower, world-famous topiary gardens, Bellingham Buttery, Potting Shed gift shop, plant centre and play area.

Muncaster Castle, Gardens, Owl Centre and Meadow Vole Maze
Ravenglass, Cumbria
Tel: (01229) 717614
www.muncaster.co.uk
Historic haunted castle with the most beautifully situated Owl Centre in the world. See the birds fly, picnic in the gardens, visit the Pennington family home.

Rheged – The Village in the Hill
Redhills, Penrith, Cumbria
Tel: (01768) 868000
www.rheged.com
Award-winning Rheged is home to a giant cinema screen showing four movies daily, the only international Everest Exhibition, speciality shops, indoor play area and café.

The Rum Story
Lowther Street, Whitehaven, Cumbria
Tel: (01946) 592933
www.rumstory.co.uk
The world's first exhibition depicting the unique and dramatic story of the UK rum trade, set in the original Jefferson's wine merchant premises.

Rydal Mount and Gardens
Rydal, Cumbria
Tel: (015394) 33002
www.rydalmount.co.uk
Nestling between the majestic fells, Lake Windermere and Rydal Water lies the most beloved home of William Wordsworth from 1813-1850.

Left still waters, Ambleside; spellbinding views at Borrowdale

Places to visit

Awarded VisitBritain's
Quality Assured Visitor
Attraction marque.

Sellafield Visitors Centre
Sellafield, Cumbria
Tel: (01946) 727027
www.sparkingreaction.info
Sellafield's new exhibition, produced and written by the
Science Museum in London, explores the complex issues
around nuclear power.

Sizergh Castle and Garden (National Trust)
Sizergh, Kendal, Cumbria
Tel: (015395) 60070
www.nationaltrust.org.uk
The Strickland family home for 750 years with 14thC pele
tower, 15thC great hall, 16thC wings and Stuart
connections. Rock garden, rose garden, daffodils.

South Tynedale Railway
Railway Station, Alston, Cumbria
Tel: (01434) 381696
www.strps.org.uk
Narrow-gauge steam and diesel railway along part of the
route of the former Alston to Haltwhistle branch line,
through the beautiful scenery of the South Tynedale valley.

Steam Yacht Gondola (National Trust)
Pier Cottage, Coniston, Cumbria
Tel: (015394) 41288
www.nationaltrust.org.uk/gondola
View Coniston Water from the elegant, Victorian steam-
powered yacht Gondola, now completely renovated with
an opulently-upholstered saloon.

Theatre by the Lake
Lakeside, Keswick, Cumbria
Tel: (017687) 74411
www.theatrebythelake.com
Year-round programme of drama, music, dance and
comedy, with a summer season of plays, Christmas and
Easter shows and festivals of film, literature and jazz.

Tullie House Museum and Art Gallery
Castle Street, Carlisle, Cumbria
Tel: (01228) 534781
www.tulliehouse.co.uk
Georgian mansion housing a magnificent pre-Raphaelite
collection, Victorian childhood gallery, 1689 fireplace and
Jacobean oak staircase.

Ullswater 'Steamers'
Penrith, Cumbria
Tel: (017684) 82229
www.ullswater-steamers.co.uk
Relax and enjoy a beautiful Ullswater cruise with walks
and picnic areas. Boat services operating all year round.

Windermere Lake Cruises
Lakeside, Newby Bridge, Cumbria
Tel: (015395) 31188
www.windermere-lakecruises.co.uk
Steamers and launches sail daily throughout the year
between Ambleside, Lakeside and Bowness. Seasonal
sailings to Brockhole, Lakeside and Haverthwaite Steam
Railway and Aquarium of the Lakes.

Windermere Steamboats & Museum
Rayrigg Road, Bowness-on-Windermere, Cumbria
Tel: (015394) 45565
www.steamboat.co.uk
A wealth of interest and information about life on bygone
Windermere. Regular steam launch trips, vintage vessels
and classic motorboats. Model boat pond, lakeside
picnic area.

The World of Beatrix Potter Attraction
The Old Laundry, Bowness-on-Windermere, Cumbria
Tel: (015394) 88444
www.hop-skip-jump.com
The life and works of Beatrix Potter brought to life,
with three dimensional scenes from the delightful
children's stories.

Above great views from the Settle to Carlise Railway, Dent; the centre of town, Keswick **Right** stunning scenery at Ullswater

This is just a selection of attractions available. Contact any Tourist Information Centre in the region for more ideas.

Cumbria Tourist Board

Ashleigh, Holly Road, Windermere, Cumbria LA23 2AQ
T: (015394) 44444 F: (015394) 44041
E: info@golakes.co.uk
www.golakes.co.uk www.lakedistrictoutdoors.co.uk

The following publications are available from Cumbria Tourist Board:

Cumbria – The Lake District Holidays & Breaks Guide (free) T: 0870 513 3059

The Hidden Treasures of Cumbria Guide (free) T: 0870 070 2199

The Gardens, Parks and Wildlife of Cumbria – The Lake District (free)
T: (015394) 44444

The Caravan and Camping Guide of Cumbria – the Lake District (free)
T: (015394) 44444

The Taste District Food & drink guide (free) T: (015394) 44444

Events Listing (free) T: (015394) 44444

Travel information

By road:
The M1/M6/M25/M40 provide a link with London and the South East and the M5/M6 provide access from the South West. The M6 links the Midlands and North West and the M62/M6 links the East of England and Yorkshire. Approximate journey time from London is five hours, from Manchester one hour 30 minutes.

By rail:
From London (Euston) to Oxenholme (Kendal) takes approximately three hours 30 minutes. From Oxenholme (connecting station for all main line trains) to Windermere takes approximately 20 minutes. From Carlisle to Barrow-in-Furness via the coastal route, with stops at many of the towns in between, takes approximately two hours. Trains from Edinburgh to Carlisle take approximately two hours 15 minutes. The historic Settle-Carlisle line also runs through the county bringing passengers from Yorkshire via the Eden Valley.

www.golakes.co.uk/transport.html

Where to stay in
Cumbria –
The Lake District

All place names in the blue bands, under which accommodation is listed, are shown on the maps at the front of this guide.

A complete listing of all VisitBritain assessed accommodation covered by this guide appears at the back.

Accommodation symbols

Symbols give useful information about services and facilities. Inside the back cover flap you can find a key to these symbols. Keep it open for easy reference.

BOUTH, Cumbria Map ref 6A3

★★★★★
**HOLIDAY &
TOURING PARK**

BLACK BECK CARAVAN PARK
Bouth, Ulverston LA12 8JN
T: (01229) 861274
F: (01229) 861041
E: reception@blackbeck.net

Payment accepted: Delta, Mastercard, Switch, Visa

24		£13.25–£21.20
4		£12.00–£20.20
3		£180.00–£470.00
30 touring pitches		

Leave M6 at jct 36, follow A590, go through Newby Bridge, pass steam railway on right, take next right signposted Bouth, at T-jct turn left, follow road along, entrance immediate right after bridge.

CARLISLE, Cumbria Map ref 6A2 *Tourist Information Centre Tel: (01228) 625600*

★★★★
**HOLIDAY, TOURING
& CAMPING PARK**

BH&HPA

DALSTON HALL CARAVAN PARK
Dalston Hall, Carlisle CA5 7JX
T: (01228) 710165

Payment accepted: Delta, Mastercard, Switch, Visa, Euros

30		£12.00–£14.00
5		£12.00–£14.00
15		£5.00–£14.00
35 touring pitches		

Leave the M6 at jct 42, take road to Dalston. At Dalston turn onto the B5299, site on right after 1.5 miles.

★★★★
**TOURING &
CAMPING PARK**

BH&HPA

DANDY DINMONT CARAVAN AND CAMPING SITE
Blackford, Carlisle CA6 4EA
T: (01228) 674611
F: (01228) 674611
E: dandydinmont@btopenworld.com
I: www.caravan-camping-carlisle.itgo.com

27		£8.75–£9.00
27		£8.75–£9.00
20		£7.50–£8.00
47 touring pitches		

Exit the M6 at jct 44. Take A7 north, 1.5 miles. After Blackford sign follow the road directional signs to site. Site is on the right-hand side of the A7.

CONISTON, Cumbria Map ref 6A3

★ ★ ★ ★ ★
HOLIDAY PARK

ROSE AWARD

BH&HPA

CRAKE VALLEY HOLIDAY PARK
Lake Bank, Water Yeat, Ulverston LA12 8DL
T: (01229) 885203
F: (01229) 885203
E: crakevalley@coniston1.fslife.co.uk
I: www.crakevalley.co.uk

6	▲	£9.50
15	⛺	£190.00–£500.00

Leave M6 at jct 30 and take A590 towards Barrow. Turn right off the A590, Barrow road at Greenodd. Go onto the A5092, within 2 miles fork right onto the A5084 for Coniston. The park is 3 miles along on your left-hand side.

★ ★ ★ ★ ★
TOURING PARK

BH&HPA

See Ad on inside back cover

PARK COPPICE CARAVAN CLUB SITE
Park Gate, Coniston LA21 8LA
T: (015394) 41555
I: www.caravanclub.co.uk

Landscaped site set in 63 acres of NT woodland. Lake for watersports, on-site play areas, orienteering courses and Red Squirrel Nature Trail. Open 26 March to 1 November. Special member rates mean you can save your membership subscription in less than a week. Visit www.caravanclub.co.uk to find out more.

280	⛃	£14.60–£20.60
280	⛃	£14.60–£20.60
	▲	On application
280 touring pitches		

Payment accepted: Delta, Mastercard, Switch, Visa

Follow A593, 1.5 miles south of Coniston village. Final approach from the north or south is narrow in places.

GRANGE-OVER-SANDS, Cumbria Map ref 6A3 *Tourist Information Centre Tel: (015395) 34026*

★ ★ ★ ★
HOLIDAY &
TOURING PARK

ROSE AWARD

GREAVES FARM CARAVAN PARK
Field Broughton, Grange-over-Sands
LA11 6HR
T: (015395) 36329

3	⛃	£8.00–£11.00
3	⛃	£8.00–£11.00
5	▲	£8.00–£10.00
2	⛺	£190.00–£260.00
8 touring pitches		

Leave M6 at jct 36 and take A590. Leave the A590 1 mile south of Newby Bridge, signed Cartmel 4. Proceed 2 miles to 3 bungalows on the left. Approximately 200yds before Field Broughton church.

★ ★ ★ ★ ★
TOURING PARK

BH&HPA

See Ad on inside back cover

MEATHOP FELL CARAVAN CLUB SITE
Meathop, Grange-over-Sands LA11 6RB
T: (015395) 32912
F: (015395) 32243
I: www.caravanclub.co.uk

Peaceful site, ideal for exploring the southern Lake District. Kendal, famous for its mint cake, is within easy reach; Grange-over-Sands and Ulverston are close by. Special member rates mean you can save your membership subscription in less than a week. Visit www.caravanclub.co.uk to find out more.

130	⛃	£14.60–£20.60
130	⛃	£14.60–£20.60
130 touring pitches		

OPEN All Year
Payment accepted: Delta, Mastercard, Switch, Visa

Exit the M6 at jct 36 and follow the A590 to Barrow. After about 3.25 miles take the slip road and follow the A590 to Barrow. At the 1st roundabout follow the International Camping signs. Steep approach.

 Prices Please check prices and other details at the time of booking.

HAWKSHEAD, Cumbria Map ref 6A3

★★★★
HOLIDAY, TOURING
& CAMPING PARK

BH&HPA

THE CROFT CARAVAN AND CAMP SITE
North Lonsdale Road, Hawkshead,
Ambleside LA22 0NX
T: (015394) 36374
F: (015394) 36544
E: enquiries@hawkshead-croft.com
I: www.hawkshead-croft.com

Payment accepted: Delta,
Mastercard, Switch, Visa

From Ambleside follow B5286, 5 miles to Hawkshead.

25	🚐	£15.50–£18.50
	🚐	£12.50–£14.75
75	⛺	£12.50–£14.75
20	🏠	£205.00–£425.00
100 touring pitches		

KENDAL, Cumbria Map ref 6B3 *Tourist Information Centre Tel: (01539) 725758*

★★★★
TOURING PARK

BH&HPA

See Ad on inside back cover

LOW PARK WOOD CARAVAN CLUB SITE
Sedgwick, Kendal LA8 0JZ
T: (015395) 60186
I: www.caravanclub.co.uk

This peaceful country site is a haven for bird-watchers, freshwater fishermen and wild-flower enthusiasts. A dog-friendly site with extensive woodland to walk them in. Open 26 March to 1 November. Special member rates mean you can save your membership subscription in less than a week. Visit www.caravanclub.co.uk to find out more.

Payment accepted: Delta, Mastercard, Switch, Visa

Leave the M6 and go onto the A590 signed South Lakes. After approximately 3.25 miles leave via the slip road (signed Milnthorpe, Barrow) at the roundabout and follow caravan signs.

161	🚐	£12.50–£17.60
161	🚐	£12.50–£17.60
161 touring pitches		

THE CARAVAN CLUB

★★★★
HOLIDAY, TOURING
& CAMPING PARK

BH&HPA

WATERS EDGE CARAVAN PARK
Crooklands, Milnthorpe LA7 7NN
T: (015395) 67708
F: (015395) 67610
I: www.watersedgecaravanpark.co.uk

Payment accepted:
Mastercard, Visa

Leave M6 at jct 36. Take A65 to Crooklands. Site about 0.75 miles on the right.

27	🚐	£11.00–£16.00
27	🚐	£11.00–£16.00
5	⛺	£5.50–£16.00
27 touring pitches		

KESWICK, Cumbria Map ref 6A3 *Tourist Information Centre Tel: (017687) 72645*

★★★★
HOLIDAY, TOURING
& CAMPING PARK

BH&HPA

See Ad below

CASTLERIGG HALL CARAVAN AND CAMPING PARK
Castlerigg, Keswick CA12 4TE
T: (017687) 74499
F: (017687) 74499
E: info@castlerigg.co.uk
I: www.castlerigg.co.uk

Payment accepted:
Mastercard, Switch, Visa

Leave M6 at jct 40 and follow signs for Keswick. About 1.5 miles south east of Keswick off A591, turn right 100yds on the right.

53	🚐	£12.95–£15.20
53	🚐	£11.50–£13.90
120	⛺	£9.60–£12.10
7	🏠	£170.00–£420.00

NB
Important note Information on accommodation listed in this guide has been supplied by the proprietors. As changes may occur you are advised to check details at the time of booking.

KESWICK continued

★★★★
**HOLIDAY &
TOURING PARK**

BH&HPA

LAKESIDE HOLIDAY PARK
Norman Garner Ltd, Crow Park Road,
Keswick CA12 5EW
T: (017687) 72878
F: (017687) 72017
E: welcome@lakesideholidaypark.co.uk
I: www.lakesideholidaypark.co.uk

OPEN All Year except
Christmas and New Year
Payment accepted: Delta,
Mastercard, Switch, Visa

10 £110.00–£476.00

Leave the M6 at jct 40. Exit A66 at roundabout near Keswick, 16 miles. Follow signs for town centre. Follow camping and caravan signs.

KIRKBY STEPHEN, Cumbria Map ref 6B3 *Tourist Information Centre Tel: (017683) 71199*

★★★★★
**TOURING &
CAMPING PARK**

PENNINE VIEW CARAVAN PARK
Station Road, Kirkby Stephen CA17 4SZ
T: (017683) 71717

Payment accepted: Delta,
Mastercard, Switch, Visa

43		£14.50–£15.80
43		£14.50–£15.80
15	Å	£11.75–£13.60

58 touring pitches

Just off A685.

NEWBY BRIDGE, Cumbria Map ref 6A3

★★★★★
HOLIDAY PARK

BH&HPA

NEWBY BRIDGE CARAVAN PARK
Canny Hill, Newby Bridge, Ulverston
LA12 8NF
T: (015395) 31030
F: (015395) 30105
E: info@cumbriancaravans.co.uk
I: www.cumbriancaravans.co.uk

Payment accepted: Delta,
Mastercard, Switch, Visa,
Euros

7 £175.00–£470.00

Leave M6 at jct 36 and follow A590 in the direction of Barrow. Just before entering Newby Bridge about 2.25 miles beyond High Newton turn left off the A590 signposted Canny Hill. Park entrance 200yds on the right-hand side.

PENRITH, Cumbria Map ref 6B2 *Tourist Information Centre Tel: (01768) 867466*

★★★★★
TOURING PARK

BH&HPA

See Ad on inside back cover

TROUTBECK HEAD CARAVAN CLUB SITE
Troutbeck Head, Penrith CA11 0SS
T: (017684) 83521
F: (017684) 83839
I: www.caravanclub.co.uk

Classic Lakeland country. Attractive site sitting in a valley with spectacular views of Blencathra. Numerous attractions and activities within 10-mile radius. Open 1 March to 14 January 2006. Special member rates mean you can save your membership subscription in less than a week. Visit www.caravanclub.co.uk to find out more.

Payment accepted: Delta, Mastercard, Switch, Visa

From north or south on the M6, leave at jct 40 onto the A66 signposted Keswick. In about 7.25 miles turn left onto A5091, signposted Dockray/Ullswater, site on right after 1.5 miles.

119		£17.00–£22.00
119		£17.00–£22.00
119 touring pitches		

Map references
The map references refer to the colour maps at the front of this guide. The first figure is the map number; the letter and figure which follow indicate the grid reference on the map.

SILLOTH, Cumbria Map ref 6A2 *Tourist Information Centre Tel: (016973) 31944*

★★★★★
HOLIDAY, TOURING
& CAMPING PARK

BH&HPA
NCC

STANWIX PARK HOLIDAY CENTRE

Greenrow, Silloth, Wigton CA7 4HH
T: (016973) 32666
F: (016973) 32555
E: enquiries@stanwix.com
I: www.stanwix.com

Situated on the Solway coast, popular touring site with leisure and entertainment facilities for all ages. All pitches have hook-ups. Base to explore the Lake District. Check our website for special deals during certain periods. You could save up to 25% off your next holiday.

OPEN All Year except Christmas
Payment accepted: Mastercard, Switch, Visa

Leave M6 at jct 44, follow signs to Carlisle, Wigton and Silloth. From south leave M6 at jct 41, follow signs to Wigton and Silloth.

121	🚐	£15.25–£18.55
121	🚐	£15.25–£18.55
121	▲	£15.25–£18.55
77	⌗	£190.00–£555.00
121 touring pitches		

Country Code

Always follow the Country Code • Enjoy the countryside and respect its life and work • Guard against all risk of fire • Fasten all gates • Keep your dogs under close control • Keep to public paths across farmland • Use gates and stiles to cross fences, hedges and walls • Leave livestock, crops and machinery alone • Take your litter home • Help to keep all water clean • Protect wildlife, plants and trees • Take special care on country roads • Make no unnecessary noise.

A brief guide to the main towns and villages offering accommodation in **Cumbria – The Lake District**

CARLISLE, Cumbria
Cumbria's only city is rich in history. Attractions include the small red sandstone cathedral and 900-year-old castle with magnificent view from the keep. Award-winning Tullie House Museum and Art Gallery brings 2000 years of Border history dramatically to life. Excellent centre for shopping.

CONISTON, Cumbria
The 803m fell Coniston Old Man dominates the skyline to the east of this village at the northern end of Coniston Water. Arthur Ransome set his Swallows and Amazons stories here. Coniston's most famous resident was John Ruskin, whose home, Brantwood, is open to the public. Good centre for walking.

GRANGE-OVER-SANDS, Cumbria
Set on the beautiful Cartmel Peninsula, this tranquil resort, known as Lakeland's Riviera, overlooks Morecambe Bay. Pleasant seafront walks and beautiful gardens. The bay attracts many species of wading birds.

HAWKSHEAD, Cumbria
Lying near Esthwaite Water, this village has great charm and character. Its small squares are linked by flagged or cobbled alleys and the main square is dominated by the market house, or Shambles, where the butchers had their stalls in days gone by.

KENDAL, Cumbria
The Auld Grey Town lies in the valley of the river Kent with a backcloth of limestone fells. Situated just outside the Lake District National Park, it is a good centre for touring the Lakes and surrounding country. Ruined castle, reputed birthplace of Catherine Parr.

KESWICK, Cumbria
Beautifully positioned town beside Derwentwater and below the mountains of Skiddaw and Blencathra. Excellent base for walking, climbing, watersports and touring. Motor-launches operate on Derwentwater and motor boats, rowing boats and canoes can be hired.

KIRKBY STEPHEN, Cumbria
Old market town close to the river Eden, with many fine Georgian buildings and an attractive market square. St Stephen's Church is known as the Cathedral of the Dales. Good base for exploring the Eden Valley and the Dales.

NEWBY BRIDGE, Cumbria
At the southern end of Windermere on the river Leven, this village has an unusual stone bridge with arches of unequal size. The Lakeside and Haverthwaite Railway has a stop here, and steamer cruises on Lake Windermere leave from nearby Lakeside.

PENRITH, Cumbria
Ancient and historic market town, the northern gateway to the Lake District. Penrith Castle was built as a defence against the Scots. Its ruins, open to the public, stand in the public park. High above the town is the Penrith Beacon, made famous by William Wordsworth.

SILLOTH, Cumbria
Small port and coastal resort on the Solway Firth with wide cobbled roads and an attractive green leading to the promenade and seashore known for its magnificent sunsets.

Below, from left visit the Citadel, Carlisle; take a stroll over Watendlath Bridge

Invigorate your senses and free your mind. There's so much **diversity** in this corner of England you'll want to come back for **more**.

Northumbria

Looking for some inspiration? Here are a few ideas to get you started in Northumbria. **experience** the splendour of Alnwick Castle and Garden or Sunderland Museum & Winter Gardens, one of the finest new hothouses in the country. **discover** Hartlepool Historic Quay, a museum dedicated to seafaring experiences at the time of Nelson and Trafalgar. **explore** Roman remains along the Hadrian's Wall Path National Trail. **relax** and unwind in the sanctuary of senses at Seaham Hall, Excellence in England 2004 Small Hotel of the Year, Silver Winner.

THE REGION
County Durham, Tees Valley, Tyne and Wear (including NewcastleGateshead), Northumberland (including Hadrian's Wall Country)

CONTACT
▸ **One NORTHEAST TOURISM TEAM**
 Aykley Heads,
 Durham DH1 5UX
 T: (0191) 375 3050
 F: (0191) 386 0899
 www.visitnorthumbria.com

Northumbria will stir your soul and relax your mind. Enjoy lively cities with fantastic nightlife, discover the sheer beauty of empty beaches and breathtaking countryside and get the taste for Craster kippers. There's so much diversity in this corner of England you'll want to come back for more.

Feel the city vibe

Shop in designer outlets or splash out in one of Europe's biggest indoor shopping complexes, the MetroCentre. Head for Eldon Square or Northumberland Street in Newcastle for all the major high street names. At weekends, the clubs, pubs and restaurants are buzzing and eating out is a favourite pastime for city visitors, with a host of international flavours on offer. Enjoy your choice of cuisine from tapas to teriyaki before stepping out to sample world-class entertainment. Take in a show from the Royal Shakespeare Company, a smash-hit West End musical or one of the latest films. Check out the magnificent Angel of the North, the inspiring BALTIC Centre for Contemporary Art, the Biscuit Factory and the amazing Gateshead Millennium Bridge to return home culturally hip.

Relax and indulge

The north-east air will invigorate your senses and free your mind as you walk through picture-postcard vistas. Miles and miles of empty sandy beaches are overlooked by stunning castles, and picturesque villages are dotted along the unspoilt coastline. Reflect and reminisce on your favourite moments in quaint pubs. Absorb the region's distinctiveness from bespoke handmade jewellery to medieval fairs and music festivals.

Stroll around Durham City with its amazing castle and cathedral or visit Beamish, The North of England Open Air Museum, which re-creates the years of 1825 and 1913. Then join in the exciting hustle and bustle of the farmers' markets where you can indulge in local specialities like Northumberland hill lamb, cheese and a wide range of exotic jams and jellies.

Activity Utopia

Outdoor life is a big part of Northumbria. With two National Parks, two Areas of Outstanding Natural Beauty, acres of forests and Europe's biggest man-made lake at Kielder, it's the perfect place to enjoy your favourite activities, from walking to horse-riding. And remember to keep your eyes peeled for abundant wildlife – from otters to puffins. Championship-standard golf courses will challenge your game and the C2C cycle route will test your determination. There are plenty of relaxing cycle routes too, suitable for families or those wanting a bit of gentle exercise, with a rewarding pub meal to round off your adventure.

Left, from top unwind at Seaham Hall and Serenity Spa, Seaham; imposing Alnwick Castle; NewcastleGateshead Quaysides **Right** shoreside at Saltburn

Places to visit

 Awarded VisitBritain's Quality Assured Visitor Attraction marque.

Alnwick Castle
Alnwick, Northumberland
Tel: (01665) 510777
www.alnwickcastle.com
Imposing Alnwick Castle is the largest inhabited castle in England after Windsor Castle. It has been home of the Percys, Dukes of Northumberland, since 1309 and a film location for the Harry Potter movies.

Alnwick Garden
Alnwick, Northumberland
Tel: (01665) 511350
www.alnwickgarden.com
Take pleasure in this beautiful 5-ha (12-acre) garden with dramatic grand cascade, rose garden, ornamental garden with over 15,000 plants, water features and woodland walk.

BALTIC Centre for Contemporary Art
South Shore Road, Gateshead, Tyne and Wear
Tel: (0191) 478 1810
www.balticmill.com
Don't miss this major international centre for contemporary art with an ever changing programme of exhibitions in five galleries plus artists' studios, cinema and Rooftop Restaurant with stunning views.

Bamburgh Castle
Bamburgh, Northumberland
Tel: (01668) 214515
www.bamburghcastle.com
Stand in awe at this magnificent coastal castle, completely restored in 1900. Collections of china, porcelain, furniture, paintings, arms and armour.

Beamish The North of England Open Air Museum
Beamish, County Durham
Tel: (0191) 370 4000
www.beamish.org.uk
Plenty to see and do here – wander around the town, colliery village, working farm, Pockerley Manor and 1825 railway, recreating life in the North East in the early 1800s and 1900s.

Bede's World
Jarrow, Tyne and Wear
Tel: (0191) 489 2106
www.bedesworld.co.uk
Discover the exciting world of the Venerable Bede, early-medieval Europe's greatest scholar. Church, monastic site, museum with exhibitions and recreated Anglo-Saxon farm.

Blue Reef Aquarium
Grand Parade, Tynemouth, Tyne and Wear
Tel: (0191) 258 1031
www.bluereefaquarium.co.uk
Marvel at more than 30 living displays exploring the drama of the North Sea and the dazzling beauty of a spectacular coral reef with its own underwater tunnel.

Bowes Museum
Barnard Castle, County Durham
Tel: (01833) 690606
www.bowesmuseum.org.uk
Outstanding collections of art, ceramics and textiles – take the time to call into this world-class visitor attraction and centre for major exhibitions.

Captain Cook Birthplace Museum
Stewart Park, Marton, Middlesbrough, Cleveland
Tel: (01642) 311211
www.captaincook-ne.co.uk
Discover why Captain Cook is the world's most famous navigator and explorer, and shudder at the hardships of life below decks in the 18thC.

Cherryburn: Thomas Bewick Birthplace Museum
Cherryburn, Station Bank, Stocksfield, Northumberland
Tel: (01661) 843276
Birthplace cottage of artist Thomas Bewick (1700) and farmyard, with a printing house using original printing blocks. Introductory exhibition of his life, work and countryside.

Chesters Roman Fort (Cilurnum) Hadrian's Wall
Chollerford, Humshaugh, Northumberland
Tel: (01434) 681379
www.english-heritage.org.uk
Hear the rumble of distant hooves in the remains of this fort built for 500 cavalrymen. Five gateways, barrack blocks, commandant's house and headquarters, and the finest military bath house in Britain to explore.

Chillingham Castle
Chillingham, Northumberland
Tel: (01668) 215359
www.chillingham-castle.com
Be sure to avoid the torture chamber in this medieval fortress with Tudor additions, shop, dungeon, tearoom, woodland walks, furnished rooms and topiary garden.

Cragside House, Gardens and Estate (National Trust)
Cragside, Rothbury, Northumberland
Tel: (01669) 620333
www.nationaltrust.org.uk
Revolutionary home of Lord Armstrong, Victorian inventor and landscape genius – as amazing today as it was then. House, gardens, red squirrels, woodland and lakeside walks.

Discovery Museum
Blandford House, Newcastle upon Tyne, Tyne and Wear
Tel: (0191) 232 6789
www.twmuseums.org.uk
A wide variety of experiences for all the family to enjoy. Check out the Newcastle Story, Live Wires, Science Maze and Fashion Works.

Dunstanburgh Castle (English Heritage)
Craster, Alnwick, Northumberland
Tel: (01665) 576231
www.english-heritage.org.uk
Feel the drama in the romantic ruins of this extensive 14thC castle built by Thomas, Earl of Lancaster. In a stunning coastal setting on 30.5m (100ft) cliffs.

Durham Castle
Durham, County Durham
Tel: (0191) 334 4106
www.durhamcastle.com
This fine example of a motte-and-bailey castle, founded in 1072, evokes a real sense of history. The Norman chapel dates from 1080 and the kitchens and great hall from 1499 and 1284 respectively.

Durham Cathedral
Durham, County Durham
Tel: (0191) 386 4266
www.durhamcathedral.co.uk
Thought by many to be the finest example of Norman church architecture in England. Contains the tombs of St Cuthbert and The Venerable Bede.

Guisborough Priory
Church Street, Guisborough, Cleveland
Tel: (01287) 633801
Remains of a priory for Augustinian canons founded by Robert de Brus in AD1119, in the grounds of Guisborough Hall. A sanctuary from busy market day shopping.

Hall Hill Farm
Lanchester, County Durham
Tel: (01388) 731333
www.hallhillfarm.co.uk
Family fun set in attractive countryside with an opportunity to see and touch the animals at close quarters. Farm trailer ride, gift shop, tearoom, picnic and play area.

Hartlepool Historic Quay
Maritime Avenue, Hartlepool, Cleveland
Tel: (01429) 860006
www.destinationhartlepool.com

Hartlepool Historic Quay is an exciting reconstruction of a seaport of the 1800s with buildings and lively quayside, authentically reconstructed.

Housesteads Roman Fort, Hadrian's Wall (English Heritage)
Haydon Bridge, Northumberland
Tel: (01434) 344363
www.english-heritage.org.uk
Best preserved and most impressive of the Roman forts. Vercovicium was a five-acre fort for an extensive 800 civil settlement. See the only example of a Roman hospital.

Killhope, The North of England Lead Mining Museum
Cowshill, County Durham
Tel: (01388) 537505
www.durham.gov.uk/killhope
Don a hard hat and go underground at Britain's most complete lead mining site. Mine tours available, 34ft diameter waterwheel, reconstruction of Victorian machinery, miner's lodging and woodland walks.

Life Science Centre
Centre for Life, Newcastle upon Tyne, Tyne and Wear
Tel: (0191) 243 8223
www.lifesciencecentre.org.uk
Meet your four billion-year-old family, explore what makes us all different, test your brain power and enjoy the thrill of the crazy motion ride.

Lindisfarne Castle (National Trust)
Holy Island, Northumberland
Tel: (01289) 389244
www.nationaltrust.org.uk
Built in 1550 and perched atop a rocky crag, this miniature castle was converted into a private home for Edward Hudson by the architect Sir Edwin Lutyens in 1903.

Left majestic Bamburgh Castle; picturesque Kielder

Places to visit

Awarded VisitBritain's Quality Assured Visitor Attraction marque.

Locomotion The National Railway Museum at Shildon
Soho Cottages, Shildon, County Durham
Tel: (01388) 777999
www.locomotion.uk.com
Get on the right track at Shildon Railway Village. Free admission to visitors who will be able to view 60 vehicles, a workshop and education centre. Shop and refreshments.

National Glass Centre
Liberty Way, Sunderland, Tyne and Wear
Tel: (0191) 515 5555
www.nationalglasscentre.com
A unique attraction presenting the best in contemporary glass. Watch live glass-making demostrations by master craftspeople or attend classes and workshops.

Nature's World at the Botanic Centre
Ladgate Lane, Acklam, Middlesbrough, Cleveland
Tel: (01642) 594895
www.naturesworld.org.uk
Pioneering eco-experience, with new futuristic Hydroponicum and Eco centre, plus demonstration gardens, wildlife pond, white garden, environmental exhibition hall, shop and tearoom.

Otter Trust's North Pennines Reserve
Vale House Farm, Bowes, County Durham
Tel: (01833) 628339
www.ottertrust.org.uk/pennine.htm
Animal lovers will delight in this branch of the famous Otter Trust. Spot Asian and British otters, red and fallow deer and rare breeds of farm animals in this 93-ha (230-acre) wildlife reserve.

Raby Castle

Staindrop, County Durham
Tel: (01833) 660202
www.rabycastle.com
Dramatic medieval castle, home of Lord Barnard's family since 1626, with deer park, walled gardens, carriage collection, adventure playground, shop and tearoom.

South Shields Museum and Art Gallery
Ocean Road, South Shields, Tyne and Wear
Tel: (0191) 456 8740
www.twmuseums.org.uk
Discover how the area's development has been influenced by its natural and industrial past through lively displays in this recently refurbished museum.

Wallington House, Walled Garden and Grounds (National Trust)
Wallington, Morpeth, Northumberland
Tel: (01670) 773600
www.nationaltrust.org.uk
17thC country house set in 40ha (100 acres) of lawns, lakes and woodlands, with beautiful walled garden and conservatory.

Washington Old Hall
The Avenue, Washington, Tyne and Wear
Tel: (0191) 416 6879
Home to George Washington's ancestors from 1183 to 1399, the manor remained in the family until 1613 and was saved in 1936.

Wet 'N Wild
Rotary Way, North Shields, Tyne and Wear
Tel: (0191) 296 1333
www.wetnwild.co.uk
Tropical indoor water park, a fun water playground providing the wildest and wettest indoor rapids experience. Whirlpools, slides and meandering lazy river. Don't forget your towel!

Wildfowl and Wetlands Trust

Washington Pattinson, Washington, Tyne and Wear
Tel: (0191) 416 5454
www.wwt.org.uk
Binoculars at the ready. Nature reserve with 1000 wildfowl of 85 varieties. Viewing gallery, picnic areas, hides and winter wild bird-feeding station, flamingos and wild grey heron. Waterside café.

Above contemporary day out at BALTIC Centre for Contemporary Art, Gateshead; inviting countryside near Ireshopeburn
Right shopping spree in the MetroCentre, Newcastle upon Tyne

One NorthEast Tourism Team

Aykley Heads, Durham DH1 5UX
T: (0191) 375 3050 F: (0191) 386 0899
www.visitnorthumbria.com

The following publications are available from One NorthEast Tourism Team unless otherwise stated:

Northumbria 2005 – information on the region, including hotels, bed and breakfast and self-catering accommodation, caravan and camping parks, attractions, shopping, eating and drinking.

Group Travel Guide – packed with everything tour planners need to know when planning a group visit – group hotels, attractions, destinations, itinerary suggestions, Blue Badge Guides, coach parking locations and events.

Educational Visits Guide – information for teachers planning school visits including attractions with links to National Curriculum subjects, suitable accommodation, itinerary suggestions and events.

Northumbria's Top Tours – a selection of themed itineraries offering suggestions for day tours, short breaks and long stay holidays which can be tailored to suit the needs of the group.

Cycle Northumbria – for information on day rides, traffic free trails and challenging routes call (0191) 375 3044 for your free cycling guide.

Travel information

By road:
The north/south routes on the A1 and A19 thread the region as does the A68. East/west routes like the A66 and A69 easily link with the western side of the country. Within Northumbria you will find fast, modern interconnecting roads between all the main centres, a vast network of scenic, traffic-free country roads to make motoring a pleasure and frequent local bus services operating to all towns and villages.

By rail:
London to Edinburgh InterCity service stops at Darlington, Durham, Newcastle and Berwick upon Tweed. Trains make the journey between London and Newcastle in around three hours. The London to Middlesbrough journey (changing at Darlington) takes three hours. Birmingham to Darlington just under three hours. Bristol to Durham five hours and Sheffield to Newcastle just over two hours. Direct services operate to Newcastle from Liverpool, Manchester, Glasgow and Carlisle. Regional services to areas of scenic beauty operate frequently, allowing the traveller easy access. The Tyne & Wear Metro makes it possible to travel to many destinations within the Tyneside area, such as Gateshead, South Shields, Whitley Bay, Sunderland, Newcastle City Centre and Newcastle International Airport, in minutes.

Where to stay in
Northumbria

All place names in the blue bands, under which accommodation is listed, are shown on the maps at the front of this guide.

A complete listing of all VisitBritain assessed accommodation covered by this guide appears at the back.

Accommodation symbols
Symbols give useful information about services and facilities. Inside the back cover flap you can find a key to these symbols. Keep it open for easy reference.

BAMBURGH, Northumberland Map ref 6C1

★★★

HOLIDAY, TOURING
& CAMPING PARK

GLORORUM CARAVAN PARK
Glororum, Bamburgh NE69 7AW
T: (01668) 214457
F: (01668) 214622
E: info@glororum-caravanpark.co.uk
I: www.glororum-caravanpark.co.uk

50	🚐	£15.00–£17.00
20	🚐	£15.00–£17.00
30	▲	£15.00–£17.00
100 touring pitches		

From the A1 take the B1341 at Adderstone Garage, signposted.

★★★★

HOLIDAY, TOURING
& CAMPING PARK

BH&HPA

MEADOWHEAD'S WAREN CARAVAN AND CAMPING PARK
Waren Mill, Belford NE70 7EE
T: (01668) 214366   Payment accepted:
F: (01668) 214224   Mastercard, Switch, Visa
E: waren@meadowhead.co.uk
I: www.meadowhead.co.uk

150	🚐	£9.50–£18.00
150	🚐	£9.50–£18.00
30	▲	£9.50–£18.00
27	🏠	£230.00–£495.00
150 touring pitches		

Follow B1342 from A1 to Waren Mill towards Bamburgh. By Budle turn right, follow Meadowhead's Waren Caravan and Camping Park signs.

BARDON MILL, Northumberland Map ref 6B2

★★

CAMPING PARK

WINSHIELDS CAMP SITE, CAMPING BARN
Bardon Mill, Hexham NE47 7AN
T: (01434) 344243

60	▲	£8.50–£10.50

Take A69 to Bardon Mill. Turn off for Hadrian's Wall at Once Brewed Youth Hostel. Turn left on B6318, 0.5 miles.

BEADNELL, Northumberland Map ref 6C1

★★★★

HOLIDAY, TOURING
& CAMPING PARK

BH&HPA

BEADNELL LINKS CARAVAN PARK
Beadnell Harbour, Chathill NE67 5BN   Payment accepted: Delta,
T: (01665) 720526   Mastercard, Switch, Visa
F: (01665) 720526
E: b.links@talk21.com
I: www.caravanningnorthumberland.com

17	🚐	£14.50–£17.00
17	🚐	£14.50–£17.00
17 touring pitches		

Follow roads B6347 or B1342 from A1. Signed thereafter.

BEAL, Northumberland Map ref 6B1

★★★★★
HOLIDAY, TOURING
& CAMPING PARK

BH&HPA

HAGGERSTON CASTLE

Haggerston, Berwick-upon-Tweed TD15 2PA
T: (01289) 381333
F: (01289) 381433
E: enquiries@british-holidays.co.uk
I: www.british-holidays.co.uk/haggerstoncastle

Situated in landscaped parklands with fantastic on-park facilities. Full family entertainment programme, golf, horse-riding, tennis, boats, bikes, and kids' and teens' clubs. Open March to November.

Payment accepted: Delta, Mastercard, Switch, Visa

The park is signposted from the A1, 7 miles south of Berwick-upon-Tweed. Situated just off the A1 between Edinburgh and Newcastle.

150		£23.00–£50.00
150		£23.00–£50.00
500		£69.00–£750.00
150 touring pitches		

BELFORD, Northumberland Map ref 6B1

★★★
HOLIDAY, TOURING
& CAMPING PARK

BRADFORD KAIMS CARAVAN PARK
Bradford House, Belford NE70 7JT
T: (01668) 213432
F: (01668) 213891
E: lwrob@tiscali.co.uk
I: www.bradford-leisure.co.uk

Payment accepted: Delta, Mastercard, Switch, Visa

80		£12.00–£15.00
80		£12.00–£15.00
80	A	£12.00–£15.00
80 touring pitches		

Exit the A1 onto the B1341. Stay on the road for approx 2 miles. Bradford Kaims is signposted from here.

BELLINGHAM, Northumberland Map ref 6B2 Tourist Information Centre Tel: (01434) 220616

★★★★
TOURING &
CAMPING PARK

BH&HPA

BROWN RIGG CARAVAN & CAMPING PARK

Bellingham, Hexham NE48 2JY
T: (01434) 220175
E: ross@brcaravanpark.fsbusiness.co.uk
I: www.northumberlandcaravanparks.com

Quiet rural setting in Northumberland National Park. Near to Hadrian's Wall and Kielder Water. Many local walks and cycle routes. Open 31 March to 31 October. Family deal for 2 adults and up to 4 children.

Payment accepted: Delta, Mastercard, Switch, Visa

From A69 near Hexham take A68 north then left on B6318. Then B6320 to Bellingham.

60		£9.00–£14.50
60		£9.00–£14.50
20	A	£8.00–£14.50
80 touring pitches		

BERWICK-UPON-TWEED, Northumberland Map ref 6B1 Tourist Information Centre Tel: (01289) 330733

★★★★★
TOURING &
CAMPING PARK

BH&HPA

See Ad on inside back cover

SEAVIEW CARAVAN CLUB SITE

Billendean Road, Spittal, Berwick-upon-Tweed TD15 1QU
T: (01289) 305198
I: www.caravanclub.co.uk

Spectacular scenery of Northumberland, wonderful views of Holy Island, miles of safe, unspoilt beaches, small castles, pele towers and romantic ruins. Edinburgh within easy reach. Open 26 March to 1 November. Special member rates mean you can save your membership subscription in less than a week. Visit www.caravanclub.co.uk to find out more.

Payment accepted: Delta, Mastercard, Switch, Visa

From A1(M) from north avoiding the town centre stay on the A1 Berwick bypass for about 4.5 miles. Turn left onto the A1167 signposted Tweedmouth, Spittal. In about 1.5 miles at the roundabout into Billendean Terrace, site on the right.

100		£14.60–£20.60
100		£14.60–£20.60
	A	On application
100 touring pitches		

THE CARAVAN CLUB

CORBRIDGE, Northumberland Map ref 6B2

★★★
TOURING &
CAMPING PARK

NCC

WELL HOUSE FARM – CORBRIDGE

Newton, Stocksfield NE43 7UY
T: (01661) 842193

Peaceful family-run site on a farm near Corbridge one mile south of Hadrian's Wall. Ideal for exploring Northumberland and surrounding areas.

Turn off the A69 (north) at Stocksfield/Mowden Hall crossroads onto B6309. Straight over crossroads. The site is down bank on left, signposted or 1 mile south of B6318 Hadrian's Wall.

40	🚐	£8.00–£15.00
40	🚙	£8.00–£15.00
40	⛺	£4.00–£10.00
40 touring pitches		

DURHAM, County Durham Map ref 6C2 *Tourist Information Centre Tel: (0191) 384 3720*

★★★★
TOURING &
CAMPING PARK

BH&HPA

See Ad on inside back cover

GRANGE CARAVAN CLUB SITE

Meadow Lane, Carrville, Durham DH1 1TL
T: (0191) 384 4778
F: (0191) 383 9161
I: www.caravanclub.co.uk

An open, level site, this is a lovely location for a short break and an ideal stopover en route to or from Scotland. Special member rates mean you can save your membership subscription in less than a week. Visit www.caravanclub.co.uk to find out more.

OPEN All Year
Payment accepted: Delta, Mastercard, Switch, Visa

Leave the A1(M) at jct 62, take the A690, towards Durham. Turn right after 50m. Signposted Maureen Terrace and brown caravan sign.

102	🚐	£14.60–£20.60
102	🚙	£14.60–£20.60
102 touring pitches		

★★★★
HOLIDAY, TOURING
& CAMPING PARK

BH&HPA

STRAWBERRY HILL FARM CAMPING & CARAVANNING PARK
Running Waters, Old Cassop, Durham
DH6 4QA
T: (0191) 372 3457
F: (0191) 372 2512
E: howarddunkerley@strawberryhillfarm.
freeserve.co.uk

Payment accepted: Delta,
Mastercard, Switch, Visa,
Euros

20	🚐	£12.50–£14.50
20	🚙	£12.50–£14.50
10	⛺	£10.00–£11.50
1	🏕	£275.00–£325.00
30 touring pitches		

Exit A1(M) at jct 61, on roundabout take exit signed take A177 Peterlee. Take 1st right before The Jennings Pub to staggered crossroad. Turn right A181. Park on left 1.5 miles.

Credit card bookings

If you book by telephone and are asked for your credit card number it is advisable to check the proprietor's policy should you cancel your reservation.

You're welcome at our Sites!

For details of Caravan Club sites in this region, where high standards, excellent facilities and a warm welcome are assured, please see our website

THE CARAVAN CLUB

www.caravanclub.co.uk

HEXHAM, Northumberland Map ref 6B2 *Tourist Information Centre Tel: (01434) 652220*

★★★
TOURING &
CAMPING PARK

HEXHAM RACECOURSE CARAVAN SITE
Yarridge Road, High Yarridge, Hexham
NE46 2JP
T: (01434) 606847
F: (01434) 605814
E: hexrace@aol.com
I: www.hexham-racecourse.co.uk

40	🚐	£12.00
30	🚏	£12.00
16	⛺	£9.00–£12.00
40 touring pitches		

From A1(M) leave A69 at Bridge End roundabout and follow signs for Allendale. Turn left at traffic lights. Follow B6305 for 3 miles to signed T-jct on left. About 1.5 miles to site.

KIELDER, Northumberland Map ref 6B1

★★★★
TOURING PARK

BH&HPA

See Ad on inside back cover

KIELDER WATER CARAVAN CLUB SITE

Leaplish Waterside Park, Falstone, Hexham NE48 1AX
T: (01434) 250278
I: www.caravanclub.co.uk

This is a gently sloping site, with some pitches overlooking the beautiful Kielder Water - Britain's largest man-made lake. A fabulous site for an active holiday. Open 26 March to 29 October. Special member rates mean you can save your membership subscription in less than a week. Visit www.caravanclub.co.uk to find out more.

Payment accepted: Delta, Mastercard, Switch, Visa

From east on A69. Past Hexham, right onto A6079. Approximately 3 miles, left onto B6320. In Bellingham, turn left and follow signs to Kielder Water. Turn right signposted Leaplish Waterside Park. Site on right.

80	🚐	£12.50–£16.00
80	🚏	£12.50–£16.00
	⛺	On application
80 touring pitches		

KIELDER FOREST

See under Bellingham, Kielder

LONGHORSLEY, Northumberland Map ref 6C1

★★★★
HOLIDAY, TOURING
& CAMPING PARK

BH&HPA

FORGET-ME-NOT HOLIDAY PARK
Croftside, Longhorsley, Morpeth NE65 8QY
T: (01670) 788364
F: (01670) 788715
E: info@forget-me-notholidaypark.co.uk
I: www.forget-me-notholidaypark.co.uk

Payment accepted: Delta,
Mastercard, Switch, Visa

26	🚐	£12.50–£17.00
	🚏	£12.50–£17.00
30	⛺	£10.50–£15.00
56 touring pitches		

From north: follow A1 south, take B6525 – Wooler, then left onto A697 – Longhorsley village. From south: follow A1 north, take A697 – Coldstream and continue into Longhorsley village. Find us approximately 1.5 miles from the village.

NEWTON-BY-THE-SEA, Northumberland Map ref 6C1

★★★★
HOLIDAY, TOURING
& CAMPING PARK

BH&HPA

NEWTON HALL CARAVAN PARK
Newton-by-the-Sea, Alnwick NE66 3DZ
T: (01665) 576239
F: (01665) 576900
E: ianpatterson@newtonholidays.co.uk
I: www.newtonholidays.co.uk

OPEN All Year
Payment accepted: Delta,
Mastercard, Switch, Visa

15	🚐	£10.00–£16.00
15	🚏	£10.00–£16.00
3	🏠	£230.00–£530.00
15 touring pitches		

Turn off A1 trunk road, take the B1430, and then the unclassified road to Newton-by-the-Sea.

NB **Important note** Information on accommodation listed in this guide has been supplied by the proprietors. As changes may occur you are advised to check details at the time of booking.

OTTERBURN, Northumberland Map ref 6B1 *Tourist Information Centre Tel: (01830) 520093*

★★★★
HOLIDAY, TOURING
& CAMPING PARK

BH&HPA

BORDER FOREST CARAVAN PARK
Cottonshopeburnfoot, Nr Otterburn
NE19 1TF
T: (01830) 520259
I: www.borderforestcaravanpark.co.uk

36	🚐	£9.50–£15.00
36	🚏	£9.50–£15.00
36	⛺	£8.40–£12.00
2	🏠	£300.00–£400.00
36 touring pitches		

Leave A1(M) at jct 58 towards Jedburgh. The park lies adjacent to A68, 6 miles south of Scottish Border. Alternatively, leave A1, join A696 towards Jedburgh and join the A68 north.

SEAHOUSES, Northumberland Map ref 6C1 *Tourist Information Centre Tel: (01665) 720884*

★★
TOURING PARK

ELFORD CARAVAN PARK
Crackpool Cottage, Elford Farm,
Seahouses NE68 7UT
T: (01665) 720244
F: (01665) 720244
E: bill@elfordcaravanpark.co.uk
I: www.elfordcaravanpark.co.uk

🚐	£8.50–£13.50
🚏	£8.50–£13.50
25 touring pitches	

From the south, 10 miles north of Alnwick, turn right at sign Elford 4 miles. From the north, turn left as above.

★★★★★
HOLIDAY &
TOURING PARK

BH&HPA

SEAFIELD CARAVAN PARK
Seafield Road, Seahouses NE68 7SP
T: (01665) 720628
F: (01665) 720088
E: info@seafieldpark.co.uk
I: www.seafieldpark.co.uk

Luxurious holiday homes for hire on Northumberland's premier park. Fully appointed caravans. Superior touring facilities including fully serviced pitches. Open February 2005. Indoor swimming pool available summer 2005. Seasonal discounts available on 3-, 4- and 7-day breaks.

Payment accepted: Delta, Mastercard, Switch, Visa

Take the B1340 from Alnwick for 14 miles. East to coast.

25	🚐	£15.00–£28.00
25	🚏	£15.00–£28.00
37	🏠	£230.00–£550.00
25 touring pitches		

STOCKTON-ON-TEES, Stockton–on–Tees Map ref 6C3 *Tourist Information Centre Tel: (01642) 528130*

★★★★★
TOURING &
CAMPING PARK

BH&HPA

See Ad on inside back cover

WHITE WATER CARAVAN CLUB PARK
Tees Barrage, Stockton-on-Tees TS18 2QW
T: (01642) 634880
I: www.caravanclub.co.uk

Pleasantly landscaped site, part of the largest white-water canoeing and rafting course built to an international standard in Britain. Nearby Teesside Park for shopping, restaurants etc. Special member rates mean you can save your membership subscription in less than a week. Visit www.caravanclub.co.uk to find out more.

OPEN All Year
Payment accepted: Delta, Mastercard, Switch, Visa

Come off the A66 Teesside Park. Follow Teesdale sign, go over Tees Barrage Bridge, turn right. Site 200yds on the left.

117	🚐	£12.10–£16.00
117	🚏	£12.10–£16.00
	⛺	On application
117 touring pitches		

THE CARAVAN CLUB

Map references The map references refer to the colour maps at the front of this guide. The first figure is the map number; the letter and figure which follow indicate the grid reference on the map.

A brief guide to the main towns and villages offering accommodation in **Northumbria**

BAMBURGH, Northumberland
Village with a spectacular red sandstone castle standing 150 ft above the sea. On the village green the magnificent Norman church stands opposite a museum containing mementoes of the heroine Grace Darling.

BARDON MILL, Northumberland
Small hamlet midway between Haydon Bridge and Haltwhistle, within walking distance of Vindolanda, an excavated Roman settlement, and near the best stretches of Hadrian's Wall.

BEADNELL, Northumberland
Charming fishing village on Beadnell Bay. Seashore lime kilns (National Trust), dating from the 18thC, recall busier days as a coal and lime port and a pub is built on to a medieval pele tower which survives from days of the border wars.

BEAL, Northumberland
Tiny hamlet with an inn at the junction of the A1 which leads on to the causeway to Holy Island. Some farmhouses and buildings are dated 1674.

BELFORD, Northumberland
Small market town on the old coaching road, close to the coast, the Scottish border and the north-east flank of the Cheviots. Built mostly in stone and very peaceful now that the A1 has by-passed the town, Belford makes an ideal centre for excursions to the moors and coast.

BELLINGHAM, Northumberland
Set in the beautiful valley of the North Tyne close to the Kielder Forest, Kielder Water and lonely moorland below the Cheviots. The church has an ancient stone wagon roof fortified in the 18thC with buttresses.

BERWICK-UPON-TWEED, Northumberland
Guarding the mouth of the Tweed, England's northernmost town with the best 16thC city walls in Europe. The handsome Guildhall and barracks date from the 18thC. Three bridges cross to Tweedmouth, the oldest built in 1634.

CORBRIDGE, Northumberland
Small town on the river Tyne. Close by are extensive remains of the Roman military town Corstopitum, with a museum housing important discoveries from excavations. The town itself is attractive with shady trees, a 17thC bridge and interesting old buildings, notably a 14thC vicarage.

DURHAM, County Durham
Ancient city with its Norman castle and cathedral, now a World Heritage site, set on a bluff high over the Wear. A market and university town and regional centre, spreading beyond the marketplace on both banks of the river.

HEXHAM, Northumberland
Old coaching and market town near Hadrian's Wall. Since pre-Norman times a weekly market has been held in the centre with its marketplace

and abbey park, and the richly-furnished 12thC abbey church has a superb Anglo-Saxon crypt.

NEWTON-BY-THE-SEA, Northumberland
Attractive hamlet at the south end of Beadnell Bay with a sandy beach and splendid view of Dunstanburgh Castle. In a designated Area of Outstanding Natural Beauty, Low Newton, part of the village, is now owned by the National Trust.

OTTERBURN, Northumberland
Small village set at the meeting of the river Rede with Otter Burn, the site of the Battle of Otterburn in 1388. A peaceful tradition continues in the sale of Otterburn tweeds in this beautiful region, which is ideal for exploring the Border country and the Cheviots.

SEAHOUSES, Northumberland
Small modern resort developed around a 19thC herring port. Just offshore, and reached by boat from here, are the rocky Farne Islands (National Trust) where there is an important bird reserve. The bird observatory occupies a medieval pele tower.

Below, from left cycle near Dunstanburgh; admire Tynemouth Priory and Castle

This **proud** corner of England boasts **heritage**, **hills** and **lively cities** with a **cutting-edge** arts scene.

Yorkshire

Looking for some inspiration? Here are a few ideas to get you started in Yorkshire. experience life as a Viking at JORVIK – The Viking City. discover the story of the world's oceans on a dramatic underwater journey at The Deep in Kingston upon Hull. explore the most beautiful corners of The Yorkshire Dales National Park via 26 pubs on The Inn Way. relax at the Turkish Baths & Health Spa in Harrogate for that elusive feeling of total wellbeing.

THE REGION
Yorkshire and North & North East Lincolnshire

CONTACT
▸ YORKSHIRE TOURIST BOARD
312 Tadcaster Road,
York YO24 1GS
T: (01904) 707070
(24-hour brochure line)
F: (01904) 701414
E: info@ytb.org.uk
www.yorkshirevisitor.com

England's biggest county boasts heritage, hills and historical grandeur. Dramatic abbeys, picturesque villages, modern art, local and international cuisine: you'll find them all in this proud corner of England.

Green and pleasant land

For diverse landscape and inspiring scenery, Yorkshire really takes the biscuit. Relax in over 1000 square miles of National Parks (The Yorkshire Dales, the North York Moors and the Peak District) as well as the Pennines and a stretch of Heritage Coast, or cycle the Trans Pennine Trail to enjoy spectacular views.

At Xscape in Castleford you can put your climbing, skiing and skating skills to the test. Sheffield Winter Garden is an impressive cathedral of plants, creating a temperate green world in the city centre.

Huge heritage

Yorkshire's rich cultural and industrial heritage has given rise to an incredible number of historic houses, castles, abbeys and gardens. Fountains Abbey & Studley Royal Water Garden is rightly a World Heritage Site, and Harewood House and Whitby Abbey offer more treasures to discover. For atmosphere alone, impressive Rievaulx Abbey and Castle Howard are well worth a visit and give a glimpse of what life was like in days gone by. Stunning stained glass and 1000 years of history may entice you to York Minster, the largest medieval Gothic cathedral in northern Europe. And for free family entertainment, visit the National Railway Museum which tells the story of the train. Peep inside royal carriages with sumptuous bedrooms and dining rooms. Or plan an experimental day out at Magna – the UK's first science adventure centre.

Left, from top ornate architecture at Castle Howard, York; the enchanting Yorkshire Dales; shopping in the Corn Exchange, Leeds **Right** the past comes to life at JORVIK Viking Festival, York

For a more spiritual experience take a tour of Epworth Old Rectory, the house where John Wesley, founder of the Methodist Church, grew up.

Cultural landscape

Yorkshire boasts lively cities with a cutting-edge arts scene. If you're an opera buff, Leeds is home to Opera North. You'll also find top-class entertainment at the two theatres of the West Yorkshire Playhouse. In Bradford, the National Museum of Photography, Film & Television is the most visited museum outside London – which should come as no surprise since Yorkshire has been the inspiration for some of England's greatest films, books and TV series. Visit the locations for yourself as you explore the living sets of Emmerdale, The Full Monty, Wuthering Heights, Jane Eyre and, most recently, Calendar Girls. For modern culture, Bradford, Sheffield and Leeds are shopping heaven.

Places to visit

Awarded VisitBritain's
Quality Assured Visitor
Attraction marque.

Beningbrough Hall & Gardens (National Trust)

Beningbrough, York
Tel: (01904) 470666
www.nationaltrust.org.uk
Contemplate 100 pictures from the National Portrait Gallery hung in this final example of a Baroque house, built in 1716. Victorian laundry, potting shed and restored walled garden.

Bolton Abbey Estate

Bolton Abbey, Skipton, North Yorkshire
Tel: (01756) 718009
www.boltonabbey.com
Ruins of 12thC priory in a park setting by the river Wharfe. Feeling energetic? Walk some of the 80 miles of footpaths through spectacular scenery. Tearooms, nature trails, fishing.

Colour Museum

Perkin House, Bradford, West Yorkshire
Tel: (01274) 390955
www.sdc.org.uk
Ever wondered how colours came about? The only museum of its kind in Europe, dedicated to the history, development and technology of colour.

Cusworth Hall Museum of South Yorkshire Life

Cusworth Hall, Doncaster, South Yorkshire
Tel: (01302) 782342
Georgian mansion in landscaped park containing displays illustrating everyday life in South Yorkshire over the last 200 years, from childhood to costumes and transport.

The Deep

Hull
Tel: (01482) 381000
www.thedeep.co.uk
Glimpse the world's oceans from the beginning of time and into the future using interactives and live aquaria exhibits, including the world's deepest underwater tunnel. Spellbinding.

Eureka! The Museum for Children

Discovery Road, Halifax, West Yorkshire
Tel: (01422) 330069
www.eureka.org.uk
The first museum of its kind designed especially for children up to the age of 12 – stimulate all the senses as you touch, listen, feel, and smell as well as look.

Flamingo Land Theme Park, Zoo and Holiday Village

Kirby Misperton, North Yorkshire
Tel: (01653) 668287
www.flamingoland.co.uk
One-price family fun park with over 100 attractions and six shows. Europe's largest privately owned zoo and only triple looping coaster, Magnum Force. Feel your heart race!

Fountains Abbey and Studley Royal Water Garden (National Trust)

Ripon, North Yorkshire
Tel: (01765) 608888
www.fountainsabbey.org.uk
Stunning, World Heritage Site including the largest monastic ruin in Britain, founded by Cistercian monks in 1132. Landscaped garden laid between 1720-40 with lake, water garden, temples and deer park.

Freeport Hornsea Outlet Village

Rolston Road, Hornsea, East Riding of Yorkshire
Tel: (01964) 534211
www.freeporthornsea.com
Set in landscaped gardens with over 40 quality high-street names all selling stock with discounts of up to 50%, plus licensed restaurant and leisure attractions. Shop until you drop!

Helmsley Castle (English Heritage)

Helmsley, York
Tel: (01439) 770442
www.english-heritage.org.uk/yorkshire
Explore the changing military defences of this castle with its 12thC keep, Tudor mansion and spectacular earthworks cut from solid rock. Exhibitions and excavated artefacts.

Last of the Summer Wine Exhibition
Huddersfield Road, Holmfirth, Huddersfield
Tel: (01484) 681408
www.summerwineexhibition.com
Check out the collection of photographs and memorabilia commemorating the world's longest running television comedy series, Last of the Summer Wine.

Leeds City Art Gallery
The Headrow, Leeds
Tel: (0113) 247 8248
www.leeds.gov.uk/artgallery
Art gallery containing British paintings, sculptures, prints and drawings of the 19th/20thC. Henry Moore gallery with permanent collection of 20thC sculpture.

Lightwater Valley
North Stainley, North Yorkshire
Tel: 0870 458 0040
www.lightwatervalley.net
Hang onto your hat! Set in 70ha (175 acres) of parkland, Lightwater Valley features white-knuckle rides and attractions for all the family, shopping, a restaurant and picnic areas.

Magna

Sheffield Road, Rotherham, South Yorkshire
Tel: (01709) 720002
www.magnatrust.org.uk
The UK's first Science Adventure Centre set in the vast Templeborough steelworks in Rotherham. Amusement guaranteed with giant interactives.

Mother Shipton's Cave & the Petrifying Well
Prophecy Lodge, Knaresborough, North Yorkshire
Tel: (01423) 864600
www.mothershipton.co.uk
Beware the prophecies of Mother Shipton! Her birthplace cave and the Petrifying Well are the oldest tourist attractions in Britain, opened in 1630. Well, museum, playground and 12 acres of riverside grounds.

National Fishing Heritage Centre
Alexandra Dock, Grimsby, North East Lincolnshire
Tel: (01472) 323345
www.nelincs.gov.uk/Tourism/Attractions
Sign on as a crew member and experience the reality of life on a deep-sea trawler. Interactive games and displays.

National Museum of Photography, Film & Television
Bradford, West Yorkshire
Tel: 0870 701 0200
www.nmpft.org.uk
Ten, free, interactive galleries will take you on a tour of the past, present and future of photography, film and television. Catch a screening at the spectacular 3D IMAX cinema.

National Railway Museum

Leeman Road, York
Tel: (01904) 621261
www.nrm.org.uk
The story of the train is brought to life in a great day out for all the family. Three enormous galleries to explore with interactive exhibits and working engines.

Newby Hall & Gardens

Ripon, North Yorkshire
Tel: (01423) 322583
www.newbyhall.com
Late 17thC house with additions, interior by Robert Adam, classical sculpture, Gobelins tapestries, 10ha (25 acres) of gardens, miniature railway, children's adventure garden.

North Yorkshire Moors Railway
Pickering , North Yorkshire
Tel: (01751) 472508
www.northyorkshiremoorsrailway.com
Jump aboard Britain's most popular heritage railway travelling through the beautiful North York Moors National Park.

Nunnington Hall (National Trust)
Nunnington, York
Tel: (01439) 748283
www.nationaltrust.org.uk
Large 17thC manor house situated on banks of river Rye. With hall, bedrooms, nursery and Carlisle collection of miniature rooms. Watch out for the haunted maid's room.

Piece Hall
Halifax, West Yorkshire
Tel: (01422) 358087
www.calderdale.gov.uk
Built in 1779 and restored in 1976, this Grade I Listed building forms a unique and striking monument to the wealth and importance of the wool trade.

Ripley Castle
Ripley, North Yorkshire
Tel: (01423) 770152
www.ripleycastle.co.uk
An adventure through English history, Ripley Castle, home to the Ingilby family since 1308, is set in the heart of a delightful estate with Victorian walled gardens, deer park and pleasure grounds.

Royal Armouries Museum
Armouries Drive, Leeds
Tel: (0113) 220 1916
www.armouries.org.uk
Traverse more than 3000 years of history covered by over 8000 spectacular items of arms and armour, jousting displays and falconry, all in stunning surroundings.

Left dramatic ruins of Fountains Abbey, Ripon; awe-inspiring Hardraw Force, Wensleydale

Places to visit

Awarded VisitBritain's Quality Assured Visitor Attraction marque.

Sea Life and Marine Sanctuary
Scalby Mills, Scarborough, North Yorkshire
Tel: (01723) 373414
www.sealifeeurope.com
Meet creatures that live in and around the oceans of the British Isles, ranging from starfish to sharks. The comic inhabitants of the penguin sanctury will no doubt keep you amused.

Sheffield Botanical Gardens
Clarkehouse Road, Sheffield
Tel: (0114) 267 6496
www.sbg.org.uk
Extensive gardens with over 5500 species of plants and Grade II Listed garden pavilion. Fully restored and containing a temperate plant collection.

Skipton Castle
Skipton, South Yorkshire
Tel: (01756) 792442
www.skiptoncastle.co.uk
Skipton was the last Royalist stronghold in the North during the Civil War and is one of the best preserved, complete medieval castles in England. A formidable fortification!

Thackray Museum
Beckett Street, Leeds
Tel: (0113) 244 4343
www.thackraymuseum.org
Award-winning collections and interactive displays bring to life the history of medicine from a Victorian operating theatre to the wonders of modern surgery. Not for the squeamish.

Thirsk Museum
Kirkgate, Thirsk, North Yorkshire
Tel: (01845) 527707
www.thirskmuseum.org
Exhibits of local life, industry and cricket memorabilia. The building was the home of Thomas Lord, founder of Lords cricket ground in London.

Thrybergh Country Park
Doncaster Road, Thrybergh, South Yorkshire
Tel: (01709) 850353
Twenty-eight hectare (70-acre) country park with a vast lake and bird reserve. Fly-fishing. Caravan and camping site. Take a picnic and contemplate the scenery.

The World of James Herriot
Kirkgate, Thirsk, North Yorkshire
Tel: (01845) 524234
www.worldofjamesherriot.org
Visit the original home and surgery of vet and author James Herriot, with 1950s themed rooms and the Austin Seven car used in the TV series.

Wensleydale Cheese Visitor Centre
Wensleydale Creamery, Hawes, North Yorkshire
Tel: (01969) 667664
www.wensleydale.co.uk
Observe Wensleydale cheese being made by hand and sample a range of cheeses too. Museum, shop and café.

York Minster
Deangate, York
Tel: (01904) 557200
www.yorkminster.org
Simply awe-inspiring, York Minster is the largest medieval gothic cathedral in northern Europe, and a treasure house of 800 years of stained glass. Take the audio tour to discover 2000 years of history.

Yorkshire Lavender
Terrington, York
Tel: (01653) 648430
www.lavenderland.co.uk
Probably Europe's most northerly lavender farm. Discover the many varieties of lavender and be amazed at their versatile uses.

Above spoilt for choice in York; journey through English history at Ripley Castle **Right** experience the age of steam on board the North York Moors Railway

Yorkshire Tourist Board

312 Tadcaster Road, York YO24 1GS
T: (01904) 707070 (24-hour brochure line) F: (01904) 701414
E: info@ytb.org.uk
www.yorkshirevisitor.com

The following publications are available from Yorkshire Tourist Board:

Yorkshire Visitor Guide – information on Yorkshire and Northern Lincolnshire, including hotels, self-catering, camping and caravan parks. Also attractions, shops, restaurants and major events

For information about Yorkshire outdoors, heritage breaks and seasonal breaks in Yorkshire, please visit www.yorkshirevisitor.com

Travel information

By road:
Motorways: M1, M62, M606, M621, M18, M180, M181, A1(M). Trunk roads: A1, A19, A57, A58, A59, A61, A62, A63, A64, A65, A66.

By rail:
InterCity services to Bradford, Doncaster, Harrogate, Kingston upon Hull, Leeds, Sheffield, Wakefield and York. Frequent regional railway services city centre to city centre including Manchester Airport service to Scarborough, York and Leeds.

Where to stay in
Yorkshire

All place names in the blue bands, under which accommodation is listed, are shown on the maps at the front of this guide.

A complete listing of all VisitBritain assessed accommodation covered by this guide appears at the back.

Accommodation symbols
Symbols give useful information about services and facilities. Inside the back cover flap you can find a key to these symbols. Keep it open for easy reference.

BEVERLEY, East Riding of Yorkshire Map ref 5C1 *Tourist Information Centre Tel: (01482) 867430*

★★★★★
HOLIDAY PARK

BARMSTON FARM STATIC CARAVAN PARK
Barmston Farm, Barmston Lane, Woodmansey, Beverley HU17 0TP
T: (01482) 863566 & 07970 042587
I: www.barmstonfarm.co.uk

Small, quiet, friendly site. Caravans positioned around a pond with open countryside views. In an adjacent field there is a well-stocked two-acre fishing lake.

OPEN All Year
Payment accepted: Amex, Delta, Diners, Mastercard, Switch, Visa, Euros

Follow A1174 from Beverley 3 miles to Woodmansey. Church on sharp bend, site at bottom of lane, next to church.

5	£170.00

FILEY, North Yorkshire Map ref 6D3

★★★★★
HOLIDAY, TOURING
& CAMPING PARK

BH&HPA

ORCHARD FARM HOLIDAY VILLAGE
Stonegate, Hunmanby, Filey YO14 0PU
T: (01723) 891582
F: (01723) 891582

	£11.00–£15.00
	£11.00–£15.00
25	£11.00–£15.00
60 touring pitches	

At Staxton roundabout take Filey Road, pick up signs for Hunmanby and then follow brown tourist signs for caravan park.

FLAMBOROUGH, East Riding of Yorkshire Map ref 6D3

★★★★
HOLIDAY, TOURING
& CAMPING PARK

BH&HPA

THORNWICK & SEA FARM HOLIDAY CENTRE
North Marine Road, Flamborough,
Bridlington YO15 1AU
T: (01262) 850369
F: (01262) 851550
E: enquiries@thornwickbay.co.uk
I: www.thornwickbay.co.uk

Payment accepted: Delta, Diners, Mastercard, Switch, Visa

	£12.50–£16.50
	£12.50–£14.50
	£12.50–£14.50
60	£150.00–£420.00
200 touring pitches	

From M62 jct 16. Follow the B1255 from Bridlington to Flamborough, the park is approximately 1 mile farther towards North Landing.

GILLING WEST, North Yorkshire Map ref 6C3

★★★★
TOURING PARK

BH&HPA

See Ad on inside back cover

HARGILL HOUSE CARAVAN CLUB SITE

Gilling West, Richmond DL10 5LJ
T: (01748) 822734
I: www.caravanclub.co.uk

This is an intimate, gently sloping site in the old town of Richmond. Breathtaking views over the Yorkshire Dales National Park. Open 26 March to 1 November. Special member rates mean you can save your membership subscription in less than a week. Visit www.caravanclub.co.uk to find out more.

Payment accepted: Delta, Mastercard, Switch, Visa

Leave the A1 at Scotch Corner and go onto the A66. After 1.5 miles turn left at the crossroads. Site entrance is a further 100yds on left.

63	🚐	£12.50–£17.60
63	🚏	£12.50–£17.60
63 touring pitches		

HARROGATE, North Yorkshire Map ref 5B1 *Tourist Information Centre Tel: (01423) 537300*

★★★★★
HOLIDAY, TOURING & CAMPING PARK

BH&HPA
NCC

RUDDING HOLIDAY PARK

Rudding Lane, Harrogate HG3 1JH
T: (01423) 870439
F: (01423) 870859
E: holiday-park@ruddingpark.com
I: www.ruddingpark.com

Award-winning campsite. Three miles south of Harrogate, in peaceful setting, offering Deer House Pub, swimming pool, golf course, driving range and shop. Closed February. Self-catering timber lodges available. Peak season: 7 nights for the price of 6. Off-peak season: 4 nights for the price of 3.

Payment accepted: Delta, Mastercard, Switch, Visa, Euros

Three miles south of Harrogate, to the north of the A658 between its junction with the A61 to Leeds and the A661 to Wetherby.

141	🚐	£12.00–£29.00
141	🚏	£12.00–£29.00
141	🛆	£8.50–£12.50
15	🛏	£260.00–£760.00
141 touring pitches		

HAWES, North Yorkshire Map ref 6B3 *Tourist Information Centre Tel: (01969) 667450*

★★
HOLIDAY, TOURING & CAMPING PARK

BAINBRIDGE INGS CARAVAN AND CAMPING SITE
Hawes DL8 3NU
T: (01969) 667354
E: janet@bainbridge-ings.co.uk
I: www.bainbridge-ings.co.uk

Approaching Hawes from the east on the A684 turn left at signpost marked Gayle.

25	🚐	£9.50
5	🚏	£9.00
40	🛆	£9.00
2	🛏	£150.00–£195.00
70 touring pitches		

Credit card bookings

If you book by telephone and are asked for your credit card number it is advisable to check the proprietor's policy should you cancel your reservation.

HELMSLEY, North Yorkshire Map ref 6C3

★★★★★
TOURING &
CAMPING PARK

BH&HPA

FOXHOLME TOURING CARAVAN PARK
Harome, York YO62 5JG
T: (01439) 770416
F: (01439) 771744

60	🚐	£8.50–£10.00
60	🚚	£8.50–£10.00
60	⛺	£8.50–£10.00
60 touring pitches		

Leave Helmsley on the A170 in the direction of Scarborough. After 0.5 miles turn right for Harome. Turn left at the church, through the village and then follow the caravan signs.

★★★★★
TOURING &
CAMPING PARK

BH&HPA

GOLDEN SQUARE CARAVAN AND CAMPING PARK

Oswaldkirk, York YO62 5YQ
T: (01439) 788269
F: (01439) 788236
E: barbara@goldensquarecaravanpark.freeserve.co.uk
I: www.goldensquarecaravanpark.com

Secluded site with magnificent view of the North Yorks Moors. Superb facilities. Indoor and outdoor play areas. Sports centre nearby. Seasonal pitches. Winter/summer storage. 7 nights for the price of 6 (excl Bank Holidays and high season).

Payment accepted: Euros

From Helmsley A170 (Thirsk) 1st left onto B1257 to York. 1st right Ampleforth. Turning 0.5 miles on right. From Thirsk 'caravan route' A19 to York. Left for Coxwold, then Byland Abbey, Wass, Ampleforth.

	🚐	£9.00–£13.00
	🚚	£9.00–£13.00
	⛺	£9.00–£13.00
1	🏠	£90.00–£180.00
129 touring pitches		

KNARESBOROUGH, North Yorkshire Map ref 5B1

★★★★★
TOURING PARK

BH&HPA

See Ad on inside back cover

KNARESBOROUGH CARAVAN CLUB SITE

New Road, Scotton, Knaresborough HG5 9HH
T: (01423) 860196
I: www.caravanclub.co.uk

Popular family destination located in Lower Nidderdale, gateway to the Yorkshire Dales. Knaresborough and the city of Harrogate are within easy reach. Open 1 March to 14 January 2006. Special member rates mean you can save your membership subscription in less than a week. Visit www.caravanclub.co.uk to find out more.

Payment accepted: Delta, Mastercard, Switch, Visa

Turn right off the A59 onto the B6165. After approximately 1.5 miles turn right immediately after the petrol station into New Road. The site is on the right hand side after 50yds.

62	🚐	£16.10–£21.50
62	🚚	£16.10–£21.50
	⛺	On application
62 touring pitches		

THE CARAVAN CLUB

LEEDS, West Yorkshire Map ref 5B1 *Tourist Information Centre Tel: (0113) 242 5242*

★★★★
HOLIDAY, TOURING
& CAMPING PARK

BH&HPA

ST HELENA'S CARAVAN SITE
Otley Old Road, Horsforth, Leeds LS18 5HZ
T: (0113) 284 1142

30	🚐	£7.00–£10.00
15	🚚	£7.00–£10.00
15	⛺	£6.00–£8.00
60 touring pitches		

Follow the A65 to the A658 past the airport to Carlton crossroads, then turn right at sign for Cookridge and Horsforth down Otley Old Road for 0.75 miles.

Confirm your booking You are advised to confirm your booking in writing.

LEEDS/BRADFORD AIRPORT

See under Leeds

MASHAM, North Yorkshire Map ref 6C3

★★★
TOURING PARK

BH&HPA

BLACK SWAN HOLIDAY PARK

Rear Black Swan Hotel, Fearby, Masham, Ripon HG4 4NF
T: (01765) 689477
F: (01765) 689477
E: info@blackswanholiday.co.uk
I: www.blackswanholiday.co.uk

The holiday park is in an Area of Outstanding Natural Beauty designated by the Countryside Commission. Pub and restaurant on park. Ideal for walking. Special offers on website.

Payment accepted: Amex, Delta, Diners, Mastercard, Switch, Visa

Over Masham bridge keep on A6108 past the garage on the right, take 2nd turning on the left to Fearby. Park is 2.25 miles on left, at the rear of Black Swan Hotel.

50	⊞	£10.00–£15.00
5	⊞	£10.00–£15.00
20	▲	£4.50–£15.00
3	⊞	£105.00–£195.00
75 touring pitches		

OXENHOPE, West Yorkshire Map ref 5B1

★★★★
HOLIDAY, TOURING
& CAMPING PARK

BH&HPA

UPWOOD HOLIDAY PARK

Blackmoor Road, Oxenhope, Keighley
BD22 9SS
T: (01535) 644242
F: (01535) 643254
E: caravans@upwoodholidaypark.fsnet.co.uk
I: www.upwoodholidaypark.fsnet.co.uk

OPEN All Year

From A629 Halifax – Keighley road turn left at Flappit pub. Down B6144 and then 1 mile on left is Blackmoor Road. Park 1 mile on left.

	⊞	£10.00–£15.00
2	⊞	£10.00–£15.00
10	▲	£7.50
60 touring pitches		

PICKERING, North Yorkshire Map ref 6D3 Tourist Information Centre Tel: (01751) 473791

★★★★
HOLIDAY, TOURING
& CAMPING PARK

BH&HPA

WAYSIDE CARAVAN PARK

Wrelton, Pickering YO18 8PG
T: (01751) 472608
F: (01751) 472608
E: waysideparks@freenet.co.uk
I: www.waysideparks.co.uk

Payment accepted: Delta, Mastercard, Switch, Visa

Situated 2.5 miles west of Pickering, 250yds off the A170 by the village of Wrelton. For correct turning watch for signs.

55	⊞	£13.50
55	⊞	£13.00
20	▲	£8.50–£12.00
75 touring pitches		

RICHMOND, North Yorkshire Map ref 6C3 Tourist Information Centre Tel: (01748) 850252

★★★★★
HOLIDAY, TOURING
& CAMPING PARK

BH&HPA

BROMPTON CARAVAN PARK

Easby, Richmond DL10 7EZ
T: (01748) 824629
F: (01748) 826383
E: brompton.caravanpark@btinternet.com
I: www.bromptoncaravanpark.co.uk

Payment accepted: Delta, Mastercard, Switch, Visa

On the B6271 halfway between Brompton-on-Swale and Richmond on the left-hand side.

	⊞	£12.50–£19.50
	⊞	£12.50–£19.50
	▲	£12.50–£19.50
2	⊞	£100.00–£360.00
217 touring pitches		

RIPON, North Yorkshire Map ref 6C3

★★★★
HOLIDAY, TOURING
& CAMPING PARK

BH&HPA

WOODHOUSE FARM CARAVAN & CAMPING PARK

Winksley, Ripon HG4 3PG
T: (01765) 658309
E: woodhouse.farm@talk21.com
I: www.woodhousewinksley.com

Payment accepted: Mastercard, Switch, Visa

From Ripon take the B6265 Pateley Bridge. After Fountains Abbey take 2nd right and follow site signs.

60	⊞	£9.50–£15.00
5	⊞	£9.50–£15.00
40	▲	£9.50–£14.00
100 touring pitches		

SCARBOROUGH, North Yorkshire Map ref 6D3 *Tourist Information Centre Tel: (01723) 373333*

★★★★★
TOURING &
CAMPING PARK

BH&HPA

CAYTON VILLAGE CARAVAN PARK

Mill Lane, Cayton Bay, Scarborough YO11 3NN
T: (01723) 583171
E: info@caytontouring.co.uk
I: www.caytontouring.co.uk

Adjoining church, 0.5 miles from beach. Two inns, bus services. Scarborough three miles, Filey four miles. Free shower, dish-washing facilities, family bathroom. Four-acre dog walk. Open 1 March to 4 January. Low-season offers – any 4 nights Sun-Thu inclusive £5 discount, 1 week £7 discount, 1 week (Senior Citizen) £10 discount.

Payment accepted: Delta, Mastercard, Switch, Visa

A165, south of Scarborough, turn inland at Cayton Bay, traffic lights, 0.5 miles on the right. A64, take B1261 at McDonalds roundabout. In Cayton turn 2nd left after Blacksmiths. Signposted.

200	🚐	£11.00–£17.00
200	🚐	£11.00–£17.00
200	▲	£9.00–£14.00
200 touring pitches		

★★★★★
HOLIDAY, TOURING
& CAMPING PARK

CROWS NEST CARAVAN PARK
Gristhorpe, Filey YO14 9PS
T: (01723) 582206
F: (01723) 582206
E: enquiries@crowsnestcaravanpark.com
I: www.crowsnestcaravanpark.com

On the A165, 5 miles south of Scarborough, 2 miles north of Filey.

50	🚐	£12.00–£20.00
50	🚐	£12.00–£20.00
100	▲	£12.00–£15.00
40	🏠	£110.00–£440.00
150 touring pitches		

★★★★★
HOLIDAY, TOURING
& CAMPING PARK

NCC

FLOWER OF MAY HOLIDAY PARK

Lebberston, Scarborough YO11 3NU
T: (01723) 584311
F: (01723) 581361
E: info@flowerofmay.com
I: www.flowerofmay.com

Excellent facilities on family-run park. Luxury indoor pool, golf course. Ideal for coast and country. Prices based per pitch, per night for four people with car. Early-booking discount: £25 off full week's hire. 10% discount off full week's pitch fees booked by post in advance.

From A64 take the A165 Scarborough/Filey coast road. Well signposted at Lebberston.

220	🚐	£12.00–£16.50
30	🚐	£12.00–£16.50
50	▲	£9.00–£16.50
37	🏠	£180.00–£460.00
300 touring pitches		

★★★★★
TOURING PARK

BH&HPA

LEBBERSTON TOURING PARK

Lebberston, Scarborough YO11 3PE
T: (01723) 585723
E: info@lebberstontouring.co.uk
I: lebberstontouring.co.uk

Quiet country location. Well-spaced pitches. Extensive south-facing views. Ideal park for a peaceful, relaxing break. Fully modernised amenity blocks. Dogs on lead.

Payment accepted: Delta, Mastercard, Switch, Visa

From the A64 or the A165 take the B1261 to Lebberston and follow the signs for Lebberston Touring Park.

125	🚐	£11.50–£17.00
40	🚐	£11.50–£17.00
125 touring pitches		

SLINGSBY, North Yorkshire Map ref 6C3

★★★★★
HOLIDAY, TOURING
& CAMPING PARK

ROBIN HOOD CARAVAN & CAMPING PARK
Green Dyke Lane, Slingsby, York YO62 4AP
T: (01653) 628391
F: (01653) 628391
E: info@robinhoodcaravanpark.co.uk
I: www.robinhoodcaravanpark.co.uk

32	🚐	£10.00–£18.00
32	🚛	£10.00–£18.00
32	⛺	£10.00–£15.00
22	🏠	£130.00–£430.00
32 touring pitches		

The caravan park is situated on the edge of the village of Slingsby with access off the B1257 Malton to Helmsley road.

SNAINTON, North Yorkshire Map ref 6D3

★★★★★
HOLIDAY, TOURING
& CAMPING PARK

ROSE AWARD

BH&HPA

JASMINE PARK

Cross Lane, Snainton, Scarborough YO13 9BE
T: (01723) 859240
F: (01723) 859240
E: info@jasminepark.co.uk
I: www.jasminepark.co.uk

Picturesque and peaceful park between Pickering and Scarborough. Winner of Yorkshire Caravan Park of the Year and Yorkshire in Bloom. Gold David Bellamy Conservation Award. Storage available.

Payment accepted: Delta, Mastercard, Switch, Visa

Turn south off the A170 in Snainton opposite the junior school, signposted.

74	🚐	£11.00–£16.00
74	🚛	£11.00–£16.00
20	⛺	£9.00–£16.00
1	🏠	£160.00–£300.00
94 touring pitches		

WHITBY, North Yorkshire Map ref 6D3 *Tourist Information Centre Tel: (01947) 602674*

★★★★
HOLIDAY PARK

BH&HPA

FLASK HOLIDAY HOME PARK

Robin Hood's Bay, Fylingdales, Whitby YO22 4QH
T: (01947) 880592
F: (01947) 880592
E: flaskinn@aol.com
I: www.flaskinn.com

Small, family-run site between Whitby and Scarborough, in the North York Moors. All super-luxury caravans have central heating and double glazing. Rose Award.

Payment accepted: Switch, Visa

Situated on the A171, 7 miles to Whitby and 12 miles to Scarborough.

10	🏠	£180.00–£330.00

★★★★★
TOURING &
CAMPING PARK

BH&HPA

LADYCROSS PLANTATION CARAVAN PARK
Egton, Whitby YO21 1UA
T: (01947) 895502
E: enquiries@ladycrossplantation.co.uk
I: www.ladycrossplantation.co.uk

Payment accepted: Delta,
Mastercard, Switch, Visa

	🚐	£12.00–£15.50
6	🚛	£12.00–£15.50
4	⛺	£10.00–£13.50
100 touring pitches		

From Whitby to Guisborough (A171) take turning signed Egton/North York Moors Railway/Grosmont/Glaisdale. The caravan site is 200yds on the right. Avoid minor roads from A169.

Important note Information on accommodation listed in this guide has been supplied by the proprietors. As changes may occur you are advised to check details at the time of booking.

WHITBY continued

★★★★★

**HOLIDAY, TOURING
& CAMPING PARK**

BH&HPA

MIDDLEWOOD FARM HOLIDAY PARK

Middlewood Lane, Fylingthorpe, Robin Hood's Bay, Whitby
YO22 4UF
T: (01947) 880414
F: (01947) 880871
E: info@middlewoodfarm.com
I: www.middlewoodfarm.com

*Small, peaceful, award-winning family park. A walker's paradise with
magnificent panoramic coastal and moorland views! Hardstandings, heated
facilities. 10 minutes' walk to pub/shops/beach.*

OPEN All Year
Payment accepted: Delta, Mastercard, Switch, Visa

*Follow A171 Scarborough to Whitby road signposted from Fylingthorpe
junction. In Fylingthorpe turn onto Middlewood Lane. Park is 500yds. Follow
brown tourist signs.*

20	🚐	£7.50–£13.50
20	🚐	£7.50–£13.50
80	▲	£7.50–£13.50
30	🏠	£129.00–£499.00
100 touring pitches		

YORK, York Map ref 5C1 *Tourist Information Centre Tel: (01904) 621756*

★★★★★

**TOURING &
CAMPING PARK**

BH&HPA

ALDERS CARAVAN PARK
Home Farm, Monk Green, Alne, York
YO61 1RY
T: (01347) 838722
F: (01347) 838722
E: enquiries@homefarm.co.uk
I: www.alderscaravanpark.co.uk

Situated 2 miles west of the A19 and 9 miles north of York. In the centre of the village of Alne.

	🚐	£9.00–£11.25
	🚐	£9.00–£11.25
40 touring pitches		

★★★★

**HOLIDAY, TOURING
& CAMPING PARK**

BH&HPA

ALLERTON PARK CARAVAN PARK
Allerton Park, Knaresborough HG5 0SE
T: (01423) 330569
F: (01759) 371377
E: enquiries@yorkshireholidayparks.co.uk
I: www.yorkshireholidayparks.co.uk

Site is 0.25 miles east of the A1(M) leading from the A59 York to Harrogate road.

20	🚐	£11.00–£13.00
20	🚐	£11.00–£13.00
20	▲	£11.00–£13.00
5	🏠	£180.00–£425.00
20 touring pitches		

★★★★★

TOURING PARK

BH&HPA

See Ad on inside back cover

BEECHWOOD GRANGE CARAVAN CLUB SITE

Malton Road, York YO32 9TH
T: (01904) 424637
I: www.caravanclub.co.uk

*Situated just outside York in countryside. Plenty of space for children to play.
Ideal for families. Open 26 March to 1 November. Special member rates
mean you can save your membership subscription in less than a week. Visit
www.caravanclub.co.uk to find out more.*

Payment accepted: Delta, Mastercard, Switch, Visa

*From A64 on the junction of the A1237 York ring road and the A1036 leading
to the A64, north of York. At 3rd roundabout turn right onto road signed
local traffic only. Site at end of drive.*

111	🚐	£16.10–£21.50
111	🚐	£16.10–£21.50
111 touring pitches		

Map references The map references refer to the colour maps at the front of
this guide. The first figure is the map number; the letter and figure which follow
indicate the grid reference on the map.

YORK continued

★★★★
HOLIDAY, TOURING
& CAMPING PARK

CASTLE HOWARD LAKESIDE HOLIDAY PARK

Coneysthorpe, York YO60 7DD
T: (01653) 648316
E: lakeside@castlehoward.co.uk
I: www.castlehoward.co.uk

This peaceful lakeside site has views of Castle Howard which is within walking distance. Pitches available for touring caravans and tents with electrical hook-up.

Fifteen miles north of York on the A64, follow Castle Howard signs from the main roads.

30	🚐	£9.50–£12.50
	🚐	£9.50–£12.50
30	▲	£4.00–£5.00

★★★★★
TOURING PARK

BH&HPA

See Ad on inside back cover

ROWNTREE PARK CARAVAN CLUB SITE

Terry Avenue, York YO23 1JQ
T: (01904) 658997
I: www.caravanclub.co.uk

On the banks of the river Ouse in the heart of York, this popular site is just a few minutes' walk from the city centre. Special member rates mean you can save your membership subscription in less than a week. Visit www.caravanclub.co.uk to find out more.

OPEN All Year
Payment accepted: Delta, Mastercard, Switch, Visa

Turn off A64 (Tadcaster-York) onto A19 signposted York centre. After 2 miles join one-way system. Keep left over river bridge. Left after 200yds at International Caravan Club site. Turn right onto Terry Avenue. Site on right in 0.25 miles.

102	🚐	£17.00–£22.00
102	🚐	£17.00–£22.00
	▲	On application
102 touring pitches		

★★★★
HOLIDAY, TOURING
& CAMPING PARK

BH&HPA

WEIR CARAVAN PARK
Buttercrambe Road, Stamford Bridge, York
YO41 1AN
T: (01759) 371377
F: (01759) 371377
E: enquiries@yorkshireholidayparks.co.uk
I: www.yorkshireholidayparks.co.uk

From York on the A166 turn left before bridge.

	🚐	£11.00–£13.00
	🚐	£11.00–£13.00
8	🏠	£190.00–£420.00
25 touring pitches		

★★★★
TOURING PARK

YORK TOURING CARAVAN SITE

Towthorpe Lane, Towthorpe, York YO32 9ST
T: (01904) 499275
F: (01904) 499271
E: info@yorkcaravansite.co.uk
I: www.yorkcaravansite.co.uk

Small, family-run, secluded park in an idyllic countryside setting, only five miles from York centre. Spacious pitches and superior facilities. Book 7 nights in advance and only pay for 6 (excl Bank Holidays).

OPEN All Year
Payment accepted: Mastercard, Switch, Visa

Travelling on the A64 towards Scarborough/Malton take the turn-off to the left signposted Strensall/Haxby. We are 1 mile down that road on the left.

20	🚐	£9.00–£17.00
20	🚐	£9.00–£17.00
10	▲	£9.00–£17.00
40 touring pitches		

A brief guide to the main towns and villages offering accommodation in **Yorkshire**

BEVERLEY,
East Riding of Yorkshire
Beverley's most famous landmark is its beautiful medieval Minster dating from 1220, with Percy family tomb. Many attractive squares and streets, notably Wednesday and Saturday Market and North Bar Gateway. Famous racecourse. Market cross dates from 1714.

FILEY, **North Yorkshire**
Resort with elegant Regency buildings along the front and six miles of sandy beaches bounded by natural breakwater, Filey Brigg. Starting point of the Cleveland Way. St Oswald's church, overlooking a ravine, belonged to Augustinian canons until the Dissolution.

FLAMBOROUGH,
East Riding of Yorkshire
Village with strong seafaring tradition, high on chalk headland dominated by cliffs of Flamborough Head, a fortress for over 2000 years. St Oswald's Church is in the oldest part of Flamborough. A nature trail follows the Iron Age earthworks known as Danes Dyke.

HARROGATE, **North Yorkshire**
Major conference, exhibition and shopping centre, renowned for its spa heritage and award-winning floral displays, spacious parks and gardens. Famous for antiques, toffee, fine shopping and excellent tea shops, also its Royal Pump Rooms and Baths. Annual Great Yorkshire Show in July.

HAWES, **North Yorkshire**
The capital of Upper Wensleydale on the famous Pennine Way, Yorkshire's highest market town and renowned for great cheeses. Popular with walkers. Dales National Park Information Centre and Folk Museum. Nearby is spectacular Hardraw Force waterfall.

HELMSLEY, **North Yorkshire**
Delightful small market town with red roofs, warm stone buildings and cobbled market square, on the river Rye at the entrance to Ryedale and the North York Moors. Remains of 12thC castle, several inns and All Saints' Church.

KNARESBOROUGH,
North Yorkshire
Picturesque market town on the river Nidd. The 14thC keep is the best-preserved part of John of Gaunt's castle, and the manor-house with its chequerboard walls was presented by James I to his son Charles as a fishing lodge. Prophetess Mother Shipton's cave. Boating on river.

LEEDS, **West Yorkshire**
Large city with excellent modern shopping centre and splendid Victorian architecture. Museums and galleries including Temple Newsam House (the Hampton Court of the North), Tetley's Brewery Wharf and the Royal Armouries Museum; also home of Opera North.

PICKERING, **North Yorkshire**
Market town and tourist centre on edge of North York Moors. Parish church has complete set of 15thC wall paintings depicting lives of saints. Part of 12thC castle still stands. Beck Isle Museum. The North York Moors Railway begins here.

RICHMOND, **North Yorkshire**
Market town on edge of Swaledale with 11thC castle, Georgian and Victorian buildings surrounding cobbled marketplace. Green Howards' Museum is in the former Holy Trinity Church. Attractions include the Georgian Theatre, restored Theatre Royal, Richmondshire Museum, Easby Abbey.

RIPON, **North Yorkshire**
Ancient city with impressive cathedral containing Saxon crypt which houses church treasures from all over Yorkshire. Charter granted in 886 by Alfred the Great. Setting the Watch tradition kept nightly by horn-blower in Market Square. Fountains Abbey nearby.

Above picturesque Thixendale in the Wolds

SCARBOROUGH,
North Yorkshire
Large, popular East Coast seaside resort, formerly a spa town. Beautiful gardens and two splendid sandy beaches. Castle ruins date from 1100; fine Georgian and Victorian houses. Scarborough Millennium depicts 1000 years of town's history. Sea Life Centre.

SLINGSBY, **North Yorkshire**
Large, attractive village with ruined castle and village green, on Castle Howard estate.

WHITBY, **North Yorkshire**
Holiday town with narrow streets and steep alleys at the mouth of the river Esk. Captain James Cook, the famous navigator, lived in Grape Lane. 199 steps lead to St Mary's Church and St Hilda's Abbey overlooking harbour. Dracula connections. Gothic weekend every April.

YORK, **York**
Ancient walled city nearly 2000 years old, containing many well-preserved medieval buildings. Its Minster has over 100 stained glass windows and is the largest Gothic cathedral in England. Attractions include Castle Museum, National Railway Museum, Jorvik Viking Centre and York Dungeon.

Ratings **you** can trust

STAR QUALITY

★★★★★	Exceptional quality
★★★★	Excellent quality
★★★	Very good quality
★★	Good quality
★	Acceptable quality

When you're looking for a place to stay, you need a rating system you can trust. The British Graded Holiday Parks Scheme, operated jointly by the national tourist boards for England, Scotland and Wales, gives you a clear guide of what to expect.

Based on the internationally recognised rating of one to five stars, the system puts great emphasis on quality and reflects customer expectations.

Parks are visited annually by trained, impartial assessors who award a rating based on cleanliness, environment and the quality of services and facilities provided.

Explore at your leisure the **extensive canal** and river networks that are a legacy of the region's **industrial heritage**.

Heart of England

Looking for some inspiration? Here are a few ideas to get you started in the Heart of England. **experience** a Shakespeare play, performed in the great bard's birthplace. **discover** medieval history inside the ramparts of Warwick Castle. **explore** black-and-white villages in Shropshire and Herefordshire. **relax** with a drink at a canalside café in Birmingham's Brindleyplace.

THE REGION
Black Country, Herefordshire, Shropshire, Staffordshire, Warwickshire, Birmingham, Worcestershire

CONTACT
▸ HEART OF ENGLAND TOURISM
   Larkhill Road, Worcester WR5 2EZ
   T: (01905) 761100
   F: (01905) 763450
   www.visitheartofengland.com

The Heart of England is full of contrasts – you'll find England's second-largest city, historic towns, cathedrals, mighty battlements and ruined castles. Search out the region's industrial past or thrill to the excitement of a white-knuckle ride.

Big city buzz

Hit the pavements of Birmingham and you feel it instantly. The buzz of a great city. Start in the Bullring, the city's newly created retail experience the size of 26 football pitches in the centre of town! A stimulating glass-covered environment where you can shop, eat or just be. At one end is the bizarre, shimmering Selfridges building covered in over 15,000 aluminium-spun disks. Then head for the canalside bars and restaurants of Brindleyplace or the historic Jewellery Quarter.

Or opt for Coventry instead. A thousand years of history have left their imprint on the city, from the superb 14th-century guildhall to streets of timber-framed buildings and soaring church spires. But it's never been a city content to just look backwards. It boasts architect Sir Basil Spence's extraordinary modern cathedral and, like Birmingham, it is renewing and re-fashioning its city centre. With two world-renowned motor museums and the majestic ruins of medieval Kenilworth Castle in the surrounding area, you're guaranteed a great city break.

On the trail

By contrast, your jeans and trainers can feel rather out of place against the higgledy-piggledy backdrop of Tudor half-timbered buildings in the historic towns of Shrewsbury and Worcester. For more beautiful buildings, follow a trail of black-and-white villages in Shropshire and Herefordshire – they make wonderful photographs!

Or in spring, signposts will guide you through the stunning pink-and-white froth of the Blossom Trail, threading its way through the thousands of orchards in the Vale of Evesham.

In search of history

Head for Stratford-upon-Avon, Shakespeare's birthplace. With five houses associated with the bard, there is almost too much to see. Browse the antique shops before thrilling to a production performed by the Royal Shakespeare Company, the greatest exponent of his works. Then make your way to Warwick. Massive, brooding, battle-scarred. The temperature seems to drop and the hairs on the back of your neck rise as you enter England's bloody past inside the impenetrable ramparts of Warwick Castle.

Spend a day at Ironbridge Gorge, wandering among its many fascinating museums or at the Black Country Museum where electric tramcars and trolleybuses transport you back in time to the canalside village to watch costumed craftsmen bring the buildings to life with their local knowledge, practical skills and unique Black Country humour.

If it's historic houses and gardens that interest you, you're spoilt for choice in the Heart of England. Visit the great mansion at Shugborough, begun in 1693, or stroll through the parkland and woodlands of Trentham Gardens, both in Staffordshire.

Food for thought

Feeling hungry? Then you should visit the pretty market town of Ludlow on the Welsh borders. Here in the shadow of Ludlow Castle, are some of the best restaurants in the UK, and specialist food shops bursting with luscious British produce such as Evesham Asparagus.

Left, from top pedal your way around the region; peaceful countryside, Shropshire; reflecting on history, Ironbridge

Places to visit

Awarded VisitBritain's Quality Assured Visitor Attraction marque.

Acton Scott Historic Working Farm
Wenlock Lodge, Acton Scott, Shropshire
Tel: (01694) 781306
www.actonscottmuseum.co.uk
Living history in the Shropshire Hills. This working farm demonstrates farming and rural life in south Shropshire at the close of the 19thC.

Alton Towers
Alton, Staffordshire
Tel: 0870 520 4060
www.altontowers.com
Experience the thrills and excitement of Britain's No 1 theme park with rides and attractions such as Air, Oblivion, Nemesis, Congo River Rapids, Log Flume and the Tweenies live show.

Amazing Hedge Puzzle
The Jubilee Park, Symonds Yat, Herefordshire
Tel: (01600) 890360
Loose yourself in this traditional hedge maze, created to celebrate the Queen Elizabeth Jubilee in 1977. Visit the world's only hands-on interactive Museum of Mazes.

AZTEC Watersports
The Spring Holiday Park, Lower Moor, Worcestershire
Tel: (01386) 860013
An ideal learning environment with safe, shallow, clean, spring water and professional instructors for windsurfing, sailing, canoeing and lots more.

Birmingham Botanical Gardens and Glasshouses
Westbourne Road, Edgbaston, West Midlands
Tel: (0121) 454 1860
www.birminghambotanicalgardens.org.uk
Six hectares (15 acres) of ornamental gardens and glasshouses featuring the widest range of plants in the Midlands from tropical rainforest to arid desert. Aviaries with exotic birds, and a children's play area.

Black Country Living Museum
Tipton Road, Dudley, West Midlands
Tel: (0121) 557 9643
www.bclm.co.uk
Wander around original shops and houses, ride on a tramcar or fairground swingboat, chat by the coal-fired kitchen ranges, go down the mine or just soak up the atmosphere.

Cadbury World
Linden Road, Bournville, West Midlands
Tel: (0121) 451 4180
www.cadburyworld.co.uk
Indulge in the story of Cadbury's chocolate which includes a chocolate-making demonstration. Enjoy attractions for all ages, with free samples, free parking, shop and restaurant.

Coventry Cathedral
Priory Street, Coventry, West Midlands
Tel: (024) 7652 1200
www.coventrycathedral.org
This glorious 20thC cathedral rises above the stark ruins of the medieval cathedral which was destroyed in 1940. The visitor centre includes audio-visual shows.

Coventry Transport Museum
Hales Street, Coventry, West Midlands
Tel: (024) 7683 2425
www.mbrt.co.uk
A fascinating collection of cars and commercial vehicles from 1896, cycles from 1818, motorcycles from 1920 and Thrust 2 and Thrust SSC land speed record cars.

The Crystal Glass Centre
Churton House, Audnam, West Midlands
Tel: (01384) 354400
See the best of British and European crystal on show. The exhibition reveals the history of glass from its earliest days to the present.

Drayton Manor Family Theme Park
Tamworth, Staffordshire
Tel: 0870 872 5252
www.draytonmanor.co.uk
Over 100 rides and attractions featuring some of the biggest, wettest and scariest rides around, including Apocalypse, the world's first stand up tower drop.

Droitwich Spa Brine Baths Complex
St Andrews Road, Droitwich, Worcestershire
Tel: (01905) 794894
www.brinebath.co.uk
Try a unique experience – floating weightless in natural Droitwich brine. Spa treatments plus fitness and health facilities such as physiotherapy, hydrotherapy and sports injury.

The Elgar Birthplace Museum
Crown East Lane, Lower Broadheath, Worcestershire
Tel: (01905) 333224
www.elgarfoundation.org
Country cottage birthplace of Sir Edward Elgar and the new Elgar Centre, giving a fascinating insight into his life, music, family, friends, musical development and inspirations.

Farncombe Estate Centre
Broadway, Worcestershire
Tel: 0845 230 8590
www.farncombeestate.co.uk
Music, writing, art, singing, meditation and yoga are just a selection of courses available for all throughout the year on this 120-ha (300-acre) private estate in the beautiful Cotswolds.

Hoar Park Craft Village and Antiques Centre
Hoar Park Farm, Nuneaton, Warwickshire
Tel: (024) 7639 4433
Craft and Antiques Centre, Garden Centre, Children's Farm, licensed restaurant, country walks, fishing pools and children's play area will keep you entertained. Regular craft and antique fairs are also held.

Ikon Gallery
Oozells Square, Brindleyplace, Birmingham
Tel: (0121) 248 0708
www.ikon-gallery.co.uk
One of Europe's foremost contemporary art galleries, presenting the work of national and international artists within an innovative educational framework.

Ironbridge Gorge Museums
Coalbrookdale, Telford, Shropshire
Tel: (01952) 435900
www.ironbridge.org.uk
See the world's first cast-iron bridge and visit the Museum of the Gorge, Tar Tunnel, Jackfield Tile Museum, Coalport China Museum, Rosehill House, Blists Hill Victorian Town and Iron and Enginuity Museum.

Ludlow Castle (ruin)
Castle Square, Ludlow, Shropshire
Tel: (01584) 873355
www.ludlowcastle.com
A former royal castle, these impressive ruins date from the 11th to the16thC. It includes towers, a great hall and chambers as well as a shop and gallery.

Mamble Craft Centre Limited
Hall Farm, Mamble, Worcestershire
Tel: (01299) 832834
www.mamblecraftcentre.co.uk
Craft centre consisting of four workshops, gallery, tearoom, gift shop and courses room, housed in 17thC barns on an ancient medieval site with stunning views of Clee Hills.

Manor Farm Animal Centre and Donkey Sanctuary
Manor Farm, East Leake, Leicestershire
Tel: (01509) 852525
www.manorfarmanimalcentre.co.uk
A wide variety of animals and birds, small donkey sanctuary, nature trail, willow dens, adventure playgrounds, art and activity centre and straw maze will keep the family entertained.

National Sea Life Centre
The Water's Edge, Birmingham
Tel: (0121) 643 6777
www.sealifeeurope.com
Come face-to-face with hundreds of fascinating sea creatures from sharks to shrimps. Discover the pioneering seahorse breeding programme, and watch otters in their enclosure.

Newnham Paddox Gardens and Art Park
Newnham Paddox House, Monks Kirby, Warwickshire
Tel: (01788) 833513
www.newnhampaddox.com
12-ha (30-acre) open-air sculpture gallery set in idyllic 18thC landscaped park created by Capability Brown with woods, rare trees and lakes. Sculpture to view or buy.

Royal Brierley Crystal Experience
Tipton Road, Dudley, West Midlands
Tel: (0121) 530 5600
www.royalbrierley.com
Factory tours to see crystal being hand-made. Museum, factory shopping and attractive coffee shop open all year.

Secret Hills – The Shropshire Hill Discovery Centre
School Road, Craven Arms, Shropshire
Tel: (01588) 676000
www.shropshireonline.gov.uk/discover.nsf
All-weather, all-year-round family fun day out. Enjoy a simulated balloon ride over the Shropshire Hills and see the famous Shropshire mammoth. Café and shop.

Left tickle your taste buds at Cadbury World, Bournville; make a splash at Drayton Manor, Tamworth

Places to visit

Awarded VisitBritain's Quality Assured Visitor Attraction marque.

Severn Valley Railway
The Railway Station, Bewdley, Worcestershire
Tel: (01299) 403816
www.svr.co.uk
Take a ride on the standard-gauge steam railway running 16 miles between Kidderminster, Bewdley and Bridgnorth. Also see the collection of locomotives and passenger coaches.

Shakespeare's Birthplace
Henley Street, Stratford-upon-Avon, Warwickshire
Tel: (01789) 2040161
www.shakespeare.org.uk
Visit the world-famous house where William Shakespeare was born in 1564 and where he grew up. See the highly acclaimed Shakespeare Exhibition.

Shugborough Estate (National Trust)
Shugborough, Milford, Staffordshire
Tel: (01889) 881388
www.staffordshire.gov.uk/shugborough
18thC mansion with fine collections of furniture, paintings, silver and ceramics. Gardens and park with neo-classical monuments plus a Georgian farmstead and servants' quarters.

The Snowdome Leisure Island
River Drive, Tamworth, Staffordshire
Tel: 0870 500 0011
www.snowdome.co.uk
Real snow centre where you can ski, snowboard and toboggan indoors. Tuition and equipment provided. Bars, restaurants and other leisure activities available.

Walsall Arboretum
Lichfield Street, Walsall, West Midlands
Tel: (01922) 653148
www.walsallarboretum.co.uk
Picturesque Victorian park with over 70ha (170 acres) of gardens, lakes and parkland. Home to the famous Walsall Illuminations lights and laser show each autumn.

Walsall Leather Museum
Littleton Street West, Walsall, West Midlands
Tel: (01922) 721153
www.walsall.gov.uk/leathermuseum
Award-winning working museum in the saddlery and leathergoods 'capital' of Britain. Watch skilled craftsmen and women at work in this restored Victorian leather factory.

Warwick Castle
Warwick, Warwickshire
Tel: 0870 442 2000
www.warwick-castle.co.uk
Meet Warwick the Kingmaker in this mighty medieval castle with state rooms, armoury, dungeon, torture chamber and the Mill and Engine House attraction.

The Wedgwood Visitor Centre

Barlaston, Stoke-on-Trent, Staffordshire
Tel: (01782) 204218
www.thewedgwoodvisitorcentre.com
New £4.5 million visitor centre showing centuries of craftmanship on a plate. Audio-guided tour includes exhibition and demonstration areas. Shop and restaurants.

West Midland Safari and Leisure Park
Spring Grove, Bewdley, Worcestershire
Tel: (01299) 402114
www.wmsp.co.uk
See Britain's only pride of rare white lions. There's something for everyone: drive-through safari, pets corner, reptile house, sea lion theatre, hippo lakes, and family amusement rides.

Worcester Cathedral
College Green, Worcester, Worcestershire
Tel: (01905) 611002
www.cofe-worcester.org.uk
England's loveliest cathedral, with royal tombs, Medieval cloisters, an ancient crypt and magnificent Victorian stained glass. Refreshments and gift shop. Disabled access.

Above imposing Worcester Cathedral; state dining at Warwick Castle **Right** view a glass figure of Shakespeare in Stratford-upon-Avon

This is just a selection of attractions available. Contact any Tourist Information Centre in the region for more ideas.

Heart of England Tourism

Larkhill Road, Worcester WR5 2EZ
T: (01905) 761100 F: (01905) 763450
www.visitheartofengland.com

The following publications are available from Heart of England Tourism

Bed & Breakfast Touring Map including Camping and Caravan Parks 2005

Escape 2005/6 (Accommodation in the Heart of England)

Visit the Heart of England 2005 (Attractions in the Heart of England)

Travel information

By road:
Britain's main motorways (M1/M6/M5) meet in the Heart of England; the M40 links with the M42 south of Birmingham while the M4 provides fast access from London to the south of the region. These road links ensure that the Heart of England is more accessible by road than any other region in the UK.

By rail:
The Heart of England is served by an excellent rail network. InterCity rail services are fast and frequent from London and other major cities into the region. Trains run from Euston to Birmingham, Coventry, Rugby; from Paddington to the Cotswolds, Stratford-upon-Avon and Worcester; and from Marylebone to Birmingham and Stourbridge. From the main stations a network of regional routes takes you around the Heart of England.

Where to stay in
Heart of England

All place names in the blue bands, under which accommodation is listed, are shown on the maps at the front of this guide.

A complete listing of all VisitBritain assessed accommodation covered by this guide appears at the back.

Accommodation symbols
Symbols give useful information about services and facilities. Inside the back cover flap you can find a key to these symbols. Keep it open for easy reference.

ASTON CANTLOW, Warwickshire Map ref 3B1

★★★
HOLIDAY, TOURING
& CAMPING PARK

BH&HPA

ISLAND MEADOW CARAVAN PARK
The Mill House, Aston Cantlow B95 6JP
T: (01789) 488273
F: (01789) 488273
E: holiday@islandmeadowcaravanpark.
co.uk
I: www.islandmeadowcaravanpark.co.uk

24	£15.00–£15.00
24	£15.00–£15.00
10	£11.00–£11.00
5	£220.00–£395.00
24 touring pitches	

From the A3400 between Stratford and Henley-in-Arden or from the A46 between Stratford and Alcester follow the signs for Aston Cantlow. The park is 0.25 miles west of the village.

BIRMINGHAM, West Midlands Map ref 5B3 *Tourist Information Centre Tel: (0121) 202 5099*

★★★★★
TOURING PARK

BH&HPA

See Ad on inside back cover

CHAPEL LANE CARAVAN CLUB SITE
Chapel Lane, Wythall, Birmingham B47 6JX
T: (01564) 826483
I: www.caravanclub.co.uk

Wythall is a quiet, rural area yet convenient for Birmingham (nine miles) and the NEC (13 miles). Visit Cadbury's World or explore the surrounding countryside and local canals. Special member rates mean you can save your membership subscription in less than a week. Visit www.caravanclub.co.uk to find out more.

106	£16.10–£21.50
106	£16.10–£21.50
106 touring pitches	

OPEN All Year
Payment accepted: Delta, Mastercard, Switch, Visa

From M1 jct 23a, jct 3 off M42 then A435 to Birmingham. After 1 mile at roundabout take 1st exit, Middle Lane. Turn right at church then immediately right into site.

Credit card bookings
If you book by telephone and are asked for your credit card number it is advisable to check the proprietor's policy should you cancel your reservation.

BIRMINGHAM AIRPORT

See under Birmingham

BRIDGNORTH, Shropshire Map ref 5A3 *Tourist Information Centre Tel: (01746) 763257*

★★★★
HOLIDAY PARK

BH&HPA

PARK GRANGE HOLIDAYS
Park Grange, Morville, Bridgnorth
WV16 4RN
T: (01746) 714285
F: (01746) 714145
E: info@parkgrangeholidays.co.uk
I: www.parkgrangeholidays.co.uk

OPEN All Year
Payment accepted: Euros

4   £145.00–£322.00

On the A458 Bridgnorth to Shrewsbury road, 1.5 miles beyond Morville towards Shrewsbury, look for the signs to Park Grange Holiday Caravans.

★★★★★
**HOLIDAY &
TOURING PARK**

BH&HPA

STANMORE HALL TOURING PARK
Stourbridge Road, Bridgnorth WV15 6DT
T: (01746) 761761
F: (01746) 768069
E: stanmore@morris-leisure.co.uk
I: www.morris-leisure.co.uk

OPEN All Year
Payment accepted:
Mastercard, Switch, Visa

130   £13.80–£16.30
44   £13.80–£16.30
10
130 touring pitches

Located on the east of Bridgnorth on the Stourbridge road, A458.

ELLESMERE, Shropshire Map ref 5A2

★★★★★
**HOLIDAY &
TOURING PARK**

BH&HPA
NCC

FERNWOOD CARAVAN PARK
Lyneal, Ellesmere SY12 0QF
T: (01948) 710221
F: (01948) 710324
E: fernwood@caravanpark37.fsnet.co.uk
I: www.ranch.co.uk

Payment accepted: Delta,
Mastercard, Switch, Visa

  £14.00–£19.00
  £14.00–£19.00
1 £250.00–£360.00
60 touring pitches

Ellesmere A495 road at Welshampton B5063, after canal follow signs.

HEREFORD, Herefordshire Map ref 3A1 *Tourist Information Centre Tel: (01432) 268430*

★★★★★
**HOLIDAY &
TOURING PARK**

BH&HPA

LUCKSALL CARAVAN AND CAMPING PARK
Mordiford, Hereford HR1 4LP
T: (01432) 870213
F: (01432) 870213
I: www.lucksallpark.co.uk
Payment accepted: Mastercard, Switch,
Visa

80   £10.50–£12.00
80   £10.50–£12.00
40   £9.00–£11.00
2 £140.00–£270.00
80 touring pitches

On the B4224 between Hereford and Ross-on-Wye.

HOPTON HEATH, Shropshire Map ref 5A3

★★★★★
HOLIDAY PARK

ROSE AWARD

BH&HPA
NCC

ASHLEA POOLS COUNTRY PARK
Hopton Heath, Craven Arms SY7 0QD
T: (01547) 530430
F: (01547) 530430
E: ashleapools@surfbay.dircon.co.uk
I: www.ashleapools.co.uk

Surrounded by rolling hills and picturesque valleys, set in 11 acres of beautiful greenery with an idyllic lake. Open end of February to January. Lodges for sale or hire. 10% off your 2nd holiday. Couples discount – £20 off. Under 5's and over 55's – £10 off. Fortnight break – £25 off.

Payment accepted: Amex, Mastercard, Switch, Visa

From Craven Arms turn off at the Craven Arms Hotel on the B4368 signposted Clun. At Long Meadow End turn left onto the B4367 and follow the brown signs to village of Hopton Heath.

6 lodges £200.00–£535.00

LUDLOW, Shropshire Map ref 5A3 *Tourist Information Centre Tel: (01584) 875053*

★★★★★
**HOLIDAY &
TOURING PARK**

BH&HPA

ORLETON RISE HOLIDAY HOME PARK
Green Lane, Orleton, Ludlow SY8 4JE
T: (01584) 831617
F: (01584) 831617
I: www.lucksallpark.co.uk

16		£9.00–£14.00
16		£9.00–£14.00
16 touring pitches		

A49 Ludlow/Leominster turn at Wooferton B4362. Turn left at T-junction towards Leominster. Turn right at Maidenhead Inn and the park is 0.75 miles along Green Lane.

PEMBRIDGE, Herefordshire Map ref 3A1

★★★★★
**TOURING &
CAMPING PARK**

NCC

TOWNSEND TOURING PARK
Townsend Farm, Leominster HR6 9HB
T: (01544) 388527
F: (01544) 388527
E: info@townsend-farm.co.uk
I: www.townsend-farm.co.uk

OPEN All Year
Payment accepted: Delta,
Mastercard, Switch, Visa

60		£9.00–£16.00
60		£9.00–£16.00
60		£9.00–£16.00
60 touring pitches		

Follow the A44 into village of Pembridge. Townsend Touring Park is situated on the Leominster side of the village 50m within the village boundary.

SHREWSBURY, Shropshire Map ref 5A3 *Tourist Information Centre Tel: (01743) 281200*

★★★★★
**HOLIDAY &
TOURING PARK**

BH&HPA

OXON HALL TOURING PARK
Welshpool Road, Bicton Heath, Shrewsbury
SY3 5FB
T: (01743) 340868
F: (01743) 340869
E: oxon@morris-leisure.co.uk
I: www.morris-leisure.co.uk

OPEN All Year
Payment accepted:
Mastercard, Switch, Visa

120		£13.80–£16.30
40		£13.80–£16.30
10		
120 touring pitches		

On A458 to Welshpool, 1.5 miles from Shrewsbury town centre, adjacent to Oxon park and ride.

STOKE-ON-TRENT, Stoke-on-Trent Map ref 5B2 *Tourist Information Centre Tel: (01782) 236000*

★★★★
**HOLIDAY, TOURING
& CAMPING PARK**

BH&HPA

THE STAR CARAVAN AND CAMPING PARK

Star Road, Cotton, Stoke-on-Trent ST10 3DW
T: (01538) 702219
F: (01538) 703704
I: www.starcaravanpark.co.uk

The closest touring park to Alton Towers, strict 11pm-all-quiet rule on site. No single-sex groups allowed. Families and mixed couples always welcomed. Early-season discounts on caravan holidays homes. Free 2nd day admission to Alton Towers for 2 persons (ring for information).

From M6 jct 16 or M1 jct 23a follow signs for Alton Towers. Go past and follow the road (Beelow Lane) for 0.75 miles to crossroads. Turn right up hill. Site on right after 400m.

60		£10.00
30		£10.00–£12.00
30		£10.00–£12.00
9		£270.00–£340.00
120 touring pitches		

Visitor attractions For ideas on places to visit refer to the introduction at the beginning of this section. Look out for the VisitBritain Quality Assured Visitor Attraction signs.

TELFORD, Telford and Wrekin Map ref 5A3 *Tourist Information Centre Tel: (01952) 238008*

★★★★★

**TOURING &
CAMPING PARK**

BH&HPA

NCC

SEVERN GORGE PARK
Bridgnorth Road, Tweedale, Telford TF7 4JB
T: (01952) 684789
E: info@severngorgepark.co.uk
I: www.severngorgepark.co.uk

OPEN All Year

Payment accepted: Amex,
Mastercard, Switch, Visa

40		£14.10–£15.75
40		£14.10–£15.75
10	▲	£9.85–£11.75
50 touring pitches		

From M54 jct 4 or 5 take the A442 south signposted Kidderminster (approximately 3 miles). Follow signs for Madeley then Tweedale.

WYE VALLEY

See under Hereford

Use your *i*s

There are more than 750
Tourist Information Centres
throughout England, Scotland
and Wales, offering friendly
help with accommodation and
holiday ideas as well as
suggestions of places to visit
and things to do. You'll find
addresses in the local
phone book.

A brief guide to the main towns and villages offering accommodation in the **Heart of England**

ASTON CANTLOW, Warwickshire

Attractive village on the river Alne, with a black and white timbered guild house and a fine old inn.

BIRMINGHAM, **West Midlands**

Britain's second city, whose attractions include Centenary Square and the ICC with Symphony Hall, the NEC, the City Art Gallery, Barber Institute of Fine Arts, 17thC Aston Hall, science and railway museums, Jewellery Quarter, Cadbury World, two cathedrals and Botanical Gardens.

BRIDGNORTH, **Shropshire**

Red sandstone riverside town in two parts – High and Low – linked by a cliff railway. Much of interest including a ruined Norman keep, half-timbered 16thC houses, Midland Motor Museum and Severn Valley Railway.

HEREFORD, **Herefordshire**

Agricultural county town, its cathedral containing much Norman work, a large chained library and the world-famous Mappa Mundi exhibition. Among the city's varied attractions are several museums including the Cider Museum and the Old House.

LUDLOW, **Shropshire**

Outstandingly interesting border town with a magnificent castle high above the river Teme, two half-timbered old inns and an impressive 15thC church. The Reader's House, with its three-storey Jacobean porch, should also be seen.

PEMBRIDGE, **Herefordshire**

Delightful village close to the Welsh border with many black and white half-timbered cottages, some dating from the 14thC. There is a market hall supported by eight wooden pillars in the marketplace, also old inns and a 14thC church with interesting separate bell tower.

SHREWSBURY, **Shropshire**

Beautiful historic town on the river Severn retaining many fine old timber-framed houses. Its attractions include Rowley's Museum with Roman finds, remains of a castle, Clive House Museum, St Chad's 18thC round church, rowing on the river and the Shrewsbury Flower Show in August.

STOKE-ON-TRENT, Stoke-on-Trent

Famous for its pottery. Factories of several famous makers, including Josiah Wedgwood, can be visited. The City Museum has one of the finest pottery and porcelain collections in the world.

TELFORD, **Telford and Wrekin**

New Town named after Thomas Telford, the famous engineer who designed many of the country's canals, bridges and viaducts. It is close to Ironbridge with its monuments and museums to the Industrial Revolution, including restored 18thC buildings.

Below, from left visit historic Shrewsbury; peaceful Shropshire countryside

Tourist Information Centres

When it comes to your next British break, the first stage of your journey could be closer than you think. You've probably got a tourist information centre nearby which is there to serve the local community – as well as visitors. Knowledgeable staff will be happy to help you, wherever you're heading.

Many tourist information centres can provide you with maps and guides, and often it's possible to book accommodation and travel tickets too.

Across Britain there are more than 750 TICs. You'll find the address of your nearest centre in your local phone book.

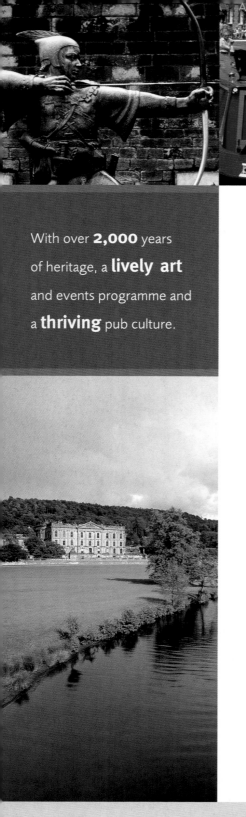

With over **2,000** years of heritage, a **lively art** and events programme and a **thriving** pub culture.

East Midlands

Looking for some inspiration? Here are a few ideas to get you started in the East Midlands. **experience** food from around the world in Nottingham. **discover** the hidden gardens at Belvoir Castle. **explore** the limestone caves of the Peak District. **relax** on a boat on the Grand Union Canal.

THE REGION
Leicestershire and Rutland, Lincolnshire, Northamptonshire, Nottinghamshire, Peak District and Derbyshire

CONTACT

▸ **EAST MIDLANDS TOURISM**
www.enjoyeastmidlands.com
Leicestershire and Rutland
www.goleicestershire.com
Lincolnshire
www.visitlincolnshire.com
Northamptonshire
www.enjoynorthamptonshire.com
Nottinghamshire
www.experiencenottinghamshire.com
Peak District and Derbyshire
www.derbyshirethepeakdistrict.com
www.visitpeakdistrict.com

Do you love that adrenalin rush or are you more into a laid back holiday? Whether your idea of perfect happiness is cave diving or watching the world go by very slowly from a canal-boat, you will find it in the East Midlands.

Break out in the city

East Midlands' cities make perfect short breaks. Visit Lincoln's cathedral and castle and then absorb the vibrant atmosphere along Brayford waterfront as the city comes to life. With a lively art and events programme, you can indulge in all your favourite pleasures. While here sample some Lincolnshire plumbread and Lincolnshire Poacher cheeses.

Or go in search of Robin Hood, and the story of lace-making in Nottingham. A medieval city with a thoroughly modern heart, Nottingham is one of the clubbing capitals of the Midlands and has more bars, restaurants and clubs than you've had hot cappuccinos.

In Leicester, get a flavour of the city in Belgrave Road, a street saturated in colourful silks, saris and spices and enjoy the buzz of the lively, covered market – just the place to sample a tasty Melton Mowbray pork pie, or Stilton and Red Leicester cheeses.

You are guaranteed a warm welcome in the great multicultural city of Derby, bursting with entertainment venues, museums, parks and shops. Fans of real ale should come in July for the annual CAMRA festival.

Wealth and power

Wealth and power simply ooze from the very foundations of great houses like Elizabethan Hardwick Hall and Chatsworth House, the Palace of the Peaks, where the gardens are as magnificent as the house. Nearby, taste some delicious Bakewell pudding in the village where it originated. Other fantastic gardens from all periods include Althorp (the final resting place of Princess Diana) and Belvoir Castle where you'll find the hidden Spring Gardens.

On the waterfront

Get the wind in every kind of sail along the Lincolnshire coast; water-ski or row at the National Watersports Centre at Holme Pierrepont in Nottinghamshire or try white-water rafting at Nene Whitewater Centre. Something less energetic? Stroll around the shore and watch the activity at Rutland Water, one of the largest man-made lakes in Western Europe, or take a gentle cruise on the Grand Union Canal, the river Nene or Soar. Discover special wildlife habitats throughout the intricate waterways of the Lincolnshire Fens. The Fens Discovery Centre at Spalding explains how man overcame nature and tamed the inhospitable marshland.

Plenty of activity

Walking, cycling, climbing, potholing. Enjoy them all in the East Midlands. Completing even a small section of the Pennine Way Long Distance Footpath will lift your spirits and make you crave for more and what could be more appropriate than to bowl through the picturesque Derwent Valley, a World Heritage Site, on a bike, one of its most important inventions.

Left, from top Robin Hood statue, Nottingham; drifting along the Grand Union Canal, Stoke Bruerne; be amazed at Chatsworth House in the Peak District

Places to visit

Awarded VisitBritain's Quality Assured Visitor Attraction marque.

78 Derngate
Northampton
Tel: (01604) 603407
www.78derngate.org.uk
Discover the Charles Ronnie Mackintosh designed interior and supporting exhibition, including life and work of patron WJ Bassett-Lowke, maker of engineering models. Strictly by pre-booked timed entry only.

American Adventure
Ilkeston, Derbyshire
Tel: 0845 330 2929
www.americanadventure.co.uk
Action and entertainment for all ages, including The Missile white-knuckle rollercoaster, Europe's tallest skycoaster and the world's wettest log flume.

Belton House, Park and Gardens (National Trust)
Belton, Lincolnshire
Tel: (01476) 566116
www.nationaltrust.org.uk
Magnificent restoration country house, with fine plasterwork ceilings and woodcarvings, portraits and oriental porcelain. Formal gardens, orangery and landscaped park.

Belvoir Castle
Belvoir, Leicestershire
Tel: (01476) 871002
www.belvoircastle.com
Enjoy magnificent views of the Vale of Belvoir. Art treasures include works by Poussin, Rubens, Holbein and Reynolds. See also the Queen's Royal Lancers display.

Berzerk Leisure
Moulton Park, Northamptonshire
Tel: (01604) 647213
Large indoor activity centre featuring inflatables, ballponds and slides, where children aged 12 months to 10 years will enjoy letting off steam. Restaurant and ample free parking.

Bosworth Battlefield Visitor Centre and Country Park
Sutton Cheney, Leicestershire
Tel: (01455) 290429
www.leics.gov.uk
Site of the Battle of Bosworth Field between Richard II and Henry VII in 1485. Explore the visitor centre with models, exhibitions, flags, armour, a film theatre and illustrated battle trails.

Brocks Hill Environment Centre and Country Park
Oadby, Leicester
Tel (0116) 271 4514
www.brockshill.co.uk
Be amazed at this environmentally friendly building promoting energy efficiency and sustainability set in 67 acres of country park. Play area, café and human sundial.

Butlins
Skegness, Lincolnshire
Tel: (01754) 762311
www.butlinsonline.co.uk
A feast of fun, magic and laughter with the Redcoats, Skyline Pavilion, Toyland, Sub Tropical Waterworld, tenpin bowling and entertainment centre with live shows.

Chatsworth House, Garden, Farmyard & Adventure Playground
Chatsworth, Derbyshire
Tel: (01246) 582204
www.chatsworth.org
One of the great Treasure Houses of England. More than 30 richly decorated rooms, garden with fountains, a cascade and maze. Farmyard and Adventure Playground.

Conkers: at the Heart of the National Forest
Near Ashby, Leicestershire
Tel: (01283) 216633
www.visitconkers.com
Innovative indoor exhibitions, including the Tree Top Adventure Walk, are complemented by 120-acres of trails, sculpture and habitats. Restaurants, shops and crafts, plus fantastic playpark and a train. Year-round activities.

Crich Tramway Village
Crich, Derbyshire
Tel: (01773) 854321
www.tramway.co.uk

A collection of over 70 trams from Britain and overseas from 1873-1969 with tram rides, a period street scene, depots, a power station, workshops and exhibitions.

Denby Pottery Visitor Centre
Denby, Derbyshire
Tel: (01773) 740799
www.denbypottery.co.uk
See how pottery is made on one of the daily factory tours. Museum, Denby and Dartington Crystal factory shops, garden centre, gift shop, Cookery Emporium and Courtyard Restaurant.

The Galleries of Justice
Shire Hall, Nottingham
Tel: (0115) 952 0555
www.galleriesofjustice.org.uk
An atmospheric experience of justice over the ages located in and around an original 19thC courthouse and county gaol, brought to life by live actors.

Great Central Railway
Great Central Station, Loughborough
Tel: (01509) 230726
www.greatcentralrailway.com
Britain's only double track, mainline heritage railway running through eight miles of scenic Leicestershire countryside.

Grimsthorpe Castle, Park and Gardens
Bourne, Lincolnshire
Tel: (01778) 591205
www.grimsthorpe.co.uk
Visit the castle which features four periods of architecture and a collection of 18thC portraits and furniture. Young children will enjoy the adventure playground and can help feed the reed deer.

Gulliver's Kingdom
Matlock Bath, Derbyshire
Tel: (01629) 580540
www.gulliversfun.co.uk
Enjoy a great family day out at this theme park with rides and attractions including Little Switzerland, Fantasy Terrace, Royal Cave, chair lift and a cycle monorail.

Hartsholme Country Park
Skellingthorpe Road, Lincoln
Tel: (01522) 873577
Woodland, lakes and open grassland with a visitor centre and ranger service. Nearby is a local nature reserve, Swanholme Park.

The Heights of Abraham Cable Cars, Caverns and Hilltop Park
Matlock Bath, Derbyshire
Tel: (01629) 582365
www.heights-of-abraham.co.uk
A spectacular cable car ride takes you to the summit where, within the grounds, there are a wide variety of attractions for young and old alike. Gift shop and coffee shop.

Horse World
Market Rasen, Lincolnshire
Tel: (01673) 849967
See horses at work, rest and play with forest walks, a conservation area, educational visits, riding and hacking.

Indian Chief Cruises
The Boat Inn, Stoke Bruerne, Northamptonshire
Tel: (01604) 862428
www.boatinn.co.uk
Cruises on the Grand Union canal for up to 40 passengers, sailing through Northamptonshire countryside, through the famous Blisworth tunnel or up a flight of seven locks.

Lincoln Castle
Castle Hill, Lincoln
Tel: (01522) 511068
www.lincolnshire.gov.uk/lincolncastle
Walk the walls of this medieval castle, view the Magna Carta exhibition and reconstructed Westgate, experience a prison chapel, and enjoy popular events throughout the summer.

Lincoln Cathedral
Minster Yard, Lincoln
Tel: (01522) 544544
www.lincolncathedral.com
A medieval Gothic cathedral of outstanding historical and architectural merit. Must-sees include Katherine Swynford's tomb, St Hugh's Shrine and the Lincoln Imp.

Making It! Discovery Centre
Mansfield, Nottinghamshire
Tel: (01623) 473297
www.makingit.org.uk
Interactive galleries describing the process of making things. You can design and make a model to take away.

Midland Railway-Butterley
Butterley Station, Butterley, Derbyshire
Tel: (01773) 747674
Over 50 steam and diesel locomotives and over 100 items of historic Midland and LMS rolling stock with a steam-hauled passenger service, museum site, country and farm park.

Above left step back in time at Bosworth Battlefield, Sutton Cheney; drop in at Rockingham Castle

Places to visit

Awarded VisitBritain's Quality Assured Visitor Attraction marque.

Peak District Mining Museum
Matlock Bath, Derbyshire
Tel: (01629) 583834
www.peakmines.co.uk
A large exhibition illustrating 3500 years of lead mining with displays on geology, mines and miners, tools and engines. Go underground and pan for gold and other minerals.

Rockingham Castle
Rockingham, Northamptonshire
Tel: (01536) 770240
www.rockinghamcastle.com
An Elizabethan house within the walls of a Norman castle with fine pictures and china, extensive views and gardens with roses, a tilting lawn and an ancient yew hedge.

Royal Crown Derby Visitor Centre
Osmaston Road, Derby
Tel: (01332) 712800
www.royal-crown-derby.co.uk
A museum of Derby and Royal Crown Derby china dating from 1750. Take a guided tour of the working factory and see demonstrations of key skills. Museum, demonstrations and factory shop open daily.

Safari Parties at Grange Wood Zoo
Grangewood, Netherseal, Derbyshire
Tel: (01283) 760541
www.safari-parties.co.uk
Small rainforest zoo situated at Netherseal in Derbyshire, with a collection of small exotic rainforest animals, birds, reptiles and insects birds, mammals, reptiles and insects. Parties, open days and events.

The Seal Sanctuary
Mablethorpe, Lincolnshire
Tel: (01507) 473346
A wildlife sanctuary in gardens and natural dunes with the emphasis on Lincolnshire wildlife, past and present, and the Seal Trust Wildlife Hospital.

Skegness Natureland Seal Sanctuary
Skegness, Lincolnshire
Tel: (01754) 764345
www.skegnessnatureland.co.uk
Sanctuary for seals and baby seals, many rescued from beaches around the Wash, plus penguins, aquarium, crocodiles, snakes, terrapins, scorpions, tropical birds, butterflies and pets.

Snibston Discovery Park
Coalville, Leicestershire
Tel: (01530) 278444
www.leics.gov.uk/museums
An all-weather and award-winning science and technology heritage museum exploring Leicestershire's industrial past, where visitors can get 'hands-on'.

Twycross Zoo
Twycross, Leceistershire
Tel: (01827) 880250
www.twycrosszoo.com
A zoo with gorillas, orang-utans, chimpanzees, a modern gibbon complex, elephants, lions, giraffes, a reptile house, pets' corner and rides.

The Workhouse
Southwell, Nottinghamshire
Tel: (01636) 817250
www.nationaltrust.org.uk/workhouse
Explore the segregated rooms, stairways and the master's quarters of the best surviving workhouse in England. Built in 1824, it was a prototype for similar 'welfare' institutions throughout the country.

The Yard Gallery
Wollaton Hall, Nottingham
Tel: (0115) 915 3920
www.nottinghamcity.gov.uk
A vibrant art gallery housed in an old stableblock, hosting an exciting programme of contemporary art exhibitions exploring themes of natural history and science.

Above admire the views at Rushup Edge, the Peak District; admire Belvoir Castle, Leicestershire

East Midlands Tourism

Apex Court, City Link,
Nottingham NG2 4LA
www.enjoyeastmidlands.com

Further publications are available from the following organisations:

Experience Nottinghamshire
www.experiencenottinghamshire.com
Nottingham and Nottinghamshire Short Break and Visitor Guide
Nottingham and Nottinghamshire Places to visit

Peak District and Derbyshire
www.derbyshirethepeakdistrict.com or
www.visitpeakdistrict.com
Peak District Walking Guide
Peak District Visitor Guide
Savour the Flavour of the Peak District
Derbyshire – the Peak District Visitor Guide
Derbyshire – the Peak District Attractions Guide

Lincolnshire
www.visitlincolnshire.com
Visit Lincolnshire - Places to stay
Tastes of Lincolnshire
Visit Lincolnshire – Things to do
Visit Lincolnshire – Great days out
Visit Lincolnshire – Gardens and Nurseries

Northamptonshire Tourism
www.enjoynorthamptonshire.com
Enjoy Northamptonshire Visitor Guide

Leicestershire and Rutland
www.goleicestershire.com
Leicestershire 05
Cream of Leicestershire and Rutland
Rutland Guide

Travel information

The central location of the East Midlands makes it easily accessible from all parts of the UK.

By road:
From the North and South, the M1 bisects the East Midlands with access to the region from junctions 14 through to 31. The A1 offers better access to the eastern part of the region, particularly Lincolnshire and Rutland. From the west the M69, M/A42 and A50 provide easy access.

By rail:
The region is well served by three main line operators – GNER, Midland Mainline and Virgin, each offering direct services from London and the north of England and Scotland to the East Midlands' major cities and towns. East/west links are provided by Central Trains, offering not only access to the region but also travel within it.

By air:
Nottingham East Midlands airport is located centrally in the region, with scheduled domestic flights from Aberdeen, Belfast, Edinburgh, Glasgow, Isle of Man and the Channel Islands. Manchester, Birmingham, Luton, Stansted and Humberside airports also offer domestic scheduled routes with easy access to the region by road and rail.

Where to stay in
East Midlands

All place names in the blue bands, under which accommodation is listed, are shown on the maps at the front of this guide.

A complete listing of all VisitBritain assessed accommodation covered by this guide appears at the back.

Accommodation symbols
Symbols give useful information about services and facilities. Inside the back cover flap you can find a key to these symbols. Keep it open for easy reference.

ALSOP-EN-LE-DALE, Derbyshire Map ref 5B2

★★★★
HOLIDAY, TOURING
& CAMPING PARK

BH&HPA

See Ad opposite

RIVENDALE CARAVAN AND LEISURE PARK
Buxton Road, Alsop-en-le-Dale, Ashbourne
DE6 1QU
T: (01335) 310311
F: (01335) 310311
E: greg@rivendalecaravanpark.co.uk
I: www.rivendalecaravanpark.co.uk

Payment accepted:
Mastercard, Switch, Visa

81	🚐	£8.00–£13.50
81	🚚	£8.00–£13.50
30	⛺	£8.00–£13.50
111 touring pitches		

From A515 Rivendale is situated 6.5 miles north of Ashbourne, directly off the A515 Buxton road on the right-hand side.

ASHBOURNE, Derbyshire Map ref 5B2 *Tourist Information Centre Tel: (01335) 343666*

★★★★
TOURING PARK

BH&HPA

See Ad on inside back cover

BLACKWALL PLANTATION CARAVAN CLUB SITE
Kirk Ireton, Ashbourne DE6 3JL
T: (01335) 370903
I: www.caravanclub.co.uk

Beautifully landscaped, within walking distance of Carsington Reservoir. Good walking and cycling area, ideal for exploring the Peak District National Park. Alton Towers 15 miles. Open 26 March to 1 November. Special member rates mean you can save your membership subscription in less than a week. Visit www.caravanclub.co.uk to find out more.

Payment accepted: Delta, Mastercard, Switch, Visa

Take the A517 from Ashbourne. In 4.5 miles, turn left at the signpost to Carsington Water/Atlow/Hognaston. In 0.75 miles at the crossroads, turn right signposted to Carsington Water. The site is on the right after 1 mile.

134	🚐	£14.60–£20.60
134	🚚	£14.60–£20.60
134 touring pitches		

THE CARAVAN CLUB

NB **Important note** Information on accommodation listed in this guide has been supplied by the proprietors. As changes may occur you are advised to check details at the time of booking.

BAKEWELL, Derbyshire Map ref 5B2 *Tourist Information Centre Tel: (01629) 813227*

★★★★★
TOURING PARK

BH&HPA

See Ad on inside back cover

CHATSWORTH PARK CARAVAN CLUB SITE

Chatsworth, Bakewell DE45 1PN
T: (01246) 582226
I: www.caravanclub.co.uk

120 £17.00–£22.00
120 £17.00–£22.00
120 touring pitches

Breathtaking setting in walled garden on the Estate. Farmyard and adventure playground for children. The Peak District National Park's towns are nearby. Open 26 March 2005 to 3 January 2006. Special member rates mean you can save your membership subscription in less than a week. Visit www.caravanclub.co.uk to find out more.

Payment accepted: Delta, Mastercard, Switch, Visa

From Bakewell on A619. In 3.75 miles on the outskirts of Baslow turn right at roundabout (signposted Sheffield). Site entrance on right in 150yds.

THE CARAVAN CLUB

BOSTON, Lincolnshire Map ref 4A1 *Tourist Information Centre Tel: (01205) 356656*

★★★
HOLIDAY & TOURING PARK

BH&HPA

ORCHARD CARAVAN PARK

Frampton Lane, Hubberts Bridge, Boston
PE20 3QU
T: (01205) 290328
F: (01205) 290247
I: www.orchardpark.co.uk

£12.00–£14.00
3 £170.00–£220.00
87 touring pitches

From A17 take the A1121 towards Boston and at the junction with the B1192 take the Hubberts Bridge turn. Frampton Lane is 1st on the left and the park is 0.25 miles down the lane.

BUXTON, Derbyshire Map ref 5B2 *Tourist Information Centre Tel: (01298) 25106*

★★★
TOURING & CAMPING PARK

BH&HPA

COTTAGE FARM CARAVAN PARK

Blackwell in the Peak, Buxton SK17 9TQ
T: (01298) 85330
E: mail@cottagefarmsite.co.uk
I: www.cottagefarmsite.co.uk

30 £7.00
30 £7.00
30 £7.00
30 touring pitches

Off A6 midway between Buxton and Bakewell. Site signposted.

Map references The map references refer to the colour maps at the front of this guide. The first figure is the map number; the letter and figure which follow indicate the grid reference on the map.

BUXTON continued

★★★★★
**TOURING &
CAMPING PARK**

BH&HPA

See Ad on inside back cover

GRIN LOW CARAVAN CLUB SITE

Grin Low Road, Ladmanlow, Buxton SK17 6UJ
T: (01298) 77735
I: www.caravanclub.co.uk

Attractively landscaped site ideally situated for Buxton, at the centre of the Peak District National Park, and for visiting Chatsworth and Haddon Hall. Open 26 March to 1 November. Special member rates mean you can save your membership subscription in less than a week. Visit www.caravanclub.co.uk to find out more.

Payment accepted: Delta, Mastercard, Switch, Visa

From Buxton turn left off the A53 Buxton to Leek road. Within 1.5 miles at Grin Low signpost, in 300yds turn left into the site approach road; the site entrance is 0.25 miles away.

117	£14.60–£20.60
117	£14.60–£20.60
▲	On application
117 touring pitches	

★★★★
**HOLIDAY, TOURING
& CAMPING PARK**

BH&HPA

LIME TREE PARK
Dukes Drive, Buxton SK17 9RP
T: (01298) 22988
F: (01298) 22988
E: limetreebuxton@dukesso.fsnet.co.uk
I: www.ukparks.co.uk/limetree

Payment accepted: Amex, Delta, Mastercard, Switch, Visa

From M1 jct 29. One mile south of Buxton centre between A6 and A515.

65	£13.00–£16.00
15	£13.00–£16.00
70 ▲	£12.00–£16.00
12	£180.00–£445.00
65 touring pitches	

★★★
**HOLIDAY, TOURING
& CAMPING PARK**

BH&HPA

NEWHAVEN CARAVAN AND CAMPING PARK
Newhaven, Buxton SK17 0DT
T: (01298) 84300
F: (01332) 726027

Payment accepted: Delta, Mastercard, Switch, Visa

Halfway between Ashbourne and Buxton on A515 at the jct with the A5012.

95	£8.00–£9.50
95	£8.00–£9.50
30 ▲	£8.00–£9.50
125 touring pitches	

CASTLETON, Derbyshire Map ref 5B2

★★★★★
**TOURING &
CAMPING PARK**

BH&HPA

See Ad on inside back cover

LOSEHILL CARAVAN CLUB SITE

Castleton, Hope Valley S33 8WB
T: (01433) 620636
I: www.caravanclub.co.uk

This popular site, set in the north of the Peak District National Park, is an excellent base for outdoor activities. Rock-climbing, potholing, biking and horse-riding. Special member rates mean you can save your membership subscription in less than a week. Visit www.caravanclub.co.uk to find out more.

OPEN All Year
Payment accepted: Delta, Mastercard, Switch, Visa

From Hathersage on the B6001 in about 2.5 miles, turn left onto the A6187 (signposted Castleton), site on right in 5m.

78	£16.10–£21.50
78	£16.10–£21.50
▲	On application
78 touring pitches	

Credit card bookings

If you book by telephone and are asked for your credit card number it is advisable to check the proprietor's policy should you cancel your reservation.

INGOLDMELLS, Lincolnshire Map ref 5D2

★★★
HOLIDAY PARK

BH&HPA

INGOLDALE PARK
Beach Estate, Roman Bank, Ingoldmells,
Skegness PE25 1LL
T: (01754) 872335
F: (01754) 873887
E: ingoldalepark@btopenworld.com
I: www.ingoldmells.net

14 £160.00–£450.00

From M180 jct 1. From Skegness follow A52 to Ingoldmells, bear right after Funcoast World, on Roman Bank. 0.75 miles straight on, over Fantasy Island crossroads, Ingoldale is the first drive on left.

LINCOLN, Lincolnshire Map ref 5C2 *Tourist Information Centre Tel: (01522) 873213*

★★★
TOURING PARK

HARTSHOLME COUNTRY PARK
Skellingthorpe Road, Lincoln LN6 0EY
T: (01522) 873578
I: www.lincoln.gov.uk

£9.30–£16.00
£9.30–£16.00
14 £6.00–£11.50
36 touring pitches

Signposted from A46 Lincoln bypass, brown signs. Entrance on B1378.

METHERINGHAM, Lincolnshire Map ref 5C2

★★★
**HOLIDAY, TOURING
& CAMPING PARK**

THE WHITE HORSE CARAVAN PARK
Dunston Fen, Metheringham, Lincoln
LN4 3AP
T: (01526) 399919
F: (01526) 399919
E: whitehorse@dunstonfen.co.uk
I: www.dunstonfen.co.uk

8 £9.50–£13.00
8 £9.50–£13.00
8 £4.00–£9.50
1 £180.00–£210.00
8 touring pitches

Take the turn off the B1188 towards Dunston. Continue into village and follow signs for the River Witham, and Dunston Fen and White Horse Inn.

PEAK DISTRICT

See under Alsop-en-le-Dale, Ashbourne, Bakewell, Buxton, Castleton

SHERWOOD FOREST

See under Worksop

SUTTON IN ASHFIELD, Nottinghamshire Map ref 5C2

★★★★★
**TOURING &
CAMPING PARK**

BH&HPA

SHARDAROBA CARAVAN PARK
Shardaroba, Silverhill Lane, Teversal,
Nr Sutton in Ashfield NG17 3JJ
T: (01623) 551838
F: (01623) 552174
E: stay@shardaroba.co.uk
I: www.shardaroba.co.uk

OPEN All Year
Payment accepted: Amex,
Mastercard, Switch, Visa

100 £12.00–£16.00
95 £12.00–£16.00
23 £12.00–£14.00
100 touring pitches

M1 jct 28, take A38 towards Mansfield. At traffic lights left B6027, over 2 mini-roundabouts, at top of hill straight over crossroads. Next crossroads turn left, T-junction turn right B6014, at Carnarvon Arms turn left onto Silverhill Lane.

Important note Information on accommodation listed in this guide has been supplied by the proprietors. As changes may occur you are advised to check details at the time of booking.

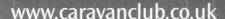

SUTTON ST JAMES, Lincolnshire Map ref 4A1

★★★★
HOLIDAY, TOURING
& CAMPING PARK

BH&HPA

FOREMAN'S BRIDGE CARAVAN PARK
Sutton Road, Spalding PE12 0HU
T: (01945) 440346
F: (01945) 440346
I: www.foremans-bridge.co.uk

40	🚐	£8.50
40	🚑	£8.50
40	▲	£6.00
7	🏕	£155.00–£240.00
40 touring pitches		

Two miles from A17 onto B1390. The park is 2 miles on the left.

🔌 📺 ⊕ 🚗 🏕 🚻 WP 🅿 🎱 🎰 🗄 ☺ 🚲 🦆 ▶ 🐕

WOODHALL SPA, Lincolnshire Map ref 5D2

★★★★★
HOLIDAY &
TOURING PARK

BH&HPA

BAINLAND COUNTRY PARK
Horncastle Road, Woodhall Spa LN10 6UX
T: (01526) 352903
F: (01526) 353730
E: bookings@bainland.com
I: www.bainland.com

OPEN All Year
Payment accepted: Delta,
Mastercard, Switch, Visa

160	🚐	£11.50–£31.00
160	🚑	£11.50–£31.00
16	▲	£9.50–£24.50
10	🏕	£210.00–£500.00
160 touring pitches		

One-and-a-half miles from the centre of Woodhall Spa, going towards Horncastle, on the right just before the petrol station, on the B1191.

🔌 📺 ⊕ 🚗 🏕 🚻 WP 🅿 🎱 ✕ 🍴 TV 🗄 ☺ 🔍 ⛰ 📶 ✂ 🦆 ▶ 🐕 ☀

WORKSOP, Nottinghamshire Map ref 5C2 *Tourist Information Centre Tel: (01909) 501148*

★★★★
TOURING PARK

BH&HPA

See Ad on inside back cover

CLUMBER PARK CARAVAN CLUB SITE

Lime Tree Avenue, Clumber Park, Worksop S80 3AE
T: (01909) 484758
I: www.caravanclub.co.uk

Set in the heart of Sherwood Forest and redeveloped to a high standard in 2002. Visit Nottingham Castle and the watersports centre at Holme Pierrepont. Special member rates mean you can save your membership subscription in less than a week. Visit www.caravanclub.co.uk to find out more.

OPEN All Year
Payment accepted: Delta, Mastercard, Switch, Visa

From the junction of the A1 and A57, take the A614 signposted to Nottingham for 0.5 miles. Turn right into Clumber Park site. The club is signposted thereafter.

183	🚐	£17.00–£22.00
183	🚑	£17.00–£22.00
183 touring pitches		

THE CARAVAN CLUB

📺 ⊕ 🚗 🏕 🚻 WP 🅿 🗄 🎱 ☺ ⛰ 🐕

David Bellamy Conservation Awards

If you are looking for a site that's environmentally friendly, look for those that have achieved the David Bellamy Conservation Award. Launched in conjunction with the British Holiday & Home Parks Association, this award is given to sites which are committed to protecting and enhancing the environment – from care of the hedgerows and wildlife to recycling waste – and are members of the Association. More information about the award scheme can be found at the back of the guide.

A brief guide to the main towns and villages offering accommodation in the **East Midlands**

ASHBOURNE, Derbyshire
Market town on the edge of the Peak District National Park and an excellent centre for walking. Its impressive church with 212-ft spire stands in an unspoilt old street. Ashbourne is well-known for gingerbread and its Shrovetide football match.

BAKEWELL, Derbyshire
Pleasant market town, famous for its pudding. It is set in beautiful countryside on the river Wye and is an excellent centre for exploring the Derbyshire Dales, the Peak District National Park, Chatsworth and Haddon Hall.

BOSTON, Lincolnshire
Historic town famous for its church tower, the Boston Stump, 272 ft high. Still a busy port, the town is full of interest and has links with Boston, Massachusetts, through the Pilgrim Fathers. The cells where they were imprisoned can be seen in the medieval Guildhall.

BUXTON, Derbyshire
The highest market town in England and one of the oldest spas, with an elegant Crescent, Poole's Cavern, Opera House and attractive Pavilion Gardens. An excellent centre for exploring the Peak District.

HORNCASTLE, Lincolnshire
Pleasant market town near the Lincolnshire Wolds, which was once a walled Roman settlement. It was the scene of a decisive Civil War battle, relics of which can be seen in the church. Tennyson's bride lived here.

LINCOLN, Lincolnshire
Ancient city dominated by the magnificent 11thC cathedral with its triple towers. A Roman gateway is still used and there are medieval houses lining narrow, cobbled streets. Other attractions include the Norman castle, several museums and the Usher Gallery.

WOODHALL SPA, Lincolnshire
Attractive town which was formerly a spa. It has excellent sporting facilities with a championship golf course and is surrounded by pine woods.

WORKSOP, Nottinghamshire
Market town close to the Dukeries, where a number of Ducal families had their estates, some of which, like Clumber Park, may be visited. The upper room of the 14thC gatehouse of the priory housed the country's first elementary school in 1628.

Below, from left relax by the river Wye, Bakewell; admire crescent architecture, Buxton

A **quarter** of England's market towns are crammed into this **fertile corner** of the country.

East of England

Looking for some inspiration? Here are a few ideas to get you started in the East of England. **experience** classic flying legends at the Imperial War Museum Duxford. **discover** how Nelson came to be England's greatest naval hero at the Nelson Museum. **explore** the countryside that inspired Constable on the 81-mile Essex Way. **relax** while the children build sandcastles on the beach.

THE REGION
Bedfordshire, Cambridgeshire, Essex, Hertfordshire, Norfolk, Suffolk

CONTACT
▸ **EAST OF ENGLAND TOURIST BOARD**
Toppesfield Hall, Hadleigh,
Suffolk IP7 5DN
T: 0870 225 4800
F: 0870 225 4890
E: information@eetb.org.uk
www.visiteastofengland.com

The gently rolling countryside, historic market towns, traditional seaside resorts and unspoilt coastline of the East of England make it quintessentially English. Sailors, cyclists, hikers and bird-watchers will find it a natural haven.

Spinning wheels

With cycle tracks running along former railway lines, around reservoirs and through forests, this is the place to be on two wheels. Hire a bike and go where the mood takes you: follow specially-tailored cycle tours down quiet country lanes, or along one of the many cycle routes such as the Fens Cycle Way, the Suffolk Coastal Cycle Route or the Norfolk Coast Cycleway. Special maps are also available to guide you round a choice of Discovery Routes. The level terrain in the East of England means the views – and not the hills! – will take your breath away, making it perfect for cyclists of all ages.

Traditional England

A quarter of England's market towns are crammed into this fertile corner of the country that has somehow resisted the relentless march of time. Wander around colourful market stalls and take your pick of the local produce, experience the timeless atmosphere of the ancient market town of Woburn, visit Cromwell's birthplace at Huntingdon or make a bid at an antiques auction in Coggeshall. Many traditional crafts, such as glassblowing, can still be seen at Barleylands Craft Village in Billericay.

For aviation history visit the Imperial War Museum at Duxford, home to a fascinating display of historic aircraft including Spitfires and Gulf War jets – some of which still fly – as well as tanks and guns. For true wartime spirit, get along to one of the nostalgic events at Twinwood Airfield in 2005.

Left, from top take-off at the Shuttleworth Collection, Biggleswade; family fun in Southwold; admire Norwich Cathedral **Right** traditional entertainment in Great Yarmouth

Sail away

Over 250 miles of coastline and more than 50 rivers make this the ideal place for boating, sailing and fishing. Experience the calm of the reed-fringed waterways in the Norfolk Broads and enjoy the unique panorama of rivers and dykes in the Fens. The area is renowned for bird-watching, with plenty of wildlife to observe all year round at Minsmere, Titchwell, Berney Marshes and the Ouse Washes. The journey continues where rivers meet the sea. At the Norfolk Nelson Museum in Great Yarmouth the new interactive below-decks experience shows you how seamen lived in the 1800s. All along the coast there are many more places to stay and discover. From intimate fishing villages to the bustling seaside resorts of Felixstowe, Southend-on-Sea and Great Yarmouth, you're sure to find your ideal holiday destination.

Places to visit

Audley End House and Park (English Heritage)
Audley End, Saffron Walden, Essex
Tel: (01799) 522399

www.english-heritage.org.uk
Palatial Jacobean house remodelled in the 18th-19thC with a magnificent great hall featuring 17thC plaster ceilings. Rooms and furniture by Robert Adam and park by Capability Brown.

Banham Zoo
The Grove, Banham, Norfolk
Tel: (01953) 887771
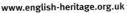
www.banhamzoo.co.uk
A wildlife spectacular which will take you on a journey to experience tigers, leopards and zebra plus some of the world's most exotic, rare and endangered animals.

Barleylands Craft Village and Farm Centre
Barleylands Road, Billericay, Essex
Tel: (01268) 290229
www.barleylands.co.uk
Stroll around over 20 impressive individual specialist workshops, including blacksmiths and glassblowing. Cuddle a rabbit and feed the animals.

Blickling Hall (National Trust)
Blickling, Norfolk
Tel: (01263) 738030
www.nationaltrust.org.uk
Jacobean redbrick mansion with garden, orangery, parkland and lake. Spectacular long gallery and interesting collections of furniture, pictures and books.

Bure Valley Railway: Aylsham Station
Norwich Road, Aylsham, Norfolk
Tel: (01263) 733858
www.bvrw.co.uk
A 15-inch narrow-gauge steam railway covering nine miles of track from Wroxham in the heart of the Norfolk Broads to the bustling market town of Aylsham.

Colchester Castle
Colchester, Essex
Tel: (01206) 282939
www.colchestermuseums.org.uk
A Norman keep on the foundations of a Roman temple. The archaeological material includes much on Roman Colchester (Camulodunum). Exciting hands-on displays.

Colchester Zoo
Maldon Road, Stanway, Colchester, Essex
Tel: (01206) 331292

www.colchester-zoo.co.uk
Zoo with 200 species and some of the best cat and primate collections in the UK, 24ha (60 acres) of gardens and lakes, award-winning animal enclosures and picnic areas.

Ely Cathedral
Chapter House, Ely, Cambridgeshire
Tel: (01353) 667735
www.cathedral.ely.anglican.org
One of England's finest cathedrals with guided tours and tours of the Octagon and West Tower. Monastic precincts, brass rubbing centre and The Stained Glass Museum.

Fritton Lake Country World
Church Lane, Fritton, Norfolk
Tel: (01493) 488208
www.frittonlake.co.uk
A 100-ha (250-acre) centre with a children's assault course, adventure playground, golf, fishing, boating, wildfowl, heavy horses, cart rides, falconry and flying displays.

Hatfield House, Park and Gardens
Hatfield, Hertfordshire
Tel: (01707) 287010
www.hatfield-house.co.uk
A magnificent Jacobean house, childhood home of Queen Elizabeth I and now home of the Marquess of Salisbury. Exquisite formal gardens, model soldiers and park trails.

Hedingham Castle
Castle Hedingham, Essex
Tel: (01787) 460261
www.hedinghamcastle.co.uk
The finest Norman keep in England, built in 1140 by the de Veres, Earls of Oxford. Visited by Kings Henry VII and VIII and Queen Elizabeth I and besieged by King John.

Holkham Hall
Wells-next-the-Sea, Norfolk
Tel: (01328) 710227
www.holkham.co.uk

A classic 18thC Palladian-style mansion. Part of a great agricultural estate and a living treasure house of artistic and architectural history along with a bygones collection.

Ickworth House, Park and Gardens (National Trust)
The Rotunda, Horringer, Suffolk
Tel: (01284) 735270
www.nationaltrust.org.uk
An extraordinary oval house begun in 1795. View fine paintings, a beautiful collection of Georgian silver, an Italian garden and stunning parkland.

Imperial War Museum Duxford
Duxford, Cambridgeshire
Tel: (01223) 835000
www.iwm.org.uk
With its airshows, unique history and atmosphere, Duxford combines the sights, sounds and power of aircraft.

Knebworth House, Gardens and Park
Knebworth, Hertfordshire
Tel: (01438) 812661
www.knebworthhouse.com
15thC manor house, altered in the 19thC, with a Jacobean banquet hall and collections of manuscripts and portraits. Formal gardens, parkland and adventure playground.

Marsh Farm Country Park
Marsh Farm Road, South Woodham Ferrers, Essex
Tel: (01245) 321552
www.marshfarmcountrypark.co.uk
Working farm with sheep, a pig unit, free-range chickens, milking demonstrations, indoor and outdoor adventure play areas, nature reserve, walks, picnic area and pets' corner.

National Horseracing Museum and Tours
High Street, Newmarket, Suffolk
Tel: (01638) 667333
www.nhrm.co.uk
Award-winning display of the people and horses involved in racing's amazing history. Minibus tours of the gallops, stables and equine pool. Test your skills on the horse simulator in the hands-on gallery.

National Stud
Newmarket, Suffolk
Tel: (01638) 663464
www.nationalstud.co.uk

A conducted tour which includes top thoroughbred stallions, mares and foals, and gives an insight into the day-to-day running of a modern stud farm.

Norfolk Lavender Limited
Caley Mill, Heacham, Norfolk
Tel: (01485) 570384
www.norfolk-lavender.co.uk
Lavender is distilled from the flowers grown here and the oil is made into a wide range of gifts. There is a slide show when the distillery is not in action.

Norwich Cathedral
The Close, Norwich, Norfolk
Tel: (01603) 218321
www.cathedral.org.uk
A Norman cathedral dating from 1096 with 14thC roof bosses depicting bible scenes from Adam and Eve to the Day of Judgement. Shop and restaurant.

Oliver Cromwell's House
St Marys Street, Ely, Cambridgeshire
Tel: (01353) 662062
www.eastcambs.gov.uk

Explore the family home of Oliver Cromwell with its 17thC kitchen, parlour, Cromwell's study and a haunted bedroom. Tourist Information Centre, souvenirs and gift shop.

Peter Beales Roses
London Road, Attleborough, Norfolk
Tel: (01953) 454707
www.classicroses.co.uk
Large, world-famous collection of roses featuring over 1100 rare, unusual and beautiful varieties of which more than 250 are unique.

Pleasure Beach
South Beach Parade, Great Yarmouth, Norfolk
Tel: (01493) 844585
www.pleasure-beach.co.uk
Seafront leisure park with over 70 rides including Rollercoaster, Terminator, log flume, Twister, monorail, galloping horses, caterpillar, ghost train and fun house.

The Royal Air Force Air Defence Radar Museum
RAF Neatishead, Norwich, Norfolk
Tel: (01692) 633309
www.radarmuseum.co.uk
Discover the history of the development and use of radar in the UK and overseas from 1935 to date. Winner of the Regional Visitor Attraction (under 100,000 visitors), National Silver Award.

Left re-enactment of the past at Hedingham Castle; enjoy a visit to Holkham Hall, Wells-next-the-Sea

Places to visit

Awarded VisitBritain's Quality Assured Visitor Attraction marque.

RSPB Minsmere Nature Reserve
Westleton, Suffolk
Tel: (01728) 648281
www.rspb.org.uk/reserves/minsmere
This RSPB reserve is located on the Suffolk coast with bird-watching hides and trails, year-round events and guided walks. Visitor centre with a large shop and welcoming tearoom.

Sainsbury Centre for Visual Arts
University of East Anglia, Norwich, Norfolk
Tel: (01603) 593199
www.uea.ac.uk/scva
Housed in a breathtaking Norman Foster building, the Sainsbury Collection includes works by artists such as Picasso, Bacon and Henry Moore, alongside art from across cultures and time.

Sandringham
Sandringham, Norfolk
Tel: (01553) 612908
www.sandringhamestate.co.uk
The country retreat of HM The Queen. A delightful house set in 24ha (60 acres) of grounds and lakes, with a museum of royal vehicles and memorabilia.

Shuttleworth Collection
Old Warden Aerodrome, Biggleswade, Bedfordshire
Tel: (01767) 627288
www.shuttleworth.org
A unique historical collection of aircraft – from a 1909 Bleriot to a 1942 Spitfire in flying condition – plus cars in running order dating from an 1898 Panhard.

Somerleyton Hall and Gardens
Somerleyton, Suffolk
Tel: (01502) 730224
www.somerleyton.co.uk

Early Victorian stately mansion in Anglo-Italian style, with lavish features and fine state rooms. Beautiful 5-ha (12-acre) gardens, with historic yew hedge maze. Gift shop.

Stondon Museum
Station Road, Henlow Camp, Bedfordshire
Tel: (01462) 850339
www.transportmuseum.co.uk
A museum with transport exhibits from the early 1900s to the 1980s. The largest private collection in England of bygone vehicles from the beginning of the century.

Thursford Collection
Thursford Green, Thursford, Norfolk
Tel: (01328) 878477
A live musical show with nine mechanical organs and a Wurlitzer show starring Robert Wolfe, plus fairground rides and traction engines.

Wimpole Hall and Home Farm (National Trust)
Arrington, Hertfordshire
Tel: (01223) 206000
www.wimpole.org
A 18thC house with a yellow drawing room by Sir John Soane, set in a landscaped park with a folly and Chinese bridge. Home Farm has a rare breeds centre.

Woburn Abbey
Woburn, Bedfordshire
Tel: (01525) 290666
www.woburnabbey.co.uk
18thC Palladian mansion, altered by Henry Holland, the Prince Regent's architect, containing collections of English silver, French and English furniture and Old Master paintings.

Woburn Safari Park
Woburn Park, Woburn, Bedfordshire
Tel: (01525) 290407
www.woburnsafari.co.uk
Drive through the safari park with 30 species of animals in natural groups just a windscreen's width away, then venture into the action-packed Wild World Leisure Area.

Above bright lights in Great Yarmouth; come face-to-face with a tiger at Woburn Safari Park **Right** Sandringham, HM The Queen's country retreat

East of England Tourist Board

Toppesfield Hall, Hadleigh, Suffolk IP7 5DN
T: 0870 225 4800 F: 0870 225 4890
E: information@eetb.org.uk
www.visiteastofengland.com

The following publications are available from the East of England Tourist Board:

Great days out in the East of England 2005 – an information-packed A5 guide featuring all you need to know about places to visit and things to see and do in the East of England. From historic houses to garden centres, from animal collections to craft centres – this guide has it all, including film and TV locations, city, town and village information, events, shopping, car tours plus lots more! (£4.50 excl p&p).

England's Cycling Country – the East of England offers perfect cycling country – from quiet country lanes to ancient trackways. This free publication promotes the many Cycling Discovery Maps that are available to buy (£1.50 excl p&p), as well as providing useful information for anyone planning a cycling tour of the region.

Travel information

By road:
The region is easily accessible. From London and the south via the A1(M), M11, M25, A10, M1, A46 and A12. From the north via the A1(M), A15, A5, M1 and A6. From the west via the A14, A47, A421, A428, A418, A41, A422, A17 and A427.

By rail:
Regular fast trains run to all major cities and towns in the region. London stations which serve the region are Liverpool Street, Kings Cross, Fenchurch Street, St Pancras, London Marylebone and London Euston. Bedford, Luton and St Albans are on the Thameslink line which runs to Kings Cross and on to London Gatwick Airport. There is also a direct link between London Stansted Airport and Liverpool Street. Through the Channel Tunnel, there are trains direct from Paris and Brussels to Waterloo Station, London. A short journey on the Underground will bring passengers to those stations operating services into the East of England. Further information on rail journeys in the East of England can be obtained on 0845 748 4950.

Where to stay in
East of England

All place names in the blue bands, under which accommodation is listed, are shown on the maps at the front of this guide.

A complete listing of all VisitBritain assessed accommodation covered by this guide appears at the back.

Accommodation symbols
Symbols give useful information about services and facilities. Inside the back cover flap you can find a key to these symbols. Keep it open for easy reference.

ASHILL, Norfolk Map ref 4B1

★★★
TOURING &
CAMPING PARK

BRICK KILN FARM
Swaffham Road, Thetford IP25 7BT
T: (01760) 441300
E: brickkiln@onetel.com

OPEN All Year

37	🚐	£6.20–£9.20
8	🚏	£6.20–£9.20
20	▲	£3.70–£9.20
45 touring pitches		

From M11 jct 9. Leave the A47 at Swaffham, follow B1077 for 5 miles to Ashill. Alternatively, leave A11 at Mildenhall and take A1065 to Swaffham, follow B1077 for 5 miles to Ashill.

BAWBURGH, Norfolk Map ref 4B1

★★★★
TOURING PARK

BH&HPA

See Ad on inside back cover

NORFOLK SHOWGROUND CARAVAN CLUB SITE

Royal Norfolk Showground, Long Lane, Bawburgh,
Norwich NR9 3LX
T: (01603) 742708
I: www.caravanclub.co.uk

A charming and secluded site set adjacent to the Norfolk showground, this is an ideal escape. Golf course and well-stocked fishing lakes nearby. Open 26 March to 25 October. Special member rates mean you can save your membership subscription in less than a week. Visit www.caravanclub.co.uk to find out more.

60	🚐	£13.35–£17.60
60	🚏	£13.35–£17.60
60 touring pitches		

Payment accepted: Delta, Mastercard, Switch, Visa

Turn off A47 Norwich Southern Bypass at Longwater intersection (Bawburgh). Follow signpost Bawburgh, site entrance on right 0.25 miles.

BUNGAY, Suffolk Map ref 4C1

★★★
TOURING &
CAMPING PARK

BH&HPA

OUTNEY MEADOW CARAVAN PARK
Outney Meadow, Bungay NR35 1HG
T: (01986) 892338
F: (01986) 896627
E: c.r.hancy@ukgateway.net
I: www.outneymeadow.co.uk

45	🚐	£9.00–£14.00
45	🚏	£9.00–£14.00
45	▲	£9.00–£14.00
45 touring pitches		

Follow direction signs from roundabout at jct of A143 and A144 at Bungay.

BURNHAM DEEPDALE, Norfolk Map ref 4B1

★★★★
CAMPING PARK

BH&HPA

DEEPDALE CAMPING
Deepdale Farms, Burnham Deepdale, King's
Lynn PE31 8DD
T: (01485) 210256
F: (01485) 210158
E: info@deepdalefarm.co.uk
I: www.deepdalefarm.co.uk

OPEN All Year
Payment accepted: Delta,
Mastercard, Switch, Visa

22	🚐	£6.00–£13.00
22	▲	£6.00–£13.00

From King's Lynn, take A149 coast road towards Cromer. Continue past Hunstanton for approximately 8 miles until you enter Burnham Deepdale. Deepdale Farm is opposite the church.

🚗 🏕 🖐 🅿 ✕ 🏬 🔲 ⊙ 🚲 ∪ ℘ ✈ ► 🐕 ☼

CAISTER-ON-SEA, Norfolk Map ref 4C1

★★★★
HOLIDAY PARK

BH&HPA

ELM BEACH CARAVAN PARK
Manor Road, Caister-on-Sea, Great Yarmouth NR30 5HG
T: (01493) 721630
F: (01493) 721640
E: enquiries@elmbeachcaravanpark.com
I: www.elmbeachcaravanpark.com

Quiet caravan park situated on clean, sandy beach. Open from March through to the New Year. All caravans heated and fully equipped.

OPEN All Year
Payment accepted: Delta, Mastercard, Switch, Visa

A47 to Great Yarmouth then A149 to Caister-on-Sea. Turn right into Beach Road, 3rd turning on the left is Manor Road.

30	🏠	£95.00–£460.00

🚗 🏬 🔲 ∪ ✈ ► 🐕

CAMBRIDGE, Cambridgeshire Map ref 3D1 *Tourist Information Centre Tel: (01223) 322640*

★★★★★
TOURING &
CAMPING PARK

BH&HPA

See Ad on inside back cover

CHERRY HINTON CARAVAN CLUB SITE
Lime Kiln Road, Cherry Hinton, Cambridge CB1 8NQ
T: (01223) 244088
I: www.caravanclub.co.uk

Imaginatively landscaped site set in old quarry workings, bordered by a nature trail. 0.5 miles Cambridge (Park & Ride bus), Newmarket 14 miles. Open 26 March to 3 January 2006. Special member rates mean you can save your membership subscription in less than a week. Visit www.caravanclub.co.uk to find out more.

Payment accepted: Delta, Mastercard, Switch, Visa

M11 jct 9 onto A11. After 7 miles slip road signposted Fulbourn and Tevisham. In Fulbourn continue to roundabout signposted Cambridge. At traffic lights turn left. Left again into Lime Kiln Road.

76	🚐	£14.60–£20.60
76	🚐	£14.60–£20.60
	▲	On application
76 touring pitches		

🚐 🚗 🏕 ▼ 🅦🅟 🖐 🏬 🔲 ⊙ 🐕

Map references The map references refer to the colour maps at the front of this guide. The first figure is the map number; the letter and figure which follow indicate the grid reference on the map.

CAMBRIDGE continued

★★★★★

**TOURING &
CAMPING PARK**

BH&HPA

HIGHFIELD FARM TOURING PARK

Long Road, Comberton, Cambridge CB3 7DG
T: (01223) 262308
F: (01223) 262308
E: enquiries@highfieldfarmtouringpark.co.uk
I: www.highfieldfarmtouringpark.co.uk

A popular family-run park with excellent facilities close to the university city of Cambridge, Imperial War Museum, Duxford. Ideally situated for touring East Anglia. Open April to October. Low-season rate for Senior Citizens – 10% discount for stay of 3 nights or longer.

Payment accepted: Euros

From Cambridge, take A428 to Bedford. After 3 miles, turn left at roundabout and follow sign to Comberton. From M11 jct 12, take A603 to Sandy for 0.5 miles. Then take B1046 to Comberton.

60	🚐	£8.75–£12.25
60	🚏	£8.75–£12.25
60	▲	£8.50–£12.00
120 touring pitches		

**TOURING &
CAMPING PARK**

STANFORD PARK

Weirs Drove, Burwell, Cambridge CB5 0BP
T: (01638) 741547
E: enquiries@stanfordcaravanpark.co.uk
I: www.stanfordcaravanpark.co.uk

A family-run caravan park with modern facilities and children's play area. Conveniently situated for Cambridge and Newmarket. Excellent for dog walking, cycling and nearby fishing. Seasonal pitches from only £360, includes winter storage. Also, discounted rates on long-term stays.

OPEN All Year

From A14 turn off at Newmarket jct. Turn left to Exning and follow signs to Burwell on B1102.

🚐	£10.00
🚏	£10.00
▲	£10.00
300 touring pitches	

CROMER, Norfolk Map ref 4C1 *Tourist Information Centre Tel: (01263) 512497*

★★★

**TOURING &
CAMPING PARK**

BH&HPA

FOREST PARK CARAVAN SITE

Northrepps Road, Northrepps, Cromer NR27 0JR
T: (01263) 513290
F: (01263) 511992
E: forestpark@netcom.co.uk
I: www.forest-park.co.uk

Quiet, picturesque park for tourers and holiday homes. Situated in the centre of a large forest with extensive, charming walks. Open 15 March to 15 January.

Payment accepted: Mastercard, Switch, Visa

Turn right off A140 at Northrepps, turn immediately left under railway bridge to T-jct and turn left. Forest Park entrance on right.

238	🚐	£9.50–£17.00
55	🚏	£9.50–£17.00
85	▲	£9.50–£17.00
338 touring pitches		

GREAT YARMOUTH, Norfolk Map ref 4C1

★★★
TOURING PARK

BH&HPA

GRASMERE CARAVAN PARK (T.B)
Bultitudes Loke, Yarmouth Road,
Caister-on-Sea, Great Yarmouth NR30 5DH
T: (01493) 720382
F: (01493) 377573
I: www.ukparks.co.uk/grasmere

Payment accepted: Delta,
Mastercard, Switch, Visa

40	🚐	£9.00–£12.00
6	🚐	£9.00–£12.00
10	🏠	£90.00–£330.00
46 touring pitches		

Take the A149 from Great Yarmouth and enter Caister at the roundabout by Yarmouth Stadium. After 0.5 miles turn left, just before bus stop. Signposted.

★★★★
TOURING PARK

BH&HPA

See Ad on inside back cover

GREAT YARMOUTH CARAVAN CLUB SITE

Great Yarmouth Racecourse, Jellicoe Road, Great
Yarmouth NR30 4AU
T: (01493) 855223
I: www.caravanclub.co.uk

Spacious, level site in a very popular family resort offering wide sandy beaches, countless seaside attractions and fishing, golf, sailboarding, ballroom dancing and bowls. Open 26 March to 8 November. Special member rates mean you can save your membership subscription in less than a week. Visit www.caravanclub.co.uk to find out more.

Payment accepted: Delta, Mastercard, Switch, Visa

122	🚐	£14.60–£20.60
122	🚐	£14.60–£20.60
122 touring pitches		

Travel north on A149 and turn left at lights (within 1 mile past 40mph sign on southern outskirts of Caister) into Jellicoe Road. Within 0.25 miles, turn left into racecourse entrance and continue to site.

★★★★
HOLIDAY PARK

BH&HPA

See Ad below

LIFFENS HOLIDAY PARK
Butt Lane, Burgh Castle, Great Yarmouth
NR31 9QB
T: (01493) 780357
F: (01493) 782383
I: www.liffens.co.uk

Payment accepted: Delta,
Mastercard, Switch, Visa

150	🚐	£10.00–£21.00
150	🚐	£10.00–£21.00
150	⛺	£10.00–£21.00
30	🏠	£100.00–£475.00
150 touring pitches		

From Great Yarmouth, follow signs for Beccles and Lowestoft. Watch for left turn signed for Burgh Castle, follow for 2 miles to T-junction and turn right. Then follow signs to holiday park.

Credit card bookings

If you book by telephone and are asked for your credit card number it is advisable to check the proprietor's policy should you cancel your reservation.

GREAT YARMOUTH continued

★★★★
HOLIDAY PARK

BH&HPA

LIFFENS WELCOME HOLIDAY CENTRE
Butt Lane, Burgh Castle, Great Yarmouth
NR31 9PY
T: (01493) 780481
F: (01493) 781627
I: www.liffens.co.uk

Payment accepted: Delta, Mastercard, Switch, Visa

150		£10.00–£21.00
150		£10.00–£21.00
150		£10.00–£21.00
20		£100.00–£475.00
150 touring pitches		

On A143 from Great Yarmouth to Beccles road. Proceed through village of Bradwell to start of dual carriageway. Take first right, next on right. Holiday Centre is along on the right.

HADLEIGH, Suffolk Map ref 4B2

★★★★
TOURING &
CAMPING PARK

BH&HPA

POLSTEAD TOURING PARK
Holt Road, Polstead, Colchester CO6 5BZ
T: (01787) 211969
F: (01787) 211969

OPEN All Year

30		£10.00–£11.00
30		£10.00–£11.00
30		£8.00–£10.00
30 touring pitches		

Off A1071 between Boxford and Hadleigh opposite the Brewers Arms pub, follow signs.

HEMEL HEMPSTEAD, Hertfordshire Map ref 3D1 *Tourist Information Centre Tel: (01442) 234222*

★★★
TOURING PARK

BH&HPA

See Ad on inside back cover

BREAKSPEAR WAY CARAVAN CLUB SITE

Buncefield Lane, Breakspear Way, Hemel Hempstead
HP2 4TZ
T: (01442) 268466
I: www.caravanclub.co.uk

The site is a green oasis screened from the surrounding countryside by trees, yet within a mile of the M1. Ideally situated to explore London. Special member rates mean you can save your membership subscription in less than a week. Visit www.caravanclub.co.uk to find out more.

OPEN All Year
Payment accepted: Delta, Mastercard, Switch, Visa

M1 jct 8, onto A414, signposted Hemel Hempstead. At 2nd roundabout (about 1 mile) turn and return on A414 towards M1. Within 0.5 miles, turn left immediately past petrol station into Buncefield Lane. Site on left, 100yds.

60		£12.50–£17.60
60		£12.50–£17.60
60 touring pitches		

NB **Important note** Information on accommodation listed in this guide has been supplied by the proprietors. As changes may occur you are advised to check details at the time of booking.

HEMINGFORD ABBOTS, Cambridgeshire Map ref 4A2

★★★★
HOLIDAY, TOURING & CAMPING PARK

BH&HPA

QUIET WATERS CARAVAN PARK
Hemingford Abbots, Huntingdon PE28 9AJ
T: (01480) 463405
F: (01480) 463405
E: quietwaters.park@btopenworld.com
I: www.quietwaterscaravanpark.co.uk

Payment accepted: Delta, Mastercard, Switch, Visa

20		£11.00–£14.00
20		£11.00–£14.00
20	▲	£11.00–£14.00
9		£220.00–£330.00
20 touring pitches		

End of M11 onto A14, 12 miles from Cambridge. Turn at Hemingford Abbots jct 25 and follow signs in village. One mile north of A14 Huntingdon and Cambridge.

KESSINGLAND, Suffolk Map ref 4C2

★★★★★
HOLIDAY, TOURING & CAMPING PARK

ROSE AWARD

BH&HPA

HEATHLAND BEACH CARAVAN PARK
London Road, Kessingland, Lowestoft
NR33 7PJ
T: (01502) 740337
F: (01502) 742355
E: heathlandbeach@btinternet.com
I: www.heathlandbeach.co.uk

Payment accepted: Delta, Mastercard, Switch, Visa

		£16.50–£20.50
		£16.50–£20.50
	▲	£8.00–£20.50
6		£280.00–£500.00
63 touring pitches		

One mile north of Kessingland village, off old A12, now B1437, and 3 miles from Lowestoft.

KING'S LYNN, Norfolk Map ref 4B1 *Tourist Information Centre Tel: (01553) 763044*

★★★
TOURING PARK

BANK FARM CARAVAN PARK
Bank Farm, Fallow Pipe Road, King's Lynn
PE34 3AS
T: (01553) 617305
F: (01553) 617305
I: www.caravancampingsites.co.uk/norfolk/bankfarm.htm

Payment accepted: Euros

15		£7.50
15		£7.50
2	▲	£5.00
15 touring pitches		

Off King's Lynn southern bypass (A47) via slip road signposted Saddlebow. Once in the village, cross the river bridge and after 1 mile fork right into Fallow Pipe Road. The farm is 0.66 miles, by the River Great Ouse.

LITTLE CORNARD, Suffolk Map ref 4B2

★★★
TOURING & CAMPING PARK

BH&HPA

WILLOWMERE CARAVAN PARK
Bures Road, Little Cornard, Sudbury
CO10 0NN
T: (01787) 375559
F: (01787) 375559

15		£11.00
15		£11.00
15	▲	£9.00–£11.00
35 touring pitches		

From Sudbury, take B1508 to Colchester, 1.5 miles, site on left.

LOWESTOFT, Suffolk

See display advertisement below

Official guide to quality
Please mention this guide when making your booking.

MERSEA ISLAND, Essex Map ref 4B3

★★★
HOLIDAY, TOURING & CAMPING PARK

BH&HPA

WALDEGRAVES HOLIDAY AND LEISURE PARK
Mersea Island, Colchester CO5 8SE
T: (01206) 382898
F: (01206) 385359
E: holidays@waldegraves.co.uk
I: www.waldegraves.co.uk

Payment accepted: Delta, Mastercard, Switch, Visa

60	£16.00–£22.00
60	£16.00–£22.00
60	£16.00–£22.00
25	£195.00–£500.00
60 touring pitches	

Take the B1025 from Colchester then left to East Mersea, 2nd right then follow the brown tourist signs.

MUNDESLEY, Norfolk Map ref 4C1

★★★
HOLIDAY & TOURING PARK

BH&HPA

SANDY GULLS CLIFF TOP TOURING PARK
Cromer Road, Mundesley, Norwich NR11 8DF
T: (01263) 720513

The area's only cliff-top park. Easy access to clean beaches. New caravans for sale and hire. Ideal for North Norfolk's amenities and managed by the owning family. 7 days for the price of 4, Apr–Jun and Sep–Oct, for 2 adults with a touring caravan.

From Cromer drive south along coast road for 5 miles.

40	£8.00–£18.00
40	£8.00–£18.00
2	£200.00–£360.00
40 touring pitches	

NORFOLK BROADS

See under Bungay, Caister-on-Sea, Great Yarmouth, Lowestoft, Norwich

NORWICH, Norfolk Map ref 4C1 *Tourist Information Centre Tel: (01603) 666071*

★★★
TOURING & CAMPING PARK

See Ad p155

REEDHAM FERRY TOURING AND CAMPING PARK
Ferry Road, Reedham, Norwich NR13 3HA
T: (01493) 700999
F: (01493) 700999
E: reedhamferry@aol.com
I: www.archerstouringpark.co.uk

Payment accepted: Delta, Mastercard, Switch, Visa

	£11.00–£16.50
	£11.00–£16.50
20	£11.00–£16.50
30 touring pitches	

From A47 B1140 declassified – follow signs to Reedham. From Acle – follow signs to Reedham. From Beccles – follow ferry signs.

PETERBOROUGH, Peterborough Map ref 4A1 *Tourist Information Centre Tel: (01733) 452336*

★★★★★
TOURING PARK

BH&HPA

See Ad on inside back cover

FERRY MEADOWS CARAVAN CLUB SITE
Ham Lane, Orton Waterville, Peterborough PE2 5UU
T: (01733) 233526
F: (01733) 233526
I: www.caravanclub.co.uk

Set in 500-acre Nene Country Park. Plenty of activities including canoeing, windsurfing and sailing. Also nature trails, two golf courses, pitch and putt and bird sanctuary. Special member rates mean you can save your membership subscription in less than a week. Visit www.caravanclub.co.uk to find out more.

OPEN All Year
Payment accepted: Delta, Mastercard, Switch, Visa

From any direction, on approaching Peterborough, follow the brown signs to Nene Park and Ferry Meadows.

254	£14.60–£20.60
254	£14.60–£20.60
	On application
254 touring pitches	

Star Ratings were correct at the time of going to press but are subject to change.
Please check at the time of booking.

Set sail beside chalk-white cliffs or drift inland through historic towns and cities such as Oxford and Canterbury. Walk the rolling downlands, then stretch out and soak up the sun on golden sands and shingle bays. Wild ponies tug at the grass on village greens in the tranquil New Forest.

Café culture

Step out in any of the major towns or cities of the South East to experience the history that has made each one unique. Enjoy the arts that have enriched it, the culture that has shaped it, the food and drink that keeps us all so nicely nourished! And of course there is the shopping, hard to match elsewhere.

You'll find a tempting choice of excellent cafés and restaurants in the South East. In many of the historic cities and towns, such as Windsor, Oxford and Canterbury, some of the age-old buildings have been given a new lease of life. Now they are cool cafés, restaurants and bars, all stripped floors and neat furnishings and it's great that they can continue to be an everyday part of our lives.

Green fingers

Blessed with a rich soil and a favourable climate, the South East has been home to many of Britain's top gardens for centuries. Explore the region's parklands and enjoy classic designs by famous landscapers – then marvel at the contemporary gardens laid out by modern masters. Be inspired by the variety and the rich tapestry of colours that change with the seasons.

You're spoilt for choice if you enjoy visiting stately homes and castles, set in magnificent surroundings. They are in abundance. Blenheim Palace, Churchill's birthplace in Oxfordshire, for example, has over 2000 acres of landscaped parkland while Hever Castle in Kent, childhood home of Anne Boleyn, boasts Tudor Gardens with a yew-hedge maze.

Go with the flow!

The South East is packed to the gunnels with maritime heritage and plays host to many flagship SeaBritain events. Soak up the fascinating history of seafaring in Portsmouth or Chatham, and watch great sporting events like the Henley Royal Regatta and Cowes Week. Brighton's seawater was once medically prescribed – offering so much fun in the sun, perhaps it still should be!

Stride out along the Thames Path National Trail through rural Oxfordshire to Henley, sit on the banks of the Thames, and enjoy a spot of fishing. Try your hand at rowing, punting or canoeing or take to the water yourself and enjoy a boat ride from Windsor, Wallingford or Oxford to see a different perspective of the towns and cities along the Thames.

Left, from top a gentle day on the river, Oxfordshire; be entertained on Brighton beach; admire the State Rooms at Blenheim Palace, Woodstock **Right** picturesque gardens of Scotney Castle, Lamberhurst

Places to visit

Awarded VisitBritain's
Quality Assured Visitor
Attraction marque.

Alfriston Clergy House (National Trust)
The Tye, Alfriston, East Sussex
Tel: (01323) 870001
www.nationaltrust.org.uk
A beautiful thatched medieval hall house, the first
building to be acquired by the National Trust in 1896.
Idyllic riverside setting, pretty cottage garden and
charming gift shop.

Amberley Working Museum
Houghton Bridge, Amberley, West Sussex
Tel: (01798) 831370
www.amberleymuseum.co.uk
Touch the past at this open-air industrial history centre in
a chalk quarry. Working craftsmen, narrow-gauge railway,
early buses, working machines and other exhibits. Nature
trail/visitor centre.

Arundel Wildfowl and Wetlands Centre
Mill Road, Arundel, West Sussex
Tel: (01903) 883355
www.wwt.org.uk
Get nose to beak with nature! Over 24ha (60 acres) of
ponds, lakes and reedbeds, home to hundreds of wetland
birds and wildlife. Restaurant, gift shop, wildlife art gallery.

Basingstoke Canal Visitor Centre
Mytchett Place Road, Mytchett, Surrey
Tel: (01252) 370073
www.basingstoke-canal.org.uk
Soak up the peace and tranquillity on one of the most
beautiful waterways in the country. Canal visitor centre
offers information, boat trips, narrowboat hire, floating
art gallery and tearoom.

Battle Abbey and Battlefield (English Heritage)
High Street, Battle, East Sussex
Tel: (01424) 773792
www.english-heritage.org.uk
Atmospheric ruins of the abbey founded by William the
Conqueror on the site of the 1066 Battle of Hastings.
Look out over the battlefields and imagine the scene.

Bentley Wildfowl and Motor Museum
Bentley, Halland, East Sussex
Tel: (01825) 840573
www.bentley.org.uk
Something for everyone – over 1000 wildfowl in parkland
with lakes, a motor museum with vintage cars, house with
antique furniture and collection of wildlife paintings,
children's play facilities and woodland walk.

Birdworld
Holt Pound, Farnham, Surrey
Tel: (01420) 22140
www.birdworld.co.uk
Ten and a half hectares (26 acres) of gardens and
parkland with an impressive collection of birds. Seashore
walk, penguin island, aquarium, children's farm and
tropical walk. Heron theatre with regular shows.

Blenheim Palace
Woodstock, Oxfordshire
Tel: 0870 060 2080
www.blenheimpalace.com
Home of the Duke of Marlborough and birthplace of
Sir Winston Churchill. Designed by Vanbrugh in the
English baroque style with magnificent state rooms.
Stunning parkland by Capability Brown.

Bletchley Park
The Mansion, Milton Keynes, Buckinghamshire
Tel: (01908) 640404
www.bletchleypark.org.uk
Learn about the secret history of Bletchley Park and its
pioneering WWII codebreakers Alan Turing and Dilly
Knox, as shown in the major film Enigma.

Borde Hill Garden
Balcombe Road, Haywards Heath, West Sussex
Tel: (01444) 450326
www.bordehill.co.uk
A plantsman's paradise with rare trees and shrubs
amassed by the great plant collectors from all corners of
the world. Formal and informal garden rooms. Woodland
and parkland walks.

Broadlands
Romsey, Hampshire
Tel: (01794) 505010
www.broadlands.net
Experience part of English history in this magnificent 18thC house, home of the late Lord Mountbatten. Superb views across river Test, Mountbatten exhibition and audiovisual presentation.

Brooklands Museum
Brooklands Road, Weybridge, Surrey
Tel: (01932) 857381
www.brooklandsmuseum.com
Evoking thrills on land or in the air, this original 1907 motor racing circuit was the birthplace of British motorsport and aviation. Collection of historic racing and sports cars, and aircraft. Motoring village and Grand Prix exhibition.

Charleston
Firle, East Sussex
Tel: (01323) 811265
www.charleston.org.uk
Charming farmhouse home of Vanessa Bell and Duncan Grant of the Bloomsbury Set, with interiors and furniture decorated by the artists. Traditional walled garden.

Chartwell (National Trust)
Mapleton Road, Westerham, Kent
Tel: (01732) 866368
www.nationaltrust.org.uk
Delightful home of Sir Winston Churchill, still much as he left it. Enter his study and studio, and visit the museum rooms with gifts, uniforms and photos. Garden, Golden Rose Walk, lakes and exhibition.

Dover Castle and Secret Wartime Tunnels (English Heritage)
Dover, Kent
Tel: (01304) 211067
www.english-heritage.org.uk
Secret tunnels bring wartime activities vividly to life at one of the most powerful medieval fortresses in Western Europe. St Mary-in-Castro Saxon church, Roman lighthouse and Henry II Great Keep.

Drusillas Park
Alfriston, East Sussex
Tel: (01323) 874100
www.drusillas.co.uk

All whole day's entertainment awaits at Drusillas. Known as the best small zoo in England with animals in natural habitats. Playland is masses of fun for children from three to 12 – they'll insist you return!

English Wine Centre
Alfriston, East Sussex
Tel: (01323) 870164
www.weddingwine.co.uk
Connoisseurs or not, the English Wine Centre will appeal to lovers of wine. It stocks a large selection of wines (English and world) plus beers and ciders. Tours and tastings available.

Explosion! Museum of Naval Firepower
Priddy's Hard, Gosport, Hampshire
Tel: (023) 9250 5600
www.explosion.org.uk
The amazing story of naval firepower, from gunpowder to the Exocet, in an exciting new visitor experience for all the family, on the shores of Portsmouth Harbour.

Goodwood House
Goodwood, West Sussex
Tel: (01243) 755040
www.goodwood.co.uk
Magnificent Regency house, home of the Dukes of Richmond, set on one of the world's finest sporting estates. Major collection of paintings, fine furnishings, tapestries and porcelain.

Hastings Castle and 1066 Story
West Hill, Hastings, East Sussex
Tel: (01424) 781112
www.discoverhastings.co.uk
Enter the dungeons carved out of rock and tread the fragmentary remains of this Norman castle set high on West Hill. 1066 Story audiovisual interpretation centre in siege tent.

Hatchlands Park (National Trust)
East Clandon, Surrey
Tel: (01483) 222482
www.nationaltrust.org.uk
Built in 1758 and set in a Repton park, Hatchlands has splendid interiors by Robert Adam and houses the Cobbe collection of keyboard musical instruments. Gertrude Jekyll garden.

High Beeches Woodland & Water Gardens
Handcross, West Sussex
Tel: (01444) 400589
www.highbeeches.com
Unearth the pleasures of the peaceful, landscaped woodland and water gardens with many rare plants, tree trail, wildflower meadow, spring bulbs and glorious autumn colour.

Left experience English history at Broadlands, Romsey; be inspired by Duncan Grant's fireplace at Charleston, Firle

Places to visit

Awarded VisitBritain's Quality Assured Visitor Attraction marque.

Isle of Wight Zoo, Home of the Tiger Sanctuary and Lemurland
Sandown, Isle of Wight
Tel: (01983) 403883
www.isleofwightzoo.com
This seafront zoo specialises in breeding and caring for some of the planet's most severely threatened creatures. Admire some of the most beautiful and dangerous tigers, big cats and primates.

Kent & East Sussex Railway
Tenterden Town Station, Tenterden, Kent
Tel: (01580) 765155
www.kesr.org.uk
Designed with the enthusiast in mind, a full-size heritage railway. Restored Edwardian stations, 14 steam engines, Victorian coaches and Pullman carriages. Museum. Children's play area.

National Motor Museum
John Montagu Building, Beaulieu, Hampshire
Tel: (01590) 612345
www.beaulieu.co.uk
Motoring memories abound in this museum with over 250 exhibits dating from 1896. Also Palace House, Wheels Experience, Beaulieu Abbey ruins and a display of monastic life.

Painshill Park
Portsmouth Road, Cobham, Surrey
Tel: (01932) 868113
www.painshill.co.uk
Unique, award-winning restoration of England's Georgian heritage. Discover true peace and inspiration in this 65-ha (160-acre) landscaped park created by Charles Hamilton.

Port Lympne Wild Animal Park, Mansion and Gardens
Aldington Road, Lympne, Kent
Tel: (01303) 264647
www.howletts.net
Take a trip on the safari trailer and see many rare and endangered species, including the largest herd of captive-bred black rhino in the world outside Africa.

Portsmouth Historic Dockyard
Porter's Lodge, Portsmouth,
Tel: (023) 9286 1533
www.historicdockyard.co.uk
Too much on offer for just one day out – Action Stations, Mary Rose, HMS Victory, HMS Warrior 1860, Royal Naval Museum, Warships by water harbour tours, Dockyard Apprentice exhibition.

Royal Marines Museum
Southsea, Hampshire
Tel: (023) 9281 9385
www.royalmarinesmuseum.co.uk
The history of the intrepid Royal Marines, 1664 to present day, set in what was one of the most stately Officers' Messes in England. Jungle and trench warfare sight and sound exhibitions among others.

Royal Navy Submarine Museum
Haslar Jetty Road, Gosport, Hampshire
Tel: (023) 9252 9217
www.rnsubmus.co.uk
Learn all there is to know about the Royal Navy Submarine Service, with models of submarines from earliest days to present nuclear age, including HM Submarine No 1 and midget submarines.

Above keeping guard at Windsor Castle; relax on the Basingstoke Canal **Right** a fun-filled visit to Portsmouth Historic Dockyard

St Mary's House and Gardens
Bramber, West Sussex
Tel: (01903) 816205
www.stmarysbramber.co.uk
A medieval timber-framed Grade I house with rare
16thC wall-leather, fine panelled rooms and a unique
painted room. Enchanting topiary gardens and Victorian
Secret Gardens.

Scotney Castle Garden and Estate
(National Trust)
Lamberhurst, Kent
Tel: (01892) 891081
www.nationaltrust.org.uk
Romantic gardens created around the ruins of a 14thC
moated castle containing exhibitions. Gardens created
by the Hussey family with shrubs, winding paths and
superb views.

South of England Rare Breeds Centre
Highlands Farm, Woodchurch, Kent
Tel: (01233) 861493
www.rarebreeds.org.uk
Visit this working farm and see the large collection of rare
and traditional farm breeds. Home to the Tamworth Two.
Woodland walks and children's play activities.

The Savill Garden, Windsor Great Park
Wick Lane, Windsor, Berkshire
Tel: (01753) 847518
www.savillgarden.co.uk
Woodland garden with formal rose gardens and
herbaceous borders. Something of interest and beauty to
behold in all seasons. Plant centre, gift shop, restaurant.

Ventnor Botanic Garden and Visitor Centre
The Undercliff Drive, Ventnor, Isle of Wight
Tel: (01983) 855397
www.botanic.co.uk
Escape overseas in nine hectares (22 acres) of world-
themed gardens including Mediterranean, The Americas
and New Zealand. Visitor centre, gift shop, café, two
semi-permanent exhibitions and plant sales.

Weald and Downland Open Air Museum
Singleton, West Sussex
Tel: (01243) 811348
www.wealddown.co.uk
Rescued and rebuilt, a fascinating insight into dwellings
from the past with over 45 historic buildings spanning
more than 500 years, including a medieval farmstead,
17thC watermill and Tudor kitchen.

West Dean Gardens
West Dean, West Sussex
Tel: (01243) 818210
www.westdean.org.uk
Historic garden with specimen trees, 300ft pergola,
rustic summerhouses and restored walled kitchen
garden with splendid Victorian glasshouses. Parkland
and arboretum walks.

Winchester Cathedral
The Close, Winchester, Hampshire
Tel: (01962) 857225
www.winchester-cathedral.org.uk
Magnificent medieval cathedral with a soaring Gothic
nave. Inside are ancient and modern art treasures, 12thC
illuminated Winchester Bible, Jane Austen's tomb, crypt
and chapels.

Windsor Castle
Windsor, Berkshire
Tel: (020) 7766 7304
www.royal.gov.uk
Fit for a queen! Official residence of HM The Queen and
royal residence for nine centuries. State apartments
contain treasures from the Royal Collection as well as
Queen Mary's Doll's House.

Tourism South East

40 Chamberlayne Road, Eastleigh, Hampshire SO50 5JH
T: (023) 8062 5505 F: (023) 8062 0010
E: enquiries@tourismse.com
www.visitsoutheastengland.com

Travel information

By road:
From the north east – M1 & M25; the north west – M6, M40 & M25; the west and Wales – M4 & M25; the east – M25; the south west – M5, M4 & M25; London – M25, M2, M20, M23, M3, M4 or M40.

By rail:
Regular services from London's Charing Cross, Victoria, Waterloo and Waterloo East stations to all parts of the South East. Further information on rail journeys in the South East can be obtained on 0845 748 4950.

The following publications are available from Tourism South East:

Escape into the Countryside

Waterside

Cities

Horse Racing

Gardens

Great Value Touring Guide

Great Days Out

Regional Visitor Guide

Right wander around Nymans Gardens, Handcross

Where to stay in
South East England

All place names in the blue bands, under which accommodation is listed, are shown on the maps at the front of this guide.

A complete listing of all VisitBritain assessed accommodation covered by this guide appears at the back.

Accommodation symbols

Symbols give useful information about services and facilities. Inside the back cover flap you can find a key to these symbols. Keep it open for easy reference.

ANDOVER, Hampshire Map ref 3C2 *Tourist Information Centre Tel: (01264) 324320*

★★★
TOURING &
CAMPING PARK

WYKE DOWN TOURING CARAVAN & CAMPING PARK
Picket Piece, Andover SP11 6LX
T: (01264) 352048
F: (01264) 324661
E: wykedown@wykedown.co.uk
I: www.wykedown.co.uk

OPEN All Year
Payment accepted: Delta,
Mastercard, Switch, Visa

	£12.00–£16.00
	£12.00–£16.00
	£12.00–£16.00
69 touring pitches

Follow Tourist Information camping signs from A303 trunk road, Andover ring road, then through village. Picket Piece is signposted, approximately 2 miles from ring road.

ARUNDEL, West Sussex Map ref 3D3 *Tourist Information Centre Tel: (01903) 882268*

★★
TOURING &
CAMPING PARK

BH&HPA

SHIP & ANCHOR MARINA
Heywood and Bryett Ltd, Ford, Arundel
BN18 0BJ
T: (01243) 551262
F: (01243) 555256
E: ysm36b@dsl.pipex.com

Payment accepted: Euros

	£11.00–£14.00
	£11.00–£14.00
	£11.00–£14.00
160 touring pitches

From A27 at Arundel take road south signposted Ford. Site 2 miles on the left, after level crossing. Also signposted from A259 between Littlehampton and Bognor Regis.

ASHURST, Kent Map ref 3D2 *Tourist Information Centre Tel: (01892) 515675*

★★★
TOURING &
CAMPING PARK

MANOR COURT FARM
Ashurst, Tunbridge Wells TN3 9TB
T: (01892) 740279
F: (01892) 740919
E: jsoyke@jsoyke.freeserve.co.uk
I: www.manorcourtfarm.co.uk

Four acres of secluded, informal camping in garden, meadow or near ponds on 350-acre mixed farm. Lovely views. Fire sites. Riding, fishing nearby (3 miles). Reduced rates for longer stays and reduced rates for children. Babies free.

OPEN All Year
Payment accepted: Euros

5	£12.00–£15.50
5	£12.00–£15.50
15	£12.00–£15.50
25 touring pitches

On A264, 5 miles west of Tunbridge Wells, between Stonecross and Ashurst villages.

BATTLE, East Sussex Map ref 4B4 *Tourist Information Centre Tel: (01424) 773721*

★★★★★
HOLIDAY PARK

BH&HPA
NCC

See Ad below

CROWHURST PARK

Telham Lane, Battle TN33 0SL
T: (01424) 773344
F: (01424) 775727
E: enquiries@crowhurstpark.co.uk
I: www.crowhurstpark.co.uk

Quality development of luxury Scandinavian-style pine lodges within the grounds of a 17thC country estate. Facilities include leisure club with indoor swimming pool. Christmas and New Year breaks available.

Payment accepted: Mastercard, Switch, Visa

Two miles south of Battle on A2100.

54		£250.00–£880.00

★★★★★
TOURING PARK

BH&HPA

See Ad on inside back cover

NORMANHURST COURT CARAVAN CLUB SITE

Stevens Crouch, Battle TN33 9LR
T: (01424) 773808
I: www.caravanclub.co.uk

An elegant site, set in the heart of 1066 country. Visit historic Battle Abbey or picturesque Rye, littered with antique shops and tea rooms. Open 26 March to 1 November. Special member rates mean you can save your membership subscription in less than a week. Visit www.caravanclub.co.uk to find out more.

Payment accepted: Delta, Mastercard, Switch, Visa

From Battle, turn left onto A271. Site is 3 miles on left.

152		£14.60–£20.60
152		£14.60–£20.60
152 touring pitches		

Quality Assurance Standard

For an explanation of the quality and facilities represented by the stars please refer to the front of this guide. A more detailed explanation can be found in the information pages at the back.

BEACONSFIELD, Buckinghamshire Map ref 3C2

★★★★
TOURING &
CAMPING PARK

BH&HPA

HIGHCLERE FARM COUNTRY TOURING PARK

Newbarn Lane, Seer Green, Beaconsfield HP9 2QZ
T: (01494) 874505
F: (01494) 875238
E: highclerepark@aol.com
I: www.highclerefarmpark.co.uk

Quiet meadowland park, low-cost tube prices to London (25 minutes). Eleven miles Legoland. Launderette, showers, play area. New toilet block 2003. Open March to January inclusive.

Payment accepted: Delta, Mastercard, Switch, Visa

A40 to Potkiln Lane and follow signs up to site. M40 jct 2 to Beaconsfield, A355 signed Amersham 1 mile, right to Seer Green.

60	🚐	£13.00–£18.00
60	🚗	£13.00–£18.00
35	▲	£10.00–£18.00
95 touring pitches		

BEMBRIDGE, Isle of Wight Map ref 3C3

★★★★
HOLIDAY PARK

BH&HPA
NCC

WHITECLIFF BAY HOLIDAY PARK

Hillway Road, Bembridge PO35 5PL
T: (01983) 872671
F: (01983) 872941
E: holiday@whitecliff-bay.com
I: www.whitecliff-bay.com

Situated in an Area of Outstanding Natural Beauty, the park offers great-value family holidays. There are facilities on site for all ages. Special offers are available from time to time – please visit our website for full details.

Payment accepted: Delta, Mastercard, Switch, Visa, Euros

From A3055 turn onto B3395 at Brading and follow signposts.

400	🚐	£8.50–£18.50
400	🚗	£8.50–£18.50
400	▲	£8.50–£18.50
230	🏠	£220.00–£580.00
400 touring pitches		

BEXHILL-ON-SEA, East Sussex Map ref 4B4 *Tourist Information Centre Tel: (01424) 732208*

★★★★
HOLIDAY, TOURING
& CAMPING PARK

COBBS HILL FARM CARAVAN & CAMPING PARK
Watermill Lane, Sidley, Bexhill-on-Sea
TN39 5JA
T: (01424) 213460
F: (01424) 221358
E: cobbshillfarmuk@hotmail.com
I: www.cobbshillfarm.co.uk

Turn off the A269 into Watermill Lane, 1 mile on left.

55	🚐	£5.70–£6.50
55	🚗	£5.50–£6.20
55	▲	£5.70–£6.50
2	🏠	£98.00–£255.00
55 touring pitches		

★★★★★
TOURING &
CAMPING PARK

BH&HPA

KLOOFS CARAVAN PARK

Sandhurst Lane, Whydown, Bexhill-on-Sea TN39 4RG
T: (01424) 842839
F: (01424) 845669
E: camping@kloofs.com
I: www.kloofs.com

Freedom all year round, whatever the weather! Fully serviced, hard, extra-large pitches. Modern facilities, private washing, central heating. In a quiet, rural setting. Further upgraded 2004/5.

OPEN All Year

From A259 Bexhill/Little Common roundabout turn into Peartree Lane. At crossroads turn left into Whydown Road.

	🚐	£15.00
	🚗	£15.00
	▲	£12.50
50 touring pitches		

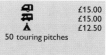

BIRCHINGTON, Kent Map ref 4C3

★★★★★
HOLIDAY, TOURING
& CAMPING PARK

BH&HPA
NCC

TWO CHIMNEYS HOLIDAY PARK

Shottendane Road, Birchington CT7 0HD
T: (01843) 841068
F: (01843) 848099
E: info@twochimneys.co.uk
I: www.twochimneys.co.uk

A friendly, family-run country site near sandy beaches. Spacious, level pitches. Modern WC/shower and laundry facilities including disabled. Children's play and ball-games areas.

Payment accepted: Delta, Mastercard, Switch, Visa

A2 then A28 to Birchington. Turn right into Park Lane, bear left into Manston Road, left at crossroads B2049, site on right.

100	🚐	£11.00–£18.00
100	🚎	£11.00–£18.00
100	⛺	£11.00–£18.00
3	🏠	£180.00–£500.00
300 touring pitches		

BOGNOR REGIS, West Sussex Map ref 3C3 *Tourist Information Centre Tel: (01243) 823140*

★★★
TOURING PARK

THE LILLIES CARAVAN PARK
Yapton Road, Barnham, Bognor Regis
PO22 0AY
T: (01243) 552081
F: (01243) 552081
E: thelillies@hotmail.com
I: lilliescaravanpark.co.uk

OPEN All Year
Payment accepted: Delta,
Mastercard, Switch, Visa

34	🚐	£10.00–£14.00
34	🚎	£10.00–£14.00
16	⛺	£10.00–£14.00
8	🏠	£190.00–£340.00
34 touring pitches		

Three miles north of Bognor Regis. Take the A29 to Westergate bearing right at Labour in Vain public house to Eastergate and onto B2233. From A27 Fontwell roundabout onto A29 then B2233 to park. Signposted.

★★★★★
HOLIDAY PARK

BH&HPA

See Ad on inside back cover

ROWAN PARK CARAVAN CLUB SITE

Rowan Way, Bognor Regis PO22 9RP
T: (01243) 828515
I: www.caravanclub.co.uk

A small, recently redeveloped site just two miles from Bognor. Award-winning beach, seaside attractions. Chichester, Arundel and Brighton within easy reach; also NT properties including Petworth. Open 26 March to 1 November. Special member rates mean you can save your membership subscription in less than a week. Visit www.caravanclub.co.uk to find out more.

Payment accepted: Delta, Mastercard, Switch, Visa

From roundabout on A29, 1 mile north of Bognor, turn left into Rowan Way, site 100yds on right, opposite Halfords superstore.

109	🚐	£14.60–£20.60
109	🚎	£14.60–£20.60
109 touring pitches		

Credit card bookings

If you book by telephone and are asked for your credit card number it is advisable to check the proprietor's policy should you cancel your reservation.

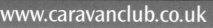

You're welcome at our Sites!

For details of Caravan Club sites in this region, where high standards, excellent facilities and a warm welcome are assured, please see our website

THE CARAVAN CLUB

www.caravanclub.co.uk

BRIGHTON & HOVE, Brighton & Hove Map ref 3D3 *Tourist Information Centre Tel: 0906 711 2255*

★★★★★
TOURING & CAMPING PARK

BH&HPA

See Ad on inside back cover

SHEEPCOTE VALLEY CARAVAN CLUB SITE

Sheepcote Valley, Brighton BN2 5TS
T: (01273) 626546
F: (01273) 682600
I: www.caravanclub.co.uk

Located on the South Downs, just two miles from Brighton. Visit the Marina, with its shops, pubs, restaurants and cinema, and take a tour of the exotic Royal Pavilion. Special member rates mean you can save your membership subscription in less than a week. Visit www.caravanclub.co.uk to find out more.

OPEN All Year

Payment accepted: Delta, Mastercard, Switch, Visa

M23/A23, join A27 (signposted Lewes) turn off at B2123 (signposted Falmer and Rottingdean). At top turn right onto B2123 to Woodingdean. In 2 miles at traffic lights turn right into Warren Road, after 1 mile turn left into Wilson Avenue.

170	(caravan)	£17.00–£22.00
170	(motor caravan)	£17.00–£22.00
	(tent)	On application

170 touring pitches

THE CARAVAN CLUB

BURFORD, Oxfordshire Map ref 3B1 *Tourist Information Centre Tel: (01993) 823558*

★★★★★
TOURING PARK

BH&HPA

See Ad on inside back cover

BURFORD CARAVAN CLUB SITE

Bradwell Grove, Burford OX18 4JJ
T: (01993) 823080
I: www.caravanclub.co.uk

Attractive, spacious site opposite Cotswold Wildlife Park. Burford has superb Tudor houses, a museum and historic inns. A great base to explore the Cotswolds. Open 26 March to 1 November. Special member rates mean you can save your membership subscription in less than a week. Visit www.caravanclub.co.uk to find out more.

Payment accepted: Delta, Mastercard, Switch, Visa

From roundabout at A40/A361 junction in Burford, take A361 signposted Lechlade. Site on right after 2.5 miles. Site signposted from roundabout.

120	(caravan)	£14.60–£20.60
120	(motor caravan)	£14.60–£20.60

120 touring pitches

THE CARAVAN CLUB

CANTERBURY, Kent Map ref 4B3 *Tourist Information Centre Tel: (01227) 378100*

★★★★
HOLIDAY, TOURING & CAMPING PARK

BH&HPA

YEW TREE PARK

Stone Street, Petham, Canterbury CT4 5PL
T: (01227) 700306
F: (01227) 700306
E: info@yewtreepark.com
I: www.yewtreepark.com

Picturesque country park close to Canterbury, centrally located for exploring Kent. Naturally landscaped touring and camping facilities. Self-catering (not assessed) apartments and holiday units. Outdoor pool.

Payment accepted: Delta, Mastercard, Switch, Visa

On B2068, 4 miles south of Canterbury, 9 miles north of M20, jct 11.

15	(caravan)	£13.00–£19.50
5	(motor caravan)	£13.00–£19.50
25	(tent)	£11.00–£16.00
7	(holiday unit)	£175.00–£395.00

45 touring pitches

NB

Important note **Information on accommodation listed in this guide has been supplied by the proprietors. As changes may occur you are advised to check details at the time of booking.**

CHICHESTER, West Sussex Map ref 3C3 *Tourist Information Centre Tel: (01243) 775888*

★★
**HOLIDAY &
TOURING PARK**

BH&HPA

BELL CARAVAN PARK
Bell Lane, Birdham, Chichester PO20 7HY
T: (01243) 512264

15	🚐	£12.00
15	🚏	£12.00

Take A286 south from Chichester for 5 miles, turn left into Bell Lane, park is 500yds on left.

★★★★★
CAMPING PARK

BH&HPA

WICKS FARM CAMPING PARK
West Wittering, Chichester PO20 8QD
T: (01243) 513116
F: (01243) 511296
I: www.wicksfarm.co.uk

Payment accepted:
Mastercard, Switch, Visa

40	🚐	£12.00–£15.00
40	⛺	£12.00–£15.00

From Chichester take A286/B2179 for 6 miles, straight on towards West Wittering. Wicks Farm is 2nd on the right just past Lamb pub.

COTSWOLDS

See under Burford, Standlake

See also Cotswolds in the South West England section

DYMCHURCH, Kent Map ref 4B4

★★★★
HOLIDAY PARK

E & J PIPER CARAVAN PARK
St Marys Road, Dymchurch, Romney Marsh
TN29 0PN
T: (01303) 872103
F: (01303) 872020

6	🏠	£151.00–£270.00

From A259 follow sign for Romney, Hythe, Dymchurch railway from motorway.

EASTBOURNE, East Sussex Map ref 4B4 *Tourist Information Centre Tel: 0906 711 2212*

★★★★
**TOURING &
CAMPING PARK**

FAIRFIELDS FARM CARAVAN & CAMPING PARK

Eastbourne Road, Westham, Pevensey BN24 5NG
T: (01323) 763165
F: (01323) 469175
E: enquiries@fairfieldsfarm.com
I: www.fairfieldsfarm.com

A warm welcome awaits you at this delightful, quiet, touring park with clean facilities, lakeside walk and fishing. An excellent location for exploring many attractions. 3-night, mid-week stay for the price of 2 – Apr, May, Jun, Sep and Oct. Contact us for more details.

Payment accepted: Amex, Delta, Mastercard, Switch, Visa

Signposted off A27 Pevensey roundabout. Straight through Pevensey and Westham villages towards castle. Then B2191 (left) to Eastbourne east, over level crossing on the left.

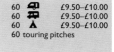

60	🚐	£9.50–£10.00
60	🚏	£9.50–£10.00
60	⛺	£9.50–£10.00
60 touring pitches		

Map references
The map references refer to the colour maps at the front of this guide. The first figure is the map number; the letter and figure which follow indicate the grid reference on the map.

★★★★★
TOURING &
CAMPING PARK

BH&HPA

See Ad on inside back cover

THE *Caravan Club*

BLACK HORSE FARM
CARAVAN CLUB SITE

385 Canterbury Road, Densole, Folkestone CT18 7BG
T: (01303) 892665
I: www.caravanclub.co.uk

Landscaped, peaceful, rural site set on the Downs. Folkestone four miles, Dover eight miles, Canterbury 11 miles. Why not stop here en route to Europe? Special member rates mean you can save your membership subscription in less than a week. Visit www.caravanclub.co.uk to find out more.

OPEN All Year
Payment accepted: Delta, Mastercard, Switch, Visa

From M20 jct 13 on A260 to Canterbury, 2 miles from junction with A20, site on left 200yds past Black Horse inn.

80	🚐	£14.60–£20.60
80	🚚	£14.60–£20.60
	▲	On application
80 touring pitches		

★★★★★
HOLIDAY PARK

BH&HPA

SANDY BALLS HOLIDAY
CENTRE

Godshill, Fordingbridge SP6 2JZ
T: (01425) 653042
F: (01425) 653067
E: post@sandy-balls.co.uk
I: www.sandy-balls.co.uk

Nestled in 120 acres of glorious parks and woodland on the river Avon, Sandy Balls offers an idyllic retreat, with the New Forest on its doorstep.
OPEN All Year
Payment accepted: Delta, Mastercard, Switch, Visa
Located on B3078 to Fordingbridge.

	🚐	£12.75–£25.50
	🚚	£12.75–£25.50
	▲	£12.75–£25.50
131	🏚	£110.00–
		£1,040.00
233 touring pitches		

See under Horsham, Redhill

★★★★
HOLIDAY, TOURING
& CAMPING PARK

BH&HPA

PEEL HOUSE FARM
CARAVAN PARK

Sayerland Lane, Polegate BN26 6QX
T: (01323) 845629
F: (01323) 845629
E: peelhocp@tesco.net

Friendly, peaceful, rural site with resident proprieters. Views to South Downs. Good walking and cycling. Eastbourne 5 miles. Many attractions in area. Open April to October.

From A22 take A295 to Hailsham then sharp right at mini-roundabout signed Pevensey (Ersham Road). Park is 1.25 miles on right.

14	🚐	£10.00–£12.00
2	🚚	£10.00–£12.00
4	▲	£4.00–£12.00
3	🏚	£160.00–£200.00
20 touring pitches		

Credit card bookings
If you book by telephone and are asked for your credit card number it is advisable to check the proprietor's policy should you cancel your reservation.

SOUTH EAST ENGLAND

HASTINGS

See display advertisement below

HORSHAM, West Sussex Map ref 3D2 *Tourist Information Centre Tel: (01403) 211661*

★★★
HOLIDAY PARK

BH&HPA
NCC

HONEYBRIDGE PARK

Honeybridge Lane, Dial Post, Horsham RH13 8NX
T: (01403) 710923
F: (01403) 710923
E: enquiries@honeybridgepark.co.uk
I: www.honeybridgepark.co.uk

Delightfully situated, spacious 15-acre park adjacent to woodlands. Relaxed and informal atmosphere. Convenient for coast and theme parks. Heated amenity blocks. Licensed shop/takeaway. 10% discount on pitch fees for Senior Citizens, foreign Camping Carnet holders and 7 nights or more. Mid-week special: £6 off (incl Tue).

OPEN All Year
Payment accepted: Delta, Mastercard, Switch, Visa, Euros

On A24 travelling south, turn left 1 mile past Dial Post turning. At Old Barn Nurseries continue for 300yds and site is on the right.

200	🚐	£15.00–£20.00
100	🚍	£15.00–£20.00
80	▲	£13.00–£18.00
200 touring pitches		

HOVE

See under Brighton & Hove

HURLEY, Windsor and Maidenhead Map ref 3C2 *Tourist Information Centre Tel: (01628) 796502*

★★★★
HOLIDAY, TOURING
& CAMPING PARK

ROSE AWARD

BH&HPA

HURLEY RIVERSIDE PARK
Hurley, Maidenhead SL6 5NE
T: (01628) 823501
F: (01628) 825533
E: info@hurleyriversidepark.co.uk
I: www.hurleyriversidepark.co.uk

Payment accepted: Delta, Mastercard, Switch, Visa

138	🚐	£9.50–£15.50
138	🚍	£9.50–£15.50
62	▲	£8.25–£14.25
10	🏕	£230.00–£450.00
200 touring pitches		

From M4, jct 8/9, take A404M, then A4130 towards Henley. From M40 jct 4, take A404 south, then A4130 towards Henley. 1 mile past Hurley Village, turn right into Shepherds Lane.

ISLE OF WIGHT

See under Bembridge, St Helens

See display advertisement opposite

LINGFIELD, Surrey Map ref 3D2

★★★
TOURING PARK

BH&HPA

LONG ACRES CARAVAN & CAMPING PARK
Newchapel Road, Lingfield RH7 6LE
T: (01342) 833205   OPEN All Year
F: (01622) 735038
I: www.ukparks.co.uk/longacres

🚐	£11.00
🚍	£11.00
▲	£11.00
60 touring pitches	

South on A22 for 6 miles towards East Grinstead. At Newchapel roundabout turn left onto B2028 to Lingfield. Site is 700yds on the right.

 Symbols The symbols in each entry give information about services and facilities. A key to these symbols appears at the back of this guide.

5993498498

SHEAR BARN HOLIDAY PARK

Overlooking Hastings Country Park and to the sea beyond is the family holiday that has it all, with fully serviced pitches and facilities for all the family to enjoy.

Tel: 01424 423583 www.haulfryn.co.uk

178

MARDEN, Kent Map ref 4B4 *Tourist Information Centre Tel: (01732) 770929*

★★★★★
TOURING &
CAMPING PARK

BH&HPA

TANNER FARM TOURING CARAVAN & CAMPING PARK

Goudhurst Road, Tonbridge TN12 9ND
T: (01622) 832399
F: (01622) 832472
E: enquiries@tannerfarmpark.co.uk
I: www.tannerfarmpark.co.uk

Immaculate, secluded park surrounded by beautiful countryside on family farm. Ideal touring base for the area. Gold David Bellamy Conservation Award. Bed and Breakfast also available. Caravan club MUC.

OPEN All Year
Payment accepted: Delta, Mastercard, Switch, Visa

From A21 or A229 onto B2079 midway between Marden and Goudhurst.

100	🚐	£10.00–£17.00
26	🚎	£10.00–£17.00
20	⛺	£10.00–£13.00
100 touring pitches		

At-a-glance symbols

Symbols at the end of each entry give useful information about services and facilities. A key to symbols can be found inside the back cover flap. Keep this open for easy reference.

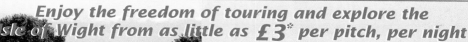

MILFORD ON SEA, Hampshire Map ref 3C3

★★★★
HOLIDAY PARK

BH&HPA

DOWNTON HOLIDAY PARK

Shorefield Road, Milford on Sea, Lymington SO41 0LH
T: (01425) 476131 & (01590) 642515
F: (01590) 642515
E: info@downtonholidaypark.co.uk
I: www.downtonholidaypark.co.uk

A small, peaceful park on the edge of the New Forest, within easy reach of picturesque villages. Near to coast. Pets welcome in some caravans.

Payment accepted: Delta, Mastercard, Switch, Visa

Turn from B3058 into Downton Lane, then 1st right, or from A337 into Downton Lane, then 1st left.

22	⊞	£130.00–£280.00

★★★★
TOURING PARK

BH&HPA
NCC

See Ad p18

LYTTON LAWN TOURING PARK
Lymore Lane, Milford on Sea, Lymington
SO41 0TX
T: (01590) 648331
F: (01590) 645610
E: holidays@shorefield.co.uk
I: www.shorefield.co.uk

OPEN All Year
Payment accepted: Delta,
Mastercard, Switch, Visa

136	🚐	£9.50–£30.00
136	🚙	£9.50–£30.00
83	▲	£9.50–£28.00
136 touring pitches		

Take A337 from Cadnam (jct 1, M27) through Lyndhurst and Brockenhurst to Lymington. Proceed to Everton and turn left on to B3058. Lytton Lawn is on the left.

★★★★★
HOLIDAY PARK

BH&HPA
NCC

See Ad p18

SHOREFIELD COUNTRY PARK
Shorefield Road, Milford on Sea, Lymington
SO41 0LH
T: (01590) 648331
F: (01590) 645610
E: holidays@shorefield.co.uk
I: www.shorefield.co.uk

OPEN All Year
Payment accepted: Delta,
Mastercard, Switch, Visa

150	⊞	£175.00–£1,216.00

From M27 jct 1 take A337 through Lyndhurst, Brockenhurst and Lymington to Downton, turn left at Royal Oak public house.

NEW FOREST

See under Ashurst, Fordingbridge, Milford on Sea, Ringwood

READING, Reading Map ref 3C2 *Tourist Information Centre Tel: (0118) 956 6226*

★★★★
TOURING &
CAMPING PARK

BH&HPA

WELLINGTON COUNTRY PARK

Odiham Road, Riseley, Reading RG7 1SP
T: (0118) 932 6444
F: (0118) 932 3445
E: camping@wellington-country-park.co.uk
I: www.wellington-country-park.co.uk

A wealth of enjoyment. Nature trails, barbecue, picnic areas, adventure playground, crazy golf, sandpit, animal farm, fishing lake. Special events throughout the season.

OPEN All Year except Christmas and New Year
Payment accepted: Mastercard, Switch, Visa

Between Reading and Basingstoke, signposted from the A33.

58	🚐	£16.00–£25.00
58	🚙	£16.00–£25.00
14	▲	£16.00–£20.00
58 touring pitches		

Important note Information on accommodation listed in this guide has been supplied by the proprietors. As changes may occur you are advised to check details at the time of booking.

REDHILL, Surrey Map ref 3D2

★★★★
TOURING PARK

BH&HPA

See Ad on inside back cover

THE CARAVAN CLUB

ALDERSTEAD HEATH CARAVAN CLUB SITE

Dean Lane, Redhill RH1 3AH
T: (01737) 644629
I: www.caravanclub.co.uk

Quiet site with views over rolling, wooded North Downs. Denbies Wine Estate nearby. For day trips try Chessington and Thorpe Park and the lively city of Brighton. Non-members welcome. Special member rates mean you can save your membership subscription in less than a week. Visit www.caravanclub.co.uk to find out more.

OPEN All Year
Payment accepted: Delta, Mastercard, Switch, Visa

From M25 jct 8 onto A217 towards Reigate, fork left after 300yds towards Merstham. 2.5 miles turn left at T-junction onto A23. 0.5 miles turn right into Shepherds Hill (B2031). 1 mile turn left into Dean Lane. Site on right.

85	🚐	£14.60–£20.60
85	🚐	£14.60–£20.60
85 touring pitches		

RINGWOOD, Hampshire

See display advertisement below

ROMSEY, Hampshire Map ref 3C3 *Tourist Information Centre Tel: (01794) 512987*

★★★★
HOLIDAY, TOURING & CAMPING PARK

BH&HPA

HILL FARM CARAVAN PARK
Branches Lane, Sherfield English, Romsey
SO51 6FH
T: (01794) 340402
F: (01794) 342358
E: gjb@hillfarmpark.com
I: www.hillfarmpark.com

Directions given at time of booking.

70	🚐	£15.00–£24.00
70	🚐	£15.00–£24.00
40	▲	£11.00–£18.00
6	🏠	£160.00–£400.00
70 touring pitches		

ST HELENS, Isle of Wight

See display advertisement below

ST NICHOLAS AT WADE, Kent Map ref 4C3

★★★
TOURING & CAMPING PARK

ST NICHOLAS CAMPING SITE
Court Road, St Nicholas at Wade,
Birchington CT7 0NH
T: (01843) 847245

Village signposted off A299 and off the A28, near Birchington.

15	🚐	£10.00–£14.00
5	🚐	£10.00–£12.00
55	▲	£7.00–£14.00
75 touring pitches		

SELSEY, West Sussex Map ref 3C3 *Tourist Information Centre Tel: (01243) 775888*

★★★★★
TOURING PARK

NCC

WARNER FARM TOURING PARK
Warners Lane, Selsey, Chichester PO20 9EL
T: (01243) 608440
F: (01243) 604499
E: touring@bunnleisure.co.uk
I: www.bunnleisure.co.uk

Payment accepted: Amex, Delta, Mastercard, Switch, Visa

250	🚐	£15.00–£27.25
250	🚐	£15.00–£27.25
50	▲	£13.00–£25.25
250 touring pitches		

B2145 into Selsey, turn right into School Lane, 1st right off School Lane, 1st left, proceed until you see sign for all touring caravans.

STANDLAKE, Oxfordshire

See display advertisement below

WARSASH, Hampshire Map ref 3C3 *Tourist Information Centre Tel: (023) 8083 3333*

★★★★
TOURING PARK

BH&HPA

DIBLES PARK
Dibles Road, Warsash, Southampton
SO31 9SA
T: (01489) 575232

OPEN All Year

14	🚐	£8.00–£12.00
14	🚐	£8.00–£12.00
14	▲	£7.00
14 touring pitches		

From M27 junction J8 A27 to Park Gate, right into Brook Lane 2nd turning off at roundabout, Lockwoods Road. At bottom turn left then right at Fleet End Road, 2nd turning on right.

WASHINGTON, West Sussex Map ref 3D3

★★★★
**TOURING &
CAMPING PARK**

WASHINGTON CARAVAN & CAMPING PARK
London Road, Washington, Pulborough
RH20 4AJ
T: (01903) 892869
F: (01903) 893252
E: washcamp@amserve.com
I: www.washcamp.com

OPEN All Year
Payment accepted: Delta, Mastercard, Switch, Visa

21	🚐	£12.00
5	🚐	£12.00
80	▲	£12.00
21 touring pitches		

A24 – A283 signposted.

WINCHESTER, Hampshire Map ref 3C3 *Tourist Information Centre Tel: (01962) 840500*

★★★★
TOURING PARK

BH&HPA

See Ad on inside back cover

MORN HILL CARAVAN CLUB SITE

Alresford Road, Winchester SO21 1HL
T: (01962) 869877
I: www.caravanclub.co.uk

Large, split-level site from which to explore Winchester. Oxford, Chichester, the New Forest and Salisbury are all within an hour's drive. Open 26 March to 1 November. Special member rates mean you can save your membership subscription in less than a week. Visit www.caravanclub.co.uk to find out more.

Payment accepted: Delta, Mastercard, Switch, Visa

From M3 jct 10 A31 (signposted Alton). Turn left at roundabout with Percy Hobbs sign, signposted Easton. Immediate turn in front of pub, top of lane for Caravan Club.

150	🚐	£12.50–£17.60
150	🚐	£12.50–£17.60
	▲	On application
150 touring pitches		

THE CARAVAN CLUB

WORTHING, West Sussex Map ref 3D3 *Tourist Information Centre Tel: (01903) 221307*

★★★★
TOURING PARK

BH&HPA

See Ad on inside back cover

NORTHBROOK FARM CARAVAN CLUB SITE

Titnore Way, Worthing BN13 3RT
T: (01903) 502962
I: www.caravanclub.co.uk

An attractive grassy site in open countryside with good trees, and only two miles from the coast. Open 26 March to 18 October. Special member rates mean you can save your membership subscription in less than a week. Visit www.caravanclub.co.uk to find out more.

Payment accepted: Delta, Mastercard, Switch, Visa

From A24 follow signs for Chichester/Littlehampton approx 4 miles on, far side of bridge, signposted Ferring and Goring. After 0.75 miles turn left, caravan site sign Titnore Way is on left. Site entrance on left in 200 yds.

132	🚐	£13.35–£17.60
132	🚐	£13.35–£17.60
132 touring pitches		

THE CARAVAN CLUB

WROTHAM HEATH, Kent Map ref 4B3 *Tourist Information Centre Tel: (01732) 450305*

★★★★★
**TOURING &
CAMPING PARK**

BH&HPA

GATE HOUSE WOOD TOURING PARK
Ford Road, Wrotham Heath, Sevenoaks
TN15 7SD
T: (01732) 843062

56	🚐	£9.00–£13.50
56	🚐	£9.00–£13.50
56	⛺	£9.00–£13.50
56 touring pitches		

From M26 jct 2a take A20 south towards Maidstone. Through traffic lights at Wrotham Heath. Take 1st left signposted Trottiscliffe. Left at next junction. Gate House Wood is within 100yds on left.

Use your *i*s

There are more than 750 Tourist Information Centres throughout England, Scotland and Wales, offering friendly help with accommodation and holiday ideas as well as suggestions of places to visit and things to do. You'll find addresses in the local phone book.

A brief guide to the main towns and villages offering accommodation in **South East England**

ANDOVER, Hampshire
Town that achieved importance from the wool trade and now has much modern development. A good centre for visiting places of interest.

ARUNDEL, West Sussex
Picturesque, historic town on the river Arun, dominated by Arundel Castle, home of the Dukes of Norfolk. There are many 18thC houses, the Wildfowl and Wetlands Centre and Museum and Heritage Centre.

ASHURST, Kent
Small hamlet on a hill, at the top of which is the church with its unusual weatherboarded bellcote. The Wealdway long-distance footpath passes nearby at Stone Cross.

BATTLE, East Sussex
The Abbey at Battle was built on the site of the Battle of Hastings, when William defeated Harold II and so became the Conqueror in 1066. The museum has a fine collection relating to the Sussex iron industry and there is a social history museum – Buckleys Yesterday's World.

BEACONSFIELD, Buckinghamshire
Former coaching town with several inns still surviving. The old town has many fine houses and an interesting church. Beautiful countryside and beech woods nearby.

BEMBRIDGE, Isle of Wight
Village with harbour and bay below Bembridge Down – the most easterly village on the island.

Bembridge Sailing Club is one of the most important in southern England.

BEXHILL-ON-SEA, East Sussex
Popular resort with beach of shingle and firm sand at low tide. The impressive 1930s designed De la Warr Pavilion has good entertainment facilities. Costume Museum in Manor Gardens.

BOGNOR REGIS, West Sussex
Five miles of firm, flat sand has made the town a popular family resort. Well supplied with gardens.

BRIGHTON & HOVE, Brighton & Hove
Brighton's attractions include the Royal Pavilion, Volks Electric Railway, Sea Life Centre and Marina Village, Conference Centre, The Lanes and several theatres.

BURFORD, Oxfordshire
One of the most beautiful Cotswold wool towns with Georgian and Tudor houses, many antique shops and a picturesque High Street sloping to the river Windrush.

CANTERBURY, Kent
Place of pilgrimage since the martyrdom of Becket in 1170 and the site of Canterbury Cathedral. Visit St Augustine's Abbey, St Martin's (the oldest church in England), Royal Museum and Art Gallery and the Canterbury Tales. Nearby is Howletts Wild Animal Park. Good shopping centre.

CHICHESTER, West Sussex
The county town of West Sussex with a beautiful Norman cathedral. Noted for its Georgian architecture but also has modern buildings like the Festival Theatre. Surrounded by places of interest, including Fishbourne Roman Palace, Weald and Downland Open Air Museum and West Dean Gardens.

DYMCHURCH, Kent
For centuries the headquarters of the Lords of the Level, the local government of this area. Probably best known today because of the fame of its fictional parson, the notorious Dr Syn, who has inspired a regular festival.

EASTBOURNE, East Sussex
One of the finest, most elegant resorts on the south-east coast situated beside Beachy Head. Long promenade, well known Carpet Gardens on the seafront, Devonshire Park tennis and indoor leisure complex, theatres, Towner Art Gallery, How We Lived Then Museum of Shops and Social History.

FOLKESTONE, Kent
Popular resort. The town has a fine promenade, the Leas, from where orchestral concerts and other entertainments are presented. Horse-racing at Westenhanger Racecourse nearby.

Below, from left step back in time at Leeds Castle, Maidstone; hop on board HMS Victory, Portsmouth

FORDINGBRIDGE, Hampshire
On the north-west edge of the New Forest. A medieval bridge crosses the Avon at this point and gave the town its name. A good centre for walking, exploring and fishing.

HORSHAM, West Sussex
Busy town with much modern development but still retaining its old character. The museum in Causeway House is devoted chiefly to local history and the agricultural life of the county.

LINGFIELD, Surrey
Wealden village with many buildings dating back to the 15thC. Nearby there is year-round horse racing at Lingfield Park.

MARDEN, Kent
The village is believed to date back to Saxon times, though today more modern homes surround the 13thC church.

MILFORD-ON-SEA, Hampshire
Victorian seaside resort with shingle beach and good bathing, set in pleasant countryside and looking out over the Isle of Wight. Nearby is Hurst Castle, built by Henry VIII. The school chapel, former abbey church, can be visited.

READING, Reading
Busy, modern county town with large shopping centre and many leisure and recreation facilities. There are several interesting museums and the Duke of Wellington's Stratfield Saye is nearby.

REDHILL, Surrey
Part of the borough of Reigate and now the commercial centre with good shopping facilities. Gatwick Airport is three miles to the south.

ROMSEY, Hampshire
Town grew up around the important abbey and lies on the banks of the river Test, famous for trout and salmon. Broadlands House, home of the late Lord Mountbatten, is open to the public.

ST NICHOLAS AT WADE, Kent
Village in the Isle of Thanet with ancient church built of knapped flint.

SELSEY, West Sussex
Almost surrounded by water, with the English Channel on two sides and an inland lake, once Pagham Harbour, and the Brook on the other two. Ideal for yachting, swimming, fishing and wildlife.

WARSASH, Hampshire
On the edge of Southampton Water. Warships were built here in Napoleonic times.

WASHINGTON, West Sussex
Near the village is the famous Chanctonbury Ring, an Iron Age camp on a rise nearly 800 ft above sea level.

WINCHESTER, Hampshire
King Alfred the Great made Winchester the capital of Saxon England. A magnificent Norman cathedral, with one of the longest naves in Europe, dominates the city. Home of Winchester College founded in 1382.

WORTHING, West Sussex
Town in the West Sussex countryside and by the South Coast, with excellent shopping and many pavement cafés and restaurants. Attractions include the award-winning Museum and Art Gallery, beautiful gardens, pier, elegant town houses, Cissbury Ring hill fort and the South Downs.

David Bellamy Conservation Awards

If you are looking for a site that's environmentally friendly, look for those that have achieved the David Bellamy Conservation Award. Launched in conjunction with the British Holiday & Home Parks Association, this award is given to sites which are committed to protecting and enhancing the environment – from care of the hedgerows and wildlife to recycling waste – and are members of the Association. More information about the award scheme can be found at the back of the guide.

A mix of **sandy** beaches and **sheltered** bays, **wild moors,** buzzing nightlife and **relaxing** resorts.

South West England

Looking for some inspiration? Here are a few ideas to get you started in South West England. **experience** the amazing surfing championships at Newquay. **discover** The Lost Gardens of Heligan, 80 acres of the largest garden restoration project in Europe. **explore** the origins of life to the ends of the earth at Wildwalk, one of At-Bristol's three magical attractions **relax** in a honey-coloured Cotswolds village.

THE REGION
Bristol & Bath, Cornwall & the Isles of Scilly, Devon, Dorset, Gloucestershire & the Cotswolds, Somerset, Wiltshire

CONTACT
▸ SOUTH WEST TOURISM
  Woodwater Park,
  Exeter EX2 5WT
  T: 0870 442 0880
  www.visitsouthwest.co.uk

Awe-inspiring cliffs, warm sandy beaches, rolling farmland and wild moors, buzzing nightlife and relaxing resorts: the many faces of the South West ensure every visitor is enthralled, and every visit is as different as you want it be.

Sand, surf and seals

The South West coast is always a popular holiday choice with its mix of safe, sandy beaches, sheltered bays and wilder stretches that are perfect for watersports. If you're a novice there are plenty of places to learn – try Bude, Croyde or Woolacombe for surfing or Poole for windsurfing and sailing. Check out the progress of Torquay's waterfront which is currently undergoing a £21 million facelift. Or watch penguins, seals and puffins in the re-created environment at Living Coasts. Divers can even explore an artificial reef which has been created off the coast in Whitsand Bay, Cornwall.

Dramatic coasts and moors

Enjoy breathtaking views along the South West Coast Path, a 630-mile continuous coastal trail. For the less adventurous there are plenty of shorter strolls in the National Parks of Exmoor and Dartmoor. Or if you don't feel like getting out of the car at all, the Royal Forest route is a 20-mile car trail designed to take visitors around the prettiest parts of the Forest of Dean.

In Dorset and East Devon, the Jurassic Coast Natural World Heritage Site offers a unique voyage back in time through 185 million years of the earth's history. Exposed rocks along 95 miles of beautiful coastline reveal the secrets of the past.

Good at any time

The sub-tropical climate of the South West ensures an early spring each year. Be among the first to catch a glimpse of the colourful buds as they burst into flower at Tresco Abbey Gardens on the Isles of Scilly, or at Westonbirt Arboretum with its acres of bluebells, giant rhododendrons and azaleas. All year round a visit to the Eden Project promises colour and fragrance, including a tropical rainforest. In Falmouth, be sure to visit the National Maritime Museum Cornwall. Interactive displays, small boats and windows looking under the ocean will bring out the sea salt in your blood! After a day's exploring, enjoy a meal of fresh, local ingredients home-cooked in a local pub. Or try an exciting new restaurant, such as Damien Hirst's at 11 The Quay, Ilfracombe. For a souvenir of your stay, visit Bristol Blue Glass where you can see glass pieces being blown in the traditional way.

Left, from top explore and discover At-Bristol; admire the great and ancient circle of Stonehenge; tranquil surroundings at the Roman Baths in Bath **Right** life's a beach in Newquay

Places to visit

At-Bristol
Anchor Road, Bristol
Tel: 0845 345 1235
www.at-bristol.org.uk
For the interactive adventure of a lifetime, visit At-Bristol's three award-winning attractions – Explore, Wildwalk and the IMAX Theatre. Amazing experiences every day.

Atwell-Wilson Motor Museum Trust
Calne, Wiltshire
Tel: (01249) 813119
www.atwell-wilson.org
Impressive motor museum with vintage, post-vintage and classic cars, including American models. Classic motorbikes. A 17thC water meadow walk. Play area.

Babbacombe Model Village
Hampton Avenue, Babbacombe, Devon
Tel: (01803) 315315
www.babbacombemodelvillage.co.uk
Over 400 models, many with sound and animation, set in award-winning gardens. See modern towns, villages and rural areas, and Aquaviva, a light, laser, sound and water show. An enchanting experience.

Bristol City Museum & Art Gallery
Queen's Road, Bristol
Tel: (0117) 922 3571
www.bristol-city.gov.uk/museums
An outstanding museum housing a diverse range of objects from sea dinosaurs to magnificent art. Dynamic temporary exhibitions complement the museum's vast permanent collections. Guaranteed to inspire.

Bristol Zoo Gardens
Clifton, Bristol
Tel: (0117) 974 7300
www.bristolzoo.org.uk
See over 300 species of wildlife from the smallest, rarest tortoise to the largest ape, in beautiful gardens. Voted Zoo of the Year by the Good Britain Guide 2004.

Buckland Abbey
Yelverton, Devon
Tel: (01822) 853607
www.nationaltrust.org.uk
Originally a Cistercian monastery, then home of Sir Francis Drake. Ancient buildings, exhibitions, herb garden, Elizabethan garden , craft workshops and estate walks.

Cheddar Caves and Gorge
Cheddar, Somerset
Tel: (01934) 742343
www.cheddarcaves.co.uk
Beautiful caves located in Cheddar Gorge. Stand in awe at Gough's Cave with its cathedral-like caverns and Cox's Cave with stalagmites and stalactites. Also The Crystal Quest fantasy adventure.

Children's Farm and Smugglers Barn
New Barn Road, Abbotsbury, Dorset
Tel: (01305) 871130
www.abbotsbury-tourism.co.uk
For those wet days, a soft play, undercover adventure with a smuggling theme for children under 11 years. Other activities include rabbit and guinea pig cuddling. Pony rides (extra charge).

Combe Martin Wildlife and Dinosaur Park
Combe Martin, Devon
Tel: (01271) 882486
www.dinosaur-park.com
The land that time forgot. A subtropical paradise with hundreds of birds and animals, and animatronics dinosaurs, so real they're alive!

Compton Acres
Canford Cliffs Road, Poole, Dorset
Tel: (01202) 700778
www.comptonacres.co.uk
Surprise, drama, romance and delight at every turn. Ten distinctive gardens of the world – themes include Italian, Japanese and Roman. Restaurants, craft centre and extensive retail development.

Cotswold Farm Park
Guiting Power, Gloucestershire
Tel: (01451) 850307
www.cotswoldfarmpark.co.uk
Fun on the farm! Observe 50 flocks and herds of British
rare breeds of farm animals and watch seasonal farming
demonstrations. Children's activities, café and gift shop.

Crealy Adventure Park
Sidmouth Road, Clyst St Mary, Devon
Tel: (01395) 233200
www.crealy.co.uk
Crealy offers an unforgettable day packed with magic, fun
and adventure for all the family, with exciting rides, all-
weather attractions and the friendliest animals.

Dairyland Farm World
Tresillian Barton, Summercourt, Cornwall
Tel: (01872) 510246
www.dairylandfarmworld.com
Meet lots of beautiful animals, including lambs, rabbits,
donkeys and llamas, and have a go milking Clarabelle the
Cybercow. Adventure playground, country life museum,
nature trail.

Eden Project
Bodelva, St Austell, Cornwall
Tel: (01726) 811911
www.edenproject.com
An unforgettable experience in a breathtaking, epic
location. Eden is a gateway into the fascinating world
of plants and people.

Exmoor Falconry & Animal Farm
West Lynch Farm, Allerford, Somerset
Tel: (01643) 862816
www.exmoorfalconry.co.uk
Creatures galore – farm animals, rare breeds, pets corner,
birds of prey and owls. Fabulous flying displays daily.
Historic farm buildings. Short activity breaks.

Flambards Village
Culdrose Manor, Helston, Cornwall
Tel: (01326) 573404
www.flambards.co.uk
Let your imagination lead you through the lamp-lit streets
of a full-size reconstuction of a Victorian village with 50 fully
stocked shops, homes, carriages and fashions. Also Britain
in the Blitz wartime street, historic aircraft, science centre
and rides.

Heale Garden & Plant Centre
Middle Woodford, Wiltshire
Tel: (01722) 782504
Mature traditional garden with shrubs, musk and other
roses, and kitchen garden. Authentic Japanese teahouse
in water garden with magnolias and acers. Snowdrops and
aconites in winter. Heavenly.

Jamaica Inn & Daphne du Maurier Smuggling Museum
Jamaica Inn Courtyard, Bolventor, Cornwall
Tel: (01566) 86250
www.jamaicainn.co.uk
High on wild and beautiful Bodmin Moor, visit the famous
Jamaica Inn featuring the Daphne du Maurier smuggling
museum.

Kingston Lacy (National Trust)
Wimborne Minster, Dorset
Tel: (01202) 883402
www.nationaltrust.org.uk
17thC house designed for Sir Ralph Bankes by Sir Roger
Pratt, altered in 19thC. Outstanding collection of paintings,
100-ha (250-acre) wooded park, herd of Devon cattle.

Longleat
Warminster, Wiltshire
Tel: (01985) 844400
www.longleat.co.uk
One not to miss – Elizabethan stately home and safari park
plus a wonderland of 10 family attractions. World's Longest
Hedge Maze, Safari Boats, Pets Corner, Longleat railway
and Adventure Castle.

The Lost Gardens of Heligan
Heligan, Pentewan, Cornwall
Tel: (01726) 845100
www.heligan.com
Justifiably nominated the Nation's Favourite Garden by
viewers of BBC Gardener's World. This world-famous
restoration now extends to over 80ha (200 acres) of superb
working Victorian gardens.

Lyme Regis Philpot Museum
Bridge Street, Lyme Regis, Dorset
Tel: (01297) 443370
www.lymeregismuseum.co.uk
Lots of good tales to tell from fossils to geology, local
history and literary connections – the story of Lyme in
its landscape.

Left visit Buckland Abbey in Yelverton, the home of Sir Francis Drake; journey through gardens of the world at Compton Acres, Poole

Places to visit

Awarded VisitBritain's Quality Assured Visitor Attraction marque.

National Marine Aquarium
Rope Walk, Plymouth
Tel: (01752) 600301
www.national-aquarium.co.uk
A fascinating journey through an amazing underwater world in Britain's biggest aquarium. Discover a mountain stream, wave tank and Caribbean reef complete with sharks.

Newquay Zoo
Trenance Park, Newquay, Cornwall
Tel: (01637) 873342
www.newquayzoo.co.uk
A modern award-winning zoo, where you can have fun and learn at the same time. Hundreds of animals in sub-tropical lakeside gardens.

Oceanarium
Pier Approach, Bournemouth
Tel: (01202) 311993
www.oceanarium.co.uk
Take a thrilling voyage across the oceans of the world to discover a dazzling array of underwater life from elegant seahorses to sinister sharks.

Paignton Zoo Environmental Park
Totnes Road, Paignton, Devon
Tel: (01803) 697500
www.paigntonzoo.org.uk
One of England's largest zoos with over 1200 animals in the beautiful setting of 30ha (75 acres) of botanical gardens. An educational experience for all the family.

Plant World
St Marychurch Road, Newton Abbot, Devon
Tel: (01803) 872939
www.plantworld-devon.co.uk
One and a half hectares (4 acres) of gardens including the unique map of the world gardens and cottage garden. Panoramic views. Comprehensive nursery of rare and more unusual plants.

Powderham Castle
Kenton, Devon
Tel: (01626) 890243
www.powderham.co.uk
Built c1390, restored in 18thC, with Georgian interiors, china, furnishings and paintings. Home of the Courtenays for over 600 years. Take time to enjoy the fine views across the deer park and river Exe.

Roman Baths
Pump Room, Bath
Tel: (01225) 477785
www.romanbaths.co.uk
The birthplace of Bath, one of the country's finest ancient monuments. Wonder at the great Roman temple and bathing complex built around natural hot springs almost 2000 years ago.

St Michael's Mount
Marazion, Cornwall
Tel: (01736) 710507
www.stmichaelsmount.co.uk
A must for every visitor to the area, this atmospheric island with 14thC castle, was originally the site of a Benedictine chapel. Reached by foot, or ferry at high tide in summer.

Steam – Museum of the Great Western Railway

Kemble Drive, Swindon, Wiltshire
Tel: (01793) 466646
www.steam-museum.org.uk
Displays celebrating the Great Western Railway include footplate access on locomotives, detailed reconstructions of life on the railways, people's stories, film and interactive displays.

Above be spooked by the Witch of Wookey at Wookey Hole Caves and Papermill at Wookey Hole; celebrate the Great Western Railway at Steam – Museum of the Great Western Railway **Right** be inspired at the Tate St Ives

This is just a selection of attractions available. Contact any Tourist Information Centre in the region for more ideas.

Stonehenge
Amesbury, Wiltshire
Tel: (01980) 624715
www.english-heritage.org.uk
A real sense of mysticism at this dramatic prehistoric monument, built as a ceremonial centre 5000 years ago. It was remodelled several times in the next 1500 years.

Stourhead House and Garden (National Trust)
Stourton, Wiltshire
Tel: (01747) 841152
www.nationaltrust.org.uk
World-famous landscaped garden laid out c1741-80, with lakes, temples, rare trees and plants. Palladian mansion with magnificent interiors, fine paintings and Chippendale furniture.

The Tank Museum
Bovington, Dorset
Tel: (01929) 405096
www.tankmuseum.co.uk
You can't fail to be impressed by the world's finest display of armoured fighting vehicles from World War I tanks to Challenger, the latest main battle tank of the British Army.

Tate St Ives
Porthmeor Beach, St Ives, Cornwall
Tel: (01736) 796226
www.tate.org.uk
Opened in 1993, the gallery offers a unique introduction to modern art. Changing displays focus on St Ives' renowned modern movement. Major contemporary exhibitions.

Teignmouth Museum
French Street, Teignmouth, Devon
Tel: (01626) 777041
www.lineone.net/~teignmuseum/
A truly local museum whose exhibits include a 16thC cannon and artefacts from Armada wreck, c1920s pier machines and c1877 cannon.

Tintagel Castle (English Heritage)
Tintagel, Cornwall
Tel: (01840) 770328
www.english-heritage.org.uk/tintagel
Awe-inspiring, romantic and a place of Arthurian legend. A medieval ruined castle on wild, wind-swept coast, built largely in 13thC by Richard, Earl of Cornwall.

Totnes Costume Museum – Devonshire Collection of Period Costume
Bogan House, Totnes, Devon
Tel: (01803) 863821
This museum in Bogan House, an historic merchant's house, shows a new exhibition of costumes and accessories each season.

Woodlands Leisure Park
Blackawton, Devon
Tel: (01803) 712598
www.woodlandspark.com

All-weather fun guaranteed with this unique combination of indoor and outdoor attractions – three water coasters, toboggan run, indoor venture centre with rides. Falconry and animals.

Wookey Hole Caves and Papermill
Wookey Hole, Somerset
Tel: (01749) 672243
www.wookey.co.uk
Spectacular caves, the legendary home of the Witch of Wookey. Spooky! Working Victorian paper mill including Old Penny Arcade, Magical Mirror Maze and Cave Diving Museum.

WWT Slimbridge Wetlands Centre
Slimbridge, Gloucestershire
Tel: (01453) 891900
www.wwt.org.uk
Founded by Sir Peter Scott, the centre is home to over 2300 waterbirds of 180 different species. £6.2 million visitor centre, 17m (55ft) observation tower, hides and heated observatory.

South West Tourism

Woodwater Park, Exeter EX2 5WT
T: 0870 442 0880
www.visitsouthwest.co.uk

Travel information

By road:
The region is easily accessible from London, the South East, the North and Midlands by the M6/M5 which extends just beyond Exeter, where it links in with the dual carriageways of the A38 to Plymouth, A380 to Torbay and the A30 into Cornwall. The North Devon Link Road A361 joins junction 37 with the coast of North Devon and the A39, which then becomes the Atlantic Highway into Cornwall.

By rail:
The main towns in the South West are served throughout the year by fast, direct and frequent rail services from all over the country. Trains operate from London (Paddington) to Chippenham, Swindon, Bath, Bristol, Weston-super-Mare, Taunton, Exeter, Plymouth and Penzance, and also from Scotland, the North East and the Midlands to the South West.

A service runs from London (Waterloo) to Exeter, via Salisbury, Yeovil and Crewkerne. Sleeper services operate between Devon and Cornwall and London as well as between Bristol and Glasgow and Edinburgh. Motorail services operate from strategic points to key South West locations.

Visit the following websites for further information on South West England:

www.visitsouthwest.co.uk

www.sw-watersports.com

www.accessiblesouthwest.co.uk

www.swcp.org.uk

Also available from South West Tourism:

Trencherman's Restaurant Guide

Right majestic views across Dartmoor

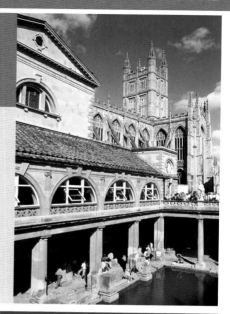

Where to stay in
South West England

All place names in the blue bands, under which accommodation is listed, are shown on the maps at the front of this guide.

A complete listing of all VisitBritain assessed accommodation covered by this guide appears at the back.

Accommodation symbols
Symbols give useful information about services and facilities. Inside the back cover flap you can find a key to these symbols. Keep it open for easy reference.

ASHBURTON, Devon

See display advertisement below

AXMINSTER, Devon Map ref 2D2

★★★★
HOLIDAY PARK

BH&HPA

ANDREWSHAYES CARAVAN PARK

Dalwood, Axminster EX13 7DY
T: (01404) 831225
F: (01404) 831893
E: enquiries@andrewshayes.co.uk
I: www.andrewshayes.co.uk

Friendly, family, countryside park, a short drive to the coast. Outdoor pool, bar and bistro. Seasonal pitches available. Static holiday homes for hire and sale. Short breaks and special offers for camping and holiday-home hire in low season.

Located 150yds off A35 signposted Dalwood, Stockland, at Taunton Cross. Three miles Axminster, 6 miles Honiton.

116	🚐	£9.00–£15.50
4	🚍	£9.00–£15.50
10	⛺	£9.00–£15.50
24	🏠	£115.00–£490.00
130 touring pitches		

193

AXMINSTER continued

★★★★
HOLIDAY PARK

HUNTERS MOON COUNTRY ESTATE
Hawkchurch, Axminster EX13 5UL
T: (01297) 678402
F: (01297) 678720
I: www.ukparks.co.uk/huntersmoon

Payment accepted:
Mastercard, Visa

159		£10.00–£20.00
		£10.00–£20.00
60	▲	£8.00–£14.00
10		£160.00–£460.00
159 touring pitches		

Take A358 to A35 past Axminster; head east for 2 miles, turn left onto B3165; park is on left after 1.5 miles.

BATH, Bath and North East Somerset Map ref 3B2 *Tourist Information Centre Tel: 0906 711 2000 (50p per minute)*

★★★★
TOURING &
CAMPING PARK

BH&HPA

NEWTON MILL CAMPING

Newton Road, Bath BA2 9JF
T: (01225) 333909
E: newtonmill@hotmail.com
I: www.campinginbath.co.uk

In beautiful hidden valley close to city centre (frequent buses). Restaurant/bar beside mill stream. Superior heated amenities including bathrooms. Nearby traffic-free cycle path. Gold conservation award. 10% discount on stays of 7 days (selected periods). New Year package.

OPEN All Year
Payment accepted: Delta, Mastercard, Switch, Visa

On A4 on the outskirts of Bath towards Bristol, take the exit signposted Newton St Loe at the roundabout by the Globe pub. Site is 1 mile on the left.

90		£13.95–£17.50
90		£13.95–£17.50
105	▲	£11.00–£14.50
195 touring pitches		

BEETHAM, Somerset Map ref 2D2

★★★★
TOURING PARK

BH&HPA

See Ad on inside back cover

THE CARAVAN CLUB

FIVE ACRES CARAVAN CLUB SITE
Beetham, Chard
T: (01460) 234519
I: www.caravanclub.co.uk

This peaceful, open site is near Chard (6 miles) - a busy market town. A wonderful spot from which to explore the lovely south Somerset countryside. Open 26 March to 4 October. Special member rates mean you can save your membership subscription in less than a week. Visit www.caravanclub.co.uk to find out more.

Payment accepted: Delta, Mastercard, Switch, Visa

From east on A303, 5.25 miles past roundabout at end of Ilminster bypass, turn left at crossroads into narrow lane signposted Crickleaze, Whitestaunton. Site 2nd entrance on left in 250 yds.

74	🚐	£13.35–£17.60
74	🚙	£13.35–£17.60
74 touring pitches		

BERE REGIS, Dorset Map ref 3B3

★★★
TOURING &
CAMPING PARK

BH&HPA

ROWLANDS WAIT TOURING PARK
Rye Hill, Bere Regis, Wareham BH20 7LP
T: (01929) 472727
F: (01929) 472275
E: bta@rowlandswait.co.uk
I: www.rowlandswait.co.uk

Payment accepted: Amex, Delta, Mastercard, Switch, Visa

71	🚐	£9.50–£12.50
71	🚙	£9.50–£12.50
71	▲	£7.50–£10.50
71 touring pitches		

From A35 (Poole/Dorchester road) at Bere Regis take Wool/ Bovington Tank Museum road. About 0.5 mile up Rye Hill turn right, site 300 yds.

BICKINGTON, Devon Map ref 2D2

★★★★★
HOLIDAY, TOURING
& CAMPING PARK

BH&HPA

LEMONFORD CARAVAN PARK
Bickington, Newton Abbot TQ12 6JR
T: (01626) 821242
F: (01626) 821242
E: mark@lemonford.co.uk
I: www.lemonford.co.uk

50	🚐	£7.50–£11.00
15	🚙	£7.50–£11.00
20	▲	£7.50–£11.00
12	🏠	£140.00–£400.00
85 touring pitches		

From Exeter take A38 towards Plymouth. Take A382 (Drumbridges) turn off to Bickington, 3rd exit. After 3 miles site is on left at bottom of the hill.

David Bellamy Conservation Awards

If you are looking for a site that's environmentally friendly, look for those that have achieved the David Bellamy Conservation Award. Launched in conjunction with the British Holiday & Home Parks Association, this award is given to sites which are committed to protecting and enhancing the environment – from care of the hedgerows and wildlife to recycling waste – and are members of the Association. More information about the award scheme can be found at the back of the guide.

BLACKWATER, Cornwall Map ref 2B3

★★★★
HOLIDAY PARK

BH&HPA

TREVARTH HOLIDAY PARK

Blackwater, Truro TR4 8HR
T: (01872) 560266
F: (01872) 560379
E: trevarth@lineone.net
I: www.ukparks.co.uk/trevarth

Luxury caravan holiday homes, touring and camping. A small, quiet park conveniently situated for north-and south-coast resorts. Level touring and tent pitches with electric hook-up.

Payment accepted: Delta, Mastercard, Switch, Visa

Three hundred metres from Blackwater exit off Chiverton roundabout on A30. Four and a half miles north east of Redruth.

30	🚐	£8.30–£11.50
30	🚗	£8.30–£11.50
30	⛺	£8.30–£11.50
20		£115.00–£490.00
30 touring pitches		

BLANDFORD FORUM, Dorset Map ref 3B3 *Tourist Information Centre Tel: (01258) 454770*

★★★★
TOURING &
CAMPING PARK

BH&HPA

THE INSIDE PARK
Blandford Forum DT11 9AD
T: (01258) 453719
F: (01258) 459921
E: inspark@aol.com
I: members.aol.com/inspark/inspark

Payment accepted:
Mastercard, Switch, Visa

	🚐	£9.50–£16.00
	🚗	£9.50–£16.00
	⛺	£9.50–£16.00
125 touring pitches		

Follow signs from Blandford St Mary, exit off Blandford bypass, 1.75 miles from roundabout.

BOURNEMOUTH, Bournemouth Map ref 3B3 *Tourist Information Centre Tel: (01202) 451700*

★★★★★
HOLIDAY, TOURING
& CAMPING PARK

BH&HPA

MEADOW BANK HOLIDAYS

Stour Way, Christchurch BH23 2PQ
T: (01202) 483597
F: (01202) 483878
E: enquiries@meadowbank-holidays.co.uk
I: www.meadowbank-holiday.co.uk

Bournemouth's closest combined holiday and touring park. Ideally located on the pretty river Stour, between Christchurch, Bournemouth and the New Forest. Open March to October.

Payment accepted: Delta, Mastercard, Switch, Visa

From A35 from Christchurch, west 1.5 miles, turn right at Crooked Beam Restaurant into the Grove, site 3rd left.

41	🚐	£7.00–£25.00
41	🚗	£7.00–£25.00
136		£160.00–£650.00
41 touring pitches		

BRAUNTON, Devon Map ref 2C1 *Tourist Information Centre Tel: (01271) 816400*

★★★★
TOURING &
CAMPING PARK

BH&HPA

LOBB FIELDS CARAVAN AND CAMPING PARK
Saunton Road, Braunton EX33 1EB
T: (01271) 812090
F: (01271) 812090
E: info@lobbfields.com
I: www.lobbfields.com

Payment accepted: Delta,
Mastercard, Switch, Visa

100	🚐	£7.50–£19.00
40	🚗	£7.50–£19.00
40	⛺	£6.00–£19.00
180 touring pitches		

From M5 jct27 A361 from Barnstaple to Ilfracombe. In Braunton take B3231 towards Croyde and Saunton. One mile from Braunton centre on right.

Credit card bookings

If you book by telephone and are asked for your credit card number it is advisable to check the proprietor's policy should you cancel your reservation.

BREAN, Somerset Map ref 2D1

★★★★
TOURING &
CAMPING PARK

BH&HPA
NCC

NORTHAM FARM TOURING PARK
Brean Sands, Burnham-on-Sea TA8 2SE
T: (01278) 751244
F: (01278) 751150
E: enquiries@northamfarm.co.uk
I: www.northamfarm.co.uk

Payment accepted: Delta,
Mastercard, Switch, Visa

350	🚐	£5.00–£16.50
350	🚙	£5.00–£16.50
150	⛺	£5.00–£15.00
350 touring pitches		

From M5 jct 22 follow signs to Brean. Half a mile past Brean Leisure Park through village on right.

🔌 🚗 🏠 🍴 🌳 🗳 ✕ 🖥 🔘 ☺ 🥾 🐕 ☼

BRIDPORT, Dorset Map ref 3A3 *Tourist Information Centre Tel: (01308) 424901*

★★★
HOLIDAY &
CAMPING PARK

BH&HPA

EYPE HOUSE CARAVAN PARK

Eype, Bridport DT6 6AL
T: (01308) 424903
F: (01308) 424903
E: enquiries@eypehouse.co.uk
I: www.eypehouse.co.uk

Small, quiet site, situated 200yds from sea and coastal path. Exceptional views of sea and countryside. No touring caravans.

From Bridport take A35 west, signposted to Eype 1 mile. Follow signs to the sea.

20	🚙	£8.50–£14.50
20	⛺	£8.50–£14.50
35	🏠	£150.00–£400.00
20 touring pitches		

🚗 🏠 🍴 🌳 🗳 ✕ 🖥 🔘 ☺ 🥾 🐕 ☼

★★★★
HOLIDAY, TOURING
& CAMPING PARK

BH&HPA

See Ad below

FRESHWATER BEACH HOLIDAY PARK
Burton Bradstock, Bridport DT6 4PT
T: (01308) 897317
F: (01308) 897336
E: office@freshwaterbeach.co.uk
I: www.freshwaterbeach.co.uk

Payment accepted: Delta,
Mastercard, Switch, Visa,
Euros

350	🚐	£8.00–£26.00
50	🚙	£8.00–£26.00
100	⛺	£8.00–£26.00
60	🏠	£220.00–£650.00
500 touring pitches		

From Bridport take B3157, situated 2 miles on the right.

📺 🔌 🚗 🏠 🍴 🌳 🗳 ✕ 🍴 📺 🖥 🔘 ☺ 🔍 ⛰ 〜 ∪ 🥾 🐕 ♫ ☼

★★★★★
HOLIDAY PARK

GOLDEN CAP HOLIDAY PARK
Seatown, Chideock, Bridport DT6 6JX
T: (01308) 422139
F: (01308) 425672
E: holidays@wdlh.co.uk
I: www.wdlh.co.uk

Payment accepted: Delta,
Mastercard, Switch, Visa

108	🚐	£11.50–£20.00
108	🚙	£11.50–£20.00
159	⛺	£8.50–£15.00
12	🏠	£220.00–£520.00
108 touring pitches		

Continue along the A35 into Chideock, take the turning signposted Seatown (south), follow the signposts for the park.

🔌 🚗 🏠 🍴 🌳 🗳 🖥 🔘 ☺ ⛰ ∪ 🥾 🐕 ☼

Colour maps Colour maps at the front of this guide pinpoint all places in which you will find parks listed.

BRIDPORT continued

★★★★★
HOLIDAY PARK

BH&HPA
NCC

HIGHLANDS END HOLIDAY PARK
Eype, Bridport DT6 6AR
T: (01308) 422139
F: (01308) 425672
E: holidays@wdlh.co.uk
I: www.wdlh.co.uk

Payment accepted: Delta,
Mastercard, Switch, Visa

🚐	£11.50–£20.00	
🚐	£11.50–£20.00	
75	▲	£8.50–£15.00
18	⬜	£175.00–£520.00
120 touring pitches		

One mile west of Bridport along A35, take the first turning on the left signposted Eype. Park is signposted on the right-hand side.

🔌 🔋 🚗 🏠 📶 🚰 🅿️ 🔧 ✕ ⛽ 💻 ☺ 🔍 ⛰ 🔁 ∪ ⚲ 🎣 ▶ 🐕 ☀

BRISTOL, City of Bristol Map ref 3A2 *Tourist Information Centre Tel: 0906 711 2191 (Premium rate number)*

★★★★
TOURING PARK

BH&HPA

See Ad on inside back cover

BALTIC WHARF CARAVAN CLUB SITE

Cumberland Road, Bristol BS1 6XG
T: (0117) 926 8030
I: www.caravanclub.co.uk

A waterside site, right in the heart of Bristol's beautifully redeveloped dockland. Linked in the summer by a river ferry to the city centre. Special member rates mean you can save your membership subscription in less than a week. Visit www.caravanclub.co.uk to find out more.

OPEN All Year
Payment accepted: Delta, Mastercard, Switch, Visa

Leave M5 jct 18 onto A4, under bridge, left lane and follow signs for Historic Harbour/SS Great Britain, into Hotwells Road. Right lane at lights, left lane after pedestrian crossing. Pass over dock bridge. Site on left in about 500yds.

58	🚐	£17.00–£22.00
58	🚐	£17.00–£22.00
58 touring pitches		

🔋 🚗 🏠 📶 🚰 🅿️ 💻 🔲

BRIXHAM, Torbay Map ref 2D2 *Tourist Information Centre Tel: 0906 680 1268 (Premium rate number)*

★★★★
**TOURING &
CAMPING PARK**

BH&HPA

GALMPTON TOURING PARK

Greenway Road, Galmpton, Brixham TQ5 0EP
T: (01803) 842066
F: (01803) 844458
E: galmptontouringpark@hotmail.com
I: www.galmptontouringpark.co.uk

Overlooking the River Dart with superb views from pitches. A quiet base for families and couples to explore Torbay and South Devon. Open Easter to September. Off-peak reductions.

Payment accepted: Delta, Mastercard, Switch, Visa

Take A380 Torbay ring road then A379 to Brixham. Take 2nd right to Galmpton Park through village to park. Site signposted.

60	🚐	£8.30–£14.80
10	🚐	£8.30–£14.80
60	▲	£8.30–£14.80
4	⬜	£180.00–£450.00
120 touring pitches		

🔌 🔋 🚗 🏠 🚰 🅿️ 💻 🔲 ⛰ ⚲ 🐕 ☀

★★★★★
**TOURING &
CAMPING PARK**

BH&HPA

See Ad on inside back cover

HILLHEAD HOLIDAY PARK

Hillhead, Brixham TQ5 0HH
T: (01803) 853204
I: www.caravanclub.co.uk

In a great location with many pitches affording stunning sea views. Swimming pool, evening entertainment, bar, restaurant and much more! Open 8 April to 4 October. Special member rates mean you can save your membership subscription in less than a week. Visit www.caravanclub.co.uk to find out more.

Right off A380 (Newton Abbot). 3 miles onto ring road signposted Brixham. 7 miles turn right, A3022. In 0.75 miles, right onto A379. 2 miles keep left onto B3025. Site entrance on left within 0.25 miles.

230	🚐	£18.00–£23.00
230	🚐	£18.00–£23.00
	▲	On application
230 touring pitches		

🔋 🚗 🏠 📶 🚰 🅿️ 🔧 ✕ ⛽ 💻 🔲 ☺ 🔍 ⛰ 🔁 ∪ 🐕 🎵

★ ★ ★ ★ ★
TOURING PARK

BUDEMEADOWS TOURING HOLIDAY PARK

Budemeadows, Bude EX23 0NA
T: (01288) 361646
F: (01288) 361646
E: holiday@budemeadows.com
I: www.budemeadows.com

Superb centre for surfing, scenery and sightseeing. All usual facilities including heated pool, licensed bar, shop, launderette, playground. Large pitches-no overcrowding.

OPEN All Year
Payment accepted: Mastercard, Switch, Visa

Signposted on A39, 3 miles south of Bude, 200yds past crossroads to Widemouth Bay.

145	🚐	£7.40–£17.00
145	🚙	£7.40–£17.00
145	⛺	£7.40–£17.00
145 touring pitches		

★ ★ ★
TOURING & CAMPING PARK

PENHALT FARM HOLIDAY PARK

Widemouth Bay, Poundstock, Bude EX23 0DG
T: (01288) 361210
F: (01288) 361210
E: den&jennie@penhaltfarm.fsnet.co.uk
I: www.holidaybank.co.uk/penhaltfarmholidaypark

Spectacular, panoramic sea views from most pitches. Friendly, family-run site, ideal for walking, surfing, touring. Site shop, play area, games room. Dogs welcome.

Payment accepted: Delta, Mastercard, Switch, Visa

Travelling south, 4.5 miles from Bude on A39. Take 2nd right into Widemouth Bay, left at bottom. Widemouth Manor Hotel on your left. Our sign is 0.75 miles on the right.

30	🚐	£6.00–£15.00
30	🚙	£6.00–£15.00
78	⛺	£6.00–£13.00
2	🏠	£100.00–£370.00
98 touring pitches		

★ ★ ★ ★
HOLIDAY, TOURING & CAMPING PARK

BH&HPA

UPPER LYNSTONE CARAVAN AND CAMPING SITE
Upton, Bude EX23 0LP
T: (01288) 352017
F: (01288) 359034
E: reception@upperlynstone.co.uk
I: www.upperlynstone.co.uk

Payment accepted:
Mastercard, Switch, Visa

65	🚐	£7.50–£14.00
65	🚙	£7.50–£14.00
65	⛺	£7.50–£14.00
18	🏠	£139.50–£381.00
65 touring pitches		

0.5 miles south of Bude on coastal road to Widemouth Bay. Signposted.

★ ★ ★
HOLIDAY, TOURING & CAMPING PARK

BH&HPA

COASTAL CARAVAN PARK
Annings Lane, Burton Bradstock, Bridport
DT6 4QP
T: (01308) 422139
F: (01308) 425672
E: holidays@wdlh.co.uk
I: www.wdlh.co.uk

	🚐	£11.50–£20.00
	🚙	£11.50–£20.00
	⛺	£8.50–£15.00
40 touring pitches		

From A35 from Bridport follow signs to Burton Bradstock, turn left past the Anchor Hotel. Annings Lane 2nd on right; park is one mile on.

Important note Information on accommodation listed in this guide has been supplied by the proprietors. As changes may occur you are advised to check details at the time of booking.

CAMELFORD, Cornwall Map ref 2B2

★★★
HOLIDAY, TOURING & CAMPING PARK

BH&HPA

JULIOT'S WELL HOLIDAY PARK

Camelford PL32 9RF
T: (01840) 213302
F: (01840) 212700
E: juliotswell@holidaysincornwall.net
I: www.holidaysincornwall.net

Quiet park in 31 acres of beautiful woodland and meadows. Facilities include a swimming pool, bar and restaurant plus more. Close to beach and moor. Open March to October.

Payment accepted: Delta, Mastercard, Switch, Visa

Through Camelford towards Wadebridge on A39, right after Valley Truckle Road sign, then 1st left.

86	£5.00–£10.00
86	£5.00–£10.00
51	£5.00–£10.00
65	£129.00–£559.00
86 touring pitches	

CHARMOUTH, Dorset Map ref 2D2

★★★★
TOURING & CAMPING PARK

BH&HPA

MONKTON WYLD FARM CARAVAN & CAMPING PARK

Monkton Wyld, Bridport DT6 6DB
T: (01297) 34525
F: (01297) 33594
E: holidays@monktonwyld.co.uk
I: www.monktonwyld.co.uk

Beautifully landscaped, level, 60-pitch park. Only three miles from sandy beaches and surrounded by lovely countryside. All the amenities you would expect to find in a quality park. Weekly special-offer rates: £58 low season, £68 mid-season.

A35 from west towards Charmouth, cross Dorset county boundary, next lane left (brown tourist sign), 2nd campsite on left.

£7.40–£15.40
£7.40–£15.40
£7.40–£15.40
60 touring pitches

★★★★★
HOLIDAY, TOURING & CAMPING PARK

See Ad below

SEADOWN HOLIDAY PARK

Bridge Road, Charmouth, Bridport DT6 6QS
T: (01297) 560154
F: (01297) 561130
I: www.seadownholidaypark.co.uk

Payment accepted: Mastercard, Switch, Visa

40	£12.00–£16.00
10	£12.00–£16.00
10	£12.00–£16.00
62	£200.00–£440.00
60 touring pitches	

Leave A35 Bridport to Axminster road, to Charmouth. Turn left into Bridge Road. The site is 100yds directly in front of you.

Map references **The map references refer to the colour maps at the front of this guide. The first figure is the map number; the letter and figure which follow indicate the grid reference on the map.**

CHARMOUTH continued

★★★★★
HOLIDAY, TOURING
& CAMPING PARK

BH&HPA

WOOD FARM CARAVAN AND CAMPING PARK

Charmouth, Bridport DT6 6BT
T: (01297) 560697
F: (01297) 561243
E: holidays@woodfarm.co.uk
I: www.woodfarm.co.uk

Breathtaking views and superb facilities are both on offer at Wood Farm. Our Heritage Coast and spectacular rural scenery are just waiting to amaze you. Senior Citizen offer in low and mid-season for 1-and 2-week stays.

Payment accepted: Delta, Mastercard, Switch, Visa

Off the main A35 to the west of Charmouth. From M5 jct 25 follow A358 to Chard then Axminster. Join A35 towards Bridport. After 4 miles, at roundabout take first exit to Wood Farm.

181	🚐	£10.50–£18.00
	🚐	£10.50–£18.00
35	⛺	£10.50–£15.00
3	🛖	£200.00–£480.00
216 touring pitches		

CHEDDAR, Somerset Map ref 2D1

★★★★
HOLIDAY, TOURING
& CAMPING PARK

BH&HPA

CHEDDAR BRIDGE TOURING PARK

Draycott Road, Cheddar BS27 3RJ
T: (01934) 743048
E: tracy@cheddarbridge.co.uk
I: www.cheddarbridgepark.co.uk

For a peaceful break, just for adults. Five minutes' walk to village, Gorge, caves, Mendip Hills. Luxury heated facilities. Open March to October. Oct rates – £10pn for pitch with hook-up. Shavers/hairdryer use free. Short breaks for static holiday homes Mar/Apr/Oct.

From south west (M5) exit at jct 22. A38 towards Cheddar/Bristol for approx 5 miles. Turn right onto A371 at Cross. Follow signs for Cheddar. We are between St Andrews church and Cheddar football club.

	🚐	£13.00–£15.00
	🚐	£13.00–£15.00
10	⛺	£12.00–£14.00
3	🛖	£225.00–£375.00
45 touring pitches		

CHRISTCHURCH, Dorset Map ref 3B3 *Tourist Information Centre Tel: (01202) 471780*

★★★
CAMPING PARK

BH&HPA

HARROW WOOD FARM CARAVAN PARK
Poplar Lane, Bransgore, Christchurch
BH23 8JE
T: (01425) 672487
F: (01425) 672487
E: harrowwood@caravan-sites.co.uk
I: www.caravan-sites.co.uk

Payment accepted: Delta, Mastercard, Switch, Visa

From A35 Lyndhurst to Christchurch road, turn right at Cat and Fiddle pub, 1.5 miles to Bransgore.

60	🚐	£10.00–£21.00
60	🚐	£10.00–£21.00
14	⛺	£10.00–£15.00
60 touring pitches		

COMBE MARTIN, Devon Map ref 2C1

★★★★
TOURING &
CAMPING PARK

BH&HPA

STOWFORD FARM MEADOWS

Combe Martin, Ilfracombe EX34 0PW
T: (01271) 882476
F: (01271) 883053
E: enquiries@stowford.co.uk
I: www.stowford.co.uk

Recent winner of numerous awards and situated on the fringe of the Exmoor National Park, this park has a reputation for superb facilities and unrivalled value. Open Easter to end October. Low season: one week, only £38.00 (incl electric hook-up). Mid season: one week, only £58.00 (incl electric hook-up).

Situated on the A3123 Woolacombe to Combe Martin road 4 miles west of Combe Martin.

610	🚐	£6.50–£17.00
50	🚐	£6.50–£17.00
50	⛺	£6.50–£20.00
710 touring pitches		

COTSWOLDS

See under Moreton-in-Marsh, Tewkesbury

See also Cotswolds in the South East England section

CROYDE BAY, Devon Map ref 2C1

★★★★
HOLIDAY, TOURING & CAMPING PARK

ROSE AWARD

BH&HPA
NCC

RUDA HOLIDAY PARK

Croyde, Braunton EX33 1NY
T: 0870 420 2997 & (01271) 890671
E: enquiries@parkdeanholidays.co.uk
I: www.parkdeanholidays.co.uk

Set on a superb Blue Flag beach, Croyde Bay. Surf schools, kids' club, family entertainment. Cascades tropical indoor pool. Luxury caravans, lodges and touring. Short breaks available.

OPEN All Year
Payment accepted: Delta, Mastercard, Switch, Visa

From M5 jct 27, take A361 to Barnstaple. Continue on A361 to Braunton. In the centre of Braunton, turn left after 2nd traffic lights onto B3231. Enter Croyde Village and follow signs.

92		£10.00–£30.00
92		£7.00–£30.00
220		£7.00–£26.00
260		£175.00–£865.00
92 touring pitches		

DARTMOOR

See under Bickington, Tavistock

DAWLISH, Devon Map ref 2D2 *Tourist Information Centre Tel: (01626) 215665*

★★★
TOURING & CAMPING PARK

LEADSTONE CAMPING
Warren Road, Dawlish EX7 0NG
T: (01626) 864411
F: (01626) 873833
E: info@leadstonecamping.co.uk
I: www.leadstonecamping.co.uk

Payment accepted: Amex, Delta, Mastercard, Switch, Visa, Euros

28		£13.20–£14.70
28		£10.00–£11.20
109		£10.00–£11.20
137 touring pitches		

Leave M5 motorway at jct 30, take A379 towards Dawlish. As you approach Dawlish turn left on brow of hill signposted Dawlish Warren. Our site is 0.5 miles on right.

★★★★
HOLIDAY PARK

BH&HPA

OAKCLIFF HOLIDAY PARK

Mount Pleasant Road, Dawlish Warren, Dawlish EX7 0ND
T: (01626) 863347
F: (01626) 866636
E: info@oakcliff.co.uk
I: www.oakcliff.co.uk

Award-winning family park in beautiful grounds of elegant Georgian house, only 600yds from Blue Flag beach. Swimming pool, club, entertainment, bistro. Beautiful views. Short breaks available (excl Aug). Over-50s weeks. Gardens week.

Payment accepted: Delta, Mastercard, Switch, Visa, Euros

From M5 jct 30 take A379 to Dawlish. At Dawlish turn left to Dawlish Warren.

50		£175.00–£600.00

DORCHESTER, Dorset Map ref 3B3 *Tourist Information Centre Tel: (01305) 267992*

★★
TOURING & CAMPING PARK

BH&HPA

GIANTS HEAD CARAVAN & CAMPING PARK
Old Sherborne Road, Dorchester DT2 7TR
T: (01300) 341242
E: holidays@giantshead.co.uk
I: www.giantshead.co.uk

50		£7.00–£11.00
50		£7.00–£11.00
50		£7.00–£11.00
50 touring pitches		

Into Dorchester avoiding bypass; at top of town roundabout take Sherbourne Road. After 500yds take right-hand fork at Loders Esso garage. Park is signposted. From Cerne Abbas take Buckland Newton Road.

DULVERTON, Somerset Map ref 2D1

★★★★
TOURING PARK

BH&HPA

See Ad on inside back cover

EXMOOR HOUSE CARAVAN CLUB SITE
Dulverton TA22 9HL
T: (01398) 323268
I: www.caravanclub.co.uk

Very quiet and secluded, in the heart of Lorna Doone country. Shops and pubs within walking distance, Exmoor is on the doorstep. Open 26 March to 2 January 2006. Special member rates mean you can save your membership subscription in less than a week. Visit www.caravanclub.co.uk to find out more.

Payment accepted: Delta, Mastercard, Switch, Visa

From M5 jct 27, B3222 to Dulverton, left over river bridge, 200yds on. Note: two narrow hump bridges on B3222, approach carefully.

64	🚐	£14.60–£20.60
64	🚐	£14.60–£20.60
64 touring pitches		

EXMOOR

See under Combe Martin, Dulverton, Winsford

EXMOUTH, Devon Map ref 2D2 *Tourist Information Centre Tel: (01395) 222299*

Rating
Applied For

BH&HPA

See Ad below

WEBBERS FARM CARAVAN & CAMPING PARK
Castle Lane, Woodbury, Exeter EX5 1EA
T: (01395) 232276
F: (01395) 233389
E: reception@webberspark.co.uk
I: www.webberspark.co.uk

	🚐	£12.00–£16.00
	🚐	£12.00–£16.00
	▲	£12.00–£16.00
2	🛖	£200.00–£450.00
115 touring pitches		

Leave M5 at jct 30 and follow A376 to Exmouth. At 2nd roundabout take B3179 to Budleigh Salterton and Woodbury. From Woodbury village centre follow official brown signs.

FOWEY, Cornwall Map ref 2B3 *Tourist Information Centre Tel: (01726) 833616*

★★★
HOLIDAY, TOURING & CAMPING PARK

BH&HPA

PENHALE CARAVAN AND CAMPING PARK
Penhale, Fowey PL23 1JU
T: (01726) 833425
F: (01726) 833425
E: info@penhale-fowey.co.uk
I: www.penhale-fowey.co.uk

Small, uncrowded park overlooking unspoilt farmland and coast. Close to sandy beaches and many lovely walks. Laundry, free hot showers, small shop for basics.

From A30 West from Lostwithiel, on A390 turn left after 1 mile onto B3269, after 3 miles turn right onto A3082. Penhale 600yds on left.

35	🚐	£5.75–£11.00
16	🚐	£5.75–£11.00
56	▲	£5.75–£11.00
10	🛖	£110.00–£365.00
56 touring pitches		

Credit card bookings
If you book by telephone and are asked for your credit card number it is advisable to check the proprietor's policy should you cancel your reservation.

GLASTONBURY, Somerset Map ref 3A2 *Tourist Information Centre Tel: (01458) 832954*

★★★★★

TOURING &
CAMPING PARK

BH&HPA

THE OLD OAKS TOURING PARK

Wick, Glastonbury BA6 8JS
T: (01458) 831437
F: (01458) 833238
E: info@theoldoaks.co.uk
I: www.theoldoaks.co.uk

An award-winning park, exclusively for adults, set in tranquil, unspoilt countryside with panoramic views, offering spacious, landscaped pitches and excellent amenities. Open 18 March to 2 October. £1pn discount for Senior Citizens (excl high season). No extra charge for serviced pitch for disabled persons.

Payment accepted: Delta, Mastercard, Switch, Visa

From Glastonbury 2 miles towards Shepton Mallet on A361, signed for Wick, site 1 mile. From Wells left after roundabout entering Glastonbury at sign for Wick. Site 1.5 miles.

40		£9.00–£13.00
20		£9.00–£13.00
20	A	£9.00–£13.00
80 touring pitches		

HAYLE, Cornwall Map ref 2B3

★★★★

HOLIDAY PARK

BH&HPA

BEACHSIDE HOLIDAY PARK
Lethlean Lane, Phillack, Hayle TR27 5AW
T: (01736) 753080
F: (01736) 757252
E: reception@beachside.demon.co.uk
I: www.beachside.co.uk

Leave A30 at the large roundabout at the approach to Hayle, take the Hayle road, turn right beside the putting green and signpost showing 'Beachside'. Situated approximately 0.5 miles on right.

		£8.00–£22.00
		£8.00–£22.00
	A	£8.00–£22.00
84 touring pitches		

★★★★

HOLIDAY PARK

BH&HPA

ST IVES BAY HOLIDAY PARK
73 Loggans Road, Loggans, Hayle
TR27 5BH
T: (01736) 752274
F: (01736) 754523
E: stivesbay@bt.connect.com
I: www.stivesbay.co.uk

Payment accepted:
Mastercard, Switch, Visa,
Euros

Exit A30 at Hayle, turn immediately right. Park entrance 500m on the left.

250		£6.50–£23.00
250		£6.50–£23.00
250	A	£6.50–£23.00
250		£125.00–£750.00
250 touring pitches		

HIGHCLIFFE, Dorset Map ref 3B3

★★★★

HOLIDAY PARK

BH&HPA

COBB'S HOLIDAY PARK

32 Gordon Road, Highcliffe, Christchurch BH23 5HN
T: (01425) 273301
F: (01425) 276090

Pleasant family park, enviable location, near New Forest and beaches. Well-stocked shop, launderette, children's playground, licensed club with entertainment. Full-facility units. Colour TV.

Payment accepted: Mastercard, Switch, Visa

Leave A35 near Christchurch, take A337 to Highcliffe, follow brown tourist signs, turn left at traffic lights in village centre. Park is situated 200yds on the left.

45		£220.00–£500.00

Important note Information on accommodation listed in this guide has been supplied by the proprietors. As changes may occur you are advised to check details at the time of booking.

HOLTON HEATH, Dorset Map ref 3B3

★★★★★
TOURING &
CAMPING PARK

BH&HPA

PEAR TREE TOURING PARK

Organford Road, Holton Heath, Poole BH16 6LA
T: (01202) 622434
E: info@visitpeartree.co.uk
I: www.visitpeartree.co.uk

A quiet, family park, laid out with terraces and good natural landscaping. Ideal for relaxing or exploring the Purbeck World Heritage Coastline. Low-season discounts available – please call for details.

Payment accepted: Delta, Mastercard, Switch, Visa

From Poole follow A35 until A351. Follow A351 to Wareham, after 2 miles turn right at first traffic lights. Park is 0.5 miles on left.

76	🚐	£11.50–£17.00
38	🚙	£11.50–£17.00
49	⛺	£10.00–£15.00
125 touring pitches		

ILFRACOMBE, Devon Map ref 2C1 *Tourist Information Centre Tel: (01271) 863001*

★★★★★
HOLIDAY PARK

BH&HPA

BEACHSIDE HOLIDAY PARK
33 Beach Road, Hele, Ilfracombe EX34 9QZ
T: (01271) 863006
F: (01271) 867296
E: enquiries@beachsidepark.co.uk
I: www.beachsidepark.co.uk

OPEN All Year
Payment accepted: Amex, Delta, Diners, Mastercard, Switch, Visa, Euros

27	🏠	£150.00–£620.00

From M5 jct 27. From Ilfracombe take A399 Combe Martin road for 1 mile. Pass Hele Bay Hotel on the left and turn next left (after 100 yds) into Beachside.

★★★★
TOURING &
CAMPING PARK

BH&HPA

HIDDEN VALLEY TOURING & CAMPING PARK

West Down, Ilfracombe EX34 8NU
T: (01271) 813837
F: (01271) 814041
E: relax@hiddenvalleypark.com
I: www.hiddenvalleypark.com

A warm welcome awaits at this beautiful owner-run touring park which offers first-class amenities, including bar. Ideally located for exploring coast and countryside. Look on our website for our special offers and events.

OPEN All Year
Payment accepted: Delta, Mastercard, Switch, Visa

From M5 jct 27 follow A361 to Barnstaple, pass through Barnstaple on A361, signed towards Ilfracombe. We are directly off the A361, 3.5 miles from Braunton, on left.

120	🚐	£7.00–£18.00
60	🚙	£7.00–£18.00
60	⛺	£7.00–£18.00
120 touring pitches		

Town index

This can be found at the back of the guide. If you know where you want to stay the index will give you the page number listing accommodation in your chosen town, city or village.

★★★★
HOLIDAY PARK

BH&HPA

FOREST GLADE HOLIDAY PARK

Kentisbeare, Cullompton EX15 2DT
T: (01404) 841381
F: (01404) 841593
E: nwellard@forest-glade.co.uk
I: www.forest-glade.co.uk

Free indoor heated pool on small, family-managed park surrounded by forest with deer. Large, flat, sheltered pitches. Luxury, all-serviced holiday homes for hire. Club members £1 per night discount on pitch fees. Short breaks available in holiday homes during most of season. Pet-free and non-smoking holiday homes available.

Payment accepted: Delta, Mastercard, Switch, Visa

From Honiton take Dunkerswell road and follow Forest Glade signs. From M5, A373, 2.5 miles at Keepers Cottage Inn then 2.5 miles on Sheldon road. Touring caravans from Honiton direction only via Dunkerswell road.

	£11.00–£14.50
	£11.00–£14.50
	£9.00–£11.00
26	£170.00–£415.00
80 touring pitches	

★★★★★
TOURING & CAMPING PARK

BH&HPA

PICCADILLY CARAVAN PARK
Folly Lane (West), Lacock, Chippenham
SN15 2LP
T: (01249) 730260
E: piccadillylacock@aol.com

39	£10.50–£12.00
39	£10.50–£12.00
4	£10.50–£12.00
43 touring pitches	

Turn right off A350 Chippenham to Melksham road, signposted to Gastard (Folly Lane West), with caravan symbol, situated 300yds on the left.

★★★★
TOURING & CAMPING PARK

BH&HPA

DOLBEARE CARAVAN AND CAMPING PARK
St Ive Road, Saltash PL12 5AF
T: (01752) 851332   OPEN All Year
F: (01752) 851332
E: dolbeare@btopenworld.com
I: www.dolbeare.co.uk

60	£9.50–£15.50
60	£9.50–£15.50
11	£3.50–£15.50
60 touring pitches	

Across Tamar bridge; follow A38 for approximately 4 miles; as you enter Landrake, signpost on A38 giving directions to Dolbeare park.

★★★
TOURING PARK

BH&HPA
NCC

CARDINNEY CARAVAN AND CAMPING PARK
Penberth Valley, St Buryan, Penzance
TR19 6HJ   OPEN All Year except
T: (01736) 810880   Christmas and New Year
F: (01736) 810998   Payment accepted: Delta,
E: cardinney@btinternet.com   Mastercard, Switch, Visa
I: www.cardinney-camping-park.co.uk

	£8.00–£12.00
	£12.00
	£8.00–£12.00
	£84.00–£112.00
105 touring pitches	

On the main A30, signposted 5 miles past Penzance. Large name board on right-hand side.

★★★
HOLIDAY, TOURING & CAMPING PARK

BH&HPA

BOWDENS CREST CARAVAN AND CAMPING PARK
Bowdens, Langport TA10 0DD
T: (01458) 250553   OPEN All Year
F: (01458) 253360   Payment accepted: Delta,
E: bowcrest@btconnect.com   Mastercard, Switch, Visa
I: www.Bowdenscrest.co.uk

	£10.00–£16.00
	£10.00–£16.00
	£8.00–£16.00
10	£135.00–£425.00
30 touring pitches	

From M5 jct 23 A372 out of Langport, north for 1.5 miles. Right on unclassified road.

LANGTON MATRAVERS, Dorset Map ref 3B3

★★★
CAMPING PARK

BH&HPA

TOM'S FIELD CAMPSITE & SHOP
Tom's Field Road, Langton Matravers,
Swanage BH19 3HN
T: (01929) 427110
F: (01929) 427110
E: tomsfield@hotmail.com
I: www.tomsfieldcamping.co.uk

Payment accepted: Amex,
Delta, Switch, Visa, Euros

| 100 | 🚐 | £7.00–£10.50 |
| 100 | ▲ | £7.00–£10.50 |

*Approaching Swanage on A351, turn right onto B3069. At Langton Matravers turn right into Tom's Field Road.
Site at end of road.*

LUXULYAN, Cornwall Map ref 2B2

★★★★
**HOLIDAY, TOURING
& CAMPING PARK**

BH&HPA

CROFT FARM HOLIDAY PARK
Luxulyan PL30 5EQ
T: (01726) 850228
F: (01726) 850498
E: lynpick@ukonline.co.uk
I: www.croftfarm.co.uk

Payment accepted: Delta,
Mastercard, Switch, Visa

52	🚐	£9.20–£13.20
52	🚐	£9.20–£13.20
52	▲	£6.40–£8.40
22	🏠	£139.00–£410.00
52 touring pitches		

*From A390 Liskeard to St Austell road, turn right just past level crossing in St Blazey (signed Luxulyan). Turn
right after 1.25 miles, right again at next T-jct. Park is on your left approximately 0.5 miles on.*

LYME REGIS, Dorset

See display advertisement below

MALMESBURY, Wiltshire Map ref 3B2 *Tourist Information Centre Tel: (01666) 823748*

★★
**TOURING &
CAMPING PARK**

BH&HPA

BURTON HILL CARAVAN AND CAMPING PARK
Arches Lane, Malmesbury SN16 0EH
T: (01666) 826880
F: (01666) 826880
E: stay@burtonhill.co.uk
I: www.burtonhill.co.uk

Payment accepted: Delta,
Mastercard, Switch, Visa

30	🚐	£9.00–£12.00
30	🚐	£9.00–£12.00
30	▲	£9.00–£12.00
30 touring pitches		

*M4 jct 17, take A429 north towards Cirencester. Left into Arches Lane on approaching Malmesbury. From the
north, A429 from Circester towards Chippenham. Right into Arches Lane on leaving Malmesbury.*

MARTOCK, Somerset Map ref 3A3

Rating
Applied For

BH&HPA
NCC

SOUTHFORK CARAVAN PARK
Parrett Works, Martock TA12 6AE
T: (01935) 825661
F: (01935) 825122
E: southfork.caravans@virgin.net
I: www.ukparks.co.uk/southfork

OPEN All Year
Payment accepted: Amex,
Delta, Mastercard, Switch,
Visa

23	🚐	£8.00–£11.00
23	🚐	£8.00–£11.00
7	▲	£8.00–£11.00
3	🏠	£150.00–£280.00
30 touring pitches		

*From East – A303. Take exit signposted Stoke-sub-Hamdon and Martock. At T-jct turn left and follow camping
signs. From West – A303. 6 miles east of Ilminster at roundabout take 1st exit, signposted South Petherton,
follow signs.*

Map references The map references refer to the colour maps at the front of
this guide. The first figure is the map number; the letter and figure which follow
indicate the grid reference on the map.

MORETON-IN-MARSH, Gloucestershire Map ref 3B1

★★★★★
TOURING &
CAMPING PARK

BH&HPA

See Ad on inside back cover

MORETON-IN-MARSH CARAVAN CLUB SITE

Bourton Road, Moreton-in-Marsh GL56 0BT
T: (01608) 650519
I: www.caravanclub.co.uk

An attractive, well-wooded site within easy walking distance of market town of Moreton-in-Marsh. On-site facilities include crazy golf, volleyball and boules. Large dog-walking area. Special member rates mean you can save your membership subscription in less than a week. Visit www.caravanclub.co.uk to find out more.

OPEN All Year
Payment accepted: Delta, Mastercard, Switch, Visa

From Moreton-in-Marsh on A44 the site entrance is on the right 250yds past the end of the speed limit sign.

182	🚐	£16.10–£21.50
182	🚏	£16.10–£21.50
182 touring pitches		

THE CARAVAN CLUB

MORTEHOE, Devon Map ref 2C1

★★★★
HOLIDAY, TOURING
& CAMPING PARK

BH&HPA

NORTH MORTE FARM CARAVAN AND CAMPING PARK

North Morte Road, Mortehoe,
Woolacombe EX34 7EG
T: (01271) 870381
F: (01271) 870115
E: info@northmortefarm.co.uk
I: www.northmortefarm.co.uk

Payment accepted: Delta,
Mastercard, Switch, Visa

25	🚐	£9.00–£15.00
		£9.00–£15.00
150	⛺	£9.00–£15.00
24	🏠	£200.00–£460.00

6 miles from Ilfracombe, near to the sea. Take B3343 to Mortehoe, turn right at post office, park 500yds on left.

MUCHELNEY, Somerset Map ref 2D1

★★★
TOURING &
CAMPING PARK

BH&HPA

THORNEY LAKES AND CARAVAN PARK

Thorney West Farm, Langport TA10 0DW
T: (01458) 250811
E: enquiries@thorneylakes.co.uk
I: www.thorneylakes.co.uk

36	🚐	£10.00–£12.00
36	🚏	£10.00–£12.00
36	⛺	£10.00–£12.00
36 touring pitches		

Turn off A303 signposted Kingsbury Episcopi. In village turn right at T-jct signposted Muchelney, Langport. Site on right after about 1.25 miles.

NEWQUAY, Cornwall Map ref 2B2 *Tourist Information Centre Tel: (01637) 854020*

★★★★
HOLIDAY PARK

BH&HPA

See Ad below

HENDRA HOLIDAY PARK

Lane, Newquay TR8 4NY
T: (01637) 875778
F: (01637) 879017
E: hendra.cornwall@dial.pipex.com
I: www.hendra-holidays.com

Payment accepted:
Mastercard, Switch, Visa

588	🚐	£8.40–£14.00
588	🚏	£8.40–£14.00
588	⛺	£8.40–£14.00
254	🏠	£139.00–£795.00

Take A30 to the Highgate Hill junction, follow the signs for the A392 to Newquay. At Quintrell Downs go straight across the roundabout, Hendra is 0.5 miles on the left.

⭐ **Ratings** All accommodation in this guide has been rated, or is awaiting a rating, by a trained VisitBritain assessor.

NEWQUAY continued

★★★★
HOLIDAY PARK

BH&HPA
NCC

HOLYWELL BAY HOLIDAY PARK

Holywell Bay, Newquay TR8 5PR
T: 0870 420 2997 & (01637) 871111
E: enquiries@parkdeanholidays.co.uk
I: www.parkdeanholidays.co.uk

Family park nestling in the Ellenglaze Valley, a short stroll to the stunning beach. Luxury caravans and touring. Kids' club, live family entertainment, heated pool and waterslide. Short breaks available.

OPEN All Year except Christmas and New Year
Payment accepted: Mastercard, Switch, Visa

Turn right off the A3075, signposted Holywell Bay, 3 miles west of Newquay.

244		£9.00–£26.00
244		£7.00–£26.00
244		£7.00–£23.00
166		£145.00–£725.00
244 touring pitches		

★★★★★
HOLIDAY PARK

BH&HPA

MAWGAN PORTH HOLIDAY PARK

Mawgan Porth, Newquay TR8 4BD
T: (01637) 860322
E: mawganporthhp@fsbdial.co.uk
I: www.mawganporth.co.uk

Between Padstow and Newquay, luxury caravans and bungalows landscaped amongst trees and equipped to high standard. Beach 400m, heated outdoor pool, shop, play area, laundry. Couple's discount on selected accommodation. Discount on 2-week holidays, selected dates.

OPEN All Year
Payment accepted: Mastercard, Switch, Visa

A30 (Reduth) follow signs to Newquay and Airport. Follow B3276, passing airport on left. At T-junction turn right to Mawgan Porth. In village cross bridge, first right, 400m on left.

27		£220.00–£670.00

Credit card bookings

If you book by telephone and are asked for your credit card number it is advisable to check the proprietor's policy should you cancel your reservation.

NEWQUAY continued

★★★★
HOLIDAY PARK

BH&HPA
NCC

NEWQUAY HOLIDAY PARK

Newquay TR8 4HS
T: 0870 420 2997 & (01637) 871111
E: enquiries@parkdeanholidays.co.uk
I: www.parkdeanholidays.co.uk

A beautiful location. Set in 60 acres of countryside near the Cornish coastline, only a short distance from Newquay. Short breaks available.

OPEN All Year except Christmas and New Year
Payment accepted: Mastercard, Switch, Visa

Follow A30 Bodmin to Redruth road, after iron bridge turn right signed RAF St Mawgan. After 7 miles and 1 mile roundabout, signs to Newquay Holiday Park.

60	£9.00–£26.00
60	£7.00–£26.00
60	£7.00–£23.00
140	£135.00–£715.00

60 touring pitches

★★★★
TOURING PARK

BH&HPA

PORTH BEACH TOURIST PARK
Alexandra Road, Porth, Newquay TR7 3NH
T: (01637) 876531
F: (01637) 871227
E: info@porthbeach.co.uk
I: www.porthbeach.co.uk

Payment accepted: Delta, Mastercard, Switch, Visa

102	£9.00–£26.00
74	£9.00–£26.00
175	£9.00–£26.00
18	£220.00–£660.00

201 touring pitches

Take A392 from Indian Queens A30. At mini-roundabout turn right, B3276.

★★★★
**TOURING &
CAMPING PARK**

BH&HPA

TRELOY TOURIST PARK
Newquay TR8 4JN
T: (01637) 872063 & 876279
E: holidays@treloy.co.uk
I: www.treloy.co.uk

Payment accepted: Delta, Mastercard, Switch, Visa

140	£8.00–£13.00
140	£8.00–£13.00
140	£8.00–£13.00

140 touring pitches

A30 into Cornwall. End of dual carriageway follow A30 Newquay/Redruth road, pass Little Chef on left and after iron bridge then right, (Highgate Hill). After 3 miles at roundabout follow A3059. Signposted after 4 miles.

NEWTON ABBOT, Devon

See display advertisement below

ORCHESTON, Wiltshire Map ref 3B2

★★★
**TOURING &
CAMPING PARK**

BH&HPA

STONEHENGE TOURING PARK
Orcheston, Salisbury SP3 4SH
T: (01980) 620304
E: stonehengetouringpark@supanet.com
I: stonehengetouringpark.supanet.com

OPEN All Year
Payment accepted: Delta, Mastercard, Switch, Visa

30	£6.50–£11.50
30	£6.50–£11.50
30	£6.50–£11.50

30 touring pitches

A360 from Shrewton to Devizes, after 0.5 miles turn right to Orcheston past Crown Cottage.

NB

Important note Information on accommodation listed in this guide has been supplied by the proprietors. As changes may occur you are advised to check details at the time of booking.

ORGANFORD, Dorset Map ref 3B3

★★★
TOURING &
CAMPING PARK

BH&HPA

ORGANFORD MANOR CARAVANS & HOLIDAYS

The Lodge, Organford, Poole BH16 6ES
T: (01202) 622202
F: (01202) 623278
E: organford@lds.co.uk

A quiet, country site in the wooded grounds of the manor-house, level and grassy. Good facilities; surrounded by farmland but centrally placed. 10% discount off a 4-night stay in May, Jun and Sep, low season times only (not Bank Holiday weeks).

From Poole A35 towards Dorchester. First turning left off A35 after roundabout, junction with A351 to Wareham. First drive entrance on right.

30	🚐	£9.00–£10.50
10	🚐	£8.00–£9.50
30	⛺	£9.00–£10.50
4	🏠	£170.00–£220.00
70 touring pitches		

OWERMOIGNE, Dorset Map ref 3B3

★★★★
HOLIDAY, TOURING
& CAMPING PARK

BH&HPA

SANDYHOLME HOLIDAY PARK
Moreton Road, Owermoigne, Dorchester DT2 8HZ
T: (01305) 852677
F: (01305) 854677
E: smeatons@sandyholme.co.uk
I: www.sandyholme.co.uk

Payment accepted: Delta, Mastercard, Switch, Visa

One mile inland off A352. Through village of Owermoigne, 1 mile.

50	🚐	£9.00–£16.00
52	🚐	£9.00–£16.00
70	⛺	£9.00–£13.50
26	🏠	£160.00–£500.00
50 touring pitches		

PADSTOW, Cornwall Map ref 2B2 *Tourist Information Centre Tel: (01841) 533449*

★★★★
HOLIDAY, TOURING
& CAMPING PARK

BH&HPA

CARNEVAS FARM HOLIDAY PARK

Carnevas Farm, St Merryn, Padstow PL28 8PN
T: (01841) 520230
F: (01841) 520230

Family-run park for families. Situated on the North Cornish coast. Padstow four miles. Nearest beach 0.5 miles. Great surfing. Excellent facilities. Cleanliness assured.

At end of Bodmin bypass, on A30 carry on under iron bridge. Turn right towards Newquay Airport. Turn onto A39, then left onto B3271, Padstow. At St Merryn turn left onto B3276. Two miles, towards Porthcothan Bay, opposite Tredrea Inn.

	🚐	£6.50–£13.00
	🚐	£6.50–£13.00
	⛺	£6.50–£13.00
9	🏠	£160.00–£500.00
198 touring pitches		

★★★★
TOURING &
CAMPING PARK

BH&HPA

THE LAURELS HOLIDAY PARK

Whitecross, Wadebridge PL27 7JQ
T: (01208) 813341
F: (01208) 816590
E: anicholson@thelaurelsholidaypark.co.uk
I: www.thelaurelsholidaypark.co.uk

Small, relaxing park with individual, shrub-lined pitches. All with electric, grass and level in beautiful surroundings. Ideal touring centre. Open Easter to October.

Turn onto A389 for Padstow off A39 west of Wadebridge. Entrance 20yds from junction.

30	🚐	£5.00–£14.00
30	🚐	£5.00–£14.00
30	⛺	£5.00–£14.00
30 touring pitches		

PAIGNTON, Torbay Map ref 2D2 *Tourist Information Centre Tel: 0906 680 1268 (Premium rate number)*

★★★★

HOLIDAY, TOURING & CAMPING PARK

BH&HPA

HIGHER WELL FARM HOLIDAY PARK
Waddeton Road, Stoke Gabriel, Totnes
TQ9 6RN
T: (01803) 782289
E: higherwell@talk21.com
I: www.ukparks.co.uk/higherwell

Payment accepted:
Mastercard, Switch, Visa

80		£7.50–£12.00
80		£7.50–£12.00
80		£7.50–£12.00
18		£140.00–£400.00
80 touring pitches		

From Paignton, A385 to Totnes turn left at Parkers Arms for Stoke Gabriel, 1.5 miles turn left to Waddeton, situated 200yds down the road.

PENZANCE, Cornwall Map ref 2A3 *Tourist Information Centre Tel: (01736) 362207*

★★★

HOLIDAY & TOURING PARK

BH&HPA

TOWER PARK CARAVANS AND CAMPING
St Buryan, Penzance TR19 6BZ
T: (01736) 810286
F: (01736) 810286
E: enquiries@towerparkcamping.co.uk
I: www.towerparkcamping.co.uk

Payment accepted: Delta,
Mastercard, Switch, Visa

		£6.50–£10.90
		£6.50–£10.90
		£6.50–£9.00
5		£128.00–£295.00
102 touring pitches		

Off A30 3 miles west of Penzance, B3283 to St Buryan, fork right and keep right for 400yds.

POLRUAN-BY-FOWEY, Cornwall Map ref 2B3

★★★★

HOLIDAY, TOURING & CAMPING PARK

BH&HPA

POLRUAN HOLIDAYS (CAMPING & CARAVANNING)
Townsend, Polruan, Fowey PL23 1QH
T: (01726) 870263
F: (01726) 870263
E: polholiday@aol.com

7		£9.00–£13.00
7		£9.00–£13.00
40		£7.00–£11.00
11		£110.00–£380.00
47 touring pitches		

A38 to Dobwalls, left on A390 to East Taphouse. Left on B3359 after 4.5 miles turn right signposted Polruan.

£ Prices Please check prices and other details at the time of booking.

POLZEATH, Cornwall Map ref 2B2

★★
HOLIDAY PARK

VALLEY CARAVAN PARK
Polzeath, Wadebridge PL27 6SS
T: (01208) 862391
F: (01208) 869231
E: valleypark@tiscali.co.uk
I: www.valleycaravanpark.co.uk

OPEN All Year
Payment accepted: Delta,
Mastercard, Switch, Visa

	£10.00–£20.00
	£10.00–£17.00
	£5.00–£20.00
50	£125.00–£635.00
65 touring pitches	

From Wadebridge, take the B3314 to Polzeath – 7 miles. Our entrance is opposite the beach between the shops.

POOLE, Poole Map ref 3B3 *Tourist Information Centre Tel: (01202) 253253*

★★★
**TOURING &
CAMPING PARK**

BH&HPA

BEACON HILL TOURING PARK
Blandford Road North, Nr Lytchett Minster,
Poole BH16 6AB
T: (01202) 631631
F: (01202) 625749
E: bookings@beaconhilltouringpark.co.uk
I: www.beaconhilltouringpark.co.uk

120	£11.50–£23.00
50	£10.00–£23.00
50	£10.00–£23.00
170 touring pitches	

On A350, 0.25 miles from junction of A35 and A350 towards Blandford. Approximately 3 miles north of Poole.

PORTLAND, Dorset Map ref 3B3

★★★★★
HOLIDAY PARK

COVE HOLIDAY PARK
Pennsylvania Road, Portland DT5 1HU
T: (01305) 821286
F: (01305) 823224
E: coveholidaypark@onetel.net.uk

Payment accepted:
Mastercard, Switch, Visa

| 25 | £140.00–£470.00 |

From A35 from Weymouth, follow signs for Portland; proceed to top of isle; Cove Park is approximately 0.5 miles past Easton Square, heading towards Portland Bill.

PORTREATH, Cornwall Map ref 2B3

★★★
TOURING PARK

CAMBROSE TOURING PARK
Portreath Road, Cambrose, Redruth
TR16 4HT
T: (01209) 890747
F: (01209) 891665
E: cambrosetouringpark@supanet.com
I: www.cambrosetouringpark.co.uk

	£7.50–£12.50
	£7.50–£12.50
	£7.50–£12.50
	£80.00–£165.00
60 touring pitches	

From new A30, 3 miles north on B3300 Portreath/Redruth road. Turn right, 100yds on left.

★★★★
HOLIDAY PARK

TEHIDY HOLIDAY PARK
Harris Mill, Redruth TR16 4JQ
T: (01209) 216489
F: (01209) 216489
E: holiday@tehidy.co.uk
I: www.tehidy.co.uk

18	£7.50–£11.00
3	£7.50–£11.00
18	£7.50–£11.00
20	£120.00–£395.00

South on A30 take Porthtowan exit. Right at 1st roundabout, 1st left to Portreath.

Special breaks

Many establishments offer special promotions and themed breaks. These are highlighted in red. (All such offers are subject to availability.)

★★★★
HOLIDAY PARK

BH&HPA

LANYON HOLIDAY PARK

Loscombe Lane, Four Lanes, Redruth TR16 6LP
T: (01209) 313474
F: (01209) 313422
E: jamierielly@btconnect.com
I: www.lanyonholidaypark.co.uk

Lovely friendly park, in the heart of West Cornwall. Ideal touring base, heated shower block, bar/restaurant, launderette, play park, pets welcome. Open mid-February to mid-January.

Payment accepted: Amex, Delta, Diners, Mastercard, Switch, Visa

From A30 turn off signposted for Redruth. Follow signs Redruth/Helston. Take B3297 towards Helston, enter Four Lanes village and follow signs to Lanyon Park.

25	⌷	£12.00–£18.00
25	⌷	£12.00–£18.00
50	▲	£6.00–£8.00
16	⌷	£140.00–£500.00
25 touring pitches		

★★★★★
HOLIDAY PARK

ROSE AWARD

BH&HPA
NCC

RIVER VALLEY COUNTRY PARK

Relubbus, Penzance TR20 9ER
T: (01736) 763398
F: (01736) 763398
E: rivervalley@surfbay.dircon.co.uk
I: www.rivervalley.co.uk

Partly wooded park alongside luxury lodges and caravan holiday homes for sale or hire. Spacious pitches for touring caravans, motor homes or tents. Open March to December. Couple's discount, subject to availability.

Payment accepted: Amex, Mastercard, Switch, Visa

From A394 A30 St Michael's Mount roundabout, left A394 Helston road, left next roundabout B3280. Straight through to Relubbus.

70	⌷	£8.50–£13.50
10	⌷	£8.50–£13.50
19	▲	£7.00–£12.00
45	⌷	£135.00–£620.00

★★★★
HOLIDAY PARK

ROSE AWARD

BH&HPA

KENNEGGY COVE HOLIDAY PARK

Higher Kenneggy, Penzance TR20 9AU
T: (01736) 763453
E: enquiries@kenneggycove.co.uk
I: www.kenneggycove.co.uk

Quiet site in magnificent situation. Sea views. Ten minutes' walk to coastal path and secluded beach. Shop and take-away service. French and German spoken. 10% discount for Senior Citizens Mar-May and Sep-Oct. No single-sex groups or large parties.

Take the lane to Higher Kenneggy, south off the A394 at the Helston end of Rosudgeon. The park is 0.5 miles down the lane on the left.

	⌷	£7.00–£14.00
	⌷	£7.00–£14.00
	▲	£7.00–£14.00
9	⌷	£150.00–£450.00
60 touring pitches		

Map references The map references refer to the colour maps at the front of this guide. The first figure is the map number; the letter and figure which follow indicate the grid reference on the map.

RUAN MINOR, Cornwall Map ref 2B3

★★★★
HOLIDAY PARK

BH&HPA
NCC

SEA ACRES HOLIDAY PARK

Kennack Sands, Ruan Minor, Helston TR12 7LT
T: 0870 420 2997 & (01326) 290064
E: enquiries@parkdeanholidays.co.uk
I: www.parkdeanholidays.co.uk

Situated in a magnificent location on the Lizard Peninsula and close to Helston, this park overlooks Kennack Sands beach. Luxury holiday homes, kids' club and family entertainment. Short breaks available.

OPEN All Year except Christmas and New Year
Payment accepted: Mastercard, Switch, Visa

Take the A3083 from Helston, then the B3293 to Coverack, turn right at crossroads signed Kennack Sands, site on right overlooking beach.

132	⌂	£120.00–£725.00

★★★
HOLIDAY &
TOURING PARK

BH&HPA

SILVER SANDS HOLIDAY PARK
Gwendreath, Kennack Sands, Ruan Minor,
Helston TR12 7LZ
T: (01326) 290631
F: (01326) 290631
E: enquiries@silversandsholidaypark.co.uk
I: www.silversandsholidaypark.co.uk

15		£11.00–£16.50
15		£11.00–£16.50
20	▲	£9.50–£13.70
14	⌂	£130.00–£390.00
35 touring pitches		

A3083 from Helston past RNAS Culdrose, left onto B3293 (St Keverne). Right turn after passing Goonhilly satellite station. Left after 1.5 miles to Gwendreath.

ST AGNES, Cornwall Map ref 2B3

★★★★
TOURING PARK

BH&HPA

BEACON COTTAGE FARM TOURING PARK
Beacon Drive, St Agnes TR5 0NU
T: (01872) 552347
E: beaconcottagefarm@lineone.net
I: www.beaconcottagefarmholidays.co.uk

Payment accepted: Amex,
Delta, Mastercard, Switch,
Visa

60		£8.00–£16.00
60		£8.00–£16.00
60	▲	£8.00–£16.00
60 touring pitches		

From A30 take B3277 to St Agnes, follow signs to park.

ST AUSTELL, Cornwall Map ref 2B3 *Tourist Information Centre Tel: (01726) 879500*

★★★★★
HOLIDAY, TOURING
& CAMPING PARK

ROSE AWARD

BH&HPA

RIVER VALLEY HOLIDAY PARK

Pentewan Road, London Apprentice, St Austell PL26 7AP
T: (01726) 73533
F: (01726) 73533
E: river.valley@tesco.net
I: www.cornwall-holidays.co.uk

Peace and tranquillity reign in this family-owned, secluded and immaculate park. Lots of lovely woodland walks and cycle trails.

Take B3273 from St Austell to Mevagissey. When entering London Apprentice, park is on left-hand side.

		£8.00–£20.00
		£8.00–£20.00
	▲	£8.00–£20.00
40	⌂	£200.00–£575.00
45 touring pitches		

Credit card bookings

If you book by telephone and are asked for your credit card number it is advisable to check the proprietor's policy should you cancel your reservation.

ST AUSTELL continued

★★★★★
HOLIDAY PARK

ROSE AWARD

BH&HPA

SUN VALLEY HOLIDAY PARK

Pentewan Road, St Austell PL26 6DJ
T: (01726) 843266
F: (01726) 843266
E: reception@sunvalley-holidays.co.uk
I: www.sunvalley-holidays.co.uk

Family-run park in wooded valley one mile from sea. Holiday homes, apartments or timber bungalows. Ideal touring centre. Seven miles to Eden Project. Open March to October.

Payment accepted: Delta, Mastercard, Switch, Visa, Euros

From A30 take A391 to St Austell, then B3273 to Mevagissey. Site is 2 miles on right.

🚐		£12.00–£26.00
🚛		£12.00–£26.00
▲		£12.00–£26.00
65	🛏	£140.00–£630.00
22 touring pitches		

★★★★
HOLIDAY PARK

BH&HPA
NCC

TREWHIDDLE HOLIDAY ESTATE

Trewhiddle, St Austell PL26 7AD
T: (01726) 879420
F: (01726) 879421
E: dmcclelland@btconnect.com
I: www.trewhiddle.co.uk

Ideally situated for touring Cornwall, 15 minutes from the Eden Project and Heligan Gardens. Three beaches within four miles. Touring and camping from £50 per week. Discounts for 2-week bookings in static caravans during low and mid-season.

OPEN All Year
Payment accepted: Delta, Mastercard, Switch, Visa

From the A390 turn south on B3273 to Mevagissey, site 0.75 miles from the roundabout on the right.

105	🚐	£10.00–£20.00
105	🚛	£10.00–£20.00
105	▲	£10.00–£20.00
40	🛏	£140.00–£550.00
105 touring pitches		

ST IVES, Cornwall Map ref 2B3 *Tourist Information Centre Tel: (01736) 796297*

★★★★★
TOURING PARK

BH&HPA

POLMANTER TOURIST PARK
Halsetown, St Ives TR26 3LX
T: (01736) 795640
F: (01736) 793607
E: reception@polmanter.com
I: www.polmanter.com

Payment accepted: Delta, Mastercard, Switch, Visa

🚐		£10.00–£23.00
🚛		£10.00–£23.00
▲		£10.00–£18.00
260 touring pitches		

A3074 to St Ives from A30, 1st left at mini-roundabout take route to St Ives (Halsetown). Turn right at inn, signposted.

ST JUST IN ROSELAND, Cornwall Map ref 2B3

★★★★★
TOURING PARK

BH&HPA

TRETHEM MILL TOURING PARK

St Just in Roseland, Nr St Mawes, Truro TR2 5JF
T: (01872) 580504
F: (01872) 580968
E: reception@trethem.com
I: www.trethem.com

We offer peace and tranquillity with an exceptional standard of facilities. Caravan Park of the year 2002, Cornwall Tourist Board. Open April to mid-October.

Payment accepted: Delta, Mastercard, Switch, Visa, Euros

A3078 towards Tregony/St Mawes, over Tregony bridge. After 5 miles follow brown caravan and camping signs from Trewithian. Look for the site 2 miles beyond Trewithian on the right-hand side.

84	🚐	£10.00–£14.00
84	🚛	£10.00–£14.00
84	▲	£10.00–£14.00
84 touring pitches		

ST LEONARDS, Dorset Map ref 3B3

★★★★
TOURING &
CAMPING PARK

BH&HPA
NCC

See Ad p18

FOREST EDGE TOURING PARK
229 Ringwood Road, St Leonards,
Ringwood BH24 2SD
T: (01590) 648331
F: (01590) 645610
E: holidays@shorefield.co.uk
I: www.shorefield.co.uk

OPEN All Year
Payment accepted: Delta,
Mastercard, Switch, Visa

167		£7.50–£25.00
167		£7.50–£25.00
167		£7.50–£25.00
167 touring pitches		

From M27 jct 1. Off A31, 3 miles west of Ringwood.

★★★★
HOLIDAY, TOURING
& CAMPING PARK

BH&HPA
NCC

See Ad p18

OAKDENE FOREST PARK
St Leonards, Ringwood BH24 2RZ
T: (01590) 648331
F: (01590) 645610
E: holidays@shorefield.co.uk
I: www.shorefield.co.uk

OPEN All Year
Payment accepted: Delta,
Mastercard, Switch, Visa

90		£7.50–£30.00
90		£7.50–£30.00
53		£7.50–£28.00
117		£175.00–£1,216.00
90 touring pitches		

On A31, 3 miles west of Ringwood. After 2nd roundabout look for footbridge over road, then turn left down lane.

SALCOMBE, Devon Map ref 2C3 *Tourist Information Centre Tel: (01548) 843927*

★★★★
TOURING &
CAMPING PARK

BH&HPA

KARRAGEEN CARAVAN AND CAMPING PARK

Bolberry, Malborough, Kingsbridge TQ7 3EN
T: (01548) 561230
F: (01548) 560192
E: phil@karrageen.co.uk
I: www.karrageen.co.uk

Small park with character overlooking a valley, with sea views. Gently terraced, level, tree-lined pitches. Beach one mile. Site shop. Hot take-away food. Open 15 March to 30 September. Discounted weekly rates for over 50s (excl high season) from £45.

Take A381 Kingsbridge to Salcombe road, turn sharp right through Malborough village, following signs to Bolberry, for 0.6 miles. Turn right to Bolberry, after 0.9 miles park is on right.

20		£8.00–£14.00
65		£8.00–£14.00
65		£8.00–£14.00
6		£250.00–£450.00
70 touring pitches		

SALISBURY PLAIN

See under Orcheston, Warminster

SIDBURY, Devon Map ref 2D2

★★★★★
TOURING PARK

BH&HPA

See Ad on inside back cover

PUTTS CORNER CARAVAN CLUB SITE

Putts Corner, Sidbury, Sidmouth EX10 0QQ
T: (01404) 42875
I: www.caravanclub.co.uk

A quiet site in pretty surroundings, with a private path to the local pub. Bluebells create a sea of blue in spring, followed by foxgloves. Open 26 March to 1 November. Special member rates mean you can save your membership subscription in less than a week. Visit www.caravanclub.co.uk to find out more.

Payment accepted: Delta, Mastercard, Switch, Visa

From M5 jct 25, A375 signposted Sidmouth in 2.5 miles. Turn right at Hare and Hounds Inn onto B3174. In about 0.25 miles turn right into site entrance.

113		£14.60–£20.60
113		£14.60–£20.60
113 touring pitches		

 Confirm your booking  You are advised to confirm your booking in writing.

SIDMOUTH, Devon Map ref 2D2 *Tourist Information Centre Tel: (01395) 516441*

★★★★★

**HOLIDAY &
TOURING PARK**

BH&HPA

SALCOMBE REGIS CAMPING AND CARAVAN PARK
Salcombe Regis, Sidmouth EX10 0JH
T: (01395) 514303
F: (01395) 514314   Payment accepted: Delta,
E: info@salcombe-regis.co.uk   Mastercard, Switch, Visa
I: www.salcombe-regis.co.uk

40	🚐	£8.00–£13.50
40	🚐	£8.00–£13.50
60	⛺	£8.00–£13.50
10	🏠	£145.00–£500.00
100 touring pitches		

One and a half miles east of Sidmouth, signposted off the A3052 road.

SOUTH MOLTON, Devon Map ref 2C1

★★★

**HOLIDAY, TOURING
& CAMPING PARK**

BH&HPA

YEO VALLEY HOLIDAY PARK

c/o Blackcock Inn, Molland, South Molton EX36 3NW
T: (01769) 550297
F: (01769) 550101
E: lorna@yeovalleyholidays.com
I: www.yeovalleyholidays.com

In a beautiful, secluded valley on the edge of Exmoor, this small, family-run park is the ideal place to relax or enjoy many activities. 10% discount off a 4-night stay in Jun, Sep or Oct.

OPEN All Year
Payment accepted: Delta, Mastercard, Switch, Visa

Follow signs to Blackcock Inn from A361 near South Molton on B3227.

45	🚐	£12.50–£15.00
5	🚐	
10	⛺	
65 touring pitches		

SWANAGE, Dorset Map ref 3B3 *Tourist Information Centre Tel: (01929) 422885*

★★★★★

TOURING PARK

BH&HPA

See Ad on inside back cover

HAYCRAFT CARAVAN CLUB SITE

Haycrafts Lane, Swanage BH19 3EB
T: (01929) 480572
I: www.caravanclub.co.uk

Peaceful site located five miles from Swanage, with its safe, sandy beach. Spectacular cliff-top walks, Corfe Castle, Lulworth Cove and Durdle Door within easy reach. Open 26 March to 1 November. Special member rates mean you can save your membership subscription in less than a week. Visit www.caravanclub.co.uk to find out more.

Payment accepted: Delta, Mastercard, Switch, Visa

Midway between Corfe Castle and Swanage. Take A351 from Wareham to Swanage, at Harmans Cross turn right into Haycrafts Lane, site 0.5 miles on the left.

53	🚐	£16.10–£21.50
53	🚐	£16.10–£21.50
53 touring pitches		

THE CARAVAN CLUB

TAUNTON, Somerset Map ref 2D1 *Tourist Information Centre Tel: (01823) 336344*

★★★
HOLIDAY, TOURING
& CAMPING PARK

ASHE FARM CARAVAN AND CAMPSITE
Thornfalcon, Taunton TA3 5NW
T: (01823) 442567
F: (01823) 443372
E: camping@ashe-frm.fsnet.co.uk

20	🚐	£9.00–£12.00
10	🚗	£9.00–£12.00
10	⛺	£8.00–£10.00
2	🏠	£120.00–£170.00
30 touring pitches		

M5 jct 25. Take A358 south-east for 2.5 miles, turn right at Nags Head, site 0.25 miles on right.

TAVISTOCK, Devon Map ref 2C2 *Tourist Information Centre Tel: (01822) 612938*

★★★★
HOLIDAY, TOURING
& CAMPING PARK

ROSE AWARD

BH&HPA

HARFORD BRIDGE HOLIDAY PARK

Harford Bridge, Tavistock PL19 9LS
T: (01822) 810349
F: (01822) 810028
E: enquiry@harfordbridge.co.uk
I: www.harfordbridge.co.uk

Beautiful, level, sheltered park set in Dartmoor with delighful views of Cox Tor. The River Tavy forms a boundary. Ideal for exploring Devon and Cornwall. Camping: 10% discount for week paid in full on arrival. Holiday let: £15 off 2-week booking. £10 Senior Citizen discount.

OPEN All Year
Payment accepted: Delta, Mastercard, Switch, Visa

M5 onto A30 to Sourton Cross; take left turn onto A386 Tavistock Road; 2 miles north of Tavistock, take the Peter Tavy; entrance 200yds on left; clearly marked and easy access.

40	🚐	£7.50–£15.00
40	🚗	£7.50–£15.00
40	⛺	£7.50–£12.50
12	🏠	£180.00–£420.00
120 touring pitches		

★★★★
HOLIDAY, TOURING
& CAMPING PARK

ROSE AWARD

BH&HPA

LANGSTONE MANOR CARAVAN AND CAMPING PARK

Moortown, Tavistock PL19 9JZ
T: (01822) 613371
F: (01822) 613371
E: jane@langstone-manor.co.uk
I: www.langstone-manor.co.uk

Fantastic location with direct access onto moor. Peace and quiet, with secluded pitches. Bar and restaurant. Excellent base for South Devon and Cornwall. Discover Dartmoor's secret! £15 discount for 2-week booking in holiday homes. 25% discount for 2 people sharing, on weekly bookings, booked on certain weeks.

Payment accepted: Delta, Mastercard, Switch, Visa, Euros

Take the B3357 Princetown road from Tavistock. After approximately 1.5 miles you will see signs to Langstone Manor. Turn right, go over cattle grid, up the hill, turn left following signs.

	🚐	£8.00–£10.00
40	🚗	£8.00–£10.00
	⛺	£8.00–£10.00
7	🏠	£160.00–£410.00
40 touring pitches		

TEIGNGRACE, Devon Map ref 2D2

★★★★
TOURING PARK

TWELVE OAKS FARM CARAVAN PARK
Teigngrace, Newton Abbot TQ12 6QT
T: (01626) 352769
F: (01626) 352769
E: info@twelveoaksfarm.co.uk
I: www.twelveoaksfarm.co.uk

OPEN All Year
Payment accepted:
Mastercard, Switch, Visa

25	🚐	£6.50–£10.00
25	🚗	£6.50–£10.00
25 touring pitches		

Turn left off A38 Expressway at international caravan sign at beginning of road to Teigngrace. After approximately 1.75 miles, turn left immediately past farm entrance into drive. Site on right.

★★★★
**TOURING &
CAMPING PARK**

BH&HPA

See Ad on inside back cover

TEWKESBURY ABBEY
CARAVAN CLUB SITE

Gander Lane, Tewkesbury GL20 5PG
T: (01684) 294035
I: www.caravanclub.co.uk

Impressive location next to Tewkesbury Abbey. Only a short walk into the old town of Tewkesbury where there is much to explore. Open 26 March to 1 November. Special member rates mean you can save your membership subscription in less than a week. Visit www.caravanclub.co.uk to find out more.

Payment accepted: Delta, Mastercard, Switch, Visa

From M5 leave by exit 9 onto A438. In about 3 miles in town centre, at cross-junction turn right. After 200yds turn left into Gander Lane. From M50 leave by exit 1 on A38.

170	🚐	£14.60–£20.60
170	🚍	£14.60–£20.60
	⛺	On application
170 touring pitches		

★★★★★
TOURING PARK

BH&HPA

See Ad on inside back cover

TREWETHETT FARM
CARAVAN CLUB SITE

Trethevy, Tintagel PL34 0BQ
T: (01840) 770222
I: www.caravanclub.co.uk

Cliff-top site with breathtaking views. Walk to Boscastle, with its pretty harbour and quayside, or Tintagel to see its dramatic castle. Non-members welcome. Open 2 April to 1 November. Special member rates mean you can save your membership subscription in less than a week. Visit www.caravanclub.co.uk to find out more.

Payment accepted: Delta, Mastercard, Switch, Visa

From A30 onto A395 signposted Camelford. Right onto A39 signposted Bude. Left just before transmitter. Right onto B3266 signposted Boscastle. Left onto B3263. Site entrance is on the right in about 2 miles.

125	🚐	£16.10–£21.50
125	🚍	£16.10–£21.50
	⛺	On application
125 touring pitches		

★★★★★
**TOURING &
CAMPING PARK**

BH&HPA
NCC

WAREHAM FOREST TOURIST
PARK

Bere Road, North Trigon, Wareham BH20 7NZ
T: (01929) 551393
F: (01929) 558321
E: holiday@wareham-forest.co.uk
I: www.wareham-forest.co.uk

A friendly, family-run woodland park with spacious, level pitches (many hardstanding), conveniently situated in the tranquil Wareham Forest. Excellent facilities. Good location for walks.

OPEN All Year
Payment accepted: Delta, Mastercard, Switch, Visa

Located off A35 between Wareham and Bere Regis. At Woodbury Cross junction turn south, signposted Wareham. Park is situated 3 miles on left-hand side.

200	🚐	£11.00–£16.00
200	🚍	£11.00–£16.00
200	⛺	£11.00–£16.00
200 touring pitches		

Visitor attractions For ideas on places to visit refer to the introduction at the beginning of this section. Look out for the VisitBritain Quality Assured Visitor Attraction signs.

WARMINSTER, Wiltshire Map ref 3B2 *Tourist Information Centre Tel: (01985) 218548*

★ ★ ★ ★ ★
TOURING PARK

BH&HPA

See Ad on inside back cover

LONGLEAT CARAVAN CLUB SITE

Longleat, Warminster BA12 7NL
T: (01985) 844663
I: www.caravanclub.co.uk

Close to Longleat House, this is the only site where you can hear lions roar at night! Cafés, pubs and restaurants within walking distance. Non-members welcome. Open 26 March to 1 November. Special member rates mean you can save your membership subscription in less than a week. Visit www.caravanclub.co.uk to find out more.

Payment accepted: Delta, Mastercard, Switch, Visa

Take A362, signed for Frome, 0.5 miles at roundabout turn left (2nd exit) onto Longleat Estate. Through toll booths, follow caravan and camping pennant signs for 1 mile.

165		£17.00–£22.00
165		£17.00–£22.00
165 touring pitches		

WESTON-SUPER-MARE, North Somerset Map ref 2D1 *Tourist Information Centre Tel: (01934) 888800*

★ ★ ★
TOURING & CAMPING PARK

BH&HPA

DULHORN FARM CAMPING SITE
Weston Road, Lympsham, Weston-super-Mare BS24 0JQ
T: (01934) 750298
F: (01934) 750913

57		£10.00–£14.00
5		£8.00–£12.00
25	A	£5.00–£10.00
87 touring pitches		

From M5 jct 22, take the A38 towards Bristol and then A370 to Weston-super-Mare, 1.25 miles on left.

David Bellamy Conservation Awards

If you are looking for a site that's environmentally friendly, look for those that have achieved the David Bellamy Conservation Award. Launched in conjunction with the British Holiday & Home Parks Association, this award is given to sites which are committed to protecting and enhancing the environment – from care of the hedgerows and wildlife to recycling waste – and are members of the Association. More information about the award scheme can be found at the back of the guide.

WESTWARD HO!, Devon Map ref 2C1

★★★★
HOLIDAY PARK

BH&HPA
NCC

BEACHSIDE HOLIDAY PARK

Merley Road, Westward Ho!, Bideford EX39 1JX
T: (01237) 421163
F: (01237) 472100
E: beachside@surfbay.dircon.co.uk
I: www.beachsideholidays.co.uk

Superbly presented and well-maintained park. Caravan holiday homes commanding spectacular views of sandy beach and the sea as it stretches out to the Atlantic. Open March to October. 15% couple's discount: 3 Apr–22 May, 5 Jun–10 July, 11 Sep–9 Oct.

Payment accepted: Amex, Mastercard, Switch, Visa

From M5 jct 27 A39 Bideford/Bude road. Over bridge, straight across at roundabout. After 0.25 miles, turn right for Westward Ho! Follow road for approximately 1 mile. Down Stanwell Hill, turn left onto Merley Road.

50   £99.00–£495.00

★★★★
HOLIDAY PARK

BH&HPA
NCC

SURF BAY HOLIDAY PARK

Golf Links Road, Westward Ho!, Bideford EX39 1HD
T: (01237) 471833
F: (01237) 474387
E: surfbayholidaypark@surfbay.dircon.co.uk
I: www.surfbay.co.uk

The park, which is situated just a few minutes' walk from Westward Ho!, has its own access to the glorious beach of Westward Ho! Open March to October. Discounts for 'out of peak season' bookings – ask for details.

Payment accepted: Amex, Mastercard, Switch, Visa

From M5 jct 27 take A39 over Torridge Bridge. On roundabout head to Westward Ho! After passing Westward Ho! sign take 2nd turning on right (Beach Road). Drive to bottom, turn right, 50 yds on left.

54   £99.00–£495.00

WEYMOUTH, Dorset Map ref 3B3 *Tourist Information Centre Tel: (01305) 785747*

★★★★
TOURING PARK

BH&HPA

See Ad on inside back cover

CROSSWAYS CARAVAN CLUB SITE

Moreton, Dorchester DT2 8BE
T: (01305) 852032
I: www.caravanclub.co.uk

Set in 35 acres of woodland. Dorchester is nearby, also Weymouth's award-winning, sandy beach. Visit Lawrence of Arabia's house at Cloud's Hill. Open 9 April to 4 October. Special member rates mean you can save your membership subscription in less than a week. Visit www.caravanclub.co.uk to find out more.

Payment accepted: Delta, Mastercard, Switch, Visa

North from A35 or south from A352, join B3390. Site on right within 1 mile. Entrance to site by forecourt of filling station.

122   £13.35–£17.60
122   £13.35–£17.60
122 touring pitches

NB **Important note** Information on accommodation listed in this guide has been supplied by the proprietors. As changes may occur you are advised to check details at the time of booking.

WHITE CROSS, Cornwall Map ref 2B2

★★★★★
HOLIDAY PARK

BH&HPA
NCC

WHITE ACRES HOLIDAY PARK

White Cross, Newquay TR8 4LW
T: 0870 420 2997 & (01726) 862100
E: enquiries@parkdeanholidays.co.uk
I: www.parkdeanholidays.co.uk

Set in 167 acres of glorious countryside. Five-star facilities, luxury caravans, lodges and touring, family entertainment, children's clubs, coarse fishing lakes.......great family holidays! Short breaks available.

OPEN All Year
Payment accepted: Delta, Mastercard, Switch, Visa

Take the Indian Queens exit from A30. Follow A392 towards Newquay. White Acres Holiday Park is approximately 1 mile on right-hand side.

40	🚐	£9.00–£26.00
40	🚏	£7.00–£26.00
40	⛺	£7.00–£23.00
300	🏠	£150.00–£1,095.00
40 touring pitches		

WIMBORNE MINSTER, Dorset Map ref 3B3 *Tourist Information Centre Tel: (01202) 886116*

★★★★★
TOURING &
CAMPING PARK

BH&HPA

MERLEY COURT TOURING PARK
Merley House Lane, Merley, Wimborne
Minster BH21 3AA
T: (01202) 881488
F: (01202) 881484
E: holidays@merley-court.co.uk
I: www.merley-court.co.uk

Payment accepted: Delta,
Mastercard, Switch, Visa

A31 to Wimborne bypass then A349 Poole road, signposted.

145	🚐	£10.50–£15.50
145	🚏	£10.50–£15.50
80	⛺	£10.50–£15.50
160 touring pitches		

★★★★★
TOURING &
CAMPING PARK

BH&HPA

SPRINGFIELD TOURING PARK

Candys Lane, Corfe Mullen, Wimborne BH21 3EF
T: (01202) 881719

Family-run park overlooking the Stour Valley. Convenient for coastal resorts, New Forest. Many attractions nearby. Free showers, awnings. Some hardstanding. Tarmac roads. Open March to October only. Low season: any 7 days £45 (incl electricity).

Close to main A31 trunk road, 1.5 miles west of Wimborne.

30	🚐	£11.50–£13.50
10	🚏	£11.50–£13.50
5	⛺	£7.00–£13.50

WINSFORD, Somerset Map ref 2D1

★★★★
TOURING &
CAMPING PARK

BH&HPA

HALSE FARM CARAVAN & TENT PARK

Winsford, Minehead TA24 7JL
T: (01643) 851259
F: (01643) 851592
E: brown@halsefarm.co.uk
I: www.halsefarm.co.uk

Exmoor National Park, small, peaceful, working farm with spectacular views. Paradise for walkers and country lovers. David Bellamy Gold Conservation Award. Open 21 March to 31 October. 10% discount for 1 week or more, paid 10 days in advance.

Payment accepted: Delta, Mastercard, Switch, Visa

Signposted from A396 Minehead to Tiverton road. Turn off A396 for Winsford. In the village turn left and bear left in front of the Royal Oak Inn. Keep up hill for 1 mile; our entrance is immediately after the cattle grid on the left.

22	🚐	£8.50–£10.50
22	🚏	£8.50–£10.50
22	⛺	£8.50–£10.50
44 touring pitches		

WOOL, Dorset Map ref 3B3

★★★★
TOURING &
CAMPING PARK

BH&HPA

WHITEMEAD CARAVAN PARK
East Burton Road, Wool, Wareham
BH20 6HG
T: (01929) 462241
F: (01929) 462241
E: whitemeadcp@aol.com
I: www.whitemeadcaravanpark.co.uk

On A352 from Wareham turn right before Wool level crossing 350yds.

95	£7.20–£11.50
95	£7.20–£11.50
95	£7.20–£11.50
95 touring pitches	

WOOLACOMBE

See display advertisement below

Use your *i*s

There are more than 750
Tourist Information Centres
throughout England, Scotland
and Wales, offering friendly
help with accommodation and
holiday ideas as well as
suggestions of places to visit
and things to do. You'll find
addresses in the local
phone book.

A brief guide to the main towns and villages offering accommodation in **South West England**

AXMINSTER, Devon
This tree-shaded market town on the banks of the river Axe was one of Devon's earliest West Saxon settlements, but is better known for its carpet making. Based on Turkish methods, the industry began in 1755, declined in the 1830s and was revived in 1937.

BATH, Bath and North East Somerset
Georgian spa city beside the river Avon. Important Roman site with impressive reconstructed baths, uncovered in 19thC. Bath Abbey built on site of monastery where first king of England was crowned (AD 973). Fine architecture in mellow local stone. Pump Room and museums.

BERE REGIS, Dorset
This watercress-growing village was famed in the Middle Ages for its fairs and being a resort of kings on their way to the south west; its former splendour is well commemorated by the medieval church.

BLANDFORD FORUM, Dorset
Almost completely destroyed by fire in 1731, the town was rebuilt in a handsome Georgian style. The church is large and grand and the town is the hub of a rich farming area.

BOURNEMOUTH, Bournemouth
Seaside town set among the pines with a mild climate, sandy beaches and fine coastal views. The town has wide streets with excellent shops, a pier, a pavilion, museums and conference centre.

BREAN, Somerset
Caravans and holiday bungalows by sand dunes on the flat shoreline south of Brean Down. This rocky promontory has exhilarating cliff walks, bird-watching and an Iron Age fort.

BRIDPORT, Dorset
Market town and chief producer of nets and ropes just inland of dramatic Dorset coast. Old, broad streets built for drying and twisting and long gardens for rope-walks. Grand arcaded Town Hall and Georgian buildings. Local history museum has Roman relics.

BRISTOL, City of Bristol
Famous for maritime links, historic harbour, Georgian terraces and Brunel's Clifton suspension bridge. Many attractions including ss Great Britain, Bristol Zoo, museums and art galleries, and top name entertainments. Events include Balloon Fiesta and Regatta.

BRIXHAM, Torbay
Famous for its trawling fleet in the 19thC, a steeply built fishing port overlooking the harbour and fish market. A statue of William of Orange recalls his landing here before deposing James II. There is an aquarium and museum. Good cliff views and walks.

BUDE, Cornwall
Resort on dramatic Atlantic coast. High cliffs give spectacular sea and inland views. Golf course, cricket pitch, folly, surfing, coarse-fishing and boating. Mother-town Stratton was base of Royalist Sir Bevil Grenville.

BURTON BRADSTOCK, Dorset
Lying amid fields beside the river Bride, a village of old stone houses, a 14thC church and a village green. The beautiful coast road from Abbotsbury to Bridport passes by and Iron Age forts top the surrounding hills. The sheltered river valley makes a staging post for migrating birds.

CHARMOUTH, Dorset
Set back from the fossil-rich cliffs, a small coastal town where Charles II came to the Queen's Armes when seeking escape to France. Just south at low tide, the sandy beach rewards fossil-hunters; at Black Ven an ichthyosaurus (now in London's Natural History Museum) was found.

CHEDDAR, Somerset
Large village at foot of Mendips just south of the spectacular Cheddar Gorge. Close by are Roman and Saxon sites and famous show caves. Traditional Cheddar cheese is still made here.

CHRISTCHURCH, Dorset
Tranquil town lying between the Avon and Stour just before they converge and flow into Christchurch Harbour. A fine 11thC church and the remains of a Norman castle and house can be seen.

Below, from left admire the Cornish coastline at Bude; enjoy a day out by the sea in Bournemouth

COMBE MARTIN, Devon

On the edge of the Exmoor National Park, this seaside village is set in a long narrow valley with its natural harbour lying between towering cliffs. The main beach is a mixture of sand, rocks and pebbles and the lack of strong currents ensures safe bathing.

DAWLISH, Devon

Small resort, developed in Regency and Victorian periods beside Dawlish Water. One of England's most scenic stretches of railway was built by Brunel alongside jagged red cliffs between the sands and the town.

DORCHESTER, Dorset

Busy medieval county town destroyed by fires in 17th and 18thC. Cromwellian stronghold and scene of Judge Jeffreys' Bloody Assize after Monmouth Rebellion of 1685. Tolpuddle Martyrs were tried in Shire Hall. Museum has Roman and earlier exhibits and Hardy relics.

DULVERTON, Somerset

Set among woods and hills of south-west Exmoor, a busy riverside town with a 13thC church. The rivers Barle and Exe are rich in salmon and trout. The information centre at the Exmoor National Park Headquarters at Dulverton is open throughout the year.

EXMOUTH, Devon

Developed as a seaside resort in George III's reign, set against the woods of the Exe estuary and red cliffs of Orcombe Point. Extensive sands, small harbour, chapel and almshouses, a model railway and A la Ronde, a 16-sided house.

FOWEY, Cornwall

Set on steep slopes at the mouth of the Fowey river, important clayport and fishing town. Ruined forts guarding the shore recall days of Fowey Gallants who ruled local seas. The lofty church rises above the town. Ferries to Polruan and Bodinnick.

GLASTONBURY, Somerset

Market town associated with Joseph of Arimathea and the birth of English Christianity. Built around its 7thC abbey said to be the site of King Arthur's burial. Glastonbury Tor with its ancient tower gives panoramic views over the Mendip Hills.

HAYLE, Cornwall

Former mining town with modern light industry on the Hayle estuary. Most buildings are Georgian or early Victorian, with some Regency houses along the canal.

HIGHCLIFFE, Dorset

Seaside district of Christchurch some three miles to the east. Highcliffe Castle is of interest.

ILFRACOMBE, Devon

Resort of Victorian grandeur set on hillside between cliffs with sandy coves. At the mouth of the harbour stands an 18thC lighthouse, built over a medieval chapel. There are fine formal gardens and a museum. Chambercombe Manor, an interesting old house, is nearby.

KENTISBEARE, Devon

Pretty village at the foot of the Blackdown Hills. The church has a magnificent carved 15thC screen, and nearby is a medieval priest's house with a minstrels' gallery.

LACOCK, Wiltshire

Village of great charm. Medieval buildings of stone, brick or timber-frame have jutting storeys, gables, oriel windows. Magnificent church has perpendicular fan-vaulted chapel with grand tomb to benefactor who, after Dissolution, bought Augustinian nunnery, Lacock Abbey.

LANDS END, Cornwall

The most westerly point of the English mainland, eight miles south-west of Penzance. Spectacular cliffs with marvellous views. Exhibitions and multi-sensory Last Labyrinth Show.

LANGPORT, Somerset

Small market town with Anglo-Saxon origins, sloping to river Parrett. Well-known for glove making and, formerly, for eels. Interesting old buildings include some fine local churches.

LANGTON MATRAVERS, Dorset

18thC Purbeck stone village surrounded by National Trust downland, about a mile from the sea and 350 ft above sea level. Excellent walking.

MALMESBURY, Wiltshire

Overlooking the river Avon, an old town dominated by its great church, once a Benedictine abbey. The surviving Norman nave and porch are noted for fine sculptures, 12thC arches and musicians' gallery.

MARTOCK, Somerset

Large village with many handsome buildings of hamstone and a beautiful old church with tie-beam roof. Medieval treasurer's house where a large medieval mural has recently been discovered during National Trust restoration work. Georgian market house, 17thC manor.

MORETON-IN-MARSH, Gloucestershire

Attractive town of Cotswold stone with 17thC houses, an ideal base for touring the Cotswolds. Some of the local attractions include Batsford Park Arboretum, the Jacobean Chastleton House and Sezincote Garden.

NEWQUAY, Cornwall

Popular resort spread over dramatic cliffs around its old fishing port. Many beaches with abundant sands, caves and rock pools; excellent surf. Pilots' gigs are still raced from the harbour and on the headland stands the stone Huer's House from the pilchard-fishing days.

OWERMOIGNE, Dorset

Village six miles east of Dorchester, within easy reach of the Dorset coast and the family resort of Weymouth.

PADSTOW, Cornwall

Old town encircling its harbour on the Camel estuary. The 15thC church has notable bench-ends. There are fine houses on North Quay and Raleigh's Court House on South Quay. Tall cliffs and golden sands along the coast and ferry to Rock.

PAIGNTON, Torbay

Lively seaside resort with a pretty harbour on Torbay. Bronze Age and Saxon sites are occupied by the 15thC church, which has a Norman door and font. The beautiful Chantry Chapel was built by local landowners, the Kirkhams.

PENZANCE, Cornwall

Resort and fishing port on Mount's Bay with mainly Victorian promenade and some fine Regency terraces. Former prosperity came from tin trade and pilchard fishing. Grand Georgian style church by harbour. Georgian Egyptian building at head of Chapel Street and Morrab Gardens.

POLRUAN-BY-FOWEY, Cornwall
Old village linked to Fowey across its estuary by a passenger ferry. Twin medieval forts guard village and town at the river's mouth.

POOLE, Poole
Tremendous natural harbour makes Poole a superb boating centre. The harbour area is crowded with historic buildings including the 15thC Town Cellars housing a maritime museum.

PORTLAND, Dorset
Joined by a narrow isthmus to the coast, a stony promontory sloping from the lofty landward side to a lighthouse on Portland Bill at its southern tip.

PORTREATH, Cornwall
Formerly developed as a mining port, small resort with some handsome 19thC buildings. Cliffs, sands and good surf.

ST AGNES, Cornwall
Small town in a once-rich mining area on the north coast. Terraced cottages and granite houses slope to the church. Some old mine workings remain, but the attraction must be the magnificent coastal scenery and superb walks. St Agnes Beacon offers one of Cornwall's most extensive views.

ST AUSTELL, Cornwall
Leading market town, the meeting point of old and new Cornwall. One mile from St Austell Bay with its sandy beaches, old fishing villages and attractive countryside. Ancient narrow streets, pedestrian shopping precincts. Fine church of Pentewan stone and Italianate Town Hall.

ST IVES, Cornwall
Old fishing port, artists' colony and holiday town with good surfing beach. Fishermen's cottages, granite fish cellars, a sandy harbour and magnificent headlands typify a charm that has survived since the 19thC pilchard boom. Tate Gallery opened in 1993.

SALCOMBE, Devon
Sheltered yachting resort of whitewashed houses and narrow streets in a balmy setting on the Salcombe estuary. Mediterranean plants flourish and there are sandy bays and creeks for boating.

SIDMOUTH, Devon
Charming resort set amid lofty red cliffs where the river Sid meets the sea. The wealth of ornate Regency and Victorian villas recalls the time when this was one of the south coast's most exclusive resorts.

SWANAGE, Dorset
Began life as an Anglo-Saxon port, then a quarrying centre of Purbeck marble. Now the safe, sandy beach set in a sweeping bay and flanked by downs is good walking country, making it an ideal resort.

TAUNTON, Somerset
County town, well-known for its public schools, sheltered by gentle hill-ranges on the river Tone. Medieval prosperity from wool has continued in marketing and manufacturing and the town retains many fine period buildings. Museum.

TAVISTOCK, Devon
Old market town beside the river Tavy on the western edge of Dartmoor. Developed around its 10thC abbey, of which some fragments remain, it became a stannary town in 1305 when tin-streaming thrived on the moors. Tavistock Goose Fair, October.

TEWKESBURY, Gloucestershire
Tewkesbury's outstanding possession is its magnificent church, built as an abbey, with a great Norman tower and beautiful 14thC interior. The town stands at the confluence of the Severn and Avon and has many medieval houses, inns and several museums.

TINTAGEL, Cornwall
Coastal village near the legendary home of King Arthur. There is a lofty headland with the ruin of a Norman castle and traces of a Celtic monastery are still visible in the turf.

WAREHAM, Dorset
This site has been occupied since pre-Roman times and has a turbulent history. In 1762 fire destroyed much of the town, so the buildings now are mostly Georgian.

WARMINSTER, Wiltshire
Attractive stone-built town high up to the west of Salisbury Plain. A market town, it originally thrived on cloth and wheat. Many prehistoric camps and barrows nearby, along with Longleat House and Safari Park.

WESTON-SUPER-MARE, North Somerset
Large, friendly resort developed in the 19thC. Traditional seaside attractions include theatres and a dance hall. The museum has a Victorian seaside gallery and Iron Age finds from a hill fort on Worlebury Hill in Weston Woods.

WESTWARD HO!, Devon
Small resort, whose name comes from the title of Charles Kingsley's famous novel, on Barnstaple Bay, close to the Taw and Torridge estuary. There are good sands and a notable golf course.

WEYMOUTH, Dorset
Ancient port and one of the south's earliest resorts. Curving beside a long, sandy beach, the elegant Georgian esplanade is graced with a statue of George III and a cheerful Victorian Jubilee clock tower. Museum, Sea Life Centre.

WIMBORNE MINSTER, Dorset
Market town centred on the twin-towered Minster Church of St Cuthberga which gave the town the second part of its name. Good touring base for the surrounding countryside, depicted in the writings of Thomas Hardy.

WINSFORD, Somerset
Small village in Exmoor National Park, on the river Exe in splendid walking country under Winsford Hill. On the other side of the hill is a Celtic standing stone and nearby across the river Barle stretches an ancient packhorse bridge, Tarr Steps.

WOOL, Dorset
On the river Frome with a mainline station. Woolbridge Manor is of interest and occupies a prominent position.

Scotland is a **unique** country of **soaring** peaks, **sparkling** lochs and fairytale castles.

Scotland

Looking for some inspiration? Here are a few ideas to get you started in Scotland. **experience** the military spectacle and the massed pipes and drums at the Edinburgh Tattoo. **discover** the huge variety of tastes on a malt whisky trail. **explore** castles and abbeys in the Scottish Borders. **relax** in the renowned Willow Tea Rooms in Glasgow.

CONTACT

▶ **VISITSCOTLAND**

**6 Fairways Business Park,
Deer Park Road,
Livingstone EH54 8AF
T: 0845 225 5121
E: info@visitscotland.com
www.visitscotland.com**

Dramatic landscapes and mist on the lochs. Or world-class shopping and an unrivalled arts festival. Can you stay the course at St Andrews, or indeed on the malt whisky trail? Rediscover yourself in some of Europe's finest landscapes and enjoy a leisurely break or an action-packed holiday.

Take the high road

Scotland's easy to get to, with excellent motorway links from most parts of the UK, and wherever your journey in Scotland takes you, you're in for a treat. You might linger in the Borders to explore the dignified ruins of once-powerful abbeys or follow in the footsteps of Rob Roy and Walter Scott through the Trossachs. Perhaps you'll potter around colourful fishing villages in the Kingdom of Fife and tee off on the legendary Old Course in St Andrews. Or venture into Speyside to tickle your tastebuds on the malt whisky trail.

If it's drama you're after, you'll head for the Highlands, a vast swathe of untamed wilderness where land and sea collide to create stunning perspectives. Discover the most perfect vista at Eilean Donan where the dramatic castle ruins and surrounding mountains are reflected in the waters of the loch. Both landscapes and wildlife are at their most spectacular in Scotland's two National Parks – Loch Lomond and Cairngorm.

Ancient heritage

Whichever part of Scotland takes your fancy, history is never far away – from the Neolithic ruins of Skara Brae on Orkney to Scotland's dramatic capital city. Here you can stroll through the cobbled streets of the medieval Old Town, visit the castle and uncover 1000 years of Scotland's tumultuous past or stop for refreshment in Deacon Brodie's Tavern and learn about the devious Edinburgh citizen who inspired Robert Louis Stevenson's tale of Dr Jekyll and Mr Hyde.

Highland fling

And if it's festivals you want – they're here in abundance. Apart from Edinburgh's celebrated arts and fringe festivals, there's traditional music and celebration at the Shetland Folk Festival, caber tossing and games aplenty at the Cowal Highland Gathering and Scotland's national poet Robert Burns is celebrated at venues throughout the Scottish Borders in May each year.

The Scots are fiercely proud of their heritage, which they celebrate in a thousand different ways, from the pomp and splendour of the Edinburgh Tattoo to the more intimate appeal of an impromptu ceilidh in a cosy pub. If this leads you to assume that they only look back to the past, a trip to Glasgow will set you straight. Scotland's largest city has reinvented itself to become one of Europe's great cultural capitals. It also has shopping to rival London's best and an abundance of stylish restaurants and café bars that will seduce the most adventurous gourmet.

Left, from top watch the sun go down in Dumfries and Galloway; history at its best in Edinburgh; idyllic countryside at Rannoch Moor **Right** enjoy spectacular views of Culzean Castle, Maybole

Places to visit

VisitScotland star graded attraction

Auld Reekie Tours

Niddry Street, Edinburgh
Tel: (0131) 557 4700
www.auldreekietours.co.uk
A taste of Edinburgh's grisly past – a visitor attraction with medieval torture dungeon and gallery, legendary haunted vault and two working pagan temples. Historical tours of the city's old and new town.

Balmoral Castle
Balmoral, Aberdeenshire
Tel: (013397) 42534
www.balmoralcastle.com
World-famous Scottish holiday home of the Royal Family. Wander through the grounds and visit the exhibitions, gift shops and self-service caféteria.

Bannockburn Heritage Centre
Glasgow Road, Stirling
Tel: (01786) 812664
www.nts.org.uk
Imagine the battle cries at this historic battlefield, with famous Bruce statue. Living history presentation, exhibition of Scottish wars of independence and audiovisual film of the Battle of Bannockburn. Gift shop. Café.

Benmore Botanic Garden
Dunoon, Argyll
Tel: (01369) 706261
www.rbge.org.uk
Marvel at Benmore's magnificent trees and unrivalled collection of flowering shrubs in their dramatic mountainside setting on the Cowal peninsula. Shop and café.

Blair Castle
Blair Atholl, Pitlochry, Perthshire
Tel: (01796) 481207
www.great-houses-scotland.co.uk/blair
Step inside Scotland's most visited, private historic house. This castle features 30 rooms of exhibition displays, a gift shop, restaurant and grounds.

Braemar Castle
Braemar, Aberdeenshire
Tel: (013397) 41219
www.braemarcastle.co.uk
Impressive Braemar castle, built in 1628, is now owned by the Farquharson family. The central tower has furnished rooms with many valuable paintings, furniture and interesting curios.

British Golf Museum
Bruce Embankment, St Andrews, Fife
Tel: (01334) 460046
www.britishgolfmuseum.co.uk
Trace the history and development of golf from its medieval origins to the global, multi-million pound business it is today, in St Andrews, home of golf.

Caledonian Railway
Park Road, Brechin, Angus
Tel: (01356) 622992
www.caledonianrailway.co.uk
Steam enthusiasts will appreciate this heritage railway, running four miles from Brechin to Bridge of Dun. Special events held during the season.

Clydebuilt
(Scottish Maritime Museum Braehead)
Kings Inch Road, Glasgow
Tel: (0141) 885 1441
www.scottishmaritimemuseum.org
This dynamic new attraction on the river Clyde brings to life the story of Glasgow's development, from the tobacco lords in the 1700s, right up to the 21stC.

Culzean Castle & Country Park

Maybole, Ayrshire
Tel: (01655) 884455
www.nts.org.uk
Robert Adam's final masterpiece, this Italianate castle is perched on a cliff top. Enjoy the spectacular sea views to Arran, Kintyre and Alisa Craig.

Dunvegan Castle and Gardens
Dunvegan, Isle of Skye
Tel: (01470) 521206
www.dunvegancastle.com
Historic building with extensive private gardens, shop and restaurant complex on the magical Isle of Skye. Children and adults will be fascinated by a boat trip to a seal colony.

Edinburgh Castle
Castle Hill, Edinburgh
Tel: (0131) 225 9846
www.historicscotland.gov.uk/edinburghcastle
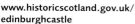
This imposing castle features magnificently restored Laich Hall, Scotland's Crown Jewels and Mons Meg, the enormous 500-year-old siege cannon.

Edinburgh Crystal Visitor Centre
Eastfield Industrial Estate, Penicuik, Midlothian
Tel: (01968) 675128
www.edinburgh-crystal.com
A stunning exhibition and video presentation reveals the heritage of Edinburgh Crystal. Join a guided tour of the factory and watch the glass blowers, cutters and engravers at work.

Edinburgh Dungeon
Market Street, Edinburgh
Tel: (0131) 240 1000
www.thedungeons.com
Bring your garlic! Explore the facts that surround Edinburgh's myths, from local legends to world-famous vampires.

Edinburgh Zoo
Corstorphine Road, Edinburgh
Tel: (0131) 314 0300
www.edinburghzoo.org.uk
Scotland's largest and most popular wildlife attraction. See over 1000 animals, furry, feathery and scaly, from the tiny blue poison arrow frog to the massive white rhino.

Elgin Museum
High Street, Elgin, Morayshire
Tel: (01343) 543675
www.elginmuseum.org.uk
Award-winning, friendly museum, internationally important for fossil reptiles. Don't miss the Pictish stones and a set of miniatures of the Parthenon Frieze (The Elgin Marbles).

Glamis Castle
Glamis, Forfar, Angus
Tel: (01307) 840393
www.glamis-castle.co.uk
Family home of the Earls of Strathmore and Kinghorne and the childhood home of Queen Elizabeth The Queen Mother. Admirers of Shakespeare's plays will recognise it as the legendary setting of Macbeth.

Glenmorangie Distillery
Tain, Ross-shire
Tel: (01862) 892477
www.glenmorangie.com

Partake of a dram at the distillery which creates Scotland's favourite whisky. Set in a tranquil glen overlooking the shores of the Dornoch Firth. Visitor Centre and shop.

Gordon Highlanders Museum
Viewfield Road, Aberdeen
Tel: (01224) 311200
www.gordonhighlanders.com
Re-live the compelling and dramatic story of one of the British Army's most famous regiments as you survey the regimental collection of the Gordon Highlanders.

Hunterian Art Gallery
University of Glasgow, Glasgow
Tel: (0141) 330 5431
www.hunterian.gla.ac.uk
The gallery houses the University of Glasgow's outstanding art collections. The Mackintosh House comprises rooms from the home of the architect Charles Rennie Mackintosh.

Islay Woollen Mill Co Ltd
Bridgend, Isle of Islay
Tel: (01496) 810563
www.islaywoollenmill.co.uk
Check out the tartans at these woollen manufacturers weaving a wide range of wool, cashmere and silk. Try on a kilt at the factory shop.

Laphroaig Distillery
Port Ellen, Isle of Islay
Tel: (01496) 302418
www.laphroaig.com
Discover the unique peat reek of Laphroaig whisky and the Islay Islanders who have made it for over 200 years on this very hands-on guided tour of the distillery.

Lochwinnoch RSPB Nature Reserve
Largs Road, Lochwinnoch, Renfrewshire
Tel: (01505) 842663
www.rspb.org.uk/reserves/lochwinnoch
One of the few remaining wetland sites in west Scotland, this nature reserve offers ground level and tower viewing areas in the visitor centre as well as nature trails and hides.

Mallaig Heritage Centre
Station Road, Mallaig, Inverness-shire
Tel: (01687) 462085
www.mallaigheritage.org.uk
Comprehensive local history exhibition, covering crofting, fishing, the Fort William-Mallaig railway, ferries and steamers, the Mallaig lifeboat and social history.

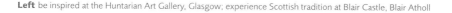
Left be inspired at the Huntarian Art Gallery, Glasgow; experience Scottish tradition at Blair Castle, Blair Atholl

Places to visit

VisitScotland star graded attraction

Mercat Walking Tours of Edinburgh

Niddry Street South, Edinburgh
Tel: (0131) 557 6464
www.mercattours.com
Scotland's oldest, award-winning walking tour company offers trips into the dark, magical history of Edinburgh. Tours by day or night... if you dare!

Museum of Scottish Lighthouses Kinnaird Head
Fraserburgh, Aberdeenshire
Tel: (01346) 511022
www.lighthousemuseum.co.uk
Light displays, multi-screen projector show and touch-screen technology. Follow the guide to the top of Kinnaird Head Lighthouse, Scotland's first mainland lighthouse.

National Gallery of Scotland
The Mound, Edinburgh
Tel: (0131) 624 6200
www.nationalgalleries.org
One of the very finest of its size in the world, the gallery is home to Scotland's greatest collection of paintings and sculpture from the Renaissance to Post-Impressionism.

National Museum of Scotland

Chambers Street, Edinburgh
Tel: (0131) 247 4422
www.nms.ac.uk
Dig back deep in time. This new museum contains the nation's most precious artefacts and tells the story of Scotland's past over 3000 million years.

National Wallace Monument
Abbey Craig, Causewayhead, Stirling
Tel: (01786) 472140
www.nationalwallacemonument.co.uk
Spectacular 67m- (220ft-) high 19thC tower built to commemorate Scotland's Braveheart, William Wallace. Experience his life through exhibitions and audiovisuals as you climb the tower.

Nevis Range Cable Cars
Nevis Range, Torlundy, Fort William
Tel: (01397) 705825
www.nevisrange.co.uk
Reach the dizzy height of 655m (2150ft) on Aonach Mor beside Ben Nevis, via Britain's only mountain gondala system. Walks, restaurants, forest trails, and skiing and snowboarding in winter.

Our Dynamic Earth
Holyrood Road, Edinburgh
Tel: (0131) 550 7800
www.dynamicearth.co.uk
Experience the planet as it was thousands of years ago, from boiling volcanoes to the freezing Ice Age and travel from the dawn of time right into the future.

Palace of Holyroodhouse
Edinburgh
Tel: (0131) 556 5100
www.royal.gov.uk
The Queen's official residence in Scotland, Holyrood was founded in 1128 by King David I and was home to Mary Queen of Scots from 1561-67. The Baroque palace was built in 1680.

The Royal Yacht Britannia
Leith Docks, Edinburgh
Tel: (0131) 555 5566
www.royalyachtbritannia.co.uk
Step on board Britannia and imagine the glittering state visits, receptions, honeymoons and relaxing family holidays the Royal Family enjoyed for over 40 years.

Scone Palace

Scone, Perth
Tel: (01738) 552300
www.scone-palace.co.uk
This historic house is situated at the heart of Scottish history, on the site of the crowning place of the Kings of Scotland, and contains treasures collected over the past 400 years.

Above step aboard The Royal Yacht Britannia in Edinburgh; wander around the grounds of Balmoral Castle, the world-famous Scottish holiday home of the Royal Family **Right** experience the Military Tattoo at Edinburgh Castle

This is just a selection of attractions available. Contact any Tourist Information Centre in Scotland for more ideas.

Scottish Crannog Centre

Kenmore, Aberfeldy, Perthshire
Tel: (01887) 830583
www.crannog.co.uk
Find out all about Scotland's Iron Age loch dwellers and their crannogs – round, wooden houses built on piles driven into the loch bed – on this fascinating guided tour.

Scottish Fisheries Museum

St Ayles, Anstruther, Fife
Tel: (01333) 310628
www.scottish-fisheries-museum.org
The many facets of the lives of Scottish fisher-folk, including the tragedies they face, are portrayed here, along with 15 full-size fishing boats in the boatyard and harbour.

Scottish National Portrait Gallery

Queen Street, Edinburgh
Tel: (0131) 624 6200
www.natgalscot.ac.uk
Face to face with a unique visual history of Scotland, told through portraits of the figures who shaped it: royals and rebels, poets and philosophers, heroes and villains.

Speyside Heather Centre

Dulnain Bridge, Grantown-on-Spey, Morayshire
Tel: (01479) 851359
www.heathercentre.com
Originally a small nursery specialising in heather, this attraction now includes a unique exhibition featuring the historical story of heather. Show garden. Restaurant.

Stirling Castle

Castle Wynd, Stirling
Tel: (01786) 450000
www.historic-scotland.gov.uk/stirlingcastle
A grand castle with outstanding architecture, including the renaissance palace of James V. Learn about the many royal connections, including strong links with Mary Queen of Scots.

The Tall Ship at Glasgow Harbour

Clyde Maritime Centre Ltd, Stobcross Road, Glasgow
Tel: (0141) 222 2513
www.glenlee.co.uk

Welcome aboard the 103-year-old tall ship Glenlee, one of only five Clyde-built sailing ships afloat in the world. Exhibitions, nautical souvenirs and children's activities.

VisitScotland

6 Fairways Businees Park, Deer Park Road, Livingstone EH54 8AF
T: 0845 225 5121 E: info@visitscotland.com www.visitscotland.com

London
Scotland's National Office
19 Cockspur Street (off Trafalgar Square) London SW1Y 4XT

The following publications are available from VisitScotland:

Where to Stay Guide, Hotels & Guest Houses £9.99 (incl p&p)

Over 800 places to stay in Scotland from luxury town houses and country hotels to budget-priced guest houses. Details of prices and facilities, with location maps.

Where to Stay Guide, Bed and Breakfast £7.99 (incl p&p)

Over 1000 Bed and Breakfast establishments throughout Scotland offering inexpensive accommodation – the perfect way to enjoy a budget trip and meet Scottish folk in their own homes. Details of prices and facilities, with location maps.

Where to Stay Guide, Caravan and Camping Parks £5.99 (incl p&p)

Over 100 parks detailed with prices, available facilities and lots of other useful information. Parks inspected by the British Holiday Parks Grading Scheme. Also includes caravan homes for hire. Location maps.

Where to Stay Guide, Self-Catering £6.99 (incl p&p)

Over 700 cottages, apartments and chalets to let – many in scenic areas. Details of prices and facilities, with location maps.

Touring Guide to Scotland £9.50 (incl p&p)

A fully revised edition of this popular guide which now lists over 1500 things to do and places to visit in Scotland. Easy to use index and locater maps. Details of opening hours, admission charges, general description and information on disabled access.

Touring Map of Scotland £5.50 (incl p&p)

An up-to-date touring map of Scotland. Full colour with comprehensive motorway and road information, the map details over 20 categories of tourist information and names over 1500 things to do and places to visit in Scotland.

Travel information

By road:
The A1 and M6 bring you quickly over the border and immerse you in beautiful scenery. Scotland's network of excellent roads span out from Edinburgh – Glasgow takes approximately one hour and 15 minutes by car; Aberdeen two hours 30 minutes and Inverness three hours.

By rail:
The cross-border service from England and Wales to Scotland is fast and efficient, and Scotrail trains offer overnight Caledonian sleepers to make the journey even easier.

Telephone 0845 748 4950 for further details.

Where to stay in
Scotland

All place names in the blue bands, under which accommodation is listed, are shown on the maps at the front of this guide.

Accommodation symbols

Symbols give useful information about services and facilities. Inside the back cover flap you can find a key to these symbols. Keep it open for easy reference.

AYR, South Ayrshire Map ref 7B2

★★★★★
TOURING PARK

BH&HPA

See Ad on inside back cover

THE CARAVAN CLUB

CRAIGIE GARDENS
CARAVAN CLUB SITE

Craigie Road, Ayr KA8 0SS
T: (01292) 264909
I: www.caravanclub.co.uk

Set in a beautiful park, a short walk from Ayr. This area, known as 'The Golf Coast', has 40 golf courses! Firth of Clyde cruises, Culzean Castle (NT). Open 26 May to 25 October. Special member rates mean you can save your membership subscription in less than a week. Visit www.caravanclub.co.uk to find out more.

Payment accepted: Delta, Mastercard, Switch, Visa

Take A77 Ayr bypass to Whitletts roundabout, then A719 via racecourse. Left at traffic lights into Craigie Road. Drive 0.5 miles, then after right-hand bend turn left into Craigie Gardens. Site 400yds on right.

90	£15.50–£20.60
90	£15.50–£20.60
90 touring pitches	

★★★★
HOLIDAY PARK

BH&HPA

NCC

HEADS OF AYR CARAVAN PARK
Dunure Road, Ayr KA7 4LD
T: (01292) 442269
F: (01292) 500298

20	£11.00–£15.00
8	£9.00–£14.00
8	£9.00–£14.00
10	£160.00–£450.00
36 touring pitches	

Five miles (8km) south of Ayr on A719. Site overlooking Arran and the Firth of Clyde. Signposted.

BALLOCH, West Dunbartonshire Map ref 7B2

★★★★★
HOLIDAY PARK

THISTLE AWARD

BH&HPA

LOMOND WOODS HOLIDAY PARK
Balloch G83 8QP
T: (01389) 755000
F: (01389) 755563
E: lomondwoods@holiday-parks.co.uk
I: www.holiday-parks.co.uk

OPEN All Year
Payment accepted: Delta, Mastercard, Switch, Visa, Euros

	£13.00–£18.00
	£13.00–£18.00
15	£13.00–£18.00
6	£200.00–£400.00
120 touring pitches	

17 miles north of Glasgow take right off A82 to Balloch/Stirling on A811. Park is on left next to Loch Lomond Shores Visitor Centre and Loch Lomond.

BALMACARA, Highland Map ref 8B3

★★★★
TOURING PARK

RERAIG CARAVAN SITE
Balmacara IV40 8DH
T: (01599) 566215
E: warden@reraig.com
I: www.reraig.com

Payment accepted:
Mastercard, Switch, Visa

40	🚐	£9.50
40	🚏	£9.50
5	▲	£9.50
45 touring pitches		

1.75 miles (3km) west of junction of A87 and A890 behind Balamacara Hotel. 4 miles east of bridge to Isle of Skye.

BLAIR ATHOLL, Perth and Kinross Map ref 7C1

★★★★★
HOLIDAY PARK

THISTLE AWARD

BH&HPA
NCC

BLAIR CASTLE CARAVAN PARK
Blair Atholl PH18 5SR
T: (01796) 481263
F: (01796) 481587
E: mail@blaircastlecaravanpark.co.uk
I: www.blaircastlecaravanpark.co.uk

Payment accepted: Delta,
Mastercard, Switch, Visa

150	🚐	£10.00–£13.00
65	🚏	£10.00–£13.00
65	▲	£10.00–£13.00
27	🏠	£190.00–£400.00
280 touring pitches		

Take A9 north from Pitlochry. Turn off for Blair Atholl after 6 miles.

BOAT OF GARTEN, Highland Map ref 8C3

★★★★
HOLIDAY PARK

THISTLE AWARD

BH&HPA
NCC

CAMPGROUNDS OF SCOTLAND
Boat of Garten PH24 3BN
T: (01479) 831652
F: (01479) 831652

OPEN All Year
Payment accepted: Euros

37	🚐	£12.50–£17.50
37	🚏	£12.50–£17.50
37	▲	£7.50–£15.50
5	🏠	£240.00–£450.00
37 touring pitches		

From the A9 take the A95 to Grantown-on-Spey then follow the signs for Boat of Garten Park situated in the centre of the village.

BRAEMAR, Aberdeenshire Map ref 8C3

★★★★
TOURING PARK

BH&HPA

See Ad on inside back cover

INVERCAULD CARAVAN CLUB SITE

Glenshee Road, Ballater AB35 5YQ
T: (01339) 741373
I: www.caravanclub.co.uk

Set on the edge of Braemar village, gateway to the Cairngorms. Ideal centre for mountain lovers. See red deer, capercaillie and golden eagles. Open 12 December 2004 to 11 October 2005. Special member rates mean you can save your membership subscription in less than a week. Visit www.caravanclub.co.uk to find out more.

Payment accepted: Delta, Mastercard, Switch, Visa

On A93 on southern outskirts of village.

100	🚐	£14.60–£20.60
100	🚏	£14.60–£20.60
	▲	On application
100 touring pitches		

Map references The map references refer to the colour maps at the front of this guide. The first figure is the map number; the letter and figure which follow indicate the grid reference on the map.

BRORA, Highland Map ref 8C2

★★★★★
TOURING PARK

BH&HPA

See Ad on inside back cover

DALCHALM CARAVAN CLUB SITE

Dalchalm, Brora KW9 6LP
T: (01408) 621479

A sheltered site where you can play golf or relax on the nearby sandy beach. Marvellous walking, bird-watching, sea and loch fishing. Open 9 April to 27 September. Special member rates mean you can save your membership subscription in less than a week. Visit www.caravanclub.co.uk to find out more.

Payment accepted: Delta, Mastercard, Switch, Visa

1.25 miles (2km) north of Brora on A9, turn right at Dalchalm.

52	🚐	£15.50–£20.60
52	🚎	£15.50–£20.60
	▲	On application
52 touring pitches		

CALLANDER, Stirling Map ref 7B1

★★★★★
HOLIDAY PARK

BH&HPA

GART CARAVAN PARK

Stirling Road, Callander FK17 8LE
T: (01877) 330002
F: (01877) 330002
E: enquiries@gart-caravan-park.co.uk
I: www.gart-caravan-park.co.uk

A peaceful and spacious park maintained to a very high standard with modern, heated shower block facilities. The ideal centre for cycling, walking and fishing. Reduced rates for the over 50s. Winner – Calor Gas Best Park in Britain 2003.

Payment accepted: Delta, Mastercard, Switch, Visa

Leave jct 10 of the M9, west to Callander.

128	🚐	£16.00
128	🚎	£16.00
128 touring pitches		

COLDINGHAM, Scottish Borders Map ref 7D2

★★★★★
HOLIDAY PARK

THISTLE AWARD

BH&HPA

SCOUTSCROFT HOLIDAY CENTRE
St Abbs Road, Coldingham TD14 5NB
T: (018907) 71338
F: (018907) 71746
E: holidays@scoutscroft.co.uk
I: www.scoutscroft.co.uk

Payment accepted: Delta, Mastercard, Switch, Visa

40	🚐	£12.00–£17.00
2	🚎	£12.00–£14.00
40	▲	£8.00–£10.00
20	🏠	£160.00–£390.00
50 touring pitches		

Twelve miles (20km) north of Berwick-upon-Tweed, turn north off A1 at Reston to Coldingham. Park on St Abbs side of Coldingham village.

CONTIN, Highland Map ref 8C3

★★
TOURING PARK

RIVERSIDE CHALETS AND CARAVAN PARK

Strathpeffer IV14 9ES
T: (01997) 421351
F: (01463) 232502

Quiet riverside site. Excellent location for touring the scenic west coast and close to Inverness. Fishing, forest walks and golf nearby.

OPEN All Year except Christmas and New Year

In Contin village, on A835 between Inverness and Ullapool at Strathpeffer junction.

	🚐	£10.00
	🚎	£10.00
	▲	£10.00
30 touring pitches		

CULLODEN, Highland Map ref 8C3

★★★★★
TOURING PARK

BH&HPA

See Ad on inside back cover

CULLODEN MOOR CARAVAN CLUB SITE

Newlands, Inverness IV2 5EF
T: (01463) 790625
I: www.caravanclub.co.uk

A gently sloping site with glorious views over the Nairn Valley. Inverness, with impressive castle, great shops and fascinating museums, is six miles away. Open 26 March to 25 October. Special member rates mean you can save your membership subscription in less than a week. Visit www.caravanclub.co.uk to find out more.

Payment accepted: Delta, Mastercard, Switch, Visa

From A9 south of Inverness, take B9006 signposted Croy, site on left 1 mile past Culloden field memorial.

97	🚐	£15.50–£20.60
97	🚗	£15.50–£20.60
	▲	On application
97 touring pitches		

THE CARAVAN CLUB

DIRLETON, East Lothian Map ref 7D2

★★★★★
TOURING PARK

BH&HPA

See Ad on inside back cover

YELLOWCRAIG CARAVAN CLUB SITE

North Berwick EH39 5DS
T: (01620) 850217
I: www.caravanclub.co.uk

This is a great choice for family holidays with acres of golden sands and rock pools close by. Open 26 March to 25 October. Special member rates mean you can save your membership subscription in less than a week. Visit www.caravanclub.co.uk to find out more.

Payment accepted: Delta, Mastercard, Switch, Visa

From North Berwick take A198, signposted Edinburgh. Turn right off bypass for Dirleton, then right again at International Camping sign.

116	🚐	£17.00–£21.50
116	🚗	£17.00–£21.50
116 touring pitches		

THE CARAVAN CLUB

DUMFRIES, Dumfries & Galloway Map ref 7C3

★★★
HOLIDAY PARK

BH&HPA

BARNSOUL FARM

Irongray, Shawhead, Dumfries DG2 9SQ
T: (01387) 730249
F: (01387) 730453
E: barnsouldg@aol.com
I: barnsoulfarm.co.uk

Barnsoul is one of Galloway's most scenic farms. 200 acres of meadows, ponds, woodlands and heath. Includes two Iron Age forts and medieval farm settlement. Special offers for small groups in bothies, tents or caravans.

Off A75 at sign for Shawhead. At Shawhead take right, then within 50m bear left. After 1.5 miles Barnsoul is on left.

10	🚐	£8.00–£12.00
10	🚗	£8.00–£12.00
10	▲	£7.00–£12.00
	🛖	£150.00–£225.00
30 touring pitches		

DUNBAR, East Lothian Map ref 7D2

★★★★
HOLIDAY PARK

THISTLE AWARD

BH&HPA

BELHAVEN BAY CARAVAN PARK
Belhaven Bay EH42 1TU
T: (01368) 865956
F: (01368) 865022
E: belhaven@meadowhead.co.uk
I: www.meadowhead.co.uk

Payment accepted:
Mastercard, Switch, Visa

53	🚐	£9.00–£17.00
53	🚗	£9.00–£17.00
53	▲	£9.00–£17.00
5	🛖	£190.00–£500.00
53 touring pitches		

From the A1 exit on north side of Dunbar. Park is about 5 miles along the A1087 on left (signed from A1).

DUNDONNELL, Highland Map ref 8B2

★★★★
CAMPING PARK

BADRALLACH BOTHY & CAMP SITE

Croft No 9, Badrallach, Garve IV23 2QP
T: (01854) 633281
E: michael.stott2@virgin.net
I: www.badrallach.com

Walk Antealloch or just sit and watch otters, porpoises, golden eagles and abundant wild flora. In the evenings relax in the gas-lit bothy by the peat stove. Canoe, boat and kite hire.

OPEN All Year

Off A832. One mile east of Dundonnell Hotel take single-track road; 7 miles to lochside site.

3	🚐	£7.50
3	🚏	£7.50
12	▲	£7.50
1	⊞	£195.00–£300.00
15 touring pitches		

DUNKELD, Perth and Kinross Map ref 7C1

★★★★
TOURING PARK

INVERMILL FARM CARAVAN PARK

Inver PH8 0JR
T: (01350) 727477
F: (01350) 727477
E: invermill@talk21.com
I: www.visitdunkeld.com/
perthshire-caravan-park.htm

Turn off the A9 onto the A822 (signposted Crieff). Immediately turn right following the sign to Inver for 0.5 miles past the static site and cross the bridge. We are the first on the left.

	🚐	£12.00–£13.00
	🚏	£12.00–£13.00
15	▲	£10.00–£11.00
50 touring pitches		

EDINBURGH, Edinburgh Map ref 7C2

★★★★
TOURING PARK

BH&HPA

LINWATER CARAVAN PARK

West Clifton, Livingston EH53 0HT
T: (0131) 333 3326
F: (0131) 333 1952
E: linwater@supanet.com
I: www.linwater.co.uk

A peaceful park seven miles west of Edinburgh. Excellent facilities. Ideal for visiting Edinburgh, Royal Highland Showground, Falkirk Wheel, or as a stop-over on your way north or south.

Payment accepted: Mastercard, Switch, Visa, Euros

At jct 1 of M9 at Newbridge or at Wilkieston on A71, follow signposts along B7030.

50	🚐	£11.00–£13.00
50	🚏	£11.00–£13.00
10	▲	£9.00–£11.00
60 touring pitches		

Credit card bookings

If you book by telephone and are asked for your credit card number it is advisable to check the proprietor's policy should you cancel your reservation.

DRUMMOHR CARAVAN PARK

Levenhall, Musselburgh, Edinburgh EH21 8JS T: (0131) 665 6867 F: (0131) 653 6859

Premier park close to Princes Street, Edinburgh, and the coast of East Lothian. Excellent bus service to city with many retail outlets in the area.

E: bookings@drummohr.org www.drummohr.org

EDINBURGH continued

★★★★
HOLIDAY PARK

THISTLE AWARD

BH&HPA

MORTONHALL CARAVAN PARK
38 Mortonhall Gate, Frogston Road East
EH16 6TJ
T: (0131) 664 1533
F: (0131) 664 5387
E: mortonhall@meadowhead.co.uk
I: www.meadowhead.co.uk

Payment accepted:
Mastercard, Switch, Visa

100	🚐	£10.00–£20.00
100	🚙	£10.00–£20.00
150	▲	£10.00–£20.00
19	🚐	£195.00–£595.00

250 touring pitches

From the city bypass at Lothianburn junction, follow signs for Mortonhall. From city centre take the roads at the east or west ends of Princes Street, heading south (A701 or A702).

FORDOUN, Aberdeenshire Map ref 7D1

★★★
HOLIDAY PARK

BROWNMUIR CARAVAN PARK
Laurencekirk AB30 1SJ
T: (01561) 320786
F: (01561) 320786
E: brownmuircaravanpark@talk21.com
I: www.brownmuircaravanpark.co.uk

10	🚐	£9.00–£10.50
10	🚙	£9.00–£10.50
5	▲	£7.00–£9.00
2	🚐	£230.00–£250.00

10 touring pitches

4 miles north of Laurencekirk, on A90 turn left at Fordoun over bridge, park 1 mile on right.

FORT WILLIAM, Highland Map ref 7B1

★★★★★
HOLIDAY PARK

BH&HPA

LINNHE LOCHSIDE HOLIDAYS

Corpach PH33 7NL
T: (01397) 772376
F: (01397) 772007
E: holidays@linnhe.demon.co.uk
I: www.linnhe-lochside-holidays.co.uk

Almost a botanical garden. Winner of 'Best Park in Scotland 1999' award. Free fishing. Colour brochure sent with pleasure. Also self-catering. Open mid-March to 31 October. Discounts for Senior Citizen groups and for 2nd week. Rallies – no charge for awnings.

Payment accepted: Delta, Mastercard, Switch, Visa, Euros

On A830 1.5 miles (3km) west of Corpach village, 5 miles from Fort William.

65	🚐	£13.50–£16.50
65	🚙	£13.50–£16.50
15	▲	£10.50–£12.50
60	🚐	£195.00–£475.00

80 touring pitches

GAIRLOCH, Highland Map ref 8B2

★★★★
HOLIDAY PARK

THISTLE AWARD

NCC

SANDS HOLIDAY CENTRE
Gairloch IV21 2DL
T: (01445) 712152
F: (01445) 712518
E: Litsands@aol.com
I: www.highlandcaravancamping.co.uk

Payment accepted: Amex,
Mastercard, Switch, Visa

120	🚐	£8.50–£11.50
40	🚙	£8.50–£11.00
120	▲	£8.50–£11.50
5	🚐	£290.00–£470.00

280 touring pitches

At Gairloch turn on to B8021 (Melvaig). Site 3 miles on, beside sandy beach.

GLENCOE, Highland Map ref 7B1

★★★★★
HOLIDAY PARK

THISTLE AWARD

BH&HPA
NCC

INVERCOE CARAVAN & CAMPING PARK
Invercoe, Glencoe PH49 4HP
T: (01855) 811210
F: (01855) 811210
E: invercoe@sol.co.uk
I: www.invercoe.co.uk

	🚐	£14.00–£16.00
	🚙	£14.00–£16.00
	▲	£14.00–£16.00
	🚐	£285.00–£420.00

60 touring pitches

Site is 0.25 miles from Glencoe crossroads (A82) on the Kinlochleven road B863.

Official guide to quality
Please mention this guide when making your booking.

INVERBEG, Argyll & Bute Map ref 7B1

★★★★
HOLIDAY PARK

THISTLE AWARD

BH&HPA

INVERBEG HOLIDAY PARK

Inverbeg, Nr Luss, Argyll G83 8PD
T: (01436) 860267
F: (01436) 860266
E: info@lochlomondholidays.co.uk
I: www.lochlomondholidays.co.uk

Beautiful holiday park on the banks of Lomond with luxury caravans and lodges for hire. Short breaks also available. Closed February. Ideal for water-sports and touring.

Payment accepted: Delta, Mastercard, Switch, Visa

4 miles north of Luss on A82.

8	⊞	£220.00–£530.00

INVERNESS, Highland Map ref 8C3

★★★★
HOLIDAY PARK

BH&HPA

AUCHNAHILLIN CARAVAN AND CAMPING PARK
Daviot East, Inverness IV2 5XQ
T: (01463) 772286
F: (01463) 772282
E: info@auchnahillin.co.uk
I: www.auchnahillin.co.uk

Payment accepted: Amex, Delta, Mastercard, Switch, Visa

	⊟	£8.00–£10.00
	⊞	£8.00–£10.00
30	▲	£7.00–£9.00
12	⊞	£135.00–£437.00
75 touring pitches		

Off A9, approximately 7 miles south of Inverness. Take B9154 east towards Moy and Daviot East.

JOHN O'GROATS, Highland Map ref 8D1

★★★
TOURING PARK

JOHN O'GROATS CARAVAN PARK
Wick KW1 4YS
T: (01955) 611329 & 611744
E: info@johnogroatscampsite.co.uk
I: www.johnogroatscampsite.co.uk

90	⊟	£8.00
90	⊞	£8.00
90	▲	£8.00
90 touring pitches		

Site on the seashore at the north end of the A99 beside the Last House in Scotland.

KENMORE, Perth and Kinross Map ref 7C1

★★★★
HOLIDAY PARK

BH&HPA

KENMORE CARAVAN AND CAMPING PARK
Aberfeldy PH15 2HN
T: (01887) 830226
F: (01887) 829059
E: info@taymouth.co.uk
I: www.taymouth.co.uk

Payment accepted: Mastercard, Visa, Euros

80	⊟	£13.00–£16.00
10	⊞	£13.00–£16.00
60	▲	£12.00–£15.00
150 touring pitches		

From A9 west on A827 at Ballinluig, 15 miles through Aberfeldy to Kenmore. Over the bridge on right-hand side.

KILLIN, Stirling Map ref 7B1

★★★★★
TOURING PARK

See Ad on inside back cover

MARAGOWAN CARAVAN CLUB SITE

Aberfeldy Road, Stirling FK21 8TN
T: (01567) 820245
I: www.caravanclub.co.uk

Set on the river Lochay, this site provides all the ingredients for a marvellous outdoor holiday and a good family base. Open 26 March to 25 November. Special member rates mean you can save your membership subscription in less than a week. Visit www.caravanclub.co.uk to find out more.

Payment accepted: Delta, Mastercard, Switch, Visa

Just north of Killin on A827.

100	⊟	£17.00–£21.50
100	⊞	£17.00–£21.50
100 touring pitches		

THE CARAVAN CLUB

KINLOCHEWE, Highland Map ref 8B3

★★★★
TOURING PARK

BH&HPA

See Ad on inside back cover

KINLOCHEWE CARAVAN CLUB SITE

Achnasheen IV22 2PA
T: (01445) 760239
I: www.caravanclub.co.uk

Peaceful site near Loch Maree. A rare and very special place with lochs, woodland and mountains - a paradise for climbers and walkers. Non-members welcome. Open 26 March to 27 September. Special member rates mean you can save your membership subscription in less than a week. Visit www.caravanclub.co.uk to find out more.

Payment accepted: Delta, Mastercard, Switch, Visa

Just north of Kinlochewe at junction of A832 and A896. Signposted.

56	🚐	£12.75–£16.00
56	🚏	£12.75–£16.00
56 touring pitches		

LAUDER, Scottish Borders Map ref 7C2

★★★★
TOURING PARK

BH&HPA

THIRLESTANE CASTLE CARAVAN AND CAMPING PARK
Thirlstone Castle, Lauder TD2 6RU
T: (01578) 722254 & 07976 231032
F: (01578) 718749
E: maitland_carew@compuserve.com

	🚐	£10.00
	🚏	£10.00
	▲	£9.00
1	🚽	£200.00–£300.00
50 touring pitches		

0.25 miles (0.5km) south of Lauder, just off A68 and A697. Edinburgh 28 miles (45km), Newcastle 68 miles (109km).

LAURENCEKIRK, Aberdeenshire Map ref 7D1

★★★★
HOLIDAY PARK

BH&HPA

DOVECOT CARAVAN PARK
Northwaterbridge AB30 1QL
T: (01674) 840630
F: (01674) 840630
E: info@dovecotcaravanpark.com
I: www.dovecotcaravanpark.com

25	🚐	£9.50–£10.50
25	🚏	£9.50–£10.50
25	▲	£7.00–£8.00
1	🚽	£200.00–£220.00
25 touring pitches		

From Laurencekirk (A90) 5 miles south at Northwater Bridge, turn right to Edzell. Site is 300m on left.

LINLITHGOW, West Lothian Map ref 7C2

★★★★
TOURING PARK

BEECRAIGS CARAVAN AND CAMPING SITE

Beecraigs Country Park, The Park Centre EH49 6PL
T: (01506) 844516
F: (01506) 846256
E: mail@beecraigs.com
I: www.beecraigs.com

Open all year. Situated near historic Linlithgow town. On-site facilities include electric hook-ups, barbecues, play area, modern toilet facilities and laundry. Pets welcome. Leaflets available. Sep 2004-Mar 2005: 10% discount for Senior Citizens (proof required) and 10% discount for 7-night stay if paid in advance (excl Senior Citizens).

OPEN All Year
Payment accepted: Delta, Mastercard, Switch, Visa

From Linlithgow, follow Beecraigs Country Park and International Caravan Park signposts. Park is 2 miles south of Linlithgow. From M8, follow B792. From M9, follow A803.

36	🚐	£10.80–£14.80
36	🚏	£10.80–£14.80
20	▲	£9.70–£10.80
56 touring pitches		

Star Ratings were correct at the time of going to press but are subject to change.
Please check at the time of booking.

LOCKERBIE, Dumfries & Galloway Map ref 7C3

★ ★ ★ ★ ★
HOLIDAY PARK

HODDOM CASTLE CARAVAN PARK
Hoddom DG11 1AS
T: (01576) 300251
F: (01576) 300757
E: hoddomcastle@aol.com
I: www.hoddomcastle.co.uk

Payment accepted:
Mastercard, Switch, Visa

100	🚐	£6.50–£12.00
100	🚙	£6.50–£12.00
30	⛺	£6.00–£12.00
130 touring pitches		

From M74 turn off at jct 19. Follow signs to Hoddom Castle from A75. Take B723 west of Annan to Lockerbie. Follow signs to Hoddom Castle.

MARKINCH, Fife Map ref 7C2

★ ★ ★ ★
TOURING PARK

BH&HPA

See Ad on inside back cover

BALBIRNIE PARK CARAVAN CLUB SITE

Balbirnie Road, Glenrothes KY7 6NR
T: (01592) 759130
I: www.caravanclub.co.uk

Attractive site set in 400 acres of parkland. Thirty golf courses, including one on site. Swimming pool, ice rink, ten-pin bowling, children's farm close by. Open 26 March to 18 October. Special member rates mean you can save your membership subscription in less than a week. Visit www.caravanclub.co.uk to find out more.

Payment accepted: Delta, Mastercard, Switch, Visa

From A92, follow signs to Markinch, then signs to Balbirnie Park Craft Centre. Site entrance is just inside park on right, 0.5 miles west of Markinch.

77	🚐	£13.35–£17.60
77	🚙	£13.35–£17.60
	⛺	On application
77 touring pitches		

THE CARAVAN CLUB

MELROSE, Scottish Borders Map ref 7C2

★ ★ ★ ★ ★
TOURING PARK

BH&HPA

See Ad on inside back cover

GIBSON PARK CARAVAN CLUB SITE

High St, Melrose TD6 9RY
T: (01896) 822969
I: www.caravanclub.co.uk

Peaceful, award-winning site on edge of town. Adjacent tennis courts and playing fields. Melrose Abbey, where Robert the Bruce's head is buried, is within walking distance. Non-members welcome. Special member rates mean you can save your membership subscription in less than a week. Visit www.caravanclub.co.uk to find out more.

OPEN All Year
Payment accepted: Delta, Mastercard, Switch, Visa

Site adjacent to main road (A6091) close to centre of town. Approximately 6 miles (10km) from A68 Edinburgh/Newcastle road.

60	🚐	£16.10–£21.50
60	🚙	£16.10–£21.50
	⛺	On application
60 touring pitches		

THE CARAVAN CLUB

NEWTONGRANGE, Midlothian Map ref 7C2

★ ★ ★ ★
TOURING PARK

LOTHIAN BRIDGE CARAVAN PARK
Lothian Bridge, Dalkeith EH22 4TP
T: (0131) 663 6120

46	🚐	£12.00–£14.00
46	🚙	£12.00–£14.00
30	⛺	£8.00–£10.00
46 touring pitches		

Campsite 7 miles south of Edinburgh on A7.

Symbols The symbols in each entry give information about services and facilities. A key to these symbols appears at the back of this guide.

NORTH BERWICK, East Lothian Map ref 7D2

★★★★★
HOLIDAY PARK

THISTLE AWARD

BH&HPA

TANTALLON CARAVAN PARK
Dunbar Road, North Berwick EH39 5NJ
T: (01620) 893348
F: (01620) 895623
E: tantallon@meadowhead.co.uk
I: www.meadowhead.co.uk

Payment accepted:
Mastercard, Switch, Visa

147	🚐	£10.00–£19.00
147	🚏	£10.00–£19.00
40	⛺	£10.00–£19.00
10	🏠	£200.00–£500.00
147 touring pitches		

From North Berwick take A198 towards Dunbar. From the south, turn off at A1 north of Dunbar and follow signs for North Berwick and Tantallon Park. Situated on east side of town.

PORT LOGAN, Dumfries & Galloway Map ref 7B3

★★★★
TOURING PARK

BH&HPA

See Ad on inside back cover

NEW ENGLAND BAY CARAVAN CLUB SITE
Stranraer DG9 9NX
T: (01776) 860275
I: www.caravanclub.co.uk

On the edge of Luce Bay, an ideal site for children with direct access to a safe, clean, sandy beach. Sailing, sea-angling, golf, green bowling, pony-trekking. Open 26 March to 25 October. Special member rates mean you can save your membership subscription in less than a week. Visit www.caravanclub.co.uk to find out more.

Payment accepted: Delta, Mastercard, Switch, Visa

From Newton Stewart take A75, then A715, then A716. Site on left 2.7 miles past Ardwell Filling Station.

150	🚐	£13.35–£17.60
150	🚏	£13.35–£17.60
	⛺	On application
150 touring pitches		

ST ANDREWS, Fife Map ref 7C1

★★★★★
HOLIDAY PARK

THISTLE AWARD

BH&HPA

CRAIGTOUN MEADOWS HOLIDAY PARK
Mount Melville, St Andrews KY16 8PQ
T: (01334) 475959
F: (01334) 476424
E: craigtoun@aol.com
I: www.craigtounmeadows.co.uk
Contact us for prices during British Golf Open.

Payment accepted: Delta,
Mastercard, Switch, Visa

58	🚐	£15.50–£22.00
58	🚏	£15.50–£22.00
9	⛺	£13.50–£16.50
27	🏠	£260.00–£490.00
67 touring pitches		

From M90 jct 8 take A91 to St Andrews. Turn right 436 yds (400m) after Guardbridge, signed Strathkinness. Turn left at 2nd crossroads after Strathkinness.

SHIEL BRIDGE, Highland Map ref 8B3

★★★★★
TOURING PARK

BH&HPA

See Ad on inside back cover

MORVICH CARAVAN CLUB SITE
Kyle Of Lochalsh IV40 8HQ
T: (01599) 511354
I: www.caravanclub.co.uk

An ideal holiday base and a paradise for walkers and climbers, with dazzling scenery, hills and mountains (much of it owned by the National Trust). Open 26 March to 25 October. Special member rates mean you can save your membership subscription in less than a week. Visit www.caravanclub.co.uk to find out more.

Payment accepted: Delta, Mastercard, Switch, Visa

From A87 at head of Loch Duich turn onto unclassified road signposted Morvich, after 1 mile turn onto side road into site.

76	🚐	£15.50–£20.60
76	🚏	£15.50–£20.60
30	⛺	On application
106 touring pitches		

Colour maps Colour maps at the front of this guide pinpoint all places in which you will find parks listed.

STIRLING, Stirling Map ref 7C2

★★★★
TOURING PARK

BH&HPA

See Ad on inside back cover

BLAIR DRUMMOND CARAVAN CLUB SITE

Cuthill Brae, Stirling FK9 4UX
T: (01786) 841208
I: www.caravanclub.co.uk

Set in the walled garden of Blair Drummond House at Doune. Centrally located for east and west coasts. Golf courses at Stirling and Gleneagles (20 miles). Open 26 March to 3 January 2006. Special member rates mean you can save your membership subscription in less than a week. Visit www.caravanclub.co.uk to find out more.

Payment accepted: Delta, Mastercard, Switch, Visa

From Stirling take A84 signposted Crianlarich after passing over M9 at jct 10. Turn right within 3 miles after passing A873 on left. Past church on left.

88	🚐	£14.60–£20.60
88	🚏	£14.60–£20.60
88 touring pitches		

★★★★★
TOURING PARK

BH&HPA

WITCHES CRAIG CARAVAN PARK
Blairlogie, Stirling FK9 5PX
T: (01786) 474947
F: (01786) 447286
E: info@witchescraig.co.uk
I: www.witchescraig.co.uk

Stirling – St Andrews road, A91. 3 miles north-east of Stirling.

60	🚐	£11.00–£13.00
60	🚏	£11.00–£13.00
60	⛺	£11.00–£13.00
60 touring pitches		

ULLAPOOL, Highland Map ref 8B2

★★★★
TOURING PARK

BH&HPA

ARDMAIR POINT HOLIDAY PARK
Ardmair Point, Ullapool IV26 2TN
T: (01854) 612054
F: (01854) 612757
E: sales@ardmair.com
I: www.ardmair.com

Payment accepted: Delta, Mastercard, Switch, Visa, Euros

Situated 3.5 miles north of Ullapool on A835. Entrance next to telephone kiosk at Ardmair beach.

45	🚐	£10.00
45	🚏	£10.00
45	⛺	£10.00
45 touring pitches		

WICK, Highland Map ref 8D2

★★★★
TOURING PARK

BH&HPA

See Ad on inside back cover

RIVERSIDE CARAVAN CLUB SITE

Janetstown, Wick KW1 5SR
T: (01955) 605420
E: www.caravanclub.co.uk

Nature lovers will enjoy the seabirds and seal colonies off the coast at this excellent away-from-it-all site set in a meadow alongside the river Wick. Open 9 April to 27 September. Special member rates mean you can save your membership subscription in less than a week. Visit www.caravanclub.co.uk to find out more.

Payment accepted: Delta, Mastercard, Switch, Visa

On southern outskirts of Wick. From A9 take A882 signposted Thurso. Site on right after 500yds (480m) along Riverside Drive.

90	🚐	£12.75–£16.00
90	🚏	£12.75–£16.00
	⛺	On application
90 touring pitches		

NB

Important note Information on accommodation listed in this guide has been supplied by the proprietors. As changes may occur you are advised to check details at the time of booking.

A brief guide to the main towns and villages offering accommodation in **Scotland**

AYR, Ayrshire
One of Scotland's brightest seaside resorts. Also a Royal Burgh and noted centre for the manufacture of carpets and fabrics. Many associations with the poet Robert Burns. Faces the Isle of Arran across the Firth of Clyde.

BALLOCH, West Dunbartonshire
Situated at the southern end of Loch Lomond, an ideal starting place for touring the loch.

BALMACARA, Highland
Small village on the north shore of Loch Alsh with views towards the Sound of Sleat and Skye.

BLAIR ATHOLL, Perth and Kinross
Highland village at the foot of the Grampian mountains.

CALLANDER, Central
A favourite centre for exploring the Trossachs and the Highlands, beautifully situated at the entrance to the Pass of Leny.

DUMFRIES, Dumfries & Galloway
Fascinating town with old five-arched bridge spanning the river Nith. County capital and Royal Burgh with associations with Robert Burns, James Barrie and Robert Bruce. Burns died here and the house he occupied contains interesting personal relics. His tomb is in St Michaels.

DUNBAR, Lothian
Popular seaside resort at the foot of the Lammermuir Hills. Good bathing from extensive sands. On the rock above the harbour are the remains of Dunbar Castle. Mary Queen of Scots fled here with Darnley in 1566, immediately after the murder of Rizzio, her secretary.

DUNDONNELL, Highland
Locality of scattered crofting hamlets round the shores of Little Loch Broom, dominated by the magnificent ridge of An Teallach. Glorious scenery, mountaineering and sea angling.

DUNKELD, Perth and Kinross
Picturesque cathedral town beautifully situated in the richly wooded valley of the river Tay on the edge of the Perthshire Highlands. Salmon and trout fishing.

EDINBURGH, Lothian
Scotland's capital and international festival city. Dominated by its ancient fortress, the city is surrounded by hills, woodlands and rivers. Good shopping on Princes Street.

FORT WILLIAM, Highland
One of the finest touring centres in the Western Highlands. A busy holiday town set on the shores of Loch Linnhe at the western end of the Great Glen almost in the shadow of Ben Nevis, the highest mountain in the British Isles. Nearby are fishing, climbing, walking and steamer trips to the islands.

GLENCOE, Highland
Village at the foot of Glen Coe, a deep and rugged defile enclosed by towering mountains. Scene of massacre of MacDonalds of Glencoe by the Campbells of Glen Lyon in 1692. A valley of haunting beauty offering winter sports.

LAUDER, Scottish Borders
Royal Burgh with quaint old tolbooth, 16thC church and medieval Thirlstane Castle.

LINLITHGOW, West Lothian
Historic town west of Edinburgh whose industries include electronics, distilling and manufacturing. Close by stand the ruins of Linlithgow Palace, birthplace of Mary Queen of Scots.

LOCKERBIE, Dumfries & Galloway
Market town in the beautiful Valley of Annandale.

NORTH BERWICK, Lothian
Holiday resort on the Firth of Forth with sandy beaches, golf and a picturesque harbour.

STIRLING, Central
Ancient town with a long and turbulent history. The famous castle perched on its towering rock was a vital stronghold which became the scene of several battles, notably the Battle of Bannockburn in 1314.

Below, from left historic Edinburgh; take a nostalgic journey on the West Highland Line

enjoyEngland™
official guides to quality

Hotels, Townhouses,
Travel Accommodation
and Restaurants with
Rooms in England 2005
£10.99

Bed & Breakfasts,
Guesthouses, Small Hotels,
Farmhouses, Inns, Campus
Accommodation and Hostels
in England 2005
£11.99

Self-Catering
Holiday Homes and Boat
Accommodation
in England 2005
£11.99

Touring Parks, Camping, Holiday Parks
and Villages in Britain 2005
£8.99

Somewhere Special
in England 2005
£8.99

Families and Pets Welcome
in England 2005
£11.99

INFORMATIVE • EASY TO USE • GREAT VALUE FOR MONEY

The guides include:

- **Accommodation entries packed with information**
- **Full colour maps**
- **Places to visit**
- **Tourist Information Centres**

From all good bookshops or by mail order from:

VisitBritain Fulfilment Centre,
c/o Westex Ltd, 7 St Andrews Way,
Devons Road, Bromley-by-Bow, London E3 3PA
Tel: 0870 606 7204
Fax: (020) 7987 6505
Email: fulfilment@visitbritain.org

Wales

Looking for some inspiration? Here are a few ideas to get you started in Wales. **experience** something new and go coasteering in quirky Pembrokeshire. **explore** the stunning Snowdonian landscape of mountains and lakes. **discover** alternative lifestyles at Mid Wales' Centre for Alternative Technology. **relax** with a cocktail in hand, watching the sun set over cosmopolitan Cardiff Bay.

CONTACT

▸ WALES TOURIST BOARD
Brunel House, 2 Fitzalan Road,
Cardiff CF24 OUY
T: 0870 121 1251
F: 0870 121 1259
Minicom: 0870 121 1255
E: info@visitwales.com
www.visitwales.com

For a small country Wales is big on things to see and do. To start with it has three National Parks, each one featuring very different landscapes, and a turbulent history which comes alive in its many castles. Search out Wales' fascinating industrial heritage and discover its myths and legends.

Nature at its best

In big, bold Snowdonia National Park walk to the summit of Mount Snowdon, or take the little mountain railway. Pembrokeshire has Britain's only coastal-based National Park where the sea air fills your lungs and the wildlife captures your attention. The Brecon Beacons National Park is filled with the greenest, grassiest hills you'll ever see. Walk, cycle, or take a trip on a canal-boat, whichever you prefer.

Cappuccinos and citadels

Europe's youngest capital, Cardiff is just a stone's throw from the Beacons' wide, open spaces. It's cosmopolitan, lively and busy. Join in the café culture and don't miss the stunning new waterfront along Cardiff Bay. Make sure you visit the fabulous city-centre castle. Castles, of course, are what Wales does very well. There are hundreds of them, ranging from Harlech, Beaumaris, Caernarfon and Conwy, part of Edward I's mighty iron ring of castles in the north, to romantic hilltop fortresses such as Carreg Cennen near Llandeilo. Here it's easy to conjure up tales of princes, wizards and dragons as you climb its ramparts or explore the eerie underground passage.

Experience the country's fascinating industrial heritage first-hand in places like the Big Pit at Blaenavon and the Llechwedd Slate Caverns where you go underground and find out exactly what it was like to work there.

Left, from top hands-on at Techniquest, Cardiff; picturesque coastline at Three Cliffs Bay, Gower; gallop through beautiful countryside in Harlech Right savour deserted beaches at Pembrey Country Park, Cefn Sidan

Get up and go

For all its history, Wales doesn't live in the past. It's an exciting, forward-looking country, full of zest, activity and adventure. You can go mountain biking or try parascending and white-water rafting. For quieter exploration walk, cycle or ride on waymarked trails through hill and vale. At the Centre for Alternative Technology in mid Wales you'll find the village of the future with lots of child-friendly exhibits and events throughout the year. Hold your breath as you shoot down Europe's largest wooden rollercoaster at Oakwood Theme Park or ride gently on Wales' charming Great Little Trains – scenic narrow-gauge railways that puff their way to the loveliest corners of the country.

And there's plenty going on all over Wales. Give your tastebuds a treat in September at the Abergavenny Food Festival or at Caerphilly's Big Cheese extravaganza in July. Or for something completely different watch the extraordinary World Bog Snorkelling Championships near Llanwrtyd Wells on August Bank Holiday Monday. As you would expect, there is music everywhere. Tap your feet to the beat of jazz at the renowned Brecon Jazz Festival in August or immerse yourself in all things Welsh at the National Eisteddfod.

Places to visit

Alice in Wonderland Centre

The Rabbit Hole, Llandudno, Conwy
Tel: (01492) 860082
www.wonderland.co.uk
Follow in Alice's footsteps – go through the rabbit hole to see life-size scenes from Lewis Carroll's famous book. Books and memorabilia sold at the shop.

The Animalarium
Ynys Fergi, Borth, Ceredigion
Tel: (01970) 871224
www.animalarium.co.uk
Unusual and interesting collection of exotic and domestic creatures to amuse and delight, including monkeys, lemurs, snakes and crocodiles. Animal petting barn, snake handling, pony rides, play areas and café.

Big Pit National Mining Museum of Wales
Blaenavon, Torfaen
Tel: (01495) 790311
www.nmgw.ac.uk/bigpit
Experience the atmosphere of a real mine. Enter the pit cage to travel down 300ft and walk through underground roadways with an ex-miner as your guide.

Brecon Mountain Railway
Pant Station, Pontsticill, Merthyr Tydfil
Tel: (01685) 722988
www.breconmountainrailway.co.uk
Narrow-gauge steam railway running into the Brecon Beacons National Park, giving wonderful mountain, lakeside and forest views.

Caerleon Roman Fortress Baths
Broadway, Caerleon, Newport
Tel: (01633) 422518
www.cadw.wales.gov.uk
Travel back in time at the site of the Roman legionary fortress Isca, base of the elite 2nd Augustan legion in Britain from about AD75. Impressive remains of baths, amphitheatre, barracks and fortress walls.

Caernarfon Castle
Castle Ditch, Caernarfon, Gwynedd
Tel: (01286) 677617
www.cadw.wales.gov.uk
Famous as the setting for the investiture of HRH Prince Charles as Prince of Wales, now a World Heritage Site, this majestic medieval fortress was originally built for King Edward I.

Caerphilly Castle
Caerphilly
Tel: (029) 2088 3143
www.cadw.wales.gov.uk
Reminiscent of history lessons, massive 13thC Caerphilly Castle is a superb example of the concentric walls-within-walls system of defence, and has four gatehouses, and lake and island water defences.

Carew Castle & Tidal Mill
Carew, Tenby, Pembrokeshire
Tel: (01646) 651782
www.carewcastle.com
This magnificent Norman castle later became an Elizabethan residence with royal links to Henry Tudor, and was the setting for the Great Tournament of 1507, drawing 600 knights to the contest.

Castell Coch
Tongwynlais, Cardiff
Tel: (029) 2081 0101
www.cadw.wales.gov.uk
The ultimate fairytale castle with conical towers and turrets, Castell Coch was built in 1875 by eccentric architect William Burgess for the Marquess of Bute.

Celtica
Y Plas, Machynlleth, Powys
Tel: (01654) 702702
www.celticawales.com
They rattled the Romans, stunned the Saxons and nobbled the Normans. Celtica is an unique interpretive centre looking at the history and culture of the Celts.

Conwy Castle

Rosehill Street, Conwy
Tel: (01492) 592358
www.cadw.wales.gov.uk
Now a World Heritage Site, this imposing fortress was
built between 1283 and 1287. Relish the breathtaking
views from the battlements across mountains and the sea.

Dan-yr-Ogof: the National Showcaves Centre for Wales

Glyntawe, Abercraf, Swansea
Tel: (01639) 730801
www.showcaves.co.uk
Experience three award-winning show caves and dinosaur
park and meet the gentle giants of the horse world at the
Shire Horse Centre. Barney Owl's covered play area.

Felinwynt Rainforest Centre

Felinwynt, Cardigan, Ceredigion
Tel: (01239) 810250
www.felinwyntrainforest.co.uk
Be transported to a rainforest – this mini version displays
exotic plants, houses free flying tropical butterflies and
resonates with the sounds of the Amazon.

Ffestiniog Railway
Harbour Station, Porthmadog, Gwynedd
Tel: (01766) 516024
www.festrail.co.uk
Narrow-gauge steam and diesel railway service from
Porthmadog to Blaenau Ffestiniog, and between
Caernarfon and Waunfawr, with wonderful views.

Folly Farm

Begelly, Kilgetty, Pembrokeshire
Tel: (01834) 812731
www.folly-farm.co.uk
Enjoy the magical fun of the farm, with bottle-feeding,
hand-milking and birds of prey. Vintage fun fair, go-karts,
adventure play, restaurants and shops.

Gower Heritage Centre

Parkmill, Swansea
Tel: (01792) 371206
www.gowerheritagecentre.co.uk
Set in the beautiful Gower Peninsula, the centre is based
around a 12thC water-powered corn and saw mill, with
craft workshops, tearooms and children's puppet theatre.

Harlech Castle

Castle Square, Harlech, Gwynedd
Tel: (01766) 780552
www.harlech.com
An imposing edifice, this magnificent 13thC castle, now a
World Heritage Site, was built by King Edward I to defend
Snowdonia and has spectacular views across land and sea.

Kidwelly Castle

Castle Road, Kidwelly, Carmarthenshire
Tel: (01554) 890104
www.cadw.wales.gov.uk
Remarkably complete Norman stronghold built in 1106 to
a concentric walls-within-walls design with round towers
and a massive twin-towered gatehouse.

Llangollen Motor Museum
Pentrefelin, Llangollen, Denbighshire
Tel: (01978) 860324
www.llangollenmotormuseum.co.uk
Choose from four wheels or two. On display are classic
cars, more than 30 British motorcycles and fascinating
automobilia. Reference library and canal exhibition.

Museum of Welsh Life

St Fagans, Cardiff
Tel: (029) 2057 3500
www.nmgw.ac.uk
See Wales in a day from Celtic times to the present at
Europe's leading open air museum. Over 40 historic
buildings rebuilt here to recreate 500 years of Welsh
history.

National Cycle Collection
The Automobile Palace, Llandrindod Wells, Powys
Tel: (01597) 825531
www.cyclemuseum.org.uk
Journey through the lanes of cycle history and see over
200 machines from 1818 like the hobby horse,
boneshaker and penny farthing, up to the most modern
cycles of today.

National Museum and Gallery of Wales

Cathays Park, Cardiff
Tel: (029) 2039 7951
www.nmgw.ac.uk
Unrivalled in Britain, this museum houses dazzling
displays of art, natural history and science. World-class art
galleries include one of the finest Impressionist collections
outside Paris.

Left be amazed at the elegant drawing room at Castell Coch, Tongwynlais; take a train ride into the Brecon Beacons

Places to visit

Accredited with the Wales Tourist Board Visitor Attraction Assurance Service marque

National Wetlands Centre, Wales
Llanelli Centre, Llwynhendy, Carmarthenshire
Tel: (01554) 741087
www.wwt.org.uk
Visit this wetlands reserve in Llanelli, facing the Gower Peninsula, teeming with hundreds of waterfowl and wildlife. The only centre of its kind in Wales.

Pembroke Castle
Main Street, Pembroke, Pembrokeshire
Tel: (01646) 681510
www.pembrokecastle.co.uk
This early 13thC Norman castle was the birthplace of Henry VII, and has a 22m- (75ft-) high circular great tower. Browse the exhibitions which give an insight into both county history and national heritage.

Powis Castle and Garden (National Trust)
Powis Castle and Garden, Welshpool, Powys
Tel: (01938) 551944
www.nationaltrust.org.uk
Stunning, world-famous Italian and French style terraced garden to admire. The medieval castle perched above the garden contains fine collections of paintings and furniture, and treasures from India.

Raglan Castle
Raglan, Usk, Monmouthshire
Tel: (01291) 690228
www.cadw.wales.gov.uk
Raglan is the finest late medieval fortress-palace in the British Isles, preserving a wealth of decorative detail in its beautifully dressed sandstone walls.

Rhiannon Welsh Gold Centre
Canolfan Aur Cymru, Tregaron, Ceredigion
Tel: (01974) 298415
www.rhiannon.co.uk
Watch goldsmiths at work at this craft design centre and jewellery workshop specialising in the Welsh and Celtic heritage.

Rhondda Heritage Park
Lewis Merthyr Colliery, Trehafod, Rhondda, Cynon, Taff
Tel: (01443) 682036
www.rhonddaheritagepark.com
Helmets compulsory! Ex-miners will guide you around this award-winning underground mining attraction based at the former Lewis Merthyr Colliery.

Roman Legionary Museum
High Street, Caerleon, Newport
Tel: (01633) 423134
www.nmgw.ac.uk/rlm
See all aspects of a Roman soldier's life from his arms, armour and equipment to his religious beliefs, leisure time and even his death.

St Davids Cathedral
The Close, St Davids, Haverfordwest, Pembrokeshire
Tel: (01437) 720691
www.stdavidscathedral.org.uk
Built on the site where St David founded a monastic settlement in the 6thC, the outstanding features of this cathedral are the magnificent ceilings and sloping floor.

Snowdon Mountain Railway
Llanberis, Caernarfon, Gwynedd
Tel: 0870 458 0033
www.snowdonrailway.co.uk
An amazing feat of engineering, Britain's only rack and pinion mountain railway rises from the lakeside village of Llanberis and almost reaches the summit of Snowdon.

Talyllyn Railway
Wharf Station, Tywyn, Gwynedd
Tel: (01654) 710472
www.talyllyn.co.uk
A great day out. Coal-fired, steam-operated, narrow-gauge railway running 7.5 miles into Snowdonia National Park. Forest walks, museum, waterfalls, cafés and shops.

Techniquest

Stuart Street, Cardiff
Tel: (029) 2047 5475
www.techniquest.org
Launch a hot air balloon, create your own shadow in colour or film your own animation! All this and more in the UK's most visited hands-on science discovery centre.

Tintern Abbey

Tintern, Chepstow, Monmouthshire
Tel: (029) 2050 0200
www.cadw.wales.gov.uk
The sublime beauty of Tintern, the best preserved medieval abbey in Wales, has brought travellers to this river bank in the wooded Wye Valley for hundred of years.

Zoological Society of Wales
Welsh Mountain Zoo

Flagstaff Gardens, Colwyn Bay, Conwy
Tel: (01492) 532938
www.welshmountainzoo.org
Set in a lovely location on the North Wales coast, the zoo is within a large wooded estate with a formal terraced garden and informal woodland garden.

Left majestic St Davids Cathedral, Haverfordwest; step back in time at Pembroke Castle **Below** take a well-earned break while watching the sun go down in Llyn Mymbyr

Wales Tourist Board

Brunel House, 2 Fitzalan Road, Cardiff CF24 OUY
T: 0870 121 1251   F: 0870 121 1259
Minicom: 0870 121 1255
E: info@visitwales.com
www.visitwales.com

Travel information

By road:

Travelling to South and West Wales is easy on the M4 and the dual carriageway network. The new Second Severn Crossing gives two ways to enter Wales, but those wishing to visit Chepstow and the Wye Valley should use the original Severn Bridge and the M48 (originally part of the M4). In North Wales the A55 'Expressway' has made travelling speedier, whilst mid Wales is accessible via the M54 which links with the M6, M5 and M1.

By rail:

Fast and frequent Great Western Intercity trains travel between London Paddington and Cardiff, departing hourly and half-hourly at peak times, and taking only two hours. Newport, Bridgend, Port Talbot, Neath and Swansea are also accessible through this service, which encompasses most of West Wales. London Euston links to the North Wales coast via Virgin Trains, who also run a service between the North East of England and South Wales. In addition, Wales and West Passenger Trains run Alphaline services from London Waterloo, Manchester and the North East, Brighton and the South, and Nottingham and the Heart of England.

For further rail enquiries, please telephone 0845 748 4950.

Wales on the web www.visitwales.com

Find out all you need to know from the Wales Tourist Board website. It's your instant route to up-to-the-minute information on accommodation, attractions, activities and events. It's also full of ideas for travel itineraries and themes to explore – and you can use it to book online.

Below a gentle ride though stunning Snowdonian scenery

Where to stay in
Wales

All place names in the blue bands, under which accommodation is listed, are shown on the maps at the front of this guide.

Accommodation symbols

Symbols give useful information about services and facilities. Inside the back cover flap you can find a key to these symbols. Keep it open for easy reference.

ABERAERON, Ceredigion Map ref 1A2

★★★★
HOLIDAY, TOURING & CAMPING PARK

BH&HPA

AERON COAST CARAVAN PARK
North Road, Aberaeron SA46 0JF
T: (01545) 570349
E: aeroncoastcaravanpark@aberaeron.
freeserve.co.uk

Payment accepted:
Mastercard, Switch, Visa

100	🚐	£10.50–£14.00
100	🚐	£10.50–£14.00
100	⛺	£10.50–£14.00
100 touring pitches		

Situated on main coastal A487 road on northern edge of Aberaeron. Filling station at entrance. Signposted.

🔌 🚗 📶 ♿ 🅿️ 🔥 🛒 🍴 📺 ⬛🔘⊙ ● ⚡ ☕ 🎣 🐕 🎵 ☀

ABERGAVENNY, Monmouthshire Map ref 1B3

★★★★
TOURING PARK

BH&HPA

See Ad on inside back cover

PANDY CARAVAN CLUB SITE
Abergavenny NP7 8DR
T: (01873) 890370
I: www.caravanclub.co.uk

Attractively landscaped site where you can fish (by permit from the site), pony trek or walk on Offa's Dyke or in the Brecon Beacons National Park. Open 26 March to 1 November. Special member rates mean you can save your membership subscription in less than a week. Visit www.caravanclub.co.uk to find out more.

Payment accepted: Delta, Mastercard, Switch, Visa

From south do not go into Abergavenny, continue onto A465 (signposted Hereford). In 6.25 miles turn left by The Old Pandy Inn, onto minor road. Site on left after passing under railway bridge. Signposted.

53	🚐	£14.60–£20.60
53	🚐	£14.60–£20.60
53 touring pitches		

THE CARAVAN CLUB

🔌 🚗 📶 ♿ 🅿️ 🔥 ⬛🔘⊙ 🐕

255

ABERGELE

See display advertisement below

BARMOUTH, Gwynedd Map ref 1A2

★★★★
HOLIDAY PARK

BH&HPA
NCC

PARC CAERELWAN
Talybont, Nr Barmouth LL43 2AX
T: (01341) 247236
F: (01341) 247711
E: parc@porthmadog.co.uk
I: www.porthmadog.co.uk/parc/

OPEN All Year
Payment accepted: Amex,
Delta, Mastercard, Switch,
Visa

70 ⊞ £244.00–£450.00

On the A496 coast road 5 miles north of Barmouth. Signposted.

BRECON, Powys Map ref 1B3

★★★★★
**TOURING &
CAMPING PARK**

BH&HPA

BRYNICH CARAVAN PARK
Brecon LD3 7SH
T: (01874) 623325
F: (01874) 623325
E: holidays@brynich.co.uk
I: www.brynich.co.uk

Payment accepted: Delta,
Mastercard, Switch, Visa

50		£13.00–£18.00
20		£13.00–£18.00
60	▲	£8.00–£13.00
130 touring pitches		

The caravan park is situated on the A470, 200yds from the junction with the A40, 2km east of Brecon. Signposted.

CAERNARFON, Gwynedd Map ref 1A1

★★★
**TOURING &
CAMPING PARK**

BH&HPA

CWM CADNANT VALLEY
Llanberis Road, Caernarfon LL55 2DF
T: (01286) 673196
F: (01286) 675941
E: etc@cwmcadnant.co.uk
I: www.cwmcadnant.co.uk

Payment accepted: Delta,
Mastercard, Switch, Visa

35		£10.00–£14.00
5		£10.00–£14.00
25	▲	£8.00–£12.00
60 touring pitches		

A487 to Caernarfon then A4086 for Llanberis – we are opposite the school. Signposted.

Quality Assurance Standard

For an explanation of the quality and facilities represented by the stars please refer to the front of this guide. A more detailed explanation can be found in the information pages at the back.

CAERNARFON continued

★★★
TOURING &
CAMPING PARK

BH&HPA

TY'N YR ONNEN HOLIDAY PARK

Waunfawr, Caernarfon LL55 4AX
T: (01286) 650281
F: (01286) 650043
E: tom.griffith1@btopenworld.com
I: tyn-yr-onnen.co.uk

Ty'n yr Onnen is a paradise for walkers, on the edge of the Snowdonia range. High-quality facilities. Central, convenient to find from motorway. Camp fires. Donkeys, nature trail. Donkeys, nature trail, other animals to cuddle. Footpath to Snowdon summit from park. Fishing, walkers' paradise.

Payment accepted: Delta, Mastercard, Switch, Visa, Euros

Take the A4085 from Caernarfon. Turn left at Waunfawr fish and chip shop (near church). We are located on the left-hand side.

20	£8.00–£10.00	
10	£6.00–£8.00	
30	£7.00–£10.00	
3	£150.00–£350.00	
60 touring pitches		

CARDIGAN, Ceredigion Map ref 1A2

★★★★★
HOLIDAY PARK

BH&HPA

CENARTH FALLS HOLIDAY PARK
Newcastle Emlyn SA38 9JS
T: (01239) 710345
F: (01239) 710344
E: enquiries@cenarth-holipark.co.uk
I: www.cenarth-holipark.co.uk

Payment accepted: Delta, Mastercard, Switch, Visa

30	£13.00–£22.00	
30	£13.00–£22.00	
30	£13.00–£22.00	
4	£200.00–£550.00	
30 touring pitches		

After 0.25 miles from Cenarth bridge turn right at park signs. Situated off A484 Cardigan-Carmarthen Road. Signposted for Holiday Park and Corades Health and Leisure Club.

COLWYN BAY, Conwy Map ref 1B1

★★★★★
TOURING PARK

BRON-Y-WENDON TOURING CARAVAN PARK
Wern Road, Llanddulas, Colwyn Bay
LL22 8HG
T: (01492) 512903
F: (01492) 512903
E: bron-y-wendon@northwales-holidays.co.uk
I: www.northwales-holidays.co.uk

OPEN All Year
Payment accepted:
Mastercard, Switch, Visa

120	£13.00–£16.00	
10	£13.00–£16.00	
130 touring pitches		

Leave the A55 at the Llanddulas interchange, jct 23 (A547) and follow the Tourist Information signs to the Park.

Map references The map references refer to the colour maps at the front of this guide. The first figure is the map number; the letter and figure which follow indicate the grid reference on the map.

CWMCARN, Newport Map ref 1B3

★★★
TOURING &
CAMPING PARK

CWMCARN FOREST DRIVE CAMP SITE
Nantcarn Road, Nr Newport NP11 7FA
T: (01495) 272001
F: (01495) 271403
E: cwmcarn-vc@caerphilly.gov.uk
I: www.caerphilly.gov.uk/visiting

OPEN All Year except
Christmas and New Year
Payment accepted:
Mastercard, Switch, Visa

4	🚐	£8.50–£10.00
	�	£8.50–£10.00
	▲	£6.00–£9.00
37 touring pitches		

M4 jct 28, follow A467 for 7 miles to Cwmcarn, follow brown tourism signs.

FISHGUARD, Pembrokeshire Map ref 1A2

★★★★
HOLIDAY, TOURING
& CAMPING PARK

DRAGON AWARD

BH&HPA

FISHGUARD BAY CARAVAN & CAMPING PARK
Garn Gelli, Fishguard SA65 9ET
T: (01348) 811415
F: (01348) 811425
E: inquiries@fishguardbay.com
I: www.fishguardbay.com

OPEN All Year except
Christmas and New Year
Payment accepted: Delta,
Mastercard, Switch, Visa

	🚐	£11.50–£13.50
30	�	£11.50–£13.50
8	▲	£10.50–£12.50
	🏠	£195.00–£440.00
20 touring pitches		

Take A487 Cardigan Road from Fishguard, 3 miles outside Fishguard, turning on left. Signposted.

★★★★
TOURING PARK

BH&HPA

GWAUN VALE TOURING PARK
Fishguard SA65 9TA
T: (01348) 874698
E: margaret.harries@talk21.com

19	🚐	£11.00–£12.50
20	�	£11.00–£12.50
8	▲	£9.50–£11.00
28 touring pitches		

From Fishguard, take B4313 for 1.5 miles. The site is on the right. Signposted.

HORTON, Swansea Map ref 1A3

★★
HOLIDAY, TOURING
& CAMPING PARK

NCC

BANK FARM
Horton, Swansea SA3 1LL
T: (01792) 390228
F: (01792) 391282
E: bankfarmleisure@aol.com
I: bankfarmleisure.co.uk

Payment accepted: Amex,
Delta, Mastercard, Switch,
Visa

	🚐	£10.00–£19.00
	�	£10.00–£13.00
	▲	£10.00–£19.00
230 touring pitches		

End of A4118 from Swansea. Turn left for Horton.

KEESTON, Pembrokeshire Map ref 1A3

★★★★
HOLIDAY PARK

DRAGON AWARD

BH&HPA

SCAMFORD CARAVAN PARK
Keeston, Haverfordwest SA62 6HN
T: (01437) 710304
F: (01437) 710304
E: holidays@scamford.com
I: www.scamford.com

Payment accepted: Delta,
Mastercard, Switch, Visa

5	🚐	£6.50–£8.50
5	�	£6.50–£8.50
25	🏠	£128.00–£393.00
5 touring pitches		

A487 Haverford west to St Davids road. In village of Keeston.

At-a-glance symbols

Symbols at the end of each entry give useful information
about services and facilities. A key to symbols can be found
inside the back cover flap. Keep this open for easy reference.

LLANDOVERY, Carmarthenshire Map ref 1B3

★★★
TOURING &
CAMPING PARK

BH&HPA

ERWLON CARAVAN & CAMPING

Brecon Road, Llandovery SA20 0RD
T: (01550) 720332

Erwlon is a family-run park located at the foothills of the Brecon Beacons. Ideal touring base for south and west Wales. New facilities for 2005. Seasonal touring pitches available from £400.

OPEN All Year

One mile east of Llandovery, off A40 towards Brecon.

40	🚐	£8.00–£10.00
40	🚙	£8.00–£10.00
35	▲	£8.00–£10.00
75 touring pitches		

LLANELLI, Carmarthenshire Map ref 1A3

★★★★★
TOURING PARK

BH&HPA

See Ad on inside back cover

PEMBREY COUNTRY PARK CARAVAN CLUB SITE

Factory Road, Llanelli SA16 0EJ
T: (01554) 834369
I: www.caravanclub.co.uk

Site set in a large country park with extensive forest walks, cycle tracks, an adventure playground and miles of Blue Flag sandy beaches. Open 26 March 2005 to 4 January 2006. Special member rates mean you can save your membership subscription in less than a week. Visit www.caravanclub.co.uk to find out more.

Payment accepted: Delta, Mastercard, Switch, Visa

From M4, leave at jct 48 onto A4138. After 4 miles turn right onto A484 and continue towards Camarthen. Within 7 miles in Pembrey Village turn right before park gates. Signposted.

125	🚐	£16.10–£21.50
125	🚙	£16.10–£21.50
	▲	On application
125 touring pitches		

THE CARAVAN CLUB

LLANGADOG, Carmarthenshire Map ref 1B3

★★★★
TOURING &
CAMPING PARK

BH&HPA

ABERMARLAIS CARAVAN PARK

Llangdog SA19 9NG
T: (01550) 777868 & 777797

A tranquil site in a beautiful woodland valley at the western end of the Brecon National Park, ideal for nature lovers and bird-watchers.

Payment accepted: Delta, Mastercard, Switch, Visa

Situated on A40, 6 miles west of Llandovery or 6 miles east of Llandeilo. Signposted.

60	🚐	£9.00
60	🚙	£9.00
28	▲	£8.50–£9.00
88 touring pitches		

LLANGORSE, Powys Map ref 1B3

★★★★
HOLIDAY, TOURING
& CAMPING PARK

BH&HPA

LAKESIDE CARAVAN & CAMPING PARK

Llangorse Lake, Brecon LD3 7TR
T: (01874) 658226
F: (01874) 658430
E: holidays@lakeside.zx3.net
I: www.lakeside-holidays.net

Payment accepted: Delta,
Mastercard, Switch, Visa

50	🚐	£7.50–£9.50
50	🚙	£7.50–£9.50
50	▲	£7.50–£9.50
10	🏠	£175.00–£325.00
50 touring pitches		

From Abergavenny A40 to Bwlch, turn right onto B4560 to Llangorse. Head for the lake.

WALES

LLIGWY BAY, Isle of Anglesey Map ref 1A1

★★★★★
HOLIDAY PARK

DRAGON AWARD

MINFFORDD CARAVAN PARK
Lligwy LL70 9HJ
T: (01248) 410678
F: (01248) 410378
E: enq@minffordd.holidays.com
I: www.minffordd-holidays.com

Payment accepted: Euros

4 ⊡ £135.00–£540.00

At roundabout at Llanallgo keep left on A5025 for approx 2 miles. Reception on right-hand side before sharp left-hand bend.

NEWPORT, Newport Map ref 1B3

★★★★★
TOURING PARK

BH&HPA

See Ad on inside back cover

TREDEGAR HOUSE & PARK CARAVAN CLUB SITE
Newport NP10 8T
T: (01633) 815600
I: www.caravanclub.co.uk

High-standard site within the park, bordering one of the ornamental lakes. Just off the M4, seven miles from Cardiff. Non-members welcome. Open 26 March to 13 December. Special member rates mean you can save your membership subscription in less than a week. Visit www.caravanclub.co.uk to find out more.

Payment accepted: Delta, Mastercard, Switch, Visa

Exit M4 at jct 28 via slip road. At roundabout turn onto A48 (signposted Tredegar House) Roundabout 0.25 miles, turn left. Next roundabout, turn left into Tredegar House. Signposted.

82	🚐	£14.60–£20.60
82	⛺	£14.60–£20.60
	▲	On application
82 touring pitches		

PEMBROKE, Pembrokeshire Map ref 1A3

★★★★★
TOURING & CAMPING PARK

BH&HPA

See Ad on inside back cover

FRESHWATER EAST CARAVAN CLUB SITE
Trewent Hill, Freshwater East, Pembroke SA71 5LJ
T: (01646) 672341
I: www.caravanclub.co.uk

Situated a few minutes from a safe, sandy beach and close to 180-mile coastal path with magnificent views. You can visit Ireland for the day! Open 26 March to 1 November. Special member rates mean you can save your membership subscription in less than a week. Visit www.caravanclub.co.uk to find out more.

Payment accepted: Delta, Mastercard, Switch, Visa

Take M4 to Carmarthen, then follow signs to Pembroke. Go under railway bridge, take left onto A4139, in Lamphey continue onto B4584, after 1.75 miles turn right, sign after 0.25 miles at foot of hill. Signposted.

130	🚐	£14.60–£20.60
130	⛺	£14.60–£20.60
	▲	On application
130 touring pitches		

ST DAVIDS, Pembrokeshire Map ref 1A3

★★★★
HOLIDAY, TOURING & CAMPING PARK

BH&HPA

CAERFAI BAY CARAVAN & TENT PARK
St Davids, Haverfordwest SA62 6QT
T: (01437) 720274
F: (01437) 720577
E: info@caerfaibay.co.uk
I: www.caerfaibay.co.uk

Payment accepted: Delta, Mastercard, Switch, Visa

28	🚐	£8.50–£14.00
15	⛺	£7.50–£14.00
77	▲	£7.50–£10.00
8	⊡	£175.00–£390.00
120 touring pitches		

Turn off A487 (Haverfordwest to St Davids) in St Davids at Visitor Centre. The Park is at road end, 1 mile, on the right. Signposted.

 Ratings All accommodation in this guide has been rated, or is awaiting a rating, by a trained VisitBritain assessor.

★★★★
TOURING PARK

BH&HPA

See Ad on inside back cover

LLEITHYR MEADOW CARAVAN CLUB SITE
Whitesands, St Davids, Haverfordwest SA62 6PR
T: (01437) 720401
I: www.caravanclub.co.uk

Set on a peninsula, surrounded by the Pembrokeshire Coast National Park with its wonderful walks, wild coves and sandy bays. Visit the picturesque harbour village of Solva. Open 2 April to 11 October. Special member rates mean you can save your membership subscription in less than a week. Visit www.caravanclub.co.uk to find out more.

Payment accepted: Delta, Mastercard, Switch, Visa

Take M4 to Carmarthen, then A40 to Haverfordwest, then A487 towards St Davids. Before entering St Davids turn right onto B4583, crossroads. Turn sharp right oppposite entrance to St Davids golf club. Signposted.

120		£15.50–£20.60
120		£15.50–£20.60
120 touring pitches		

THE CARAVAN CLUB

★★★★
TOURING PARK

BH&HPA

See Ad on inside back cover

GOWERTON CARAVAN CLUB SITE
Pont-Y-Cob Road, Swansea SA4 3QP
T: (01792) 873050
I: www.caravanclub.co.uk

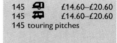

Safe, clean, sandy beaches, sightseeing, spectacular falls and the Brecon Beacons National Park make this a perfect, all-round destination. Swansea six miles. Open 10 May to 1 November. Special member rates mean you can save your membership subscription in less than a week. Visit www.caravanclub.co.uk to find out more.

Payment accepted: Delta, Mastercard, Switch, Visa

Take B4296 towards Gower and then Gowerton. In 0.5 miles, 100yds after passing under railway bridge (height restriction of 11ft), turn right onto B4295. Turn after 0.5 miles. Signposted Pont-Y-Cob Road.

145		£14.60–£20.60
145		£14.60–£20.60
145 touring pitches		

THE CARAVAN CLUB

261

A brief guide to the main towns and villages offering accommodation in **Wales**

BARMOUTH, Gwynedd
Popular seaside resort at the mouth of the beautiful Mawddach estuary, on the edge of the Snowdonia National Park.

BRECON, Powys
Market town situated at the junction of the rivers Usk and Honddu. Excellent base for exploring the Brecon Beacons National Park.

CAERNARFON, Gwynedd
Ancient county town famous for its magnificent and well preserved medieval castle, the birthplace of Edward I and scene of the investiture of the Prince of Wales in 1969.

FISHGUARD, Pembrokeshire
Picturesque little town perched high above its harbour. Fine cliff scenery.

LLANELLI, Carmarthenshire
Industrial centre on the Burry inlet, with beautiful surrounding countryside. Kidwelly Castle and Wildlife and Wetlands Centre nearby.

PEMBROKE, Pembrokeshire
Historic county town, dominated by its fine old castle, birthplace of Henry VII. Remains of Monkton Priory.

ST DAVIDS, Pembrokeshire
A place of pilgrimage for over eight centuries, situated on the rugged western peninsula within easy reach of some of Britain's finest cliffs and bays. Interesting cathedral.

SWANSEA, Swansea
Large seaport and modern industrial city with a university and extensive parks and gardens. Swansea is also a seaside resort and a good centre for exploring the Gower Peninsula.

Above imposing Criccieth Castle

Tourist Information Centres

When it comes to your next English break, the first stage of your journey could be closer than you think. You've probably got a tourist information centre nearby which is there to serve the local community – as well as visitors. Knowledgeable staff will be happy to help you, wherever you're heading.

Many tourist information centres can provide you with maps and guides, and often it's possible to book accommodation and travel tickets too.

Across the country there are more than 550 TICs. You'll find the address of your nearest centre in your local phone book.

Further information

Left, from top master the locks on the River Wey; relax and enjoy the beautiful countryside at Big Sands, Gairloch

Useful addresses

Automobile Association

Routes can be prepared avoiding unsuitable routes for caravans if specified. Visit www.theaa.com

British Holiday & Home Parks Association

Chichester House, 6 Pullman Court, Great Western Road, Gloucester GL1 3ND
Enquiries and brochure requests: (01452) 526911
Fax: (01452) 508508

Professional UK park owners are represented by the British Holiday and Home Parks Association. Almost 2000 parks are in membership, and each year welcome millions of visitors seeking quality surroundings in which to enjoy a good value stay.

Parks provide caravan holiday homes and lodges for hire, and pitches for your own touring caravan, motorhome or tent. On many, you can opt to buy your own holiday home.

A major strength of the UK's park industry is its diversity. Whatever your idea of holiday pleasure, there's sure to be a park which can provide it. If your preference is for a quiet, peaceful holiday in tranquil rural surroundings, you'll find many idyllic locations.

Alternatively, many parks are to be found at our most popular resorts – and reflect the holiday atmosphere with plenty of entertainment and leisure facilities. And for more adventurous families, parks often provide excellent bases from which to enjoy outdoor activities.

Literature available from BH&HPA (call (01452) 526911) includes a guide to over 450 parks which have this year achieved the David Bellamy Conservation Award for environmental excellence.

The Caravan Club

East Grinstead House, East Grinstead, West Sussex RH19 1UA
Tel: (01342) 326944 Fax: (01342) 410258
www.caravanclub.co.uk

The Caravan Club offers around 200 sites in the United Kingdom and Ireland. These include city locations such as London, Edinburgh, York and Chester, plus sites near leading heritage attractions such as Longleat, Sandringham, Chatsworth and Blenheim Palace.

The Camping and Caravanning Club

Greenfields House, Westwood Way, Coventry CV4 8JH
Tel: (024) 7947 5448
Advance bookings: 0870 243 333
Fax: (024) 7647 5418
www.campingandcaravanningclub.co.uk

We have over 90 sites covering the length and breath of the country in locations that will take your breath away.

With excellent grades from VisitBritain, you are guaranteed quality facilities. We also have a legendary reputation for cleanliness, as well as great value for money. All our guests receive a warm and friendly welcome from our Holiday Site Managers.

The majority of our sites are open to non-members, with special deals available for families, backpackers and reduced site fees if you are 55 or over. Overseas visitors are also catered for with a go as you please Freedom UK Pass or Temporary Overseas Membership.

For more details send for your free guide to the Camping and Caravanning Club Sites.
Tel: (024) 7647 5442

A further 20 sites are in National Parks. Over 90% of pitches have an electric hook-up point and most sites offer emptying points for motor caravanners. Foreign visitors are welcomed and holders of International Camping Cards (CCIs) qualify for pitch discounts on selected sites. Non-member caravanners pay a supplement (£5 per pitch per night in 2004), refunded against the membership fee (£31 in 2004 plus £5 joining fee) which adds access to a further 2600 small five-van sites. A 656-page Sites Directory and UK Location Map gives clear directions whilst towing. Tent campers are welcome on 70 sites.

Forestry Commission

231 Corstorphine Road, Edinburgh EH12 7AT
Tel: 0845 FORESTS (367 3787)
www.forestry.gov.uk

Forest Holidays, run by Forest Enterprise, an executive agency of the Forestry Commission, have almost 30 camping and caravan sites in the scenic forest locations throughout the UK. Choose from the Scottish Highlands, the New Forest, Snowdonia National Park, the Forest of Dean, or the banks of Loch Lomond. Some sites are open all year.

Advance bookings are accepted for many sites. Dogs are also welcome on most sites. For a unique forest experience, call Forest Holidays for a brochure on Tel: (0131) 314 6505 or visit www.forestholidays.co.uk

The Motor Caravanners' Club Ltd

22 Evelyn Close, Twickenham TW2 7BN
Tel: (020) 8893 3883 Fax: (020) 8893 8324
Email: info@motorcaravanners.org.uk
www.motorcaravanners.org.uk

The Motor Caravanners' Club is authorised to issue the Camping Card International (CCI). It also produces a monthly magazine, Motor Caravanner, for all members. Member of The Federation Internationale de Camping et de Caravanning (FICC).

Left cycling through Cumbria **Below** fishing at Crowhurst Park, Battle

Standards for caravan and camping parks

Normes requises pour les terrains de camping et pour caravanes
Regeln für camping- und caravanplätze
Aan caravan en campingparken gestelde eisen
Norme imposte ai campeggi per tende e roulottes

These standards should be read in conjunction, where applicable, with the Caravan Sites and Control of Development Act 1960, and, where applicable, the Public Health Act 1936.

A The park

1 The park must have planning permission and site licence readily available, if applicable.

2 Facilities must be clean and in wholesome condition.

3 The park must be well managed and maintained and kept in a clean and presentable manner and attention paid to the road-side sign and entrance.

4 The park must have reception arrangements at appropriate times where advice and assistance can be obtained if necessary.

5 The park operator must be capable of arranging or carrying out repairs to caravans and equipment.

6 Supplies of gas and replacement bottles together with essential (where applicable) spares must be available at all reasonable times.

7 Where provided, all toilet blocks and washing facilities must be lit internally and externally during the hours of darkness, whilst the park is open.

8 All shower blocks must have internal lighting.

9 Where washing and/or shower facilities are provided, an adequate supply of hot and cold water must be available at all reasonable times.

10 A proprietary first-aid kit must be readily available. Emergency notices must be prominently displayed giving details and location of park, contact, telephone, doctor, fire service, local hospital and other essential services.

11 Parks open in the shoulder season (Oct-Mar) must provide adequate heating in at least one toilet, washing and shower facility (both male and female).

12 The park owner must have fire fighting equipment and notices which conform with the conditions of the site licence.

13 All electricity installations on the park, both internally and externally, must have the appropriate safety certification.

14 Parks providing pitches for touring units must provide facilities for chemical disposal unless specifically prohibited by local authorities.

15 Lighting should be appropriate to the size and type of park.

16 Adequate provision to be made for refuse disposal.

17 The intended use of facilities must be indicated by signage.

NB: Parks providing NO toilet facilities make this clear in all promotional literature and advertising.

B Visitor information

The booking form must be accompanied by details of the park, stating clearly:

1   A description of the park and its amenities, eg:

a)   Whether cars park by caravans or in a car park.

b)   Whether or not pets are allowed.

c)   Details of shower and bath facilities.

d)   Whether a grocery shop is on site or the distance to nearest shop.

e)   Licensed bar.

f)   Laundry facilities.

g)   Dancing, entertainments.

h)   Television room.

i)   Sports facilities.

j)   Public transport to and from park.

k)   Distance from sea and accessibility to beach (coastal parks only).

2   The prices for the pitch for the period booked and details of any further charges, eg electricity, gas, showers, awnings as well as any optional charges, eg holiday insurance.

NB: If Value Added Tax (VAT) is not included in the total charge, this must be clearly stated.

3   Any special conditions for payment of deposits or balance.

4   Wherever possible, a map showing the location of the park and its proximity to main centres and attractions.

5   If bookings in advance are necessary during the summer months.

C Caravan holiday homes and chalets

1   All caravans must be of proprietary make.

2   All caravans/chalets must be in good state of internal and external repair and decoration with no internal dampness.

3   The caravans/chalets must not be occupied by more than the number of persons for which they are designed by the manufacturer ie four persons in a four-berth.

4   It is the park operator's responsibility to ensure that all caravans offered for hire on the park have insurance cover for public liability as letting caravans and comply with the Consumer Protection Act.

5   Equipment must be provided as listed opposite. An inventory of this equipment must be available for each caravan/chalet.

6   All caravans/chalets must have adequate storage space for luggage and food for the maximum number of occupants.

7   All doors, windows, skylights and all ventilation in the caravan/chalet must function correctly. All windows must be properly fitted with opaque curtains or blinds.

8   All caravans/chalets must have adequate internal lighting.

9   All caravans/chalets must be thoroughly cleaned and checked before every letting and equipment maintained and replaced as necessary.

10   Where linen is provided it must be changed on each change of occupier and as appropriate during lets of two weeks or more. All mattresses must be in sound condition.

11   The sink and its waste pipe must be in sound condition with a draining board. A fixed impervious work top for food preparation must be provided.

12   All caravans/chalets must have a fridge and a cooker with at least two boiling rings. The cooker must be in a sound and clean condition and functioning properly.

13   All caravans/chalets must have adequate heating.

14   All caravans must have safe steps or equivalent, to each external door.

15 All caravans must have a supply of hot and cold water.

16 All caravan holiday homes must be fully serviced with water, drainage, mains WC, shower and/or bath.

D Inventory of equipment for caravan holiday-homes and chalets

The accommodation should contain the following:

- **One per caravan/chalet**
  Ladle
  Grater
  Plastic/wooden spoon
  Potato masher
  Cleaning agents
  Carpet sweeper or vacuum available
  Toilet brush and holder, toilet roll and holder
  Kettle
  Teapot
  Saucepan and lid (large, medium, small)
  Frying pan
  Colander
  Oven roasting tray
  Casserole dish
  Carving knife and fork
  Bread knife
  Bread/cake container
  Bread/chopping board
  Fish slice
  Small vegetable knife
  Tin opener
  Corkscrew/bottle opener
  Potato peeler
  Large fruit dish
  Butter dish
  Sugar bowl
  Tray
  Milk jug
  Mixing bowl or basin
  Bread/cake plate
  Condiment set (two-piece)
  Washing-up bowl
  Dustpan and brush
  Broom
  Floor cloth
  Pot scourer/dish mop
  Bucket
  Mirror
  Doormat
  Covered kitchen refuse container
  Fire extinguisher/blanket
  Smoke detector

- **Two per caravan/chalet**
  Table spoons
  Dusters
  Ash trays

- **Per bed**
  Three blankets or one continental quilt and cover (for winter lettings, or letting very early or late in the season the scale of bedding to be increased and adequate heating provided)
  One pillow per person

- **One per person**
  Knife (table and dessert)
  Fork (table and dessert)
  Spoon (dessert and tea)
  Plate (large and small)
  Tea cup and saucer
  Cereal/soup plate
  Tumbler
  Egg cup

- **Four per person**
  Coat-hangers

E Information for hirers

The booking form should be accompanied by details of the park and caravan(s)/chalet(s) stating clearly:

1 The accommodation size (length and width) of the caravan and the number of berths. This shall not exceed the maximum number of berths as defined by the manufacturer.

2 Whether caravans are connected to:
   Mains water
   Mains drainage
   Mains sewerage
   Electricity (stating voltage)
   Piped gas (stating LPG or Natural)

3 Type of lighting: Electricity or Gas

4 Type of cooking: Electricity or Gas

5 A full description of park and its amenities.

6 Wherever possible a map showing the location of the park and its proximity to main centres and attractions.

7 The charges for the accommodation/pitch for the period booked and details of any further additional charges, for example, electricity, gas, showers etc, as well as any optional charges, eg holiday insurance.

NB: If VAT is payable it must be included in the quoted price.

F The Caravan Parks Standard for guests with disabilities

The National Accessible Scheme is operated by VisitBritain and the National and Regional Tourist Boards throughout Britain. They assess places to stay that provide accommodation for wheelchair users or others who may have difficulty walking. The tourist organisations recognise three categories of accessibility:

 Category 1 Accessible to a wheelchair user travelling independently.

 Category 2 Accessible to a wheelchair user travelling with assistance.

 Category 3 Accessible to a wheelchair user able to walk a few paces and up a maximum of three steps.

For holiday home parks, the rating will depend upon access to reception, route to the caravan, food shop and telephone (where provided), and the holiday home itself.

For touring/camping parks, it will depend upon access to reception, routes to pitches, food shop and telephone (where provided), toilet and washing facilities. Please contact individual park operators for more detailed information you may require. A list of parks offering accessible accommodation featured in this guide can be found on page 283.

Code of conduct & conditions for participation for caravan & camping parks

In addition to fulfilling its statutory obligations, including having applied for a certificate under the Fire Precautions Act 1971 (if applicable) and holding public liability insurance, and ensuring that all caravan holiday homes/chalets for hire and the park and all buildings and facilities thereon, the fixtures, furnishings, fittings and décor are maintained in sound and clean condition and are fit for the purposes intended, the management undertakes to observe the following code of conduct:

- To ensure high standards of courtesy and cleanliness; catering and service appropriate to the type of park.

- To describe to all visitors and prospective visitors the amenities, facilities and services provided by the park and/or caravan holiday homes/chalets whether by advertisement, brochure, word of mouth or other means.

- To allow visitors to see the park or caravan holiday homes/chalets for hire, if requested, before booking.

- To present grading awards and/or any other National Tourist Board awards unambiguously.

- To make clear to visitors exactly what is included in prices quoted for the park or caravan holiday homes/chalets, meals and refreshments, including service charge, taxes and other surcharges. Details of charges, if any, for heating or for additional services or facilities available should also be made clear.

- To adhere to, and not to exceed, prices current at time of occupation for caravan holiday homes/chalets or other services.

- To advise visitors at the time of booking, and subsequently of any change, if the caravan holiday home/chalet or pitch offered is in a different location or on another park, and to indicate the location of this and any difference in comfort and amenities.

- To give each visitor, on request, details of payments due and a receipt if required.

- To advise visitors at the time of booking of the charges that might be incurred if the booking is subsequently cancelled.

- To deal promptly and courteously with all visitors and prospective visitors, including enquiries, requests, reservations, correspondence and complaints.

- To allow a National Tourist Board representative reasonable access to the park and/or caravan holiday homes/chalet whether by prior appointment or on an unannounced assessment, to confirm that the Code of Conduct is being observed and that the appropriate quality standard is being maintained.

- The operator must comply with the provision of the caravan industry Codes of Practice.

Code of conduct & conditions for participation for Holiday Villages

The operator/manager is required to observe the following Code of Conduct:

- To maintain standards of guest care, cleanliness, and service appropriate to the type of establishment;

- To describe accurately in any advertisement, brochure, or other printed or electronic media, the facilities and services provided;

- To make clear to visitors exactly what is included in all prices quoted for accommodation, including taxes, and any other surcharges. Details of charges for additional services/facilities should also be made clear;

- To give a clear statement of the policy on cancellations to guests at the time of booking ie by telephone, fax, email as well as information given in a printed format;

- To adhere to, and not to exceed prices quoted at the time of booking for accommodation and other services;

- To advise visitors at the time of booking, and subsequently of any change, if the accommodation offered is in an unconnected annexe or similar, and to indicate the location of such accommodation and any difference in comfort and/or amenities from accommodation in the establishment;

- To give each visitor, on request, details of payments due and a receipt, if required;

- To deal promptly and courteously with all enquiries, requests, bookings and correspondence from visitors;

- Ensure complaint handling procedures are in place and that complaints received are investigated promptly and courteously and that the outcome is communicated to the visitor;

- To give due consideration to the requirements of visitors with special needs, and to make suitable provision where applicable;

- To provide public liability insurance or comparable arrangement and to comply with applicable planning, safety and other statutory requirements;

- To allow a VisitBritain representative reasonable access to the establishment, on request, to confirm the Code of Conduct is being observed.

enjoy**England**™

official guides to **quality**

Hotels, Townhouses,
Travel Accommodation
and Restaurants with
Rooms in England 2005
£10.99

Bed & Breakfasts,
Guesthouses, Small Hotels,
Farmhouses, Inns, Campus
Accommodation and Hostels
in England 2005
£11.99

Self-Catering
Holiday Homes and Boat
Accommodation
in England 2005
£11.99

Touring Parks, Camping, Holiday Parks
and Villages in Britain 2005
£8.99

Somewhere Special
in England 2005
£8.99

Families and Pets Welcome
in England 2005
£11.99

INFORMATIVE • EASY TO USE • GREAT VALUE FOR MONEY

The guides include:

- **Accommodation entries packed with information**
- **Full colour maps**
- **Places to visit**
- **Tourist Information Centres**

From all good bookshops or by mail order from:

VisitBritain Fulfilment Centre,
c/o Westex Ltd, 7 St Andrews Way,
Devons Road, Bromley-by-Bow, London E3 3PA
Tel: 0870 606 7204
Fax: (020) 7987 6505
Email: fulfilment@visitbritain.org

A selection of events for 2005

This is a selection of the many cultural, sporting and other events that will be taking place throughout Britain during 2005. Please note, as changes often occur after press date, it is advisable to confirm the date and location before travelling.

JANUARY

1 Jan – 9 Jan
Lakeside World Professional Darts Championships
Lakeside Country Club
Wharf Road, Frimley Green, Camberley, Surrey
Tel: (020) 8883 5544
Bookings: (01252) 836464
www.bdodarts.com

12 Jan – 30 Jan
Festival: Celtic Connections
Glasgow Royal Concert Hall
Sauchiehall Street, Glasgow
Tel: (0141) 353 8000
www.celticconnections.co.uk

15 Jan – 16 Jan
Autosports International 2005
National Exhibition Centre
Birmingham, West Midlands
Tel: 0870 902 0444
www.autosport-international.com

15 Jan – 16 Jan
Motorbike 2005
Springfields Exhibition Centre
Camelgate, Spalding, Lincolnshire
Tel: (01775) 724843
www.springfields.mistral.co.uk

16 Jan
Antique and Collectors Fair
Alexandra Palace
Alexandra Palace Way, London
Tel: (020) 8883 7061
www.allypally-uk.com

30 Jan
Charles I Commemoration
Banqueting House
Whitehall, London
Tel: (01430) 430695

FEBRUARY

13 Feb
Chinese New Year Celebrations
Chinatown, London
Tel: (020) 7292 2877
www.chinatownchinese.com

13 Feb
Youth Brass Band Entertainment Festival of Great Britain
Winter Gardens, Opera House and Empress Ballroom
Church Street, Blackpool, Lancashire
Tel: (01706) 373911
Bookings: (01706) 373911 x 213

MARCH

1 Mar – 6 Mar
Fine Art and Antiques Fair
Olympia
Hammersmith Road, London
Tel: 0870 736 3105
www.olympia-antiques.co.uk

Above Chinese New Year 2004, Chinatown, London

* provisional date at time of going to press

2 Mar – 28 Mar
Daily Mail Ideal Home Show
Earls Court Exhibition Centre
Warwick Road, London
Tel: 0870 606 6080

13 Mar
Antique and Collectors' Fair
Alexandra Palace and Park
Alexandra Palace Way, Wood Green, London
Tel: (020) 8883 7061
www.allypally-uk.com

25 Mar – 28 Mar
Easter Trails
Petworth House and Park
Petworth, West Sussex
Tel: (01798) 342207
www.nationaltrust.org.uk/petworth

28 Mar
Trigg Morris Men's Easter Monday Tour
Various venues starting in the Market Square
Launceston, Cornwall
Tel: (01637) 880394
www.triggmorris.freeserve.co.uk

APRIL

17 Apr
Flora London Marathon
Greenwich Park to The Mall
London
Tel: (020) 7902 0199
www.london-marathon.co.uk

28 Apr – 1 May
Harrogate Spring Flower Show
Great Yorkshire Showground
Harrogate, North Yorkshire
Tel: (01423) 561049
www.flowershow.org.uk

29 Apr – 2 May
Spirit of Speyside: Scotland's Whisky Festival
Various venues across Speyside
Elgin, Morayshire
Tel: (01343) 542666
www.spiritofspeyside.com

MAY

1 May
Old Custom: Mayday Celebrations
Town Centre
Padstow, Cornwall
Tel: (01841) 533449

1 May – 2 May *
Carlisle and Borders Spring Flower Show
Bitts Park, Carlisle
Tel: (01228) 817359

7 May – 21 May
Newbury Spring Festival
Various venues
Newbury, Berkshire
Tel: (01635) 528766
Bookings: (01635) 522733
www.newburyspringfestival.org.uk

8 May
Antique and Collectors' Fair
Alexandra Palace and Park
Alexandra Palace Way, Wood Green, London
Tel: (020) 8883 7061
www.allypally-uk.com

14 May – 15 May
Newark and Nottinghamshire County Show
County Showground
Drove Lane, Winthorpe, Newark
Tel: (01636) 702627
www.newarkshowground.com

24 May – 27 May*
Chelsea Flower Show
Royal Hospital Chelsea
Royal Hospital Road, Chelsea, London
Tel: (020) 7649 1885
Bookings: 0870 906 3781
www.rhs.org.uk

27 May – 3 Jun
Blackpool Dance Festival
Winter Gardens, Opera House and Empress Ballroom
Church Street, Blackpool, Lancashire
Tel: (01253) 625252

28 May – 30 May
Kent Garden Show
Kent County Showground
Detling, Maidstone, Kent
Tel: (01795) 474660
www.kentgardenshow.com

29 May – 4 Jun
Pennine Spring Music Festival
Parish Church
Heptonstall, Hebden Bridge, West Yorkshire
Tel: (01422) 845023
Bookings: (01422) 843831

MAY continued

30 May
Northumberland County Show
Tynedale Park
Corbridge, Northumberland
Tel: (01697) 747848
Bookings: 0870 011 5007
www.northcountyshow.co.uk

JUNE

1 Jun – 19 Jun
BBC Singer of the World in Cardiff
St David's Hall
The Hayes, Cardiff
Tel: (029) 2032 2820
Bookings: (029) 2087 8437
www.bbc.co.uk/singeroftheworld

3 Jun
Robert Dover's Cotswold Olimpick Games
Dovers Hill
Weston Subedge, Chipping Campden, Gloucestershire
Tel: (01384) 274041
www.olimpickgames.co.uk

3 Jun – 5 Jun
The Garden Festival at Holker Hall
Holker Hall and Gardens
Cark in Cartmel, Grange-over-Sands, Cumbria
Tel: (015395) 58328
www.holker-hall.co.uk

9 Jun – 12 Jun
Blenheim Palace Flower Show
Blenheim Palace
Woodstock, Oxfordshire
Tel: 0845 644 5145
Bookings: 0870 906 3805
www.blenheimpalaceflowershow.co.uk

18 Jun*
Trooping the Colour – The Queen's Birthday Parade
Horse Guards Parade Headquarters Household Division
Horse Guards, Whitehall, London
Tel: (020) 7414 2479

18 Jun – 26 Jun
Otley Walking Festival 2005
Various locations around Otley
Otley, West Yorkshire
Tel: (01943) 851166
www.chevintrek.co.uk

20 Jun – 3 Jul
Tennis: Wimbledon Lawn Tennis Championships
All England Lawn Tennis & Croquet Club
Church Road, Wimbledon
Bookings: (020) 8946 2244
www.wimbledon.org

21 Jun – 23 Aug
The Highland Dancing and Pipe Band Display
Stirling Castle Esplanade
Stirling
Tel: (01786) 450000

22 Jun - 23 Jul
Bard in the Botanics 2005
Glasgow Botanic Gardens
Great Western Road, Glasgow
Tel: (0141) 334 3995
Bookings: (0141) 3311 3995
www.glasgowrep.org

24 Jun – 27 Jun
The Mersey River Festival
Albert Dock
Edward Pavilion, Albert Dock, Liverpool, Merseyside
Tel: (0151) 233 3007

Left Hampton Court Palace, London **Right** Mersey River Festival, Liverpool

* provisional date at time of going to press

25 Jun – 26 Jun
Whitehaven Maritime Festival
Whitehaven Harbour
Whitehaven, Cumbria
Tel: (01946) 696346

29 Jun – 3 Jul
Henley Royal Regatta
Henley Reach
Regatta Headquarters, Henley-on-Thames, Oxfordshire
Tel: (01491) 572153
www.hrr.co.uk

JULY

1 Jul – 10 Jul
Ledbury Poetry Festival
Various venues
Church Street, Ledbury, Herefordshire
Tel: 0845 458 1743
www.poetry-festival.com

2 Jul*
Alnwick Fair
Market Square
Alnwick, Northumberland
Tel: (01665) 711397

2 Jul – 3 Jul
Chiltern Traction Engine Steam Rally
The Hangings
Honor End Road, Prestwood, Great Missenden,
Buckinghamshire
Tel: 07889 965604

2 Jul – 3 Jul*
Sunderland International Kite Festival
Northern Area Playing Fields
Stephenson, Washington,
Tyne and Wear
Tel: (0191) 514 1235
www.sunderland.gov.uk/kitefestival

5 Jul – 10 Jul
Hampton Court Palace Flower Show
Hampton Court Palace
Hampton Court, East Molesey, Surrey
Tel: (020) 7649 1885
Bookings: 0870 906 3791
www.rhs.org.uk

5 Jul – 10 Jul
Llangollen International Musical Eisteddfod
Royal International Pavilion
Abbey Road, Llangollen, Denbighshire
Tel: (01978) 862001
www.international-eisteddfod.co.uk

8 Jul - 17 Jul
Lichfield Festival
Throughout City of Lichfield
Lichfield, Staffordshire
Tel: (01543) 306270
Bookings: (01543) 306543
www.lichfieldfestival.org

9 Jul – 10 Jul
Americana International
County Showground
Drove Lane, Winthorpe, Newark
Tel: (0115) 939 0595
www.americana-international.co.uk/

9 Jul – 10 Jul*
Beaulieu 4 x 4 Show
National Motor Museum
John Montagu Building, Beaulieu, Brockenhurst,
Hampshire
Tel: (01590) 612345
Bookings: (01590) 612888
www.beaulieu.co.uk

9 Jul – 16 Jul*
Carlisle International Summer Festival
Carlisle Cathedral
The Abbey, Castle Street, Carlisle, Cumbria
Bookings: (01228) 625600

10 Jul
Burton Constable Country Fair
Burton Constable Hall
Burton Constable, Hull, East Yorkshire
Tel: (01964) 562400
www.burtonconstable.com

10 Jul – 17 Jul
Golf: The Open Championship
The Old Course
St Andrews, Fife
Tel: (01334) 460000
Bookings: (01334) 460010
www.opengolf.com

12 Jul – 14 Jul
Great Yorkshire Show
Great Yorkshire Showground
Harrogate, North Yorkshire
Tel: (01423) 541000
Bookings: (01423) 541000
www.yas.co.uk

15 Jul – 17 Jul
Kent County Show
Kent County Showground
Detling, Maidstone, Kent
Tel: (01622) 630975
Bookings: (01622) 630030
www.kentshowground.co.uk

JULY continued

15 Jul – 10 Sep*
The Proms
Royal Albert Hall
Kensington Gore, London
Tel: (020) 7765 5575
www.bbc.co.uk/proms

15 Jul – 31 Jul*
Ryedale Festival
Various venues in the Ryedale area
North Yorkshire
Tel: (01751) 475777
www.ryedalefestival.co.uk

16 Jul
Beaulieu Village Fete
Palace House Lawns
Beaulieu, Brockenhurst, Hampshire
Tel: (01590) 614621

17 Jul
Battle Abbey Classic Car and Motorcycle Show
Battle Abbey and Battlefield
High Street, Battle, East Sussex
Tel: (01424) 211334

18 Jul - 21 Jul*
Royal Welsh Show
Royal Welsh Showground
Llanelwedd, Builth Wells, Powys
Tel: (01982) 553683
www.rwas.co.uk

29 Jul – 2 Aug
Class 1 Powerboats World Championships
Plymouth Sound
Plymouth, Devon
Tel: (01752) 304849

29 Jul – 31 Jul
Gateshead Summer Flower Show
Gateshead Central Nurseries
Whickham Highway, Lobley Hill, Gateshead,
Tyne and Wear
Tel: (0191) 433 3838

29 Jul – 31 Jul*
Potfest in the Park
Hutton-in-the-Forest
Penrith, Cumbria
Tel: (017684) 83820
www.potfest.co.uk

29 Jul
Stranraer Show
London Road Playing Fields
Stranraer, Wigtownshire
Tel: (01581) 500309
www.stranraershow.com

30 Jul – 31 Jul*
Cumbria Steam Gathering
Cark Airfield
Flookburgh, Grange-over-Sands, Cumbria
Tel: (015242) 71584

30 Jul – 6 Aug
Skandia Cowes Week 2005
The Solent
Cowes, Isle of Wight
Tel: (01983) 29330330

Jul – 31 Jul*
Sunderland International Air Show Promenade
Sea Front, Seaburn, Sunderland
Tel: (0191) 553 2000
www.sunderland.gov.uk/airshow

AUGUST

4 Aug
Burwarton Show
Burwarton Showground
Cleobury North, Bridgnorth, Shropshire
Tel: (01746) 787535
www.burwartonshow.co.uk

* provisional date at time of going to press

5 Aug – 27 Aug
Edinburgh Military Tattoo
Edinburgh Castle Esplanade
Castle Hill, Edinburgh
Tel: (0131) 225 1188
Bookings: 0870 7555 1188
www.edintattoo.co.uk

5 Aug – 7 Aug
Lowther Horse Driving Trials and Country Fair
Lowther Castle
Lowther Estate, Lowther, Penrith, Cumbria
Tel: (01931) 712378
www.lowther.co.uk

6 Aug
Aboyne Highland Games
The Green
Aboyne, Aberdeenshire
Tel: (01333) 981209

7 Aug – 13 Aug
Falmouth Regatta Week
Helford River
Carrick Roads and Falmouth Bay, Cornwall
Tel: (01326) 211555
www.falmouth-week.co.uk

9 Aug – 10 Aug*
The Anglesey County Show
Anglesey County Showground
Ty Glyn Williams, Gwalchmai, Holyhead, Ynys Mon
Tel: (01407) 720880

12 Aug – 14 Aug*
Brecon Jazz Festival
Various venues
Brecon, Powys
Tel: (01874) 622838
Bookings: (01874) 625557
www.breconjazz.co.uk

12 Aug – 14 Aug
Weymouth Sailing Regatta
Weymouth Bay
Weymouth, Dorset
Tel: (01305) 838501
www.weymouth.gov.uk

14 Aug – 3 Sep
Edinburgh International Festival
Various venues
Edinburgh
Tel: (0131) 473 2000
www.eif.co.uk

20 Aug – 21 Aug
Saddleworth Rushcart Festival
Saddleworth Villages of Uppermill, Greenfield,
Dobcross and Delph Uppermill, Saddleworth,
Tel: (01457) 876198
www.saddleworthrushcart.mysite.
freeserve.com

24 Aug*
Vale of Glamorgan Agricultural Show
Fonmon Castle
Fonmon, Barry, Vale of Glamorgan
Tel: (01446) 710099

27 Aug – 29 Aug*
England's Medieval Festival
Gardens and Grounds of Herstmonceux Castle
Herstmonceux, Hailsham, East Sussex
Tel: (020) 8416 0398
Bookings: (01323) 834489 (Advance ticket sales)
www.mgel.com

28 Aug
Grasmere Lakeland Sports and Show
Sports Field
Stock Lane, Grasmere, Ambleside, Cumbria
Tel: (015394) 32127

28 Aug – 29 Aug
Notting Hill Carnival
Streets around Ladbroke Grove
London
Tel: (020) 8964 0544

29 Aug
Corsley Show
Corsley Showfield
Corsley, Warminster, Wiltshire
Tel: (01373) 832418

29 Aug
Keswick Agricultural Show
Keswick Showground
Crossings Field, High Hill, Keswick, Cumbria
Tel: (016973) 23418

29 Aug – 1 Sep
International Beatles Festival
Various venues
Liverpool
Tel: (0151) 236 9091
www.caverncitytours.com

31 Aug*
Port of Dartmouth Royal Regatta
Various venues
Dartmouth, Devon
www.dartmouthregatta.co.uk

Left Notting Hill Carnival, London **Right** Herstmonceux Castle, Herstmonceux

SEPTEMBER

2 Sep – 6 Nov 2005
Blackpool Illuminations
Blackpool Promenade
Blackpool
Tel: (01253) 478222
www.blackpooltourism.com

3 Sep 2005*
Braemar Gathering
Princess Royal and Duke of Fife Memorial Park
Braemar, Ballater, Aberdeenshire
Tel: (01339) 755377
www.braemargathering.org

8 Sep 2005*
Westmorland County Show
Westmorland County Showfield
Lane Farm, Crooklands, Milnthorpe, Cumbria
Tel: (015395) 67804
www.westmorland-county-show.co.uk

9 Sep 2005*
36th Annual Kendal Torchlight Carnival
Town Centre Streets
Kendal, Cumbria
Tel: (015395) 63018
www.kendaltorchlightcarnival.co.uk

10 Sep – 11 Sep 2005*
Beaulieu International Autojumble and Automart
National Motor Museum
John Montagu Building, Beaulieu, Brockenhurst,
Hampshire
Tel: (01590) 612345
Bookings: (01590) 612888
www.beaulieu.co.uk

10 Sep – 11 Sep 2005
Caravan Extravaganza
The Lawns
University of Hull, Harland Way, Cottingham,
East Riding of Yorkshire
Tel: (01276) 686654
www.hercma.co.uk

15 Sep 2005
Thame and Oxfordshire County Show
The Showground
Kingsey Road, Thame, Oxfordshire
Tel: (01844) 212737
www.thameshow.co.uk

16 Sep - 18 Sep 2005
Harrogate Autumn Flower Show
Great Yorkshire Showground
Harrogate, North Yorkshire
Tel: (01423) 561049
www.flowershow.org.uk

17 Sep – 18 Sep 2005
Mayor's Thames Festival
River Thames
London
Tel: (020) 7928 0960
www.ThamesFestival.org

17 Sep – 18 Sep 2005*
The Royal County of Berkshire Show
Newbury Showground
Priors Court, Hermitage, Thatcham, Berkshire
Tel: (01635) 247111
www.newburyshowground.co.uk

24 Sep – 25 Sep 2005
Malvern Autumn Garden and Country Show
Three Counties Showground
The Showground, Malvern, Worcestershire
Tel: (01684) 584900
www.threecounties.co.uk

OCTOBER

7 Oct – 15 Oct 2005
Hull Fair
Walton Street Fairground
Walton Street, Hull
Tel: (01482) 615625

13 Oct – 16 Oct 2005
Falmouth Oyster Festival
Falmouth, Cornwall
Tel: (01326) 375309

23 Oct 2005*
Trafalgar Day Parade
Trafalgar Square
London
Tel: (020) 7928 8978

NOVEMBER

5 Nov 2005
The City of Liverpool Fireworks Display
Sefton Park, Liverpool
Tel: (0151) 233 3007

12 Nov 2005
Lord Mayor's Show
London
Tel: (020) 7606 3030
www.lordmayorsshow.org

* provisional date at time of going to press

Ratings **you** can trust

STAR QUALITY

★★★★★   **Exceptional quality**

★★★★   **Excellent quality**

★★★   **Very good quality**

★★   **Good quality**

★   **Acceptable quality**

When you're looking for a place to stay, you need a rating system you can trust. The British Graded Holiday Parks Scheme, operated jointly by the national tourist boards for England, Scotland and Wales, gives you a clear guide of what to expect.

Based on the internationally recognised rating of one to five stars, the system puts great emphasis on quality and reflects customer expectations.

Parks are visited annually by trained, impartial assessors who award a rating based on cleanliness, environment and the quality of services and facilities provided.

In which region is the county I wish to visit?

English counties and unitary authorities can be found in the following regions in this guide:

County/Unitary Authority	Region	County/Unitary Authority	Region
Bath and North East Somerset (U)	South West England	Hampshire	South East England
Bedfordshire	East of England	Hartlepool (U)	Northumbria
Blackburn with Darwen (U)	England's Northwest	Herefordshire (U)	Heart of England
Blackpool (U)	England's Northwest	Hertfordshire	East of England
Bournemouth (U)	South West England	Isle of Wight (U)	South East England
Bracknell Forest (U)	South East England	Isles of Scilly	South West England
Brighton & Hove (U)	South East England	Kent	South East England
Buckinghamshire	South East England	Kingston upon Hull (U)	Yorkshire
Cambridgeshire	East of England	Lancashire	England's Northwest
Cheshire	England's Northwest	Leicester (U)	East Midlands
City of Bristol (U)	South West England	Leicestershire	East Midlands
Cornwall	South West England	Lincolnshire	East Midlands
County Durham	Northumbria	Luton (U)	East of England
Cumbria	Cumbria – The Lake District	Medway (U)	South East England
Darlington (U)	Northumbria	Merseyside	England's Northwest
Derby (U)	East Midlands	Middlesbrough (U)	Northumbria
Derbyshire	East Midlands	Milton Keynes (U)	South East England
Devon	South West England	Norfolk	East of England
Dorset	South West England	North East Lincolnshire (U)	Yorkshire
Durham	Northumbria	North Lincolnshire (U)	Yorkshire
East Riding of Yorkshire (U)	Yorkshire	North Somerset (U)	South West England
East Sussex	South East England	North Yorkshire	Yorkshire
Essex	East of England	Northamptonshire	East Midlands
Gloucestershire	South West England	Northamptonshire	East Midlands
Greater London	London	Northumberland	Northumbria
Greater Manchester	England's Northwest	Nottingham City (U)	East Midlands
Halton (U)	England's Northwest	Nottinghamshire	East Midlands

Above Rochdale Canal, Greater Manchester **Right** enjoy summer sun in Southwold, Suffolk

County/Unitary Authority	Region	County/Unitary Authority	Region
Oxfordshire	South East England	Surrey	South East England
Peterborough (U)	East of England	Swindon (U)	South West England
Plymouth (U)	South West England	Telford and Wrekin (U)	Heart of England
Poole (U)	South West England	Thurrock (U)	East of England
Portsmouth (U)	South East England	Torbay (U)	South West England
Reading (U)	South East England	Tyne and Wear	Northumbria
Redcar and Cleveland (U)	Northumbria	Warrington (U)	England's Northwest
Rutland (U)	East Midlands	Warwickshire	Heart of England
Shropshire	Heart of England	West Berkshire (U)	South East England
Slough (U)	South East England	West Midlands	Heart of England
Somerset	South West England	West Sussex	South East England
South Gloucestershire (U)	South West England	West Yorkshire	Yorkshire
South Yorkshire	Yorkshire	Wiltshire	South West England
Southampton (U)	South East England	Windsor and Maidenhead (U)	South East England
Southend-on-Sea (U)	East of England	Wirral	England's Northwest
Staffordshire	Heart of England	Wokingham (U)	South East England
Stockton-on-Tees (U)	Northumbria	Worcestershire	Heart of England
Stoke-on-Trent (U)	Heart of England	York (U)	Yorkshire
Suffolk	East of England		

(U) Unitary Authority

National Accessible Scheme

VisitBritain has a variety of accessible parks in its National Accessible Scheme for Caravan Holiday Homes and Parks for wheelchair users and those with limited mobility. The different accessible ratings will help you choose the one that best suits your needs.

Holiday Parks that display one of these three signs are committed to accessibility. When you see them, you can be sure that the park has been thoroughly assessed against demanding criteria. If you have additional needs or special requirements we strongly recommend that you make sure these can be met by your chosen establishment before confirming your booking.

 Category 1 Accessible to a wheelchair user travelling independently.

 Category 2 Accessible to a wheelchair user travelling with assistance.

 Category 3 Accessible to a wheelchair user able to walk a few paces and up a maximum of three steps.

Accommodation taking part in the National Accessible Scheme, and which appears in the regional sections of this guide, is listed below. Use the town index at the back to find the page numbers for their full entries. The National Accessible Scheme for Caravan Holiday Homes and Parks is currently in the process of being updated.

Above Blakebeck Farm, Blakebeck **Below** take in the magnificent scenery, Snowdonia

Accessible parks

Category 2

Stanmore Hall Touring Park	Bridgnorth	**Heart of England**
Oxon Hall Touring Park	Shrewsbury	**Heart of England**
Severn Gorge Park	Telford	**Heart of England**
Yew Tree Park	Canterbury	**South East England**
Tanner Farm Touring Caravan & Camping Park	Marden	**South East England**
Beacon Hill Touring Park	Poole	**South West England**
Tehidy Holiday Park	Portreath	**South West England**
Halse Farm Caravan & Tent Park	Winsford	**South West England**
Kenmore Caravan and Camping Park	Kenmore	**Scotland**

The National Accessible Scheme forms part of the Tourism for All Campaign that is being promoted by VisitBritain and national and regional tourism organisations. Additional help and guidance on finding suitable holiday accommodation for those with special needs can be obtained from:

Tourism for All UK
(formerly Holiday Care Service)
Hawkins Suite, Enham Place,
Enham Alamein, Andover,
Hampshire SP11 6JS

Admin/consultancy: 0845 124 9974
Information helpline: 0845 124 9971
(9-5 Mon, Tue and 9-1 Wed-Fri)
Reservation/Friends: 0845 124 9973
Fax: 0845 124 9972
Minicom: 0845 124 9976
Email: info@holidaycare.org
Web: www.tourismforall.info

Tourist information in Britain

Information pour les touristes en Grande-Bretagne
Touristen-information in Grossbritannien
Toeristische informatie In Groot-Brittannie
Informazioni per turisti in Gran Bretagna

To help you explore Britain, to see both the major sites and the fascinating attractions off the beaten track, there is a country-wide service of Tourist Information Centres (TICs), each ready and able to give advice and directions on how best to enjoy your holiday in Britain. A comprehensive list can be obtained from VisitBritain offices overseas.

Call in at these centres while travelling – you'll find them in most towns and many villages – and make use of the help that awaits you. Much development of Tourist Information Centre services has taken place in recent years and you should have no difficulty in locating them as most are well signposted and the use of the following international direction sign is becoming more common:

You can rest assured that the Tourist Information Centres in the places you visit will be ready to give you all the help you need when you get to Britain, particularly on matters of detailed local information.

Accommodation reservation services

Wherever you go in Britain, you will find TICs which can help and advise you about all types of accommodation. Details of Park-Finding Services are outlined on page 37.

Britain and London Visitor Centre

1 Regent Street London SW1Y 4XT
(No telephone enquiries. Walk-in centre only)
Monday 09.30 – 18.30
Tuesday to Friday 09.00 – 18.30
Weekends 10.00 – 16.00
Saturdays on summer weekends
(June to Oct) 09.00 – 17.00

Her Majesty The Queen opened the revamped Britain and London Visitor Centre in June 2003. At the height of the summer season up to 2000 visitors a day will come to plan and book their trips around Britain and London.

The BLVC is a one-stop shop for visitors, providing free information on everything from tourist attractions and cultural events to travel and destination advice, and itinerary planning. The centre also provides the opportunity to book travel, tours, accommodation, tourist attractions and tickets to theatre shows and other events. Special offers are available every day of the week. The Great British Heritage Pass and the London Pass can be bought or redeemed at the BLVC and there is also a currency exchange office with VAT refund. Free access to the VisitBritain and Visit London websites allow visitors to search for even more information for themselves in the newly installed internet lounge.

Our highly trained information staff can speak many languages including French, German, Spanish, Italian, Japanese, Portuguese, Dutch and Hindi. All staff receive Welcome All Training, and constantly look to ways of improving customer care for visitors with disabilities. We have a large spacious centre with hard floors suitable for wheelchairs, lift (with Braille buttons), accessible lower desk for helping customers in wheelchairs, large print literature, magnifying sheets and a hearing loop. Chairs are available for customers on the ground and first floors.

There are also a number of marketing opportunities within the centre such as exhibition space, events programmes, evening receptions and large fully equipped conference room facilities. The Britain and London Visitor Centre is located just two minutes' walk south of Piccadilly Circus tube.

Tourist organisations

The following official tourist organisations in all parts of Britain welcome personal callers, except where indicated:

London

Visit London
6th Floor, 2 More London Riverside,
London SE1 2RR
(no personal callers please).
www.visitlondon.com
For further information on London Tourist Information Centres please refer to page 70.

VisitScotland
19 Cockspur Street, London SW1Y 5BL
(personal callers only)
Telephone enquiries: (0131) 332 2433

VisitBritain
Thames Tower, Blacks Road,
Hammersmith, London W6 9EL
(written enquiries only)

England

Information is available from the 10 regional tourism areas in England (contact details can be found at the beginning of each regional section), and a network of around 550 Tourist Information Centres. Look out for the sign shown above.

Scotland

VisitScotland has a substantial network of local tourist boards, backed up by more than 140 information centres.

VisitScotland
23 Ravelston Terrace, Edinburgh EH4 3TP
Tel: (0131) 332 2433

Wales

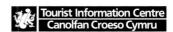

There are three Regional Tourism Companies and over 82 information centres to help you.

Wales Tourist Board
Brunel House, 2 Fitzalan Road, Cardiff CF24 0UY
Tel: (029) 2049 9909
(telephone and written enquiries only)

Information on the internet

Browse VisitBritain's website for a wealth of information including travel information, places to visit and events.
www.visitbritain.com

VisitBritain offices

Contact your local VisitBritain office

ARGENTINA
VisitBritain
Avenida Córdoba 645, 2 piso
C1054AAF Buenos Aires
T/F: 011 4314 6735 / 8955
T/F: 011 4315 3161
E: buenos.aires@visitbritain.org
www.visitbritain.com/ar

AUSTRALIA
VisitBritain
Level 2, 15 Blue Street
North Sydney NSW 2060
T: 1300 85 85 89 (toll-free)
E: visitbritainaus@visitbritain.org
www.visitbritain.com.au

BELGIË/BELGIQUE
VisitBritain Centre
Louizalaan/Avenue Louise 140
2 de verdieping/2ème étage
1050 Brussel/Bruxelles
T: 02 646 35 10
F: 02 646 39 86
E: british.be@visitbritain.org
www.visitbritain.com/be (Flemish)
www.visitbritain.com/be2 (French)

BRASIL
VisitBritain
Rua da Assembléia 10 / 3707
Rio de Janeiro - RJ - 20011-901
T: 21 2531 1717
F: 21 2531 0383
E: brasil@visitbritain.org
www.visitbritain.com/br

CANADA
VisitBritain
5915 Airport Road, Suite 120
Mississauga, Ontario L4V 1T1
T: 1 888 VISIT UK
F: 905 405 8490
E: britinfo@visitbritain.org
www.visitbritain.com/ca

DANMARK
VisitBritain
T: 70 21 50 11
E: dkweb@visitbritain.org
www.visitbritain.com/dk

DEUTSCHLAND
VisitBritain & Britain Visitor Centre
Hackescher Markt 1
10178 Berlin
T: 01801-46 86 42 (Ortstarif)
F: 030-31 57 19 10
E: gb-info@visitbritain.org
www.visitbritain.com/de

ESPAÑA
Turismo Británico
Apartado de Correos 19205
28080 Madrid (dirección postal)
T: 902 171 181
E: turismo.britanico@visitbritain.org
www.visitbritain.com/es

FRANCE
Office de Tourisme de Grande-Bretagne
BP 154-08
75363 Paris Cedex 08
T: 01 58 36 50 50
F: 01 58 36 50 51
E: gbinfo@visitbritain.org
www.visitbritain.com/fr (en français)

HONG KONG
VisitBritain
7/F British Council
3 Supreme Court Road
Admiralty
Hong Kong
T: 3515 7755
F: 3515 7700
E: hongkong@visitbritain.org
www.visitbritain.com/hk

INDIA
VisitBritain
B1106 Millennium Plaza
Sector 27, Gurgaon 122002
Haryana
T: 124 280 6180
F: 124 280 6187
E: india@visitbritain.org
www.visitbritain.com/in

IRELAND
VisitBritain
18/19 College Green
Dublin 2
T: 01 670 8000
F: 01 670 8244
E: contactus@visitbritain.org
www.visitbritain.ie

ITALIA
VisitBritain
Ente Nazionale Britannico per il Turismo
Corso Magenta 32
20123 Milano
T: 02 88 08 151
F: 02 7201 0086
E: milanenquiry@visitbritain.org
www.visitbritain.com/ciao

JAPAN
VisitBritain
Akasaka Twin Tower 1F
2-17-22 Akasaka
Minato-ku
Tokyo 107-0052
T: 03 5562 2550
www.visitbritain.com/jp (English)
www.uknow.or.jp (Japanese/English)
NEDERLAND

VisitBritain
Stadhouderskade 2 (5e)
1054 ES Amsterdam
T: 020 689 0002
F: 020 689 0003
E: nl@visitbritain.org
www.visitbritain.com/nl

NEW ZEALAND
VisitBritain
PO Box 105-652, Auckland
T: 0800 700 741 (toll-free)
E: newzealand@visitbritain.org
www.visitbritain.co.nz

NORGE
VisitBritain
PB 1554 Vika
0117 Oslo
T: 22 01 20 80 (contact center)
F: 22 01 20 84
E: britisketuristkontor@visitbritain.org
www.visitbritain.com/no

ÖSTERREICH
Britain Visitor Centre
c/o British Council
Siebensterngasse 21
1070 Wien
T: 0800-150 170 (gebührenfrei)
F: 01-5 33 26 16 85
E: a-info@visitbritain.org
www.visitbritain.com/at

POLEN
Turystyczna Informacja Wielka Brytania
c/o British Council
ul. Al. Jerozolimskie 59
00-697 Warszawa
www.visitbritain.com/pl

PORTUGAL
Turismo Británico
Apartado 24195
1251 - 901 Lisboa
T: 808 201 273
F: 21 324 0191
E: britanicoturismo@visitbritain.org
www.visitbritain.com/pt
RUSSLAND

c/o British Council
Ulitsa Nikoloyamskaya 1, VGBIL
Moscow 109189
www.visitbritain.com/ru

SCHWEIZ/SUISSE/SVIZZERA
Britisches Verkehrsbüro
Badenerstr. 21
8004 Zürich
T: 0844-007 007 (Ortstarif)
F: 043-3 22 20 01
E: ch-info@visitbritain.org
www.visitbritain.com/chde

SINGAPORE
VisitBritain
108 Robinson Road
GMG Building #01-00
Singapore 068900
T: 6227 5400
F: 6227 5411
E: singapore@visitbritain.org
www.visitbritain.com/sg

SOUTH AFRICA
VisitBritain
(public address)
Lancaster Gate
Hyde Park Lane
Hyde Lane
Hyde Park, Sandton 2196
(postal address)
PO Box 41896, Craighall 2024
T: 011 325 0343
F: 011 325 0344
E: johannesburg@visitbritain.org
W: www.visitbritain.com/za

SUOMI
VisitBritain
Box 3102, 103 62 Stockholm
T: 9 2512 2422
F: 00 468 21 31 29
E: suomi@visitbritain.org
www.visitbritain.com/suomi

SVERIGE:
Brittiska Turistbyrån
(public address)
Klara Norra Kyrkogata 29
S 111 22 Stockholm
(postal address)
Box 3102, 103 62 Stockholm
T: 08 4401 700
F: 08 21 31 29
E: sverige@visitbritain.org
www.visitbritain.com/sverige

UNITED ARAB EMIRATES
VisitBritain
Tariq Bin Zaid Street
Near Rashid Hospital
Al Maktoum Roundabout
PO Box 33342
Dubai
T: 04 3350088
F: 04 3355335
E: dubai@visitbritain.org
www.visitbritain.com/meast
(English language site)
www.visitbritain.com/ahlan
(Arabic language site)

USA
VisitBritain
551 Fifth Avenue, Suite 701
New York, NY 10176-0799
T: 1 800 462 2748
F: 212 986 1188
E: travelinfo@visitbritain.org
www.visitbritain.com/usa

The David Bellamy Conservation Award

"These well-deserved awards are a signpost to parks which are making real achievements in protecting our environment. Go there and experience wrap-around nature....you could be amazed at what you find!" says Professor David Bellamy.

Many of Britain's holiday parks have become 'green champions' of conservation in the countryside, according to leading conservationist David Bellamy. More than 450 gold, silver and bronze parks were this year named in the David Bellamy Conservation Awards, organised in conjunction with the British Holiday and Home Parks Association. These parks are recognised for their commitment to conservation and the environment through their management of landscaping, recycling policies, waste management, the cultivation of flora and fauna and the creation of habitats designed to encourage a variety of wildlife onto the park. Links with the local community and the use of local materials is also an important consideration.

Parks participating in the scheme are assessed for the awards by holidaymakers who complete postcards to be returned to David Bellamy, an independent inspection by a representative from the local Wildlife Trust and David Bellamy's own study of the parks environmental audit completed when joining the scheme. Parks with Bellamy Awards offer a variety of accommodation from pitches for touring caravans, motorhomes and tents, to caravan holiday homes, holiday lodges and cottages for rent. Holiday parks with these awards are not just those in quiet corners of the countryside. Amongst the winners are much larger centres in popular holiday areas that offer a wide range of entertainments and attractions.

Turn over the page for a list of award-winning parks featured in this guide.

Left, from top peaceful views in Dumfries and Galloway; reflections in the river Yare, Norfolk

The following parks, which are all featured in this guide, have received a Gold, Silver or Bronze David Bellamy Conservation Award.

For a free brochure featuring a full list of award winning parks please contact:
BH&HPA 6 Pullman Court, Great Western Road, Gloucester GL1 3ND
Tel: (01452) 526911 Fax: (01452) 508508
Email: enquiries@bhhpa.org.uk www.ukparks.com/bellamy.htm

Crake Valley Holiday Park GOLD	Coniston	**Cumbria – The Lake District**
Castlerigg Hall Caravan and Camping Park GOLD	Keswick	**Cumbria – The Lake District**
Beadnell Links Caravan Park GOLD	Beadnell	**Northumbria**
Haggerston Castle GOLD	Beal	**Northumbria**
Seafield Caravan Park SILVER	Seahouses	**Northumbria**
Thornwick & Sea Farm Holiday Centre SILVER	Flamborough	**Yorkshire**
Rudding Holiday Park GOLD	Harrogate	**Yorkshire**
Golden Square Caravan and Camping Park GOLD	Helmsley	**Yorkshire**
St Helena's Caravan Site GOLD	Leeds	**Yorkshire**
Upwood Holiday Park GOLD	Oxenhope	**Yorkshire**
Lebberston Touring Park SILVER	Scarborough	**Yorkshire**
Jasmine Park GOLD	Snainton	**Yorkshire**
Ladycross Plantation Caravan Park GOLD	Whitby	**Yorkshire**
Middlewood Farm Holiday Park GOLD	Whitby	**Yorkshire**
Allerton Park Caravan Park GOLD	York	**Yorkshire**
Island Meadow Caravan Park GOLD	Aston Cantlow	**Heart of England**
Fernwood Caravan Park GOLD	Ellesmere	**Heart of England**
Ashlea Pools Country Park SILVER	Hopton Heath	**Heart of England**
Rivendale Caravan and Leisure Park GOLD	Alsop-en-le-Dale	**East Midlands**
Orchard Caravan Park GOLD	Boston	**East Midlands**
Foreman's Bridge Caravan Park GOLD	Sutton St James	**East Midlands**
Forest Park Caravan Site GOLD	Cromer	**East of England**
Grasmere Caravan Park (TB) BRONZE	Great Yarmouth	**East of England**
Vauxhall Holiday Park SILVER	Great Yarmouth	**East of England**
Heathland Beach Caravan Park GOLD	Kessingland	**East of England**
Waldegraves Holiday and Leisure Park SILVER	Mersea Island	**East of England**
Sandy Gulls Cliff Top Touring Park SILVER	Mundesley	**East of England**
Crowhurst Park GOLD	Battle	**South East England**
Whitecliff Bay Holiday Park SILVER	Bembridge	**South East England**
Rowan Park Caravan Club Site GOLD	Bognor Regis	**South East England**
Wicks Farm Camping Park GOLD	Chichester	**South East England**
Sandy Balls Holiday Centre GOLD	Fordingbridge	**South East England**
Honeybridge Park SILVER	Horsham	**South East England**
Hurley Riverside Park GOLD	Hurley	**South East England**
Tanner Farm Touring Caravan & Camping Park GOLD	Marden	**South East England**
Shorefield Country Park GOLD	Milford on Sea	**South East England**
Hillgrove Park GOLD	St Helens	**South East England**
Parkers Farm Holiday Park SILVER	Ashburton	**South West England**

Newton Mill Camping GOLD	Bath	**South West England**
Freshwater Beach Holiday Park BRONZE	Bridport	**South West England**
Golden Cap Holiday Park GOLD	Bridport	**South West England**
Highlands End Holiday Park GOLD	Bridport	**South West England**
Coastal Caravan Park SILVER	Burton Bradstock	**South West England**
Monkton Wyld Farm Caravan & Camping Park GOLD	Charmouth	**South West England**
Wood Farm Caravan and Camping Park SILVER	Charmouth	**South West England**
Cheddar Bridge Touring Park SILVER	Cheddar	**South West England**
Ruda Holiday Park SILVER	Croyde Bay	**South West England**
Oakcliff Holiday Park GOLD	Dawlish	**South West England**
Penhale Caravan and Camping Park BRONZE	Fowey	**South West England**
The Old Oaks Touring Park GOLD	Glastonbury	**South West England**
Hidden Valley Touring & Camping Park GOLD	Ilfracombe	**South West England**
Forest Glade Holiday Park GOLD	Kentisbeare	**South West England**
Croft Farm Holiday Park GOLD	Luxulyan	**South West England**
Thorney Lakes and Caravan Park GOLD	Muchelney	**South West England**
Holywell Bay Holiday Park SILVER	Newquay	**South West England**
Newquay Holiday Park GOLD	Newquay	**South West England**
Sandyholme Holiday Park SILVER	Owermoigne	**South West England**
Beverley Holidays GOLD	Paignton	**South West England**
Whitehill Country Park GOLD	Paignton	**South West England**
Polruan Holidays (Camping & Caravanning) SILVER	Polruan-by-Fowey	**South West England**
Beacon Hill Touring Park GOLD	Poole	**South West England**
River Valley Country Park SILVER	Relubbus	**South West England**
Sea Acres Holiday Park BRONZE	Ruan Minor	**South West England**
Silver Sands Holiday Park SILVER	Ruan Minor	**South West England**
Sun Valley Holiday Park GOLD	St Austell	**South West England**
Oakdene Forest Park SILVER	St Leonards	**South West England**
Yeo Valley Holiday Park SILVER	South Molton	**South West England**
Ulwell Cottage Caravan Park SILVER	Swanage	**South West England**
Harford Bridge Holiday Park GOLD	Tavistock	**South West England**
Wareham Forest Tourist Park SILVER	Wareham	**South West England**
White Acres Holiday Park SILVER	White Cross	**South West England**
Merley Court Touring Park GOLD	Wimborne Minster	**South West England**
Halse Farm Caravan & Tent Park GOLD	Winsford	**South West England**
Lomond Woods Holiday Park GOLD	Balloch	**Scotland**
Barnsoul Farm GOLD	Dumfries	**Scotland**
Belhaven Bay Caravan Park SILVER	Dunbar	**Scotland**
Linwater Caravan Park SILVER	Edinburgh	**Scotland**
Linnhe Lochside Holidays GOLD	Fort William	**Scotland**
Dovecot Caravan Park SILVER	Laurencekirk	**Scotland**
Craigtoun Meadows Holiday Park GOLD	St Andrews	**Scotland**
Witches Craig Caravan Park GOLD	Stirling	**Scotland**
Cenarth Falls Holiday Park GOLD	Cardigan	**Wales**
Scamford Caravan Park BRONZE	Keeston	**Wales**
Lakeside Caravan & Camping Park SILVER	Llangorse	**Wales**
Caerfai Bay Caravan & Tent Park SILVER	St Davids	**Wales**

Travel information by car and by train

Distance chart

The distances between towns on the chart below are given to the nearest mile, and are measured along routes based on the quickest travelling time, making maximum use of motorways or dual-carriageway roads. The chart is based upon information supplied by the Automobile Association.

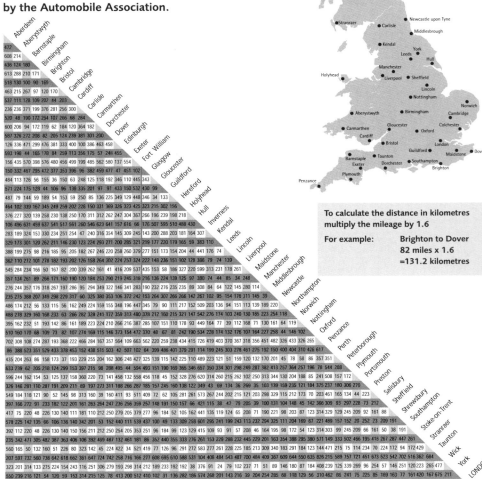

Town labels (diagonal, in order):
Aberdeen, Aberystwyth, Barnstaple, Birmingham, Brighton, Bristol, Cambridge, Cardiff, Carlisle, Carmarthen, Dorchester, Dover, Edinburgh, Exeter, Fort William, Glasgow, Gloucester, Guildford, Hereford, Holyhead, Hull, Inverness, Kendal, Leeds, Lincoln, Liverpool, Maidstone, Manchester, Middlesbrough, Newcastle, Northampton, Norwich, Nottingham, Oxford, Penzance, Perth, Peterborough, Plymouth, Portsmouth, Preston, Salisbury, Sheffield, Shrewsbury, Southampton, Stoke-on-Trent, Stranraer, Taunton, Wick, York, LONDON

```
472
608 214
436 124 180
613 288 210 171
518 130 100  90 169
463 215 267  97 120 170
537 111 128 109 202  44 203
236 236 371 199 376 281 256 300
520  48 190 172 254 107 266  68 284
600 206  94 172 119  62 184 120 364 182
587 326 272 208  82 205 124 239 381 301 200
126 336 471 299 476 381 333 400 100 386 463 458
593 198  44 165 178  84 259 113 356 175  57 248 455
156 435 570 398 576 480 456 499 199 485 562 580 137 554
150 332 467 295 472 377 353 396  96 382 459 477  47 451 102
484 113 126  56 155  36 150  63 248 125 118 192 346 110 445 343
571 224 175 128  44 106  96 139 335 201  97  97 433 150 532 430  99
487  79 144  59 189  54 153  59 250  85 136 225 349 129 448 346  34 133
464 102 339 167 345 249 259 202 228 150 331 369 326 323 425 323 215 302 156
376 227 320 139 258 230 138 250 170 311 312 262 247 304 367 266 196 239 198 218
106 496 631 459 637 541 517 561 260 546 623 641 157 616 176 507 595 510 488 430
283 189 324 153 330 234 251 254  47 240 316 354 145 309 245 143 200 288 203 181 164 307
329 173 301 120 262 211 146 230 123 224 293 271 200 285 321 219 177 220 179 165  59 383 110
388 199 275  98 216 185  95 205 182 267 246 220 268 260 379 277 151 173 154 204  44 441 176  74
362 110 272 101 278 182 193 202 126 158 264 302 224 257 324 222 148 236 151 102 128 386  79  74 139
545 284 234 166  50 167  82 200 339 262 161  41 416 209 537 435 153  58 186 327 220 599 313 231 178 261
357 134 261  89 266 171 160 190 120 184 253 290 219 245 318 216 136 224 139 125  97 380  74  44  85  34 248
276 244 357 176 318 267 197 286  95 294 349 322 146 341 283 190 232 276 235  89 308  84  64 122 146 280 114
235 275 368 207 349 298 229 317  60 325 380 353 106 372 242 153 264 307 266 142 267 102  95 154 176 311 145  39
486 174 212  56 133 115  56 162 249 224 159 155 348 196 447 345  79  90 111 217 152 509 203 136  94 151 113 139 189 220
488 278 329 160 168 233  63 266 282 328 241 172 359 313 480 378 212 160 215 321 147 542 276 174 103 240 130 185 223 254 118
395 162 232  51 193 142  86 161 189 223 224 210 266 218 385 107 151 110 178  93 449 164  77  39 112 168  71 130 161  64 119
510 160 170  68 109  73  82 107 274 169 115 146 373 154 472 370  48  67  81 242 190 534 234 172 136 107 164 127 258  44 146 102
702 308 108 274 287 193 368 222 466 284 167 357 564 109 663 562 220 259 238 434 415 726 419 403 370 318 356 451 482 326 433 326 265
 86 388 523 351 529 433 378 453 152 438 515 503  47 507 102  64 399 486 401 379 241 199 245 303 278 461 275 192 100 400 404 310 426 617
435 204 263  86 158 173  37 193 229 255 204 162 306 248 427 325 159 115 142 225 110 489 221 121  51 159 120 170 201  45  78  58  88 357 351
633 239  62 205 218 124 299 153 397 215  98 288 495  41 544 454 209 213 305 346 657 350 304 298 287 382 413 257 364 257 196  78 544 298
596 244 162 154  53 125 137 158 360 220  73 141 458 132 558 456 118  45 152 328 276 620 314 260 215 262 102 250 313 344 130 204 188  85 241 508 157 172
326 146 281 110 287 191 209 211  89 197 273 311 188 266 287 185 157 245 160 138 122 349  43  69 134  36 269  35 103 139 159 235 121 184 375 237 180 306 270
549 184 118 121  90  52 145  98 313 160  39 160 401  93 511 409  72  62 105 281 573 267 244 202 215 121 203 298 329 115 212 173  70 203 461 165 134  44 223
397 166 272  91 233 182 122 201 161 263 264 247 236 256 359 257 148 191 150 157  66 421 115  38  47  79 205  39 100 131 104 148  45 142 366 309  93 297 228  73 212
417  75 220  48 226 130 140 111 181 110 212 250 219 205 379 277  96 184  52 105 162 441 135 119 124  65 208  71 190 221  98 203  87 123 314 329 129 245 209  92 161  88
578 225 142 135  86 116 140 142 340 200  49 143 440 111 539 437 100  49 133 309 268 620 295 241 199 241 130 232 294 325 111 204 293 209 191 157  67 221 489 157 152  20 252  23 209 191
392 112 220  48 226 130 140 150 156 211 212 250 254 205 353 251  96 184  99 123 129 415 109  93  91  57 208  46 194 195  98 172  54 123 314 303  99 245 209  66 161  50  38 191
235 342 477 305 482 387 363 406 106 392 469 487 132 461 181  86 352 440 355 333 276 261 153 229 288 232 445 229 201 163 354 388 295 380 571 149 333 502 466 195 418 267 287 447 261
560 165  50 132 160  51 226  80 323 142  45 224 422  34 521 419  77 126  96 291 272 583 277 261 228 225 185 213 309 340 183 291 184 123 144 471 215  75 114 234  70 224 172  94 172 429
207 537 732 560 738 642 618 662 361 647 724 742 258 716 166 277 608 695 610 588 531 104 408 484 543 487 700 484 409 367 609 644 550 635 826 215 589 757 721 451 673 523 542 702 516 362 684
323 201 314 133 275 224 154 243 116 251 306 279 193 298 314 212 189 233 192 192  38 376  91  24  79 102 237  71  51  89 146 180  87 184 408 239 125 339 269  96 254  57 146 251 120 223 265 477
550 239 216 121  54 120  59 153 314 215 125  78 413 200 512 410 102  31 136 282 186 574 268 201 143 216  39 204 254 285  68 118 129  56 310 462  86 241  75 225  85 169 163  77 161 420 167 675 211
```

To calculate the distance in kilometres multiply the mileage by 1.6

For example: Brighton to Dover
                 82 miles x 1.6
                 =131.2 kilometres

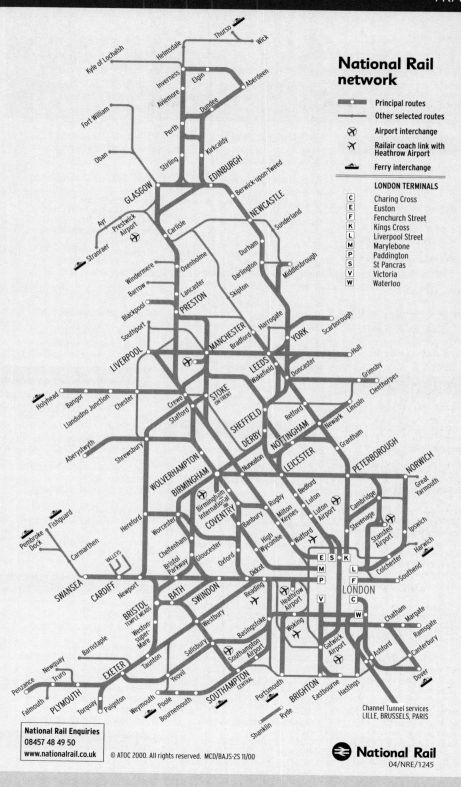

National Rail network

▬▬▬	Principal routes
─●─	Other selected routes
✈	Airport interchange
✈	Railair coach link with Heathrow Airport
⛴	Ferry interchange

LONDON TERMINALS

C	Charing Cross
E	Euston
F	Fenchurch Street
K	Kings Cross
L	Liverpool Street
M	Marylebone
P	Paddington
S	St Pancras
V	Victoria
W	Waterloo

Channel Tunnel services
LILLE, BRUSSELS, PARIS

National Rail Enquiries
08457 48 49 50
www.nationalrail.co.uk

© ATOC 2000. All rights reserved. MCD/BAJS-2S 11/00

National Rail
04/NRE/1245

Index to parks
Repertoire des terrains/platzverzeichnis/register van campings/indice dei campeggi

Index to towns
Annuaire par villes/städteverzeichnis/index van steden/indice delle citta

Tourist Information Centres

When it comes to your next British break, the first stage of your journey could be closer than you think. You've probably got a tourist information centre nearby which is there to serve the local community – as well as visitors. Knowledgeable staff will be happy to help you, wherever you're heading.

Many tourist information centres can provide you with maps and guides, and often it's possible to book accommodation and travel tickets too.

Across Britain there are more than 750 TICs. You'll find the address of your nearest centre in your local phone book.

Index to advertisers

enjoyEngland™
official guides to quality

Hotels, Townhouses,
Travel Accommodation
and Restaurants with
Rooms in England 2005
£10.99

Bed & Breakfasts,
Guesthouses, Small Hotels,
Farmhouses, Inns, Campus
Accommodation and Hostels
in England 2005
£11.99

Self-Catering
Holiday Homes and Boat
Accommodation
in England 2005
£11.99

Touring Parks, Camping, Holiday Parks
and Villages in Britain 2005
£8.99

Somewhere Special
in England 2005
£8.99

Families and Pets Welcome
in England 2005
£11.99

enjoyEngland™
official guides to **quality**

Published by: VisitBritain, Thames Tower, Blacks Road,
London W6 9EL in partnership with England's tourism
industry www.visitengland.com
Publishing Manager: Tess Lugos
Production Manager: Iris Buckley
Compilation, design, copywriting, production and
advertisement sales: Jackson Lowe Marketing,
173 High Street, Lewes, East Sussex BN7 1YE
Tel: (01273) 487487 www.jacksonlowe.com
Typesetting: Tradespools Ltd, Somerset and Jackson
Lowe Marketing
Maps: Based on digital map data © ESR Cartography, 2004
Printing and binding: Emirates Printing Press, Dubai,
United Arab Emirates
Cover design: Eugenie Dodd Typographics

Photography credits: Cumbria Tourist Board; Drayton
Manor; East Midlands Tourism; East of England Tourist
Board; Heart of England Tourism; Zac Macaulay; The
National Trust; Northwest Development Agency; One
Northeast Tourism Team/Alex Telfer/Carlton Reid;
Portsmouth Historic Dockyard; South West Tourism; Tourism
South East; Visit London; VisitScotland; Wales Tourist Board
Photo Library; www.britainonview.com/Martin Brent/Rod
Edwards/Graham Gough/Klaus Hagmeier/David Hal/Grant
Pritchard/Ingrid Rasmussen; Yorkshire Tourist Board

Important note: The information contained in this guide has
been published in good faith on the basis of information
submitted to VisitBritain by the proprietors of the premises
listed, who have paid for their entries to appear. VisitBritain
cannot guarantee the accuracy of the information in this
guide and accepts no responsibility for any error or
misrepresentation. All liability for loss, disappointment,
negligence or other damage caused by reliance on the
information contained in this guide, or in the event of
bankruptcy, or liquidation, or cessation of trade of any
company, individual or firm mentioned, is hereby excluded
to the fullest extent permitted by law. Please check
carefully all prices, ratings and other details before
confirming a reservation.

© British Tourist Authority (trading as VisitBritain) 2005
ISBN 0 7095 7934 9
Product code C5CAMEN

A VisitBritain Publishing guide

Ratings **you** can trust

When you're looking for a place to stay, you need a rating system you can trust. The British Graded Holiday Parks Scheme, operated jointly by the national tourist boards for England, Scotland and Wales, gives you a clear guide of what to expect.

Based on the internationally recognised rating of one to five stars, the system puts great emphasis on quality and reflects customer expectations.

Parks are visited annually by trained, impartial assessors who award a rating based on cleanliness, environment and the quality of services and facilities provided.

STAR QUALITY

★★★★★   **Exceptional quality**

★★★★   **Excellent quality**

★★★   **Very good quality**

★★   **Good quality**

★   **Acceptable quality**

British Graded
Holiday Parks Scheme

★ ★ ★ ★ ★

HOLIDAY PARK

On the following pages you will find brief contact details for each park, together with its star rating and type of site. The listing also shows if an establishment has a National Accessible rating (see the front of the guide for further information). Parks are listed by region and then alphabetically by place name. They may be located in, or a short distance from, the places in the blue bands.

Quality-Assessed Parks

More detailed information on all the places shown in blue can be found in the regional sections (where establishments have paid to have their details included). To find these entries please refer to the appropriate regional section, or look in the town index.

The list which follows was compiled slightly later than the regional sections. For this reason you may find that, in a few instances, a star rating may differ between the two sections. This list contains the most up-to-date information and was correct at the time of going to press. Please note that it does not include parks in Scotland and Wales.

Holiday Villages

This section includes details for holiday villages quality-rated by VisitBritain.

LONDON

INNER LONDON
E4
Lee Valley Campsite ★★★★
Touring and Camping Park
Sewardstone Road, Chingford,
London E4 7RA
T: (020) 8529 5689
F: (020) 8559 4070
E: scs@leevalleypark.org.uk
I: www.leevalleypark.org.uk

N9
**Lee Valley Camping and
Caravan Park ★★★★**
Touring and Camping Park
Picketts Lock Lane, London
N9 0AS
T: (020) 8803 6900
F: (020) 8884 4975
E: leisurecentre@leevalleypark.
org.uk
I: www.leevalleypark.org.uk

SE2
**Abbey Wood Caravan Club
Site ★★★★★**
Touring and Camping Park
Federation Road, Abbey Wood,
London SE2 0LS
T: (020) 8311 7708
F: (020) 8311 1465
I: www.caravanclub.co.uk

SE19
**Crystal Palace Caravan Club
Site ★★★★★**
Touring and Camping Park
Crystal Palace Parade, London
SE19 1UF
T: (020) 8778 7155
F: (020) 8676 0980
I: www.caravanclub.co.uk

OUTER LONDON
LOUGHTON
**Debden House Camp Site
★★★**
Touring and Camping Park
Debden Green, Loughton
IG10 2NZ
T: (020) 8508 3008
F: (020) 85080284

STANSTED
**Thriftwood Caravan &
Camping Park ★★★★★**
*Holiday, Touring and Camping
Park*
Plaxdale Green Road, Sevenoaks
TN15 7PB
T: (01732) 822261
F: (01732) 824636
E: booking@thriftwoodleisure.
co.uk
I: www.thriftwoodleisure.co.uk

ENGLAND'S NORTHWEST

AINSDALE
Merseyside
**Willowbank Holiday Home
and Touring Park ★★★★★**
*Holiday, Touring and Camping
Park*
Coastral Road, Southport
PR8 3ST
T: (0170) 457 1566
F: (0170) 457 1566
E: mail@willowbankcp.co.uk
I: www.willowbankcp.co.uk

ALVANLEY
Warrington
**Ridgeway Country Holiday
Park ★★★★**
Holiday Park
The Ridgeway, Frodsham
WA6 6XQ
T: (0192) 873 4981
F: (0192) 873 4981
E: enquiries@ridgewaypark.com
I: www.ridgewaypark.com

BLACKPOOL
Blackpool
**Marton Mere Holiday
Village ★★★**
*Holiday, Touring and Camping
Park*
Mythop Road, Blackpool
FY4 4XN
T: (01253) 767544
F: (01253) 791544
E: enquiries@british-holidays.
co.uk
I: www.british-holidays.co.uk/
martonmere

**Newton Hall Holiday Park
★★★★**
Holiday and Touring Park
Staining Road, Blackpool
FY3 0AX
T: (01253) 882512
F: (01253) 893101
E: sales@partingtons.
fsbusiness.co.uk
I: www.partingtons.com

**Pipers Height Caravan &
Camping Park ★★★★**
*Holiday, Touring and Camping
Park*
Peel Road, Blackpool FY4 5JT
T: (01253) 763767

**Richmond Hill Caravan Park
★★★**
Touring Park
352 St Annes Road, South
Shore, Blackpool FY4 2QN
T: (01253) 344266
E: bookings@richmond-hill.
freeserve.co.uk
I: www.richmond-hill.freeserve.
co.uk

Sunset Park ★★★★★
Holiday Park
Hambleton, Poulton-le-Fylde
FY6 9EQ
T: (01253) 700222
F: (01253) 701756
E: sunset@caravans.com
I: www.caravans.
com/parks/sunset

**Windy Harbour Holiday
Centre ★★★**
*Holiday, Touring and Camping
Park*
Little Singleton, Blackpool
FY6 8NB
T: (01253) 883064
E: info@windyharbour.net
I: www.windyharbour.net

CABUS
Lancashire
**Claylands Caravan Park
★★★★**
*Holiday, Touring and Camping
Park*
Claylands Farm, Preston PR3 1AJ
T: (01524) 791242
F: (01524) 792406
E: alan@
claylands-caravan-park.co.uk
I: www.claylands-caravan-park.
co.uk

CAPERNWRAY
Lancashire
**Old Hall Caravan Park
★★★★★**
Holiday and Touring Park
Carnforth LA6 1AD
T: (01524) 733276
F: (01524) 734488
E: oldhall@charis.co.uk
I: www.oldhall.uk.com

CARNFORTH
Lancashire
**Netherbeck Holiday Home
Park ★★★★★**
Holiday Park
North Road, Carnforth LA5 9NG
T: (01524) 735133
F: (01524) 735133
E: info@netherbeck.co.uk
I: www.netherbeck.co.uk

Redwell Fisheries ★★★
Touring and Camping Park
Kirkby Lonsdale Road, Arkholme,
Carnforth LA6 1BQ
T: (01524) 221979
E: kenanddiane@
redwellfisheries.co.uk
I: www.redwellfisheries.co.uk

CHESTER
Cheshire
**Chester Fairoaks Caravan
Club Site ★★★★★**
Touring and Camping Park
Rake Lane, Chester CH2 4HS
T: (0151) 355 1600
I: www.caravanclub.co.uk

CLITHEROE
Lancashire
**The Camping and
Caravanning Club Site
Clitheroe ★★★**
Touring and Camping Park
Edisford Road, Clitheroe
BB7 3LA
T: (01200) 425294
I: www.
campingandcaravanningclub.
co.uk

COCKERHAM
Lancashire
**Moss Wood Caravan Park
★★★★★**
Holiday and Touring Park
Crimbles Lane, Lancaster
LA2 0ES
T: (01524) 791041
F: (01524) 792444
E: info@mosswood.co.uk
I: www.mosswood.co.uk

FLEETWOOD
Lancashire
Cala Gran ★★★★
Holiday Park
Fleetwood Road, Fleetwood
FY7 8JX
T: (01253) 872555
F: (01253) 771288
E: enquiries@british-holidays.
co.uk
I: www.british-holidays.co.uk

HEYSHAM
Lancashire
**Ocean Edge Leisure Park
★★★**
*Holiday, Touring and Camping
Park*
Moneyclose Lane, Heysham,
Morecambe LA3 2XA
T: (01524) 855553
F: (01524) 855884

HEYWOOD
Greater Manchester
**Gelder Wood Country Park
★★★★★**
Touring and Camping Park
Oak Leigh Cottage, Ashworth
Road, Rochdale OL11 5UP
T: (01706) 364858
F: (01706) 364858
E: gelderwood@aol.com
I: www.adultstouring.co.uk

KIRKHAM
Lancashire

Mowbreck Holiday and Residential Park ★★★★★
Holiday Park
Mowbreck Lane, Preston
PR4 3HA
T: (01772) 682494
F: (01772) 672986

LANCASTER
Lancashire

New Parkside Farm Caravan Park ★★★
Touring and Camping Park
Denny Beck, Caton Road,
Lancaster LA2 9HH
T: (01524) 770723
I: www.ukparks.
co.uk/newparkside

Wyreside Lakes Fishery ★★★
Touring and Camping Park
Sunnyside Farmhouse, Gleaves
Hill Road, Lancaster LA2 9DQ
T: (01524) 792093
F: (01524) 792093
E: wyreside2003@yahoo.co.uk
I: www.wyresidelakes.co.uk

LYTHAM ST ANNES
Lancashire

Eastham Hall Caravan Park ★★★
Holiday and Touring Park
Saltcotes Road, Lytham St Annes
FY8 4LS
T: (0125) 373 7907

MACCLESFIELD
Cheshire

Strawberry Wood Caravan Park ★★★
Touring Park
Home Farm, Farm Lane, Lower
Withington, Macclesfield
SK11 9DU
T: (01477) 571407
E:
strawberrywoodcaravanpark@
yahoo.co.uk

MIDDLETON
Lancashire

Melbreak Caravan Park ★★★
Holiday, Touring and Camping Park
Carr Lane, Middleton,
Morecambe LA3 3LH
T: (01524) 852430

MORECAMBE
Lancashire

Regent Leisure Park ★★★★
Holiday Park
Westgate, Morecambe LA3 3DF
T: (01524) 413940
F: (01524) 832247

Venture Caravan Park
★★★★
Holiday, Touring and Camping Park
Langridge Way, Westgate,
Morecambe LA4 4TQ
T: (01524) 412986
F: (01524) 422029
E: mark@venturecaravanpark.
co.uk
I: www.venturecaravanpark.
co.uk

Westgate Caravan Park ★★★★
Holiday and Touring Park
Westgate, Morecambe LA3 3DE
T: (01524) 411448
F: (01524) 414226
I: www.ukparks.co.uk/westgate

NATEBY
Lancashire

Bridge House Marina and Caravan Park ★★★★
Holiday and Touring Park
Nateby Crossing Lane, Preston
PR3 0JJ
T: (01995) 603207
F: (01995) 601612

NETHER KELLET
Lancashire

The Hawthorns Caravan Park ★★★★★
Holiday Park
Carnforth LA6 1EA
T: (01524) 732079
F: (01524) 732079

ORMSKIRK
Lancashire

Abbey Farm Caravan Park ★★★★★
Holiday, Touring and Camping Park
Dark Lane, Ormskirk L40 5TX
T: (01695) 572686
F: (01695) 572686
E: abbeyfarm@yahoo.com
I: www.abbeyfarmcaravanpark.
co.uk
&

PILLING
Lancashire

Fold House Caravan Park ★★★★★
Holiday Park
Head Dyke Lane, Preston
PR3 6SJ
T: (01253) 790267
F: (01253) 790157
E: fhcp@foldhouse.co.uk
I: www.foldhouse.co.uk

RIMINGTON
Lancashire

Rimington Caravan Park ★★★★★
Holiday, Touring and Camping Park
Hardcacre Lane, Clitheroe
BB7 4EE
T: (01200) 445355
F: (01200) 445355

ROCHDALE
Greater Manchester

Hollingworth Lake Caravan Park ★★★
Touring and Camping Park
Roundhouse Farm, Hollingworth
Lake, Littleborough OL15 0AT
T: (01706) 378661

SCARISBRICK
Lancashire

Hurlston Hall Country Caravan Park ★★★★
Holiday and Touring Park
Southport Road, Ormskirk
L40 8HB
T: (01704) 841064
F: (01704) 841700

SILVERDALE
Lancashire

Far Arnside Caravan Park ★★★★★
Holiday Park
Holgates Caravan Parks Ltd,
Middlebarrow Plain, Carnforth
LA5 0SH
T: (01524) 701508
F: (01524) 701580
E: caravan@holgates.co.uk
I: www.holgates.co.uk

Holgates Caravan Park ★★★★★
Holiday, Touring and Camping Park
Cove Road, Carnforth LA5 0SH
T: (01524) 701508
F: (01524) 701580
E: caravan@holgates.co.uk
I: www.holgates.co.uk

THURSTASTON
Wirral

Wirral Country Park Caravan Club Site ★★★★
Touring and Camping Park
Station Road, Thurstaston,
Wirral CH61 0HN
T: (0151) 648 5228
I: www.caravanclub.co.uk

TOSSIDE
Lancashire

Crowtrees Park ★★★★★
Holiday Park
Rose Award
Skipton BD23 4SD
T: (01729) 840278
F: (01729) 840863
E: hol@crowtreespark.co.uk
I: www.crowtreespark.co.uk

WARRINGTON
Warrington

Holly Bank Caravan Park ★★★★
Touring Park
Warburton Bridge Road, Rixton,
Warrington WA3 6HU
T: (0161) 775 2842

WEST BRADFORD
Lancashire

Three Rivers Woodland Park ★★★★
Holiday, Touring and Camping Park
Eaves Hall Lane, Clitheroe
BB7 3JG
T: (01200) 423523
F: (01200) 442383
E: enquiries@threeriverspark.
co.uk
I: www.threeriverspark.co.uk

WHITEGATE
Cheshire

Lamb Cottage Caravan Park ★★★★★
Touring Park
Dalefords Lane, Northwich
CW8 2BN
T: (01606) 882302
F: (01606) 888491
E: lynn@lccp.fsworld.co.uk
I: www.lambcottage.co.uk

WINSFORD
Cheshire

Lakeside Caravan Park ★★★★
Holiday Park
Stockhill, Winsford CW7 4EF
T: (01606) 861043
F: (01606) 861043
E: enquiries@thornleyleisure.
co.uk
I: www.thornleyleisure.co.uk

WREA GREEN
Lancashire

Ribby Hall Village ★★★
Holiday Village
Ribby Road, Preston PR4
T: (01772) 671111
F: (01772) 673113
E: enquiries@ribbyhall.co.uk
I: www.ribbyhall.co.uk

CUMBRIA – THE LAKE DISTRICT

ALLONBY
Cumbria

Manor House Caravan Park
★★★
Holiday, Touring and Camping Park
Maryport CA15 6RA
T: (01900) 881236
F: (01900) 881199
E: holidays@manorhousepark.co.uk
I: www.manorhousepark.co.uk

Spring Lea Caravan Park
★★★★
Holiday, Touring and Camping Park
Main Road, Maryport CA15 6QF
T: (01900) 881331
F: (01900) 881209
E: mail@springlea.co.uk
I: www.springlea.co.uk

AMBLESIDE
Cumbria

Greenhowe Caravan Park
★★★★
Holiday Park
Rose Award
Ambleside LA22 9JU
T: (015394) 37231
F: (015394) 37464
I: www.greenhowe.com

Skelwith Fold Caravan Park
★★★★★
Holiday and Touring Park
Ambleside LA22 0HX
T: (015394) 32277
F: (015394) 34344
E: info@skelwith.com
I: www.skelwith.com

APPLEBY-IN-WESTMORLAND
Cumbria

Wild Rose Park ★★★★★
Holiday, Touring and Camping Park
Appleby-in-Westmorland CA16 6EJ
T: (017683) 51077
F: (017683) 52551
E: hs@wildrose.co.uk
I: www.wildrose.co.uk

BASSENTHWAITE
Cumbria

Bassenthwaite Lakeside Lodges ★★★★★
Holiday Park
Scarness, Keswick CA12 4QZ
T: (017687) 76641
F: (017687) 76919
E: enquiries@bll.ac
I: www.bll.ac

BOTHEL
Cumbria

Skiddaw View Caravan Park
Rating Applied For
Keswick CA7 2JG
T: (016973) 20919
E: office@skiddawview.com
I: www.skiddawview.co.uk

BOUTH
Cumbria

Black Beck Caravan Park
★★★★★
Holiday and Touring Park
Bouth, Ulverston LA12 8JN
T: (01229) 861274
F: (01229) 861041
E: reception@blackbeck.net

BRAMPTON
Cumbria

Cairndale Caravan Park
★★★
Holiday and Touring Park
Cumwhitton, Headsnook, Carlisle CA8 9BZ
T: (01768) 896280

BRAYSTONES
Cumbria

Tarnside Caravan Park
★★★★
Holiday and Touring Park
Beckermet CA21 2YL
T: (01946) 841308
E: ann@hotmail.com
I: www.ukparks.co.uk/tarnside

CARLISLE
Cumbria

Dalston Hall Caravan Park
★★★★
Holiday, Touring and Camping Park
Dalston Hall, Carlisle CA5 7JX
T: (01228) 710165

Dandy Dinmont Caravan and Camping Site ★★★★
Touring and Camping Park
Blackford, Carlisle CA6 4EA
T: (01228) 674611
F: (01228) 674611
E: dandydinmont@btopenworld.com
I: www.caravan-camping-carlisle.itgo.com

COCKERMOUTH
Cumbria

Violet Bank Holiday Home Park Ltd ★★★
Holiday, Touring and Camping Park
Simonscales Lane, Cockermouth CA13 9TG
T: (01900) 822169
F: (01900) 822169
I: www.violetbank.co.uk

CONISTON
Cumbria

Crake Valley Holiday Park
★★★★★
Holiday Park
Rose Award
Lake Bank, Water Yeat, Ulverston LA12 8DL
T: (01229) 885203
F: (01229) 885203
E: crakevalley@coniston1.fslife.co.uk
I: www.crakevalley.co.uk

Park Coppice Caravan Club Site ★★★★★
Touring Park
Park Gate, Coniston LA21 8LA
T: (015394) 41555
I: www.caravanclub.co.uk

ENDMOOR
Cumbria

Gatebeck Park ★★★★★
Holiday and Touring Park
Gatebeck Road, Kendal LA8 0HL
T: (015395) 67875
F: (015395) 67875

ESKDALE
Cumbria

Fisherground Farm Campsite ★★★
Camping Park
Boot, Holmrook CA19 1TF
T: (019467) 23349
E: karen@fishergroundcampsite.co.uk
I: www.fishergroundcampsite.co.uk

FLOOKBURGH
Cumbria

Lakeland Leisure Park
★★★★
Holiday, Touring and Camping Park
Moor Lane, Grange-over-Sands LA11 7LT
T: (015395) 58556
F: (015395) 58559
E: enquiries@british-holidays.co.uk
I: www.british-holidays.co.uk/lakeland

GRANGE-OVER-SANDS
Cumbria

Greaves Farm Caravan Park
★★★★
Holiday and Touring Park
Rose Award
Field Broughton, Grange-over-Sands LA11 6HR
T: (015395) 36329

Meathop Fell Caravan Club Site ★★★★★
Touring Park
Meathop, Grange-over-Sands LA11 6RB
T: (015395) 32912
F: (015395) 32243
I: www.caravanclub.co.uk

Old Park Wood Caravan Park ★★★★
Holiday and Touring Park
Holker, Grange-over-Sands LA11 7PP
T: (015395) 58266
F: (015395) 58101
E: pobatopw@aol.com
I: www.holker-estate-parks.co.uk

HAWKSHEAD
Cumbria

The Croft Caravan and Camp Site ★★★★
Holiday, Touring and Camping Park
North Lonsdale Road, Hawkshead, Ambleside LA22 0NX
T: (015394) 36374
F: (015394) 36544
E: enquiries@hawkshead-croft.com
I: www.hawkshead-croft.com

KENDAL
Cumbria

Ashes Exclusively Adult Caravan Park ★★★★★
Touring Park
Kendal LA8 0AS
T: (01539) 731833
E: info@ashescaravanpark.co.uk
I: www.ashescaravanpark.co.uk

Camping and Caravanning Club Site Kendal ★★★★
Touring and Camping Park
Millcrest, Shap Road, Kendal LA9 6NY
T: (01539) 741363
I: www.campingandcaravanningclub.co.uk

Low Park Wood Caravan Club Site ★★★★
Touring Park
Sedgwick, Kendal LA8 0JZ
T: (015395) 60186
I: www.caravanclub.co.uk

Waters Edge Caravan Park
★★★★
Holiday, Touring and Camping Park
Crooklands, Milnthorpe LA7 7NN
T: (015395) 67708
F: (015395) 67610
I: www.watersedgecaravanpark.co.uk

KESWICK
Cumbria

The Camping and Caravanning Club Site, Derwentwater ★★★★
Holiday and Touring Park
Crowe Park Road, Keswick CA12 5EN
T: (017687) 72579
I: www.campingandcaravanningclub.co.uk

Camping and Caravanning Club Site Keswick ★★★★
Touring and Camping Park
Derwentwater, Keswick CA12 5EP
T: (01768) 772392
I: www.campingandcaravanningclub.co.uk

Castlerigg Farm Camping & Caravan Site ★★★★
Touring and Camping Park
Keswick CA12 4TE
T: (017687) 72479
F: (017687) 74718
E: info@castleriggfarm.com
I: www.castleriggfarm.com

Castlerigg Hall Caravan and Camping Park ★★★★
Holiday, Touring and Camping Park
Castlerigg, Keswick CA12 4TE
T: (017687) 74499
F: (017687) 74499
E: info@castlerigg.co.uk
I: www.castlerigg.co.uk

Lakeside Holiday Park
★★★★
Holiday and Touring Park
Norman Garner Ltd, Crow Park
Road, Keswick CA12 5EW
T: (017687) 72878
F: (017687) 72017
E: welcome@
lakesideholidaypark.co.uk
I: www.lakesideholidaypark.
co.uk

Low Briery Holiday Village
★★★★
Holiday Park
Penrith Road, Keswick
CA12 4RN
T: (017687) 72044
E: info@lowbriery.fsnet.co.uk
I: www.keswick.uk.com

Scotgate Holiday Park
★★★★
*Holiday, Touring and Camping
Park*
Keswick CA12 5TF
T: (017687) 78343
F: (017687) 78099
I: www.scotgateholidaypark.
co.uk

KIRKBY LONSDALE
Cumbria

Woodclose Caravan Park
★★★★
*Holiday, Touring and Camping
Park*
High Casterton, Carnforth
LA6 2SE
T: (015242) 71597
F: (015242) 72301
E: info@woodclosepark.com
I: www.woodclosepark.com

KIRKBY STEPHEN
Cumbria

Pennine View Caravan Park
★★★★★
Touring and Camping Park
Station Road, Kirkby Stephen
CA17 4SZ
T: (017683) 71717

LAMPLUGH
Cumbria

Inglenook Caravan Park
★★★★
*Holiday, Touring and Camping
Park*
Workington CA14 4SH
T: (01946) 861240
E: john@inglenookcaravanpark.
fsnet.co.uk
I: www.inglenookcaravanpark.
co.uk

LOUGHRIGG
Cumbria

Neaum Crag ★★★★★
Holiday Park
Ambleside LA22 9HG
T: (015394) 33221
F: (015394) 33735
E: neaum.crag@virgin.net
I: www.neaumcrag.co.uk

MILNTHORPE
Cumbria

Fell End Caravan Park
★★★★★
*Holiday, Touring and Camping
Park*
Slack Head Road, Milnthorpe
LA7 7BS
T: (015395) 62122
F: (01524) 782243
E: enquiries@
southlakeland-caravans.co.uk
I: www.southlakeland-caravans.
co.uk

NEWBY BRIDGE
Cumbria

Newby Bridge Caravan Park
★★★★★
Holiday Park
Canny Hill, Newby Bridge,
Ulverston LA12 8NF
T: (015395) 31030
F: (015395) 30105
E: info@cumbriancaravans.
co.uk
I: www.cumbriancaravans.co.uk

ORTON
Cumbria

Tebay Caravan Site ★★★★
Holiday and Touring Park
Penrith CA10 3SB
T: (015396) 24511
F: (015396) 24944
I: www.tebaycaravanpark.co.uk

PENRITH
Cumbria

Flusco Wood Caravan Park
★★★★★
Holiday and Touring Park
Penrith CA11 0JB
T: (017684) 80020
E: admin@fluscowood.co.uk
I: www.fluscowood.co.uk

Lowther Holiday Park
★★★★★
*Holiday, Touring and Camping
Park*
Penrith CA10 2JB
T: (01768) 863631
F: (01768) 868126
E: info@lowther-holidaypark.
co.uk
I: www.lowther-holidaypark.
co.uk

Melmerby Caravan Park
★★★★
Holiday and Touring Park
Melmerby, Penrith CA10 1HE
T: (01768) 881311
F: (01768) 881311

**Troutbeck Head Caravan
Club Site ★★★★★**
Touring Park
Troutbeck Head, Penrith
CA11 0SS
T: (017684) 83521
F: (017684) 83839
I: www.caravanclub.co.uk

POOLEY BRIDGE
Cumbria

Waterside House Campsite
★★★★
Camping Park
Waterside House, Penrith
CA10 2NA
T: (017684) 86332
F: (017684) 86332
E: enquire@
watersidefarm-campsite.co.uk
I: www.watersidefarm-campsite.
co.uk

ST BEES
Cumbria

Seacote Park ★★★★
*Holiday, Touring and Camping
Park*
The Beach, St Bees CA27 0ES
T: (01946) 822777
F: (01946) 824442
E: reception@seacote.com

SILLOTH
Cumbria

Seacote Caravan Park
★★★★
Holiday and Touring Park
Skinburness Road, Wigton
CA7 4QJ
T: (016973) 31121
F: (016973) 31031

Solway Holiday Village ★★
*Holiday, Touring and Camping
Park*
Skinburness Drive, Wigton
CA7 4QQ
T: (016973) 31236
F: (028) 9334 2457
E: solway@hagansleisure.co.uk
I: www.hagansleisure.co.uk

**Stanwix Park Holiday
Centre ★★★★★**
*Holiday, Touring and Camping
Park*
Greenrow, Silloth, Wigton
CA7 4HH
T: (016973) 32666
F: (016973) 32555
E: enquiries@stanwix.com
I: www.stanwix.com

Tanglewood Caravan Park
★★★
*Holiday, Touring and Camping
Park*
Causewayhead, Wigton CA7 4PE
T: (016973) 31253
E: tanglewoodcaravanpark@
hotmail.com
I: www.tanglewoodcaravanpark.
co.uk

STAVELEY
Cumbria

**The Camping and
Caravanning Club Site**
★★★★★
*Holiday, Touring and Camping
Park*
Ashes Lane, Kendal LA8 9JS
T: (01539) 821119
F: (01539) 821282
I: www.asheslane.com

ULLSWATER
Cumbria

Quiet Site Caravan Park
★★★★★
*Holiday, Touring and Camping
Park*
Penrith CA11 0LS
T: (017684) 86337
F: (017684) 86610

Waterfoot Park ★★★★★
Holiday and Touring Park
Penrith CA11 0JF
T: (017684) 86302
F: (01539) 732048
E: waterfoot@
lakedistrictestates.co.uk
I: www.waterfootpark.co.uk

ULVERSTON
Cumbria

Bardsea Leisure Park
★★★★
Holiday and Touring Park
Priory Road, Ulverston LA12 9QE
T: (01229) 584712
F: (01229) 580413

WASDALE
Cumbria

**Church Stile Farm Holiday
Park ★★★★**
*Holiday, Touring and Camping
Park*
Church Stile Farm, Seascale
CA20 1ET
T: (019467) 26252
F: (019467) 26028
E: churchstile@campfarm.fsnet.
co.uk
I: www.churchstile.com

WATERMILLOCK
Cumbria

**Cove Caravan and Camping
Park ★★★★★**
*Holiday, Touring and Camping
Park*
Ullswater, Penrith CA11 0LS
T: (017684) 86549
E: info@cove-park.co.uk
I: www.cove-park.co.uk

WINDERMERE
Cumbria

Fallbarrow Park ★★★★★
Holiday and Touring Park
Rayrigg Road, Windermere
LA23 3DL
T: (015394) 44422
F: (01524) 782243
E: enquiries@
southlakeland-caravans.co.uk
I: www.southlakeland-caravans.
co.uk

**Hill of Oaks and Blakeholme
Caravan Estate ★★★★★**
Holiday and Touring Park
Tower Wood, Windermere
LA23 3PJ
T: (015395) 31578
F: (015395) 30431
E: lde@netcomuk.co.uk
I: www.ukparks.co.uk/hillofoaks

Limefitt Park ★★★★★
*Holiday, Touring and Camping
Park*
Patterdale Road, Windermere
LA23 1PA
T: (015394) 32300
F: (01524) 782243

Park Cliffe Caravan & Camping Estate ★★★★★
Holiday, Touring and Camping Park
Birks Road, Windermere
LA23 3PG
T: (015395) 31344
F: (015395) 31971
E: info@parkcliffe.co.uk
I: www.parkcliffe.co.uk

White Cross Bay Holiday Park and Marina ★★★★★
Holiday and Touring Park
Ambleside Road, Windermere
LA23 1LF
T: (015394) 43937
F: (01524) 782243
E: enquiries@southlakeland-caravans.co.uk
I: www.southlakeland-caravans.co.uk

NORTHUMBRIA

ALNWICK
Northumberland

Alnwick Rugby Football Club ★
Touring and Camping Park
Greensfield, Alnwick NE66 1BG
T: (01665) 602342

AMBLE
Northumberland

Amble Links Holiday Park ★★★★
Holiday Park
Links Road, Morpeth NE65 0SD
T: (01665) 710530
F: (01665) 710440
E: amble@linksholidaypark.fsnet.co.uk
I: www.amblelinksholidaypark.co.uk

ASHINGTON
Northumberland

Wansbeck Riverside Park Caravan and Camp Site ★★
Touring and Camping Park
Wansbeck Riverside Park, Ashington NE63 8TX
T: (01670) 812323
F: (01670) 812323

BAMBURGH
Northumberland

Glororum Caravan Park ★★★
Holiday, Touring and Camping Park
Glororum, Bamburgh NE69 7AW
T: (01668) 214457
F: (01668) 214622
E: info@glororum-caravanpark.co.uk
I: www.glororum-caravanpark.co.uk

Meadowhead's Waren Caravan and Camping Park ★★★★
Holiday, Touring and Camping Park
Waren Mill, Belford NE70 7EE
T: (01668) 214366
F: (01668) 214224
E: waren@meadowhead.co.uk
I: www.meadowhead.co.uk

BARDON MILL
Northumberland

Winshields Camp Site, Camping Barn ★★
Camping Park
Bardon Mill, Hexham NE47 7AN
T: (01434) 344243

BEADNELL
Northumberland

Beadnell Links Caravan Park ★★★★
Holiday, Touring and Camping Park
Beadnell Harbour, Chathill NE67 5BN
T: (01665) 720526
F: (01665) 720526
E: b.links@talk21.com
I: www.caravanningnorthumberland.com

The Camping and Caravanning Site Beadnell ★★★
Touring and Camping Park
Chathill NE67 5BX
T: (01665) 720586
I: www.campingandcaravanningclub.co.uk

BEAL
Northumberland

Haggerston Castle ★★★★★
Holiday, Touring and Camping Park
Haggerston, Berwick-upon-Tweed TD15 2PA
T: (01289) 381333
F: (01289) 381433
E: enquiries@british-holidays.co.uk
I: www.british-holidays.co.uk/haggerstoncastle

BEAMISH
County Durham

Bobby Shafto Caravan Park ★★★
Holiday, Touring and Camping Park
Money Hills, Stanley DH9 0RY
T: (0191) 3701776
F: (0191) 3701776
E: andrewpeel@harlepeel.freeserve.co.uk
I: www.ukparks.co.uk/bobbyshafto

BELFORD
Northumberland

Bradford Kaims Caravan Park ★★★
Holiday, Touring and Camping Park
Bradford House, Belford NE70 7JT
T: (01668) 213432
F: (01668) 213891
E: lwrob@tiscali.co.uk
I: www.bradford-leisure.co.uk

South Meadows Caravan Park ★★★★★
Touring and Camping Park
South Meadows, Belford NE70 7DP
T: (01668) 213326
F: (01668) 213790
E: G.McL@btinternet.com
I: www.southmeadows.co.uk

BELLINGHAM
Northumberland

Brown Rigg Caravan & Camping Park ★★★★
Touring and Camping Park
Bellingham, Hexham NE48 2JY
T: (01434) 220175
E: ross@brcaravanpark.fsbusiness.co.uk
I: www.northumberlandcaravanparks.com

Demesne Farm Campsite ★
Touring and Camping Park
Demesne Farm, Hexham NE48 2BS
T: (01434) 220258
E: telfer@demesne.plus.com
I: www.demesnefarmcampsite.co.uk

BERWICK-UPON-TWEED
Northumberland

Beachcomber Campsite ★★★
Touring and Camping Park
Goswick, Berwick-upon-Tweed TD15 2RW
T: (01289) 381217

Berwick Holiday Centre ★★★★★
Holiday Park
Magdalene Fields, Berwick-upon-Tweed TD15 1NE
T: (01289) 307113
F: (01289) 306276
E: berwick@bourne-leisure.co.uk
I: www.british-holidays.co.uk

Marshall Meadows Farm ★★★
Holiday, Touring and Camping Park
Marshall Meadows Farm, Berwick-upon-Tweed TD15 1UT
T: (01289) 307375
F: (01289) 307375

Seaview Caravan Club Site ★★★★★
Touring and Camping Park
Billendean Road, Spittal, Berwick-upon-Tweed TD15 1QU
T: (01289) 305198
I: www.caravanclub.co.uk

BIRLING
Northumberland

Rose Cottage Camp Site ★★★
Touring and Camping Park
Birling, Morpeth NE65 0XS
T: (01665) 711459
E: anne.foreman@virgin.net

CASTLESIDE
County Durham

Manor Park Caravan Park (Manor Park Ltd) ★★★
Holiday, Touring and Camping Park
Broadmeadows, Rippon Burn, Consett DH8 9HD
T: (01207) 501000
F: (01207) 599779

CORBRIDGE
Northumberland

Well House Farm - Corbridge ★★★
Touring and Camping Park
Newton, Stocksfield NE43 7UY
T: (01661) 842193

COTHERSTONE
County Durham

Doe Park Caravan Site ★★★★
Touring and Camping Park
Barnard Castle DL12 9UQ
T: (01833) 650302
F: (01833) 650302

CRASTER
Northumberland

Proctors Stead Caravan Site ★★★
Holiday, Touring and Camping Park
Dunstan Village, Alnwick NE66 3TF
T: (01665) 576613
F: (01665) 576311

CRESSWELL
Northumberland

Cresswell Towers Holiday Park ★★★
Holiday and Touring Park
Morpeth NE61 5JT
T: (01670) 860411
F: (01670) 860226
I: www.leisuregb.co.uk

Golden Sands Holiday Park ★★★★
Holiday Park
Beach Road, Morpeth NE61 5LF
T: (01670) 860256
F: (01670) 860256
E: enquiries@northumbrianleisure.co.uk
I: www.northumbrianleisure.co.uk

DUNSTAN
Northumberland

Camping and Caravan Club Site Dunstan Hill ★★★★
Touring and Camping Park
Dunstan Hill, Alnwick NE66 3TQ
T: (01665) 576310
I: www.
campingandcaravanningclub.
co.uk

DURHAM
County Durham

Grange Caravan Club Site ★★★★
Touring and Camping Park
Meadow Lane, Carrville, Durham
DH1 1TL
T: (0191) 384 4778
F: (0191) 383 9161
I: www.caravanclub.co.uk

Strawberry Hill Farm Camping & Caravanning Park ★★★★
Holiday, Touring and Camping Park
Running Waters, Old Cassop,
Durham DH6 4QA
T: (0191) 372 3457
F: (0191) 372 2512
E: howarddunkerley@
strawberryhillfarm.freeserve.
co.uk

EAST ORD
Northumberland

Ord House Country Park ★★★★★
Holiday, Touring and Camping Park
Berwick-upon-Tweed TD15 2NS
T: (01289) 305288
F: (01289) 330832
E: enquiries@ordhouse.co.uk
I: www.ordhouse.co.uk

EBCHESTER
County Durham

Byreside Caravan Site ★★★★
Holiday and Touring Park
Newcastle upon Tyne NE17 7RT
T: (01207) 560280

GREENHEAD
Northumberland

Roam-n-Rest Caravan Park ★★★
Touring and Camping Park
Raylton House, Brampton
CA8 7HA
T: (016977) 47213

HALTWHISTLE
Northumberland

Camping & Caravanning Club Site Haltwhistle ★★★★
Touring and Camping Park
Burnfoot Park Village,
Haltwhistle NE49 0JP
T: (01434) 320106
I: www.
campingandcaravanningclub.
co.uk

HAYDON BRIDGE
Northumberland

Poplars Riverside Caravan Park ★★★★
Holiday, Touring and Camping Park
East Lands Ends, Hexham
NE47 6BY
T: (01434) 684427

HEXHAM
Northumberland

Causey Hill Caravan Park ★★★
Holiday, Touring and Camping Park
Causey Hill, Hexham NE46 2JN
T: (01434) 602834
F: (01434) 609086
E: causeyhillcp@aol.com
I: www.causeyhill.co.uk

Fallowfield Dene Caravan and Camping Park ★★★★
Touring and Camping Park
Hexham NE46 4RP
T: (01434) 603553
F: (01434) 603553
E: den@fallowfielddene.co.uk
I: www.fallowfielddene.co.uk

Hexham Racecourse Caravan Site ★★★
Touring and Camping Park
Yarridge Road, High Yarridge,
Hexham NE46 2JP
T: (01434) 606847
F: (01434) 605814
E: hexrace@aol.com
I: www.hexham-racecourse.
co.uk

Riverside Leisure ★★★★★
Holiday Park
Tyne Green, Hexham NE46 3RY
T: (01434) 604705
F: (01434) 606217
E: riverleis@aol.com

KIELDER
Northumberland

Kielder Caravan & Camping Site
Rating Applied For
Kielder Campsite, Hexham
NE48 1EJ
T: (01434) 250291
E: kielder.campsite@ntlworld.
com

Kielder Water Caravan Club Site ★★★★
Touring Park
Leaplish Waterside Park,
Falstone, Hexham NE48 1AX
T: (01434) 250278
I: www.caravanclub.co.uk

LARTINGTON
County Durham

Camping and Caravanning Club Site Barnard Castle ★★★★
Touring and Camping Park
Dockenflatts Lane, Barnard
Castle DL12 9DG
T: (01833) 630228
I: www.
campingandcaravanningclub.
co.uk

LONGHORSLEY
Northumberland

Forget-Me-Not Holiday Park ★★★★
Holiday, Touring and Camping Park
Croftside, Longhorsley, Morpeth
NE65 8QY
T: (01670) 788364
F: (01670) 788715
E: info@
forget-me-notholidaypark.co.uk
I: www.
forget-me-notholidaypark.co.uk

LOWICK
Northumberland

Barmoor South Moor ★★★★
Holiday Park
Barmoor South Moor, Berwick-
upon-Tweed TD15 2QF
T: (01289) 388205
E: barryandanngold@aol.com

MELKRIDGE
Northumberland

Hadrian's Wall Caravan and Camping Site ★★★
Touring and Camping Park
Melkridge Tilery, Haltwhistle
NE49 9PG
T: (01434) 320495
E: info@romanwallcamping.
co.uk
I: www.romanwallcamping.co.uk

NEWTON-BY-THE-SEA
Northumberland

Newton Hall Caravan Park ★★★★
Holiday, Touring and Camping Park
Newton-by-the-Sea, Alnwick
NE66 3DZ
T: (01665) 576239
F: (01665) 576900
E: ianpatterson@
newtonholidays.co.uk
I: www.newtonholidays.co.uk

NORTH SEATON
Northumberland

Sandy Bay Holiday Park ★★★
Holiday and Touring Park
Ashington NE63 9YD
T: (01670) 815055
F: (01670) 812705
E: Sandybay@gbholidayparks.
co.uk
I: www.gbholidayparks.co.uk

OTTERBURN
Northumberland

Border Forest Caravan Park ★★★★
Holiday, Touring and Camping Park
Cottonshopeburnfoot, Nr
Otterburn NE19 1TF
T: (01830) 520259
I: www.borderforestcaravanpark.
co.uk

OVINGHAM
Northumberland

The High Hermitage Caravan Park ★★★
Holiday and Touring Park
The Hermitage, Main Road,
Ovingham, Prudhoe NE42 6HH
T: (01661) 832250
F: (01661) 834848
E: highhermitage@onetel.com

RAMSHAW
County Durham

Craggwood Caravan Park ★★
Holiday, Touring and Camping Park
Gordon Lane, Bishop Auckland
DL14 0NS
T: (01388) 835866
F: (01388) 835866
E: billy6482@btopenworld.com

REDCAR
Redcar and Cleveland

New Coatham Caravan Park ★★
Holiday, Touring and Camping Park
49-51 York Road, Redcar
TS10 5AJ
T: (01642) 483422

ROTHBURY
Northumberland

Coquetdale Caravan Park ★★★
Holiday, Touring and Camping Park
Whitton, Morpeth NE65 7RU
T: (01669) 620549
F: (01669) 620559
E: enquiry@
coquetdalecaravanpark.co.uk
I: www.coquetdalecaravanpark.
co.uk

SEAHOUSES
Northumberland

Elford Caravan Park ★★
Touring Park
Crackerpool Cottage, Elford
Farm, Seahouses NE68 7UT
T: (01665) 720244
F: (01665) 720244
E: bill@elfordcaravanpark.co.uk
I: www.elfordcaravanpark.co.uk

Seafield Caravan Park ★★★★★
Holiday and Touring Park
Seafield Road, Seahouses
NE68 7SP
T: (01665) 720628
F: (01665) 720088
E: info@seafieldpark.co.uk
I: www.seafieldpark.co.uk

SOUTH SHIELDS
Tyne and Wear

Lizard Lane Camping & Caravan Site ★★★
Holiday, Touring and Camping Park
Lizard Lane, South Shields
NE34 7AB
T: (0191) 4544982

Sandhaven Caravan and Camping Park ★★★
Holiday, Touring and Camping Park
Bents Park Road, South Shields
NE33 2NL
T: (0191) 4545594

STOCKTON-ON-TEES
Stockton-on-Tees

White Water Caravan Club Park ★★★★★
Touring and Camping Park
Tees Barrage, Stockton-on-Tees
TS18 2QW
T: (01642) 634880
I: www.caravanclub.co.uk

STONEHAUGH
Northumberland

Stonehaugh Campsite ★★★
Touring and Camping Park
Stonehaugh Shields,
Stonehaugh Village, Hexham
NE48 3BU
T: (01434) 230798
E: carole@stonehaugh.
fsbusiness.co.uk
I: www.stonehaugh.fsbusiness.
co.uk

WHITLEY BAY
Tyne and Wear

Whitley Bay Holiday Park Great British Holiday Parks Ltd ★★★★
Holiday and Touring Park
The Links, Whitley Bay NE26 4RR
T: (0191) 2531216
F: (0191) 2971033
E: whitleybay@gbholidayparks.
co.uk
I: www.gbholidayparks.co.uk

WINSTON
County Durham

Winston Caravan Park ★★★
Holiday, Touring and Camping Park
The Old Forge, Front Street,
Darlington DL2 3RH
T: (01325) 730228
F: (01325) 730228
E: m.willetts@ic24.net
I: www.touristnetuk.
com/ne/winston

YORKSHIRE

ACASTER MALBIS
York

Chestnut Farm Caravan Park ★★★★★
Holiday, Touring and Camping Park
York YO23 2UQ
T: (01904) 704676
F: (01904) 704676
E: enquiries@
chestnutfarmholidaypark.co.uk
I: www.
chestnutfarmholidaypark.co.uk

Moor End Farm ★★★★
Holiday, Touring and Camping Park
Moor End, York YO23 2UQ
T: (01904) 706727
E: moorendfarm@acaster99.
fsnet.co.uk
I: www.ukparks.co.uk/moorend

ALLERSTON
North Yorkshire

Vale of Pickering Caravan Park ★★★★★
Touring and Camping Park
Pickering YO18 7PQ
T: (01723) 859280
F: (01723) 850060
E: tony@valeofpickering.co.uk
I: www.valeofpickering.co.uk

BARMSTON
East Riding of Yorkshire

Barmston Beach Holiday Park ★★★★
Holiday Park
Sands Lane, Driffield YO25 8PJ
T: (01262) 468202
F: (01262) 468670

BEDALE
North Yorkshire

Pembroke Caravan Park ★★★★
Touring and Camping Park
19 Low Street, Northallerton
DL7 9BW
T: (01677) 422652

BEVERLEY
East Riding of Yorkshire

Barmston Farm Static Caravan Park ★★★★★
Holiday Park
Barmston Farm, Barmston Lane,
Woodmansey, Beverley
HU17 0TP
T: (01482) 863566 &
07970 042587
I: www.barmstonfarm.co.uk

BOLTON ABBEY
North Yorkshire

Howgill Lodge ★★★★★
Holiday, Touring and Camping Park
Skipton BD23 6DJ
T: (01756) 720655
E: enquiries@howgill-lodge.
co.uk
I: www.howgill-lodge.co.uk

Strid Wood Caravan ★★★★
Touring Park
Skipton BD23 6AN
T: (01756) 710433
I: www.caravanclub.co.uk

BRANDESBURTON
East Riding of Yorkshire

Dacre Lakeside Park ★★★★
Touring and Camping Park
Leven Road, Driffield YO25 8RT
T: (01964) 543704
F: (01964) 544040
E: dacresurf@aol.com
I: www.dacrepark.co.uk

Fosse Hill Caravan Park ★★★
Touring and Camping Park
Catwick Lane, Driffield YO25 8SB
T: (01964) 542608
F: (01964) 543010
E: tony@fossehill.co.uk
I: www.fossehill.co.uk

BRIDLINGTON
East Riding of Yorkshire

Park Estate Caravan Park ★★★★
Holiday Park
Lime Kiln Lane, Bridlington
YO16 6TG
T: (01262) 673733
F: (01262) 401851
E: admin@park-estates.co.uk
I: www.park-estates.co.uk

The Poplars Touring Park ★★★★
Touring and Camping Park
45 Jewison Lane, Bridlington
YO15 1DX
T: (01262) 677251
I: www.the-poplars.co.uk

BURTON IN LONSDALE
North Yorkshire

Gallaber Farm Caravan Park ★★★★
Holiday, Touring and Camping Park
Gallaber Farm, Burton in
Lonsdale, Carnforth LA6 3LU
T: (015242) 61361
E: gallaber@btopenworld.com
I: www.gallaber.btinternet.co.uk

BURTON UPON STATHER
North Lincolnshire

Brookside Caravan Park ★★★★★
Touring Park
Stather Road, Burton-upon-
Stather, Scunthorpe DN15 9DH
T: (01724) 721369
E: brooksidecp@aol.com

CAYTON BAY
North Yorkshire

Cayton Bay Holiday Park ★★★★
Holiday Park
Mill Lane, Scarborough
YO11 3NJ
T: (01723) 583111
F: (01723) 584863

Cliff Farm Caravan Park ★★★★★
Holiday Park
Mill Lane, Scarborough
YO11 3NN
T: (01723) 582239
F: (01723) 582239
E: sandrabrown5@btinternet.
com

CLIFFE COMMON
North Yorkshire

The Ranch Caravan Park ★★★★
Touring and Camping Park
Selby YO8 6EF
T: (01757) 638984
F: (01757) 638985

CONSTABLE BURTON
North Yorkshire

Constable Burton Hall Caravan Park ★★★★★
Touring and Camping Park
Leyburn DL8 5LJ
T: (01677) 450428

CROPTON
North Yorkshire

Spiers House Caravan and Camping Site ★★★★
Touring and Camping Park
Forestry Commission, Cropton,
Pickering YO18 8ES
T: (01751) 417591
E: fe.holidays@forestry.gov.uk
I: www.forestholidays.co.uk

FARNHAM
North Yorkshire

Kingfisher Caravan and Camping Park ★★★★
Holiday, Touring and Camping Park
Low Moor Lane, Knaresborough
HG5 9DQ
T: (01423) 869411
F: (01423) 869411

FILEY
North Yorkshire

Filey Brigg Caravan & Country Park ★★★
Touring and Camping Park
Church Cliff Drive, North Cliff,
Arndale, Filey YO14 9ET
T: (01723) 513852
E: filey@ytbic.co.uk
I: www.ycc.org.uk

Orchard Farm Holiday Village ★★★★★
Holiday, Touring and Camping Park
Stonegate, Hunmanby, Filey
YO14 0PU
T: (01723) 891582
F: (01723) 891582

Primrose Valley Holiday Park ★★★★
Holiday and Touring Park
Primrose Valley, Filey YO14 9RF
T: (01723) 513771
F: (01723) 513777
I: www.havenholidays.com/
primrosevalley

FLAMBOROUGH
East Riding of Yorkshire

Thornwick & Sea Farm Holiday Centre ★★★★
Holiday, Touring and Camping Park
North Marine Road,
Flamborough, Bridlington
YO15 1AU
T: (01262) 850369
F: (01262) 851550
E: enquiries@thornwickbay.
co.uk
I: www.thornwickbay.co.uk

FOLLIFOOT
North Yorkshire
Great Yorkshire Showground Caravan Club Site ★★★★
Touring Park
Wetherby Road, Harrogate
HG3 1TZ
T: (01423) 560470
I: www.caravanclub.co.uk

GILLING WEST
North Yorkshire
Hargill House Caravan Club Site ★★★★
Touring Park
Gilling West, Richmond
DL10 5LJ
T: (01748) 822734
I: www.caravanclub.co.uk

GLAISDALE
North Yorkshire
Hollins Farm ★★
Camping Park
Whitby YO21 2PZ
T: (01947) 897516

GRISTHORPE BAY
North Yorkshire
Blue Dolphin Holiday Park ★★★★
Holiday, Touring and Camping Park
Gristhorpe Bay, Filey YO14 9PU
T: (01723) 515155
F: (01723) 512059
I: www.havenholidays.com/bluedolphin

HARDEN
West Yorkshire
Harden & Bingley Holiday Park ★★★★
Holiday and Touring Park
Goit Stock Private Estate, Goit Stock, Bingley BD16 1DF
T: (01535) 273810
I: www.ukparks.co.uk/harden

HARROGATE
North Yorkshire
High Moor Farm Park ★★★★★
Holiday, Touring and Camping Park
Skipton Road, Harrogate
HG3 2LT
T: (01423) 563637
F: (01423) 529449

Ripley Caravan Park ★★★★★
Holiday, Touring and Camping Park
Knaresborough Road, Harrogate
HG3 3AU
T: (01423) 770050
F: (01423) 770050

Rudding Holiday Park ★★★★★
Holiday, Touring and Camping Park
Rudding Lane, Harrogate
HG3 1JH
T: (01423) 870439
F: (01423) 870859
E: holiday-park@ruddingpark.com
I: www.ruddingpark.com

Warren Forest Caravan Park
★★★★
Holiday Park
Harrogate HG3 3LH
T: (01765) 620683
F: (01765) 620683
E: enquiries@warrenforestpark.co.uk
I: www.warrenforestpark.co.uk

HATFIELD
South Yorkshire
Hatfield Water Park ★★★
Touring Park
Old Thorn Road, Doncaster
DN7 6EQ
T: (01302) 841572
F: (01302) 846368

HAWES
North Yorkshire
Bainbridge Ings Caravan and Camping Site ★★
Holiday, Touring and Camping Park
Hawes DL8 3NU
T: (01969) 667354
E: janet@bainbridge-ings.co.uk
I: www.bainbridge-ings.co.uk

Honeycott Caravan Park ★★★
Holiday, Touring and Camping Park
Ingleton Road, Hawes DL8 3LH
T: (01969) 667310
E: info@honeycott.co.uk
I: www.honeycott.co.uk

HELMSLEY
North Yorkshire
Foxholme Touring Caravan Park ★★★★★
Touring and Camping Park
Harome, York YO62 5JG
T: (01439) 770416
F: (01439) 771744

Golden Square Caravan and Camping Park ★★★★★
Touring and Camping Park
Oswaldkirk, York YO62 5YQ
T: (01439) 788269
F: (01439) 788236
E: barbara@goldensquarecaravanpark.freeserve.co.uk
I: www.goldensquarecaravanpark.com

HOLMFIRTH
West Yorkshire
Holme Valley Camping and Caravan Park ★★★★
Touring and Camping Park
Huddersfield HD9 7TD
T: (01484) 665819
F: (01484) 663870
E: enquiries@homevalleycamping.com

HORNSEA
East Riding of Yorkshire
Longbeach Leisure Park ★★★★
Holiday, Touring and Camping Park
South Cliff, Hornsea HU18 1TL
T: (01964) 532506
F: (01964) 536846
I: www.longbeach-leisure.co.uk

HUMBERSTON
North East Lincolnshire
Thorpe Park Holiday Centre ★★★★
Holiday, Touring and Camping Park
Humberston, Cleethorpes
DN35 0PW
T: (01472) 813395
F: (01472) 812146
E: enquiries@british-holidays.co.uk
I: www.british-holidays.co.uk/thorpepark

HUTTON-LE-HOLE
North Yorkshire
Hutton le Hole Caravan Park ★★★★
Touring and Camping Park
Westfield Lodge, Hutton-le-Hole, York YO62 6UG
T: (01751) 417261
F: (01751) 417876
E: rwstrickland@farmersweekly.net
I: www.westfieldlodge.co.uk

INGLETON
North Yorkshire
Parkfoot Holiday Homes ★★★★★
Holiday Park
Bentham Road, Carnforth
LA6 3HR
T: (015242) 61833
F: (015242) 61961
E: parkfoot.ingleton@virgin.net

KEARBY WITH NETHERBY
North Yorkshire
Maustin Park Ltd ★★★★★
Holiday, Touring and Camping Park
Wharfe Lane, Wetherby
LS22 4DA
T: (0113) 288 6234
F: (0113) 288 6133
E: info@maustin.co.uk
I: www.maustin.co.uk

KEIGHLEY
West Yorkshire
Bronte Caravan Park ★★★★★
Holiday, Touring and Camping Park
Lees Moor, Off Halifax Road, Keighley BD21 5QF
T: (01535) 691746
E: bronte@brontecaravanpark.co.uk
I: brontecaravanpark.co.uk

KILLINGHALL
North Yorkshire
Pinemoor Caravan Park ★★★★★
Holiday Park
Burley Bank Road, Harrogate
HG3 2RZ
T: (01423) 503980
F: (01423) 503910
E: pinemoor@aol.com

KILNSEA
East Riding of Yorkshire
Sandy Beaches Caravan Site Ltd ★★
Holiday and Touring Park
Kilnsea Road, Hull HU12 0UB
T: (01964) 650372

KNARESBOROUGH
North Yorkshire
Knaresborough Caravan Club Site ★★★★★
Touring Park
New Road, Scotton, Knaresborough HG5 9HH
T: (01423) 860196
I: www.caravanclub.co.uk

LANGTHORPE
North Yorkshire
Old Hall Caravan Park ★★★★
Holiday and Touring Park
Skelton Road, Langthorpe, York
YO51 9BZ
T: (01423) 322130
F: (01423) 322130
E: phil.brierley@which.net
I: www.yhcparks.info

LEEDS
West Yorkshire
St Helena's Caravan Site ★★★★
Holiday, Touring and Camping Park
Otley Old Road, Horsforth, Leeds
LS18 5HZ
T: (0113) 284 1142

LINTON-ON-OUSE
North Yorkshire
Linton Lock Leisure Ways ★★
Holiday, Touring and Camping Park
Linton Locks, York YO30 2AZ
T: (01347) 848486
F: (01347) 848486
E: fullerr297@aol.com
I: www.lintonlock.co.uk

LOFTHOUSE
North Yorkshire
Studfold Holdings Caravan and Camping Park ★★★
Holiday, Touring and Camping Park
Studfold Farm, Harrogate
HG3 5SG
T: (01423) 755210
F: (01423) 755311
I: www.ukparks.co.uk/studfoldfarm

LONG PRESTON
North Yorkshire
Gallaber Park ★★★★
Holiday and Touring Park
Gallaber Park, Skipton BD23 4QF
T: (01729) 851397
F: (01729) 851398
E: info@gallaberpark.com
I: www.gallaberpark.com

MALTON
North Yorkshire
Wolds Way Caravan and Camping ★★★
Touring and Camping Park
West Farm, West Knapton, Malton YO17 8JE
T: (01944) 728463
F: (01944) 728463
E: knapton.wold.farms@farming.co.uk
I: www.ryedalesbest.co.uk

MARKINGTON
North Yorkshire

Yorkshire Hussar Inn Holiday Caravan Park ★★★
Holiday, Touring and Camping Park
High Street, Harrogate HG3 3NR
T: (01765) 677327
E: yorkshirehussar@yahoo.co.uk

MASHAM
North Yorkshire

Black Swan Holiday Park ★★★
Touring Park
Rear Black Swan Hotel, Fearby,
Masham, Ripon HG4 4NF
T: (01765) 689477
F: (01765) 689477
E: info@blackswanholiday.co.uk
I: www.blackswanholiday.co.uk

NAWTON
North Yorkshire

Wrens of Ryedale Caravan and Camp Site ★★★★
Touring and Camping Park
Gale Lane, York YO62 7SD
T: (01439) 771260
F: (01439) 771260
E: dave@wrensofryedale.fsnet.co.uk
I: www.wrensofryedale.fsnet.co.uk

NEWBIGGIN
North Yorkshire

Street Head Caravan Park ★★★
Holiday, Touring and Camping Park
Leyburn DL8 3TE
T: (01969) 663571
F: (01969) 663013

NORTHALLERTON
North Yorkshire

Cote Ghyll Caravan & Camping Park ★★★
Holiday, Touring and Camping Park
Northallerton DL6 3AH
T: (01609) 883425
F: (01609) 883425
E: hills@coteghyll.com
I: www.coteghyll.com

OXENHOPE
West Yorkshire

Upwood Holiday Park ★★★★
Holiday, Touring and Camping Park
Blackmoor Road, Oxenhope,
Keighley BD22 9SS
T: (01535) 644242
F: (01535) 643254
E: caravans@upwoodholidaypark.fsnet.co.uk
I: www.upwoodholidaypark.fsnet.co.uk

PATRINGTON
East Riding of Yorkshire

Patrington Haven Leisure Park Ltd ★★★★★
Holiday Park
Patrington Haven, Hull
HU12 0PT
T: (01964) 630071
F: (01964) 631060
E: info@patringtonhavenleisurepark.co.uk
I: www.phlp.co.uk
🏃

PICKERING
North Yorkshire

Upper Carr Chalet and Touring Park ★★★★★
Holiday, Touring and Camping Park
Upper Carr Lane, Malton Road,
Pickering YO18 7JP
T: (01751) 473115
F: (01751) 473115
E: harker@uppercarr.demon.co.uk
I: www.upercarr.demon.co.uk

Wayside Caravan Park ★★★★
Holiday, Touring and Camping Park
Wrelton, Pickering YO18 8PG
T: (01751) 472608
F: (01751) 472608
E: waysideparks@freenet.co.uk
I: www.waysideparks.co.uk

POCKLINGTON
East Riding of Yorkshire

South Lea Caravan Park ★★★★
Touring and Camping Park
The Balk, York YO42 2NX
T: (01759) 303467
E: info@south-lea.co.uk
I: www.south-lea.co.uk

REIGHTON GAP
North Yorkshire

Reighton Sands Holiday Park ★★★
Holiday, Touring and Camping Park
Reighton Gap, Filey YO14 9RF
T: (01723) 890476
F: (01723) 891043
I: www.havenholidays.com/reightonsands

RICHMOND
North Yorkshire

Brompton Caravan Park ★★★★★
Holiday, Touring and Camping Park
Easby, Richmond DL10 7EZ
T: (01748) 824629
F: (01748) 826383
E: brompton.caravanpark@btinternet.com
I: www.bromptoncaravanpark.co.uk

Swaleview Caravan Site ★★★
Holiday Park
Reeth Road, Richmond DL10 4SF
T: (01748) 823106

RIPON
North Yorkshire

River Laver Holiday Park ★★★★★
Holiday and Touring Park
Studley Road, Ripon HG4 2QR
T: (01765) 690508
F: (01765) 698708
E: riverlaver@lineone.net
I: www.riverlaver.co.uk

Sleningford Watermill Caravan and Camping Park ★★★★
Touring and Camping Park
Ripon HG4 3HQ
T: (01765) 635201
I: www.ukparks.co.uk/sleningford

Woodhouse Farm Caravan & Camping Park ★★★★
Holiday, Touring and Camping Park
Winksley, Ripon HG4 3PG
T: (01765) 658309
E: woodhouse.farm@talk21.com
I: www.woodhousewinksley.com

ROECLIFFE
North Yorkshire

Camping & Caravanning Club Site Boroughbridge ★★★★★
Touring Park
Bar Lane, York YO51 9LS
T: (01423) 322683
I: www.campingandcaravanningclub.co.uk

ROOS
East Riding of Yorkshire

Sand-le-Mere Caravan & Leisure Park ★★★★
Holiday, Touring and Camping Park
Seaside Lane, Hull HU12 0JQ
T: (01964) 670403
F: (01964) 671099
E: info@sand-le-mere.co.uk
I: www.sand-le-mere.co.uk

RUDSTON
East Riding of Yorkshire

Thorpe Hall Caravan and Camping Site ★★★★
Touring and Camping Park
Thorpe Hall, Driffield YO25 4JE
T: (01262) 420393
F: (01262) 420588
E: caravansite@thorpehall.co.uk
I: www.thorpehall.co.uk

SALTWICK BAY
North Yorkshire

Whitby Holiday Park ★★★★
Holiday, Touring and Camping Park
Whitby YO22 4JX
T: (01947) 602664
F: (01947) 820356

SCARBOROUGH
North Yorkshire

Browns Caravan Park ★★★★★
Holiday and Touring Park
Mill Lane, Scarborough
YO11 3NN
T: (01723) 582303
F: (01723) 584083
E: info@brownscaravan.co.uk
I: www.brownscaravan.co.uk

Cayton Village Caravan Park ★★★★★
Touring and Camping Park
Mill Lane, Cayton Bay,
Scarborough YO11 3NN
T: (01723) 583171
E: info@caytontouring.co.uk
I: www.caytontouring.co.uk

Crows Nest Caravan Park ★★★★★
Holiday, Touring and Camping Park
Gristhorpe, Filey YO14 9PS
T: (01723) 582206
F: (01723) 582206
E: enquiries@crowsnestcaravanpark.com
I: www.crowsnestcaravanpark.com

Flower of May Holiday Park ★★★★★
Holiday, Touring and Camping Park
Lebberston, Scarborough
YO11 3NU
T: (01723) 584311
F: (01723) 581361
E: info@flowerofmay.com
I: www.flowerofmay.com

Lebberston Touring Park ★★★★★
Touring Park
Lebberston, Scarborough
YO11 3PE
T: (01723) 585723
E: info@lebberstontouring.co.uk
I: lebberstontouring.co.uk

Scalby Close Park ★★★★
Holiday, Touring and Camping Park
Burniston Road, Scarborough
YO13 0DA
T: (01723) 365908
E: info@scalbyclosepark.co.uk
I: www.scalbyclosepark.co.uk

Scalby Manor Touring Caravan & Camp Park ★★★★
Touring Park
Burniston Road, Scarborough
YO13 0DA
T: (01723) 366212
E: scarboroughtic@scarborough.gov.uk
I: www.ycc.org.uk

SEAMER
North Yorkshire

Arosa Caravan & Camping Park ★★★★
Holiday, Touring and Camping Park
Ratten Row, Scarborough
YO12 4QB
T: (01723) 862166
E: SUEBIRD@arosa131.fsnet.co.uk
I: www.mywebpage.net/arosa

SHERIFF HUTTON
North Yorkshire

Camping and Caravanning Club Site Sheriff Hutton ★★★★
Touring and Camping Park
Rose Award
Bracken Hill, York YO60 6QG
T: (01347) 878660
I: www.
campingandcaravanningclub.
co.uk

SKIPSEA
East Riding of Yorkshire

Far Grange Park Ltd ★★★★★
Holiday Park
Hornsea Road, Driffield
YO25 8SY
T: (01262) 468293
F: (01262) 468648
E: enquiries@fargrangepark.
co.uk
I: www.fargrangepark.co.uk

Skipsea Sands Holiday Village ★★★★
Holiday, Touring and Camping Park
Mill Lane, Driffield YO25 8TZ
T: (01262) 468210
F: (01262) 468454
E: info@skipseasands.co.uk

Skirlington Leisure Park ★★★★★
Holiday, Touring and Camping Park
Hornsea Road, Driffield
YO25 8SY
T: (01262) 468213
F: (01262) 468105
E: enquiries@skirlington.com
I: www.skirlington.com

SKIRLAUGH
East Riding of Yorkshire

Burton Constable Holiday Park ★★★★★
Holiday, Touring and Camping Park
Hull HU11 4LN
T: (01964) 562508
F: (01964) 563420
E: info@burtonconstable.co.uk
I: www.burtonconstable.co.uk

SLINGSBY
North Yorkshire

Camping & Caravanning Club Site Slingsby ★★★★★
Touring and Camping Park
Railway Street, York YO62 4AA
T: (01653) 628335
I: www.
campingandcaravanningclub.
co.uk

Robin Hood Caravan & Camping Park ★★★★★
Holiday, Touring and Camping Park
Green Dyke Lane, Slingsby, York
YO62 4AP
T: (01653) 628391
F: (01653) 628391
E: info@robinhoodcaravanpark.
co.uk
I: www.robinhoodcaravanpark.
co.uk

SNAINTON
North Yorkshire

Jasmine Park ★★★★★
Holiday, Touring and Camping Park
Rose Award
Cross Lane, Snainton,
Scarborough YO13 9BE
T: (01723) 859240
F: (01723) 859240
E: info@jasminepark.co.uk
I: www.jasminepark.co.uk

STAINFORTH
North Yorkshire

Knight Stainforth Hall Caravan and Camping Park ★★★★
Holiday, Touring and Camping Park
Settle BD24 0DP
T: (01729) 822200
E: info@knightstainforth.co.uk
I: www.knightstainforth.co.uk

STAXTON
North Yorkshire

Spring Willows Touring Caravan Park ★★★★★
Touring and Camping Park
Main Road, Scarborough
YO12 4SB
T: (01723) 891505
F: (01723) 892123
E: fun4all@springwillows.fsnet.
co.uk
I: www.springwillows.co.uk

STRENSALL
York

Moorside Caravan Park ★★★★★
Touring Park
Lords Moor Lane, York YO32 5XJ
T: (01904) 491208
I: www.moorsidecaravanpark.
co.uk

THIRSK
North Yorkshire

York House Caravan Park ★★★★
Holiday, Touring and Camping Park
Thirsk YO7 2AQ
T: (01845) 597495
F: (01845) 597495
E: phil.brierley@which.net
I: www.yhcparks.info

THORNE
South Yorkshire

Elder House Touring Park ★★★★
Touring Park
Elder House Farm, Sandtoft
Road, Doncaster DN8 5TD
T: (01405) 813173

THORNTON DALE
North Yorkshire

Overbrook Caravan Park ★★★
Touring Park
Maltongate, Pickering YO18 7SE
T: (01751) 474417
F: (01751) 473373
E: overbrook@breathe.com

THRESHFIELD
North Yorkshire

Long Ashes Park ★★★★
Holiday Park
Skipton BD23 5PN
T: (01756) 752261
F: (01756) 752876
E: info@longashespark.co.uk
I: www.longashespark.co.uk

Wood Nook Caravan Park ★★★★
Holiday, Touring and Camping Park
Skipton BD23 5NU
T: (01756) 752412
F: (01756) 752946
E: enquiries@woodnook.net
I: www.woodnook.net

WHITBY
North Yorkshire

Flask Holiday Home Park ★★★★
Holiday Park
Robin Hood's Bay, Fylingdales,
Whitby YO22 4QH
T: (01947) 880592
F: (01947) 880592
E: flaskinn@aol.com
I: www.flaskinn.com

Ladycross Plantation Caravan Park ★★★★★
Touring and Camping Park
Egton, Whitby YO21 1UA
T: (01947) 895502
E: enquiries@
ladycrossplantation.co.uk
I: www.ladycrossplantation.
co.uk

Middlewood Farm Holiday Park ★★★★★
Holiday, Touring and Camping Park
Middlewood Lane, Fylingthorpe,
Robin Hood's Bay, Whitby
YO22 4UF
T: (01947) 880414
F: (01947) 880871
E: info@middlewoodfarm.com
I: www.middlewoodfarm.com

Northcliffe & Seaview Holiday Parks ★★★★★
Holiday, Touring and Camping Park
Bottoms Lane, Whitby YO22 4LL
T: (01947) 880477
F: (01947) 880972
E: enquiries@
northcliffe-seaview.com
I: www.northcliffe-seaview.com

Partridge Nest Farm Holiday Caravans ★★★
Holiday Park
Eskdaleside, Whitby YO22 5ES
T: (01947) 810450
F: (01947) 811413
E: barbara@partridgenestfarm.
com
I: www.partridgenestfarm.com

Sandfield House Farm Caravan Park ★★★★★
Touring Park
Sandsend Road, Whitby
YO21 3SR
T: (01947) 602660
E: info@sandfieldhousefarm.
co.uk
I: www.sandfieldhousefarm.
co.uk

WILSTHORPE
East Riding of Yorkshire

South Cliff Caravan Park ★★★★
Holiday, Touring and Camping Park
Bridlington YO15 3QN
T: (01262) 671051
F: (01262) 605639
E: southcliff@eastriding.gov.uk
I: www.bridlington.net

The White House Caravan Park ★★★★★
Holiday Park
Bridlington YO15 3QN
T: (01262) 673894
F: (01262) 401350

WITHERNSEA
East Riding of Yorkshire

Willows Holiday Park ★★★★
Holiday, Touring and Camping Park
Hollym Road, Withernsea
HU19 2PN
T: (01964) 612233
E: info@highfield-caravans.
co.uk
I: www.highfield-caravans.co.uk

WOMBLETON
North Yorkshire

Wombleton Caravan Park ★★★★★
Touring and Camping Park
Moorfield Lane, York YO62 7RY
T: (01751) 431684
E: info@
wombletoncaravanpark.co.uk
I: www.wombletoncaravanpark.
co.uk

YORK
York

Alders Caravan Park ★★★★★
Touring and Camping Park
Home Farm, Monk Green, Alne,
York YO61 1RY
T: (01347) 838722
F: (01347) 838722
E: enquiries@homefarm.co.uk
I: www.alderscaravanpark.co.uk

Allerton Park Caravan Park ★★★★
Holiday, Touring and Camping Park
Allerton Park, Knaresborough
HG5 0SE
T: (01423) 330569
F: (01759) 371377
E: enquiries@
yorkshireholidayparks.co.uk
I: www.yorkshireholidayparks.
co.uk

Beechwood Grange Caravan Club Site ★★★★★
Touring Park
Malton Road, York YO32 9TH
T: (01904) 424637
I: www.caravanclub.co.uk

Castle Howard Lakeside Holiday Park ★★★★
Holiday, Touring and Camping Park
Coneysthorpe, York YO60 7DD
T: (01653) 648316
E: lakeside@castlehoward.co.uk
I: www.castlehoward.co.uk

Cawood Park ★★★★★
Holiday, Touring and Camping Park
Ryther Road, Cawood, Vale Of York YO8 3TT
T: (01757) 268450
F: (01757) 268537
E: info@cawoodpark.com
I: www.cawoodpark.com

Goosewood Caravan Park ★★★★★
Holiday, Touring and Camping Park
Rose Award
Goose Lane, York YO61 1ET
T: (01347) 810829
F: (01347) 811498
E: edward@goosewood.co.uk
I: www.ukparks.co.uk/goosewood

Mount Pleasant Holiday Park and Park Home Estate ★★★★
Holiday Park
York YO23 2UA
T: (01904) 707078
F: (01904) 700888
E: mountpleasant@holgates.com
I: www.holgates.com

Rowntree Park Caravan Club Site ★★★★★
Touring Park
Terry Avenue, York YO23 1JQ
T: (01904) 658997
I: www.caravanclub.co.uk

Weir Caravan Park ★★★★
Holiday, Touring and Camping Park
Buttercrambe Road, Stamford Bridge, York YO41 1AN
T: (01759) 371377
F: (01759) 371377
E: enquiries@yorkshireholidayparks.co.uk
I: www.yorkshireholidayparks.co.uk

York Touring Caravan Site ★★★★
Touring Park
Towthorpe Lane, Towthorpe, York YO32 9ST
T: (01904) 499275
F: (01904) 499271
E: info@yorkcaravansite.co.uk
I: www.yorkcaravansite.co.uk

HEART OF ENGLAND

ALREWAS
Staffordshire

Kingfisher Holiday park ★★★★
Holiday Park
Fradley Junction, Burton upon Trent DE13 7DN
T: (01283) 790407
F: 0871 242 3495
E: mail@kingfisherholidaypark.com
I: www.kingfisherholidaypark.com

ASTON CANTLOW
Warwickshire

Island Meadow Caravan Park ★★★
Holiday, Touring and Camping Park
The Mill House, Aston Cantlow B95 6JP
T: (01789) 488273
F: (01789) 488273
E: holiday@islandmeadowcaravanpark.co.uk
I: www.islandmeadowcaravanpark.co.uk

BIRMINGHAM
West Midlands

Chapel Lane Caravan Club Site ★★★★★
Touring Park
Chapel Lane, Wythall, Birmingham B47 6JX
T: (01564) 826483
I: www.caravanclub.co.uk

BODYMOOR HEATH
West Midlands

Camping & Caravanning Club Site Kingsbury Water Park ★★★★★
Touring and Camping Park
Bodymoor Heath Lane, Sutton Coldfield B76 0DY
T: (01827) 874101
I: www.campingandcaravanningclub.co.uk

BREWOOD
Staffordshire

Homestead Caravan Park ★★★★
Holiday Park
Shutt Green, Nr Brewood, Stafford ST19 9LX
T: (01902) 851302
F: (01902) 850099
E: david@caravanpark.fsbusiness.co.uk
I: www.caravanparkstaffordshire.com

BRIDGNORTH
Shropshire

Park Grange Holidays ★★★★
Holiday Park
Park Grange, Morville, Bridgnorth WV16 4RN
T: (01746) 714285
F: (01746) 714145
E: info@parkgrangeholidays.co.uk
I: www.parkgrangeholidays.co.uk

Stanmore Hall Touring Park ★★★★★
Holiday and Touring Park
Stourbridge Road, Bridgnorth WV15 6DT
T: (01746) 761761
F: (01746) 768069
E: stanmore@morris-leisure.co.uk
I: www.morris-leisure.co.uk

CHEDDLETON
Staffordshire

Glencote Caravan Park ★★★★★
Holiday, Touring and Camping Park
Station Road, Leek ST13 7EE
T: (01538) 360745
F: (01538) 361788
I: www.glencote.co.uk

EARDISLAND
Herefordshire

Arrow Bank Caravan Park ★★★★
Holiday, Touring and Camping Park
Nun House Farm, Leominster HR6 9BG
T: (01544) 388312
F: (01544) 388312
E: arrowbankcaravanpark@btopenworld.com

ELLESMERE
Shropshire

Fernwood Caravan Park ★★★★★
Holiday and Touring Park
Lyneal, Ellesmere SY12 0QF
T: (01948) 710221
F: (01948) 710324
E: fernwood@caravanpark37.fsnet.co.uk
I: www.ranch.co.uk

EVESHAM
Worcestershire

The Ranch Caravan Park ★★★★★
Holiday and Touring Park
Station Road, Evesham WR11 7PR
T: (01386) 830744
F: (01386) 833503
E: enquiries@ranch.co.uk
I: www.ranch.co.uk

HANLEY SWAN
Worcestershire

Camping & Caravanning Club Site, Blackmore ★★★★★
Touring and Camping Park
Blackmore Camp Site No 2, Blackmore End, Hanley Swan, Worcester WR8 0EE
T: (01684) 310280
I: www.campingandcaravanningclub.co.uk

HATFIELD
Herefordshire

Fairview Caravan Park ★★★
Holiday Park
c/o The Willows, Hatfield, Leominster HR6 0SF
T: (01568) 760428
F: (01568) 760428
E: fairviewcaravanpark@supanet.com

HAUGHTON
Shropshire

Camping and Caravanning Club Site Ebury Hill ★★★★
Touring and Camping Park
Ebury Hill, Ring Bank, Telford TF6 6BU
T: (01743) 709334
I: www.campingandcaravanningclub.co.uk

HEREFORD
Herefordshire

Lucksall Caravan and Camping Park ★★★★★
Holiday and Touring Park
Mordiford, Hereford HR1 4LP
T: (01432) 870213
F: (01432) 870213
I: www.lucksallpark.co.uk

HOPTON HEATH
Shropshire

Ashlea Pools Country Park ★★★★★
Holiday Park
Rose Award
Hopton Heath, Craven Arms SY7 0QD
T: (01547) 530430
F: (01547) 530430
E: ashleapools@surfbay.dircon.co.uk
I: www.ashleapools.co.uk

LEEK
Staffordshire
The Camping and Caravanning Club Site Leek. ★★★★
Touring and Camping Park
Blackshaw Grange, Leek
ST13 8TL
T: (01538) 300285
I: www.campingandcaravanningclub.co.uk

LITTLE TARRINGTON
Herefordshire
The Millpond ★★★★
Touring and Camping Park
Hereford HR1 4JA
T: (01432) 890243
F: (01432) 890243
E: ENQUIRIES @MILLPOND.CO.UK
I: WWW.MILLPOND.CO.UK

LONGNOR
Staffordshire
Longnor Wood Caravan Park ★★★★
Holiday, Touring and Camping Park
Buxton SK17 0NG
T: (01298) 83648
F: (01298) 83648
E: enquiries@longnorwood.co.uk
I: www.longnorwood.co.uk

LUDLOW
Shropshire
Orleton Rise Holiday Home Park ★★★★★
Holiday and Touring Park
Green Lane, Orleton, Ludlow
SY8 4JE
T: (01584) 831617
F: (01584) 831617
I: www.lucksallpark.co.uk

MERIDEN
West Midlands
Somers Wood Caravan and Camping Park ★★★★★
Touring Park
Somers Road, Coventry CV7 7PL
T: (01676) 522978
F: (01676) 522978
E: enquiries@somerswood.co.uk
I: www.somerswood.co.uk

PEMBRIDGE
Herefordshire
Townsend Touring Park ★★★★★
Touring and Camping Park
Townsend Farm, Leominster
HR6 9HB
T: (01544) 388527
F: (01544) 388527
E: info@townsend-farm.co.uk
I: www.townsend-farm.co.uk

PETERCHURCH
Herefordshire
Poston Mill Park ★★★★★
Holiday and Touring Park
Poston Mill Park, Goldon Valley, Hereford HR2 0SF
T: (01981) 550225
F: (01981) 550885
E: Enquiries@poston-mill.co.uk
I: www.bestparks.co.uk

ROMSLEY
Worcestershire
Camping & Caravanning Club Site, Clent Hills ★★★★★
Touring Park
Fieldhouse Lane, Halesowen
B62 0NH
T: (01562) 710015
I: www.campingandcaravanningclub.co.uk

ROSS-ON-WYE
Herefordshire
Broadmeadow Caravan Park ★★★★★
Touring and Camping Park
Broadmeadows, Ross-on-Wye
HR9 7BH
T: (01989) 768076
F: (01989) 566030
E: broadm4811@aol.com
I: www.broadmeadow.info

RUGELEY
Staffordshire
Camping and Caravanning Club Site, Cannock Chase ★★★★
Touring and Camping Park
Old Youth Hostel, Wandon, Rugeley WS15 1QW
T: (01889) 582166
I: www.campingandcaravanningclub.co.uk

Silver Trees Caravan Park
★★★★
Holiday Park
Stafford Brook Road, Penkridge Bank, Rugeley WS15 2TX
T: (01889) 582185
F: (01889) 582373
E: enquires@silvertreescaravanpark.co.uk
I: www.silvertreescaravanpark.co.uk

SHOBDON
Herefordshire
Pearl Lake Leisure Park Ltd ★★★★★
Holiday and Touring Park
Leominster HR6 9NQ
T: (01568) 708326
F: (01568) 708408
E: info@pearllake.freeserve.co.uk
I: www.bestparks.co.uk

SHREWSBURY
Shropshire
Beaconsfield Farm Caravan Park ★★★★★
Holiday and Touring Park
Shrewsbury SY4 4AA
T: (01939) 210370
F: (01939) 210349
E: mail@beaconsfield-farm.co.uk
I: www.beaconsfield-farm.co.uk

Oxon Hall Touring Park
★★★★★
Holiday and Touring Park
Welshpool Road, Bicton Heath, Shrewsbury SY3 5FB
T: (01743) 340868
F: (01743) 340869
E: oxon@morris-leisure.co.uk
I: www.morris-leisure.co.uk

STOKE-ON-TRENT
Stoke-on-Trent
The Star Caravan and Camping Park ★★★★
Holiday, Touring and Camping Park
Star Road, Cotton, Stoke-on-Trent ST10 3DW
T: (01538) 702219
F: (01538) 703704
I: www.starcaravanpark.co.uk

STOURPORT-ON-SEVERN
Worcestershire
Lickhill Manor Caravan Park ★★★★★
Holiday Park
Lickhill, Stourport-on-Severn
DY13 8RL
T: (01299) 871041
F: (01299) 824998
E: excellent@lickhillmanor.co.uk
I: www.lickhillmanor.co.uk

STRATFORD-UPON-AVON
Warwickshire
Dodwell Park ★★★
Touring and Camping Park
Evesham Rd, (B439), Stratford-upon-Avon CV37 9SR
T: (01789) 204957
F: (01926) 620199
E: enquiries@dodwellpark.co.uk
I: www.dodwellpark.co.uk

SYMONDS YAT
Herefordshire
Sterretts Caravan Park ★★★★
Holiday and Touring Park
Ross-on-Wye HR9 6BY
T: (01594) 832888

TELFORD
Telford and Wrekin
Severn Gorge Park ★★★★★
Touring and Camping Park
Bridgnorth Road, Tweedale, Telford TF7 4JB
T: (01952) 684789
E: info@severngorgepark.co.uk
I: www.severngorgepark.co.uk

TRUMPET
Herefordshire
Trumpet Inn Camping & Caravan Park ★★
Touring and Camping Park
Ledbury HR8 2RA
T: (01531) 670277
F: (01531) 670277
E: etc@trumpetinn.com
I: www.trumpetinn.com

WOLVERLEY
Worcestershire
Camping and Caravanning Club Site - Wolverley ★★★
Touring and Camping Park
Brown Westhead Park, Kidderminster DY10 3PX
T: (01562) 850909
I: www.campingandcaravanningclub.co.uk

WYRE PIDDLE
Worcestershire
Rivermead Holiday Home Park ★★★★★
Holiday Park
Church Street, Pershore
WR10 2JF
T: (01386) 555566
E: enquires@rivermeadcaravanpark.co.uk
I: www.rivermeadcaravanpark.co.uk

EAST MIDLANDS

ALSOP-EN-LE-DALE
Derbyshire
Rivendale Caravan and Leisure Park ★★★★
Holiday, Touring and Camping Park
Buxton Road, Alsop-en-le-Dale, Ashbourne DE6 1QU
T: (01335) 310311
F: (01335) 310311
E: greg@rivendalecaravanpark.co.uk
I: www.rivendalecaravanpark.co.uk

AMBERGATE
Derbyshire
The Firs Farm Caravan and Camping Park ★★★★
Holiday, Touring and Camping Park
Crich Lane, Nether Heage, Belper DE56 2JH
T: (01773) 852913

ANDERBY CREEK
Lincolnshire
Anderby Springs Caravan Estate ★★★
Holiday Park
Skegness PE24 5XW
T: (01754) 872265
F: (01507) 441333

ASHBOURNE
Derbyshire
Blackwall Plantation Caravan Club Site ★★★★
Touring Park
Kirk Ireton, Ashbourne DE6 3JL
T: (01335) 370903
I: www.caravanclub.co.uk

Callow Top Holiday Park ★★★★
Holiday, Touring and Camping Park
Callow Top Farm, Buxton Road, Ashbourne DE6 2AQ
T: (01335) 344020
F: (01335) 343726
E: callotop@talk21.com
I: www.callowtop.co.uk

BAKEWELL
Derbyshire
Chatsworth Park Caravan Club Site ★★★★★
Touring Park
Chatsworth, Bakewell DE45 1PN
T: (01246) 582226
I: www.caravanclub.co.uk

BOSTON
Lincolnshire
Orchard Caravan Park ★★★
Holiday and Touring Park
Frampton Lane, Hubberts Bridge, Boston PE20 3QU
T: (01205) 290328
F: (01205) 290247
I: www.orchardpark.co.uk

BURGH-LE-MARSH
Lincolnshire
Sycamore Lakes Touring Site ★★★★
Touring and Camping Park
Sycamore Lakes, Skegness Road, Burgh le Marsh, Skegness PE24 5LN
T: (01754) 811411
I: www.sycamorelakes.co.uk

BUXTON
Derbyshire
Cottage Farm Caravan Park ★★★
Touring and Camping Park
Blackwell in the Peak, Buxton SK17 9TQ
T: (01298) 85330
E: mail@cottagefarmsite.co.uk
I: www.cottagefarmsite.co.uk

Grin Low Caravan Club Site ★★★★★
Touring and Camping Park
Grin Low Road, Ladmanlow, Buxton SK17 6UJ
T: (01298) 77735
I: www.caravanclub.co.uk

Lime Tree Park ★★★★
Holiday, Touring and Camping Park
Dukes Drive, Buxton SK17 9RP
T: (01298) 22988
F: (01298) 22988
E: limetreebuxton@dukesso.fsnet.co.uk
I: www.ukparks.co.uk/limetree

Newhaven Caravan and Camping Park ★★★
Holiday, Touring and Camping Park
Newhaven, Buxton SK17 0DT
T: (01298) 84300
F: (01332) 726027

CASTLE DONINGTON
Leicestershire
Donington Park Farmhouse Hotel ★★★
Touring Park
Melbourne Road, Derby DE74 2RN
T: (01332) 862409
F: (01332) 862364
E: info@parkfarmhouse.co.uk
I: www.parkfarmhouse.co.uk

CASTLETON
Derbyshire
Losehill Caravan Club Site ★★★★★
Touring and Camping Park
Castleton, Hope Valley S33 8WB
T: (01433) 620636
I: www.caravanclub.co.uk

CHAPEL ST LEONARDS
Lincolnshire
Robin Hood Leisure Park ★★★★
Holiday and Touring Park
South Road, Chapel St. Leonards, Skegness PE24 5TR
T: (01754) 874444
F: (01754) 874648
I: www.robinhoodleisure.com/

EAST FIRSBY
Lincolnshire
Manor Farm Caravan and Camping Site ★★★
Touring and Camping Park
Manor Farm, Market Rasen LN8 2DB
T: (01673) 878258
F: (01673) 878310
E: info@lincolnshire-lanes.com
I: www.lincolnshire-lanes.com

FLAGG
Derbyshire
Pomeroy Caravan Park ★★
Touring and Camping Park
Street House Farm, Pomeroy, Buxton SK17 9QG
T: (01298) 83259

FLEET HARGATE
Lincolnshire
Delph Bank Touring Caravan & Camping Park - Just for Adults. ★★★★
Touring and Camping Park
Old Main Road, Fleet Hargate, Spalding PE12 8LL
T: (01406) 422910
E: enquiries@delphbank.co.uk
I: www.delphbank.co.uk

FOLKINGHAM
Lincolnshire
Low Farm Touring Park ★★★
Touring Park
Spring Lane, Sleaford NG34 0SJ
T: (01529) 497322

HADFIELD
Derbyshire
Camping & Caravanning Club Site ★★★
Touring and Camping Park
Crowden, Glossop SK13 1HZ
T: (01457) 866057
I: www.campingandcaravanningclub.co.uk

HAYFIELD
Derbyshire
Camping & Caravanning Club Site ★★★
Camping Park
Kinder Road, High Peak SK22 2LE
T: (01663) 745394
I: www.campingandcaravanningclub.co.uk

HOLBEACH
Lincolnshire
Heron Cottage Camping and Caravanning ★★★
Touring and Camping Park
Frostley Gate, Spalding PE12 8SR
T: (01406) 540435

HORNCASTLE
Lincolnshire
Ashby Park ★★★★
Holiday, Touring and Camping Park
Furze Hills, West Ashby, Horncastle LN9 5PP
T: (01507) 527966
F: (01507) 524539
E: ashbyparklakes@aol.com
I: www.ukparks.co.uk/ashby

Elmhirst Lakes Caravan Park ★★★★
Holiday Park
Elmhirst Road, Horncastle LN9 5LU
T: (01507) 527533
I: www.elmhirstlakes.co.uk

INGOLDMELLS
Lincolnshire
Coastfield Caravan Park ★★★
Holiday Park
Vickers Point, Roman Bank, Skegness PE25 1JU
T: (01754) 872592
F: (01754) 874450

Country Meadows Touring Park ★★★★
Holiday and Touring Park
Anchor Lane, Skegness PE25 1LZ
T: (01754) 874455
E: bookings@countrymeadows.co.uk
I: www.countrymeadows.co.uk

Golden Beach Holiday Park
Rating Applied For
Roman Bank, Skegness PE25 1LT
T: (01754) 873000
F: (01754) 872765
E: gb@clemco.co.uk
I: www.clemco.co.uk

Ingoldale Park ★★★
Holiday Park
Beach Estate, Roman Bank, Ingoldmells, Skegness PE25 1LL
T: (01754) 872335
F: (01754) 873887
E: ingoldalepark@btopenworld.com
I: www.ingoldmells.net

Kingfisher Park ★★★
Holiday Park
Sea Lane, Skegness PE25 1PG
T: (01754) 872465
F: (01754) 872465
E: kingfisherpark@e-lindsey.gov.uk
I: www.ukparks.co.uk/kingfisherpark

Skegness Water Leisure Park ★★★
Holiday, Touring and Camping Park
Walls Lane, Skegness PE25 1JF
T: (01754) 899400
F: (01754) 897867
E: enquiries@skegnesswaterleisurepark.co.uk
I: www.skegnesswaterleisurepark.co.uk

Heathland Beach Caravan Park ★★★★★
Holiday, Touring and Camping Park
Rose Award
London Road, Kessingland,
Lowestoft NR33 7PJ
T: (01502) 740337
F: (01502) 742355
E: heathlandbeach@btinternet.com
I: www.heathlandbeach.co.uk

Kessingland Beach Holiday Park ★★★
Holiday, Touring and Camping Park
Beach Road, Lowestoft
NR33 7RN
T: (01502) 740636
F: (01502) 740907
I: www.park-resorts.com

KING'S LYNN
Norfolk

Bank Farm Caravan Park ★★★
Touring Park
Bank Farm, Fallow Pipe Road,
King's Lynn PE34 3AS
T: (01553) 617305
F: (01553) 617305
I: www.caravancampingsites.co.uk/norfolk/bankfarm.htm

LITTLE CORNARD
Suffolk

Willowmere Caravan Park ★★★
Touring and Camping Park
Bures Road, Little Cornard,
Sudbury CO10 0NN
T: (01787) 375559
F: (01787) 375559

LOWESTOFT
Suffolk

Beach Farm Residential and Holiday Park Limited ★★★
Holiday Park
Arbor Lane, Pakefield, Lowestoft
NR33 7BD
T: (01502) 572794
F: (01502) 537460
E: beachfarmpark@aol.com
I: www.beachfarmpark.co.uk

Warner Holidays Ltd ★★★
Holiday Village
Gunton Hall Classic Resort,
Gunton Avenue, Lowestoft
NR32 5DF
T: (01502) 730288
F: (01502) 732319

MARCH
Cambridgeshire

Floods Ferry Marina Park ★★★
Touring and Camping Park
Staffurths Bridge, Floods Ferry
Road, March PE15 0YP
T: (01354) 677302
F: (01354) 677302

MERSEA ISLAND
Essex

Waldegraves Holiday and Leisure Park ★★★
Holiday, Touring and Camping Park
Mersea Island, Colchester
CO5 8SE
T: (01206) 382898
F: (01206) 385359
E: holidays@waldegraves.co.uk
I: www.waldegraves.co.uk

MUNDESLEY
Norfolk

Sandy Gulls Cliff Top Touring Park ★★★
Holiday and Touring Park
Cromer Road, Mundesley,
Norwich NR11 8DF
T: (01263) 720513

MUTFORD
Suffolk

Beulah Hall Caravan Park ★★★
Touring and Camping Park
Beulah Hall, Dairy Lane, Beccles
NR34 7QJ
T: (01502) 476609
F: (01502) 476453
E: carol.stuckey@fsmail.net

NORTH RUNCTON
Norfolk

Kings Lynn Caravan & Camping Park ★★
Touring Park
New Road, King's Lynn
PE33 0RA
T: (01553) 840004
E: klynn_campsite@hotmail.com

NORTH WALSHAM
Norfolk

North Walsham Caravan and Chalet Park ★★★
Holiday Park
Bacton Road, North Walsham
NR28 0RA
T: (01692) 501070
F: (01692) 501070

Two Mills Touring Park ★★★★★
Touring Park
Yarmouth Road, North Walsham
NR28 9NA
T: (01692) 405829
F: (01692) 405829
E: enquiries@twomills.co.uk
I: www.twomills.co.uk

NORWICH
Norfolk

Camping and Caravanning Club Site Norwich ★★★
Touring Park
Martineau Lane, Norwich
NR1 2HX
T: (01603) 620060
I: www.campingandcaravanningclub.co.uk

Reedham Ferry Touring and Camping Park ★★★
Touring and Camping Park
Ferry Road, Reedham, Norwich
NR13 3HA
T: (01493) 700999
F: (01493) 700999
E: reedhamferry@aol.com
I: www.archerstouringpark.co.uk

OULTON BROAD
Suffolk

Broadland Holiday Village ★★★★★
Holiday Park
Marsh Road, Oulton Broad,
Lowestoft NR33 9JY
T: (01502) 573033
F: (01502) 512681
E: info@broadlandvillage.co.uk
I: www.broadlandvillage.co.uk

OVERSTRAND
Norfolk

Ivy Farm Holiday Park ★★★★
Holiday, Touring and Camping Park
Cromer NR27 0AB
T: (01263) 579239
E: enquiries@ivy-farm.co.uk
I: www.ivy-farm.co.uk

PAKEFIELD
Suffolk

Pakefield Caravan Park ★★★
Holiday Park
Arbor Lane, Pakefield, Lowestoft
NR33 7BQ
T: (01502) 561136
F: (01502) 539264

PENTNEY
Norfolk

Pentney Park Caravan Site ★★★★
Touring and Camping Park
Main Road, King's Lynn
PE32 1HU
T: (01760) 337479
F: (01760) 338118
E: holidays@pentney.demon.co.uk
I: www.pentney-park.co.uk

PETERBOROUGH
Peterborough

Ferry Meadows Caravan Club Site ★★★★★
Touring Park
Ham Lane, Orton Waterville,
Peterborough PE2 5UU
T: (01733) 233526
F: (01733) 233526
I: www.caravanclub.co.uk

PIDLEY
Cambridgeshire

Stroud Hill Park ★★★★
Touring Park
Fen Road, Pidley, Huntingdon
PE28 3DE
T: (01487) 741333
E: info@stroudhillpark.co.uk
I: www.stroudhillpark.co.uk

ROYDON
Essex

Roydon Mill Leisure Park ★★★
Holiday Park
Roydon Mill Park, Harlow
CM19 5EJ
T: (01279) 792777
F: (01279) 792695
E: info@roydonpark.com
I: www.roydonpark.com

SAHAM HILLS
Norfolk

Lowe Caravan Park ★★★★
Touring and Camping Park
Ashdale, Hills Road, Saham Hills,
Thetford IP25 7EZ
T: (01953) 881051
F: (01953) 881051

ST NEOTS
Cambridgeshire

Camping and Caravanning Club Site St Neots ★★★★
Touring Park
Hardwick Road, Eynesbury,
Huntingdon PE19 2PR
T: (01480) 474404
I: www.campingandcaravanningclub.co.uk

ST OSYTH
Essex

The Orchards Holiday Village ★★★★
Holiday Park
Point Clear, Clacton-on-Sea
CO16 8LJ
T: (01255) 820651
F: (01255) 820184
E: enquiries@british-holidays.co.uk
I: www.british-holidays.co.uk

SANDRINGHAM
Norfolk

Camping and Caravanning Club Site Sandringham ★★★★★
Touring Park
Northgate Precinct,
Sandringham PE36 6EA
T: (01485) 542555
I: www.campingandcaravanningclub.co.uk

The Sandringham Estate Caravan Club Site ★★★★★
Touring Park
Glucksburg Woods,
Sandringham PE35 6EZ
T: (01553) 631614
I: www.caravanclub.co.uk

SCRATBY
Norfolk

California Cliffs Holiday Park ★★★
Holiday Park
Rottenstone Lane, Great
Yarmouth NR29 3QU
T: (01493) 730584
F: (01493) 733146
I: www.park-resorts.com

EAST OF ENGLAND

Green Farm Caravan Park
★★★★★
Holiday and Touring Park
Beach Road, Great Yarmouth
NR29 3NW
T: (01493) 730440
F: (01493) 731565
I: www.greenfarmcaravanpark.com

Scratby Hall Caravan Park
★★★★
Touring and Camping Park
Thoroughfare Lane, Great
Yarmouth NR29 3PH
T: (01493) 730283

SEA PALLING
Norfolk

Golden Beach Holiday Centre ★★★
Holiday and Touring Park
Beach Road, Sea Palling,
Norwich NR12 0AL
T: (01692) 598269
F: (01692) 598693

SNETTISHAM
Norfolk

Diglea Caravan and Camping Park ★★★
Holiday, Touring and Camping Park
Beach Road, Snettisham, King's
Lynn PE31 7RA
T: (01485) 541367

SOUTHMINSTER
Essex

Eastland Meadows Country Park ★★★
Holiday Park
East End Road, Bradwell-on-Sea,
Southminster CM0 7PP
T: (01621) 776577
F: (01621) 776332
E: enquiries@eastlandmeadows.co.uk
I: www.eastlandmeadows.co.uk

St. Lawrence Holiday Park
★
Holiday Park
10 Main Road, St Lawrence Bay,
Southminster CM0 7LY
T: (01621) 779434
F: (01621) 778311
E: gary.duce@btinternet.com
I: www.slcaravans.co.uk

Waterside Holiday Park ★★
Holiday and Touring Park
Main Road, St Lawrence Bay,
Southminster CM0 7LY
T: (01621) 779248
F: (01621) 778106
E: waterside@gbholidayparks.co.uk
I: www.gbholidayparks.co.uk

STANHOE
Norfolk

The Rickels Caravan Site
★★★★
Touring Park
Bircham Road, Stanhoe, King's
Lynn PE31 8PU
T: (01485) 518671
F: (01485) 518969

TATTERSETT
Norfolk

Manor Park Touring Caravans ★★★
Touring Park
Manor Farm, King's Lynn
PE31 8RS
T: (01485) 528310

TRIMINGHAM
Norfolk

Woodland Leisure Park ★★
Holiday and Touring Park
Church Street, Norwich
NR11 8AL
T: (01263) 579208
F: (01263) 576477
E: info@woodland-park.co.uk
I: www.woodland-park.co.uk

UPPER SHERINGHAM
Norfolk

Woodlands Caravan Park
★★★★
Holiday and Touring Park
Holt Road, Sheringham
NR26 8TU
T: (01263) 823802
F: (01263) 825797
E: enquiries@woodlandscaravanpark.co.uk
I: www.woodlandscaravanpark.co.uk

WALTHAM CROSS
Hertfordshire

Camping and Caravanning Club Site Theobalds Park
★★★
Touring and Camping Park
Bulls Cross Ride, Waltham Cross
EN7 5HS
T: (01992) 620604
I: www.campingandcaravanningclub.co.uk

WALTON-ON-THE-NAZE
Essex

Naze Marine Holiday Park
★★★
Holiday Park
Hall Lane, Walton-on-the-Naze
CO14 8HL
T: 0870 442 9292
F: (01255) 68247
I: www.gbholidayparks.co.uk

WEELEY
Essex

Homestead Lake Park ★★★
Touring Park
Thorpe Road (B1033), Weeley,
Clacton-on-Sea CO16 9JN
T: (01255) 833492
F: (01255) 831406
E: lakepark@homesteadcaravans.co.uk
I: www.homesteadlake.co.uk

Weeley Bridge Holiday Park
★★★
Holiday Park
Clacton Road, Clacton-on-Sea
CO16 9DH
T: (01255) 830403
F: (01255) 831544
E: info@weeleybridge.fsnet.co.uk
I: www.gbholidayparks.co.uk

WELLS-NEXT-THE-SEA
Norfolk

Pinewoods Holiday Park
★★★★
Holiday Park
Beach Road, Wells-Next-the-Sea
NR23 1DR
T: (01328) 710439
F: (01328) 711060
E: holiday@pinewoods.co.uk
I: www.pinewoods.co.uk

WEST ROW
Suffolk

The Willows ★★
Touring and Camping Park
Hurdle Drove, Bury St Edmunds
IP28 8RB
T: (01638) 715963
E: breezes@campsite.fsbusiness.co.uk

WEST RUNTON
Norfolk

Camping and Caravanning Club Site ★★★★
Touring and Camping Park
Holgate Lane, Cromer
NR27 9NW
T: (01263) 837544
I: www.campingandcaravanningclub.co.uk

Laburnum Caravan Park
★★★
Holiday Park
Water Lane, Cromer NR27 9QP
T: (01263) 837473
F: (01263) 837473
E: laburnum@primex.co.uk
I: www.ukparks.co.uk/laburnum

WEYBOURNE
Norfolk

Kelling Heath Holiday Park
★★★★★
Holiday, Touring and Camping Park
Sandy Hill Lane, Holt NR25 7HW
T: (01263) 588181
F: (01263) 588599
E: info@kellingheath.co.uk
I: www.kellingheath.co.uk

WISBECH
Cambridgeshire

Virginia Lake Caravan Park
★★★★
Touring Park
Smeeth Road, St Johns Fen End,
Wisbech PE14 8JF
T: (01945) 430585
F: (01945) 430585
E: mickandmarion@supanet.com

WOODBRIDGE
Suffolk

Forest Camping ★★★
Touring and Camping Park
Tangham Campsite, Rendlesham
Forest Centre, Woodbridge
IP12 3NF
T: (01394) 450707
E: admin@forestcamping.co.uk
I: www.forestcamping.co.uk

WORTWELL
Norfolk

Little Lakeland Caravan Park ★★★★
Holiday and Touring Park
Little Lakeland Caravan Park,
Harleston IP20 0EL
T: (01986) 788646
F: (01986) 788646
E: information@littlelakeland.co.uk
I: www.littlelakeland.co.uk

WYTON
Cambridgeshire

Wyton Lakes Holiday Park
★★★★
Touring Park
Banks End, Huntingdon
PE28 2AA
T: (01480) 412715
F: (01480) 412715
E: loupeter@supanet.com
I: www.wytonlakes.com

SOUTH EAST ENGLAND

ANDOVER
Hampshire

Wyke Down Touring Caravan & Camping Park ★★★
Touring and Camping Park
Picket Piece, Andover SP11 6LX
T: (01264) 352048
F: (01264) 324661
E: wykedown@wykedown.co.uk
I: www.wykedown.co.uk

APSE HEATH
Isle of Wight

Old Barn Touring Park ★★★★
Touring and Camping Park
Cheverton Farm, Newport Road,
Sandown PO36 9PJ
T: (01983) 866414
F: (01983) 865988
E: oldbarn@weltinet.com
I: www.oldbarntouring.co.uk

Village Way Camping Site ★★★
Holiday, Touring and Camping Park
Newport Road, Sandown
PO36 9PJ
T: (01983) 863279

ARUNDEL
West Sussex

Ship & Anchor Marina ★★
Touring and Camping Park
Heywood and Bryett Ltd, Ford,
Arundel BN18 0BJ
T: (01243) 551262
F: (01243) 555256
E: ysm36b@dsl.pipex.com

ASHFORD
Kent

Broadhembury Caravan & Camping Park ★★★★★
Holiday, Touring and Camping Park
Steeds Lane, Ashford TN26 1NQ
T: (01233) 620859
F: (01233) 620918
E: holidays@broadhembury.co.uk
I: www.broadhembury.co.uk

ASHURST
Hampshire

Forestry Commission Ashurst Caravan & Camping Site ★★★★
Camping Park
Lyndhurst Road, Southampton
SO40 7AR
T: (0131) 314 6505
F: (0131) 3340849
E: fe.holidays@forestry.gov.uk
I: www.forestholidays.co.uk

ASHURST
Kent

Manor Court Farm ★★★
Touring and Camping Park
Ashurst, Tunbridge Wells
TN3 9TB
T: (01892) 740279
F: (01892) 740919
E: jsoyke@jsoyke.freeserve.co.uk
I: www.manorcourtfarm.co.uk

ATHERFIELD BAY
Isle of Wight

Chine Farm Camping Site ★★
Touring and Camping Park
Chine Farm, Military Road,
Ventnor PO38 2JH
T: (01983) 740228

BANBURY
Oxfordshire

Bo-Peep Caravan Park ★★★★
Holiday and Touring Park
Aynho Road, Banbury OX17 3NP
T: (01295) 810605
F: (01295) 810605
E: warden@bo-peep.co.uk
I: www.bo-peep.co.uk

BATTLE
East Sussex

Crowhurst Park ★★★★★
Holiday Park
Telham Lane, Battle TN33 0SL
T: (01424) 773344
F: (01424) 775727
E: enquiries@crowhurstpark.co.uk
I: www.crowhurstpark.co.uk

Normanhurst Court Caravan Club Site ★★★★★
Touring Park
Stevens Crouch, Battle TN33 9LR
T: (01424) 773808
I: www.caravanclub.co.uk

BEACONSFIELD
Buckinghamshire

Highclere Farm Country Touring Park ★★★★
Touring and Camping Park
Newbarn Lane, Seer Green,
Beaconsfield HP9 2QZ
T: (01494) 874505
F: (01494) 875238
E: highclerepark@aol.com
I: www.highclerefarmpark.co.uk

BEMBRIDGE
Isle of Wight

Sandhills Holiday Park ★★★
Holiday, Touring and Camping Park
Whitecliff Bay, Bembridge
PO35 5QB
T: (01983) 872277
F: (01983) 874888

Whitecliff Bay Holiday Park ★★★★
Holiday Park
Hillway Road, Bembridge
PO35 5PL
T: (01983) 872671
F: (01983) 872941
E: holiday@whitecliff-bay.com
I: www.whitecliff-bay.com

BOGNOR REGIS
West Sussex

Copthorne Caravans ★★★★
Holiday Park
Rose Green Road, Bognor Regis
PO21 3ER
T: (01243) 262408
F: (01243) 262408
E: copthornecaravan@aol.com

BEXHILL-ON-SEA
East Sussex

Cobbs Hill Farm Caravan & Camping Park ★★★★
Holiday, Touring and Camping Park
Watermill Lane, Sidley, Bexhill-on-Sea TN39 5JA
T: (01424) 213460
F: (01424) 221358
E: cobbshillfarmuk@hotmail.com
I: www.cobbshillfarm.co.uk

Kloofs Caravan Park ★★★★★
Touring and Camping Park
Sandhurst Lane, Whydown,
Bexhill-on-Sea TN39 4RG
T: (01424) 842839
F: (01424) 845669
E: camping@kloofs.com
I: www.kloofs.com

BIDDENDEN
Kent

Woodlands Park ★★★★
Touring and Camping Park
Woodlands Park, Ashford
TN27 8BT
T: (01580) 291216
F: (01580) 291216
E: woodlandsp@aol.com
I: www.campingsite.co.uk

BIRCHINGTON
Kent

Quex Caravan Park ★★★★★
Holiday and Touring Park
Park Road, Birchington CT7 0BL
T: (01843) 841273
F: (01227) 740585
E: info@keatfarm.com
I: www.keatfarm.co.uk/

Two Chimneys Holiday Park ★★★★★
Holiday, Touring and Camping Park
Shottendane Road, Birchington
CT7 0HD
T: (01843) 841068
F: (01843) 848099
E: info@twochimneys.co.uk
I: www.twochimneys.co.uk

BLETCHINGDON
Oxfordshire

Diamond Farm Caravan & Camping Park ★★★★
Touring Park
Islip Road, Oxford OX5 3DR
T: (01869) 350909
F: (01869) 350059
E: warden@diamondpark.co.uk
I: www.diamondfarmcaravanpark.co.uk

The Lillies Caravan Park
★★★
Touring Park
Yapton Road, Barnham, Bognor
Regis PO22 0AY
T: (01243) 552081
F: (01243) 552081
E: thelillies@hotmail.com
I: lilliescaravanpark.co.uk

Riverside Caravan Centre (Bognor) Ltd ★★★★★
Holiday Park
Shripney Road, Bognor Regis
PO22 9NE
T: (01243) 865823
F: (01243) 841570
E: info@rivcentre.co.uk
I: www.rivcentre.co.uk

Rowan Park Caravan Club Site ★★★★★
Holiday Park
Rowan Way, Bognor Regis
PO22 9RP
T: (01243) 828515
I: www.caravanclub.co.uk

BRIGHSTONE
Isle of Wight

Grange Farm Brighstone Bay ★★★
Holiday and Camping Park
Military Road, Newport
PO30 4DA
T: (01983) 740296
F: (01983) 741233
E: grangefarm@brighstonebay.fsnet.co.uk
I: www.brighstonebay.fsnet.co.uk

Lower Sutton Farm ★★★
Holiday Park
Military Road, Newport
PO30 4PG
T: (01983) 740401
F: (01983) 740401
E: info@dinosaur-farm-holidays.co.uk
I: www.dinosaur-farm-holidays.co.uk

BRIGHTON & HOVE
Brighton & Hove

Sheepcote Valley Caravan Club Site ★★★★★
Touring and Camping Park
Sheepcote Valley, Brighton
BN2 5TS
T: (01273) 626546
F: (01273) 682600
I: www.caravanclub.co.uk

BROCKENHURST
Hampshire

Forestry Commission Hollands Wood Caravan & Camping Site ★★★★
Camping Park
Lyndhurst Road, Brockenhurst
SO42 7QH
T: '(0131) 314 6505
F: (0131) 3340849
E: fe.holidays@forestry.gov.uk
I: www.forestholidays.co.uk

**Forestry Commission
Roundhill Caravan &
Camping Site ★★★**
Touring and Camping Park
Beaulieu Road, Brockenhurst
SO42 7QL
T: (0131) 314 6505
F: (0131) 334 0849
E: fe.holidays@forestry.gov.uk
I: www.forestholidays.co.uk

BROOK
Isle of Wight

Compton Farm ★★
Camping Park
Military Road, Newport
PO30 4HF
T: (01983) 740215
F: (01983) 740215

BURFORD
Oxfordshire

**Burford Caravan Club Site
★★★★★**
Touring Park
Bradwell Grove, Burford
OX18 4JJ
T: (01993) 823080
I: www.caravanclub.co.uk

CAMBER
East Sussex

**Camber Sands Holiday Park
★★★**
Holiday and Touring Park
Lydd Road, Rye TN31 7RT
T: (01797) 225551
F: (01797) 225756
E: cambersands@
gbholidayparks.co.uk
I: www.gbholidayparks.co.uk

CANTERBURY
Kent

**Camping & Caravanning
Club Site Canterbury
★★★★**
Touring and Camping Park
Bekesbourne Lane, Canterbury
CT3 4AB
T: (01227) 463216
I: www.
campingandcaravanningclub.
co.uk

Yew Tree Park ★★★★
*Holiday, Touring and Camping
Park*
Stone Street, Petham,
Canterbury CT4 5PL
T: (01227) 700306
F: (01227) 700306
E: info@yewtreepark.com
I: www.yewtreepark.com

CAPEL LE FERNE
Kent

**Little Satmar Holiday Park
★★★★**
*Holiday, Touring and Camping
Park*
Winehouse Lane, Capel-le-Ferne,
Folkestone CT18 7JF
T: (01303) 251188

**Varne Ridge Holiday Park
★★★★★**
Holiday and Touring Park
Old Dover Road, Capel-le-Ferne,
Folkestone CT18 7HX
T: (01303) 251765
F: (01303) 251765
E: vrcp@varne-ridge.freeserve.
co.uk
I: www.varne-ridge.co.uk

CHADLINGTON
Oxfordshire

**Camping & Caravanning
Club Site Chipping Norton
★★★★**
Touring and Camping Park
Chipping Norton Road,
Chadlington, Chipping Norton
OX7 3PE
T: (01608) 641993
I: www.
campingandcaravanningclub.
co.uk

CHALE
Isle of Wight

**Atherfield Bay Holiday
Centre ★**
Holiday Village
Military Road, Ventnor PO38 2JD
T: (01983) 740307

CHARLBURY
Oxfordshire

**Cotswold View Caravan &
Camping Site ★★★★**
Touring and Camping Park
Enstone Road, Oxford OX7 3JH
T: (01608) 810314
F: (01608) 811891
E: cotswoldview@gfwiddows.f9.
co.uk
I: www.cotswoldview.co.uk

CHERTSEY
Surrey

**Camping & Caravanning
Club Site Chertsey ★★★★**
Camping Park
Bridge Road, Chertsey KT16 8JX
T: (01932) 562405
I: www.
campingandcaravanningclub.
co.uk

CHICHESTER
West Sussex

Bell Caravan Park ★★
Holiday and Touring Park
Bell Lane, Birdham, Chichester
PO20 7HY
T: (01243) 512264

**Wicks Farm Camping Park
★★★★★**
Camping Park
West Wittering, Chichester
PO20 8QD
T: (01243) 513116
F: (01243) 511296
I: www.wicksfarm.co.uk

COLWELL BAY
Isle of Wight

**Colwell Bay Holiday Club
★★★★**
Holiday Park
Madeira Lane, Freshwater
PO40 9SR
T: (01983) 752403
E: james.bishop1@tinyworld.
co.uk
I: www.isleofwight-colwellbay.
co.uk

COWES
Isle of Wight

**Sunnycott Caravan Park
★★★★**
Holiday Park
Rew Street, Cowes PO31 8NN
T: (01983) 292859
F: (01983) 292859
E: info@sunnycottcaravanpark.
co.uk
I: www.sunnycottcaravanpark.
co.uk

CROWBOROUGH
East Sussex

**Camping and Caravanning
Club Site Crowborough
★★★★**
Touring and Camping Park
Eridge Road, Crowborough
TN6 2TN
T: (01892) 664827
I: www.
campingandcaravanningclub.
co.uk

DORNEY REACH
Windsor and Maidenhead

**Amerden Caravan &
Camping Park ★★★★**
Touring and Camping Park
Amerden Lane, Maidenhead
SL6 0EE
T: (01628) 627461
F: (01628) 627461

DOVER
Kent

**Hawthorn Farm Caravan &
Camping Park ★★★★★**
*Holiday, Touring and Camping
Park*
Station Road, Dover CT15 5LA
T: (01304) 852658
F: (01304) 853417
E: info@keatfarm.co.uk
I: www.keatfarm.co.uk/

**Sutton Vale Country Club &
Caravan Park ★★★★**
Holiday and Touring Park
Vale Road, Sutton-by-Dover,
Dover CT15 5DH
T: (01304) 374155
F: (01304) 381132
E: office@sutton-vale.co.uk
I: www.ukparks.co.uk/suttonvale

DYMCHURCH
Kent

**Dymchurch Caravan Park
★★★★**
Holiday Park
St Mary's Road, Romney Marsh
TN29 0PW
T: (01303) 872303
F: (01303) 875179

**E & J Piper Caravan Park
★★★★**
Holiday Park
St Marys Road, Dymchurch,
Romney Marsh TN29 0PN
T: (01303) 872103
F: (01303) 872020

**New Beach Holiday Village
★★★★**
Holiday Park
Hythe Road, Romney Marsh
TN29 0JX
T: (01303) 872233
F: (01303) 872939
E: newbeachholiday@aol.com

**New Beach Holiday Village
Touring Park ★★★★**
Touring and Camping Park
Hythe Road, Romney Marsh
TN29 0JX
T: (01303) 872234
F: (01303) 872939
E: newbeachholiday@aol.com

EAST COWES
Isle of Wight

**Waverley Park Holiday
Centre ★★★★**
*Holiday, Touring and Camping
Park*
Old Road, East Cowes PO32 6AW
T: (01983) 293452
F: (01983) 200494
E: sue@waverley-park.co.uk
I: www.waverley-park.co.uk

EAST HORSLEY
Surrey

**Camping & Caravanning
Club Site Horsley ★★★★**
Touring and Camping Park
Ockham Road North,
Leatherhead KT24 6PE
T: (01483) 283273
I: www.
campingandcaravanningclub.
co.uk

EASTBOURNE
East Sussex

**Fairfields Farm Caravan &
Camping Park ★★★★**
Touring and Camping Park
Eastbourne Road, Westham,
Pevensey BN24 5NG
T: (01323) 763165
F: (01323) 469175
E: enquiries@fairfieldsfarm.com
I: www.fairfieldsfarm.com

EASTCHURCH
Kent

**Ashcroft Coast Holiday
Park ★★★★★**
Holiday Park
Plough Road, Minster-on-Sea,
Sheerness ME12 4JH
T: (01795) 880324
F: (01795) 880090
I: www.park-resorts.com

Bramley Park ★★★
Holiday Park
Second Avenue, Warden Road,
Sheerness ME12 4EP
T: (01795) 880338
F: (01795) 880629
E: bramley.park@btinternet.com
I: www.ukparks.co.uk/bramley

**Copperfields Holiday Park
★★★★**
Holiday Park
Fourth Avenue, Warden Road,
Sheerness ME12 4EW
T: (01795) 880080
F: (01795) 881198
E: copperfields@
palmtreemanagement.co.uk
I: www.palmtreemanagement.
co.uk

Palm Trees Holiday Park
★★★★
Holiday Park
Second Avenue, Warden Road,
Sheerness ME12 4ET
T: (01795) 880080
F: (01795) 881198
E: palmtrees@
palmtreemanagement.co.uk
I: www.palmtreemanagement.
co.uk

Shurland Dale Holiday Park
★★★★
Holiday Park
Warden Road, Sheerness
ME12 4EN
T: (01795) 880353
F: (01795) 881198

Warden Springs Holiday
Park ★★★
*Holiday, Touring and Camping
Park*
Warden Point, Sheerness
ME12 4HF
T: (01795) 880216
F: (01795) 880218
E: wardensprings@
gbholidayparks.co.uk
I: www.wardensprings.co.uk

FAREHAM
Hampshire

Ellerslie Touring Caravan &
Camping Park ★
Touring Park
Down End Road, Fareham
PO16 8TS
T: (01329) 822248
F: (01329) 822248

FOLKESTONE
Kent

Black Horse Farm Caravan
Club Site ★★★★★
Touring and Camping Park
385 Canterbury Road, Densole,
Folkestone CT18 7BG
T: (01303) 892665
I: www.caravanclub.co.uk

Camping & Caravanning
Club Site Folkestone
★★★★
Touring and Camping Park
The Warren, Folkestone
CT19 6NQ
T: (01303) 255093
I: www.
campingandcaravanningclub.
co.uk

FORDINGBRIDGE
Hampshire

Sandy Balls Holiday Centre
★★★★★
Holiday Park
Godshill, Fordingbridge SP6 2JZ
T: (01425) 653042
F: (01425) 653067
E: post@sandy-balls.co.uk
I: www.sandy-balls.co.uk

FRESHWATER
Isle of Wight

Heathfield Farm Camping
Site ★★★★
Touring and Camping Park
Heathfield Road, Freshwater
PO40 9SH
T: (01983) 756756
F: (01983) 756756
E: web@heathfieldcamping.
co.uk
I: www.heathfieldcamping.co.uk

FRITHAM
Hampshire

Forestry Commission
Ocknell/ Longbeech
Caravan & Camping Site
★★★
Camping Park
Lyndhurst SO43 7HH
T: (0131) 314 6505
F: (0131) 3340849
E: fe.holidays@forestry.gov.uk
I: www.forestholidays.co.uk

GOSPORT
Hampshire

Kingfisher Caravan Park
★★
*Holiday, Touring and Camping
Park*
Browndown Road, Stokes Bay,
Gosport PO13 9BG
T: (023) 9250 2611
F: (023) 92583583
E: info@
kingfisher-caravan-park.co.uk
I: www.kingfisher-caravan-park.
co.uk

GRAFFHAM
West Sussex

Camping & Caravanning
Club Site Graffham ★★★★
Touring and Camping Park
Petworth GU28 0QJ
T: (01798) 867476
I: www.
campingandcaravanningclub.
co.uk

GRAVENEY
Kent

Country View Park
★★★★★
Holiday Park
Cleve Hill, Faversham ME13 9EF
T: (01795) 530036
F: (01795) 591728

GURNARD
Isle of Wight

Gurnard Pines Holiday
Village ★★★★★
Holiday Park
Cockleton Lane, Cowes
PO31 8QE
T: (01983) 292395
F: (01983) 299415
E: info@gurnardpines.co.uk
I: www.gurnardpines.co.uk

Solent Lawn Holiday Park
★★★
Holiday Park
Worsley Road, Cowes PO31 8JX
T: (01983) 293243
E: info@isleofwightselfcatering.
co.uk
I: www.isleofwightselfcatering.
co.uk

HAILSHAM
East Sussex

Peel House Farm Caravan
Park ★★★★
*Holiday, Touring and Camping
Park*
Sayerland Lane, Polegate
BN26 6QX
T: (01323) 845629
F: (01323) 845629
E: peelhocp@tesco.net

HAMBLE
Hampshire

Riverside Park ★★★★
*Holiday, Touring and Camping
Park*
Satchell Lane, Southampton
SO31 4HR
T: (023) 8045 3220
F: (023) 80453611
E: enquiries@riversideholidays.
co.uk
I: www.riversideholidays.co.uk

HASTINGS
East Sussex

Combe Haven Holiday Park
★★★★★
Holiday Park
Harley Shute Road, Hastings
TN38 8BZ
T: (01424) 427891
F: (01424) 442991
E: combehaven@
bourne-leisure.co.uk
I: www.havenholidays.
com/combehaven

Rocklands Holiday Park
★★★★
Holiday Park
Rocklands Lane, East Hill,
Hastings TN35 5DY
T: (01424) 423097
E: rocklandspark@aol.com

Shear Barn Holiday Park
★★★★
*Holiday, Touring and Camping
Park*
Barley Lane, Hastings TN35 5DX
T: (01424) 423583
F: (01424) 718740
E: shearbarn@haulfryn.co.uk
I: www.haulfryn.co.uk

Stalkhurst Camping &
Caravan Park ★★★
*Holiday, Touring and Camping
Park*
Ivyhouse Lane, Hastings
TN35 4NN
T: (01424) 439015
F: (01424) 445206
E: stalkhurstpark@btinternet.
com

HAYLING ISLAND
Hampshire

Fishery Creek Caravan &
Camping Park ★★★
Touring and Camping Park
Fishery Lane, Hayling Island
PO11 9NR
T: (023) 9246 2164
F: (023) 92460741
E: camping@fisherycreek.fsnet.
co.uk
I: www.keyparks.co.uk

Mill Rythe Holiday Village
★★★
Holiday Park
Havant Road, Hayling Island
PO11 0PB
T: (023) 9246 3805
F: (023) 9246 4842

Warner Holidays ★★★
Holiday Village
Lakeside Classic Resort, Fishery
Lane, Hayling Island PO11 9NR
T: (023) 9246 3976
F: (023) 9246 9143

HENFIELD
West Sussex

Downsview Caravan Park
★★★★
*Holiday, Touring and Camping
Park*
Bramlands Lane, Henfield
BN5 9TG
T: (01273) 492801
F: (01273) 495214
E: phr.peter@lineone.net

HERSTMONCEUX
East Sussex

Orchard View Park
★★★★★
Holiday Park
Victoria Road, Hailsham
BN27 4SY
T: (01323) 832335
F: (01323) 832335
E: orchardviewpark@yahoo.
co.uk
I: www.orchard-view-park.com

HORAM
East Sussex

Horam Manor Touring Park
★★★★
Touring and Camping Park
Heathfield TN21 0YD
T: (01435) 813662
E: camp@horam-manor.co.uk
I: www.horam-manor.co.uk

HORSHAM
West Sussex

Honeybridge Park ★★★
Holiday Park
Honeybridge Lane, Dial Post,
Horsham RH13 8NX
T: (01403) 710923
F: (01403) 710923
E: enquiries@honeybridgepark.
co.uk
I: www.honeybridgepark.co.uk

HURLEY
Windsor and Maidenhead

Hurley Riverside Park
★★★★
*Holiday, Touring and Camping
Park*
Rose Award
Hurley, Maidenhead SL6 5NE
T: (01628) 823501
F: (01628) 825533
E: info@hurleyriversidepark.
co.uk
I: www.hurleyriversidepark.co.uk

Hurleyford Farm Ltd
★★★★
Holiday Park
Mill Lane, Maidenhead SL6 5ND
T: (01628) 829009
F: (01628) 829010
E: hurleyfordfarm@btclick.com
I: www.ukparks.co.uk/hurleyford

KINGSDOWN
Kent

Kingsdown Park Holiday Village ★★★★★
Holiday Park
Upper Street, Deal CT14 8AU
T: (01304) 361205
F: (01304) 380125
E: info@kingsdownpark.co.uk
I: www.kingsdownpark.co.uk

LINGFIELD
Surrey

Long Acres Caravan & Camping Park ★★★
Touring Park
Newchapel Road, Lingfield
RH7 6LE
T: (01342) 833205
F: (01622) 735038
I: www.ukparks.co.uk/longacres

LYMINGTON
Hampshire

Hurst View Caravan Park ★★★
Camping Park
Lower Pennington Lane,
Lymington SO41 8AL
T: (01590) 671648
F: (01590) 689244
E: enquiries@hurstviewleisure.co.uk
I: www.hurstviewleisure.co.uk

LYMINSTER
West Sussex

Brookside Holiday Caravan Park ★★★
Holiday Park
Littlehampton BN17 7QE
T: (01903) 713292
F: (01903) 713292

MAIDSTONE
Kent

Pine Lodge Touring Park ★★★★★
Touring and Camping Park
A20 Ashford Road, Maidstone
ME17 1XH
T: (01622) 730018
F: (01622) 734498
E: booking@pinelodgetouringpark.co.uk
I: www.pinelodgetouringpark.co.uk

MARDEN
Kent

Tanner Farm Touring Caravan & Camping Park ★★★★★
Touring and Camping Park
Goudhurst Road, Tonbridge
TN12 9ND
T: (01622) 832399
F: (01622) 832472
E: enquiries@tannerfarmpark.co.uk
I: www.tannerfarmpark.co.uk

MILFORD ON SEA
Hampshire

Carrington Park ★★★★★
Holiday Park
New Lane, Milford on Sea,
Lymington SO41 0UQ
T: (01590) 642654
F: (01590) 642951
I: www.ukparks.co.uk/carrington

Downton Holiday Park
★★★★
Holiday Park
Shorefield Road, Milford on Sea,
Lymington SO41 0LH
T: (01425) 476131 & (01590) 642515
F: (01590) 642515
E: info@downtonholidaypark.co.uk
I: www.downtonholidaypark.co.uk

Lytton Lawn Touring Park
★★★★
Touring Park
Lymore Lane, Milford on Sea,
Lymington SO41 0TX
T: (01590) 648331
F: (01590) 645610
E: holidays@shorefield.co.uk
I: www.shorefield.co.uk

Shorefield Country Park
★★★★★
Holiday Park
Shorefield Road, Milford on Sea,
Lymington SO41 0LH
T: (01590) 648331
F: (01590) 645610
E: holidays@shorefield.co.uk
I: www.shorefield.co.uk

MINSTER
Kent

Riverbank Park ★★★
Holiday, Touring and Camping Park
The Broadway, Minster on Sea,
Sheerness ME12 2DB
T: (01795) 870300
F: (01795) 871300
E: riverbank.park@virgin.net
I: www.ukparks.com/riverbank

MINSTER-IN-SHEPPEY
Kent

Willow Trees Holiday Park ★★★
Holiday Park
Oak Lane, Minster on Sea,
Sheerness ME12 3QR
T: (01795) 875833
F: (01795) 881198
E: willowtrees@palmtreemanagement.co.uk
I: www.palmtreemanagement.co.uk

MINSTER-IN-THANET
Kent

Wayside Caravan Park ★★★★★
Holiday Park
Way Hill, Minster, Ramsgate
CT12 4HW
T: (01843) 821272

MOLLINGTON
Oxfordshire

Anita's Touring Caravan Park ★★★★
Touring and Camping Park
The Yews, Church Farm, Banbury
OX17 1AZ
T: (01295) 750731
F: (01295) 750731
E: anitagail@btopenworld.com
I: www.ukparks.co.uk/mollington

MONKTON
Kent

The Foxhunter Park ★★★★★
Holiday Park
Foxhunter Residential Caravan,
Monkton Street, Monkton,
Ramsgate CT12 4JG
T: (01843) 821311
F: (01843) 821458
E: foxhunterpark@aol.com
I: www.saundersparkhomes.co.uk

NEW MILTON
Hampshire

Forestry Commission Setthorns Caravan and Camping Site. ★★★★
Touring and Camping Park
Wootton, New Milton
BH25 5WA
T: (0131) 314 6505
F: (0131) 334 0849
E: fe.holidays@forestry.gov.uk
I: www.forestholidays.co.uk

Glen Orchard Holiday Park
★★★★
Holiday Park
Walkford Lane, New Milton
BH25 5NH
T: (01425) 616463
F: (01425) 638655
E: enquiries@glenorchard.co.uk
I: www.glenorchard.co.uk

Hoburne Bashley ★★★★
Holiday Park
Sway Road, New Milton
BH25 5QR
T: (01425) 612340
F: (01425) 632732
E: enquires@hoburne.co.uk
I: www.hoburne.co.uk

Hoburne Naish ★★★★★
Holiday Park
Christchurch Road, New Milton
BH25 7RE
T: (01425) 273586
F: (01425) 282130
E: enquires@hoburne.com
I: www.hoburne.com

NEW ROMNEY
Kent

Romney Sands Holiday Park ★★★★
Holiday Park
The Parade, New Romney
TN28 8RN
T: (01797) 363877
F: (01797) 367497
E: romneysands@gbholidayparks.co.uk
I: www.gbholidays.co.uk

NEWCHURCH
Kent

Norwood Farm Caravan & Camping Park ★★★
Touring and Camping Park
Romney Marsh TN29 0DU
T: (01303) 873659
F: (01303) 873659
E: jameswimble@farming.co.uk

Southland Camping Park
★★★★★
Touring and Camping Park
Winford Road, Sandown
PO36 0LZ
T: (01983) 865385
F: (01983) 867663
E: info@southland.co.uk
I: www.southland.co.uk

NITON
Isle of Wight

Meadow View Caravan Site ★
Holiday Park
Newport Road, Ventnor
PO38 2NS
T: (01983) 730015

NORTH BOARHUNT
Hampshire

South Hants Country Club ★★★★
Holiday Park
Blackhouse Lane, Fareham
PO17 6JS
T: (01329) 832919
F: (01329) 834506
E: info@naturistholidays.co.uk
I: www.naturistholidays.co.uk

OLNEY
Milton Keynes

Emberton Country Park ★★★
Touring and Camping Park
Westpits, Olney MK46 5DB
T: (01234) 711575
F: (01234) 711575
E: embertonpark@milton-keynes.gov.uk
I: www.mkweb.co.uk/embertonpark

OWER
Hampshire

Green Pastures Caravan Park ★★★
Touring Park
Whitemoor Lane, Romsey
SO51 6AJ
T: (023) 8081 4444
E: enquiries@greenpasturesfarm.com
I: www.greenpasturesfarm.com

OXFORD
Oxfordshire

The Camping & Caravanning Club Site Oxford ★★★
Touring and Camping Park
426 Abingdon Road, Oxford
OX1 4XN
T: (01865) 244088
I: www.campingandcaravanningclub.co.uk

PAGHAM
West Sussex

Church Farm Holiday Village ★★★★
Holiday Park
Church Lane, Bognor Regis
PO21 4NR
T: (01243) 262635
F: (01243) 266043
E: enquiries@british-holidays.co.uk
I: www.british-holidays.co.uk

PEVENSEY
East Sussex

Camping and Caravanning Club Site Normans Bay ★★★★
Touring and Camping Park
Pevensey BN24 6PR
T: (01323) 761190
I: www.
campingandcaravanningclub.
co.uk

PEVENSEY BAY
East Sussex

Bay View Caravan & Camping Park ★★★★★
Holiday, Touring and Camping Park
Old Martello Road, Pevensey
BN24 6DX
T: (01323) 768688
F: (01323) 769637
E: holidays@bay-view.co.uk
I: www.bay-view.co.uk

Martello Beach Park ★★★★★
Holiday Park
Eastbourne Road, Pevensey
BN24 6DH
T: (01323) 761424
F: (01323) 460433
E: m.smart@martellobeachpark.
fsbusiness.co.uk
I: www.ukparks.co.uk/martello

PORTSMOUTH & SOUTHSEA
Portsmouth

Southsea Leisure Park ★★★
Holiday, Touring and Camping Park
Melville Road, Southsea PO4 9TB
T: (023) 9273 5070
F: (023) 92821302
E: info@southsealeisurepark.
com
I: www.southsealeisurepark.com

RAMSGATE
Kent

Manston Caravan & Camping Park ★★★★
Holiday, Touring and Camping Park
Manston Court Road, Ramsgate
CT12 5AU
T: (01843) 823442
E: enquiries@manston-park.
co.uk
I: www.manston-park.co.uk

Nethercourt Touring Park ★★★
Touring and Camping Park
Nethercourt Hill, Ramsgate
CT11 0RX
T: (01843) 595485
F: (01843) 595485

READING
Reading

Wellington Country Park ★★★★
Touring and Camping Park
Odiham Road, Riseley, Reading
RG7 1SP
T: (0118) 932 6444
F: (0118) 932 3445
E: camping@
wellington-country-park.co.uk
I: www.
wellington-country-park.co.uk

REDHILL
Surrey

Alderstead Heath Caravan Club Site ★★★★
Touring Park
Dean Lane, Redhill RH1 3AH
T: (01737) 644629
I: www.caravanclub.co.uk

RINGWOOD
Hampshire

Red Shoot Camping Park ★★★★
Camping Park
Ringwood BH24 3QT
T: (01425) 473789
F: (01425) 471558
E: enquiries@
redshoot-campingpark.com
I: www.redshoot-campingpark.
com

ROCHESTER
Medway

Allhallows Leisure Park ★★★★
Holiday Park
Allhallows-on-Sea, Rochester
ME3 9QD
T: (01634) 270385
F: (01634) 270081
E: enquiries@british-holidays.
co.uk
I: www.british-holidays.co.uk

Woolmans Wood Caravan Park ★★★★
Touring and Camping Park
Rochester Road, Chatham
ME5 9SB
T: (01634) 867685
F: (01634) 867685
E: woolmans.wood@
currantbun.com
I: woolmans-wood.co.uk

ROMSEY
Hampshire

Hill Farm Caravan Park ★★★★
Holiday, Touring and Camping Park
Branches Lane, Sherfield English,
Romsey SO51 6FH
T: (01794) 340402
F: (01794) 342358
E: gjb@hillfarmpark.com
I: www.hillfarmpark.com

ROOKLEY
Isle of Wight

Island View Holidays ★★★★
Holiday Park
Rookley Country Park, Main
Road, Ventnor PO38 3LU
T: (01983) 721606
F: (01983) 721607
E: info@islandviewhols.
freeserve.co.uk
I: www.islandviewhols.co.uk

RYDE
Isle of Wight

Beaper Farm Camping Site ★★★
Touring Park
Beaper Farm, Ryde PO33 1QJ
T: (01983) 615210
E: beaper@btinternet.com

Harcourt Sands Holiday Village ★★★★
Holiday Park
Puckpool Hill, Ryde PO33 1PJ
T: (01983) 567321
F: (01983) 611622

Pondwell Holiday Park ★★★
Holiday Park
Pondwell Hill, Ryde PO33 1QA
T: (01983) 612100
F: (01983) 613511
E: info@isleofwightselfcating.
co.uk
I: www.isleofwightselfcatering.
co.uk

ST HELENS
Isle of Wight

Carpenters Farm ★★
Touring and Camping Park
Carpenters Road, Ryde PO33 1YL
T: (01983) 872450

Field Lane Holiday Park ★★★★★
Holiday Park
Field Lane, St Helens, Ryde
PO33 1UX
T: (01983) 872779
F: (01983) 873000
E: office@fieldlane.com
I: www.fieldlane.com

Hillgrove Park ★★★★
Holiday Park
Field Lane, St Helens, Ryde
PO33 1UT
T: (01983) 872802
F: (01983) 872100
E: info@hillgrove.co.uk
I: www.hillgrove.co.uk

Nodes Point Holiday Park ★★★
Holiday, Touring and Camping Park
Nodes Road, St Helens, Ryde
PO33 1YA
T: (01983) 872401
F: (01983) 874696
I: www.park-resorts.com

Old Mill Holiday Park ★★★★★
Holiday Park
Mill Road, Ryde PO33 1UE
T: (01983) 872507
E: oldmill@fsbdial.co.uk
I: www.oldmill.co.uk

ST LAWRENCE
Isle of Wight

Undercliff Glen Caravan Park ★★★★★
Holiday Park
The Undercliffe Drive, Ventnor
PO38 1XY
T: (01983) 730261
F: (01983) 730261

ST MARGARETS-AT-CLIFFE
Kent

St Margarets Holiday Park ★★★★★
Holiday Park
Reach Road, St Margarets-at-
Cliffe, Dover CT15 6AE
T: (01304) 853262
F: (01304) 853434
I: www.leisuregb.co.uk

ST NICHOLAS AT WADE
Kent

St Nicholas Camping Site ★★★
Touring and Camping Park
Court Road, St Nicholas at
Wade, Birchington CT7 0NH
T: (01843) 847245

SANDOWN
Isle of Wight

The Camping & Caravanning Club Site Adgestone Club Site ★★★★
Touring and Camping Park
Lower Road, Sandown PO36 0HL
T: (01983) 403432
I: www.
campingandcaravanningclub.
co.uk

Cheverton Copse Holiday Park ★★★★
Holiday, Touring and Camping Park
Scotchells Brook Lane, Sandown
PO36 0JP
T: (01983) 403161
F: (01983) 402861
E: holidays@cheverton-copse.
co.uk
I: www.cheverton-copse.co.uk

Fairway Holiday Park ★★★
Holiday Park
The Fairway, Sandown PO36 9PS
T: (01983) 403462
F: (01983) 405713
E: enquiries@
fairwayholidaypark.co.uk
I: www.fairwayholidaypark.co.uk

Fort Holiday Park ★★
Holiday Park
Avenue Road, Sandown
PO36 8BD
T: (01983) 402858
F: (01983) 405159
E: bookings@fortholidaypark.
co.uk
I: www.fortholidaypark.co.uk

Fort Spinney Holiday Chalets ★★★★★
Holiday Park
Yaverland Road, Sandown
PO36 8QB
T: (01983) 402360
F: (01983) 404025
E: fortspinney@isle-of-wight.
uk.com
I: www.isle-of-wight.uk.
com/spinney

Sandown Holiday Chalets ★★★★
Holiday Park
Avenue Road, Sandown
PO36 9AP
T: (01983) 404025
F: (01983) 404025
E: chalets@isle-of-wight.uk.
com
I: www.isle-of-wight.uk.
com/chalets

Establishments printed in blue have a detailed entry in this guide

SANDWICH
Kent

Sandwich Leisure Park
★★★★★
Holiday, Touring and Camping Park
Woodnesborough Road,
Sandwich CT13 0AA
T: (01304) 612681
F: (01304) 615252
E: info@
coastandcountryleisure.com
I: www.coastandcountryleisure.com

SEAFORD
East Sussex

Sunnyside Caravan Park
★★★★
Holiday Park
Marine Parade, Seaford
BN25 2QW
T: (01323) 892825
F: (01323) 892825

SEAL
Kent

Camping & Caravanning Club Site Oldbury Hill
★★★★
Touring and Camping Park
Sevenoaks TN15 0ET
T: (01732) 762728
I: www.campingandcaravanningclub.co.uk

SEASALTER
Kent

Homing Leisure Park
★★★★★
Holiday, Touring and Camping Park
Church Lane, Whitstable
CT5 4BU
T: (01227) 771777
F: (01227) 273512
E: info@
coastandcountryleisure.com
I: www.coastandcountryleisure.com

SEAVIEW
Isle of Wight

Salterns Holidays ★★★
Holiday Park
Salterns Road, Seaview
PO34 5AQ
T: (01983) 612330
F: (01983) 613511
E: info@isleofwightselfcatering.co.uk
I: www.isleofwightselfcatering.co.uk

Tollgate Holiday Park ★★★
Holiday Park
Duver Road, Seaview PO34 5AJ
T: (01983) 612107
E: info@isleofwightselfcatering.co.uk
I: www.isleofwightselfcatering.co.uk

SELSEY
West Sussex

Green Lawns Caravan Park
★★★★★
Touring Park
Paddock Lane, Chichester
PO20 9EJ
T: (01243) 606080
F: (01243) 606068
E: holidays@bunnleisure.co.uk
I: www.bunnleisure.co.uk

Warner Farm Touring Park
★★★★★
Touring Park
Warners Lane, Selsey, Chichester
PO20 9EL
T: (01243) 608440
F: (01243) 604499
E: touring@bunnleisure.co.uk
I: www.bunnleisure.co.uk

West Sands Holiday Park
★★★★
Touring Park
Mill Lane, Chichester PO20 9BH
T: (01243) 606080
F: (01243) 606068
E: holidays@bunnleisure.co.uk
I: www.bunnleisure.co.uk

White Horse Caravan Park
★★★★
Touring Park
Paddock Lane, Chichester
PO20 9EJ
T: (01243) 606080
F: (01243) 606068
E: holidays@bunnleisure.co.uk
I: www.bunnleisure.co.uk

SHANKLIN
Isle of Wight

Landguard Camping Park
★★★★
Touring and Camping Park
Sandy Lane, Shanklin PO37 7PH
T: (01983) 867028
F: (01983) 865988
E: landguard@weltinet.com
I: www.landguard-camping.co.uk

Landguard Holidays ★★★★
Holiday Park
Sandy Lane, Shanklin PO37 7PH
T: (01983) 863100
F: (01983) 867896
E: enquiries@
landguardholidays.co.uk
I: www.landguardholidays.co.uk

Lower Hyde Holiday Village
★★★★
Holiday, Touring and Camping Park
Landguard Road, Shanklin
PO37 7LL
T: (01983) 866131
F: (01983) 862532
I: www.park-resorts.com

Ninham Country Holidays
★★★★
Holiday, Touring and Camping Park
Ninham, Shanklin PO37 7PL
T: (01983) 864243
F: (01983) 868881
E: office@ninham-holidays.co.uk
I: www.ninham-holidays.co.uk

SLINDON
West Sussex

Camping & Caravanning Club Site, Slindon ★★
Touring Park
Arundel BN18 0RG
T: (01243) 814387
I: www.campingandcarvanningclub.co.uk

SMALL DOLE
West Sussex

Southdown Caravan Park
★★★
Holiday and Touring Park
Henfield Road, Henfield
BN5 9XH
T: (01903) 814323
F: (01903) 812572
I: www.southdowncaravanpark.co.uk

SOUTHBOURNE
West Sussex

Camping & Caravanning Club Site Chichester
★★★★
Touring and Camping Park
Main Road, Emsworth PO10 8JH
T: (01243) 373202
I: www.campingandcaravanningclub.co.uk

SOUTHWATER
West Sussex

Raylands Park ★★★★
Holiday, Touring and Camping Park
Jackrells Lane, Horsham
RH13 9DH
T: (01403) 730218
F: (01403) 732828
E: raylands@
roundstonecaravans.com
I: www.roundstonecaravans.com

STANDLAKE
Oxfordshire

Hardwick Parks ★★★
Holiday, Touring and Camping Park
The Downs, Witney OX29 7PZ
T: (01865) 300501
F: (01865) 300037
E: info@hardwickparks.co.uk
I: www.hardwickparks.co.uk

Lincoln Farm Park Limited
★★★★★
Touring Park
High Street, Witney OX29 7RH
T: (01865) 300239
F: (01865) 300127
E: info@lincolnfarm.touristnet.uk.com
I: www.lincolnfarm.touristnet.uk.com

THORNESS BAY
Isle of Wight

Thorness Bay Holiday Park
★★★★
Holiday, Touring and Camping Park
Cowes PO31 8NJ
T: (01983) 523109
F: (01983) 822213
I: www.park-resorts.com

TOTLAND BAY
Isle of Wight

Ivylands Holiday Park
★★★★
Holiday Park
The Broadway, Totland Bay
PO39 0AN
T: (01983) 752480
F: (01983) 752480
E: web@ivylandsholidaypark.co.uk
I: www.ivylandsholidaypark.co.uk

UCKFIELD
East Sussex

Honeys Green Caravan Park
★★★
Holiday and Touring Park
Easons Green, Uckfield
TN22 5RE
T: (01732) 860205
F: (01732) 860205
E: honeysgreenpark@tiscali.co.uk

WALTON-ON-THAMES
Surrey

Camping & Caravanning Club Site Walton on Thames
★★★
Camping Park
Field Common Lane, Walton-on-Thames KT12 3QG
T: (01932) 220392
I: www.campingandcaravanningclub.co.uk

WARSASH
Hampshire

Dibles Park ★★★★
Touring Park
Dibles Road, Warsash,
Southampton SO31 9SA
T: (01489) 575232

WASHINGTON
West Sussex

Washington Caravan & Camping Park ★★★★
Touring and Camping Park
London Road, Washington,
Pulborough RH20 4AJ
T: (01903) 892869
F: (01903) 893252
E: washcamp@amserve.com
I: www.washcamp.com

WINCHESTER
Hampshire

Morn Hill Caravan Club Site
★★★★
Touring Park
Alresford Road, Winchester
SO21 1HL
T: (01962) 869877
I: www.caravanclub.co.uk

WOKINGHAM
Wokingham

California Chalet & Touring Park ★★★★
Holiday, Touring and Camping Park
Nine Mile Ride, Wokingham
RG40 4HU
T: (0118) 973 3928
F: (0118) 932 8720

Look out for establishments participating in the National Accessible Scheme

WOODGATE
West Sussex

Willows Caravan Park
★★★★
Holiday Park
Lidsey Road, Chichester
PO20 3SU
T: (01243) 543124
F: (01243) 543124
E: sales@willowscaravans.co.uk

WORTHING
West Sussex

**Northbrook Farm Caravan
Club Site ★★★★**
Touring Park
Titnore Way, Worthing
BN13 3RT
T: (01903) 502962
I: www.caravanclub.co.uk

Onslow Caravan Park ★★★
Holiday Park
Onslow Drive, Worthing
BN12 5RX
T: (01903) 243170
F: (01243) 671624
E: islandmeadow@fsmail.net.uk
I: www.islandmeadow.co.uk

WROTHAM HEATH
Kent

**Gate House Wood Touring
Park ★★★★★**
Touring and Camping Park
Ford Road, Wrotham Heath,
Sevenoaks TN15 7SD
T: (01732) 843062

WROXALL
Isle of Wight

**Appuldurcombe Gardens
Holiday Park ★★★★**
Holiday and Touring Park
Appuldurcombe Road, Ventnor
PO38 3EP
T: (01983) 852597
F: (01983) 856225
E: info@
appuldurcombegardens.co.uk
I: www.appuldurcombegardens.
co.uk

YARMOUTH
Isle of Wight

**The Orchard Holiday
Caravan Park ★★★★★**
Holiday and Touring Park
Main Road, Yarmouth PO41 0TS
T: (01983) 531331
F: (01983) 531666
E: info@orchards-holiday-park.
co.uk
I: www.orchards-holiday-park.
co.uk

Savoy Holiday Village ★★★
Holiday Park
Halletts Shute, Yarmouth
PO41 0RJ
T: (01983) 760355
F: (01983) 761277

Silver Glades Caravan Park
★★★★
Holiday Park
Solent Road, Yarmouth
PO41 0XZ
T: (01983) 760172
E: holidays@silvergladesiow.
co.uk
I: www.silvergladesiow.co.uk

Warner Holidays ★★★
Holiday Village
Norton Grange Classic Resort,
Yarmouth PO41 0SD
T: (01983) 760323
F: (01983) 760468

SOUTH WEST ENGLAND

ALDERHOLT
Dorset

**Hill Cottage Farm Touring
Caravan Park ★★★★**
Touring and Camping Park
Sandleheath Road,
Fordingbridge SP6 3EG
T: (01425) 650513
F: (01425) 652339

ASHBURTON
Devon

Ashburton Caravan Park
★★★★
*Holiday, Touring and Camping
Park*
Waterleat, Newton Abbot
TQ13 7HU
T: (01364) 652552
F: (01364) 652552
E: info@ashburtoncaravanpark.
co.uk
I: www.ashburtoncaravanpark.
co.uk

Parkers Farm Holiday Park
★★★★
*Holiday, Touring and Camping
Park*
Rose Award
Higher Mead Farm, Alston Cross,
Ashburton, Newton Abbot
TQ13 7LJ
T: (01364) 652598
F: (01364) 654004
E: parkersfarm@btconnect.com
I: www.parkersfarm.co.uk

River Dart Adventures
★★★★
Touring and Camping Park
Holne Park, Newton Abbot
TQ13 7NP
T: (01364) 652511
F: (01364) 652020
E: enquires@riverdart.co.uk
I: www.riverdart.co.uk

AXMINSTER
Devon

**Andrewshayes Caravan
Park ★★★★**
Holiday Park
Dalwood, Axminster EX13 7DY
T: (01404) 831225
F: (01404) 831893
E: enquiries@andrewshayes.
co.uk
I: www.andrewshayes.co.uk

**Hunters Moon Country
Estate ★★★★**
Holiday Park
Hawkchurch, Axminster
EX13 5UL
T: (01297) 678402
F: (01297) 678702
I: www.ukparks.
co.uk/huntersmoon

BARNSTAPLE
Devon

**Kentisbury Grange Country
Park ★★★★**
*Holiday, Touring and Camping
Park*
Barnstaple EX31 4NL
T: (01271) 883454
F: (01271) 882040
E: info@kentisburygrange.co.uk
I: www.kentisburygrange.co.uk

BARTON
Torbay

Torquay Holiday Park
★★★★
Holiday Park
Rose Award
Kingskerswell Road, Torquay
TQ2 8JU
T: (01803) 323077
F: (01803) 323503

BATH
Bath and North East Somerset

Newton Mill Camping
★★★★
Touring and Camping Park
Newton Road, Bath BA2 9JF
T: (01225) 333909
E: newtonmill@hotmail.com
I: www.campinginbath.co.uk

BEETHAM
Somerset

**Five Acres Caravan Club
Site ★★★★**
Touring Park
Beetham, Chard
T: (01460) 234519
I: www.caravanclub.co.uk

BERE REGIS
Dorset

**Rowlands Wait Touring
Park ★★★**
Touring and Camping Park
Rye Hill, Bere Regis, Wareham
BH20 7LP
T: (01929) 472727
F: (01929) 472275
E: bta@rowlandswait.co.uk
I: www.rowlandswait.co.uk

BERROW
Somerset

Sandyglade Caravan Park
★★★★
Holiday Park
Coast Road, Burnham-on-Sea
TA8 2QX
T: (01278) 751271
F: (01278) 751036
E: info@sandyglade.co.uk
I: www.sandyglade.co.uk

BERRY HEAD
Torbay

Landscove Holiday Village
★★★★
Holiday Park
Gillard Road, Brixham TQ5 9EP
T: 0870 442 9750
F: 0870 442 9757
E: bookings@landscove.biz
I: www.southdevonholidays.biz

BERRYNARBOR
Devon

**Sandaway Beach Holiday
Park ★★★★**
Holiday and Touring Park
Ilfracombe EX34 9ST
T: (01271) 866766
F: (01271) 866791
E: bookings@
johnfowlerholidays.com
I: www.johnfowlerholidays.com

BICKINGTON
Devon

The Dartmoor Halfway
★★★★
Touring Park
Newton Abbot TQ12 6JW
T: (01626) 821270
F: (01626) 821820

Lemonford Caravan Park
★★★★★
*Holiday, Touring and Camping
Park*
Bickington, Newton Abbot
TQ12 6JR
T: (01626) 821242
F: (01626) 821242
E: mark@lemonford.co.uk
I: www.lemonford.co.uk

BIDEFORD
Devon

Bideford Bay Holiday Park
★★★★
Holiday Park
Buck's Cross, Bideford EX39 5DU
T: (01237) 431331
F: (01237) 431624
E: gm.bidefordbay@
park-resorts.com

BISHOP SUTTON
Bath and North East Somerset

**Bath Chew Valley Caravan
Park ★★★★★**
Touring Park
Ham Lane, Bristol BS39 5TZ
T: (01275) 332127
F: (01275) 332664
I: www.bathchewvalley.co.uk

BLACKWATER
Cornwall

Trevarth Holiday Park
★★★★
Holiday Park
Blackwater, Truro TR4 8HR
T: (01872) 560266
F: (01872) 560379
E: trevarth@lineone.net
I: www.ukparks.co.uk/trevarth

BLANDFORD FORUM
Dorset

The Inside Park ★★★★
Touring and Camping Park
Blandford Forum DT11 9AD
T: (01258) 453719
F: (01258) 459921
E: inspark@aol.com
I: members.aol.
com/inspark/inspark

BLUE ANCHOR
Somerset

**Blue Anchor Bay Caravan
Park ★★★★**
Holiday and Touring Park
Rose Award
Blue Anchor (Hoburne),
Minehead TA24 6JT
T: (01643) 821360
F: (01643) 821572
E: enquiries@hoburne.co.uk
I: www.hoburne.co.uk

BODMIN
Cornwall

**Camping & Caravanning
Club Site Bodmin ★★★★**
Touring and Camping Park
Old Callywith Road, Bodmin
PL31 2DZ
T: (01208) 73834
I: www.
campingandcaravanningclub.
co.uk

Ruthern Valley Holidays
★★★★
*Holiday, Touring and Camping
Park*
Ruthern Bridge, Bodmin
PL30 5LU
T: (01208) 831395
F: (01208) 831395
E: enquiries@ruthernvalley.
fsnet.co.uk
I: www.self-catering-ruthern.
co.uk

BOSSINEY
Cornwall

Ocean Cove Caravan Park
★★
Holiday Park
Tintagel PL34 0AZ
T: (01840) 770325
F: (01840) 770031

BOURNEMOUTH
Bournemouth

Meadow Bank Holidays
★★★★★
*Holiday, Touring and Camping
Park*
Stour Way, Christchurch
BH23 2PQ
T: (01202) 483597
F: (01202) 483878
E: enquiries@
meadowbank-holidays.co.uk
I: www.meadowbank-holiday.
co.uk

BOVISAND
Devon

Bovisand Lodge Estate
★★★★
Holiday Park
Bovisand Lodge, Plymouth
PL9 0AA
T: (01752) 403554
F: (01752) 482646
E: blodge@netcomuk.co.uk
I: www.bovisand.com

BRATTON FLEMING
Devon

**Greenacres Farm Touring
Caravan Park ★★★★**
Touring Park
Barnstaple EX31 4SG
T: (01598) 763334

BRAUNTON
Devon

**Lobb Fields Caravan and
Camping Park ★★★★**
Touring and Camping Park
Saunton Road, Braunton
EX33 1EB
T: (01271) 812090
F: (01271) 812090
E: info@lobbfields.com
I: www.lobbfields.com

BREAN
Somerset

Beachside Holiday Park
★★★★
Holiday Park
Coast Road, Burnham-on-Sea
TA8 2QZ
T: (01278) 751346
F: (01278) 751683
E: beachside@breansands.fsnet.
co.uk
I: www.beachsideholidaypark.
co.uk

Diamond Farm ★★★
Touring and Camping Park
Weston Road, Burnham-on-Sea
TA8 2RL
T: (01278) 751263
E: trevor@diamondfarm42.
freeserve.co.uk
I: www.diamondfarm.co.uk

Dolphin Caravan Park
★★★★
Holiday Park
Coast Road, Burnham-on-Sea
TA8 2QY
T: (01278) 751258
F: (01278) 752505
I: www.dolphincaravanpark.
co.uk

Golden Sands Caravan Park
★★
Holiday Park
South Road, Burnham-on-Sea
TA8 2RF
T: (01278) 751322
E: admin@brean.com
I: www.brean.com

Isis and Wyndham Park
★★★★
Holiday Park
Rose Award
Warren Road, Brean Sands,
Burnham-on-Sea TA8 2RP
T: (01278) 751227
F: (01278) 751033
E: enquiries@warren-farm.co.uk
I: www.warren-farm.co.uk

Northam Farm Touring Park
★★★★
Touring and Camping Park
Brean Sands, Burnham-on-Sea
TA8 2SE
T: (01278) 751244
F: (01278) 751150
E: enquiries@northamfarm.
co.uk
I: www.northamfarm.co.uk

**Warren Farm Holiday
Centre ★★★**
*Holiday, Touring and Camping
Park*
Warren Road, Brean Sands,
Burnham-on-Sea TA8 2RP
T: (01278) 751227
F: (01278) 751033
E: enquiries@warren-farm.co.uk
I: www.warren-farm.co.uk

BRIDESTOWE
Devon

Glebe Park ★★★
Holiday and Touring Park
Okehampton EX20 4ER
T: (01837) 861261

BRIDGWATER
Somerset

**Fairways International
Touring Caravan and
Camping Park ★★★**
Touring and Camping Park
Bath Road, Bridgwater TA7 8PP
T: (01278) 685569
F: (01278) 685569
E: FairwaysInt@Btinternet.com
I: www.fairwaysint.btinternet.
co.uk

BRIDPORT
Dorset

**Binghams Farm Touring
Caravan Park ★★★★**
Touring and Camping Park
Binghams Farm, Bridport
DT6 3TT
T: (01308) 488234
F: (01308) 488426
E: enquiries@binghamsfarm.
co.uk
I: www.binghamsfarm.co.uk

Eype House Caravan Park
★★★
Holiday and Camping Park
Eype, Bridport DT6 6AL
T: (01308) 424903
F: (01308) 424903
E: enquiries@eypehouse.co.uk
I: www.eypehouse.co.uk

**Freshwater Beach Holiday
Park ★★★★**
*Holiday, Touring and Camping
Park*
Burton Bradstock, Bridport
DT6 4PT
T: (01308) 897317
F: (01308) 897336
E: office@freshwaterbeach.
co.uk
I: www.freshwaterbeach.co.uk

Golden Cap Holiday Park
★★★★★
Holiday Park
Seatown, Chideock, Bridport
DT6 6JX
T: (01308) 422139
F: (01308) 425672
E: holidays@wdlh.co.uk
I: www.wdlh.co.uk

Highlands End Holiday Park
★★★★★
Holiday Park
Eype, Bridport DT6 6AR
T: (01308) 422139
F: (01308) 425672
E: holidays@wdlh.co.uk
I: www.wdlh.co.uk

BRISTOL
City of Bristol

**Baltic Wharf Caravan Club
Site ★★★★**
Touring Park
Cumberland Road, Bristol
BS1 6XG
T: (0117) 926 8030
I: www.caravanclub.co.uk

BRIXHAM
Torbay

Brixham Holiday Park
★★★★
Holiday Park
Fishcombe Road, Brixham
TQ5 8RB
T: (01803) 853324
F: (01803) 853569
E: enquiries@brixhamholpk.
fsnet.co.uk
I: www.brixhamholidaypark.
co.uk

**Centry Touring Caravans &
Tents ★★**
Touring and Camping Park
Mudberry House, Centry Road,
Brixham TQ5 9EY
T: (01803) 853215
F: (01803) 853261
E: jlacentry.touring@talk21.com
I: www.english-riviera.co.uk

Galmpton Touring Park
★★★★
Touring and Camping Park
Greenway Road, Galmpton,
Brixham TQ5 0EP
T: (01803) 842066
F: (01803) 844458
E: galmptontouringpark@
hotmail.com
I: www.galmptontouringpark.
co.uk

Hillhead Holiday Park ★★★★★
Touring and Camping Park
Hillhead, Brixham TQ5 0HH
T: (01803) 853204
I: www.caravanclub.co.uk

Riviera Bay Holiday Centre ★★★★
Holiday Park
Mudstone Lane, Brixham
TQ5 9EJ
T: (01803) 856335
F: (01803) 883855
E: info@rivierabay.biz
I: www.rivierabay.biz

BUDE
Cornwall

Bude Holiday Park ★★★
Holiday, Touring and Camping Park
Maer Lane, Bude EX23 9EE
T: (01288) 355955
F: (01288) 355980
E: enquiries@budeholidaypark.co.uk
I: www.budeholidaypark.co.uk

Budemeadows Touring Holiday Park ★★★★★
Touring Park
Budemeadows, Bude EX23 0NA
T: (01288) 361646
F: (01288) 361646
E: holiday@budemeadows.com
I: www.budemeadows.com

Penhalt Farm Holiday Park ★★★
Touring and Camping Park
Widemouth Bay, Poundstock, Bude EX23 0DG
T: (01288) 361210
F: (01288) 361210
E: den†jennie@penhaltfarm.fsnet.co.uk
I: www.holidaybank.co.uk/penhaltfarmholidaypark

Penstowe Caravan & Camping Park ★★★★
Holiday Park
Bude EX23 9QY
T: (01288) 321354
F: (01288) 321273
E: info@penstoweleisure.co.uk
I: www.penstoweleisure.co.uk

Sandymouth Bay Holiday Park ★★★★
Holiday and Touring Park
Sandymouth Bay, Bude
EX23 9HW
T: (01288) 352563
F: (01288) 354822
E: sandymouth@aol.com
I: www.sandymouthbay.co.uk

Upper Lynstone Caravan and Camping Site ★★★★
Holiday, Touring and Camping Park
Upton, Bude EX23 0LP
T: (01288) 352017
F: (01288) 359034
E: reception@upperlynstone.co.uk
I: www.upperlynstone.co.uk

Wooda Farm Park ★★★★★
Holiday and Touring Park
Bude EX23 9HJ
T: (01288) 352069
F: (01288) 355258
E: enquiries@wooda.co.uk
I: www.wooda.co.uk

BURNHAM-ON-SEA
Somerset

Burnham-on-Sea Holiday Village ★★★★
Holiday, Touring and Camping Park
Marine Drive, Burnham-on-Sea
TA8 1LA
T: (01278) 783391
F: (01278) 793776
E: enquiries@british-holidays.co.uk
I: www.british-holidays.co.uk/burnhamonsea

Home Farm Holiday Park ★★★★★
Holiday and Touring Park
Edithmead, Highbridge TA9 4HD
T: (01278) 788888
F: (01278) 780113
E: office@homefarmholidaypark.co.uk
I: www.homefarmholidaypark.co.uk

Lakeside Holiday Park ★★★★
Holiday Park
Westfield Road, Burnham-on-Sea TA8 2AE
T: (01278) 792222
F: (01278) 795592
E: enquiries@lakesideholidays.co.uk
I: www.lakesideholidays.co.uk

Pontins ★★★
Holiday Village
Brean Sands Family Centre, South Road, Burnham-on-Sea
TA8 2RJ
T: (01278) 751627
F: (01278) 751754

The Retreat Caravan Park ★★★★★
Holiday Park
Berrow Road, Burnham-on-Sea
TA8 2ES
T: (01458) 860504
F: (01458) 860330

BURTON BRADSTOCK
Dorset

Coastal Caravan Park ★★★
Holiday, Touring and Camping Park
Annings Lane, Burton Bradstock, Bridport DT6 4QP
T: (01308) 422139
F: (01308) 425672
E: holidays@wdlh.co.uk
I: www.wdlh.co.uk

CAMELFORD
Cornwall

Juliot's Well Holiday Park ★★★
Holiday, Touring and Camping Park
Camelford PL32 9RF
T: (01840) 213302
F: (01840) 212700
E: juliotswell@holidaysincornwall.net
I: www.holidaysincornwall.net

CARNON DOWNS
Cornwall

Carnon Downs Caravan and Camping Park ★★★★★
Touring Park
Truro TR3 6JJ
T: (01872) 862283
E: info@carnon-downs.caravanpark.co.uk
I: www.carnon-downs-caravanpark.co.uk

CHACEWATER
Cornwall

Chacewater Park ★★★★
Touring Park
Cox Hill, Truro TR4 8LY
T: (01209) 820762
E: chacewaterpark@aol.com
I: www.chacewaterpark.co.uk

Killiwerris Touring Park ★★★★
Touring Park
Penstraze, Truro TR4 8PF
T: (01872) 561356
E: lin@killiwerristp.fsnet.co.uk

CHARD
Somerset

Alpine Grove Touring Park
Rating Applied For
Chard TA20 4HD
T: (01460) 63479
F: (01460) 239187
E: stay@alpinegrovetouringpark.com
I: www.alpinegrovetouringpark.com

CHARMOUTH
Dorset

The Camping and Caravanning Club Site Charmouth ★★★★★
Touring and Camping Park
Monkton Wylde Farm, Nr Charmouth, Bridport DT6 6DB
T: (01297) 32965
I: www.campingandcaravanningclub.co.uk

Dolphins River Park ★★★★
Holiday Park
Berne Lane, Charmouth DT6 6RD
T: 0800 074 6375
F: (01308) 868 180

Manor Farm Holiday Centre ★★★
Holiday, Touring and Camping Park
The Street, Bridport DT6 6QL
T: (01297) 560226
F: (01297) 560429
E: enq@manorfarmholidaycentre.co.uk
I: www.manorfarmholidaycentre.co.uk

Monkton Wyld Farm Caravan & Camping Park ★★★★
Touring and Camping Park
Monkton Wyld, Bridport DT6 6DB
T: (01297) 34525
F: (01297) 33594
E: holidays@monktonwyld.co.uk
I: www.monktonwyld.co.uk

Newlands Holidays ★★★★
Holiday, Touring and Camping Park
Bridport DT6 6RB
T: (01297) 560259
F: (01297) 560787
E: enq@www.newlandsholidays.co.uk
I: www.newlandsholidays.co.uk

Seadown Holiday Park ★★★★★
Holiday, Touring and Camping Park
Bridge Road, Charmouth, Bridport DT6 6QS
T: (01297) 560154
F: (01297) 561130
I: www.seadownholidaypark.co.uk

Wood Farm Caravan and Camping Park ★★★★★
Holiday, Touring and Camping Park
Charmouth, Bridport DT6 6BT
T: (01297) 560697
F: (01297) 561243
E: holidays@woodfarm.co.uk
I: www.woodfarm.co.uk

CHEDDAR
Somerset

Broadway House Holiday Touring Caravan and Camping Park ★★★★
Holiday, Touring and Camping Park
Rose Award
Axbridge Road, Cheddar
BS27 3DB
T: (01934) 742610
F: (01934) 744950
E: enquiries@broadwayhouse.uk.com
I: www.broadwayhouse.uk.com

Cheddar Bridge Touring Park ★★★★
Holiday, Touring and Camping Park
Draycott Road, Cheddar
BS27 3RJ
T: (01934) 743048
E: tracy@cheddarbridge.co.uk
I: www.cheddarbridge.co.uk

Cheddar Touring Caravan and Camping Park ★★
Touring and Camping Park
Gas House Lane, Off Draycott Road, Cheddar BS27 3RL
T: (01934) 740207
F: (01934) 740207

CHELTENHAM
Gloucestershire

Briarfields Caravan and Camping ★★★
Touring and Camping Park
Gloucester Road, Cheltenham
GL51 0SX
T: (01242) 235324
F: (01242) 262216

CHIPSTABLE
Somerset

Oxenleaze Farm Caravans
★★★★
Holiday Park
Taunton TA4 2QH
T: (01984) 623427
F: (01984) 623427
E: enquires@oxenleazefarm.
co.uk
I: www.oxenleazefarm.co.uk

CHRISTCHURCH
Dorset

Beaulieu Gardens Holiday Park ★★★★★
Holiday Park
Beaulieu Avenue, Christchurch
BH23 2EB
T: (01202) 486215
F: (01202) 483878
E: enquiries@
meadowbank-holidays.co.uk
I: www.meadowbank-holidays.
co.uk

Forestry Commission Holmsley Caravan & Camping Site ★★★
Touring and Camping Park
Forest Road, Christchurch
BH23 7EQ
T: (0131) 314 6505
F: (0131) 3340849
E: fe.holidays@forestry.gov.uk
I: www.forestholidays.co.uk

Harrow Wood Farm Caravan Park ★★★
Camping Park
Poplar Lane, Bransgore,
Christchurch BH23 8JE
T: (01425) 672487
F: (01425) 672487
E: harrowwood@caravan-sites.
co.uk
I: www.caravan-sites.co.uk

CHUDLEIGH
Devon

Holmans Wood Holiday Park ★★★★
Holiday, Touring and Camping Park
Harcombe Cross, Newton Abbot
TQ13 0DZ
T: (01626) 853785
F: (01626) 853792
E: enquiries@holmanswood.
co.uk
I: www.holmanswood.co.uk

COLEFORD
Gloucestershire

Bracelands Caravan & Camping Site ★★★
Touring and Camping Park
Bracelands Drive, Coleford
GL16 7NN
T: (0131) 314 6505
E: fe.holidays@forestry.gsi.gov.
uk
I: www.forestholidays.co.uk

Christchurch Caravan and Camping Site ★★★
Touring and Camping Park
Bracelands Drive, Coleford
GL16 7NN
T: (0131) 314 6505
E: fe.holidays@forestry.gsi.gov.
uk
I: www.forestholidays.co.uk

COLYTON
Devon

Leacroft Touring Park
★★★★
Touring Park
Colyton EX24 6HY
T: (01297) 552823

COMBE MARTIN
Devon

Manleigh Holiday Park
★★★★
Holiday Park
Rectory Road, Ilfracombe
EX34 0NS
T: (01271) 883353
E: info@manleighpark.co.uk
I: www.manleighpark.co.uk

Newberry Farm Touring Caravans and Camping
★★★★
Touring and Camping Park
Woodlands, Ilfracombe
EX34 0AT
T: (01271) 882334
F: (01271) 882880
E: enq@newberrycampsite.
co.uk
I: www.newberrycampsite.co.uk

Stowford Farm Meadows
★★★★
Touring and Camping Park
Combe Martin, Ilfracombe
EX34 0PW
T: (01271) 882476
F: (01271) 883053
E: enquiries@stowford.co.uk
I: www.stowford.co.uk

CONNOR DOWNS
Cornwall

Higher Trevaskis Caravan & Camping Park ★★★★
Touring and Camping Park
Gwinear Road, Hayle TR27 5JQ
T: (01209) 831736

COOMBE BISSETT
Wiltshire

Summerlands Caravan Park
★★★
Touring and Camping Park
College Farm, Rockbourne Road,
Coombe Bissett, Salisbury
SP5 4LP
T: (01722) 718259
E: summerlands-park@
compaquet.co.uk
I: www.summerlands-park.com

CORFE MULLEN
Dorset

Charris Camping & Caravan Park ★★★★
Touring and Camping Park
Candys Lane, Wimborne Minster
BH21 3EF
T: (01202) 885970
F: (01202) 881281
E: jandjcharris@iclway.co.uk
I: www.charris.co.uk

CROWCOMBE
Somerset

Quantock Orchard Caravan Park ★★★★★
Touring and Camping Park
Taunton TA4 4AW
T: (01984) 618618
F: (01984) 618618
E: qocp@flaxpool.freeserve.
co.uk
I: www.flaxpool.freeserve.co.uk

CROYDE BAY
Devon

Croyde Bay Holiday Village (Unison) ★★★
Holiday Village
Braunton EX33 1QB
T: (01271) 890890
F: (01271) 890888
E: s.willis@unison.co.uk
I: www.croydeholidays.co.uk

Ruda Holiday Park ★★★★
Holiday, Touring and Camping Park
Rose Award
Croyde, Braunton EX33 1NY
T: 0870 420 2997 Et
(01271) 890671
E: enquiries@parkdeanholidays.
co.uk
I: www.parkdeanholidays.co.uk

CUBERT
Cornwall

Treworgans Holiday Park
★★★★
Holiday Park
Pennros Cottage, Newquay
TR8 5HH
T: (01637) 830200

DARTMOUTH
Devon

Hillfield Holiday Park
★★★★
Holiday Park
Hillfield, Dartmouth TQ6 0LX
T: (01803) 712322
F: (01803) 712322

DAWLISH
Devon

Cofton Country Holidays
★★★★
Holiday, Touring and Camping Park
Cofton, Exeter EX6 8RP
T: (01626) 890111
F: (01626) 891572
E: info@coftonholidays.co.uk
I: www.coftonholidays.co.uk

Dawlish Sands Holiday Park
★★★★
Holiday Park
Warren Road, Dawlish EX7 0PG
T: (01626) 862038
F: (01626) 866298

Golden Sands Holiday Park
★★★★
Holiday and Touring Park
Week Lane, Dawlish EX7 0LZ
T: (01626) 863099
F: (01626) 867149
E: info@goldensands.co.uk
I: www.goldensands.co.uk

Leadstone Camping ★★★
Touring and Camping Park
Warren Road, Dawlish EX7 0NG
T: (01626) 864411
F: (01626) 873833
E: info@leadstonecamping.
co.uk
I: www.leadstonecamping.co.uk

Oakcliff Holiday Park
★★★★
Holiday Park
Mount Pleasant Road, Dawlish
Warren, Dawlish EX7 0ND
T: (01626) 863347
F: (01626) 866636
E: info@oakcliff.co.uk
I: www.oakcliff.co.uk

Peppermint Park ★★★★
Holiday, Touring and Camping Park
Warren Road, Dawlish EX7 0PQ
T: (01626) 863436
F: (01626) 866482
I: www.peppermintpark.co.uk

Welcome Family Holiday Park ★★★★
Holiday Park
Rose Award
Welcome Family Holiday Park,
Warren Road, Dawlish Warren,
Dawlish EX7 0PH
T: (01626) 862070
F: (01626) 868988
E: fun@welcomefamily.co.uk
I: www.welcomefamily.co.uk

DOBWALLS
Cornwall

Hoburne Doublebois
★★★★
Holiday Park
Dobwalls, Liskeard PL14 6LD
T: (01579) 320049
F: (01579) 321415
E: hoburne.doublebois@
hoburne.com
I: www.hoburne.com

DONIFORD
Somerset

Doniford Bay Holiday Park
★★★★
Holiday Park
Watchet TA23 0TJ
T: (01984) 632423
F: (01984) 633649

Sunnybank Caravan Park
★★★★★
Holiday Park
Watchet TA23 0UD
T: (01984) 632237
F: (01984) 634834
E: mail@sunnybankcp.co.uk
I: sunnybankcp.co.uk

DORCHESTER
Dorset

Giants Head Caravan & Camping Park ★★
Touring and Camping Park
Old Sherborne Road, Dorchester
DT2 7TR
T: (01300) 341242
E: holidays@giantshead.co.uk
I: www.giantshead.co.uk

Morn Gate Caravan Park
★★★★
Holiday Park
Bridport Road, Dorchester
DT2 9DS
T: (01305) 889284
F: (01202) 669595
E: morngate@ukonline.co.uk
I: www.morngate.co.uk

DOUBLEBOIS
Cornwall

Pine Green Caravan and Camping Park ★★★★
Holiday, Touring and Camping Park
Liskeard PL14 6LE
T: (01579) 320183
E: mary.ruhleman@btinternet.com
I: www.pinegreenpark.co.uk

DREWSTEIGNTON
Devon

Clifford Bridge Park ★★★
Touring and Camping Park
Exeter EX6 6QE
T: (01647) 24226
F: (01647) 24116
E: info@clifford-bridge.co.uk
I: www.ukparks.co.uk/cliffordbridge

Woodland Springs Touring Park ★★★
Touring and Camping Park
Venton, Exeter EX6 6PG
T: (01647) 231695
F: (01647) 231695
E: enquiries@woodlandsprings.co.uk
I: www.woodlandsprings.co.uk

DULVERTON
Somerset

Exmoor House Caravan Club Site ★★★★
Touring Park
Dulverton TA22 9HL
T: (01398) 323268
I: www.caravanclub.co.uk

Lakeside Caravan Club Site ★★★★
Touring Park
Higher Grants, Dulverton TA22 9BE
T: (01398) 324068
I: www.caravanclub.co.uk

EAST WORLINGTON
Devon

Yeatheridge Farm Caravan Park ★★★★
Touring Park
Crediton EX17 4TN
T: (01884) 860330
F: (01884) 860330

EXFORD
Somerset

Westermill Farm ★★
Camping Park
Minehead TA24 7NJ
T: (01643) 831238
F: (01643) 831216
E: holidays@westermill-exmoor.co.uk
I: www.exmoorcamping.co.uk

EXMOUTH
Devon

Webbers Farm Caravan & Camping Park
Rating Applied For
Castle Lane, Woodbury, Exeter EX5 1EA
T: (01395) 232276
F: (01395) 233389
E: reception@webberspark.co.uk
I: www.webberspark.co.uk

FALMOUTH
Cornwall

Pennance Mill Farm Touring Park ★★
Touring Park
Maenporth Road, Falmouth TR11 5HJ
T: (01326) 317431
F: (01326) 317431
I: www.pennancemill.co.uk

FERNDOWN
Dorset

St Leonards Farm Caravan and Camping Park ★★★
Touring and Camping Park
St Leonards Farm Park, Ringwood Road, West Moors, Ferndown BH22 0AQ
T: (01202) 872637
F: (01202) 855683
E: james@love5.fsnet.co.uk
I: www.stleonardsfarm.biz

FIDDINGTON
Somerset

Mill Farm Caravan and Camping Park ★★★
Touring and Camping Park
Bridgwater TA5 1JQ
T: (01278) 732286

FOWEY
Cornwall

Penhale Caravan and Camping Park ★★★
Holiday, Touring and Camping Park
Penhale, Fowey PL23 1JU
T: (01726) 833425
F: (01726) 833425
E: info@penhale-fowey.co.uk
I: www.penhale-fowey.co.uk

GLASTONBURY
Somerset

The Old Oaks Touring Park ★★★★★
Touring and Camping Park
Wick, Glastonbury BA6 8JS
T: (01458) 831437
F: (01458) 833238
E: info@theoldoaks.co.uk
I: www.theoldoaks.co.uk

GOONHAVERN
Cornwall

Silverbow Park ★★★★★
Holiday Park
Truro TR4 9NX
T: (01872) 572347

GREAT TORRINGTON
Devon

Greenways Valley Holiday Park ★★★
Holiday, Touring and Camping Park
Great Torrington, Torrington EX38 7EW
T: (01805) 622153
F: (01805) 622144
E: enquiries@greenwaysvalley.co.uk
I: www.greenwaysvalley.co.uk

Smytham Manor Leisure ★★★
Holiday, Touring and Camping Park
Torrington EX38 8PU
T: (01805) 622110
F: (01805) 625451
E: info@smytham.fsnet.co.uk
I: www.smytham.co.uk

HAMWORTHY
Poole

Rockley Park Holiday Park ★★★★★
Holiday, Touring and Camping Park
Napier Road, Poole BH15 4LZ
T: (01202) 679393
F: (01202) 683159
E: enquiries@british-holidays.co.uk
I: www.british-holidays.co.uk/rockleypark

HAYLE
Cornwall

Beachside Holiday Park ★★★★
Holiday Park
Lethlean Lane, Phillack, Hayle TR27 5AW
T: (01736) 753080
F: (01736) 757252
E: reception@beachside.demon.co.uk
I: www.beachside.co.uk

Churchtown Farm Caravan & Camping Site ★★★
Touring Park
Churchtown Road, Hayle TR27 5BX
T: (01736) 753219
E: caravanning@churchtownfarmgwithian.fsnet.co.uk
I: www.churchtownfarm.org.uk

Riviere Sands Holiday Park ★★★
Holiday Park
Riviere Towans, Hayle TR27 5AX
T: (01736) 752132
F: (01736) 756368

St Ives Bay Holiday Park ★★★★
Holiday Park
73 Loggans Road, Loggans, Hayle TR27 5BH
T: (01736) 752274
F: (01736) 754523
E: stivesbay@bt.connect.com
I: www.stivesbay.co.uk

Toms Self-Catering Holidays ★★
Holiday Park
3A Riviere Towans, Hayle TR27 5AT
T: (01736) 756086
E: sales@tomsholidays.co.uk
I: www.tomsholidays.co.uk

HELSTON
Cornwall

Poldown Caravan Park ★★★★
Holiday and Touring Park
Poldown, Carleen, Helston TR13 9NN
T: (01326) 574560
F: (01326) 574560
E: poldown@poldown.co.uk
I: www.poldown.co.uk

Seaview Holiday Park ★★★
Holiday Park
Gwendreath, Helston TR12 7LZ
T: (01326) 290635
F: (01326) 290635
E: seaviewhp@btopenworld.com
I: www.seaviewcaravanpark.com

HIGHBRIDGE
Somerset

Greenacre Place Touring Caravan Park and Holiday Cottage ★★★★
Touring Park
Bristol Road, Edithmead, Highbridge TA9 4HA
T: (01278) 785227
F: (01278) 785227
E: sm.alderton@btopenworld.com
I: www.greenacreplace.com

HIGHCLIFFE
Dorset

Cobb's Holiday Park ★★★★
Holiday Park
32 Gordon Road, Highcliffe, Christchurch BH23 5HN
T: (01425) 273301
F: (01425) 276090

HOLTON HEATH
Dorset

Pear Tree Touring Park ★★★★★
Touring and Camping Park
Organford Road, Holton Heath, Poole BH16 6LA
T: (01202) 622434
E: info@visitpeartree.co.uk
I: www.visitpeartree.co.uk

Sandford Holiday Park ★★★★
Holiday, Touring and Camping Park
Organford Road, Poole BH16 6JZ
T: 0870 444 7774
F: (01392) 445202
E: bookings@weststarholidays.co.uk
I: www.weststarholidays.co.uk

Tanglewood Holiday Park Ltd ★★★★
Holiday Park
Organford Road, Poole BH16 6JY
T: (01202) 632618
F: (01202) 632008

HORN'S CROSS
Devon

Steart Farm Touring Park ★★★
Touring and Camping Park
Horns Cross, Bideford EX39 5DW
T: (01237) 431836
F: (01237) 431836
E: steart@tiscali.co.uk

HURN
Dorset

Longfield Caravan Park ★★
Touring Park
Matchams Lane, Christchurch BH23 6AW
T: (01202) 485214

Mount Pleasant Touring Park ★★★★★
Touring and Camping Park
Matchams Lane, Christchurch BH23 6AW
T: (01202) 475474
F: 0870 460 1701
E: enq@mount-pleasant-cc.co.uk
I: www.mount-pleasant-cc.co.uk

ILFRACOMBE
Devon

Beachside Holiday Park
★★★★★
Holiday Park
33 Beach Road, Hele, Ilfracombe
EX34 9QZ
T: (01271) 863006
F: (01271) 867296
E: enquiries@beachsidepark.
co.uk
I: www.beachsidepark.co.uk

**Hidden Valley Touring &
Camping Park** ★★★★
Touring and Camping Park
West Down, Ilfracombe
EX34 8NU
T: (01271) 813837
F: (01271) 814041
E: relax@hiddenvalleypark.com
I: www.hiddenvalleypark.com

IPPLEPEN
Devon

Ross Park ★★★★★
Touring Park
Moor Road, Newton Abbot
TQ12 5TT
T: (01803) 812983
F: (01803) 812983
E: enquiries@
rossparkcaravanpark.co.uk

Woodville Touring Park
★★★★
Touring Park
Totnes Road, Newton Abbot
TQ12 5TN
T: (01803) 812240
F: (01803) 813984
E: woodvillepark@lineone.net
I: www.caravan-sitefinder.
co.uk/sthwest/devon/woodville.
html

ISLES OF SCILLY
Isles of Scilly

St Martin's Campsite
★★★★
Camping Park
Middle Town, St Martin's
TR25 0QN
T: (01720) 422888
F: (01720) 422888
E: chris@stmartinscampsite.
freeserve.co.uk
I: www.stmartinscampsite.co.uk

KENTISBEARE
Devon

Forest Glade Holiday Park
★★★★
Holiday Park
Kentisbeare, Cullompton
EX15 2DT
T: (01404) 841381
F: (01404) 841593
E: nwellard@forest-glade.co.uk
I: www.forest-glade.co.uk

KEWSTOKE
North Somerset

Ardnave Holiday Park ★★★
Holiday Park
Crookes Lane, Weston-super-
Mare BS22 9XJ
T: (01934) 622319
F: (01934) 412741

Kewside Caravans ★★
Holiday Park
Royal Oak Stores, Crookes Lane,
Weston-super-Mare BS22 9XF
T: (01934) 623237

KINGSBRIDGE
Devon

**Challaborough Bay Holiday
Park** ★★★★
Holiday Park
Challaborough Beach,
Kingsbridge TQ7 4HU
T: 0870 420 2884
F: (0191) 2685986
E: enquiries@parkdeanholidays.
co.uk
I: www.parkdeanholidays.
co.uk/home-challaborough-bay.
aspx?Park=challaborough-bay

KINGTON LANGLEY
Wiltshire

Plough Lane Caravan Site
★★★★★
Touring Park
Plough Lane, Chippenham
SN15 5PS
T: (01249) 750795
F: (01249) 750795
E: ploughlane@lineone.net
I: www.ploughlane.co.uk

LACOCK
Wiltshire

Piccadilly Caravan Park
★★★★★
Touring and Camping Park
Folly Lane (West), Lacock,
Chippenham SN15 2LP
T: (01249) 730260
E: piccadillylacock@aol.com

LANDRAKE
Cornwall

**Dolbeare Caravan and
Camping Park** ★★★★
Touring and Camping Park
St Ive Road, Saltash PL12 5AF
T: (01752) 851332
F: (01752) 851332
E: dolbeare@btopenworld.com
I: www.dolbeare.co.uk

LANDS END
Cornwall

**Cardinney Caravan and
Camping Park** ★★★
Touring Park
Penberth Valley, St Buryan,
Penzance TR19 6HJ
T: (01736) 810880
F: (01736) 810998
E: cardinney@btinternet.com
I: www.
cardinney-camping-park.co.uk

LANGPORT
Somerset

**Bowdens Crest Caravan and
Camping Park** ★★★
*Holiday, Touring and Camping
Park*
Bowdens, Langport TA10 0DD
T: (01458) 250553
F: (01458) 253360
E: bowcrest@btconnect.com
I: www.Bowdenscrest.co.uk

LANGTON MATRAVERS
Dorset

**Tom's Field Campsite &
Shop** ★★★
Camping Park
Tom's Field Road, Langton
Matravers, Swanage BH19 3HN
T: (01929) 427110
F: (01929) 427110
E: tomsfield@hotmail.com
I: www.tomsfieldcamping.co.uk

LANIVET
Cornwall

Kernow Caravan Park
Rating Applied For
Clann Lane, Bodmin PL30 5HD
T: (01208) 831343

LANTEGLOS
Cornwall

**Penmarlam Caravan and
Camping Park**
Rating Applied For
Fowey PL23 1LZ
T: (01726) 870088
F: (01726) 870082
E: info@penmarlampark.co.uk

LELANT DOWNS
Cornwall

**Sunny Meadow Holiday
Park** ★★★
Holiday Park
Hayle TR27 6LL
T: (01736) 752243
E: sunnymeadowcornwall@
hotmail.com
I: www.holiday-park-cornwall.
com

LOOE
Cornwall

Looe Bay Holiday Park
★★★★
Holiday Park
Rose Award
St Martin, Looe PL13 1NX
T: 0870 444 7774
F: (01392) 445202
E: admin@weststarholidays.
co.uk
I: www.weststarholidays.co.uk

**Polborder House Caravan
and Camping Park** ★★★★
Holiday and Touring Park
Bucklawren Road, Looe
PL13 1QR
T: (01503) 240265
E: rlf.polborder@virgin.net
I: www.peaceful-polborder.co.uk

Seaview Holiday Village
★★★★
Holiday Park
Polperro Road, Looe PL13 2JE
T: (01503) 272335
F: (01503) 272171

Tencreek Holiday Park
★★★★
Holiday Park
Polperro Road, Looe PL13 2JR
T: (01503) 262447
F: (01503) 262760
E: reception@tencreek.co.uk
I: www.dolphinholidays.co.uk

**Tregoad Park Quality
Touring Site** ★★★
Touring and Camping Park
St Martin, Looe PL13 1PB
T: (01503) 262718
F: (01503) 264777
E: tregoadfarmccp@aol.com
I: www.cornwall-online.
co.uk/tregoad

LOWER METHERELL
Cornwall

**Trehorner Farm Holiday
Park** ★★★★
Holiday Park
Callington PL17 8BJ
T: (01579) 351122
F: (01579) 351122

LUXULYAN
Cornwall

Croft Farm Holiday Park
★★★★
*Holiday, Touring and Camping
Park*
Luxulyan PL30 5EQ
T: (01726) 850228
F: (01726) 850498
E: lynpick@ukonline.co.uk
I: www.croftfarm.co.uk

LYDFORD
Devon

**Camping & Caravanning
Club Site - Lydford** ★★★★
Touring and Camping Park
Okehampton EX20 4BE
T: (01822) 820275
I: www.
campingandcaravanningclub.
co.uk

LYME REGIS
Dorset

Shrubbery Caravan Park
★★★
Touring and Camping Park
Rousdon, Lyme Regis DT7 3XW
T: (01297) 442227

LYNTON
Devon

**Camping & Caravanning
Club Site - Lynton** ★★★
Touring Park
Caffyn's Cross, Lynton EX35 6JS
T: (01598) 752379
I: www.
campingandcaravanningclub.
co.uk

**Channel View Caravan and
Camping Park** ★★★★
Holiday and Touring Park
Manor Farm, Lynton EX35 6LD
T: (01598) 753349
F: (01598) 752777
E: channelview@bushinternet.
com
I: www.channel-view.co.uk

MALMESBURY
Wiltshire

**Burton Hill Caravan and
Camping Park** ★★
Touring and Camping Park
Arches Lane, Malmesbury
SN16 0EH
T: (01666) 826880
F: (01666) 826880
E: stay@burtonhill.co.uk
I: www.burtonhill.co.uk

MARAZION
Cornwall

Mounts Bay Caravan Park
★★★★★
Holiday Park
Green Lane, Marazion TR17 0HQ
T: (01736) 710307
E: reception@
mountsbay-caravanpark.co.uk
I: www.mountsbay-caravanpark.
co.uk

MARK
Somerset
Coombes Cider Mill Caravan and Camping Park ★★★
Touring and Camping Park
Japonica Farm, The Causeway, Mark, Highbridge TA9 4QD
T: (01278) 641265
I: www.coombescidermill.co.uk

MARLDON
Devon
Widend Touring Park ★★★★
Touring Park
Totnes Road, Paignton TQ3 1RT
T: (01803) 550116
F: (01803) 550116

MARTOCK
Somerset
Southfork Caravan Park
Rating Applied For
Parrett Works, Martock
TA12 6AE
T: (01935) 825661
F: (01935) 825122
E: southfork.caravans@virgin.net
I: www.ukparks.co.uk/southfork

MAWGAN PORTH
Cornwall
Sun Haven Valley Caravan Park & Camping Park ★★★★★
Holiday and Camping Park
Newquay TR8 4BQ
T: (01637) 860373
F: (01637) 860373
E: traceyhealey@hotmail.com
I: www.sunhavenvalley.co.uk

MEVAGISSEY
Cornwall
Sea View International ★★★★★
Holiday, Touring and Camping Park
St Austell PL26 6LL
T: (01726) 843425
F: (01726) 843358
E: holidays@seaviewinternational.com
I: www.seaviewinternational.com

MINEHEAD
Somerset
Beeches Holiday Park ★★★★
Holiday Park
Rose Award
Blue Anchor Bay, Minehead
TA24 6JW
T: (01984) 640391
F: (01984) 640361
E: info@beeches-park.co.uk
I: www.beeches-park.co.uk

Camping and Caravanning Club Site Minehead ★★★★
Camping Park
Hill Road, North Hill, Minehead
TA24 5SF
T: (01643) 704138
I: www.campingandcaravanning.co.uk

MODBURY
Devon
Camping & Caravanning Club Site - California Cross ★★★★
Touring and Camping Park
Ivybridge PL21 0SG
T: (01548) 821297
I: www.campingandcaravanning.co.uk

Pennymoor Camping and Caravan Park ★★★★
Holiday, Touring and Camping Park
Ivybridge PL21 0SB
T: (01548) 830542
F: (01548) 830542
I: www.pennymoor-camping.co.uk

MORETON
Dorset
Moreton Camping & Caravanning Club Site ★★★★★
Touring and Camping Park
Station Road, Dorchester
DT2 8BB
T: (01305) 853801
I: www.campingandcaravanning.co.uk

MORETON-IN-MARSH
Gloucestershire
Moreton-in-Marsh Caravan Club Site ★★★★★
Touring and Camping Park
Bourton Road, Moreton-in-Marsh GL56 0BT
T: (01608) 650519
I: www.caravanclub.co.uk

MORTEHOE
Devon
Easewell Farm Holiday Park & Golf Club ★★★★
Holiday, Touring and Camping Park
Woolacombe EX34 7EH
T: (01271) 870343
F: 0727 1 870089
I: www.woolacombe.com

North Morte Farm Caravan and Camping Park ★★★★
Holiday, Touring and Camping Park
North Morte Road, Mortehoe, Woolacombe EX34 7EG
T: (01271) 870381
F: (01271) 870115
E: info@northmortefarm.co.uk
I: www.northmortefarm.co.uk

Twitchen Parc ★★★★
Holiday Park
Mortehoe Station Road, Woolacombe EX34 7ES
T: (01271) 870343
F: (01271) 870089
E: goodtimes@woolacombe.com
I: www.woolacombe.com

Warcombe Farm Camping Park ★★★★
Touring and Camping Park
Station Road, Woolacombe
EX34 7EJ
T: (01271) 870690
F: (01271) 871070

MUCHELNEY
Somerset
Thorney Lakes and Caravan Park ★★★
Touring and Camping Park
Thorney West Farm, Langport
TA10 0DW
T: (01458) 250811
E: enquiries@thorneylakes.co.uk
I: www.thorneylakes.co.uk

MULLION
Cornwall
Criggan Mill ★★★★★
Holiday Park
Helston TR12 7EU
T: (01326) 240496
F: 0870 164 0549
E: info@crigganmill.co.uk
I: www.crigganmill.co.uk

Mullion Holiday Park ★★★★
Holiday Park
Helston TR12 7LJ
T: 0870 444 5344
F: (01392) 445202
E: bookings@weststarholidays.co.uk
I: www.weststarholidays.co.uk

NETHER WESTCOTE
Gloucestershire
The New Inn Caravan & Camping Site ★
Touring and Camping Park
Oxford OX7 6SD
T: (01993) 830827

NEWENT
Gloucestershire
Pelerine Caravan and Camping Park
Rating Applied For
Ford House Road, Newent
GL18 1LQ
T: (01531) 822761
E: pelerine@hotmail.com
I: www.newent.biz

NEWQUAY
Cornwall
Crantock Beach Holiday Park ★★★★
Holiday Park
Newquay TR8 5RH
T: 0870 420 2884
F: (0191) 2685986
E: enquiries@parkdeanholidays.co.uk
I: www.parkdeanholidays.co.uk

Hendra Holiday Park ★★★★
Holiday Park
Lane, Newquay TR8 4NY
T: (01637) 875778
F: (01637) 879017
E: hendra.cornwall@dial.pipex.com
I: www.hendra-holidays.com

Holywell Bay Holiday Park ★★★★
Holiday Park
Holywell Bay, Newquay TR8 5PR
T: 0870 420 2997 &
(01637) 871111
E: enquiries@parkdeanholidays.co.uk
I: www.parkdeanholidays.co.uk

Mawgan Porth Holiday Park ★★★★★
Holiday Park
Mawgan Porth, Newquay
TR8 4BD
T: (01637) 860322
E: mawganporthhp@fsbdial.co.uk
I: www.mawganporth.co.uk

Nancolleth Caravan Gardens ★★★★
Holiday Park
Rose Award
Newquay TR8 4PN
T: (01872) 510236
F: (01872) 510948
E: nancolleth@summercourt.freeserve.co.uk
I: www.nancolleth.co.uk

Newperran Holiday Park ★★★★
Holiday Park
Newquay TR8 5QJ
T: (01872) 572407
F: (01872) 571254
E: holidays@newperran.co.uk
I: www.newperran.co.uk

Newquay Holiday Park ★★★★
Holiday Park
Newquay TR8 4HS
T: 0870 420 2997 &
(01637) 871111
E: enquiries@parkdeanholidays.co.uk
I: www.parkdeanholidays.co.uk

Porth Beach Tourist Park ★★★★
Touring Park
Alexandra Road, Porth, Newquay
TR7 3NH
T: (01637) 876531
F: (01637) 871227
E: info@porthbeach.co.uk
I: www.porthbeach.co.uk

Resparva House Touring Park ★★★★
Touring Park
Chapel Town, Newquay TR8 5AH
T: (01872) 510332
E: touringpark@resparva.co.uk
I: www.resparva.co.uk

Riverside Holiday Park ★★★
Holiday Park
Gwillis Lane, Newquay TR8 4PE
T: (01637) 873617
F: (01637) 877051
E: info@riversideholidaypark.co.uk
I: www.riversideholidaypark.co.uk

Trekenning Tourist Park ★★★★
Touring Park
St Columb Major, Newquay
TR8 4JF
T: (01637) 880462
F: (01637) 880500
E: holidays@trekenning.co.uk
I: www.trekenning.co.uk

Treloy Tourist Park ★★★★
Touring and Camping Park
Newquay TR8 4JN
T: (01637) 872063 & 876279
E: holidays@treloy.co.uk
I: www.treloy.co.uk

Trenance Holiday Park
★★★
Holiday Park
Edgcumbe Avenue, Newquay
TR7 2JY
T: (01637) 873447
F: (01637) 852677
E: enquiries@
trenanceholidaypark.co.uk
I: trenanceholidaypark.co.uk/

Trethiggey Touring Park
★★★★
Touring Park
Newquay TR8 4QR
T: (01637) 877672
F: (01637) 879706
E: enquiries@trethiggey.co.uk
I: www.trethiggey.co.uk

**Trevella Caravan and
Camping Park** ★★★★★
*Holiday, Touring and Camping
Park*
Newquay TR8 5EW
T: (01637) 830308
F: (01637) 830155
E: Trevellapark@aol.com
I: www.trevella.co.uk

Trevornick Holiday Park
★★★★★
Holiday Park
Newquay TR8 5PW
T: (01637) 830531
F: (01637) 831000
E: info@trevornick.co.uk
I: www.trevornick.co.uk

NEWTON ABBOT
Devon

Dornafield ★★★★★
Touring Park
Newton Abbot TQ12 6DD
T: (01803) 812732
F: (01803) 812032
E: enquiries@dornafield.com
I: www.dornafield.com

NORTH PETHERTON
Somerset

**Somerset View Caravan
Park** ★★★
Touring and Camping Park
A38 Taunton Road, Bridgwater
TA6 6NW
T: (01278) 661294
E: someview@somerset-view.
co.uk
I: www.somerset-view.co.uk

OARE
Wiltshire

Hill-View Park ★★★
Touring and Camping Park
Marlborough SN8 4JE
T: (01672) 563151

OKEHAMPTON
Devon

**Dartmoor View Holiday
Park** ★★★★★
Holiday and Touring Park
Okehampton EX20 2QL
T: (01647) 231545
F: (01647) 231654
E: jo@dartmoorview.co.uk
I: www.dartmoorview.co.uk

ORCHESTON
Wiltshire

Stonehenge Touring Park
★★★
Touring and Camping Park
Orcheston, Salisbury SP3 4SH
T: (01980) 620304
E: stonehengetouringpark@
supanet.com
I: stonehengetouringpark.
supanet.com

ORGANFORD
Dorset

**Organford Manor Caravans
& Holidays** ★★★
Touring and Camping Park
The Lodge, Organford, Poole
BH16 6ES
T: (01202) 622202
F: (01202) 623278
E: organford@lds.co.uk

OSMINGTON
Dorset

White Horse Holiday Park
★★★
Holiday Park
Osmington Hill, Weymouth
DT3 6ED
T: (01305) 832164
F: (01305) 832164
E: enquiries@whitehorsepark.
co.uk
I: www.whitehorsepark.co.uk

OWERMOIGNE
Dorset

Sandyholme Holiday Park
★★★★
*Holiday, Touring and Camping
Park*
Moreton Road, Owermoigne,
Dorchester DT2 8HZ
T: (01305) 852677
F: (01305) 854677
E: smeatons@sandyholme.co.uk
I: www.sandyholme.co.uk

PADSTOW
Cornwall

Carnevas Farm Holiday Park
★★★★
*Holiday, Touring and Camping
Park*
Carnevas Farm, St Merryn,
Padstow PL28 8PN
T: (01841) 520230
F: (01841) 520230

The Laurels Holiday Park
★★★★
Touring and Camping Park
Whitecross, Wadebridge
PL27 7JQ
T: (01208) 813341
F: (01208) 816590
E: anicholson@
thelaurelsholidaypark.co.uk
I: www.thelaurelsholidaypark.
co.uk

**Mother Ivey's Bay Caravan
Park** ★★★★
*Holiday, Touring and Camping
Park*
Trevose, Padstow PL28 8SL
T: (01841) 520990
F: (01841) 520550
E: info@motheriveysbay.com
I: www.motheriveysbay.com

Trerethern Touring Park
★★★★
Touring and Camping Park
Trerethern Touring Park,
Padstow PL28 8LE
T: (01841) 532061
F: (01841) 532061
E: camping.trerethern@
btinternet.com
I: www.trerethern.co.uk

PAIGNTON
Torbay

Ashvale Holiday Park
★★★★
Holiday Park
Goodrington Road, Paignton
TQ4 7JD
T: (01803) 843887
F: (01803) 845427
E: info@beverley-holidays.co.uk
I: www.beverley-holidays.co.uk

Beverley Park ★★★★★
Holiday and Touring Park
Rose Award
Goodrington Road, Paignton
TQ4 7JE
T: (01803) 843887
F: (01803) 845427
E: info@beverley-holidays.co.uk
I: www.beverley-holidays.co.uk

Bona Vista Holiday Park
★★★★
Holiday Park
Totnes Road, Paignton TQ4 7PY
T: (01803) 551971
E: bonavista@tiscali.co.uk
I: www.bona-vista.co.uk

**Byslades International
Touring Park** ★★★★
Touring and Camping Park
Byslades, Paignton TQ4 7PY
T: (01803) 555072
F: (01803) 555669
E: info@byslades.co.uk
I: www.byslades.co.uk

**Higher Well Farm Holiday
Park** ★★★★
*Holiday, Touring and Camping
Park*
Waddeton Road, Stoke Gabriel,
Totnes TQ9 6RN
T: (01803) 782289
E: higherwell@talk21.com
I: www.ukparks.co.uk/higherwell

Hoburne Torbay ★★★★
Holiday and Touring Park
Rose Award
Grange Road, Paignton TQ4 7JP
T: (01803) 558010
F: (01803) 696286
E: enquiries@hoburne.com
I: www.hoburne.com

Marine Park Holiday Centre
★★★★
Holiday and Touring Park
Grange Road, Paignton TQ4 7JR
T: (01803) 843887
F: (01803) 845427
E: info@beverley-holidays.co.uk
I: www.beverley-holidays.co.uk

Waterside Holiday Park
★★★★
Holiday Park
Three Beaches, Dartmouth Road,
Paignton TQ4 6NS
T: (01803) 842400
F: (01803) 844876
I: www.watersidepark.co.uk

Whitehill Holiday Park
★★★★
*Holiday, Touring and Camping
Park*
Stoke Road, Paignton TQ4 7PF
T: (01803) 782338
F: (01803) 782722
E: info@whitehill-park.co.uk
I: www.whitehill-park.co.uk

PAR
Cornwall

**Par Sands Holiday Park
Limited** ★★★★
*Holiday, Touring and Camping
Park*
Par Beach, Par PL24 2AS
T: (01726) 812868
F: (01726) 817899
E: holidays@parsands.co.uk
I: www.parsands.co.uk

PELYNT
Cornwall

Trelay Farm Park ★★★★
Holiday and Touring Park
Looe PL13 2JX
T: (01503) 220900
F: (01503) 220900

PENTEWAN
Cornwall

**Pentewan Sands Holiday
Park** ★★★★
*Holiday, Touring and Camping
Park*
St Austell PL26 6BT
T: (01726) 843485
F: (01726) 844142
E: info@pentewan.co.uk
I: www.pentewan.co.uk

PENZANCE
Cornwall

**Tower Park Caravans and
Camping** ★★★
Holiday and Touring Park
St Buryan, Penzance TR19 6BZ
T: (01736) 810286
F: (01736) 810286
E: enquiries@
towerparkcamping.co.uk
I: www.towerparkcamping.co.uk

PERRANPORTH
Cornwall

**Perran Sands Holiday
Centre Haven Holidays**
★★★
Holiday Park
Perran Sands, Perranporth
TR6 0AQ
T: 0870 405 0144
F: (01872) 571158
E: lisa.spickett@bourne-leisure.
co.uk
I: www.Haven-Holidays.
co.uk/perransands

PERROTTS BROOK
Gloucestershire

Mayfield Touring Park
★★★★
Touring Park
Cheltenham Road, Cirencester
GL7 7BH
T: (01285) 831301
E: Mayfield-park@cirencester.
fsbusiness.co.uk
I: www.mayfieldpark.co.uk

POLGOOTH
Cornwall

Saint Margaret's Holiday Bungalows ★★★★★
Holiday Park
Tregongeeves Lane, St Austell
PL26 7AX
T: (01726) 74283
F: (01726) 71680
E: reception@
stmargaretsholidays.co.uk
I: www.stmargaretsholidays.
co.uk

POLRUAN-BY-FOWEY
Cornwall

Polruan Holidays (Camping & Caravanning) ★★★★
Holiday, Touring and Camping Park
Townsend, Polruan, Fowey
PL23 1QH
T: (01726) 870263
F: (01726) 870263
E: polholiday@aol.com

POLZEATH
Cornwall

Polzeath Beach Holiday Park
Rating Applied For
Wadebridge PL27 6ST
T: (01208) 863320
F: (01208) 863320

Valley Caravan Park ★★
Holiday Park
Polzeath, Wadebridge PL27 6SS
T: (01208) 862391
F: (01208) 869231
E: valleypark@tiscali.co.uk
I: www.valleycaravanpark.co.uk

POOLE
Poole

Beacon Hill Touring Park ★★★
Touring and Camping Park
Blandford Road North, Nr Lytchett Minster, Poole
BH16 6AB
T: (01202) 631631
F: (01202) 625749
E: bookings@
beaconhilltouringpark.co.uk
I: www.beaconhilltouringpark.
co.uk

PORLOCK
Somerset

Burrowhayes Farm Caravan and Camping Site and Riding Stables ★★★★
Holiday, Touring and Camping Park
West Luccombe, Minehead
TA24 8HT
T: (01643) 862463
E: info@burrowhayes.co.uk
I: www.burrowhayes.co.uk

Porlock Caravan Park ★★★★
Holiday, Touring and Camping Park
Rose Award
Highbank, Minehead TA24 8ND
T: (01643) 862269
F: (01643) 862239
E: info@porlockcaravanpark.
co.uk
I: www.porlockcaravanpark.
co.uk

PORTESHAM
Dorset

Portesham Dairy Farm Camp Site ★★★
Touring and Camping Park
7 Bramdon Lane, Weymouth
DT3 4HG
T: (01305) 871297
F: (01305) 871297
E: malcolm.doble@talk21.com

PORTHTOWAN
Cornwall

Rose Hill Touring Park ★★★★★
Touring Park
Truro TR4 8AR
T: (01209) 890802
E: reception@rosehillcamping.
co.uk
I: www.rosehillcamping.co.uk

PORTLAND
Dorset

Cove Holiday Park ★★★★★
Holiday Park
Pennsylvania Road, Portland
DT5 1HU
T: (01305) 821286
F: (01305) 823224
E: coveholidaypark@onetel.net.
uk

PORTREATH
Cornwall

Cambrose Touring Park ★★★
Touring Park
Portreath Road, Cambrose, Redruth TR16 4HT
T: (01209) 890747
F: (01209) 891665
E: cambrosetouringpark@
supanet.com
I: www.cambrosetouringpark.
co.uk

Tehidy Holiday Park ★★★★
Holiday Park
Harris Mill, Redruth TR16 4JQ
T: (01209) 216489
F: (01209) 216489
E: holiday@tehidy.co.uk
I: www.tehidy.co.uk

PRAA SANDS
Cornwall

Lower Pentreath Caravan and Camping ★★★
Holiday, Touring and Camping Park
Lower Pentreath Farm, Penzance
TR20 9TL
T: (01736) 763221
E: andrew.wearne@tinyworld.
co.uk

PRESTON
Dorset

Seaview Holiday Park ★★★
Holiday, Touring and Camping Park
Weymouth DT3 6DZ
T: (01305) 833037
F: (01305) 833169
I: www.havenholidays.com

Weymouth Bay Holiday Park ★★★★
Holiday, Touring and Camping Park
Preston Road, Weymouth
DT3 6BQ
T: (01305) 832271
F: (01305) 835101
I: www.havenholidays.com

RATTERY
Devon

Edeswell Farm ★★★
Holiday Park
South Brent TQ10 9LN
T: (01364) 72177
F: (01364) 72177
E: welcome@edeswellfarm.
co.uk
I: www.edeswellfarm.co.uk

REDHILL
North Somerset

Brook Lodge Farm Touring Caravan & Tent Park ★★★
Touring and Camping Park
Cowslip Green, Bristol BS40 5RB
T: (01934) 862311
F: (01934) 862311
E: brooklodgefarm@aol.com
I: www.brooklodgefarm.com

REDRUTH
Cornwall

Lanyon Holiday Park ★★★★
Holiday Park
Loscombe Lane, Four Lanes, Redruth TR16 6LP
T: (01209) 313474
F: (01209) 313422
E: jamierielly@btconnect.com
I: www.lanyonholidaypark.co.uk

RELUBBUS
Cornwall

River Valley Country Park ★★★★★
Holiday Park
Rose Award
Relubbus, Penzance TR20 9ER
T: (01736) 763398
F: (01736) 763398
E: rivervalley@surfbay.dircon.
co.uk
I: www.rivervalley.co.uk

RODNEY STOKE
Somerset

Bucklegrove Caravan & Camping Park ★★★★
Holiday and Camping Park
Wells Road, Cheddar BS27 3UZ
T: (01749) 870261
F: (01749) 870101
E: info@bucklegrove.co.uk
I: www.bucklegrove.co.uk

ROSUDGEON
Cornwall

Kenneggy Cove Holiday Park ★★★★
Holiday Park
Rose Award
Higher Kenneggy, Penzance
TR20 9AU
T: (01736) 763453
E: enquiries@kenneggycove.
co.uk
I: www.kenneggycove.co.uk

ROUSDON
Devon

Pinewood Homes ★★★★★
Holiday Park
Sidmouth Road, Lyme Regis
DT7 3RD
T: (01297) 22055
E: info@pinewood.uk.net
I: www.pinewood.uk.net

Westhayes Caravan Park ★★★★
Holiday Park
Sidmouth Road, Lyme Regis
DT7 3RD
T: (01297) 23456
F: (01297) 625079

RUAN MINOR
Cornwall

Sea Acres Holiday Park ★★★★
Holiday Park
Kennack Sands, Ruan Minor, Helston TR12 7LT
T: 0870 420 2997 &
(01326) 290064
E: enquiries@parkdeanholidays.
co.uk
I: www.parkdeanholidays.co.uk

Silver Sands Holiday Park ★★★
Holiday and Touring Park
Gwendreath, Kennack Sands, Ruan Minor, Helston TR12 7LZ
T: (01326) 290631
F: (01326) 290631
E: enquiries@
silversandsholidaypark.co.uk
I: www.silversandsholidaypark.
co.uk

ST AGNES
Cornwall

Beacon Cottage Farm Touring Park ★★★★
Touring Park
Beacon Drive, St Agnes TR5 0NU
T: (01872) 552347
E: beaconcottagefarm@lineone.
net
I: www.
beaconcottagefarmholidays.
co.uk

Troytown Farm Campsite ★★★
Camping Park
St Agnes TR22 0PL
T: (01720) 422360
E: troytown@talk21.com
I: www.st-agnes-scilly.org

ST AUSTELL
Cornwall

Carlyon Bay Caravan & Camping Park ★★★★★
Touring and Camping Park
Cypress Avenue, St Austell
PL25 3RE
T: (01726) 812735
F: (01726) 815496
E: holidays@carlyonbay.net
I: www.carlyonbay.net

Duporth Holiday Park ★★★★
Holiday Park
Rose Award
St Austell PL26 6AJ
T: (01726) 65511
F: (01726) 68497
E: reception@duporth.co.uk
I: www.dolphinholidays.co.uk

River Valley Holiday Park
★★★★★
Holiday, Touring and Camping Park
Rose Award
Pentewan Road, London Apprentice, St Austell PL26 7AP
T: (01726) 73533
F: (01726) 73533
E: river.valley@tesco.net
I: www.cornwall-holidays.co.uk

Sun Valley Holiday Park
★★★★★
Holiday Park
Rose Award
Pentewan Road, St Austell PL26 6DJ
T: (01726) 843266
F: (01726) 843266
E: reception@
sunvalley-holidays.co.uk
I: www.sunvalley-holidays.co.uk

Trewhiddle Holiday Estate
★★★★
Holiday Park
Trewhiddle, St Austell PL26 7AD
T: (01726) 879420
F: (01726) 879421
E: dmcclelland@btconnect.com
I: www.trewhiddle.co.uk

ST BURYAN
Cornwall

Camping and Caravanning Club Site Sennen Cove
★★★★
Touring Park
Higher Tregiffian Farm, St Buryan, Penzance TR19 6JB
T: (01736) 871588
I: www.
campingandcaravanningclub.
co.uk

ST COLUMB MAJOR
Cornwall

Tregatillian Holiday Park
★★★★
Holiday Park
St Columb TR9 6JH
T: (01637) 880482
F: (01637) 880482
E: tregatillian@fsbdial.co.uk
I: www.chycor.
co.uk/parks/tregatillian

ST EWE
Cornwall

Heligan Woods Caravan & Camping Park ★★★★
Holiday, Touring and Camping Park
St Austell PL26 6EL
T: (01726) 843485
F: (01726) 844142
E: info@pentewan.co.uk
I: www.pentewan.co.uk

ST GENNYS
Cornwall

Camping and Caravanning Club Site ★★★★
Touring and Camping Park
Gillards Moor, St Gennys, Bude EX23 0BG
T: (01840) 230650
I: www.
campingandcaravanningclub.
co.uk

ST HILARY
Cornwall

Wayfarers Caravan and Camping Park ★★★★
Touring Park
Relubbus Lane, St Hilary, Penzance TR20 9EF
T: (01736) 763326
E: wayfarers@eurobell.co.uk
I: www.wayfarerspark.co.uk

ST IVES
Cornwall

Ayr Holiday Park ★★★★
Holiday Park
St Ives TR26 1EJ
T: (01736) 795855
F: (01736) 798797
E: recept@ayrholidaypark.co.uk
I: www.ayrholidaypark.co.uk

Little Trevarrack Touring Park ★★★★
Touring Park
Laity Lane, St Ives TR26 3HW
T: (01736) 797580
F: (01736) 797580
E: littletrevarrack@hotmail.com
I: www.littletrevarrack.com

Polmanter Tourist Park
★★★★★
Touring Park
Halsetown, St Ives TR26 3LX
T: (01736) 795640
F: (01736) 793607
E: reception@polmanter.com
I: www.polmanter.com

Trevalgan Touring Park
Rating Applied For
Trevalgan Farm, St Ives TR26 3BJ
T: (01736) 796433
F: (01736) 796433
E: camping@
trevalganholidayfarm.co.uk
I: www.trevalganholidayfarm.
co.uk

ST JUST-IN-PENWITH
Cornwall

Roselands Caravan Park
★★★
Holiday Park
Dowran, St Just, Penzance TR19 7RS
T: (01736) 788571
E: camping@roseland84.
freeserve.co.uk
I: www.roselands.co.uk

ST JUST IN ROSELAND
Cornwall

Trethem Mill Touring Park
★★★★★
Touring Park
St Just in Roseland, Nr St Mawes, Truro TR2 5JF
T: (01872) 580504
F: (01872) 580968
E: reception@trethem.com
I: www.trethem.com

ST LEONARDS
Dorset

Forest Edge Touring Park
★★★★
Touring and Camping Park
229 Ringwood Road, St Leonards, Ringwood BH24 2SD
T: (01590) 648331
F: (01590) 645610
E: holidays@shorefield.co.uk
I: www.shorefield.co.uk

Oakdene Forest Park
★★★★
Holiday, Touring and Camping Park
St Leonards, Ringwood BH24 2RZ
T: (01590) 648331
F: (01590) 645610
E: holidays@shorefield.co.uk
I: www.shorefield.co.uk

ST MERRYN
Cornwall

Trethias Farm Caravan Park
★★★
Touring Park
Trethias, St Merryn, Padstow PL28 8PL
T: (01841) 520323
F: (01841) 520055

Trevean Farm ★★★
Touring and Camping Park
St Merryn, Padstow PL28 8PR
T: (01841) 520772
F: (01841) 520722

ST MINVER
Cornwall

Little Dinham Woodland Caravan Park ★★★
Holiday Park
Wadebridge PL27 6RH
T: (01208) 812538
E: littledinham@hotmail.com
I: www.littledinham.co.uk

St Minver Holiday Park
★★★★
Holiday, Touring and Camping Park
Rose Award
Wadebridge PL27 6RR
T: 0870 420 2884
F: (01208) 268 5986
E: enquiries@parkdeanholidays.
co.uk
I: www.parkdeanholidays.co.uk

ST STEPHEN
Cornwall

Court Farm Caravan and Camping ★★★
Touring Park
St Stephen, St Austell PL26 7LE
T: (01726) 823684
F: (01726) 823684
E: truscott@ctfarm.freeserve.
co.uk
I: www.courtfarmcornwall.co.uk

ST TUDY
Cornwall

Hengar Manor ★★★★★
Holiday Park
St Tudy, Bodmin PL30 3PL
T: (01208) 850382
F: (01208) 850722
E: holidays@hengarmanor.co.uk
I: www.hengarmanor.co.uk

Michaelstow Manor Holiday Park ★★★★
Holiday Park
Michaelstow, St Tudy, Bodmin PL30 3PB
T: (01208) 850244
F: (01208) 851420
E: michaelstow@eclipse.co.uk
I: www.michaelstow-holidays.
co.uk

SALCOMBE
Devon

Bolberry House Farm ★★★
Touring and Camping Park
Bolberry, Kingsbridge TQ7 3DY
T: (01548) 561251
F: (01548) 561251
E: bolberry.house@virgin.net
I: www.bolberryparks.co.uk

Higher Rew Touring Caravan & Camping Park
★★★★
Touring and Camping Park
Malborough, Kingsbridge TQ7 3DW
T: (01548) 842681
F: (01548) 843681
E: enquiries@higherrew.co.uk
I: www.higherrew.co.uk

Karrageen Caravan and Camping Park ★★★★
Touring and Camping Park
Bolberry, Malborough, Kingsbridge TQ7 3EN
T: (01548) 561230
F: (01548) 560192
E: phil@karrageen.co.uk
I: www.karrageen.co.uk

SALCOMBE REGIS
Devon

Kings Down Tail Caravan & Camping Park ★★★★
Touring Park
Sidmouth EX10 0PD
T: (01297) 680313
F: (01297) 680313
I: www.uk.parks.
co.uk/kingsdowntail

SALISBURY
Wiltshire

Camping and Caravanning Club Site Salisbury ★★★★
Touring and Camping Park
Hudson's Field, Castle Road, Salisbury SP1 3RR
T: (01722) 320713
I: www.
campingandcaravanningclub.
co.uk

SANDY BAY
Devon

Devon Cliffs Holiday Park
★★★★
Holiday Park
Exmouth EX8 5BT
T: (01395) 226226
F: (01395) 223111
I: www.havenholiday.com/
devoncliffs

SEATON
Devon

Axe Vale Caravan Park
★★★
Holiday Park
Colyford Road, Seaton EX12 2DF
T: (01297) 21342
F: (01297) 21712
E: info@axevale.co.uk
I: www.axevale.co.uk

Lyme Bay Holiday Village
★★★
Holiday Village
87 Harbour Road, Seaton EX12 2NE
T: (01297) 21816
F: (01297) 24688

SEEND
Wiltshire

Camping and Caravanning Club Site Devizes ★★★★★
Touring and Camping Park
Spout Lane, Melksham
SN12 6RN
T: (01380) 828839
I: www.
campingandcaravanningclub.
co.uk

SENNEN
Cornwall

Sea View Holiday Park ★★
Holiday Park
Penzance TR19 7AD
T: (01736) 871266
F: (01736) 871190
I: www.seaview.org.co.uk

SHALDON
Devon

Coast View Holiday Park ★★★★
Holiday, Touring and Camping Park
Torquay Road, Teignmouth
TQ14 0BG
T: (01626) 872392
F: (01626) 872719
E: info@coast-view.co.uk
I: www.coast-view.co.uk

Devon Valley Holiday Village ★★★★
Holiday Park
Coombe Road, Ringmore,
Teignmouth TQ14 0EY
T: 0870 442 9750
F: 0870 442 9757
E: info@devonvalley.biz
I: devonvalley.biz

SIDBURY
Devon

Putts Corner Caravan Club Site ★★★★★
Touring Park
Putts Corner, Sidbury, Sidmouth
EX10 0QQ
T: (01404) 42875
I: www.caravanclub.co.uk

SIDMOUTH
Devon

Salcombe Regis Camping and Caravan Park ★★★★★
Holiday and Touring Park
Salcombe Regis, Sidmouth
EX10 0JH
T: (01395) 514303
F: (01395) 514314
E: info@salcombe-regis.co.uk
I: www.salcombe-regis.co.uk

SIXPENNY HANDLEY
Dorset

Church Farm Caravan & Camping Park ★★★
Touring and Camping Park
High Street, Salisbury SP5 5ND
T: (01725) 552563
F: (01725) 552563

SLAPTON
Devon

Camping & Caravanning Club Site - Slapton Sands ★★★★
Touring and Camping Park
Middle Grounds, Kingsbridge
TQ7 2QW
T: (01548) 580538
I: www.
campingandcaravanningclub.
co.uk

SOUTH CERNEY
Gloucestershire

Hoburne Cotswold ★★★★
Holiday, Touring and Camping Park
Broadway Lane, Cirencester
GL7 5UQ
T: (01285) 860216
F: (01285) 868010
E: cotswold@hoburne.com
I: www.hoburne.com

SOUTH MOLTON
Devon

Yeo Valley Holiday Park ★★★
Holiday, Touring and Camping Park
c/o Blackcock Inn, Molland,
South Molton EX36 3NW
T: (01769) 550297
F: (01769) 550101
E: lorna@yeovalleyholidays.com
I: www.yeovalleyholidays.com

STICKLEPATH
Devon

Olditch Holiday Park ★★★
Holiday, Touring and Camping Park
Okehampton EX20 2NT
T: (01837) 840734
F: (01837) 840877
E: info@olditch.co.uk
I: www.olditch.co.uk

STOKE GABRIEL
Devon

Broadleigh Farm Park
Rating Applied For
Coombe House Lane, Aish,
Totnes TQ9 6PU
T: (01803) 782309
F: (01803) 782422
E: enquiries@broadleighfarm.
co.uk
I: www.gotorbay.
com/accommodation

SWANAGE
Dorset

Cauldron Barn Farm Caravan Park ★★★★
Holiday, Touring and Camping Park
Cauldron Barn Road, Swanage
BH19 1QQ
T: (01929) 422080
F: (01929) 427870
E: cauldronbarn@fsbdial.co.uk

Haycraft Caravan Club Site ★★★★★
Touring Park
Haycrafts Lane, Swanage
BH19 3EB
T: (01929) 480572
I: www.caravanclub.co.uk

Priestway Holiday Park ★★★
Holiday, Touring and Camping Park
Priests Way, Swanage BH19 2RS
T: (01929) 422747
F: (01929) 421822

Swanage Caravan Park ★★★
Holiday Park
Priests Road, Swanage
BH19 2QS
T: (01929) 422130
F: (01929) 427952

Ulwell Cottage Caravan Park ★★★★
Holiday, Touring and Camping Park
Ulwell, Swanage BH19 3DG
T: (01929) 422823
F: (01929) 421500
E: enq@ulwellcottagepark.co.uk
I: www.ulwellcottagepark.co.uk

Ulwell Farm Caravan Park ★★★★
Holiday Park
Ulwell, Swanage BH19 3DG
T: (01929) 422825
F: (01929) 422825
E: ulwell.farm@virgin.net
I: www.ukparks.co.uk/ulwellfarm

TAUNTON
Somerset

Ashe Farm Caravan and Campsite ★★★
Holiday, Touring and Camping Park
Thornfalcon, Taunton TA3 5NW
T: (01823) 442567
F: (01823) 443372
E: camping@ashe-frm.fsnet.
co.uk

Holly Bush Park ★★★★
Touring and Camping Park
Taunton TA3 7EA
T: (01823) 421515
E: info@hollybushpark.com
I: www.hollybushpark.com

Tanpits Cider Farm Camping and Caravan Park ★★
Touring and Camping Park
Dyers Lane, Taunton TA2 8BZ
T: (01823) 270663
F: (01823) 270663

TAVISTOCK
Devon

Harford Bridge Holiday Park ★★★★
Holiday, Touring and Camping Park
Rose Award
Harford Bridge, Tavistock
PL19 9LS
T: (01822) 810349
F: (01822) 810028
E: enquiry@harfordbridge.co.uk
I: www.harfordbridge.co.uk

Langstone Manor Caravan and Camping Park ★★★★
Holiday, Touring and Camping Park
Rose Award
Moortown, Tavistock PL19 9JZ
T: (01822) 613371
F: (01822) 613371
E: jane@langstone-manor.co.uk
I: www.langstone-manor.co.uk

Woodovis Park ★★★★★
Holiday Park
Tavistock PL19 8NY
T: (01822) 832968
F: (01822) 832948
E: info@woodovis.com
I: www.woodovis.com

TEIGNGRACE
Devon

Twelve Oaks Farm Caravan Park ★★★★
Touring Park
Teigngrace, Newton Abbot
TQ12 6QT
T: (01626) 352769
F: (01626) 352769
E: info@twelveoaksfarm.co.uk
I: www.twelveoaksfarm.co.uk

TEWKESBURY
Gloucestershire

Croft Farm Leisure and Water Park ★★★
Holiday Park
Bredons Hardwick, Tewkesbury
GL20 7EE
T: (01684) 772321
F: (01684) 773379
E: alan@croftfarmleisure.co.uk
I: www.croftfarmleisure.co.uk

Tewkesbury Abbey Caravan Club Site ★★★★
Touring and Camping Park
Gander Lane, Tewkesbury
GL20 5PG
T: (01684) 294035
I: www.caravanclub.co.uk

THREE LEGGED CROSS
Dorset

Woolsbridge Manor Farm Caravan Park ★★★
Touring and Camping Park
Ringwood Road, Wimborne
Minster BH21 6RA
T: (01202) 826369
F: (01202) 813172

TINTAGEL
Cornwall

Bossiney Farm Caravan and Camping Park ★★★★
Holiday, Touring and Camping Park
Tintagel PL34 0AY
T: (01840) 770481
F: (01840) 770025
E: bossineyfarm@aol.com
I: www.bossineyfarm.co.uk

Trewethett Farm Caravan Club Site ★★★★★
Touring Park
Trethevy, Tintagel PL34 0BQ
T: (01840) 770222
I: www.caravanclub.co.uk

TORQUAY
Torbay

TLH Leisure Resort ★★★★
Holiday Village
Belgrave Rod, Torquay TQ2 5HT
T: (01803) 400111
F: (01803) 400150

Widdicombe Farm Touring Park ★★★★
Touring and Camping Park
Paignton TQ3 1ST
T: (01803) 558325
F: (01803) 559526
E: enquiries@torquaytouring.
co.uk
I: www.torquaytouring.co.uk

TOWEDNACK
Cornwall
Penderleath Caravan & Camping Park ★★★★
Touring Park
St Ives TR26 3AF
T: (01736) 798403
I: www.penderleath.co.uk

TREGURRIAN
Cornwall
Camping and Caravanning Club Site Tregurrian ★★★★
Touring Park
Newquay TR8 4AE
T: (01637) 860448
I: www.
campingandcaravanningclub.
co.uk

TRURO
Cornwall
Ringwell Valley Holiday Park ★★★★★
Holiday Park
Ringwell Hill, Bissoe Road,
Carnon Downs, Truro TR3 6LQ
T: (01872) 862194
F: (01872) 864343
E: keith@ringwell.co.uk
I: www.ringwell.co.uk

Summer Valley Touring Park ★★★★
Touring Park
Truro TR4 9DW
T: (01872) 277878
E: res@summervalley.co.uk
I: www.summervalley.co.uk

UMBERLEIGH
Devon
Camping & Caravanning Club Site Umberleigh ★★★★
Touring Park
Over Weir, Umberleigh
EX37 9DU
T: (01769) 560009
I: www.
campingandcaravanningclub.
co.uk

UPTON
Somerset
Lowtrow Cross Caravan & Camping Park ★★★★
Touring and Camping Park
Taunton TA4 2DB
T: (01398) 371199
E: lowtoncross@aol.com
I: www.lowtowcross.co.uk

VERYAN
Cornwall
Camping & Caravanning Club Site Veryan ★★★★
Touring Park
Tretheake Manor, Truro TR2 5PP
T: (01872) 501658
I: www.
campingandcaravanningclub.
co.uk

WADEBRIDGE
Cornwall
Little Bodieve Holiday Park ★★★★
Holiday, Touring and Camping Park
Bodieve Road, Wadebridge
PL27 6EG
T: (01208) 812323
F: (01208) 815547
E: berry@
littlebodieveholidaypark.fsnet.
co.uk
I: www.littlebodieve.co.uk

WAREHAM
Dorset
Lookout Holiday Park ★★★★
Holiday, Touring and Camping Park
Corfe Road, Stoborough,
Wareham BH20 5AZ
T: (01929) 552546
F: (01929) 556662
E: enquiries@caravan-
sites.co.uk
I: www.caravan-sites.co.uk

Birchwood Tourist Park ★★★
Touring and Camping Park
Bere Road, Wareham BH20 7PA
T: (01929) 554763
F: (01929) 556635

Wareham Forest Tourist Park ★★★★★
Touring and Camping Park
Bere Road, North Trigon,
Wareham BH20 7NZ
T: (01929) 551393
F: (01929) 558321
E: holiday@wareham-forest.
co.uk
I: www.wareham-forest.co.uk

WARMINSTER
Wiltshire
Longleat Caravan Club Site ★★★★★
Touring Park
Longleat, Warminster BA12 7NL
T: (01985) 844663
I: www.caravanclub.co.uk

WARMWELL
Dorset
Warmwell Country Touring Park ★★★
Holiday, Touring and Camping Park
Dorchester DT2 8JD
T: (01305) 852313
F: (01305) 851824
E: warmwell@btopenworld.com
I: www.warmwell.touring.20m.
com

Warmwell Leisure Resort ★★★★
Holiday Park
Dorchester DT2 8JE
T: (01305) 852911
F: (01305) 854588

WATCHET
Somerset
Helwell Bay Holidays ★
Holiday Park
Helwell Bay, Watchet TA23 0UG
T: (01984) 631781
E: helwellbay@yahoo.co.uk
I: www.helwellbay.co.uk

Lorna Doone Holiday Park ★★★★★
Holiday Park
Rose Award
Watchet TA23 0BJ
T: (01984) 631206
E: mail@lornadoone.co.uk
I: www.lornadoone.co.uk

West Bay Caravan Park ★★★★★
Holiday Park
Cleeve Hill, Watchet TA23 0BJ
T: (01984) 631261
F: (01984) 634944
E: alistair@westbay2000.
freeserve.co.uk
I: www.westbaycaravanpark.
co.uk

WATERROW
Somerset
Waterrow Touring Park ★★★★★
Touring and Camping Park
Taunton TA4 2AZ
T: (01984) 623464
F: (01984) 624280
I: www.waterrowpark.co.uk

WELLS
Somerset
Mendip Heights Camping and Caravan Park ★★★★
Touring and Camping Park
Townsend, Wells BA5 3BP
T: (01749) 870241
F: (01749) 870368
E: bta@mendipheights.co.uk
I: www.mendipheights.co.uk

WEMBURY
Devon
Churchwood Valley Holiday Cabins ★★★★
Holiday Park
Churchwood Valley, Wembury
Bay, Plymouth PL9 0DZ
T: (01752) 862382
F: (01752) 863274
E: Churchwoodvalley@
btinternet.com
I: www.churchwoodvalley.com

WEST BAY
Dorset
West Bay Holiday Park ★★★★
Holiday, Touring and Camping Park
Bridport DT6 4HB
T: 0870 420 2884
F: (0191) 2685986
E: enquiries@parkdeanholidays.
co.uk
I: www.parkdeanholidays.
co.uk/home-west-bay.
aspx?Park=west-bay

WEST BEXINGTON
Dorset
Gorselands Caravan Park ★★★★
Holiday Park
Dorchester DT2 9DJ
T: (01308) 897232
F: (01308) 897239
I: www.gorselands-uk.com

WEST LULWORTH
Dorset
Durdle Door Holiday Park ★★★★
Holiday, Touring and Camping Park
Rose Award
Wareham BH20 5PU
T: (01929) 400200
F: (01929) 400260
E: durdle.door@lulworth.com
I: www.lulworth.com

WEST QUANTOXHEAD
Somerset
St Audries Bay Holiday Club ★★★★
Holiday Park
Taunton TA4 4DY
T: (01984) 632515
F: (01984) 632785
E: mrandle@staudriesbay.
demon.co.uk
I: www.staudriesbay.co.uk

WESTON
Devon
Oakdown Touring and Holiday Home Park ★★★★★
Holiday and Touring Park
Sidmouth EX10 0PH
T: (01297) 680387
F: (01297) 680541
E: enquiries@oakdown.co.uk
I: www.oakdown.co.uk

Stoneleigh Holiday and Leisure Village ★★★★
Holiday Park
Sidmouth EX10 0PJ
T: (01395) 513619
F: (01395) 513629
I: www.stoneleighholidays.com

WESTON-SUPER-MARE
North Somerset
Camping and Caravanning Club Site Weston-super-Mare ★★★
Touring and Camping Park
West End Farm, Weston-super-
Mare BS24 8RH
T: (01934) 822548
I: www.
campingandcaravanningclub.
co.uk

Carefree Holiday Park
Rating Applied For
12 Beach Road, Weston-super-
Mare BS22 9UZ
T: (01934) 624541

Country View Holiday Park ★★★
Holiday, Touring and Camping Park
29 Sand Road, Weston-super-
Mare BS22 9UJ
T: (01934) 627595

Dulhorn Farm Camping Site ★★★
Touring and Camping Park
Weston Road, Lympsham,
Weston-super-Mare BS24 0JQ
T: (01934) 750298
F: (01934) 750913

Sand Bay Holiday Village
★★★
Holiday Village
67 Beach Road, Kewstoke,
Weston-super-Mare BS22 9UR
T: (01934) 428200
F: (01934) 428228
I: www.sandbayholidayvillage.
co.uk

Snooty Fox Resorts ★★★★
Holiday, Touring and Camping Park
Bridgwater Road, Weston-super-Mare BS24 0AN
T: (01934) 425014
F: (01934) 425015
E: purnholidaypk@aol.com
I: www.snootyfoxresorts.co.uk

WESTWARD HO!
Devon

Beachside Holiday Park
★★★★
Holiday Park
Merley Road, Westward Ho!,
Bideford EX39 1JX
T: (01237) 421163
F: (01237) 472100
E: beachside@surfbay.dircon.
co.uk
I: www.beachsideholidays.co.uk

Surf Bay Holiday Park
★★★★
Holiday Park
Golf Links Road, Westward Ho!,
Bideford EX39 1HD
T: (01237) 471833
F: (01237) 474387
E: surfbayholidaypark@surfbay.
dircon.co.uk
I: www.surfbay.co.uk

WEYMOUTH
Dorset

Chesil Beach Holiday Park
★★★★
Holiday Park
Chesil Beach, Portland Road,
Weymouth DT4 9AG
T: (01305) 773233
F: (01305) 781233
E: info@chesilholidays.co.uk
I: www.chesilholidays.co.uk

**Crossways Caravan Club
Site ★★★★**
Touring Park
Moreton, Dorchester DT2 8BE
T: (01305) 852032
I: www.caravanclub.co.uk

**East Fleet Farm Touring
Park ★★★★**
Touring and Camping Park
Fleet Lane, Weymouth DT3 4DW
T: (01305) 785768
E: richard@eastfleet.co.uk
I: www.eastfleet.co.uk

Littlesea Holiday Park ★★★
Holiday, Touring and Camping Park
Lynch Lane, Weymouth DT4 9DT
T: (01305) 774414
F: (01305) 760038
I: www.havenholidays.com/
littlesea

Pebble Bank Caravan Park
★★★
Holiday, Touring and Camping Park
90 Camp Road, Weymouth
DT4 9HF
T: (01305) 774844
F: (01305) 774844
E: info@pebblebank.co.uk
I: www.pebblebank.co.uk

Waterside Holiday Park
★★★★★
Holiday and Touring Park
Bowleaze Coveway, Weymouth
DT3 6PP
T: (01305) 833103
F: (01305) 832830
E: info@watersideholidays.co.uk
I: www.watersideholidays.co.uk

WHITE CROSS
Cornwall

**Summer Lodge Holiday
Park ★★★★**
Holiday Park
Newquay TR8 4LW
T: (01726) 860415
F: (01726) 861490
E: reservations@summerlodge.
co.uk
I: www.summerlodge.co.uk

White Acres Holiday Park
★★★★★
Holiday Park
White Cross, Newquay TR8 4LW
T: 0870 420 2997 &
(01726) 862100
E: enquiries@parkdeanholidays.
co.uk
I: www.parkdeanholidays.co.uk

WIMBORNE MINSTER
Dorset

Merley Court Touring Park
★★★★★
Touring and Camping Park
Merley House Lane, Merley,
Wimborne Minster BH21 3AA
T: (01202) 881488
F: (01202) 881484
E: holidays@merley-court.co.uk
I: www.merley-court.co.uk

Springfield Touring Park
★★★★★
Touring and Camping Park
Candys Lane, Corfe Mullen,
Wimborne BH21 3EF
T: (01202) 881719

**Wilksworth Farm Caravan
Park ★★★★★**
Touring and Camping Park
Cranborne Road, Wimborne
Minster BH21 4HW
T: (01202) 885467
E: rayandwendy@
wilksworthfarmcaravanpark.
co.uk
I: www.
wilksworthfarmcaravanpark.
co.uk

WINCHCOMBE
Gloucestershire

**Camping and Caravanning
Site Winchcombe ★★★★**
Touring and Camping Park
Brooklands Fram, Tewkesbury
GL20 8NX
T: (01242) 620259
I: www.
campingandcaravanningclub.
co.uk

WINSFORD
Somerset

**Halse Farm Caravan & Tent
Park ★★★★**
Touring and Camping Park
Winsford, Minehead TA24 7JL
T: (01643) 851259
F: (01643) 851592
E: brown@halsefarm.co.uk
I: www.halsefarm.co.uk
♿

WOODBURY
Devon

Castle Brake Holiday Park
★★★★
Holiday Park
Castle Lane, Exeter EX5 1HA
T: (01395) 232431
E: reception@castlebrake.co.uk
I: www.castlebrake.co.uk

WOODLANDS
Dorset

**Camping & Caravanning
Club Site Verwood, New
Forest ★★★★**
Touring and Camping Park
Sutton Hill, Wimborne Minster
BH21 8NQ
T: (01202) 822763
I: www.
campingandcaravanningclub.
co.uk

WOOL
Dorset

Whitemead Caravan Park
★★★★
Touring and Camping Park
East Burton Road, Wool,
Wareham BH20 6HG
T: (01929) 462241
F: (01929) 462241
E: whitemeadcp@aol.com
I: www.whitemeadcaravanpark.
co.uk

WOOLACOMBE
Devon

**Golden Coast Holiday
Village ★★★★**
Holiday Park
Golden Coast Holiday Village,
Station Road, Woolacombe
EX34 7HW
T: (01271) 870343
F: (01271) 870089
E: goodtimes@woolacombe.
com
I: www.woolacombe.com

**Woolacombe Bay Holiday
Parks ★★★★**
Holiday Park
Station Road, Woolacombe
EX34 7HW
T: (01271) 870343
F: (01271) 870089
E: goodtimes@woolacombe.
com
I: www.woolacombe.com

**Woolacombe Bay Holiday
Village ★★★★**
Holiday and Camping Park
Seymour, Sandy Lane,
Woolacombe EX34 7AH
T: (01271) 870343
F: (01271) 870089
E: goodtimes@woolacombe.
com
I: www.woolacombe.com

**Woolacombe Sands Holiday
Park ★★★**
Holiday, Touring and Camping Park
Beach Road, Woolacombe
EX34 7AF
T: (01271) 870569
F: (01271) 870606
E: lifesabeach@
woolacombe-sands.co.uk
I: www.woolacombe-sands.
co.uk

YEOVIL
Somerset

**Long Hazel International
Caravan and Camping Park**
★★★★
Holiday, Touring and Camping Park
High Street, Yeovil BA22 7JH
T: (01963) 440002
F: (01963) 440002
E: longhazelpark@hotmail.com
I: www.sparkford.f9.co.uk/lhi.
htm
♿

Holiday Villages

VisitBritain has a separate rating scheme of one to five stars for Holiday Villages. Holiday Villages usually comprise a variety of types of accommodation, with the majority provided in custom-built rooms (e.g. chalets, hotel rooms). A range of facilities and activities are also available which may, or may not, be included in the tariff. Holiday Villages meet requirements for both the provision and quality of facilities and services, including fixtures, fittings, furnishings, décor. Progressively higher levels of quality and customer care are provided for each of the star ratings. Quite simply, the more stars, the higher the overall level of quality you can expect.

What standards to expect at each rating level:

★ Acceptable ★★ Good ★★★ Very good
★★★★ Excellent ★★★★★ Exceptional

BURNHAM-ON-SEA
Somerset

Holiday Resort Unity
★★★
Coast Road, Brean Sands,
Burnham-on-Sea TA8 2RB
T: (01278) 751235
F: (01278) 751539

Pontins Ltd ★★★
Brean Sands Family Centre,
South Road, Burnham-on-Sea
TA8 2RJ
T: (01278) 751627
F: (01278) 751754
E: ellie.hindle@pontins.com
I: www.pontins.com

CORTON
Suffolk

Warner Holidays Ltd ★★
Corton Classic Resort, The
Street, Lowestoft NR32 5HR
T: 0870 601 6012
F: (01502) 732334
I: www.warnerholidays.co.uk

CROYDE
Devon

**Croyde Bay Holiday Village
(Unison) ★★★**
Braunton EX33 1QB
T: (01271) 890890
F: (01271) 890888
E: s.willis@unison.co.uk
I: www.croydeholidays.co.uk

GREAT YARMOUTH
Norfolk

Potters Leisure Resort
★★★★★
Coast Road, Hopton-on-Sea,
Great Yarmouth NR31 9BX
T: (01502) 730345
F: (01502) 731970
E: potters@pottersholidays.com
I: www.pottersholidays.com

HAYLING ISLAND
Hampshire

Warner Holidays Ltd ★★★
Lakeside Classic Resort, Fishery
Lane, Hayling Island PO11 9NR
T: 0870 601 6012
F: (023) 9246 9143

HEMSBY
Norfolk

Pontins Hemsby ★★★
Beach Road, Hemsby
NR29 4HL
T: 0870 601 0478
F: (01493) 733751
I: www.pontins.com

LOWESTOFT
Suffolk

Warner Holidays Ltd ★★★
Gunton Hall Classic Resort,
Gunton Avenue, Lowestoft
NR32 5DF
T: (01502) 730288
F: (01502) 732319

MINEHEAD
Somerset

**Butlins Minehead
Rating Applied For**
T: 0870 242 1999
I: www.butlinsonline.co.uk

SEATON
Devon

Lyme Bay Holiday Village
★★★
87 Harbour Road, Seaton
EX12 2NE
T: (01297) 626800
F: (01297) 626801
I: www.lymebayholidayvillage.
co.uk

TORQUAY
Torbay

TLH Leisure Resort
★★★★
Belgrave Road, Torquay
TQ2 5HT
T: (01803) 400111
F: (01803) 400150

WESTON-SUPER-MARE
North Somerset

Sand Bay Holiday Village
★★★
67 Beach Road, Kewstoke,
Weston-super-Mare BS22 9UR
T: (01934) 428200
F: (01934) 428228
I: www.sandbayholidayvillage.
co.uk

WREA GREEN
Lancashire

Ribby Hall Village ★★★★
Ribby Road, Preston PR4
T: (01772) 671111
F: (01772) 673113
E: enquiries@ribbyhall.co.uk
I: www.ribbyhall.co.uk

YARMOUTH
Isle of Wight

Warner Holidays Ltd ★★★
Norton Grange Classic Resort,
Yarmouth PO41 0SD
T: 0870 601 6012
F: (01983) 760468